HANDBOOK OF
EFFECTIVE LITERACY INSTRUCTION

Also from Nell K. Duke

Literacy Research Methodologies, Second Edition
Edited by Nell K. Duke and Marla H. Mallette

Handbook of Effective Literacy Instruction

RESEARCH-BASED PRACTICE K–8

EDITED BY

Barbara M. Taylor
Nell K. Duke

THE GUILFORD PRESS
New York   London

© 2013 The Guilford Press
A Division of Guilford Publications, Inc.
72 Spring Street, New York, NY 10012
www.guilford.com

Printed in the United States of America

This book is printed on acid-free paper.

Last digit is print number: 9   8   7   6   5   4   3   2   1

Library of Congress Cataloging-in-Publication Data

Handbook of effective literacy instruction : research-based practice K–8 / edited by
Barbara M. Taylor and Nell K. Duke.
     p. cm.
  Includes bibliographical references and index.
  ISBN 978-1-4625-0941-6 (hardback)
  1. Language arts (Elementary)—Handbooks, manuals, etc.   2. Language arts
(Middle school)—Handbooks, manuals, etc.   3. Effective teaching—Handbooks,
manuals, etc.   I. Taylor, Barbara M.   II. Duke, Nell K.
  LB1576.H2333 2013
  372.6—dc23
                                                                            2012032995

About the Editors

Barbara M. Taylor, EdD, is Professor Emerita of Literacy Education at the University of Minnesota, where she is also founder and past director of the Minnesota Center for Reading Research. A member of the Reading Hall of Fame, she is a recipient of the Oscar S. Causey Award from the National Reading Conference (NRC, now the Literacy Research Association) and the Albert J. Harris Award and the Outstanding Teacher Educator Award from the International Reading Association (IRA). Dr. Taylor's research interests include reading comprehension and high-level talk and writing about text, elementary schoolwide reading improvement, early reading intervention, and the elements of effective instruction that contribute to children's success in reading. She has published numerous books, book chapters, and journal articles.

Nell K. Duke, EdD, is Professor of Language, Literacy, and Culture and an affiliate of the Combined Program in Education and Psychology at the University of Michigan. She is a recipient of honors including early career awards from the American Educational Research Association and the NRC, the Dina Feitelson Research Award from the IRA, and the Promising Researcher Award from the National Council of Teachers of English. Dr. Duke's research interests include the development of informational reading and writing in young children, comprehension development and instruction in early schooling, and issues of equity in literacy education. She is coauthor or coeditor of several books and has published numerous journal articles.

Contributors

Kerry Alexander, BS, College of Education, University of Texas at Austin and Austin Independent School District, Austin, Texas

Janet Alleman, PhD, Department of Teacher Education, Michigan State University, East Lansing, Michigan

Janice F. Almasi, PhD, Department of Curriculum and Instruction, University of Kentucky, Lexington, Kentucky

Heather Augustine, MEd, Austin Independent School District, Austin, Texas

Laurie B. Bauer, EdD, Department of Education, Hanover College, Hanover, Indiana

Shannon Blady, MEd, Department of Interdisciplinary Learning and Teaching, University of Texas at San Antonio, San Antonio, Texas

Elizabeth Hammond Brinkerhoff, MA, Department of Educational Psychology and Learning Systems, College of Education, Florida State University, Tallahassee, Florida

Kristy Brugar, MEd, Division of Teacher Education, Wayne State University, Detroit, Michigan

Gina Cervetti, PhD, Program of Language, Literacy, and Culture, Department of Educational Studies, University of Michigan, Ann Arbor, Michigan

Nell K. Duke, EdD, Program in Language, Literacy, and Culture, Department of Educational Studies, University of Michigan, Ann Arbor, Michigan

Douglas Fisher, PhD, Department of Educational Leadership, San Diego State University, San Diego, California

Ellen Fogelberg MST, Evanston/Skokie School District 65, Evanston, Illinois

Nancy Frey, PhD, Department of Teacher Education, San Diego State University, San Diego, California

Keli Garas-York, PhD, Department of Elementary Education and Reading, Buffalo State College, Buffalo, New York

Anne-Lise Halvorsen, PhD, Department of Teacher Education, Michigan State University, East Lansing, Michigan

Heather Hebard, PhD, Department of Language, Literacy, and Culture, University of Washington, Seattle, Washington

Susan Dougherty Johnson, EdD, Graduate School of Education, Rutgers, The State University of New Jersey, New Brunswick, New Jersey

Linda Kucan, PhD, Department of Instruction and Learning, University of Pittsburgh, Pittsburgh, Pennsylvania

Melanie R. Kuhn, PhD, Department of Curriculum and Teaching, Boston University, Boston, Massachusetts

Tracey Kumar, PhD, Department of Interdisciplinary Learning and Teaching, University of Texas at San Antonio, San Antonio, Texas

Nan L. McDonald, EdD, School of Music and Dance, San Diego State University, San Diego, California

Ellen McIntyre, EdD, Associate Dean of Academic Affairs, North Carolina State University, Raleigh, North Carolina

Kristina Najera, PhD, Department of Curriculum, Instruction, and Technology Education, Temple University, Philadelphia, Pennsylvania

Debra S. Peterson, PhD, Minnesota Center for Reading Research, University of Minnesota, Minneapolis, Minnesota

Tim Pressley, MEd, Department of Educational Psychology and Learning Systems, College of Education, Florida State University, Tallahassee, Florida

Erik S. Rawls, BA, Department of Educational Psychology and Learning Systems, College of Education, Florida State University, Tallahassee, Florida

Kathryn Roberts, PhD, Department of Reading, Language, and Literature, Wayne State University, Detroit, Michigan

Alysia D. Roehrig, PhD, Department of Educational Psychology and Learning Systems, College of Education, Florida State University, Tallahassee, Florida

Katie Russell, MAT, Department of Curriculum and Instruction, University of Texas at Austin, Austin, Texas

Misty Sailors, PhD, Department of Interdisciplinary Learning and Teaching, University of Texas at San Antonio, San Antonio, Texas

Patti Satz, MEd, Evanston/Skokie School District 65, Evanston, Illinois

Lynn E. Shanahan, PhD, Department of Learning and Instruction, State University of New York at Buffalo, Buffalo, New York

Carole Skalinder, MST, Evanston/Skokie School District 65, Evanston, Illinois

Katherine A. Dougherty Stahl, EdD, Department of Teaching and Learning, Steinhardt School of Culture, Education, and Human Development, New York University, New York, New York

Barbara M. Taylor, EdD (retired), Department of Curriculum and Instruction, University of Minnesota, Minneapolis, Minnesota

Gary A. Troia, PhD, Department of Counseling, Educational Psychology, and Special Education, Michigan State University, East Lansing, Michigan

Jennifer Danridge Turner, PhD, Department of Teaching, Learning, Policy, and Leadership, University of Maryland, College Park, Maryland

Sheila W. Valencia, PhD, Department of Language, Literacy, and Culture, University of Washington, Seattle, Washington

Sharon Walpole, PhD, School of Education, University of Delaware, Newark, Delaware

Lynne M. Watanabe, MA, Educational Psychology and Educational Technology Program, Michigan State University, East Lansing, Michigan

Susan Watts Taffe, PhD, Literacy and Second Language Studies Program, University of Cincinnati, Cincinnati, Ohio

Catherine M. Weber, PhD, Mary Lou Fulton Teachers College, Arizona State University, Phoenix, Arizona

Angeli Willson, MEd, Department of Interdisciplinary Learning and Teaching, University of Texas at San Antonio, San Antonio, Texas

Contents

Part II. Effective Teaching and Assessment to Develop Essential Literacy Abilities in Students

Part III. Effective Integration of Literacy with Instruction in Content Areas

Part IV. Essential Collaborations for Effective Schoolwide Literacy Instruction

Introduction •

Barbara M. Taylor
Nell K. Duke

Educators have learned a great deal from research about what it takes to help all children in the elementary and middle grades succeed in reading and writing to their fullest potential. To reach this goal, teachers and administrators within schools need to work together to develop and deliver a sound schoolwide reading program. Within the confines of their own classrooms, teachers must focus and reflect equally on the content and the pedagogy of their literacy instruction. Then they must continuously make good instructional choices, based on these reflections in conjunction with ongoing pupil assessment data, to meet individual students' evolving needs.

The intent of this handbook is to provide a comprehensive, forward-looking, research-based volume for teachers, teacher educators, and researchers on the key interconnected components of effective literacy instruction. The book is designed to be an easy-to-use resource for preservice and for practicing teachers as well. Every chapter includes substantial suggestions for implementing research-based practices in the classroom and for engaging in professional learning to help teachers increase their effectiveness as literacy instructors. Each chapter in Part IV also includes substantial suggestions for fostering collaboration among staff and, when applicable, parents within schools.

The book is divided into four parts: (1) *Fundamental Components of Effective Literacy Lessons*, focusing on the pedagogy, or teaching practices, of effective literacy instruction; (2) *Effective Teaching and Assessment to Develop Essential Literacy Abilities in Students*, focusing on the content of instruction; (3) *Effective Integration of Literacy with Instruction in Content Areas*; and (4) *Essential Collaborations for Effective Schoolwide Literacy Instruction*. To help make the book coherent and consistent, all chapters contain the following elements:

- *Overview of Research*
- *Summary of Big Ideas from Research*

- *Examples of Effective Practices* (these are sometimes incorporated into other elements, rather than presented separately)
- *Looking Forward*
- *Questions for Reflection*
- *Suggestions for Ongoing Professional Learning*
- *Research-Based Resources*
- *References*

In the *Overview of Research* and/or the *Examples of Effective Practices* sections, chapters also discuss how to meet the needs of *all* students in the classroom. In addition, the *Questions for Reflection* and *Suggestions for Ongoing Professional Learning* are particularly important features of each chapter. The *Questions for Reflection* material provides an opportunity to think about chapter content in relation to your current or future teaching. Chapters will make a greater difference in your practice if you take additional time to process and reflect on them in relation to your teaching. The *Suggestions for Ongoing Professional Learning* material provides a series of activities in which professional learning communities can engage to deepen their individual and collective understanding of chapter content and apply it to their own practice. These activities are particularly well suited for study groups using the book, but they may be useful in course-based professional development as well.

In the remainder of this introduction, we provide brief summaries of research on the characteristics of schools and teachers providing effective literacy instruction, as well as initial comments on such instruction. This discussion forms a backdrop for the structure of the handbook and the topics covered in individual chapters. Because this is a handbook of research and research-based practice, we have included a brief discussion of what we believe educators need to know about research in order to be effective consumers of research and to become the most effective literacy instructors possible (Duke & Martin, 2011).

CHARACTERISTICS OF EFFECTIVE SCHOOLS

Studies of schools that are effective in teaching children to read highlight the importance of leadership, strong within-building collaboration, effective instruction and assessment, ongoing professional learning, and constructive parent partnerships. Elaborations of this research on effective schools include the following (based on Taylor, 2002a):

- The principal of a successful school is a strong leader who fosters collaborative leadership. Teachers and parents contribute to the school decision making, and teachers contribute to the school's instructional leadership (Bryk, Sebring, Allensworth, Luppescu, & Easton, 2010; Spillane, Halverson, & Diamond, 2001; Taylor, Pressley, & Pearson, 2002).
- Teachers and administrators in successful schools make improved student learning a schoolwide priority with sustained, strategic educational planning (Bryk et al., 2010; Stringfield, Millsap, & Herman, 1997; Taylor, Pearson, Clark, & Walpole, 2000).

- Teachers in successful schools have a sense of collective responsibility for increasing students' reading achievement, and they believe that they collectively have the ability to succeed (Goddard, Hoy, & Hoy, 2000; Mosenthal, Lipson, Torncello, Russ, & Mekkelsen, 2004; Taylor et al., 2002).
- Teachers in successful schools have a strong sense of professional community and collaboration. Teachers work together in their teaching of reading and writing and in professional development pertaining to literacy (Bryk et al., 2010; Langer, 2000; Mosenthal et al., 2004; Taylor et al., 2000, 2002).
- Successful schools have ongoing, building-level professional development, with teachers actively seeking out new ideas (Bryk et al., 2010; Mosenthal et al., 2004; Taylor et al., 2000; Taylor, Pearson, Peterson, & Rodriguez, 2005).
- Successful schools regularly monitor student progress and use multiple data sources to guide their change process and to plan their instruction (Hoffman & Rutherford, 1984; Paris, Paris, & Carpenter, 2002; Taylor et al., 2000, 2002).
- Successful schools provide reading and writing instruction that balances attention to basic skills with more cognitively demanding literacy activities (Pressley, 2006; Pressley et al., 2003; Taylor et al., 2000).
- Successful schools foster parent partnerships, respect for cultural differences, and community involvement (Bryk et al., 2010; Goddard, Tschannen-Moran, & Hoy, 2001; Scribner, Young, & Pedroza, 1999; Taylor et al., 2000, 2002).

CHARACTERISTICS OF EFFECTIVE TEACHERS

Effective teachers have positive effects on students' reading achievement, and these effects persist throughout the elementary grades (Konstantopoulos & Chung, 2011). Effective teachers of reading and writing provide motivating and balanced instruction, teach strategies as well as skills, encourage higher-level thinking, and coach children as they are reading and writing. Common findings across studies on effective elementary teachers of reading include the following (based on Taylor, 2002b, 2002c):

- Effective literacy teachers maintain instructional balance. They teach basic skills as needed, but do not overemphasize them (Pressley, 2006; Pressley et al., 2001; Taylor, Pearson, Peterson, & Rodriguez, 2003; Wharton-McDonald, Pressley, & Hampston, 1998).
- Effective literacy teachers stress higher-level thinking. They engage children in challenging discussions and writing in response to what they have read (Allington & Johnston, 2002; Knapp & Associates, 1995; Peterson & Taylor, 2012; Taylor et al., 2002, 2003).
- Effective literacy teachers teach word recognition and comprehension strategies as well as skills. That is, they teach children how to transfer word recognition and comprehension skills they have learned into strategies they can use when reading or writing independently (National Reading Panel, 2000; Taylor et al., 2000, 2003).
- Effective literacy teachers do not take an overly teacher-directed stance toward instruction. They provide a substantial amount of coaching in the form of support

and feedback as their students are reading and writing. They refrain from doing too much talking, allowing their students ample time to engage firsthand in literacy activities (Allington & Johnston, 2002; Pressley, 2006; Pressley et al., 2001; Taylor et al., 2000, 2002, 2003).

- Effective literacy teachers foster self-regulation in their students. They encourage students to work independently and to take responsibility for their own learning (Paris & Paris, 2001; Pressley et al., 2001, 2003; Taylor, 2002b, 2002c).
- Effective teachers of reading provide motivating instruction and foster active pupil involvement. They give their students many opportunities to engage in meaningful reading and writing activities (Allington & Johnston, 2002; Helman, 2009; Pressley, 2006; Pressley et al., 2003; Taylor et al., 2003) and integrated instruction (Guthrie, Wigfield, & VonSecker, 2000).
- Effective literacy teachers have high expectations for their students' behavior and their reading and writing growth. They believe that their students can achieve at high levels in reading and writing. They also believe that their students will work hard whether they are working with the whole class, in a small group, with a partner, or on their own (Helman, 2009; Pressley et al., 2003; Taylor, 2002; Wharton-McDonald et al., 1998).
- Effective teachers of reading are excellent classroom managers. They work with their students to develop class rules and routines, and are persistent in seeing that these rules and routines are honored in the classroom (Pressley et al., 2001, 2003; Taylor, 2002c; Wharton-McDonald et al., 1998).
- Effective literacy teachers provide culturally responsive instruction and build strong relationships with their students' parents. They communicate regularly with parents, treat them with respect, and make them feel welcome in their classrooms (Barrera & Jimenez, 2002; Li, 2011; Pressley, 2006; Taylor et al., 2000).

EFFECTIVE LITERACY INSTRUCTION AND THE ORGANIZATION OF THIS HANDBOOK

Much of the research on effective literacy instruction in the elementary grades has focused on the content of reading lessons—that is, the teaching of emergent literacy abilities, including phonemic awareness, phonics, fluency, vocabulary, and reading comprehension. However, a valuable body of research also points to the importance of the many pedagogical decisions that effective teachers make to foster students' reading and writing growth. In addition, effective teachers develop a motivating, supportive classroom atmosphere that is responsive to children's cultural backgrounds and enhances the students' reading and writing abilities and achievement. Such teachers provide an engaging print environment, including ample opportunities for students to engage in technology-based learning.

In this handbook, we first review the *pedagogy* of sound literacy instruction teaching in the classroom. Not only must teachers masterfully orchestrate their instruction and assessment related to all of the essential content components of reading and writing, and collaborate with other teachers as they are doing so; they have to teach with good pacing and clarity of purpose, tied to individual students' needs and abilities. Teachers also need to focus continually on providing intellectual challenge to all.

In the second part of this handbook, we discuss the *content* of sound literacy instruction—that is, those components of effective reading and writing instruction supported by scientifically based research that are related to the abilities that students must develop, such as decoding and comprehension, to become competent readers and writers. These components are related to the Common Core State Standards (CCSS; National Governors Association Center for Best Practices & Council of Chief State School Officers, 2010).

In the third part of the book, we discuss the *integration of literacy in the content areas* of social studies, math, science, and the arts, also related to the CCSS. This integration of literacy and content-area instruction is not only increasing, but imperative as we move forward in the age of information technology and Internet-delivered content.

In the fourth part of this handbook, we review important elements of *schoolwide literacy programs and improvement strategies* that have an impact on classroom reading and writing instruction. As we have described earlier in the Introduction, teachers in effective schools work together to develop a cohesive, schoolwide literacy program (see Taylor, Chapter 18, and Weber, Chapter 19, this volume; see also Taylor, Peterson, Marx, & Chein, 2007; Taylor et al., 2005; Taylor, Raphael, & Au, 2011). Essential aspects include, but are not limited to, the following:

1. Collaboration among classroom teachers and resource teachers (e.g., Title I, special education, English language learner teachers) in whatever delivery model is chosen to provide cohesive, exemplary reading and writing instruction that best meets students' varying needs (see Walpole & Najera, Chapter 20, and Peterson, Chapter 21, this volume; see also Taylor et al., 2000, 2002).
2. Coherence in curriculum, instruction, and assessment (see Weber, Chapter 19; see also Au, Raphael, & Mooney, 2008; Bryk et al., 2010; Taylor et al., 2011).
3. A schoolwide assessment plan in which student data are collected and used regularly to inform instruction (see Weber, Chapter 19; see also Pressley, Raphael, Gallagher, & Di Bella, 2004; Taylor et al., 2000, 2011).
4. Interventions in place to meet the needs of students who are experiencing reading difficulties, who have special education needs, and who are English language learners (see Walpole & Najera, Chapter 20; see also Foorman & Torgesen, 2001; Mathes et al., 2005; Taylor et al., 2000, 2002).

In addition, teachers in effective schools engage in productive, ongoing, school-based professional learning to improve their practice (see Peterson, Chapter 21, and Sailors, Russell, Augustine, & Alexander, Chapter 22; see also Taylor et al., 2011). And working effectively with parents as partners (see Roberts, Chapter 23) is another important characteristic of effective literacy and schoolwide improvement programs (Bryk et al., 2010; Edwards, 2004; Taylor et al., 2002) and of effective teachers (Dolezal, Welsh, Pressley, & Vincent, 2003; Taylor et al., 2000).

In sum, this handbook first addresses fundamentals of sound literacy instruction, then identifies the content and components of this instruction, and then examines how this instruction can occur in multiple disciplinary contexts. Finally, the handbook describes strategies for bringing effective literacy instruction to entire school communities.

WHY A HANDBOOK OF *RESEARCH AND* PRACTICE?

Many professional books for current and aspiring teachers are books of practice, but not *research and* practice. Why so much attention to research? We believe that research, as well as professional wisdom, is an essential guide to practice. Duke and Martin (2011) offer five reasons why attention to research is needed[1]:

Our Experiences Alone May Misguide Us

For a very long time, people believed that Earth was flat, and that was (and still is) a reasonable conclusion to draw from personal, individual observations. Research, however, eventually proved this view to be incorrect. In reading education, we have these kinds of examples as well, although perhaps not as dramatic. For instance, for a long time, we thought that persistent word reading difficulty, often called dyslexia, was primarily a visual problem. To illustrate, we thought that reading "star" as "rats" reflected a problem with the visual processing of print. We now understand that most word reading difficulties are actually caused by problems in phonological or auditory processing rather than visual processing (Snowling, 2000).

Similarly, we frequently visit classrooms in which teachers assign students to look up a list of vocabulary words in the dictionary and write the definition and a sentence containing the word. This is a very commonsense practice. If we asked people on the street to suggest a good way to teach children new vocabulary, many would no doubt recommend exactly this practice. However, as it turns out, this practice often proves to be inferior to other approaches that although less common and arguably less commonsensible, actually result in greater vocabulary learning (e.g., Bos & Anders, 1990). Just as research has limitations, so too does common sense and individual judgment.

Sometimes We Do Not Know What We Do Not Know

We may not recognize experientially that something is a problem. A practice may be so widespread that it has been accepted as conventional wisdom, whether or not it is effective or true. For example, for many years in the United States, reading materials used in the primary grades were overwhelmingly stories; informational text, among other genres, was strongly neglected (Duke, Bennett-Armistead, & Roberts, 2003). Research is an important tool for documenting phenomena such as this (e.g., Duke, 2000; Moss & Newton, 2002).

Indeed, many people have shared with us that they had not really thought about how little experience children were getting within informational text in the primary grades. Others had thought about this but operated with assumptions that young children should read stories first and that reading stories was more "natural" for children than reading other genres. It turns out that this is not the case (e.g., Duke & Kays, 1998; Pappas, 1993), and research was again an important tool for examining an assumption that was taken for granted.

Research Allows Us to Take a Longer Term View Than Our Personal Experiences May Allow

A teacher typically only has one to two years with a student, and it is difficult to systematically monitor a student's progress after that time. This means that the teacher cannot

---

[1]From Duke and Martin (2011, pp. 10–11). Copyright 2011 by the International Reading Association. Reprinted by permission.

observe the long-term outcomes of his or her practices. Research can do this. Research-ers can track students as they move through the grades, for example, by administering the same assessments over multiple timepoints to understand long-term growth.

Research Allows Us into Places and Situations That We May Not Be Able to Observe Otherwise

The constraints of daily life mean that many literacy educators simply cannot engage in practices such as spending long periods of time in a child's home or observing what students do and do not do when visiting their local library. Research can provide some of this information for us. For example, Perry (e.g., 2009) spent 18 months in the homes, churches, and other settings of Sudanese refugee families. Her research provided valu-able insights about the literacy practices in which these children were and were not engaged and ways in which these practices were and were not consistent with school literacy practices. This work would have been nearly impossible for a full-time literacy educator to conduct.

Research Allows Us to Pool Our Numbers and Experiences

As individuals, we simply may not have enough experience with a question to feel confident that we have a reasonable answer. For example, a classroom teacher may not have had enough students with disorders on the autism spectrum to feel confident about which instructional approaches might be most efficacious, or a literacy coach may not have had enough experience working with teachers to know what forms of professional development are likely to result in the greatest change in teacher practice. Research allows us to pool data across many sites and settings to address important questions about phenomena and practices. In the end, we believe that research has value. It is worth learning about. It is worth paying attention to, even when it requires sorting out misrepresentation and misuse.

In this handbook, as noted earlier, every chapter begins with an *Overview of Research* and includes a *Summary of Big Ideas from Research*. The classroom examples presented draw on and are consistent with this research base, bringing professional experience together with research to instantiate effective practice.

CONCLUSION

Teaching all children to read and write well requires excellent reading instruction. Teachers need to remind themselves that materials don't teach; teachers do (Consortium for Responsible School Change in Literacy, 2005). With that power comes the responsi-bility to teach effectively. By working together, teachers and administrators both within a school and across schools can make a real difference in their students' success as read-ers and writers.

REFERENCES

Allington, R. L., & Johnston, P. H. (2002). *Reading to learn: Lessons from exemplary fourth-grade classrooms.* New York: Guilford Press.

Au, K. H., Raphael, T. E., & Mooney, K. (2008). Improving reading achievement in elementary schools: Guiding change in a time of standards. In S. B. Wepner & D. S. Strickland (Eds.), *The administration and supervision of reading programs* (4th ed., pp. 71–89). New York: Teachers College Press.

Barrera, R., & Jimenez, R. (2002). Bilingual teachers speak about their literacy instruction. In B. M. Taylor & P. D. Pearson (Eds.), *Teaching reading: Effective schools, accomplished teachers* (pp. 335–360). Mahwah, NJ: Erlbaum.

Bos, C. S., & Anders, P. L. (1990). Effects of interactive vocabulary instruction on the vocabulary learning and reading comprehension of junior-high learning disabled students. *Learning Disability Quarterly, 13*(1), 31–42.

Bryk, A. S., Sebring, P. B., Allensworth, E., Luppescu, S., & Easton, J. Q. (2010). *Organizing schools for improvement: Lessons from Chicago.* Chicago: University of Chicago Press.

Consortium for Responsible School Change in Literacy. (2005). *Description of common findings across multiple studies on school change in reading.* Minneapolis: University of Minnesota, Minnesota Center for Reading Research.

Dolezal, S. E., Welsh, L. M., Pressley, M., & Vincent, M. M. (2003). How nine third-grade teachers motivate student academic engagement. *Elementary School Journal, 103,* 239–267.

Duke, N. K. (2000). 3.6 minutes per day: The scarcity of informational texts in first grade. *Reading Research Quarterly, 35,* 202–224.

Duke, N. K., Bennett-Armistead, V. S., & Roberts, E. M. (2003). Bridging the gap between learning to read and reading to learn. In D. M. Barone & L. M. Morrow (Eds.), *Literacy and young children: Research-based practices* (pp. 226–242). New York: Guilford Press.

Duke, N. K., & Kays, J. (1998). "Can I say 'Once upon a time'?": Kindergarten children developing knowledge of information book language. *Early Childhood Research Quarterly, 13,* 295–318.

Duke, N. K., & Martin, N. M. (2011). 10 things every literacy educator should know about research. *The Reading Teacher, 65,* 9–22.

Edwards, P. A. (2004). *Children's literacy development: Making it happen through school, family, and community involvement.* Boston: Allyn & Bacon.

Foorman, B. R., & Torgesen, J. (2001). Critical elements of classroom and small-group instruction promote reading success in all children. *Learning Disabilities Research and Practice, 16,* 203–212.

Goddard, R. D., Hoy, W. K., & Hoy, A. W. (2000). Collective teacher efficacy: Its meaning, measure, and impact on student achievement. *American Educational Research Journal, 37,* 479–507.

Goddard, R. D., Tschannen-Moran, M., & Hoy, W. K. (2001). A multilevel examination of the distribution and effects of teacher trust in students and parents in urban elementary schools. *Elementary School Journal, 102,* 3–19.

Guthrie, J. T., Wigfield, A., & VonSecker, C. (2000). Effects of integrated instruction on motivation and strategy use in reading. *Journal of Educational Psychology, 92,* 331–341.

Helman, L. (2009). Effective instructional practices for English learners. In L. Helman (Ed.), *Literacy development with English learners: Research-based instruction in grades K–6* (pp. 234–251). New York: Guilford Press.

Hoffman, J. V., & Rutherford, W. L. (1984). Effective reading programs: A critical review of outlier studies. *Reading Research Quarterly, 20,* 79–92.

Knapp, M. S., & Associates. (1995). *Teaching for meaning in high-poverty classrooms.* New York: Teachers College Press.

Konstantopoulos, S., & Chung, V. (2011). The persistence of teacher effects in elementary grades. *American Educational Research Journal, 48*(2), 361–386.

Langer, J. A. (2000). Excellence in English in middle and high schools: How teachers' professional lives support students' achievement. *American Educational Research Journal, 37*(2), 397–439.

Li, G. (2011). The role of culture in literacy, learning, and teaching. In M. L. Kamil, P. D. Pearson, E. B. Moje, & P. Afflerbach (Eds.), *Handbook of reading research* (Vol. 4, pp. 515–538). New York: Routledge.

Mathes, P. G., Denton, C. A., Fletcher, J. M., Anthony, J. L., Francis, D. J., & Schatschneider, C. (2005). The effects of theoretically different instruction and student characteristics on the skills of struggling readers. *Reading Research Quarterly, 40,* 148–182.

Mosenthal, J., Lipson, M., Torncello, S., Russ, B., & Mekkelsen, J. (2004). Contexts and practices of six schools successful in obtaining reading achievement. *Elementary School Journal, 41*(5), 343–367.

Moss, B., & Newton, E. (2002). An examination of the informational text genre in basal readers. *Reading Psychology, 23*(1), 1–13.

National Governors Association for Best Practices & Council of Chief State School Officers. (2010). Common Core State Standards for English language arts and literacy in history/ social studies, science, and technical subjects. Washington, DC: Authors. Retrived from *www.corestandards.org/thestandards/english-language-arts-standards.*

National Reading Panel. (2000). *Report of the National Reading Panel.* Washington, DC: National Institute of Child Health and Human Development.

Pappas, C. C. (1993). Is narrative "primary"?: Some insights from kindergarteners' pretend readings of stories and information books. *Journal of Reading Behavior, 25*(1), 97–129.

Paris, S. G., & Paris, A. H. (2001). Classroom applications of research on self-regulated learning. *Educational Psychologist, 36,* 89–102.

Paris, S. G., Paris, A. H., & Carpenter, R. D. (2002). Effective practices for assessing young readers. In B. M. Taylor & P. D. Pearson (Eds.), *Teaching reading: Effective schools, accomplished teachers* (pp. 141–159). Mahwah, NJ: Erlbaum.

Perry, K. H. (2009). Genres, contexts, and literacy practices: Literacy brokering among Sudanese refugee families. *Reading Research Quarterly, 44*(3), 256–276.

Peterson, D. S., & Taylor, B. M. (2012). Using higher order questioning to accelerate students' growth in reading. *The Reading Teacher, 65*(5), 295–304.

Pressley, M. (2006). *Reading instruction that works: The case for balanced teaching* (3rd ed.). New York: Guilford Press.

Pressley, M., Dolezal, S. E., Raphael, L. M., Mohan, L., Roehrig, A. D., & Bogner, K. (2003). *Motivating primary-grade students.* New York: Guilford Press.

Pressley, M., Raphael, L. M., Gallagher, J. D., & Di Bella, J. (2004). Providence–St. Mel School: How a school that works for African American students works. *Journal of Educational Psychology, 96*(2), 216–235.

Pressley, M., Wharton-McDonald, R., Allington, R., Block, C. C., Morrow, L., Tracey, D., et al. (2001). A study of effective grade-1 literacy instruction. *Scientific Studies of Reading, 5,* 35–58.

Scribner, J. D., Young, M. D., & Pedroza, A. (1999). Building collaborative relationships with parents. In P. Reyes, J. D. Scribner, & A. P. Scribner (Eds.), *Lessons from high-performing Hispanic schools* (pp. 36–60). New York: Teachers College.

Spillane, J. P., Halverson, R., & Diamond, J. B. (2001). Investigating school leadership practice: A distributive perspective. *Educational Researcher, 30*(3), 23–28.

Snowling, M. J. (2000). *Dyslexia* (2nd ed.). Malden, MA: Blackwell.

Stringfield, S., Millsap, M. A., & Herman, R. (1997). *Urban and suburban/rural special strategies for educating disadvantaged children: Findings and policy implications of a longitudinal study.* Washington, DC: U.S. Department of Education.

Taylor, B. M. (2002a). *Characteristics of schools that are effective in teaching all children to read.* Washington, DC: National Education Association.

Taylor, B. M. (2002b). *Characteristics of teachers who are effective in teaching all children to read.* Washington, DC: National Education Association.

Taylor, B. M. (2002c). Highly accomplished primary grade teachers in effective schools. In B. M. Taylor & P. D. Pearson (Eds.), *Teaching reading: Effective schools, accomplished teachers* (pp. 279–288). Mahwah, NJ: Erlbaum.

Taylor, B. M., Pearson, P. D., Clark, K., & Walpole, S. (2000). Effective schools and accomplished teachers: Lessons about primary-grade reading instruction in low-income schools. *Elementary School Journal, 101,* 121–165.

Taylor, B. M., Pearson, P. D., Peterson, D. S., & Rodriguez, M. C. (2003). Reading growth in high-poverty classrooms: The influence of teacher practices that encourage cognitive engagement in literacy learning. *Elementary School Journal, 104,* 3–28.

Taylor, B. M., Pearson, P. D., Peterson, D. S., & Rodriguez, M. (2005). The CIERA School Change Project: An evidence-based approach to professional development and school reading improvement. *Reading Research Quarterly, 40*(1), 40–69.

Taylor, B. M., Peterson, D. S., Marx, M., & Chein, M. (2007). Scaling up a reading reform effort in 23 high-poverty schools. In B. M. Taylor & J. Ysseldyke (Eds.), *Effective instruction for struggling readers, K–6* (pp. 216–234). New York: Teachers College Press.

Taylor, B. M., Pressley, M., & Pearson, P. D. (2002). Research-supported characteristics of teachers and schools that promote reading achievement. In B. M. Taylor & P. D. Pearson (Eds.), *Teaching reading: Effective schools, accomplished teachers* (pp. 361–374). Mahwah, NJ: Erlbaum.

Taylor, B. M., Raphael, T. E., & Au, K. H. (2011). Reading and school reform. In M. L. Kamil, P. D. Pearson, E. B. Moje, & P. Afflerbach (Eds.), *Handbook of reading research* (Vol. 4, pp. 594–628). New York: Routledge.

Wharton-McDonald, R., Pressley, M., & Hampston, J. M. (1998). Outstanding literacy instruction in first grade: Teacher practices and student achievement. *Elementary School Journal, 99,* 101–128.

PART I

Fundamental Components of Effective Literacy Lessons

Motivating Classroom Practices to Support Effective Literacy Instruction ● ● ● ● ● ● ● ● ● ● ● ●

ALYSIA D. ROEHRIG
ELIZABETH HAMMOND BRINKERHOFF
ERIK S. RAWLS
TIM PRESSLEY

What is *motivation*, and how do we motivate students? We used social networking with friends and colleagues to survey some educators informally about their definitions and methods. They told us that motivation is "when a student wants to do something" (grade 3 English as a second language [ESL] inclusion teacher); when students are "focusing on a task and not stopping until that task is completed" (elementary school principal); and "when they want to complete something for their own satisfaction of being successful" (middle school language arts teacher). One grade 2 general education teacher said, "I motivate my students by *loving* them, *believing* in them, and *igniting* a desire to want to learn more!"

Motivation can also be defined according to various theoretical perspectives (such as the behavioral or cognitive traditions in psychology), yet there are common elements between those and the definitions of teachers (such as learners' interest and engagement). Goals are another common element that researchers have posited may be important for defining motivation (Schunk, 2008). For example, Pintrich and Schunk (2002) defined motivation as the process of sustaining behavior and cognition in order to reach a goal. Beyond learners' interest and engagement, other factors that have an impact on motivation include variables within a learner (e.g., emotions, values) and students' interactions with the learning environment (e.g., teachers' behavior and affect). Clearly, then, effective literacy instruction practices are implemented in the context of complex, social environments that present multiple moving targets: students with different skills, backgrounds, and needs that may shift with developmental changes.

We believe that all effective teachers want to motivate their students, but, given the complex interaction between teachers and learners in the classroom environment, how do they go about doing this? What specific aspects of their own teaching behaviors, their classroom environment, and the diversity of their students should teachers keep in mind when trying to motivate their students? Although effective teachers are masters at juggling many projects and goals simultaneously, we argue that when teachers have all the elements described in this chapter in place, motivating students is easier and more achievable. In our experience, the motivating practices related to classroom atmosphere, self-regulation (i.e., teachers' monitoring and changing their own responses to try to meet goals), and engaging instructional techniques are interdependent. They reinforce each other, while also supporting classroom management and providing intellectual challenge for all students.

As educators, we seek to promote an environment in the classroom that is conducive to learning for all of our students. Some learners are at a higher risk for learning difficulties, and these "at-risk" learners may or may not have been identified and categorized with one of the following labels: *exceptional student education* (ESE), *English language learner* (ELL), or *low socioeconomic status* (low SES). Students who are identified as belonging to one of these categories are provided with additional academic and financial accommodations mandated by state and federal law. In addition, some students who don't qualify for these labels may also be at risk, perhaps because their own goals and motivations as readers and writers do not match those of mainstream education (Ivey & Broaddus, 2007). These students too may slip through our school system without the additional support that they need. Even with additional support, at-risk students have a high rate of failure throughout their educational careers, which may ultimately end with their dropping out of school. Researchers cited by Ream (2008, p. 110; see the Ream article for references) have identified

> numerous factors that contribute to students' early departure from school, including the demographic characteristics of students and their families (Alexander, Entwisle, & Kabbani, 2001; Hauser, Simmons, & Pager, 2000), parenting practices (McNeal, 1999; Teachman, Paasch, & Carver, 1996), residential and educational mobility (Ream & Stanton-Salazar, 2007; Rumberger & Larson, 1998; Swanson & Schneider, 1999), grade retention (Jimerson, Anderson, & Whipple, 2002; Stearns et al., 2007), school performance and educational aspirations (Bridgeland, Dilulio, & Morison, 2006; Rumberger, 1987), and school and community characteristics (Rumberger, 2004).

Using engaging teaching strategies to motivate and meet the needs of *all* students, regardless of learning challenges or exceptionalities (i.e., giftedness), is the educator's responsibility.

In this chapter, we describe the classroom practices that research evidence suggests support student motivation, and we focus on how to implement and adapt these for all types of learners across the elementary and middle school contexts. In the *Overview of Research* section, we first describe the practices related to classroom atmosphere that we believe are nearly universal for motivating students, emphasizing the importance of genuine concern and high expectations for all students. Goal setting in that context, as well as the context of supporting student autonomy, helps set the stage not only for positive classroom management but for the development of self-regulated learners. We then consider how students' engagement in learning can be enhanced by instructional practices that can further help teachers support students' motivation. In the sections that follow the *Overview of Research*, we consider how teachers and school leaders can work together to support each other in enhancing students' literacy engagement and learning. There we offer suggestions for questions you might want to consider as you read each section of this chapter, as well as a structure for professional learning community sessions you might use to help you implement the practices we describe.

OVERVIEW OF RESEARCH

Creating a Motivating Classroom Atmosphere

No matter the grade or subject taught, a positive classroom environment is often one of the main ingredients for providing an engaging and welcoming learning atmosphere for students. Teachers must provide a caring classroom environment with rules and routines so that all students feel safe. This environment must also meet each student's educational needs. Teachers can provide this engaging environment by promoting high expectations for academics as well as for behavior, so that all students can succeed. Providing a safe haven for students may be accomplished in many ways, such as developing positive rapport with students, having a classroom management system that is fair and consistent, and building a classroom community by establishing expectations that everyone treat one another with respect. In this section, we look at research-based programs and empirically derived techniques to help teachers foster an effective teaching environment that is mutually supportive of positive behavioral classroom management and learning outcomes (Dolezal, Welsh, Pressley, & Vincent, 2003).

Building Relationships

"Effective teaching begins with the establishment of relationships between the teacher and students" (Bondy, Ross, Gallingane, & Hambacher, 2007, p. 331). As part of building a classroom community, teachers must focus on creating relationships with their students that allow teachers to learn about their students as individuals. Knowing about students' instructional and personal needs allows

> **Community-Building Activities We've Tried**
>
> - Play "get to know you" bingo.
> - Brainstorm hopes and dreams (goals for year and future).
> - Develop classroom rules and guidelines.
>
> For more ideas, see *The First Six Weeks of School* (Denton & Kriete, 2000).

teachers to build curriculum that supports academic achievement (Bondy et al., 2007). Community building is so important that teachers should begin to make this connection with students within the first few hours of the first day of school. Bondy et al. give examples of three teachers (in diverse, urban elementary schools) sharing things about themselves, showing photos, and being candid with their new students on the first day of school to help build a connection with their students. These teachers also provided activities for the students to begin to interact with their peers and the teachers; such interaction is key to beginning to build the classroom community, especially when a class is culturally diverse. (Bondy et al., 2007, focused on the culturally responsive classroom in their study, as do McIntyre & Turner, Chapter 6, this volume.)

> **Marzano's (2007) Eight Action Steps**
>
> 1. Know something about each student.
> 2. Engage in behaviors that indicate affection for each student.
> 3. Bring student interests into the content and personalize learning activities.
> 4. Engage in physical behaviors that communicate interest in students.
> 5. Use humor when appropriate.
> 6. Consistently enforce positive and negative consequences.
> 7. Project a sense of emotional objectivity.
> 8. Maintain a cool exterior. (pp. 154–161)

Besides starting the school year by making connections with students and building community, Marzano (2007) suggests eight action steps to communicate concern and cooperation in the classroom. These steps are highlighted in the box above. One step Marzano suggests is using physical behavior to communicate interest, which can be useful when teachers are pressed for time or are working with students from different cultures. By using positive physical communication, such as smiling or leaning in when talking with a student, teachers can provide positive feedback to students as they move around the classroom.

By providing nonverbal cues to students, teachers can begin to build a positive rapport with their students through simple daily interactions. "This rapport allows teachers to better use their limited conferencing time with students by being more direct with their verbal feedback and worrying less about how their feedback will impact students' feelings" (Martin & Mottet, 2011, p. 12). For students who are labeled at risk, it is even more important for teachers to create positive relationships with their students and to push them academically. Students who do not feel cared about may be more likely to react negatively to corrective academic feedback. It has been reported that students who believe their teachers care about them are more likely to become engaged and find success in their academics, as well as to spend more time and effort on homework (Wilson & Corbett, 2001).

Managing Behavior

Besides building positive rapport with students, teachers must develop and promote a classroom management system that has well-defined routines, rules, and consequences in order to create a positive classroom community. Establishing procedures on the very first day and reviewing them repeatedly is key for developing an engaging classroom environment. The teachers observed by Bondy and colleagues (2007) established rules and routines in their own unique ways, but all three introduced them within the first 2 hours of the first day. Along with introducing each rule and routine, the teachers gave justification so students would understand why each rule and routine was important for their classroom and learning. In addition, the teachers made sure to set clear expectations by modeling positive examples and frequently reviewing these expectations with their students (Ross, Bondy, Gallingane, & Hambacher, 2008). Overall, effective teachers should strive to provide environments with a strong, proactive classroom management system, which is supported by engaging students in instruction and content (Dolezal et al., 2003). For example, the classroom contract depicted in the photo on the right makes rules and expectations clear.

Class Rules/Expectations

1) Be respectful of others
2) Listen & pay attention to speaker
3) Keep hands/feets/objects to yourself
4) Give 100% best attitude and effort
5) Give compliments for good behavior

A research-based elementary school program, which fosters a productive learning environment through daily community-building activities, is the Responsive Classroom (RC) model. This model is designed to "bolster children's academic, social, and emotional growth" (McTigue & Rimm-Kaufman, 2011, p. 6). The RC type of classroom management focuses on the needs of the students and provides an environment that allows students to grow both academically and as individuals. The RC model fosters academic, social, and emotional growth through several daily classroom practices, including the morning meeting (MM), using proactive discipline, and using descriptive language in the classroom. An example of descriptive language use is having students and teachers share specific items during MM. A teacher can welcome a student by saying, "I see John smiling at me. Good morning" (McTigue & Rimm-Kaufman, 2011, p. 16); student might use descriptive language like this when sharing at MM, "My name is Teresa Tiger, which begins with a /t/. One thing I like about tigers is that they have stripes" (p. 16).

One of the ways a teacher can promote student growth is by encouraging students to work independently or in small groups with little direction from the teacher (for more on this topic, see the discussions of student autonomy and cooperative learning in this chapter). This allows the classroom teacher to spend less time dealing with inappropriate behaviors and more time on instruction (Rimm-Kaufman & Chiu, 2007). The focus on how students learn, in the RC model, has a positive impact on students' academic achievement (McTigue & Rimm-Kaufman, 2011). The RC model has also been adapted for use in middle school with the Circle of Power and Respect. With the Circle of Power and Respect, aspects of the RC model serve the needs and challenges of middle school students. The Circle of Power and Respect also "offers middle school students stability and predictability during a time in life marked by tumultuous emotional, physical, and cognitive change" (Kriete with Bechtel, 2002, p. 105).

Positive relationships between teacher and students can stimulate student academic achievement as well as decrease disruptive classroom behavior (Hamre & Pianta, 2001). Rimm-Kaufman and Chiu (2007) found the use of the RC model effective for building student social skills; not only did students display an increase in positive social behaviors, but teachers described an increase in student assertiveness and autonomy in the classroom. We next describe an MM lesson, which shows how teachers can engage all students academically, socially, and emotionally every morning while also incorporating some literacy instruction, so no extra time is needed or wasted to implement a successful classroom management system! MM includes four components: the greeting, sharing, an activity, and the news and announcements (for MM resources, see Kriete with Bechtel, 2002). In this classroom example, we visit Ms. Johns's grade 3 class in a high-poverty, high-minority elementary school. (To protect students' privacy, all names have been changed.)

CLASSROOM EXAMPLE: MM LESSON

Ms. Johns begins each day with the MM. Students gather in a circle on the carpet at the front of the room. During MM, students start with a greeting by turning to their neighbor on either side and shaking hands while saying "Good morning" and calling the student by name. Following the greeting, Ms. Johns reviews the procedure for "sharing" and chooses the first person to share. The student proceeds to tell two or three sentences about what he or she wants to share, and other students listen attentively. When the student has finished sharing, the student calls on two people to ask questions. This sharing is repeated by another student, and then Ms. Johns leads the class in giving a cheer for those who shared. All of the students clap two times and say "Good job" and the names of the students who shared.

The next event in MM is an activity, and on this day Ms. Johns has chosen "Catch a Horse," an activity she developed with her class. Ms. Johns reviews the procedure for this activity, which involves all of the students pretending to be horses except for one student, who pretends to be the rancher. The rancher attempts to catch the horses by tagging them and sending them to the corral, which is located in a designated area in the room. During the activity, Ms. Johns monitors the students, making comments to individuals such as "Thank you for being honest," when the students move into the corral after being caught. She uses a chime to end the activity. Then Ms. Johns instructs the students to give the cheer: "Yeehaw!"

Students recreate the circle at the front of the room for the final part of MM: news and announcements. Ms. Johns chooses a student's name from a can and calls the student to read the announcement, recreated in the box on the next page, which she has written on a chart. The student reads aloud as others read silently. Following the reading, students applaud the reader, and Ms. Johns asks the class, "Are there any questions about today's message?" She answers any questions, and students return to their seats prepared for their day.

News and Announcements

Good morning, Star Students,

Today is Fabulous Friday! I'm looking forward to our day ahead. We will continue renaming numbers—no worries. It will get easier, I promise! We will also begin the exploration of the continents and oceans found on our globe! Finally, we will explore Dr. Jamie Stevens's [a student in the class who will lead the activity] baking soda and vinegar experiment together!!! Let's have a fabulous day.

♥ *Ms. Johns*

By using MM to begin each day, Ms. Johns creates an energized learning climate. Students have had the opportunity to continue building a respectful, trusting relationship with their teacher and their peers. At-risk students from low-income households, such as those in Ms. Johns's class, recognize the need to belong to their school community, however, as these students progress through school, they may see belonging to their school community as unrealistic for themselves, due to poor achievement, high-stress households, and poor peer relationships. Often these students try to acquire this sense of belonging by becoming members of other types of groups, such as gangs. Battistich, Solomon, Kim, Watson, and Schaps (1995) suggest that "a way to change this may be to create school communities in which all students feel accepted and valued and to which they feel they are making important contributions" (p. 628). In the RC model, these students become members of the class and develop a sense of community in a safe and caring environment: "Although the deleterious effects of poverty are well known, . . . some of its negative effects can be mitigated if the school is successful in creating a caring community for its members" (Battistich et al., 1995, p. 649).

Focusing on Goals

The use of goals is another way teachers can motivate and engage students. This is exemplified by one grade 4 teacher, who shared the following with us:

"I usually motivate them by reminding them of their ultimate goal, passing their grade level. But I also remind them of other goals such as TAKS [Texas Assessment of Knowledge and Skills], weekly tests, and daily assignments. I just think the main part of staying motivated for me and the kids is just being positive. If we're all positive, it makes it a lot easier. Whether a small success or a big one, just seeing them happy is important."

Goal setting in the classroom is a growing practice. Teachers identify the learning objectives and assist students in setting goals for their own learning; by doing this, students become responsible for their personal achievement. Students' identification of the learning goals and the importance of achieving these goals motivates the students to strive for mastery of these goals.

Even in a highly motivating environment, it is possible for some students to remain unengaged, and often the unengaged students are among the at-risk students in the class. When this happens, one way to motivate such students is by guiding them as they set goals for themselves. Szente (2007) advocates the use of Action Plans, a type of student contract. An Action Plan creates an opportunity for a student to identify personal goals academically, behaviorally, or both, based on self-identified need. A teacher guides the students by reviewing the observable behaviors (or academic issues), followed by a discussion with the student. With the help of the teacher, the student is able to identify a "specific, short-range goal along with certain clear steps that are needed to achieve that specific goal" (Szente, 2007, p. 4). Goal setting (for both academics and behaviors) has supported learners in achieving success and building self-efficacy at all cognitive levels in elementary school and middle school (Williams-Diehm, Palmer, Lee, & Schroer, 2010). In the following examples, the goal-setting routines of two teachers working with students who have special needs are described.

CLASSROOM EXAMPLES: GOAL-SETTING ROUTINES

When asked about her goal-setting practices in her elementary school class for students with multiple disabilities, Ms. Williamson identified strategies that she uses with her students. She began by explaining her behavior chart system, which incorporates the use of picture symbols representing activities during the day on a contract for each individual student. The class rules are listed across the top of the contract in picture format, and students earn smiley faces (and, in turn, earn rewards) by successfully accomplishing appropriate behavior for each event in the day. Before beginning the day, Ms. Williamson meets with each individual student to set a goal for the number of smiley faces that the individual will try to earn for the day. For her students with autism, she provides goal-setting guidance in the form of identifying their goal for each learning activity for each part of the day. This is challenging for the students and time-consuming for Ms. Williamson, but she states that "students are completing each task and following the rules . . . an accomplishment for my students."

Down the hall in the same elementary school is Ms. West's inclusion classroom, which includes students in ESE and those in general education. Her system for setting goals with her students focuses on student mastery of academic benchmarks from state standards. Each Friday, students have a goal-setting time where they review their own achievement for the week in a small-group meeting with the teacher. Ms. West's system provides a tabbed notebook for each student, which includes sections for setting long-term year and life goals, reading and mathematics mastery goals, and process writing goals. During the goal-setting meeting, students graph progress, set goals for their achievement in the following week, examine the progress they are making toward long-term goals, identify the strengths and weaknesses in their learning from the previous week, and decide on strategies for improvement as needed. Doing this supports students' ownership of their progress and control of their learning.

Both teachers give feedback to their students during goal-setting times. Regular feedback reinforces the importance of learning and achieving the goals, and their students are engaged and motivated to meet the goals. All in all, "by learning appropriate goal-setting procedures and receiving continuous feedback and monitoring from adults, most children can take on the academic challenges of today's schools" (Szente, 2007, p. 5).

The idea of goal setting is also related to the goal orientation of the classroom. In the current climate of standards-based testing, there is a risk that students and teachers will tend to focus more on performance goals (which emphasize scores and grades) than on mastery goals (which focus on learning and mastering content). However, "students who adopt mastery goals have been shown to choose challenging tasks (Ames & Archer, 1988), become involved in the learning process (Nicholls, Cheung, Lauer, & Patashnick, 1989), and use effective study strategies (Nolen & Haladyna, 1990)" (Hidi & Harackiewicz, 2000, p. 161; see this article for the references cited). Although performance goals are not always associated with negative outcomes (for a review, see Hidi & Harackiewicz, 2000), positive effects are most often found for mastery goals or a combination of mastery and performance goals. Students with learning disabilities (LD), however, seem to be more sensitive to the negative potential effects of performance goal structures. When comparing students in grades 4 and 5 with and without LD, Sideridis (2005) found that in classrooms with performance goal structures, the students with LD were less engaged.

Developing Independent Learners

Goals continue to play a vital role in this section, where we describe the context and practices associated with developing independent learners. Students grow into independent learners through a combination of their individual characteristics and qualities of their learning environments. Higher order skills like self-regulation are important in learners' management of goals, cognitions, and behaviors, and so are learners' basic psychological needs (Schunk, 2008). For example, learners need to feel liked, or to sense that they belong, and to feel that they have control over their own learning. Learners also need to feel that they can effectively enact common school behaviors, including (1) engaging in tasks, (2) completing tasks, and (3) performing well in school—all of which contribute to a feeling of success. One of our colleagues aptly described the role of the teacher in fostering independence in learners as "creating an authentic interpersonal academic relationship in which the impetus for personal and academic growth shifts from being primarily teacher-driven to primarily student-driven" (social studies coordinator).

As our colleague suggests, independent learners possess the outstanding quality of self-regulation, which enables them to direct their thoughts, feelings, and behaviors toward the achievement of goals. In order for teachers to develop motivated, independent learners, they must encourage self-regulation in their students. Another hallmark of independent learners is their ability to identify, set, and accomplish their own goals. Learners choose their own goals, apply strategies to accomplish their goals, and possess a metacognitive awareness of the  learning process—for instance, by monitoring their own progress toward goals (see Boekaerts, 1999). Self-regulated students evaluate their own learning by asking personally evaluative questions such as "Am I making acceptable progress?"

But how do we explain situations in which learners are able to self-regulate but choose not to do so? Boekaerts (1999) has pointed out that students may be able to plan, monitor, and evaluate, but they may also perceive that these skills require extra time or energy. Thus it is important that students value learning, which can happen when, as discussed in the previous section, teachers create positive, learning-focused classroom environments. This process involves teacher modeling of enthusiasm and what is valued (see more on modeling under *Promoting Engagement through Instructional Practices*, below). Boekaerts has recommended giving students frequent opportunities in class to reflect on and communicate their personal goals, as well as goals influenced by others (e.g., teachers, parents). Teachers can also model self-regulated thought processes by thinking aloud. For example, teachers can model identifying learning goals for a particular assignment by asking questions like "What different parts of this task should I consider in order to help me complete my goal?" or "What skills and personal qualities do I possess that will help me complete this task?" To provide optimal supports for student motivation to be self-regulated, however, educators should think about how they can support students' basic needs for *autonomy*, *relatedness*, and *competence*. This can be achieved via a combination of all the strategies covered in this chapter.

Basic Needs: Autonomy, Relatedness, and Competence

Autonomy, competence, and relatedness are connected in the learning process, and a great deal of empirical work has led researchers to conclude that all three needs should be met for optimal learning (Deci, Koestner, & Ryan, 1999b; Niemiec & Ryan, 2009; Ryan & Deci, 2000). The term *independent learners* can refer to self-regulated learners, but independent learners can also be described as having a strong sense of autonomy. *Autonomy* refers to "the sense that one's actions emanate from one's self" (Reeve & Jang, 2006, p. 209). Students who possess greater self-determination or autonomy believe that they are engaging in a learning task of their own free choice and volition (Deci et al., 1999b). In other words, they feel that they have some control over their own learning and performance.

Students choose to engage in countless behaviors every day in school. The need for *competence* refers to their belief that those behaviors have been enacted effectively; teachers can build competence in their students by providing a learning environment and activities that are optimally challenging (Niemiec & Ryan, 2009). An optimal challenge level is neither so difficult that a child cannot successfully complete a task, nor is it so easy that the child becomes bored. Therefore, teachers are challenged to monitor and promote individual students' performance, but also to consider the individual needs of a class full of diverse learners. Supporting students with appropriate feedback can effectively build competence in students (Linnebrink & Pintrich, 2003; Niemiec & Ryan, 2009; Ryan & Deci, 2000; Shute, 2008).

The need for *relatedness* is common to students and teachers alike, who all experience the basic need to belong and to form strong, stable relationships (Baumeister & Leary, 1995). Teachers foster the need for relatedness by creating positive classroom environments. The need for relatedness is important in classrooms because it has been linked to the process of internalization of values for learning (Niemiec & Ryan, 2009). We have highlighted strategies for supporting relatedness in *Creating a Motivating Classroom Atmosphere*, above, so we focus on autonomy and competence supports in this section after introducing *self-determination theory* (SDT). SDT is based on the three psychological needs of learners (i.e., autonomy, competence, and relatedness), which teachers can meet with specific practices applicable to learners. It was originally developed to explain relationships among motivation, emotion, and human development (Niemiec & Ryan, 2009). In particular, SDT focuses on learning environments (including teachers) and the effects they have on learners.

In SDT, there is an emphasis on the importance of intrinsic motivation in human development—in other words, the "evolved inner resources for personality development and behavioral self-regulation" (Ryan & Deci, 2000, p. 68). This sentiment was captured in some of the educators' definitions of motivation we have shared at the beginning of this chapter. To date, a great deal of empirical research has been conducted on the effects of extrinsic rewards on intrinsic motivation in the context of SDT (Deci, Koestner, & Ryan, 1999a). Research in this area of motivation strongly suggests that teachers should not frequently rely on tangible external rewards because they can decrease a student's preexisting intrinsic motivation or interest for a particular activity. Within the context of a positive learning environment, teachers should work to deemphasize or phase out extrinsic rewards. SDT also accounts for how a student's motivation may progress from externally manipulated and controlling sources such as rewards to internalized values that are socially acquired (Niemiec & Ryan, 2009; Ryan & Deci, 2000).

Supporting Autonomy for Students

Of particular benefit for teachers, SDT considers both positive and negative aspects of environments or social contexts, providing us with lists of "dos" and "don'ts" (i.e., teacher behaviors that have been theorized and observed to enhance or diminish a student's sense of autonomy). Autonomy-supportive instructional practices include asking students what they want, spending time listening to students as opposed to talking, and providing students with rationale for courses of action. In contrast, some prominent controlling (autonomy-thwarting) instructional practices include frequently using spoken directives or commands, giving solutions or answers rather than letting students come to them on their own, criticizing students, or using praise as a contingent reward to reinforce ability, correct answers, or compliance (Reeve & Jang, 2006). Verbal "praise" in the form of specific instructional feedback about progress or mastery, however, is less controlling. Offering hints when students are stuck, instead of giving answers, and responding to student questions can also support autonomy.

Inevitably, however, teachers must adequately manage their classrooms, so where do they draw the line between behavioral control and control that stifles the autonomy of students? A clear distinction exists between directly controlling teacher behaviors (DCTB) and behavioral control (Assor, Kaplan, Kanat-Maymon, & Roth, 2005; Nie & Lau, 2009). DCTB are "explicit attempts to fully and instantly change the behaviors children presently engage in or the opinions they hold" (Assor et al., 2005, p. 398); these are the "don'ts" that are associated with negative emotions, like anger and anxiety, in students.

> **Directly Controlling Teacher Behaviors (DCTB or "Don'ts")**
>
> - Frequently using directives.
> - Preventing students from working at the pace they prefer.
> - Prohibiting students from expressing opinions that differ from the expressed opinions of the teacher.
> - Criticizing students.
> - Providing feedback/praise on ability, correct answers, or compliance.

Behavioral control, in contrast to DCTB, can be narrowly defined as attempts to change or correct misbehavior and sustain desirable behavior. As discussed above, teachers often establish a social structure early in the school year, based on clear rules and expectations; in this case, the environment as a whole, rather than teacher behavior alone, may be said to provide control for students that does not inherently reduce autonomy or, by extension, intrinsic motivation (Nie & Lau, 2009). SDT posits that students internalize social values, and that holding such values represents a type of motivation most closely associated with intrinsic motivation. Thus teachers' attempts to foster classroom community should involve consideration of what values students can glean from the environment. Modifications of autonomy practices also need to be considered by teachers working with at-risk learners. Friend and Bursuck's (2009) book has many strategies for promoting the autonomy of students with special needs across many subject areas and levels of inclusion. Some other suggestions we have found helpful for promoting at-risk learners' autonomy are provided in the box on the right.

> **Promoting Autonomy
> for the At-Risk Learner ("Dos")**
>
> - Pair the student with a more able peer for cooperative learning activities.
> - Practice routines thoroughly and regularly.
> - For those who need it, provide high-interest, low-level reading materials.
> - Provide recorded directions for students to use as needed.
> - Teach students to use graphic organizers.
> - Differentiate assignments by using open-ended projects.
> - Use a student contract or behavior checklist (see Burke, 2000, Ch. 4, for examples).

Supporting Competence for Students

Motivating students can entail expressing high expectations to students while also drawing upon students' need for competence, as a grade 4 teacher explains:

> "I think motivation is explaining to the kids the feeling they'll have when they see how well they did, whether it's a daily assignment, [a] weekly test, or the state assessment. I let them know how awesome it is to have that feeling of success."

Learners' beliefs about their competence are conceptually very similar to their self-efficacy beliefs. Whereas *competence* refers to students' beliefs that behaviors have been successfully enacted, *self-efficacy* beliefs are larger in scope and future-focused (Bandura, 1997; Schunk, 2005, 2008); however, these concepts are often treated as roughly equivalent (e.g., Ryan & Deci, 2000). A student might have higher self-efficacy for math than writing, or for accomplishing learning goals at school than at home. Self-efficacy beliefs have been widely studied along with motivation and self-regulation (Schunk, 2005, 2008). For example, in the literature on goal orientation, self-efficacy is associated with the pursuit of learning or mastery goals (Schunk, 2008). Students' "self-efficacy is substantiated as they work on the task and assess their progress (Wentzel, 1992). Perceived progress in skill-acquisition and self-efficacy for continued learning sustain motivation and enhance skillful performance (Schunk, 1996)" (Schunk, 2008, pp. 487–488; see Schunk's book for the references cited).

Self-efficacy beliefs come into play during the planning and forethought stages of self-regulation. Learners' self-efficacy beliefs are also informed by teacher feedback during engagement in a learning task. Hattie and Timperley (2007) have noted that the most effective teacher feedback provides students with meaningful information about how they are performing on a task and how they can perform more effectively. Effective feedback can apply to information related to (1) the attainment of learning goals, (2) students' progress toward completing goals, and (3) greater possibilities for learning (Hattie & Timperley, 2007). Hattie and Timperley have recommended focusing feedback on tasks or the processes of applying skills and strategies, instead of focusing it on learners. Shute (2008) has also recommended focusing feedback on tasks and suggested using feedback to provide a learning goal orientation. Feedback should be clear and specific, and should not be confused with general praise (e.g., "Good work!"). Deci and colleagues (1999b) have observed that positive feedback can enhance intrinsic motivation to learn.

Linnenbrink and Pintrich (2003) reinforced the relationship among competence, self-efficacy, and feedback. They have summarized the importance of maintaining high expectations, and of making students aware that competence is changeable and within a student's control, not fixed (see the box on the right).

> **Linnenbrink and Pintrich's (2003) Recommendations for Supporting Positive Motivational Outcomes**
>
> 1. "Help students maintain relatively high but accurate self-efficacy beliefs" (p. 134) by providing specific feedback to the students about the task and their skills.
> 2. Give students a chance to be successful on tasks that are slightly above their level by providing "students with challenging academic tasks that most students can reach with effort" (p. 135).
> 3. "Foster the belief that competence or ability is a changeable, controllable aspect of development" by communicating "positive, high expectations for all students" (p. 135).
> 4. "Promote students' domain specific self-efficacy beliefs rather than global self-esteem" (p. 135) by providing accurate feedback about performance in the academic domain.

CLASSROOM EXAMPLE: USING DATA NOTEBOOKS WITH A READING INTERVENTION GROUP

Originally used for formative assessment in the field of science, data notebooks for student documentation of progress can be very helpful for motivating students (see Valencia and Hebard, Chapter 5, this volume, for more about ongoing assessments). Nelson (2010) has used science notebooks to help keep her students, who are ELLs, motivated during learning; she commented that "they provide a formative assessment of both writing skills in English and content mastery. We can easily analyze how a student has grasped the language and the lesson topic" (p. 51). Ms. Wood has taken the idea of notebooks a step further by modifying the use of notebooks to support student autonomy during remedial small-group instruction for students receiving ESE in her grade 2 classroom. She recognizes that her students must relate their practice work to their own competence by looking at previous pages and identifying their improvement. She supports students in their efforts by frequently reviewing previous learning and helping her students to make reflective goal statements.

Highlights!

- Data-keeping notebooks for reading
- Self-evaluation
- Reflective thinking
- Relating effort to competence
- Self-identification of strengths and weaknesses
- Specific task-focused feedback from teacher

Ms. Wood's reading intervention group includes five grade 2 students who are working below grade level. As the students gather at the small table at the back of the room, Ms. Wood begins with a review of procedures, distribution of the materials (textbooks, pencils, and data-keeping notebooks for reading), and a greeting. Ms. Wood told us, "The greeting and a minute to share are the most important part of having my students engaged and ready to begin." Students are on task as Ms. Wood greets each student individually and allows the students to share two sentences about what they are thinking about today and how they are feeling. This time of sharing creates a calm and trusting environment where students are ready to learn.

After the sharing, Ms. Wood reviews previous learning by turning to the previous page and eliciting from her students a restatement of the previous lesson, where students made a prediction, recorded new words, wrote clarification questions, and evaluated their previous work. This is the second time that students have read this story, and Ms. Wood focuses the group on the objective question for the day: "What jobs do meerkats have?" (Kovalevs & Dewsbury, 2006, p. 32). Students have the opportunity to review the main idea of the story, write the main idea, and create a "circle map" (Hyerle & Yeager, 2007, p. 7) of the jobs of meerkats, based on the story. After creating their individual graphic organizers, students take turns sharing these jobs as other students give each peer a thumbs-up in agreement, and Ms. Wood adds the job to the group map, which she creates on a dry-erase board. Following the creation of the group circle map, students make reflective comments concerning their own products. One student writes, "I had almost all of the jobs listed, but my writing is hard to read." With this statement, Ms. Wood quietly discusses what he did well and what he could do differently at the next meeting. After putting their notebooks away, students have the opportunity to choose to view a short video about meerkats or to search for additional information on the Internet about meerkats; both of these are learning activities that also act as rewards for students.

Students in Ms. Wood's intervention group stay motivated to learn because of their ability to reflect on their learning and make choices during their day. Her interaction with her small group of students keeps them on task throughout the lesson, and the use of notebooks and reflective thinking helps students to relate their effort to their progress. The relationship that she has built with her students creates an environment where students trust and respect her and each other; because of this ideal learning environment, she is able to motivate low-performing students by providing a safe place to learn, structured, well-planned lessons, and feedback in response to students' reflection on their own notebook entries.

Promoting Engagement through Instructional Practices

In this section, we focus on a few research-based instructional practices for increasing student engagement, including teacher modeling, cooperative learning, and making interdisciplinary connections. But what is student *engagement*? Engagement is a concept closely tied to motivation. Three types of engagement include positive *behaviors, cognitions,* and *motivations* that research shows are associated with better student learning and achievement (for a more detailed discussion of this framework, see Linnenbrink & Pintrich, 2003). *Behavioral engagement* includes the observable student behaviors of expending effort and avoiding distractions, persisting in tasks even when faced with difficulties, and seeking help from others in order to better learn or understand. *Cognitive engagement* is harder to observe, but is important to consider. A student might appear to be on task, but he or she might not be using appropriate cognitive and metacognitive strategies to understand what is read and to self-assess comprehension. Having students talk about what they are thinking while reading, just as teachers can model what they are thinking during strategy use as a form of instruction, is a good way to try to determine whether and how students are cognitively engaged.

We have found indicators of the third type, *motivational engagement,* to be more evident or naturally elicited, as it seems easier for students to express their interests, values, and affect in their language and emotional cues. Emotions and personal interests (see Ainley, 2006) are associated with the use of learning strategies, self-regulation, achievement, and motivation (Pekrun, Goetz, & Titz, 2002). When students are not personally interested in a subject or activity, they may choose to engage behaviorally (and may be more likely to engage cognitively) if they are persuaded that the subject/activity is important or can help them achieve a goal. Teachers should attend to all three types of engagement because it is possible, for example, to appear behaviorally engaged and yet not to be cognitively or motivationally engaged (Linnenbrink & Pintrich, 2003).

CLASSROOM EXAMPLE: AN ENGAGING READING/LANGUAGE ARTS LESSON

The following engaging lesson was recently observed in a colleague's upper elementary classroom, in which indicators of students' behavioral and motivational engagement were seen throughout. In Ms. Long's class, the students' faces were lit up and smiling, with enjoyment further expressed in laughter. The students also displayed eagerness to participate in their body language (e.g., leaning forward on their desks). Not one complaint was heard, and the students even requested favorite activities during this 50-minute writing block in a departmentalized fourth grade at a high-poverty, high-minority elementary school.

On the observation day, Ms. Long began the lesson with review and practice of previously learned skills followed by a process writing mini-lesson, modeling of the writing for the day, and student guided practice. Ms. Long kept student materials systematically organized in folders for efficiency and effective transitions. Students first participated in a poetry warm-up, reading in unison, prior to the assignment of stanzas to each cooperative team. After the students had finished the poetry reading, Ms. Long instructed the students to turn in their folders to the synonym page for the word *big*.

> ### Highlights!
>
> - Clear expectations
> - Well-organized materials
> - Cooperative groups
> - Frequent interaction with students
> - Use of voice to create interest
> - Active learning
> - Teacher modeling

On the page, students had 15 synonyms for the word *big*. During the synonym review, the students repeated after the teacher in a matching voice level and inflection: "Huge! Huge! Large! Large! [shouting] Gigantic! Gigantic! Vast! Vast! [whispering]." The students' engagement never faltered as the lesson moved on to additional guided practice. Ms. Long assigned each student one of the synonyms to say in turn. After this, students and teacher stood on chairs to shout some of the words. Next, students had 2 minutes to review synonyms for *big* (silently or through self-talk) while Ms. Long distributed ruled notecards to the students for a formative assessment. She instructed them to write their names and numbers from 1 to 15 on the cards. The students then had 2 minutes to write the 15 synonyms for *big*. The students had successfully learned these many synonyms! (See more on vocabulary instruction in Kucan, Chapter 11, this volume.)

Ms. Long next reviewed the writing process with the students. They reviewed the introduction, the events and details, and the conclusion paragraph written previously on their planning sheets, which resembled a flow map. On previous days, students had identified their topic, events, and details; composed their introductory paragraphs and conclusion paragraphs; and written their first detail paragraph. On this day, Ms. Long used a think-aloud strategy as she modeled writing her second detail paragraph while speaking aloud her thoughts about her writing. Then it was time for students to write their second detail paragraph as Ms. Long circulated and interacted with her students, giving them feedback during their quiet writing time. Students continued to be on task with the clear purpose of writing the second paragraph in their essay. (For more on written expression, see Troia, Chapter 12, this volume.)

Clearly, Ms. Long motivated her students by modeling enthusiasm as well as thought processes, while incorporating unique engagement strategies and active learning into her lesson. Below, we elaborate on the technique of teacher modeling and introduce other practices demonstrated to enhance students' engagement and learning, including those involving cooperative learning and making interdisciplinary connections.

Teacher Modeling

Teacher modeling of desired behavior and thought processes, as in think-alouds, is a powerful practice for influencing student learning. In fact, modeling and think-alouds undergird much of research-based reading comprehension instruction (Duke & Pearson, 2002; for more on reading comprehension strategies, see Stahl, Chapter 9, this volume).

Although reading researchers continue to debate the effectiveness of using sustained silent reading (SSR) and the appropriate level of teacher involvement in this process, there is growing evidence to support the idea that time spent reading has a positive impact on students' reading achievement (Garan & DeVoogd, 2008). Besides setting aside 15 or more minutes for reading during each day, how can teachers increase students' engagement in SSR? Teacher modeling has been demonstrated to increase students' on-task reading time (Methe & Hintze, 2003). Students in a grade 3 class were observed to spend a greater proportion of the allotted time reading when the teacher modeled. First, she explained how she was going to begin reading her book where she left off. Then, while the students read for SSR, she sat in front of the class reading silently to herself. Students were less likely to be on task with reading during SSR when there was no modeling (i.e., when the teacher spent the time quietly filing or grading).

Teachers can consciously choose to model particular behaviors and attitudes for their students, but in our experience students are sharp and can pick up on nonauthentic behaviors. If you don't really read or actually enjoy reading, your students might sense this. Furthermore, research and theory suggest that people's attitudes and beliefs have an impact on their behaviors (for a brief review, see McKool & Gespass, 2009). Thus we think it is important for teachers actually to value reading for pleasure and to do it daily. McKool and Gespass found that teachers in grades 4–6, who valued reading and read for pleasure in their own lives (at least 30–45 minutes per day when not at school), were more likely to use a number of effective practices related to motivating reading instruction in their classrooms. They were more likely to talk about what they themselves were learning from their own reading, to provide time for students to talk about what they were reading, to allow students to pick their own texts at an independent reading level for SSR, and to do guided reading lessons and use literature circles. (For more on fostering high-level talk and discussions, see Garas-York, Shanahan, & Almasi, Chapter 10, this volume). Those teachers, who read at least 45 minutes a day, also did not rely on extrinsic rewards to try to motivate reading; such rewards can be counterproductive, especially for students already motivated to read. Instead, they reported using intrinsic motivators such as giving choices in what to read and discussing what students were reading.

The best advice we have from our own experience to help support the positive reading practices and attitudes of teachers has also been suggested by McKool and Gespass (2009), who recommended the following: "As a community of learners, teachers in a school should be encouraged to meet regularly and discuss books they have read, both in professional study groups and in 'Oprah-like' book clubs" (p. 273).

Cooperative Learning

The idea of cooperative or collaborative learning is closely related to the effective practices described previously in this chapter. A well-established classroom community and clear expectations support students' cooperative engagement and can fulfill students' needs for relatedness, autonomy, and competence, which then function to motivate learning further. Adding cooperative learning strategies to activities like SSR can make them more powerful. We highly recommend giving students active tasks to do while reading independently (such as identifying the main idea or the characters by using sticky notes), and then following SSR with time for cooperative activities. Pairs or small groups of students can listen to each other read, question each other about what they read, and otherwise practice skills and strategies being covered. In our experience, this can help students stay engaged—in reading during SSR time, while listening to each other read, and in reading discussions with their peers. The Daily Five model (Boushey & Moser, 2006) provides helpful structures for organizing independent reading time and peer reading activities. One of the things we like about the Daily Five model (and what distinguishes it from other models for managing the reading block) is that it focuses on teaching students independence and showing them how to monitor their goals.

Another structure that takes advantage of the benefits of cooperative learning in reading is the research-tested approach called *reciprocal teaching* (RT; Palincsar & Brown, 1984; Rosenshine & Meister, 1994), which emphasizes teachers' scaffolding and gradual release of students' application of reading comprehension strategies (usually in small groups). It focuses on strategies for summarizing, questioning, clarifying, and predicting applied during discussions of texts. (For much more on RT and the group processes related to cooperative learning in general, see Webb & Palincsar, 1996.) There is strong evidence of its efficacy in grades 4 and beyond. Much less research has been conducted on the effects of RT on students in ESE or students who are ELLs (for some positive evidence, see Gerston, Fuchs, Williams, & Baker, 2001; Klingner & Vaughn, 1996). More recently, RT has been successfully adapted and enhanced for use with students in ESE and students who are ELLs; this newer approach to improving reading comprehension of expository texts is called *collaborative strategic reading* (Klingner, Vaughn, Arguelles, Hughes, & Ahwee, 2004). (See Stahl, Chapter 9, for more about RT and collaborative strategic reading. See Peterson, Chapter 4, and Duke & Watanabe, Chapter 13, for more on differentiated teaching and literacy in multiple genre.)

Other popular resources for cooperative learning that can be applied to most content areas include those originally developed by Johnson and Johnson (see Johnson, Johnson, & Holubec, 1994), as well as methods called *Kagan structures* (see Kagan & Kagan, 2009). Eight general cooperative learning methods—tested in studies conducted in grades K–12 and beyond—were evaluated by Johnson, Johnson, and Stanne (2000), who found that all these methods had a significant impact on student achievement, but that some were more powerful than others. Those with larger positive effects are listed first in the box below.

Cooperative Learning Methods and Their Researchers-Developers

- Learning Together (Johnson & Johnson)
- Constructive (or Academic) Controversy (Johnson & Johnson)
- Student Teams Achievement Divisions (STADs; Slavin & Associates)
- Teams–Games–Tournaments (TGT; DeVries & Edwards)
- Group Investigation (Sharan & Sharan)
- Jigsaw (Aronson & Associates)
- Team Assisted Individualization (TAI; Slavin & Associates)
- Cooperative Integrated Reading and Composition (CIRC; Stevens, Slavin, & Associates)

In schools that focus on providing the best opportunities for student learning, cooperative learning is often used to enhance student engagement and retention of learning. Cooperative learning with modifications is also recommended for gifted ELL and general education ELL students, students in ESE, and students working below grade level. The emphasis in these groups must be on heterogeneously grouping the more proficient English native speakers with ELLs and the more academically proficient students with those who are at a greater risk for failure. Reducing cooperative group size and varying formal and informal groups is also helpful for these at-risk students. (For more on this topic, see Taylor, Chapter 3, this volume). When cooperative learning strategies are used in classrooms focused on student learning, minority students have been found to be "able to close the performance gap with their non-minority peers" (Salinas & Garr, 2009, p. 235). Cooperative learning groups and collaborative activities are also integrated in the research-based

Concept-Oriented Reading Instruction (CORI) program (Wigfield, Guthrie, Tonks, & Perencevich, 2004), which links reading and science and has been found to increase reading comprehension, intrinsic motivation to read, and reading self-efficacy. (For more on integration of literacy and science, see Cervetti, Chapter 14, and our *Interdisciplinary Connections* section below.)

CLASSROOM EXAMPLE: KAGAN STRUCTURES

Although no peer-reviewed research exists on Kagan structures (see the *Looking Forward* section for more on what educators need to know about research), the practices are well aligned with theory, and we have found using them to be helpful in implementing cooperative learning. This classroom example depicts the use of one of the Kagan structures, Numbered Heads Together, in which students begin by sitting in numbered seats in a small group, then get up to confer with one another about the problem, and end with the teacher randomly drawing a number to select a student to share.

Ms. Adams uses cooperative learning activities with all of her grade 5 reading classes. She begins the day with a quick review of story structure elements. Following the review, students correct a previous assignment (which is a flow map of a novel they have been reading) by using Numbered Heads Together to check elements (Kagan & Kagan, 2009). Using cooperative learning strategies such as this, Ms. Adams is able to ensure that all students are participating actively rather than passively because every student is required to participate (as opposed to individuals taking turns). After the story structure elements are reviewed

Numbered Heads Together

1. Teacher poses a problem.
2. Think time.
3. Heads together, bottoms up (students get up to confer).
4. All sit when consensus is reached on answer.
5. Teacher calls on a spokesperson to answer for the group.

by using Numbered Heads Together, the lesson continues with frequent use of cooperative learning strategies to promote continued engagement and learning.

Interdisciplinary Connections

The idea of connecting or integrating literacy instruction in content-area instruction is an intuitively attractive mechanism for increasing student engagement in reading. It is more efficient than teaching each domain separately, and it provides a purpose and context for reading and writing, particularly for expository texts. In addition, reframing curriculum as inquiry can support literacy motivation and learning from elementary to high school (Pearson, Moje, & Greenleaf, 2010; Wilhelm & Wilhelm, 2010).

One of the best-researched interdisciplinary curricula is CORI (e.g., Wigfield et al., 2008):

> In CORI, teachers implement the following practices over a 12-week period in language arts blocks of 90–120 minutes per day: (a) using concept goals in a conceptual theme for reading instruction, (b) affording choices and control to students, (c) providing hands-on activities related to the content goals, (d) using interesting texts of diverse genre for instruction, and (e) organizing collaboration for learning from all texts. (Guthrie et al., 2004, pp. 11–12)

Each week, teachers incorporate reading strategy instruction, science inquiry activities, motivational support, and reading–science integration. Evidence from experimental studies supports the claims that CORI increases students' reading engagement, motivation, and comprehension (Guthrie et al., 2004; Wigfield et al., 2008). It is probably such a powerful instructional intervention because it incorporates so many of the key elements for motivating classroom instruction that we have reviewed in this chapter. CORI was primarily developed for and evaluated in upper elementary grades, and it has now been adapted for middle school. (For more about CORI, see Cervetti, Chapter 14.)

There is a huge need to engage middle school students in literacy, as the motivation of students has been found to decline dramatically over these years (Eccles & Midgley, 1989; Unrau & Schlackman, 2006). This may not be due to developmental or biological changes, but rather to the school context and goal structures, which shift from mastery to performance (Haselhuhn, Al-Mabuk, Gabriele, Groen, & Galloway, 2007). As educators, we should be heartened by our potential to control and change the demotivating conditions that tend to persist in middle schools! Consider the differences between elementary and middle school contexts. Middle schools tend to have more whole-class instruction, more public evaluation, and more emphasis on teacher control (and fewer opportunities for student choice), as well as less time for teachers to get to know and build positive, personal relationships with the many students they see each day (Eccles, Wigfield, Midgley, Reuman, & Feldaufer, 1993; Guthrie & Davis, 2003). Guthrie and Davis (2003) suggested six practices teachers can use to support engaged reading for middle school students that align with those in CORI and those we have described throughout this chapter:

> (1) construct rich knowledge goals as the basis of reading instruction, (2) use real-world interactions to connect reading to student experiences, (3) afford students an abundance of interesting books and materials, (4) provide some choice among material to read, (5) give direct instruction for important reading strategies, and (6) encourage collaboration in many aspects of learning. (p. 59)

SUMMARY OF BIG IDEAS FROM RESEARCH

Creating a Motivating Classroom Atmosphere

Motivating teachers create a positive classroom atmosphere by building relationships with students, managing their behavior, and focusing on student goals:

- Effective teachers build relationships within the greater context of developing caring classroom communities in a culturally sensitive manner. The relationships are naturally two-way; that is, the teachers share things about themselves and get to know their students as individuals, including their unique cultural backgrounds. (For example, see Bondy et al., 2007.)
- Motivating teachers understand that managing student behavior is intimately related to building relationships with students. Just as teachers should put effort into getting to know students immediately, they should also establish expectations, rules, and behavioral procedures during the first few hours of the first day of school. (For example, see Bondy et al., 2007.)
- Teachers can simultaneously support multidimensional student growth, including in emotional, academic, and social domains. The research-based RC model includes practices (e.g., the MM) designed to target these different kinds of growth. (For example, see McTigue & Rimm-Kaufman, 2011.)
- Motivating teachers engage students by guiding them in setting personal academic and behavioral goals. (For example, see Szente, 2007.)
- Goal setting can increase self-efficacy (i.e., students' beliefs that they will be successful in their future endeavors) for students of different cognitive levels in both elementary and middle school. (For example, see Williams-Diehm et al., 2010.)

Developing Independent Learners

Interdependent with developing a positive classroom atmosphere, motivating teachers develop independent learners by providing support for students' autonomy and competence:

I LS

- Independent learners are able to self-regulate, or direct their thoughts, feelings, and behaviors toward the accomplishment of goals that can be self-chosen and monitored or supported by the teacher via scaffolding. (For example, see Boekaerts, 1999.)
- Motivating teachers understand that students have the basic psychological needs of autonomy, competence, and relatedness. These needs have been extensively researched and contribute to the body of evidence for SDT, which posits a relationship between learning environments and intrinsic and extrinsic learner motivation.
- Learners' needs for relatedness can be satisfied by using the practices that contribute to a positive classroom atmosphere as described above. (For example, see Niemiec & Ryan, 2009.)
- Teachers can support student competence or self-efficacy through the use of task-focused feedback. Teachers should also set and maintain high expectations for students, as well as communicate to them that competence is changeable (i.e., within their control) rather than fixed. (For examples, see Hattie & Timperley, 2007; Linnenbrink & Pintrich, 2003; Shute, 2008.)

- Teachers can support student autonomy by distinguishing between behavioral control of students and DCTB. Behavioral control draws upon the positive environment that teachers create to prevent misbehavior and encourage positive behavior through social expectations rather than external coercion. (For examples, see Assor et al., 2005; Nie & Lau, 2009.)

Promoting Engagement through Instructional Practices

Motivating teachers foster student engagement through the use of modeling, as well as cooperative and interdisciplinary learning opportunities:

- Effective teachers model behaviors and thought processes for students. Teachers should model authentic behaviors and attitudes, such as daily reading for pleasure. Teachers can use think-alouds to model reading procedures and positive learning experiences that have resulted from their own reading. (For example, see McKool & Gepass, 2009.)
- Teachers can structure cooperative activities into the reading block after independent or SSR reading sessions. For example, students can take turns listening to one another read and engage in discussions about the reading. The Daily Five model focuses on fostering student independence and goal monitoring with lesson structures for both independent and peer reading activities. (For example, see Boushey & Moser, 2006.)
- RT, which involves scaffolding and the gradual release of reading strategies by teachers, is another form of cooperative learning that can be implemented. Comprehension strategies include summarizing, questioning, clarifying, and predicting during discussions of texts. (For examples, see Palincsar & Brown, 1984; Rosenshine & Meister, 1994.)
- Teachers can integrate literacy instruction within content-area instruction. CORI, an interdisciplinary curriculum organized around conceptual themes, has been extensively researched. CORI has been found to increase students' reading comprehension, engagement, and motivation. (For examples, see Guthrie et al., 2004; Wigfield et al., 2008.)

LOOKING FORWARD

In this chapter, we have cited many research-based practices that represent the best of what we have seen exemplary teachers do, and we have tried to provide some background about how and why these practices are effective for motivating students' literacy learning. In some cases, as with the CORI program (Wigfield et al., 2004), the program itself has been experimentally tested (i.e., research-tested). In other cases, as with the Kagan cooperative learning structures (Kagan & Kagan, 2009), the techniques themselves as packaged in the Kagan materials have not been experimentally tested; however, the development of the techniques was informed by a large body of empirical research on cooperative learning (e.g., Johnson et al., 2000). In the *Research-Based Resources* table at the end of the chapter, we refer to programs or techniques such as Kagan structures as *research-informed*. Many of the strategies identified in Marzano's widely implemented professional development materials (e.g., Marzano, 2007) also appear to be informed by research. In both cases, nonetheless, no peer-reviewed studies evaluating the effectiveness of the Marzano or Kagan programs have been published in research journals. This means that well-controlled studies of these research-informed programs are needed to determine whether they also can be characterized as research-tested.

Why does the seemingly subtle distinction between *research-informed* and *research-tested* matter when we are talking about research-based strategies or programs? Some individual strategies have been research-tested in multiple settings and with different populations, which increases our confidence in the conclusion that they have a positive impact on teacher and/or student outcomes; however, the methods/programs by which teachers in the general population then learn to use them may not be so effective. A school district may have bought into a professional development program's package, but the effectiveness of the methods used in teacher training may not have been tested experimentally. Thus it is entirely possible that money is being wasted that could be better spent on a research-tested professional development program. Furthermore, although each strategy implemented independently may have positive effects, the effects of implementing multiple strategies in combination, as packaged in professional development materials, are for the most part unknown. It is possible there could be unanticipated negative or counteracting effects. One clear exception to this is RT, which is a set of reading comprehension instruction strategies (informed by reading research and clearly aligned with motivation research) that has also been extensively research-tested as a package (for a review, see Rosenshine & Meister, 1994). Professional development related to this package, however, has not been tested on a large scale.

The problem is that there are few if any research-tested professional development programs focused specifically on student motivation. One exception is the work of Anderman, Maehr, and Midgley (1999), who worked with schools and teachers to emphasize mastery goal development in several school reform projects (for a brief review of this and related studies, as well as applications of achievement goal orientation theory, see Meece, Anderman, & Anderman, 2006). Anderman et al. and their research team worked closely with numerous instructors and leaders at only a couple of schools; thus we should use caution in extrapolating their findings to other schools. We cannot presume to know what the results would be if efforts like theirs were tested on a larger scale, with many more schools and under much less guidance from the researchers. Clearly, more scale-up research is needed in this area. By contrast, scale-up research demonstrating positive findings for CORI, which incorporates motivational elements with reading and science instruction, has been done (see Brown, McDonald, & Schneider, 2006, for a review of scale-up research projects). We only suggest that more research on CORI be conducted by researchers other than those who developed it.

One of the primary issues associated with scaling up strategies and programs that have evidence to suggest their efficacy in smaller, well-controlled studies is how to facilitate effective professional development—professional development that can be implemented in schools to help teachers learn how to implement the strategies/programs, to motivate teachers to implement them, and to sustain reform efforts. Coaching of teachers is a popular method of professional development, and some promising research findings are beginning to suggest that it may be effective in supporting teachers' learning (see the December 2010 issue of *Elementary School Journal*, which is devoted to studies of coaching). Another up-and-coming approach to professional development is the *professional learning community* (PLC; for more on PLCs, see Peterson, Chapter 21, this volume). Although PLCs are popular, little research has been conducted to test their effects on school personnel learning and student outcomes. We would like to echo the caution of Bausmith and Barry (2011) that while PLCs seem promising, more research on them is needed, and more of what we know about what expert teachers do should be incorporated into PLC efforts. Furthermore, we hope that our descriptions in this chapter of what effective/expert teachers do to motivate students in the context of literacy content can stimulate PLCs using this book to focus on pedagogical content knowledge (Bausmith & Barry, 2011).

QUESTIONS FOR REFLECTION •

Motivating Classroom Atmosphere

1. What types of activities do I use to build strong relationships with my students on the first day of school? What activities do I use to establish peer relationships?

2. How can I integrate some of Marzano's (2007) eight action steps for building relationships into a current lesson?

3. What is my description of an ideal, positive teacher–student relationship? What goals can I set for myself to create such relationships with all students?

4. When and how do I establish rules and expectations for positive behavior in my classroom? For each rule or expectation, what justification do I provide for students?

5. To what extent do I balance students' academic, emotional, and social growth? As a teacher, what challenges have I have faced in my attempts to balance these three areas of development? What actions might I take to improve the area(s) that may be weaker than the others?

6. Based on my prior knowledge and experience, what kinds of academic or behavioral objectives do I anticipate may be most appropriate for a goal contract or action plan? How do I plan on scaffolding these goal-setting behaviors for my students? What sort of feedback will I provide for students as they become more competent at setting their own goals?

7. How do I create mastery goal orientation in my classroom? What challenges have I faced in the past, or do I anticipate facing, related to balancing performance and mastery goals?

Developing Independent Learners

1. How do I model self-regulation processes, including planning, monitoring, and evaluating goal progress, for my students? What examples can I provide from my own experiences as a teacher and a learner to help them understand the goal-setting process?

2. What strategies will I use to help students avoid developing the belief/attitude that the goal-setting process requires too much extra time or energy?

3. How do/can I intrinsically motivate my students? What challenges have I experienced with balancing extrinsic and intrinsic motivation during and beyond instruction?

4. How do I distinguish between DCTB and behavioral control in my practice? What are some examples of each, and how can I change practices that are directly controlling in order to better support student autonomy?

5. What practices will I use to support students' perception that they engage in learning tasks of their own choice or volition? What challenges to supporting student autonomy do I anticipate?

Promoting Engagement through Instructional Practices

1. How do/can I assess behavioral and cognitive engagement in my students? How can I restructure my classroom and lessons in order to support engaged reading?

2. Which reading practices and thought processes do I model for my students? Of those, which have my students struggled with in the past (or which do I anticipate my future students to find difficult), and how will I change my practice to meet similar needs?

3. How will I integrate my personal values related to literacy (e.g., reading for pleasure) into my teaching practice?

4. Why is it important for teachers to use cooperative learning methods in the classroom? How can I incorporate cooperative learning methods into a current lesson?

5. How do/can I integrate reading into other subjects, such as science or social studies, in order to help students build self-efficacy and motivation for reading?

6. In what ways does using a program like CORI to integrate subjects help students with their reading skills? How do elements of CORI relate to other aspects of motivating literacy practices discussed in this chapter?

SUGGESTIONS FOR ONGOING PROFESSIONAL LEARNING • • • • • •

If you have picked up this book, then you are likely to be the kind of motivated, reflective practitioner (or prepractitioner) we hope works (or will work) with elementary and middle school students. Although in the past teachers could realistically work independently with their classroom doors closed, the increasing accountability in schools has made this less possible. The nature of educators' work in schools is inherently social; the expectations of colleagues (in grade-level teams) and administrators, as well as of students and parents, must be considered and balanced in the context of the demands of state standards. It is not surprising that teachers, who put their all into what they do, risk burning out and losing their motivation. Recent research provides evidence to support that principals' leadership style is an important predictor of their teachers' motivation (Eyal & Roth, 2011): Principals who supported the autonomy of their teachers (just as we have talked about effective teachers supporting the autonomy of their students in this chapter) were likely to have more motivated and satisfied teachers.

Perhaps you can inspire the other faculty and administrators in your school to do some cooperative learning with you. Read and study this book together, connecting what you read to reflections on practices you have used, new practices you are trying, and observations of one another's teaching. Consider the impact of changes on students' engagement and learning outcomes by collecting and analyzing data. You might do this in the context of a promising mechanism for professional development mentioned earlier: the PLC. The school-level PLC typically includes teachers, support staff, and administrators; some PLCs include faculty from local colleges and universities as well. The following are sessions for use with your PLC to aid you in implementing the practices presented in this chapter. We recommend that you keep a log of your thoughts and experiences during this process.

Creating a Motivating Classroom Atmosphere

Session 1: Where to Begin

- With your PLC, review the *Creating a Motivating Classroom Atmosphere* section in this chapter (we recommend PLC members read the entire chapter beforehand and review relevant portions during sessions). Individually answer these questions:
  - ◆ What do you do to motivate all learners?
  - ◆ Do students see your classroom as a fair and safe learning environment?
- After answering these questions individually, share your answers with a partner. Discuss changes that you might make based on this chapter to improve the atmosphere in your classroom. Keep a log of the changes that you implement as you strive to improve the atmosphere in your classroom. (For more specific questions to stimulate reflection and discussion within your PLC, you might try using or adapting some of the *Questions for Reflection* that we provide above for this session and those that follow it.)

Session 2: Building Relationships

- As you meet for this session, discuss the notes that you have kept. Share improvements and areas still in need of improvement. (We encourage you to continue to revisit areas of improvement that you set as personal or group goals across subsequent sessions.)
- Students' motivation to learn increases when the students feel safe in the classroom learning environment. It is important that teachers facilitate positive relationships within the classroom. Individually answer the following questions:
  - ◆ In what ways do you currently seek to build positive classroom relationships with and among your students?
  - ◆ What problems do you perceive currently in classroom relationships?
- With your group, discuss ideas from this chapter that you might use to improve relationships in your classroom. Keep a record of your experiences. (For this session and others, see related *Research-Based Resources* at the end of this chapter.)

Session 3: Managing Behavior

- With a partner, share your experiences as you implemented your ideas for building positive relationships in your classroom.
- Now think about classroom management. Classroom management is challenging for many teachers. Think about your own behavior management plan. Individually answer these questions:
  - ◆ What does your current classroom management plan look like?
  - ◆ What management issues currently interfere with learning in your classroom?
- Share your answers with a partner. Discuss techniques you might use to improve your behavior management system. Review the ideas in this chapter and keep a record of your experiences as you implement your ideas.

Session 4: Focusing on Goals

- As you meet with your PLC, share your experiences during the past week as you continue to improve your classroom atmosphere.
- As members of a PLC, you and your colleagues are aware of the goals that you have for your school, your instruction, and your students. It is also important for students to understand the purpose for their learning. One way of helping students to know the purpose for their learning is to use the practice of goal setting with students. As you prepare to implement the suggestions in this chapter, answer these questions individually:
  - What do you do currently to help your students with purposeful learning?
  - Do your students know why they are currently studying the topics that you present? How?
- Share your answers with a partner. Discuss the methods for goal setting described in this chapter, and choose an area for goal setting with your students. During the coming week, keep a record of your implementation and your students' responses.

Developing Independent Learners

Session 5: Supporting Autonomy for Students

- Review and discuss your notes related to focusing on goals in your classroom.
- Focusing on learning goals in your classroom increases the independence of your students. Students take responsibility for their learning and feel that they have increased control and autonomy. (Autonomy is one of the three basic needs of learners discussed in this chapter, along with relatedness and competence.) As you consider the autonomy of your students, answer the following questions independently:
  - What current procedures are your students responsible for?
  - How can you improve the autonomy of your students?
- As you review your answers with your group or partner, make a plan for increasing students' autonomy in the classroom. Keep notes about the approaches you use to improve students' autonomy.

Session 6: Supporting Competence for Students

- Take time to discuss your notes from the past week concerning student autonomy in the classroom.
- As you have read in this chapter, another of learners' basic needs in the classroom (in addition to autonomy and relatedness) is competence. Think about the following questions and record your answers:
  - What do you currently do to promote students' perceptions of competence?
  - How do you currently challenge all learners in your classroom?
  - In what areas do you feel that improvement is needed in meeting these needs for your students?
- Discuss your answers and ideas from this chapter that you will implement. Keep a record of your experience.

Promoting Engagement through Instructional Practices

Session 7: Teacher Modeling

- Review your notes about supporting students' competence from the past week, and discuss perceived strengths and weaknesses.
- Students are greatly influenced by their teachers. Teacher modeling of desired behaviors has a positive impact on student learning and attitudes in the classroom. Think about ways that you currently model behaviors for your students, and answer these questions independently:
  - ◆ In what ways do you currently think aloud while you are modeling a skill or strategy?
  - ◆ What are other areas of instruction in where you can use modeling and/or think-alouds?
- Discuss your answers with your partner. Make a plan to increase your use of modeling and think-alouds during the week. Keep a daily record of your experience and students' reactions.

Session 8: Cooperative Learning

- Discuss your experiences with using modeling and think-alouds during instruction. What worked? What didn't work? How did your students respond?
- Students have the need for autonomy, and one way to promote autonomy is to use cooperative learning strategies. Review the chapter's discussion of cooperative learning and then answer these questions individually:
  - ◆ What teaching strategies do you use to promote cooperative learning in your classroom?
  - ◆ How can you improve use of cooperative learning strategies during your instruction?
- Discuss your current use of cooperative learning strategies with the group, and then with a partner discuss plans for implementing cooperative learning strategies this week. Keep a record of your experience.

Session 9: Interdisciplinary Connections

- Review your experience with using cooperative learning strategies. What were the strengths and weaknesses you perceived while using these strategies?
- Discuss the content-area topics taught during your school day, and the relationships among them. Brainstorm ways to incorporate reading strategies into other content areas. Answer these questions individually:
  - ◆ What are some of the reading strategies you are currently teaching?
  - ◆ How can you incorporate these strategies into your content-area instruction this week?
- Discuss your answers with a partner. Record your experiences as you incorporate your reading strategies into your content-area instruction. As you continue to promote motivating classroom practices in your classroom, continue referring to *Research-Based Resources* (see below).

RESEARCH-BASED RESOURCES

Topic	Citation	Empirical study	Empirical review	Research-informed	Research-tested
Creating a Motivating Classroom Atmosphere					
Where to Begin	Dolezal et al. (2003)	×			
Building Relationships	Marzano (2007)			×	
Managing Behavior	Denton & Kriete (2000)				×
	McTigue & Rimm-Kaufman (2011)		×		
	Kriete with Bechtel (2002)				×
Developing Independent Learners					
Focusing on Goals	Szente (2007)		×		
	Niemiec & Ryan (2009)		×		
Supporting Autonomy for Students	Burke (2000, Ch. 4)			×	
Supporting Competence for Students	Linnenbrink & Pintrich (2003)		×		
	Hyerle & Yeager (2007)				×
Promoting Engagement through Instructional Practices					
Teacher Modeling	McKool & Gespass (2009)	×			
Cooperative Learning	Kagan & Kagan (2009)			×	
	Johnson et al. (2000)				×
	Wigfield et al. (2004)	×			
Interdisciplinary Connections	Guthrie & Davis (2003)		×		

REFERENCES

Ainley, M. (2006). Connecting with learning: Motivation, affect, and cognition in interest processes. *Educational Psychology Review, 18*, 391–405.

Anderman, E. M., Maehr, M. L., & Midgley, C. (1999). Declining motivation after the transition to middle school: Schools can make a difference. *Journal of Research and Development in Education, 32*(3), 131–147.

Assor, A., Kaplan, H., Kanat-Maymon, Y., & Roth, G. (2005). Directly controlling teacher behaviors as predictors of poor motivation and engagement in girls and boys: The role of anger and anxiety. *Learning and Instruction, 15*, 397–413.

Bandura, A. (1997). *Self-efficacy: The exercise of control.* New York: Freeman.

Battistich, V., Solomon, D., Kim, D., Watson, M., & Schaps, E. (1995). Schools as communities, poverty levels of student populations, and students' attitudes, motives, and performance: A multilevel analysis. *American Educational Research Journal, 32*, 627–658.

Baumeister, R., & Leary, M. R. (1995). The need to belong: Desire for interpersonal attachments as a fundamental human motivation. *Psychological Bulletin, 117*, 497–529.

Bausmith, J. M., & Barry, C. (2011). Revisiting professional learning communities to increase college readiness: The importance of pedagogical content knowledge. *Educational Researcher, 40*(4), 175–178.

Boekaerts, M. (1999). Self-regulated learning: Where we are today. *International Journal of Educational Research, 31*, 445–457.

Bondy, E., Ross, D. D., Gallingane, C., & Hambacher, E. (2007). Creating environments of success and resilience: Culturally responsive classroom management and more. *Urban Education, 42*(4), 326–348.

Boushey, G., & Moser, J. (2006). *The daily 5: Fostering literacy independence in the elementary grades.* Portland, ME: Stenhouse.

Brown, K. L., McDonald, S.-K., & Schneider, B. (2006). *Just the facts: Results from IERI scale-up research.* Chicago: Data Research and Development Center, NORC, University of Chicago. Retrieved from *http://drdc.uchicago.edu/extra/just-the-facts.pdf.*

Burke, K. (2000). *What to do with the kid who . . . : Developing cooperation, self-discipline, and responsibility in the classroom* (2nd ed.). Thousand Oaks, CA: Corwin Press.

Deci, E. L., Koestner, R., & Ryan, R. M. (1999a). A meta-analytic review of experiments examining the effects of extrinsic rewards on intrinsic motivation. *Psychological Bulletin, 125*(6), 627–668.

Deci, E. L., Koestner, R., & Ryan, R. M. (1999b). The undermining effect is a reality after all— extrinsic rewards, task interest, and self-determination: Reply to Eisenberger, Pierce, and Cameron (1999) and Lepper, Henderlong, and Gingras (1999). *Psychological Bulletin, 125*(6), 692–700.

Denton, P., & Kriete, R. (2000). *The first six weeks of school.* Greenfield, MA: Northeast Foundation for Children.

Dolezal, S. E., Welsh, L. M., Pressley, M., & Vincent, M. M. (2003). How nine third-grade teachers motivate student academic engagement. *Elementary School Journal, 103*(3), 239–267.

Duke, N., & Pearson, P. D. (2002). Effective practices for developing reading comprehension. In A. E. Farstrup & S. J. Samuels (Eds.), *What research has to say about reading* (3rd ed., pp. 205–242). Newark, DE: International Reading Association.

Eccles, J. S., & Midgley, C. (1989). Stage–environment fit: Developmentally appropriate classrooms for young adolescents. In C. Ames & R. Ames (Eds.), *Research on motivation in education: Goals and cognitions* (Vol. 3, pp. 139–186). San Diego, CA: Academic Press.

Eccles, J. S., Wigfield, A., Midgley, C., Reuman, D., & Feldaufer, H. (1993). Negative effects of traditional middle schools on students' motivation. *Elementary School Journal, 93,* 553–574.

Eyal, O., & Roth, G. (2011). Principals' leadership and teachers' motivation. *Journal of Educational Administration, 49*(3), 256–275.

Friend, M., & Bursuck, W. D. (2009). *Including students with special needs: A practical guide for classroom teachers* (5th ed.). Upper Saddle River, NJ: Pearson Education.

Garan, E. M., & DeVoogd, G. (2008). The benefits of sustained silent reading: Scientific research and common sense converge. *The Reading Teacher, 62*(4), 336–344.

Gerston, R., Fuchs, L. S., Williams, J. P., & Baker, S. (2001). Teaching reading comprehension strategies to students with learning disabilities: A review of research. *Review of Educational Research, 71,* 279–320.

Guthrie, J. T., & Davis, M. H. (2003). Motivating struggling readers in middle school through an engagement model of classroom practice. *Reading and Writing Quarterly: Overcoming Learning Difficulties, 19*(1), 59–85.

Guthrie, J. T., Wigfield, A., Barbosa, P., Perencevich, K. C., Taboada, A., Davis, M. H., et al. (2004). Increasing reading comprehension and engagement through Concept-Oriented Reading Instruction. *Journal of Educational Psychology, 96*(3), 403–423.

Hamre, B. K., & Pianta, R. C. (2001). Early teacher–child relationships and the trajectory of children's school outcomes through eighth grade. *Child Development, 72*(2), 625–638.

Haselhuhn, C. W., Al-Mabuk, R., Gabriele, A., Groen, M., & Galloway, S. (2007). Promoting positive achievement in the middle school: A look at teachers' motivational knowledge, beliefs, and teaching practices. *Research in Middle Level Education, 9,* 1–20.

Hattie, J., & Timperley, H. (2007). The power of feedback. *Review of Educational Research, 77,* 81–112.

Hidi, S., & Harackiewicz, J. M. (2000). Motivating the academically unmotivated: A critical issue for the 21st century. *Review of Educational Research, 70,* 151–179.

Hyerle, D., & Yeager, C. (2007). *Thinking maps: A language for learning.* Cary, NC: Thinking Maps.

Ivey, G., & Broaddus, K. (2007). A formative experiment investigating literacy engagement among adolescent Latina/o students just beginning to read, write, and speak English. *Reading Research Quarterly, 42*(4), 512–545.

Johnson, D. W., & Johnson, R. T. (1994). *Learning together and alone: Cooperative, competitive, and individualistic learning* (4th ed.). Needham Heights, MA: Allyn & Bacon.

Johnson, D. W., Johnson, R. T., & Holubec, E. J. (1994). *The new circles of learning: Cooperation in the classroom and school.* Alexandria, VA: Association for Supervision and Curriculum Development.

Johnson, D. W., Johnson, R. T., & Stanne, M. B. (2000). Cooperative learning methods: A meta-analysis. Retrieved from *http://tablelearning.com/uploads/File/EXHIBIT-B.pdf.*

Kagan, S., & Kagan, M. (2009). *Kagan cooperative learning.* San Clemente, CA: Kagan Publishing.

Klingner, J. K., & Vaughn, S. (1996). Reciprocal teaching of reading comprehension strategies for students with learning disabilities who use English as a second language. *Elementary School Journal, 96,* 275–293.

Klingner, J. K., Vaughn, S., Arguelles, M. E., Hughes, M. T., & Ahwee, S. (2004). Collaborative strategic reading: Real world lessons from classroom teachers. *Remedial and Special Education, 25,* 291–302.

Kriete, R., with Bechtel, L. (2002). *The morning meeting book.* Turners Falls, MA: Northeast Foundation for Children.

Kovalevs, K., & Dewsbury, A. (2006). *Making connections.* Cambridge, MA: Educators Publishing Service.

Linnenbrink, E. A., & Pintrich, P. R. (2003). The role of self-efficacy beliefs in student engagement and learning in the classroom. *Reading and Writing Quarterly: Overcoming Learning Difficulties, 19*(2), 119–137.

Martin, L., & Mottet, T. P. (2011). The effect of instructor nonverbal immediacy behaviors and feedback sensitivity on Hispanic students' affective learning outcomes in ninth-grade writing conferences. *Communication Education, 60*, 1–19.

Marzano, R. J. (2007). *The art and science of teaching: A comprehensive framework for effective instruction.* Alexandria, VA: Association for Supervision and Curriculum Development.

McKool, S. S., & Gespass, S. (2009). Does Johnny's reading teacher love to read?: How teachers' personal reading habits affect instructional practices. *Literacy Research and Instruction, 48*(3), 264–276.

McTigue, E. M., & Rimm-Kaufman, S. E. (2011). The responsive classroom approach and its implications for improving reading and writing. *Reading and Writing Quarterly: Overcoming Learning Difficulties, 27*, 5–24.

Meece, J. L., Anderman, E. M., & Anderman, L. H. (2006). Classroom goal structure, student motivation, and academic achievement. *Annual Review of Psychology, 57*, 487–503.

Methe, S. A., & Hintze, J. M. (2003). Evaluating teacher modeling as a strategy to increase student reading behavior. *School Psychology Review, 32*(4), 617–623.

Nelson, V. (2010). Learning English, learning science. *Science and Children, 48*(3), 48–51.

Nie, Y., & Lau, S. (2009). Complementary roles of care and behavioral control in classroom management: The self-determination theory perspective. *Contemporary Educational Psychology, 34*(3), 185–194.

Niemiec, C. P., & Ryan, R. M. (2009). Autonomy, competence, and relatedness in the classroom: Applying self-determination theory to educational practice. *Theory and Research in Education, 7*(2), 133–144.

Palincsar, A. S., & Brown, A. L. (1984). Reciprocal teaching of comprehension-fostering and comprehension-monitoring activities. *Cognition and Instruction, 1*(2), 117–175.

Pearson, P. D., Moje, E., & Greenleaf, C. (2010). Literacy and science: Each in the service of the other. *Science, 328*, 459–463.

Pekrun, R., Goetz, T., & Titz, W. (2002). Academic emotions in students' self-regulated learning and achievement: A program of qualitative and quantitative research. *Educational Psychologist, 37*(2), 91–105.

Pintrich, P. R., & Schunk, D. H. (2002). *Motivation in education: Theory, research, and applications* (2nd ed.). Upper Saddle River, NJ: Merrill/Prentice Hall.

Ream, R. K. (2008). Student engagement, peer social capital, and school dropout among Mexican American and non-Latino white students. *Sociology of Education, 81*(2), 109–139.

Reeve, J., & Jang, H. (2006). What teachers say and do to support students' autonomy during a learning activity. *Journal of Educational Psychology, 98*(1), 209–218.

Rimm-Kaufman, S. E., & Chiu, Y. I. (2007). Promoting social and academic competence in the classroom: An intervention study examining the contribution of the responsive classroom approach. *Psychology in the Schools, 44*(4), 397–413.

Rosenshine, B., & Meister, C. (1994). Reciprocal teaching: A review of the research. *Review of Educational Research, 64*(4), 479–530.

Ross, D. D., Bondy, E., Gallingane, C., & Hambacher, E. (2008). Promoting academic engagement through insistence: Being a warm demander. *Childhood Education, 84*(3), 142–146.

Ryan, R. M., & Deci, E. L. (2000). Self-determination theory and the facilitation of intrinsic motivation, social development and well-being. *American Psychologist, 55*, 68–78.

Salinas, M. F., & Garr, J. (2009). Effect of learner-centered education on the academic outcomes of minority groups. *Journal of Instructional Psychology, 36* (3), 226–237.

Schunk, D. H. (2005). Self-regulated learning: The educational legacy of Paul R. Pintrich. *Educational Psychologist, 40*(2), 85–94.

Schunk, D. H. (2008). *Learning theories: An educational perspective* (5th ed.). Upper Saddle River, NJ: Pearson/Merrill/Prentice Hall.

Shute, V. J. (2008). Focus on formative feedback. *Review of Educational Research, 78,* 153–189.

Sideridis, G. D. (2005). Classroom goal structures and hopelessness as predictors of day-to-day experience at school: Differences between students with and without learning disabilities. *International Journal of Educational Research, 43,* 308–328.

Szente, J. (2007). Empowering young children for success in school and in life. *Early Childhood Education Journal, 34*(6), 449–453.

Unrau, N., & Schlackman, J. (2006). Motivation and its relationship with reading achievement in an urban middle school. *Journal of Educational Research, 100*(2), 81–101.

Webb, N. M., & Palincsar, A. S. (1996). Group processes in the classroom. In D. Berliner & R. Calfee (Ed.), *Handbook of educational psychology* (pp. 841–873). New York: Macmillan.

Wigfield, A., Guthrie, J. T., Perencevich, K. C., Taboada, A., Klauda, S. L., McRae, A., et al. (2008). Role of reading engagement in mediating effects of reading comprehension instruction on reading outcomes. *Psychology in the Schools, 45*(5), 432–445.

Wigfield, A., Guthrie, J. T., Tonks, S., & Perencevich, K. C. (2004). Children's motivation for reading: Domain specificity and instructional influences. *Journal of Educational Research, 97*(6), 299–309.

Wilhelm, J. D., & Wilhelm, P. J. (2010). Inquiring minds learn to read, write, and think: Reaching "all" learners through inquiry. *Middle School Journal, 41*(5), 39–46.

Williams-Diehm, K., Palmer, S., Lee, Y., & Schroer, H. (2010). Goal content analysis for middle and high school students with disabilities. *Career Development for Exceptional Individuals, 33*(3), 132–142.

Wilson, B. L., & Corbett, H. D. (2001). Listening to urban kids: School reform and the teachers they want. *Educational Studies, 35,* 90–93.

CHAPTER 2

Literacy Tools Created and Used within Print-Rich Classroom Environments ● ● ● ● ● ● ● ●

MISTY SAILORS
TRACEY KUMAR
SHANNON BLADY
ANGELI WILLSON

In almost everything we do as individuals, as families, as communities, and as a society, we use tools. Consider those things we do on a regular basis and the tools we use, including those we use at work (a shovel, a towel for drying dishes, or a photocopier), to stay healthy (the scale that weighs us, the exercise machines that build our muscles, or the skewers on which we place vegetables for roasting), to relax (the fishing line that we cast, the CD or iPod that plays our favorite tune, or the park bench on which we sit), and to interact with others (the cell phone, the computer, the telephone, the newspaper, or language itself), just to name a few. Tools are pervasive in our daily lives. Our society would not be what it is today without these tools to support our daily activities.

Tools can be generic in nature, but specific enough to users of those tools that they are recognized as, and sometimes called, "tools of the trade." Teachers use management tools to keep track of grades (grade books) and to keep track of students (attendance records). They use instructional tools to make note of plans for upcoming days (lesson plans) and to create other instructional tools (construction paper, laptops, scissors, pencils, and pens; these are also instructional tools themselves, of course). They use tools to create learning opportunities for and with students, both during teacher-directed learning experiences (digital projectors) and during student-centered learning experiences (storyboards, literacy learning games, and listening centers inside literacy stations/centers). There are many layers to consider in examining the tools used by teachers for literacy instruction.

In this chapter, we examine and discuss tools that literacy teachers often use (and those that are supported in research) to enhance the literacy experiences of students within effective literacy instruction. We begin this chapter with a definition of *tools* as it relates to literacy instruction. We then review the research literature on the role of the print environment and literacy tools that teachers use within print-rich environments. Next, we present two extended case examples—one of an elementary principal and one of an elementary classroom teacher—and show how they structure the print environment of their school and classroom (respectively) to support literacy learning in light of the research. We end this chapter with a set of questions for teachers, instructional leaders, and teacher educators to consider for critical reflection purposes, and with suggestions for continuing professional learning.

LITERACY TOOLS WITHIN PRINT-RICH ENVIRONMENTS: A THEORETICAL FRAMEWORK

We situate our examination of literacy tools inside a framework known as *cultural historical activity theory* (CHAT). Rooted in the works of Russian scholars (Vygotsky, Leont'ev, and Luria), CHAT only recently found its way into conversations about teaching and learning in the United States (Yamagata-Lynch, 2010). It has, however, served as the inspiration of numerous publications, conferences, and professional organizations (Holzman, 2006). In this chapter, we use CHAT as the framework in which we situate our examination of the literacy tools that teachers and administrators in highly effective classrooms and schools use to scaffold literacy development with elementary school students.

Drawing from the works of a Scandinavian theorist, Yrjö Engeström, second-generation CHAT (as it is commonly referred to) urges us to think about the various systems that organize our social worlds. Classroom teaching is embedded inside one such system—that of education—and literacy instruction is one of the mechanisms used to engage students inside that system. In this theory, participants within a system (students in a classroom) are just as active in creating their environment as their teacher is—even in classrooms that offer traditional forms of literacy instruction. Engeström's model has multiple layers, including a careful look at the activities within the system: the subjects (individuals or groups of individuals) within the activity; the object (problem space) and outcomes of the activity (as well as the motives, purposes, and reasons for the activity); the rules (codes and conventions) that people within the activity adhere to; the community (people and groups) whose knowledge, interests, stakes, and goals shape the activity; the division of labor within the activity (how the work in the activity is divided among participants in the activity); and the tools used within the activity (those physical objects and systems of symbols that people use to accomplish their outcomes). It is upon this last component, focused primarily on the interpersonal plane of activities (individuals and groups engaging in collaborative inquiry) that we situate this chapter. Based on Engeström's (1993) model, the following graphic illustrates this framework.

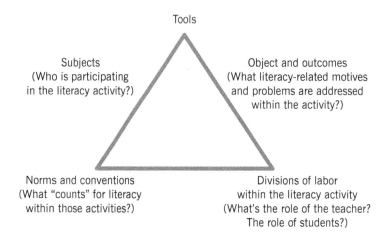

This framework provides us with an opportunity to look closely at the literacy tools that teachers and students create and use for literacy development. *Tools* are defined here as artifacts that represent the ways in which we interact with our environment, and tools used in literacy activities have developed as the literacy activities of our society have developed. For classroom instruction, this means that teachers must be very cognizant of the literacy tools they offer to and create with students, as tools (especially literacy tools) are not just items that one generation hands to the next. Rather, tools (especially literacy tools) are conceived, acquired, discarded, and replaced in each activity, allowing students to discover new tools across multiple activities. The value of a literacy tool may change over time as students engage in new activities (Bomer, 2003; Yamagata-Lynch, 2010).

In short, the CHAT framework allows us as teachers to examine the literacy tools we select to include in our literacy environments, and to make sure our students can use these tools to engage in activities that move them toward becoming literate beings. In the next section, we offer a brief look at the research that demonstrates the importance of a print-rich environment for students' literacy development. We then examine the specific types of literacy tools within print-rich environments that provide for scaffolded literacy development.

OVERVIEW OF RESEARCH

The importance of print in literacy learning is acknowledged by classroom teachers and in the literature. One would be hard pressed to find a teacher who would not agree that children must be surrounded by print as part of the literacy acquisition process. Likewise, literacy researchers also recognize the importance of print-rich environments for literacy learning. Although this is not a highly researched area, a steadily increasing number of studies have explored the role of such environments in literacy acquisition.

For example, a growing number of studies associate print-rich environments with gains in student reading achievement. Among these studies are ones conducted in early childhood (Taylor, Blum, & Logsdon, 1986), kindergarten (Neuman, 1999; Reutzel, Oda, & Moore, 1989), and elementary school classrooms (Hoffman, Sailors, Duffy, & Beretvas, 2004). Collectively, these studies have found that young and elementary-age children who are immersed in print-rich classrooms outperform their peers who are not immersed in print, especially when their teachers know what to do with that print.

Hoffman and his colleagues (2004), in a validation study of the TEX-IN3 Observation System (an instrument used to describe and measure the print environment of elementary classroom environments), reported the correlation between elements of the text environment and gains in students' scores on a measure of reading achievement. Their analysis indicated that both the holistic text environment (overall score of the quantity and qualities of the print found in the classroom) and the local print environment (those texts created within the classroom) statistically predicted gains on the comprehension test administered as part of the study. Also important to mention here were two other predictors of gains on the comprehension test: teachers' engagement with text in the classroom and students' understanding of the forms and functions of those texts. Simply stated, when classrooms are rich in print, when teachers use texts in the presence of students, and when students in those classrooms understand what those texts are and how to use them, literacy learning is greater.

How Many and What Types of Tools?

An increasing number of studies have also identified and described components of print environments that are associated with literacy learning. Print-rich classrooms are physically inviting (Morrow & Weinstein, 1982) and contain a plethora of literacy tools, especially books (McGill-Franzen, Allington, Yokoi, & Brooks, 1999; Neuman, 1999). Research has suggests that there should be at least 8–10 trade books per child—representing a variety of genres, as well as the cultural, linguistic, and reading levels of the children in the classrooms (Fractor, Woodruff, Martinez, & Teale, 1993; Hoffman et al., 2004). Especially important is the need for informational books (Duke, 2000). Other research has documented specific types of literacy tools found in classrooms, including literacy tools that are "imported" into classrooms, those that are more "local" (texts that are created in and of the classroom), and those that might be classified as either imported or local (Hoffman et al., 2004). Table 2.1 lists the various types of literacy tools found in elementary classrooms.

Recent research has investigated whether some of the tools in Table 2.1 are more important than others for effective print-rich classrooms. Further explorations of the classrooms reported in the Hoffman and colleagues' (2004) study led to the identification of literacy tools that were associated with the highest-performing classrooms. Sailors and Hoffman (2011) reported that these tools included (1) games/puzzles, (2) instructional aids, (3) leveled books, (4) limited-text process charts, (5) student/teacher-published works, and (6) trade books. As Sailors and Hoffman pointed out, these findings do not suggest that the other types of print tools are not important; they are. In fact, the authors speculated that the other literacy tools were either common across classrooms (e.g., textbooks are supplied to schools for all students) or virtually nonexistent across classrooms (e.g., portfolios).

In addition to these types of literacy tools, research has demonstrated the need for a careful consideration of qualities of texts. An early study found that texts in high-performing classrooms were student-generated, reflected ongoing activity, were displayed prominently, and represented children's interests and language and purposes (Taylor et al., 1986). Classrooms that are print-rich also contain engaging language,

TABLE 2.1. Types of Literacy Tools Found in Elementary Classrooms

Text types	Explanation	Examples
Assessments	These literacy tools include tests or testing materials used by the students in the classroom. These may appear as student testing protocols from formal or informal assessments. Assessments are used for a variety of instructional purposes and goals.	Student test protocols, end-of-book tests, spelling and grammar tests, portfolios
Computer/ electronic tools	These literacy tools include any texts that are accessed and used through an electronic medium.	Messaging systems (e-mail), Internet access (for research), software programs (reading and authoring programs), tests or test preparations, text files that are saved and accessed by students, recorded books (e.g., listening centers), and news or information shows
Extended text process charts	These literacy tools appear as connected texts (multisentence) that are usually procedural and guide students toward the use of a particular process or strategy.	Language charts, inquiry charts, writing process charts, math strategies or algorithms, rubrics
Games/puzzles/ manipulatives	These literacy tools are designed for student use (often in independent or small-group work).	Bingo, Clue, word sorts, magnetic poetry
Instructional aids	These literacy tools are used publicly and often appear as posters. They are always used to support instruction or represent past instruction. Often these instructional aid charts are used as visual aids to support direct instruction or mini-lessons.	Poems for reading together, morning message, labels, vocabulary lists, word banks, and color charts
Journals	These literacy tools are "local" texts created by the students (individuals or groups working together), based primarily on their work and writing. "Spiral folders" where students record their work in response to assignments may be considered in this category.	Personal journals, literature response logs, content inquiry logs (math, science, and social studies), draft writing
Leveled books	These literacy tools are often found in book format, but they differ from trade books because they are created explicitly for instruction and are leveled for difficulty and accessibility.	Basal readers, "little books," guided reading books, and decodable books

(continued)

TABLE 2.1. *(continued)*

Text types	Explanation	Examples
Limited-text process charts	These literacy tools include letter/word-level texts that are procedural and guide the students in the use of a particular strategy or set of strategies. These are similar to extended-text charts in purpose and design; however, they tend to focus at the letter or word level.	Word walls, alphabet charts, spelling "demon" charts
Organizational/management charts	These literacy tools are used to manage or organize the social, academic, or curricular work within the classroom. They may be enlarged or small, local or public.	"Student helpers" charts, work boards, class rules, local or state curricular objectives, a chart for multiplication facts mastered by students, a skill mastery chart, a record of number of books read
Reference materials	These literacy tools are used as resources for finding information (e.g., word spellings, geographical locations, ways to do things).	Atlas, dictionary, encyclopedia, English grammar handbook, thesaurus, globe, maps
Serials	These literacy tools are "serial" in nature; that is, they move in and out of a classroom on a regular basis.	*Ranger Rick*, *Highlights*, Scholastic newspapers, classroom newspapers, school and community newsletters
Social/personal/inspirational displays	These literacy tools motivate and inspire. They may come from a commercial source or they may be created locally.	"Star of the Week" posters, "Read, Read, Read" posters
Student/teacher-published works	These literacy tools consist of locally authored (by a student, a teacher, or a combination of the two) books or publications. These texts are on display and accessible for students to read.	Text innovations with big books, individual-student-authored books, reports/inquiry projects
Textbooks	These literacy tools are student texts that are typically identified with a subject/content area. Textbooks in this category have an instructional design for the teacher to use and the students to follow in learning new concepts and skills. These books are typically leveled by grade, and the difficulty levels increase with each grade level.	Mathematics textbooks, science textbooks, English grammar books
Trade books	These texts are typically found in book format and do not have any obvious instructional design features.	Picture books (narrative, expository, procedural, persuasive, poetry, drama, and others) and chapter books

(continued)

TABLE 2.1. *(continued)*

Text types	Explanation	Examples
Work product displays	These literacy tools are displays of teacher or student work that is being "celebrated" and set forward for others to read and enjoy. Usually these displays are rotated regularly.	Model writing samples
Writing on paper	These assignments vary across a wide spectrum of constraints. These literacy tools are conceptualized on a continuum ranging from tightly constrained text response formats (e.g., check marks, fill in the blank, multiple-choice) to entirely open-ended response/writing formats (e.g., blank paper, lined paper). The open-ended response formats may range from creative writing activities to literature responses to math problem-solving exercises.	Reading, math, phonics, and spelling workbooks/worksheets, blank paper with assigned topics, paper for creative writing

Note. Based on Hoffman and Sailors (2002).

design and content, are accessible, and represent appropriate challenge levels for all students in the classroom (Hoffman et al., 2004). In summary, research has demonstrated that print-rich classrooms—ones that provide a plethora of literacy tools for students to use and explore as they become literate—are associated with literacy acquisition.

Meeting the Needs of All Students

Research on creating print-rich environments is particularly important when we consider the lack of access to school-based print in low-income communities and neighborhoods. Past research has shown that students from ethnic-minority, low-income homes do engage in acts of literacy (Teale, 1986); those engagements simply do not occur as often as they do for white, more wealthy peers (Neuman & Celano, 2001), and those engagements do not necessarily match those of schools or other institutions (Heath, 1983). These students are often dependent on schools for reading materials that match the school discourse (Worthy, Moorman, & Turner, 1999). It takes an effective teacher to negotiate the space between the known (home literacies) and the unknown (school literacies).

From a linguistic perspective (which is one way of approaching the match or mismatch between homes and schools), for example, highly effective teachers make sure that there are support systems within the various text types to support second-language learning (such as images on the posters found around the classroom). Culturally, teachers can ensure that the materials their students are reading at home are included in the classroom. One teacher we have worked with in the past invited students to bring in reading materials (appropriate, of course) and to share them with others. This classroom thus boasted such additional reading materials as magazines about hot rods, cookbooks, and books on how to care for pets, to name a few. What is most important about the inclusion of books and other materials from homes is that teachers send a message to children that the materials they read at home are important enough to bring to school and share with others.

Similarly, we have often heard from classroom teachers that print-rich environments can "overstimulate" children who may have attention issues. We know of no research to substantiate this claim. As a matter of course, we would argue that these are the very children who should benefit from structured print-rich environments—ones containing texts that have been purposefully placed and serve as anchor texts for learning. We strongly advocate that these children be included in the placement of these texts, so that they know exactly where to look for them when they need them. Having said that, we add that teachers of children with attention issues must be mindful of extraneous texts in the classroom; ones that are there simply to decorate the room are not helpful and may get in the way of texts that are genuinely useful.

SUMMARY OF BIG IDEAS FROM RESEARCH

- The *quantity* of literacy tools offered to students is associated with literacy development.
- In addition to quantity, the *quality* of literacy tools must be considered.
- There must be a range of texts to support literacy learning.
- Finally, while quantity and quality count, the offering of *high-quality literacy instruction* centering on the use of the literacy tools is critical to literacy development.

In the next section, we present case examples of the ways in which a classroom teacher and an instructional school leader make available and use literacy tools in the environments they create for their students as a way of supporting literacy acquisition.

EXAMPLES OF EFFECTIVE PRACTICES

Using and Creating Literacy Tools with Students in a Fourth-Grade Classroom

One of us, Shannon Blady (the third author), has taught at a public school in a large metropolitan area for the past 4 years. Collaboratively designing her fourth-grade classroom with her partner teacher, Jennifer Carter, Shannon has created two distinct learning environments for her students. One of the spaces is furnished with lamps, rugs, comfortable chairs, couches, and pillows (see Figure 2.1). The other consists mainly of tables and countertops for a more structured, yet still inviting, atmosphere. While completing independent assignments, the students choose which space is more conducive to their learning. Shannon has found that most students' choice is based on their learning styles or the requirements of the assigned tasks. At the beginning of the first year of this arrangement, however, students asked for permission to move between rooms. Shannon's response was simple: "Would you ask your mom permission to walk from the living room to the kitchen at home?" One of her goals for this physical environment

FIGURE 2.1. A homelike learning environment furnished with lamps, couches, pillows, and rugs is created to make students feel comfortable to make their own choices and to take risks.

is for students to feel that school is a comfortable, enjoyable place where they are safe to take risks.

A Room with a Variety of Concrete Literacy Tools

This classroom also has a wide variety of concrete literacy tools (Bomer, 2003) that students can access on a regular basis. Shannon makes sure that she explicitly shares the expectations for the use of these tools and that she models how to take care of supplies. The classroom makes available to the students a rolling cart in one space, with pencils, scissors, pens, markers, tape, staplers, paper clips, crayons, highlighters, dry-erase boards, colored pencils, and glue sticks. There are stacks of plastic drawers in the other space with the same supplies. Each room has multiple baskets of sharpened pencils. Students are asked to bring in their own individual pencil sharpeners, to avoid foot traffic and noisy electric pencil sharpeners; because a pencil lasts only as long as its eraser, Shannon asks students to bring in erasers, too. In the more structured area, each table has a large caddy for markers, crayons, and the students' math fluency folders. There are individual hanging pockets labeled for each child with their colored pencils, a pencil sharpener, and a pair of scissors.

A Room with Different Types of Trade Books

Shannon has selected a wide variety of trade books for use in her classroom; she organizes them carefully, with attention to the purposes and uses of the books. In the less structured area, there are fiction and poetry titles, categorized and organized by author (e.g., books by Gary Paulsen; see Figure 2.2) or genre (e.g., scary stories and mysteries). The categories help students to "shop" for a book and to locate books when they want to suggest them to peers.

There is also an entire bookshelf that prominently features picture books (see Figure 2.3). Picture books are enjoyable for all ages, and students in this class read and respond to the books in small groups. A handful of students will choose to read picture books for free reading time. Most students at this age, however, have favorite chapter books that they would prefer to read.

This classroom features books that exemplify models of writing; there are a variety of books that highlight the traits of writing taught within writing workshop mini-lessons. The school year begins with explorations of why people write; this conversation continues throughout the school year. Books that illustrate these various purposes and reasons for writing (e.g., to entertain, to inform, to persuade) are prominently displayed and featured. This collection changes throughout the year.

The more structured of the two areas houses shelves of informational texts. There is a wide variety of books for students to select from, including books on Texas, dinosaurs, architecture, science experiments, space, weather, and animals, to name a few.

FIGURE 2.2. Because students begin to develop reading preferences, titles are categorized by author or genre. Students can shop for and suggest to their peers their favorite books.

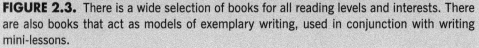

FIGURE 2.3. There is a wide selection of books for all reading levels and interests. There are also books that act as models of exemplary writing, used in conjunction with writing mini-lessons.

The books are organized for ease of selection; it is not uncommon to find students perusing and engaging with these books. Each month, the class selects picture books (focusing on nonfiction texts) to place on a shelf labeled *Books for Lessons*. These books easily lend themselves to class discussions of certain themes or help to explain certain content-area concepts. There is also a collection of biographies and some atlases, along with maps for the students to use. Dictionaries are also stored on their shelves in both rooms, but they have found that students prefer to define text vocabulary by using an application on their computer or through the Internet.

A Room That Focuses on Student Work

Next to the poetry books is a Poet's Tool Box, which stores laminated cards explaining various styles of poetry and poetic techniques. Each semester, the class hosts a Poetry Slam. Students in these two classrooms create the artistic backdrop/props and compose the event's program. Each student memorizes a favorite or original poem and performs it with expression to an invited audience of parents and students from other classes.

Students in Shannon and Jennifer's class work through their literacy rotations, including independent reading, reading with a peer, writing conferences with a peer, writing independently, and word work. They complete all written assignments or reflections on loose-leaf paper and place them in the literacy section of their binder, which also has sections for math, science, and social studies. The binder is a quick and easy way to share their progress with parents during parent–teacher conferences. Some of their written assignments are composed digitally with a word program and stored in an electronic class folder. Students can electronically submit written work, using either a Wiki or a Google document. Each student also has a composition notebook, the cover of which is designed by the student to reflect his or her unique personality. Students use these journals for creative writing and personal reflections. Shannon wants her students to feel that writing can be entertaining, heartfelt, and engaging.

A Room with Leveled Readers

Teachers and interventionists assess students' comprehension and fluency levels multiple times per year at Shannon's school. These assessments help teachers align lessons with students' instructional levels. Students choose titles from the leveled books in the school's guided reading room, where they are sure to encounter a wide range of genres. The reading specialists on Shannon's campus are available to assist teachers in selecting books and reaching the needs of readers at all levels. Many titles in the book room have multiple copies, so teachers can create small book groups with the texts. Students who read below grade level can also choose from a variety of teacher-selected texts, but the selection is slightly more limited, since Shannon wants to make sure she is covering specific reading strategies or specific genres with which these students struggle. Shannon reads with these students daily, and they may receive additional instructional time with an interventionist.

For the majority of the year, Shannon gives students the freedom to choose which books they will read. She makes sure that each book is a good fit, which means that it is not too easy or too difficult, and that the content sustains a student's interest. Sometimes students are encouraged to give a book a try, based on a recommendation by a peer or the teacher. Shannon also makes sure to expose all students to a variety of genres. If a student has been reading a lot of mysteries, she will ask the student to try historical fiction or poetry or expository texts. She keeps track of her students' reading selections with individual reading charts. Book clubs (five or six students reading the same book) have also contributed to students' motivation to read. Once a week, six or seven parent volunteers join the leveled book clubs for 20–30 minutes to discuss various elements of a book (theme, plot, characters) and their personal or intertextual connections with it. Students are more eager to read when they know that their peers and an adult will engage in text-based conversations with them.

A Room with Instructional Charts

Shannon is a self-professed lover of words! In her classroom, there is a word wall that she calls her *Lexicology Wall*. It is on this wall that they place (in alphabetical order) "dazzling" words or new vocabulary that students write on sticky notes or sentence strips. She uses the term *lexicology* to demonstrate how readers and writers use "big" words that can be broken apart and examined. She often uses elevated vocabulary in her discussions with her students, and encourages them to ask about the meanings of words and to make inferences about what the words might mean.

On the other side of her Lexicology Wall, Shannon affixes various store-bought posters, depending on the current lessons. The room has (or has had at some point) lists of prepositions, onomatopoeia words, and pronouns, for example. These lists

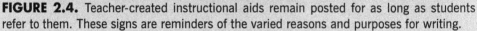

FIGURE 2.4. Teacher-created instructional aids remain posted for as long as students refer to them. These signs are reminders of the varied reasons and purposes for writing.

occasionally find their way into the classroom from the outside, but often they are created by students in the classroom. Shannon also creates instructional aids for her students (see Figure 2.4). For example, when the class was learning about parts of a letter, she wrote a sample letter to her mom and labeled the parts. Student work covers all of the other walls, including models of strong student writing. Shannon showcases the beautiful artwork that students have completed in their art classes, as she believes that a classroom should be aesthetically pleasing—a place that invites students to express themselves and that also inspires them.

A Room That Capitalizes on and Uses Computers and Digital Texts

Although Shannon's classroom is obviously a print-rich environment, filled with student- and teacher-generated literacy tools for students to use, there are tools that are less visible; these are digital literacy tools, or have been produced by using digital literacy tools. In this classroom, there are two laptop computers and six desktop computers that are all connected to the Internet. Shannon also has access to (and often uses) six additional laptops from the grade-level laptop cart.

These digital literacy tools are used in a variety of ways. For example, after interacting with trade books, students in this classroom use Google Documents to create a book review; these reviews become public texts that are used to persuade their classmates to read (or discourage them from reading) the books. Students also use Microsoft Word to type their final drafts of their compositions and to write creative stories. They often write messages to each other on their class Wiki. The public digital literacy tools are used to connect students within lessons. Students also write scripts and perform and record them, using iMovie. They pose content-area questions on Wallwisher and answer science questions after exploring modules on Discovery Education or STEM-scopes. They also use approved search engines to conduct research on independent projects.

Each quarter, Shannon assigns independent or small-group multimodal projects for content-area concepts, as well as for reading response activities. Students respond by using a self-selected literacy tool and one or more of the modalities available to them (written, artistic, and/or digital). It is not uncommon for the prolific writers (and users/creators of literacy tools) in this classroom to try a different genre of writing or perform a play, to paint a scene from the text in which a character reaches a crucial turning point, or to create a Glog or Prezi that covers the main ideas of the text.

In short, Shannon's shared classroom is a print-rich environment that provides access to numerous literacy tools. Her students take advantage of these tools and use them in ways that move them forward in their literacy development. Especially rewarding and motivating is the ready availability of digital literacy tools (which students take full advantage of) in Shannon's shared classroom. It is through the large quantity of high-quality, carefully selected student-centered tools, and through carefully scaffolded experiences with these literacy tools (high-quality instruction), that students in this classroom will grow as literacy learners.

Using and Creating Literacy Tools for Purposeful and Meaningful Literacy Events in Clifford Elementary School

Walk down the hallways of Clifford Elementary School with principal Angeli Willson (the fourth author of this chapter), and you will see products lining the hallways and classrooms. These artifacts represent the use and creation of literacy tools in ways that are typical of elementary schools throughout the nation. A welcome sign in both English and Spanish greets visitors as they come through the front door. In the main office, where visitors check in, the shelves are lined with books, magazines, and yearbooks for parents to peruse while waiting to pick up their child or for a student to read while waiting to see the principal. Around the corner is the nurse's office. The nurse has a bulletin board that has a myriad of information on keeping healthy. Next to her is the counselor's office, and the counselor too has a bulletin board, presenting information on the various programs the counseling department is offering. One can pick up brochures on parent involvement and mentoring, as well as information on getting a GED.

This hallway opens onto Wing C, where the library and several primary-grade classrooms are housed. The library is very colorful, with the different sections of the room brightly labeled. Books of many genres, as well as computers for student research and assessment, are located here. One area has tables and chairs, while another has beanbags for students to use while reading. Walking farther down the hallway, one sees student work displayed everywhere: family trees, illustrations of a book utilizing speech bubbles, essays on what they did last summer, and so on and so on. Peeking into a first-grade classroom, one sees a word wall on one side of the room, phonics sound cards above a SMART Board, an interactive calendar, and various charts used for morning meetings. These charts usually show the days of the week, the months, the date, and the weather. On the student desks, which are arranged in groups, are name plates.

The adjacent wing, which houses the intermediate grades, and its hallways still display many student work samples. There are letters to the school principal regarding bullying, recipes for homemade tortillas, and student-created lists of books that they have read. Looking into a fifth-grade classroom, one sees shelves or tubs of chapter books and reference books. Each student has an agenda or a notebook that he or she uses to write the day's homework and other important reminders.

The physical environment described above is characteristic of most schools. What makes Clifford Elementary School different is how the teachers create and use the literacy tools in their school to support literacy learning. In an era of high-stakes testing, many public school districts have required their teachers to implement a curriculum with very minimal opportunities for teacher input, choice, or creativity. At Clifford, as at a few other schools, teachers still have to follow a set curriculum, but they have their administrators' support to choose the most effective activities to attain the learning objectives. This philosophy of freedom within the parameters of a curriculum has resulted in several grade-level activities that embody the use of literacy tools for purposeful and meaningful literacy activities.

The First-Grade Reading Restaurant at Clifford Elementary

For the past 10 years, the first-grade students and their teachers at Clifford have worked hard to produce a Reading Restaurant for their parents, grandparents, and special guests. The purpose of this activity is to engage young children in purposeful and meaningful literacy events, using literacy tools found in their lived experiences outside school. Using the restaurant motif, the students choose books to read to their parents, create menus of the books they choose, and make chef's hats and placemats for their "restaurant."

USE OF LITERACY TOOLS TO MEET EDUCATIONAL OBJECTIVES

The literacy tools used in the Reading Restaurant help students meet the learning objectives set for them by their teachers and school administrators. These goals include: (1) Students will learn to speak clearly in order to discuss their opinion and ideas on the trade books that they choose to read; (2) students will learn to read the trade books with fluency; and (3) students will demonstrate an understanding of their self-selected trade books. In choosing their trade books, students make connections to their own experiences, to ideas in other texts, and to the larger community, and they discuss their reasons for their book choices. Students use artwork as one way of expressing their ideas and responses to their trade books; the placemats that are created with concrete literacy tools are displayed prominently in this Reading Restaurant.

USE OF CONCRETE TOOLS AND A "MASTER COOK" TO PLAN FOR THE ACTIVITY

With the help of the librarian, first-grade students choose 10 books—two books each for the appetizer, main entree, side dish, drink, and dessert. The first graders then practice reading the books whenever they can, so that they can "serve" a fluent reading of the books on Reading Restaurant Day itself. Each student also creates a chef's hat out of white tissue paper and cardstock. On the hem of the hat, the student writes his or her name and adorns it with drawings. On their placemats, students illustrate one of the books on the menu.

USE OF LITERACY TOOLS TO "SERVE" A WHOLESOME "MEAL"

On the day of the Reading restaurant, each first-grade classroom is set up just like a restaurant, including tablecloths and centerpieces (see Figure 2.5). Each classroom has a sign by the door that tells guests the name of the restaurant. The names are alliterations using the teachers' last names (e.g., *Collins's Café* or *Bell's Bistro*). Arriving at the door, guests are greeted by their "server," who invites them to a place in the restaurant. Guests choose a book from the menu (a type of organizational chart) and listen to their first-grader read. Guests are encouraged to ask questions about and to interact with and trade books with their "server."

As one would imagine, everyone enjoys the visit to the Reading Restaurant. Each server even receives a "tip" (a bag of goodies) for a job well done. The first-grade teachers write a news article about the event (as part of an ongoing literacy tool) and send it to the local newspaper for publication. The Reading Restaurant integrates six domains of literacy (listening, speaking, reading, writing, viewing, and visually representing) in a creative and fun way. The literacy tools used in the activity build on and support the students' concepts of print and skills of phonemic awareness, alphabetic principle, phonics, comprehension, and motivation. The literacy tools within this print environment provide multiple opportunities for students to become independent and fluent readers who see a purpose for literacy and literacy tools in their lives.

FIGURE 2.5. The Reading Restaurant is a brilliant opportunity for first-grade students at Clifford Elementary School to utilize various literacy tools to show family and friends their progress in becoming good readers.

The Second-Grade Culture Fair at Clifford Elementary

The initial inspiration for the second-grade Culture Fair came from a desire to promote the school–home relationship. The teachers wanted an event that would involve families in their classrooms. For the Culture Fair, students do research on a country of their own choosing and present their findings to parents and guests on Culture Day. Students utilize different tools, such as presentation boards and laptops, to do their presentations. They also bring artifacts related to their projects. Since the school is a culturally diverse community, the teachers felt it would be an exciting and interesting event, as well as a purposeful and meaningful way to use literacy tools. As teachers suspected, families have adopted the event, and family participation in this activity has exceeded all expectations.

USE OF LITERACY TOOLS TO MEET EDUCATIONAL OBJECTIVES

With the Culture Fair, the teachers are able to address a broad range of educational objectives. The most obvious are the integration of social studies skills and strategies pertaining to (1) following routes on a map, (2) family heritage/community celebrations, (3) expressions of culture, and (4) spreading culture. The teachers integrate the reading and language arts skills and strategies of summarization, making predictions, creating mental images, vocabulary, comparison/contrast, facts versus opinions, main ideas and details, and drawing conclusions. In short, the use of this activity allows teachers to provide integrated opportunities for students in second grade to learn how literacy tools can support content-area learning.

USE OF LITERACY TOOLS AND "MASTER COMMUNICATORS" TO PLAN FOR THE ACTIVITY

As one would expect, this event requires a tremendous amount of planning on the part of the students as well as their teachers. As a team, the second-grade teachers plan for this event weeks ahead of time. They use serial tools (letters) with their students and send them home to parents, informing them of the event and its requirements. To drum up excitement for the event, they send home follow-up notes and make phone calls. They send out special invitations to auxiliary staff members, the principal, and the vice-principal, as well as the superintendent of the school district. Students are aware that special guests will be in attendance, as many announcements and decorations appear in the second-grade hall in anticipation of this event. Parents are invited to participate fully in this activity by assisting their children in creating products for display at the fair.

USE OF LITERACY TOOLS TO "TRAVEL AROUND THE WORLD"

When the day of the Culture Fair arrives, it is show time (see Figure 2.6); students bring in the projects they have completed at home. Each project includes some form of presentation board featuring the required information (e.g., the country's population, flag, currency, famous citizens, languages spoken, etc.). The project also may include costumes, food, music, artifacts, or anything else a student wishes. Every year the teachers and administrators are pleasantly surprised at how students really get excited and go "all out!"

FIGURE 2.6. The second-grade Culture Fair is an excellent venue for students to integrate skills and strategies across content areas and to spark an interest in the different cultures of the world.

In the morning, each classroom's teacher and students transform the classroom into a "trip around the world." Desks are pushed into a circle on the outer edges of the classroom for ease of movement, allowing guests to "travel" from country to country easily and simplifying traffic flow. Countries are grouped together by continents and geographic locations. In the afternoon, guests arrive. Each guest is issued a literacy tool that will allow him or her to pass between countries—a "United States of Clifford passport." They are also given a plate for all of the delicious foods from different cultures they will be served along the way. They are encouraged to begin their journey at any point, and most parents naturally start at the country represented by their own child. Once a guest arrives at a country, the student welcomes the guest by stamping his or her passport and sharing favorite facts about the country. Students then offer guests a taste of their food or provide other artifacts or information. Once the guests are finished, students encourage them to visit the next country. Guests make the circle around the room, visiting the desk of each student in the class. The teacher acts as a facilitator of the logistics during the fair. Following the event, the teachers write a news article and send pictures to the local newspaper for publication.

As one would expect, the school receives tremendously positive feedback on the Culture Fair from students, parents, and fellow teachers. The success of the event is best measured by its continued growth and increasing level of complexity. Every year the event is more widely attended, the projects become bigger and better, and the excitement is unmatched. The Culture Fair is a literacy activity intended to motivate students, to embed and integrate skills and strategies across the content and literacy areas, and to spark an interest in cultures within and across the communities that surround Clifford Elementary. The students are fully supported by "masters" in the field; with the help of the librarian, for example, the students spend time in the library gathering books, periodicals, and documents related to their countries. Students are then asked to authenticate the information and use it in a way that gives their guests valuable information. Each student also writes and produces a display for the fair. All of these elements come together to make this an important literacy activity in which literacy tools are used in purposeful and meaningful ways.

The Fifth-Grade Poetry Slam at Clifford Elementary

The fifth-grade reading and English language arts teachers were curious about their students' interests and skills related to poetry, and decided to engage the students in a Poetry Slam. The inspiration for this activity came from a need to have the students emotionally invested in the topic of bullying. Because of the recent mass media focus on the topic (news stories were making the students well aware of the devastating effects bullying can have on a person), and because the students were talking about these events, these fifth-grade teachers decided to engage their students in explorations on the topic through the use of literacy tools found in a Poetry Slam.

USE OF LITERACY TOOLS TO MEET EDUCATIONAL OBJECTIVES

The main objective of the Poetry Slam was to explore poetry as a genre, especially as it related to the students' own experiences. Corollary objectives were for students to have opportunities for technology use, gain expertise in their research skills, and improve their oral reading (e.g., speed and clarity). Social skills, such as manners and working with a partner, were also included.

USE OF LITERACY TOOLS TO "SET THE TONE" OF THE ACTIVITY

The teachers and students searched online to determine whether Internet resources, such as poetry websites, were available. The participants (teachers and students) wanted to draw for inspiration on both classic poetry and contemporary pieces that students might find interesting. The teachers held classroom discussions to access prior knowledge. They also reminded students of where they might find poetry in modern life, and of how rhyme and rhythm are related but not the same. Teachers brought in other materials such as trade books (focused on poetry) from the library and some students brought their own poetry books from home. The students chose a name for the event and painted signs, brought in background lighting, and used battery-operated candles to add to the ambience. The students also decorated the classrooms with flowers, turned their desks into small tables, and brought in a microphone with a stand for each classroom to help set the mood.

USE OF LITERACY TOOLS TO "SLAM"

Parents and teachers were pleasantly surprised on the day of the Poetry Slam: Expecting classrooms, guests to the fifth-grade classrooms instead walked into coffee shops (see Figure 2.7). On the tables were student-made programs that had the names of the students and the titles of their poems. On a podium in front of each room was a binder that held copies of all the students' poems. Each teacher would later add this compilation to the classroom library. The students had practiced giving up their seats for visitors, as well as facilitating traffic flow into and out of each room, as teachers and parents could not always stay for the entire event. During the Poetry Slam, students took turns performing their original pieces of poetry, each with a focus on not only what they wrote (content focused on bullying—its causes, its effects, and ways in which to stave it off) but also how they performed. As performances ended, the students applauded, snapping their fingers to show their appreciation. This was a real treat (and cut down on noise in the room between performers) because the students took charge without saying anything; they eagerly snapped their fingers after each performance.

As one would expect, the Poetry Slam was a major success. The students talked about it for a long time, and even convinced their teachers to plan for another Poetry Slam in preparation for the state accountability assessment. The students actually wrote poems and performed those poems to motivate each other to perform well on the test! Parents and community members were gracious and willing to be a part of the activity. The teachers received many thank-you e-mails, and the students were anxious to perform again.

In short, Clifford Elementary is a place in which literacy tools are created and used for purposeful and meaningful literacy activities. Students are not only motivated to participate in the objectives and outcomes that their teachers structure for and with them; they are learning the rules and conventions of our written language in useful ways and in ways that will transfer to other literacy activities.

FIGURE 2.7. Fifth-grade students take a break outside the class "cafés" after performing their original poems during the Poetry Slam.

LOOKING FORWARD

Research suggests that efforts directed toward the following practices will enhance the effectiveness of instruction and improve students' literacy abilities:

- Use of digital literacy tools, such as websites that allow for creation of texts (e.g., *www.readwritethink.org*, *www.webenglishteacher.com/poetryslam.html*, *www.writing-fix.com*, and *www.kerpoof.com*).
- Selective and purposeful use of literacy tools that provide structured support for learning to take mandated state assessments (Langer, 2001).
- Use of assessment data to inform instruction (Kapinus, 2008).
- Purposeful and meaningful literacy events that mirror the social nature of literacy in students' lived worlds (Barton & Hamilton, 1998).

This chapter also raises the following questions for future research:

- What are the effects of authentic literacy events on children's reading achievement and motivation to read?
- What are the effects of active parental participation in book clubs on students' reading achievement and motivation?
- Who makes the decisions in creating a print-rich environment? How are the elements operationalized?
- Are there particular skills and strategies that children need in print-rich environments to be successful in accessing various types of text (digital vs. traditional)?

In addition, a further look into schools and classrooms such as the ones described in this chapter's vignettes could help educators answer the following questions:

- What are the teachers doing instructionally beyond the print-rich environment?
- What resources are needed so that teachers and schools can make the transition to print-rich environments?
- How do teachers negotiate the space between home literacies and school literacies?
- How do the belief systems of teachers/administrators affect the literacy outcomes of students?

QUESTIONS FOR REFLECTION •

1. What are the various literacy tools to support literacy development in my classroom? In what ways do my students use these literacy tools?

2. To what extent do I encourage the use literacy tools in my print environment as a resource for students to use in moving toward self-directed literacy learning?

3. To what extent do the literacy tools in my print environment represent not only the learning that is taking place, but also the literacy skills and strategies required for literacy development?

4. To what extent do the literacy tools in my print environment serve as both resources for my students and means of assessing what the students in my class are learning and what they can do?

5. To what extent do the literacy tools in my print environment support students who struggle with learning to read?

6. To what extent do the literacy tools in my print environment motivate and intellectually challenge students as they move forward in their literacy development?

SUGGESTIONS FOR ONGOING PROFESSIONAL LEARNING ● ● ● ● ● ●

There are several ways in which teachers can critically examine the support that their literacy tools provide to the literacy development of students. A professional learning community, or PLC, is one mechanism that offers such support (see Peterson, Chapter 21, this volume). Through regular interactions within a PLC, teachers can critically examine their own literate environment and the environment of others. Below are two examples of ways in which teachers can engage in ongoing professional learning with the assistance of a PLC. Ongoing professional learning is covered in more detail by Peterson in Chapter 21 and by Sailors, Russell, Augustine, and Alexander in Chapter 22.

Self-Evaluation of the Literacy Tools within Your Print-Rich Environment

PLCs can offer support to teachers as they become more aware of and critical about the literacy tools they provide to and create with students. Professional self-evaluation can be conducted with the assistance of other PLC members.

Session 1

Discuss this chapter and the literacy tools you offer to children in your classroom with members of a PLC. What literacy tools are most often used by students in your classroom? Are those literacy tools used equally by all children? Who creates those literacy tools? You? The students? The students, with your support and careful scaffolding? Watch the students. Talk to them about what they think about the literacy tools that are in place for them. Keep a log for 2 weeks as a way of documenting the ways in which literacy tools are created and used and by whom. Keep a careful eye on the creation and use of the literacy tools by students who are above average, average, and below average. Are the literacy tools motivating, differentiated, and intellectually challenging? To get a running start on this session, consult the *Research-Based Resources* list at the end of this chapter.

Session 2

Bring your log and some samples of the literacy tools from your classroom to your next PLC meeting. Discuss the ways in which you would like to structure the creation and use of the literacy tools in your classroom to be more meaningful to your students. Get ideas for change from your PLC group members.

Session 3

With members of a PLC, go on a scavenger hunt in each other's classrooms, looking for exemplar ways in which literacy tools are created and used in support of literacy development. You might consider using the following card as a way of structuring your *first* scavenger hunt. You may want to recreate this card and use it on other occasions, with a focus on additional types of literacy tools.

Literacy Tools Scavenger Hunt		
Literacy tools that support the *learning of new words* (word identification and word knowledge)	Literacy tools that support the *learning of various genres* (historical fiction, biographies, informational texts, science fiction, etc.)	Literacy tools that support the *learning of fix-up strategies*
Literacy tools that *organize and manage the literacy environment* (social, academic, and curricular aspects)	Literacy tools that are *motivational and inspirational* and that *build a love of reading and writing*	Literacy tools that *demonstrate an awareness of varying challenge levels in the classroom* (tools for students who are at, above, and below grade-level literacy)
Literacy tools that support the *development of cognitive strategies readers use* (you might include the name of the reading strategy, when to use it, why readers use it, and the steps involved during the use of the strategy)	Literacy tools that support the *learning of informational text structures* (descriptive, cause–effect, chronological, compare/contrast, etc.)	Literacy tools that support the *growing identity of students as readers and writers* (i.e., students were obviously involved in creating the texts)

Session 4

Discuss your findings from Session 3. What did you notice in other classrooms? Were there a variety of literacy tools? What qualities about these literacy tools did you notice? Which ones were locally created? Commercially prepared? How accessible were these literacy tools for students, both developmentally and physically? What were the purposes for these various literacy tools? Which of these literacy tools would you like to "borrow" for your own classroom? Decide upon and commit to implementing at least three new types of literacy tools in your classroom over the next few weeks. Keep notes about the positive and challenges associated with implementing these changes.

Session 5

Bring your notes on the positive and challenges associated with implementing the changes you committed to in Session 4 to your next PLC meeting. Share these notes. Discuss progress you have made in providing and creating additional literacy tools in your classroom. Seek assistance in diminishing the challenges you identified. Identify your next steps for continued improvement.

Modifying the Structure of Your Classroom to Provide for Meaningful and Purposeful Literacy Activities and Tools

Session 1

Think about the literacy activities that are in place for your students. Discuss with members of a PLC the nature of those literacy events. Are the literacy tools you use and create in your classroom part of a meaningful and purposeful context for literacy development? Do the literacy tools that you use with students mirror those literacy tools they use outside of school?

Session 2

Discuss with the members of a PLC the literacy activities described in this chapter. In what ways do your literacy activities (discussed in Session 1) mirror the activities at Clifford Elementary? How are they different?

Session 3

Poll the students in your classroom to see what types of literacy activities in which they would like to engage. With the members of a PLC, decide which of the activities mentioned by the students in your class would lead to purposeful and meaningful use and creation of literacy tools in your classroom. Make a plan for implementing at least one of these activities.

Session 4

Discuss with members of a PLC the plans you have made and the progress toward implementing the activity decided upon in Session 3. What literacy tools are required for your students during the planning stages? During the actual implementation or performance stage? How are your students responding to this activity? What literacy skills and strategies are you embedding inside the activity? What challenges do you face in implementing the activity to its fullest?

Session 5

After you have implemented (or performed) your chosen activity, discuss with a PLC the successes of the activity. Motivation of students? Success of students with embedded skills and strategies within the activity? Overall performance? Challenges? What are your next steps?

RESEARCH-BASED RESOURCES

Literacy Tools as Part of Effective Literacy Instruction

Duke, N. K., & Bennett-Armistead, V. S. (2003). *Reading and writing informational texts in the primary grades: Research-based practices.* New York: Scholastic.

Elley, W. B. (2000). The potential of book floods for raising literacy levels. *International Journal of Educational Research, 46,* 233–255.

Knapp, M. S., & Associates. (1995). *Teaching for meaning in high-poverty classrooms*. New York: Teachers College Press.

Pressley, M., Rankin, T., & Yokoi, L. (1996). A survey of instructional practices of primary teachers nominated as effective in promoting literacy. *Elementary School Journal, 96*, 363–384.

Pressley, M., Wharton-McDonald, R., Mistretta-Hampston, J., & Echevarria, M. (1998). The nature of literacy instruction in ten grade 1/5 classrooms in upstate New York. *Scientific Studies of Reading, 2*, 159–194.

Sailors, M., & Hoffman, J. V. (2010). The text environment and learning to read: Windows and mirrors shaping literate lives. In D. Wyse, R. Andrews, & J. Hoffman (Eds.), *The international handbook of English, language and literacy teaching* (pp. 294–304). New York: Routledge.

Taylor, B. M., Pearson, P. D., Clark, K. F., & Walpole, S. (2000). Effective schools and accomplished teachers: Lessons about primary-grade reading instruction in low-income schools. *Elementary School Journal, 101*, 121–165.

Observational Instruments to Evaluate Literacy Tools in Classrooms

Baker, S. K., Gersten, R., Haager, D., & Dingle, M. (2006). Teaching practice and the reading growth of first-grade English learners: Validation of an observation instrument. *Elementary School Journal, 107*, 199–221.

Hoffman, J. V., & Sailors, M. (2004). Reflecting on the literacy environment and literacy practices: The TEX-IN3 (M). In J. V. Hoffman & D. L. Schallert (Eds.), *Read this room: The role of texts in beginning reading instruction* (pp. 213–239). Ann Arbor, MI: Center for the Improvement of Early Reading Achievement.

Hoffman, J. V., Sailors, M., Duffy, G. G., & Beretvas, S. N. (2004). The effective elementary classroom literacy environment: Examining the validity of the TEX-IN3 Observation System. *Journal of Literacy Research, 36*, 303–334.

Ross, S. M., Smith, L. J., Lohr, L., & McNelis, M. (1994). Math and reading instruction in tracked first-grade classes. *Elementary School Journal, 95*, 105–119.

Wolfersberger, M. E., Reutzel, D. R., Sudweeks, R., & Fawson, P. C. (2004). Developing and validating the Classroom Literacy Environmental Profile (CLEP): A tool for examining the "print richness" of early childhood and elementary classrooms. *Journal of Literacy Research, 36*, 211–272.

REFERENCES

Barton, D., & Hamilton, M. (1998). *Local literacies: Reading and writing in one community*. New York: Routledge.

Bomer, R. (2003). Things that make kids smart: A Vygotskian perspective on concrete tool use in primary literacy classrooms. *Journal of Early Childhood Literacy, 3*, 223–247.

Duke, N. K. (2000). 3.6 minutes per day: The scarcity of informational texts in first grade. *Reading Research Quarterly, 35*, 202–224.

Engeström, Y. (1993). *Understanding practice: Perspectives on activity and context*. New York: Cambridge University Press.

Fractor, J. S., Woodruff, M., Martinez, M., & Teale, W. H. (1993). Let's not miss opportunities to promote voluntary reading: Classroom libraries in the elementary school. *Reading Teacher, 46*, 476–484.

Heath, S. B. (1983). *Ways with words: Language, life, and work in communities and classrooms*. New York: Cambridge University Press.

Hoffman, J. V., & Sailors, M. (2002). *Texts Inventory, Texts In-Use and Text Interviews Observation System*. Unpublished manuscript, University of Texas at Austin.

Hoffman, J. V., Sailors, M., Duffy, G. G., & Beretvas, S. N. (2004). The effective elementary classroom literacy environment: Examining the validity of the TEX-IN3 Observation System. *Journal of Literacy Research, 36*, 303–334.

Holzman, L. (2006). What kind of theory is activity theory?: Introduction. *Theory Psychology, 16*, 5–11.

Kapinus, B. (2008). Assessment of reading programs. In S. B. Wepner & D. S. Strickland (Eds.), *The administration and supervision of reading programs* (4th ed., pp. 144–156). New York: Teachers College Press.

Langer, J. A. (2001). Beating the odds: Teaching middle and high school students to read and write well. *American Educational Research Journal, 38*, 837–880.

McGill-Franzen, A., Allington, R. L., Yokoi, L., & Brooks, G. (1999). Putting books in the classroom seems necessary but not sufficient. *Journal of Educational Research, 93*, 67–74.

Morrow, L. M., & Weinstein, C. S. (1982). Increasing children's use of literature through program and physical design changes. *Elementary School Journal, 85*(2), 133–137.

Neuman, S. B. (1999). Books make a difference: A study of access to literacy. *Reading Research Quarterly, 34*, 286–311.

Neuman, S. B., & Celano, D. (2001). Access to print in low-income and middle-income communities: An ecological study of four neighborhoods. *Reading Research Quarterly, 36*, 8–26.

Reutzel, D. R., Oda, L. K., & Moore, B. H. (1989). Developing print awareness: The effect of three instructional approaches on kindergarteners' print awareness, reading readiness, and word reading. *Journal of Reading Behavior, 21*(3) 197–217.

Sailors, M., & Hoffman, J. V. (2011). Establishing a print-rich classroom and school environment. In R. Bean & A. S. Dagen (Eds.), *Best practices of literacy leaders in schools* (pp. 184–205). New York: Guilford Press.

Taylor, N. E., Blum, I. H., & Logsdon, D. M. (1986). The development of written language awareness: Environmental aspects and program characteristics. *Reading Research Quarterly, 21*, 132–149.

Teale, W. H. (1986). Home background and children's literacy development. In W. H. Teale & E. Sulzby (Eds.), *Emergent literacy: Writing and reading* (pp. vii–xxiv). Norwood, NJ: Ablex.

Worthy, J., Moorman, M., & Turner, M. (1999). What Johnny likes to read is hard to find in school. *Reading Research Quarterly, 34*, 12–27.

Yamagata-Lynch, L. C. (2010). *Activity systems analysis methods: Understanding complex learning environments*. New York: SpringerLink Ebooks.

CHAPTER 3

Grouping Practices, Independent Learning Activities, and Effective Instruction ● ● ● ● ● ● ● ● ● ●

BARBARA M. TAYLOR

OVERVIEW OF RESEARCH

Effective Balance in Whole-Class and Small-Group Instruction

Research suggests that it is important for teachers to reflect on grouping practices and to consider whether or not they maintain a good balance between whole-class and small-group reading instruction (Taylor, 2011a, 2011b, 2011c; Taylor, Peterson, Marx, & Chein, 2007). An excellent time to do this is when teachers meet for grade-level meetings or professional development work. Together teachers can ask, "Do we provide whole-class instruction when it is an efficient way to provide explicit instruction? Do we provide small-group instruction as a way to provide differentiated instruction that can be tailored to meet students' needs?"

Researchers found that primary-grade teachers who provided motivating instruction to their students offered a good balance between whole-class and small-group instruction, whereas primary-grade teachers who provided less motivational instruction made use of mostly whole-class instruction (Bogner, Raphael, & Pressley, 2002; Pressley et al., 2003). In a related study, teachers who provided mostly whole-class or mostly small-group instruction saw less reading growth in their students during the year than teachers who combined the two types of instruction (Taylor & Peterson, 2006a, 2006b, 2006c). A logical explanation for these findings is that with too much whole-class instruction students' minds start to wander, but with too much small-group instruction students outside the group are left on their own for too long.

Of course, there is no magic formula for the amount of whole-class versus small-group instruction a teacher should provide. Balance is the key. Depending on their

This is hardly a difference

teaching styles, teachers have success with varying amounts of whole-class and small-group instruction during their literacy blocks.

That being said, in one study of effective schools and teachers in grades 1–3 (Taylor, Pearson, Clark, & Walpole, 2000), the students of teachers in the most effective schools spent 25 minutes a day in whole-class instruction, 60 minutes a day in small-group learning activities (including guided reading groups), and 49 minutes in independent learning activities during the reading block. The students of teachers in the least effective schools spent 30 minutes a day in whole-class instruction, 38 minutes a day in small-group instruction and other learning activities, and 45 minutes in independent learning activities. When teachers, regardless of schools, were considered, students in classrooms of the most accomplished teachers spent more time in small-group than whole-class instruction, whereas students in classrooms of the least accomplished teachers spent more time in whole-class than small-group instruction (Taylor, 2011a, 2011b, 2011c; Taylor et al., 2000; see Tables 3.1 and 3.2).

Taylor and colleagues (2000) found a strong correlation between classrooms that had sufficient small-group instruction and students' reading progress. Similarly,

TABLE 3.1. Students' Time in Various Reading Activities during the Reading Block by School Effectiveness Level

	Minutes learning in whole class	Minutes learning in small group	Minutes of independent reading	Minutes writing in response to reading	Minutes in other independent activities	Total minutes in reading
Most effective schools	25	60	28	14	7	134
Moderately effective schools	37	26	27	15	7	112
Least effective schools	30	38	19	9	17	113

Note. Data from Taylor, Pearson, Clark, and Walpole (2000).

TABLE 3.2. Students' Time in Whole-Class and Small-Group Learning during the Reading Block by Level of Teacher Accomplishment

	Minutes learning in whole class	Minutes learning in small group
Most accomplished teachers	25	48
Moderately accomplished teachers	29	39
Least accomplished teachers	48	25

Note. Data from Taylor et al. (2000).

Allington and Johnston (2002) found that exemplary fourth-grade teachers provided students with more individual and small-group lessons than whole-class instruction.

As teachers consider the amount of whole-class and small-group instruction they provide, they need to make deliberate decisions about instances when one type or the other meets instructional objectives and students' needs better. For example, teachers may find it more efficient to introduce and model a comprehension strategy, such as summarizing a story, in a whole-class lesson. However, they may find that they can more effectively differentiate instruction as a follow-up to this whole-class lesson by having students practice summarizing a story in small, guided reading groups. They can use texts at students' instructional reading level in these groups, and they can provide more or less support in summarizing, depending on students' needs.

To differentiate instruction based on students' reading abilities, and to make adjustments when more or less support is required, teachers regularly need to use a variety of ongoing assessments to monitor students' progress in decoding, vocabulary, comprehension, motivation to read, and writing. (For more on balanced, differentiated instruction, see Peterson, Chapter 4, this volume. The topic of ongoing assessments to monitor students' progress and to inform practice is covered by Valencia and Hebard in Chapter 5 and by Weber in Chapter 19.)

Teachers also regularly need to reflect on the quality of their small-group lessons and independent work for students of differing reading levels, especially for those who are low-level readers. Elbaum, Vaughn, Hughes, Moody, and Schumm (2000) found that small-group instruction was more effective than whole-class instruction for students with learning disabilities. Chorzempa and Graham (2006) found that low-ability readers, compared with peers in higher-ability groups, received more unchallenging and less challenging instruction in their small groups. Below-average readers in grades 1–3 spent more time being read to by the teacher and doing worksheets, and less time reading silently, answering high-level comprehension questions, reading expository texts, and selecting their own texts, than average and above-average readers spent.

Small-Group Intervention Lessons for Struggling Readers

All classrooms have some children who are reading below grade level and need extra support in order to accelerate their reading growth. Small-group interventions and one-on-one tutoring increase the reading achievement of struggling beginning readers (Foorman & Torgesen, 2001; Gunn, Smolkowski, Biglan, Black, & Blair, 2005; Hiebert & Taylor, 1998; Mathes et al., 2005; Vaughn et al., 2006; Wasik & Slavin, 1993) and English language learner (ELL) students (Graves, Gersten, & Haager, 2004). Research suggests that it is beneficial if this additional intervention instruction is delivered either by the classroom teacher or by a resource teacher who comes into the classroom (Taylor & Peterson, 2003). Small groups receiving intervention lessons need to stay small—six or seven students, or fewer. Some children also benefit from receiving one-on-one reading support from a resource teacher (Wasik & Slavin, 1993). Foorman and Torgesen (2001) have found that children reading below grade level need additional small-group or one-on-one instruction that is more intensive, explicit, comprehensive, and supportive than the small-group instruction typically provided in guided reading groups in general.

SUMMARY OF BIG IDEAS FROM RESEARCH

- Effective teachers adjust the amount of whole-class and small-group reading instruction they provide to meet lesson objectives and students' needs effectively.
- Classroom or resource teachers provide small-group or one-on-one interventions to accelerate the reading development of students reading below grade level.

Table 3.3 shows the focus on grouping practices and interventions in the research studies.

TABLE 3.3. Grouping Practices and Interventions in the Research Studies (Taylor, 2011a, 2011b, 2011c)

Citation	Provide effective levels of whole-class and small-group instruction	Provide interventions to students needing more support in reading
Allington & Johnston (2002)	×	
Bogner, Raphael, & Pressley (2002)	×	
Foorman & Torgesen (2001)		×
Elbaum, Vaughn, Hughes, Moody, & Schumm (2000)		×
Graves, Gersten, & Haager (2004)		×
Gunn, Smolkowski, Biglan, Black, & Blair (2005)		×
Hiebert & Taylor (1998)		×
Mathes et al. (2005)		×
Pressley et al. (2003)	×	
Taylor & Peterson (2003)	×	
Taylor & Peterson (2006a, 2006b, 2006c)	×	
Taylor & Peterson (2006c)	×	
Vaughn et al. (2006)		×
Wasik & Slavin (1993)		×

EXAMPLES OF EFFECTIVE PRACTICES

Meeting All Students' Needs through Balanced Grouping Practices

Example 1

Begin with explicit instruction in a comprehension skill or strategy during a whole-class lesson, using a grade-level text. Explicitly teach (e.g., tell, model, review) one of the following:

- A comprehension concept (e.g., distinguishing between a fact and an opinion, understanding the concept of a main idea).
- A comprehension skill or process (e.g., drawing inferences, understanding main ideas, grasping themes of stories).
- A strategy (e.g., consciously engaging in comprehension monitoring during reading or summarizing after reading).

Coach students as they develop their understanding of the concept or practice the skill, process, or strategy while reading a text segment. In addition, discuss vocabulary at points of contact in the text, and engage in high-level talk about the text during or after reading.

As students finish reading the text (on their own, with a partner, or in a small group), actively engage them in learning activities in which they continue to refine their understanding of the comprehension concept or to practice the skill, process, or strategy you taught. Also have them engage in high-level talk and/or writing about text. To give students additional opportunities for practice and to differentiate instruction, continue to work on the same comprehension concept, skill, process, or strategy in guided reading groups with leveled texts at students' instructional reading level.

Example 2

To differentiate instruction to meet students' needs, teach phonics, for those who need it, in small, guided reading groups instead of in a whole-class lesson. Using texts at students' reading levels, focus on what each individual student or group of students needs to learn, not on what they already know, about symbol–sound correspondences and decoding strategies. Provide individual support by coaching students to use word

---

Using Response to Intervention to Meet Students' Needs through Collaboration among Teachers

A classroom or resource teacher should provide a second shot of high-quality, explicit response-to-intervention (RTI) instruction each day to students who are struggling with reading or who have special needs, to accelerate their literacy learning and improve their reading abilities. Students who are reading below grade level will benefit from either a daily, motivating small-group or one-on-one intervention lesson that is challenging yet supportive. (For more on collaboration among teachers to help students who need more support, see Walpole & Najera, Chapter 20, this volume.)

recognition strategies as they read appropriate leveled texts. Importantly, students who no longer need explicit phonics lessons because they are decoding well can focus on instructional activities that are more useful to them than phonics.

A Second-Grade Teacher's Whole-Class Lesson on a Comprehension Process, with Follow-up Work in Guided Reading Groups

Many effective teachers (Taylor, 2010a, 2010b, 2010c, 2011a) begin their reading blocks with a whole-class lesson in which they provide explicit instruction in a reading skill or strategy. They then provide follow-up instruction in this skill or strategy in small guided reading groups.

A second-grade teacher at a rural elementary school begins a whole-class lesson on the vital comprehension process of making inferences while reading. She asks questions related to inferences that a reader needs to make as the class reads a story from the second-grade anthology. "We see a picture of a living room and know that the story is about a character named Goldie, but does the text actually say that Goldie is a fish?" Students shake their heads no. "What clues did we use to figure this out?" Students mention the words *tank* and *wiggling* from the story. The teacher says,

> "We were making an *inference*. Some of the information came from our prior knowledge, or in other words, from ideas we already had in our heads. We already know that *tank* and *wiggling* could describe a pet fish. Making inferences as we read is an important thing to do because this helps us better understand what we are reading."

As the students read their story about the goldfish, the teacher stops to question or talk about a few other inferences they need to make to enhance their understanding of the story. At the end of the whole-class lesson, the teacher tells students that they will talk more about making inferences during their guided reading lessons. (For more on comprehension strategies instruction, see Stahl, Chapter 9, this volume.)

Small-Group Work Embedded within a Third-Grade Teacher's Whole-Class Lesson on a Comprehension Strategy

A third-grade teacher at a suburban elementary school frequently embeds partner and triad work within a whole-class lesson. For example, on one day she introduces reciprocal teaching (RT) with the whole class (Palincsar & Brown, 1986). First, she uses a few sections of the third-grade science textbook to model the RT strategies of predicting, clarifying, questioning, and summarizing. Then she has students working in triads use the strategies collaboratively as they read other sections of their science book. As the groups work, the teacher circulates among them, offering feedback and providing coaching as needed. Later, in guided reading groups, the teacher and her students again work on RT as they read texts at the students' reading levels.

A First-Grade Teacher's Small-Group Intervention Lesson

A first-grade teacher at an urban elementary school begins a 20-minute Early Intervention in Reading (EIR) lesson (Taylor, 2010a) with a group of readers who are reading below grade level. She explicitly states the lesson's purposes:

> "One of our purposes today is to work on fluency. Another is to review decoding strategies that we can use on words we don't know. A third purpose is to practice answering higher-level questions to help us better understand the story that we are reading. A fourth purpose is to review long- and short-vowel sounds that we have been learning about."

The teacher and her students talk about the value of rereading to build fluency: "What does reading with good fluency sound like?" Students take turns describing good reading fluency, and then their teacher models as she reads from the book they are reading in their EIR group. Next, the teacher and her students review peer coaching strategies they can use to help a partner who gets stuck on a word during partner reading. The teacher coaches individuals in word recognition strategies as they read their current book.

The teacher focuses on comprehension and high-level thinking related to the story they just read. She asks them to talk briefly about how they thought the main character felt when he helped others, and how they feel themselves when they are helpful.

Before the students return to their seats, the teacher does a quick activity to reinforce the short-vowel sounds the students worked on the day before. With the teacher's guidance, students make the following words from the letter cards for *a, e, d, h, m,* and *s*: *me, he, she, shed, sad, made, made.* Then they reread the words they have made. (For more on word recognition instruction, see Johnson & Kuhn, Chapter 8, this volume.)

A Third-Grade Teacher's Classroom Schedule: Planning to Achieve Effective Levels of Whole-Class and Small-Group Instruction

Although they teach at different grade levels, the three exemplary teachers highlighted above typically start their reading block with a 20- to 30-minute whole-class lesson that is often broken up with brief partner or triad work. As the teachers move into small-group, guided reading lessons, they provide instruction differentiated by students' reading levels and needs. All three teachers also provide an additional small-group reading intervention lesson to their lowest-achieving readers. In their teaching of their whole classes and small groups, the three teachers explicitly state lesson purposes and move at an efficient pace, guided by lesson goals. During blocks of time devoted to small-group lessons, students at their seats are engaged in intellectually challenging, motivating independent learning activities that meet their needs.

The third-grade teacher's schedule is included here, along with a brief discussion of how her reading block is structured. The first- and second-grade teachers have surprisingly similar schedules for their 110- to 120-minute reading blocks. However, the first-grade teacher works with her intervention group after lunch, and the other students complete morning literacy work or engage in independent reading for pleasure.

The third-grade teacher has a 110-minute reading block. She typically spends about 30 minutes a day on a whole-class lesson, 60 minutes a day on three guided reading groups, and 20 minutes on one reading intervention group to provide extra support to her lowest-performing readers. (For more on interventions, see Taylor, 2010a, 2010b, 2010c, 2011a, 2011b.)

Typically, average and above-average readers spend 60 minutes a day on four independent learning activities, and below-average readers spend about 40 minutes a day on three independent activities plus their intervention lesson. Several days a week, there is a parent or senior citizen volunteer in the classroom during the reading block who provides assistance to students as they are engaged in independent work activities.

A Third-Grade Teacher's Daily Reading Block Schedule	
9:00–9:30	Whole-class lesson
9:30–9:50	Small group 1
9:50–10:10	Small group 2
10:10–10:30	Small group 3
10:30–10:50	Intervention lesson

Typical Instructional Components of the Third-Grade Teacher's Daily Reading Block

Whole-class lesson	Small-group lessons	Intervention lesson	Activities for independent work time
Read anthology selection; teach a comprehension strategy; teach vocabulary at point of contact; discuss high-level questions; review activities for work time.	Using leveled texts, coach in word recognition strategies; discuss vocabulary at point of contact; provide follow-up to comprehension strategy taught to whole class; discuss high-level questions about leveled text.	Engage in repeated reading; read a "new" text; coach in word recognition strategies; discuss vocabulary at point of contact; engage in high-level talk about text; engage in word work.	*Activity 1*—Read or reread, write, discuss as follow-up to whole-class text. *Activity 2*—Read or reread, write, discuss as follow-up to small-group text. *Activity 3*—Read or reread, write, discuss text unrelated to whole-class or small-group lesson. *Activity 4*—Read for pleasure from book of choice.

Independent Activities in the Third-Grade Teacher's Classroom: What Students Do While the Teacher Is Working with Small Groups

The third-grade teacher featured in this chapter provides motivating, challenging learning activities for her students during independent work time. These activities include the following:

- Engaging in independent, partner, and small-group work involving high-level talk and writing about narrative and informational texts the students are reading.
- Writing in journals or on open-ended response sheets.
- Engaging in student-led book discussions.

- Using a computer, with support as needed, to read about a topic of interest or to gather new information.
- Researching and writing reports based on texts and topics of students' own choosing.
- Engaging in independent pleasure reading from self-selected books for about 20–30 minutes a day.

Specific student activities from this third-grade teacher's classroom are provided below. See Figure 3.1 for examples of open-ended response sheets that go with some of these activities. (For more on motivating learning activities, see Roehrig, Brinkerhoff, Rawls, & Pressley, Chapter 1, this volume.)

- Complete strategy work as a follow-up to a whole-class or small-group lesson:
    - ◆ With a partner, finish a topic map on a character from the story that the class began in the whole-class lesson.
    - ◆ Read and summarize a teacher-selected text on an endangered animal after practicing and summarizing an article on wolverines in a whole-class lesson.

Summary Sheet for Informational Text

Summarize the text you read by writing the main ideas and important details in complete sentences. Also write two interesting words that you did not know and what you think they might mean.

Name _____

Date _____

Part 1 main idea	
Important details	
Part 2 main idea	
Important details	
Part 3 main idea	
Important details	
First new word (page _____)	
Meaning	
Second new word (page _____)	
Meaning	

(continued)

FIGURE 3.1. Examples of open-ended response sheets.

Note-Taking Sheet to Promote Comprehension Monitoring

Name _____

Date _____

Confusing word or idea		Notes (Why is it confusing? What might it mean?)
1.	(page _____)	
2.	(page _____)	
3.	(page _____)	

Log on My Independent Reading

Name _____

Book title	Today's date	Today I read from page _____ to page _____	Ideas I had about my reading today (things I liked, things I wondered)

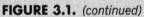

FIGURE 3.1. *(continued)*

- ◆ With a partner, read and summarize a story read in a guided reading group. Generate high-level thinking questions about this story that will be discussed during the next guided reading group lesson.
- ◆ Practice RT in triads with self-selected books on endangered animals.
- • Write in a reader response journal (and share later):
  - ◆ Respond to high-level questions that the teacher has written on the board. Make text-to-life connections in as many responses as possible.
  - ◆ Generate questions, write down interesting or unknown words, and write summaries in preparation for a book club discussion.
- • Write on sticky notes (and share later):
  - ◆ Write down meanings of unknown words from a guided reading group text.
  - ◆ Write down unfamiliar but "really useful" words to share that come from independent reading.
  - ◆ Write down ideas or vocabulary that need clarifying from texts read.
  - ◆ Make connections to these texts.

- Read, write, and discuss in book clubs:
  - ◆ Read the next chapter or two in a book club book; write good discussion questions; and jot down ideas, words, or connection to share with others in the group.
  - ◆ Discuss chapters from a book club book, using questions, words, or connections generated before the book club meeting.
- Read, write, and share ideas from informational books or articles:
  - ◆ Generate a summary of a section that comes from a social studies or science book or article.
  - ◆ Write about ideas that were interesting or surprising after reading from a social studies or science book or article.
  - ◆ Select a planet. Do additional reading about the planet in books and on the Internet, and write about the size, miles from sun and earth, number of moons, and interesting facts about this planet. Share during a whole-class meeting.
- Engage in independent reading. Read for pleasure at an independent reading level, and keep a log of pages read.

It is important to watch students closely to determine whether the independent work set up for them is both motivating and challenging. Giving them some choice of books to read or activities to engage in is also important. When students are given the opportunity to select books and to choose how to respond to these books, they become more engaged in the process, and this choice fosters independence and responsibility (Bohn, Roehrig, & Pressley, 2004; Guthrie et al., 2004; Pressley et al., 2003).

LOOKING FORWARD

Research suggests that efforts directed toward the following practices related to grouping practices and independent learning activities will be beneficial in enhancing teachers' effectiveness and improving students' literacy abilities:

- Improvements in differentiating instruction within whole-class lessons and across guided reading small-group lessons and in intervention groups focused on reading and writing. These improvements should focus on meeting the needs of above-average and average readers as well as below-average readers (Pressley, Mohan, Raphael, & Fingeret, 2007; Taylor & Peterson, 2008).
- Improvements in the quality of independent learning activities that motivate students and meet their needs (Allington & Johnston, 2002; Pressley et al., 2003).
- Increased efforts by classroom teachers to support their struggling readers (Taylor, 2010a, 2010b, 2010c), and successes in these efforts.
- Increased collaboration across classroom, special education, reading resource, and ELL teachers to accelerate the reading of students who need more support (Fuchs, Fuchs, & Vaughn, 2008; Vaughn, Wanzek, & Fletcher, 2007).
- Use of a broad range of ongoing assessments that tap into students' comprehension abilities as well as their decoding and fluency abilities (Allington & Johnston, 2002; Pressley et al., 2003).

QUESTIONS FOR REFLECTION •

1. To what extent do I, or teachers I have observed, make same-day connections between skills or strategies taught in whole-class lessons and in guided reading groups?

2. To what extent during a whole-class lesson or in guided reading groups do I (or teachers I have observed) differentiate instruction related to a specific skill or strategy?

3. To what extent do I (or teachers I have observed) use ongoing assessments—including ones that go beyond timed curriculum-based measures (CBMs)—to regularly monitor students' progress (in decoding, vocabulary, comprehension, and motivation to read), to differentiate instruction, and to make adjustments to my instruction?

4. To what extent do I (or teachers I have observed) provide motivating and intellectually challenging learning activities during independent work time to move students forward in their literacy development?

5. To what extent do I (or teachers I have observed) differentiate learning activities during independent work time to meet students' needs?

6. To what extent do I (or teachers I have observed) minimize drill and low-level repetitive work, using it only when it is necessary and useful?

7. For readers who need more support, to what extent are they receiving a research-based, daily intervention lesson in addition to their guided reading group?

8. For readers who need more support, to what extent do I (or teachers I have observed) teach them from the perspective that they need additional instruction that accelerates their learning to read before they get significantly behind—not remediation once they have fallen well behind their grade-level peers in reading ability?

9. What do I need to work on in regard to grouping practices, lessons within the whole class and small groups, and independent learning time to be a more effective teacher for students who need more reading support, as well as for students reading on and above grade level?

SUGGESTIONS FOR ONGOING PROFESSIONAL LEARNING • • • • • •

A professional learning community, or PLC, is a good venue for looking at balance in grouping practices, differentiation of instruction, and the quality of independent learning activities in your classroom or in classrooms you visit, as well as the extra support struggling readers in your classroom are receiving. Through regular, ongoing learning sessions, you can learn and share ideas with colleagues. Below, two examples of ongoing learning sessions related to grouping practices and effective instruction are provided. (Ongoing professional learning is covered in more detail by Peterson in Chapter 21, and by Sailors, Russell, Augustine, & Alexander in Chapter 22.)

Modifying the Structure of Your Whole-Class and Small-Group Lessons and Your Independent Learning Activities to Provide More Effective Instruction

Session 1

Discuss this chapter and your own current grouping practices with members of a PLC. Do you explicitly make connections between concepts, skills, strategies, or processes covered in small-group and individual work and the whole-class lesson, so that students can understand and benefit from the cycle of explicit instruction, guided practice, and independent practice you are providing for the concept, skill, process, or strategy you are teaching? Do you differentiate instruction to meet students' varying needs and abilities?

Keep notes on these aspects of your whole-class and small-group instruction, as well as the independent learning activities you provide, for the next 2 weeks. Also, keep a log for 2 weeks to determine how much time you spend on whole-class lessons and guided reading groups. Keep a list over this same 2-week period of the activities you provide for above-average, average, and below-average students during independent learning time. Are the activities motivating and differentiated?

Session 2

Bring the log, notes, and lists to share at your next monthly PLC meeting. Discuss things you'd like to change to enhance the balance and flow among whole-class, small-group, and individual learning. Get ideas for change from your PLC group members. Decide upon and implement changes over the next few weeks. Keep notes on the positive and negative aspects of your changes.

Session 3

Bring your notes on the positive and negative aspects of your changes to share these at your PLC meeting. Get help from colleagues on how to diminish the negative aspects of your changes. Decide upon and implement revised changes during the next few weeks. Keep notes to share at your next PLC meeting.

Session 4

Discuss progress you have made in your grouping practices and independent learning activities, and write down next steps for continued improvement.

Providing Supplemental Intervention Lessons to Students Who Need More Reading Support

Session 1

Consider the following questions: What data are you using to determine which students need more support in reading? What additional data would be helpful? What data are you using to monitor the progress of these students? What additional data would be helpful?

Also, consider these questions: What block of time is established to provide struggling readers with an additional shot of quality instruction? Who is providing this instruction? What is the research base behind the instruction? Is the instruction focusing on students' specific needs? What changes would help to accelerate students' learning?

Decide upon changes that you will begin to implement before your next PLC meeting on this topic. Discuss the resources that are needed to help you make these and other needed changes.

Session 2

Discuss changes you have implemented in your instruction and assessment since the last session. What are the strengths and challenges related to these changes? What are the next steps you plan to take to provided even more effective intervention lessons for your struggling readers? What additional support or resources do you need? Be prepared to talk about the instructional strategies and ongoing assessments you are using at the next session.

Session 3

Share strategies and discuss the impact of the changes you have made to support your struggling readers. What additional support or resources do you need? Be prepared to talk about instructional strategies and ongoing assessments you are using at the next session.

Session 4

Share strategies and discuss the impact of the instruction you are providing to support your struggling readers. What additional support or resources do you need? Be prepared to talk about instructional strategies and to share data on students' progress in reading at your next session.

RESEARCH-BASED RESOURCES

Fuchs, D., Fuchs, L., & Vaughn, S. (Eds.). (2008). *Response to intervention: A framework for reading educators.* Newark, DE: International Reading Association.

Gaskins, I. W. (2004). *Success with struggling readers: The Benchmark School approach.* New York: Guilford Press.

Lapp, D., Fisher, D., & Wolsey, T. D. (2009). *Literacy growth for every child: Differentiated small-group instruction, K–6.* New York: Guilford Press.

McCormick, R. L., & Paratore, J. R. (Eds.). (2005). *After early intervention, then what?: Teaching struggling readers in grades 3 and beyond.* Newark, DE: International Reading Association.

McCormick, S. (2007). *Instructing students who have literacy problems* (5th ed.). Upper Saddle River, NJ: Pearson/Merrill Prentice Hall.

Morrow, L. M. (2003). *Organizing and managing the language arts block: A professional development guide.* New York: Guilford Press.

Pressley, M. (2006). *Reading instruction that works: The case for balanced teaching* (3rd ed.). New York: Guilford Press.

Southall, M. (2009). *Differentiated small-group reading lessons.* New York: Scholastic.

Taylor, B. (2010a). *Catching readers: Grade 1.* Portsmouth, NH: Heinemann.

Taylor, B. (2010b). *Catching readers: Grade 2.* Portsmouth, NH: Heinemann.

Taylor, B. (2010c). *Catching readers: Grade 3.* Portsmouth, NH: Heinemann.

Taylor, B. (2011a). *Catching readers: Grades 4/5.* Portsmouth, NH: Heinemann.

Taylor, B. (2011b). *Catching readers: Grade K.* Portsmouth, NH: Heinemann.

Taylor, B. (2011c). *Catching schools: An action guide to schoolwide reading improvement.* Portsmouth, NH: Heinemann.

Tyner, B. (2009). *Small-group reading instruction: A differentiated teaching model for beginning and struggling readers.* Newark, DE: International Reading Association.

Tyner, B., & Green, S. E. (2005). *Small-group reading instruction: A differentiated teaching model for intermediate grade readers, grades 3–8.* Newark, DE: International Reading Association.

Vaughn, S., Wanzek, J., & Fletcher, J. M. (2007). Multiple tiers of intervention: A framework for prevention and identification of students with reading/learning disabilities. In B. M. Taylor & J. E. Ysseldyke (Eds.), *Effective instruction for struggling readers K–6* (pp. 173–95). New York: Teachers College Press.

Walpole, S., & McKenna, M. C. (2009). *How to plan differentiated reading instruction: Resources for grades K–3.* New York: Guilford Press.

REFERENCES

Allington, R. L., & Johnston, P. H. (2002). *Reading to learn: Lessons from exemplary fourth-grade classrooms.* New York: Guilford Press.

Bogner, K., Raphael, L., & Pressley, M. (2002). How grade 1 teachers motivate literate activity by their students. *Scientific Studies of Reading, 6*(2), 135–165.

Bohn, C. M., Roehrig, A. D., & Pressley, M. (2004). The first days of school in the classrooms of two more effective and four less effective primary-grade teachers. *Elementary School Journal, 104,* 271–287.

Chorzempa, B. F., & Graham, S. (2006). Primary-grade teachers' use of within-class ability grouping in reading. *Journal of Educational Psychology, 98,* 529–541.

Elbaum, B., Vaughn, S., Hughes, M. T., Moody, S. W., & Schumm, J. S. (2000). How reading outcomes of students with disabilities are related to instructional grouping formats: A meta-analytic review. In R. Gersten, E. Schiller, & S. Vaughn (Eds.), *Contemporary special education research* (pp. 95–124). Mahwah, NJ: Erlbaum.

Foorman, B. R., & Torgesen, J. (2001). Critical elements of classroom and small-group instruction promote reading success in all children. *Learning Disabilities Research and Practice, 16,* 203–212.

Fuchs, D., Fuchs, L., & Vaughn, S. (Eds.). (2008). *Response to intervention: A framework for reading educators.* Newark, DE: International Reading Association.

Graves, A. W., Gersten, R., & Haager, D. (2004). Literacy instruction in multiple-language first grade classrooms: Linking student outcomes to observed instructional practice. *Learning Disabilities Research and Practice, 19,* 262–272.

Gunn, B., Smolkowski, K., Biglan, A., Black, C., & Blair, J. (2005). Fostering the development of reading skill through supplemental instruction: Results for Hispanic and non-Hispanic students. *Journal of Special Education, 39,* 66–85.

Guthrie, J. T., Wigfield, A., Barbosa, P., Perencevich, K. C., Taboada, A., Davis, M. H., et al. (2004). Increasing reading comprehension and engagement through Concept-Oriented Reading Instruction. *Journal of Educational Psychology, 96,* 403–423.

Hiebert, E. H., & Taylor, B. M. (1998). Beginning reading instruction: Research on early interventions. In M. L. Kamil, P. B. Mosenthal, P. D Pearson, & R. Barr (Eds.), *Handbook of reading research* (Vol. 3, pp. 455–482). Mahwah, NJ: Erlbaum.

Mathes, P. G., Denton, C. A., Fletcher, J. M., Anthony, J. L., Francis, D. J., & Schatschneider, C. (2005). The effects of theoretically different instruction and student characteristics on the skills of struggling readers. *Reading Research Quarterly, 40*, 148–182.

Palincsar, A., & Brown, A. (1986). Interactive teaching to promote independent learning from text. *The Reading Teacher, 39*(8), 771–777.

Pressley, M., Dolezal, S. E., Raphael, L. M., Mohan, L., Roehrig, A. D., & Bogner, K. (2003). *Motivating primary-grade students.* New York: Guilford Press.

Pressley, M., Mohan, L., Raphael, L. M., & Fingeret, L. (2007). How does Bennett Woods Elementary School produce such high reading and writing achievement? *Journal of Educational Psychology, 99*(2), 221–240.

Taylor, B. M. (2010a). *Catching readers, grade 1.* Portsmouth, NH: Heinemann.

Taylor, B. M. (2010b). *Catching readers, grade 2.* Portsmouth, NH: Heinemann.

Taylor, B. M. (2010c). *Catching readers, grade 3.* Portsmouth, NH: Heinemann.

Taylor, B. M. (2011a). *Catching readers, grades 4/5.* Portsmouth, NH: Heinemann.

Taylor, B. M. (2011b). *Catching readers, grade K.* Portsmouth, NH: Heinemann.

Taylor, B.M. (2011c). *Catching schools: An action guide to school-wide reading improvement.* Portsmouth, NH: Heinemann.

Taylor, B. M., Pearson, P. D., Clark, K., & Walpole, S. (2000). Effective schools and accomplished teachers: Lessons about primary grade reading instruction in low-income schools. *Elementary School Journal, 101*, 121–165.

Taylor, B. M., & Peterson, D. S. (2003). *Year 1 report of the REA School Change Project.* St. Paul: University of Minnesota, Minnesota Center for Reading Research.

Taylor, B. M., & Peterson, D. S. (2006a). *The impact of the School Change Framework in twenty-three Minnesota REA schools.* St. Paul: University of Minnesota, Minnesota Center for Reading Research.

Taylor, B. M., & Peterson, D. S. (2006b). *Year 3 report of the Minnesota Reading First Cohort 1 School Change Project.* St. Paul: University of Minnesota, Minnesota Center for Reading Research.

Taylor, B. M., & Peterson, D. S. (2006c). *Year 1 report of the Minnesota Reading First Cohort 2 School Change Project.* St. Paul: University of Minnesota, Center for Reading Research.

Taylor, B. M., & Peterson, D. S. (2008). *Year 3 report of the Minnesota Reading First Cohort 2 School Change Project.* St. Paul: University of Minnesota, Minnesota Center for Reading Research.

Taylor, B. M., Peterson, D. S., Marx, M., & Chein, M. (2007). Scaling up a reading reform. In B. M. Taylor & J. E. Ysseldyke (Eds.), *Effective instruction for struggling readers, K–6* (pp. 216–234). New York: Teachers College Press.

Vaughn, S., Mathes, P., Linan-Thompson, S., Cirino, P., Carlson, C., Pollard-Durdola, S., et al. (2006). Effectiveness of an English intervention for first-grade English language learners at risk for reading problems. *Elementary School Journal, 107*, 153–181.

Vaughn, S., Wanzek, J., & Fletcher, J. M. (2007). Multiple tiers of intervention: A framework for prevention and identification of students with reading/learning disabilities. In B. M. Taylor & J. E. Ysseldyke (Eds.), *Effective instruction for struggling readers, K–6,* (pp. 173–95). New York: Teachers College Press.

Wasik, B., & Slavin, R. E. (1993). Preventing early reading failure with one-to-one tutoring: A review of five programs. *Reading Research Quarterly, 28*(2), 178–200.

CHAPTER 4

Balanced, Differentiated Teaching • • • • • • • • • • • • • • • • • •
Explicit Instruction, Scaffolded Support, and Active Student Responding

DEBRA S. PETERSON

Teaching Vignette 1

Ms. Zachary (all names are pseudonyms) is reading aloud to her third-grade class from the basal reader. After she reads a sentence with an underlined word, she asks the group, "What are *headlands*?" She calls on Abdul, who answers, "Land that goes into the water." Ms. Zachary continues to read aloud. She then stops and asks, "What are *hollows*?" She calls on Jessica, who answers, "A short, like, small valley." Ms. Zachary clarifies that it is "the area between the mountains." She continues reading aloud, stopping after reading an underlined word and asking one or two students to give meanings for the words.

Teaching Vignette 2

Ms. Ames is working with a small reading group of third-grade students. They have just independently read a section of a chapter book and have written in their response journals about the words they encountered that were difficult. Students have been asked to write down each word, the page of the text where it was found, and the strategies they used to figure out the word meaning. When the group comes together for guided reading time, Ms. Ames asks whether anyone found a challenging word.

ADAM: I have *penetrated* on page 93. (*Reads from the text.*) "The calf bellowed once more and the cry penetrated the marrow in Seth's bones."

MS. AMES: What have you tried so far to figure that word out?

ADAM: I tried to read around it, and I couldn't figure out what it meant.

Ms. AMES: All right, did anyone try something else?

SAMANTHA: It means to go into or through.

Ms. AMES: How do you know that?

SAMANTHA: I had *penetrating* and I looked it up in the dictionary.

Ms. AMES: Very good. I wonder if it would help if you thought about what was happening in the story here? "The calf bellowed . . . penetrated Seth's bones." Is there something that is actually sticking into his bones?

REBECCA: No, it means the sound is so loud it feels like it goes through his body.

Ms. AMES: Read the passage again, and see if that definition of *penetrated* seems to make sense in this context.

The first teaching vignette provides an example of a common type of instruction that is routinely used in classrooms from prekindergarten through high school. In the example, the teacher leads the students through the activity. She does most of the reading and the talking, while the students are expected to listen or take turns orally responding. The teacher then either acknowledges that the students' responses are accurate, or provides clarification to correct misunderstandings and expand upon incomplete answers. This type of exchange is repeated throughout the lesson.

The second teaching vignette shows an alternative type of instruction. In this example, students are independently reading, writing, and solving problems. The teacher asks questions that help the students elaborate on or explain their thinking as they work with one another.

OVERVIEW OF RESEARCH

Both of the types of instruction presented above are useful for teaching. In fact, research shows that effective teachers provide a balance of *teacher-directed* instruction and *student-supported* learning (Taylor, Pearson, Clark, & Walpole, 2000; Taylor, Pearson, Peterson, & Rodriguez, 2003, 2005). The teacher-directed stance is characterized by instruction that is teacher-led, with teachers telling information or leading question–answer sessions. This stance is used when teachers want to provide the explicit and direct explanation that students need to learn new material.

The student-supportive stance is evident when teachers use modeling, coaching, listening, and giving feedback as the primary modes of instruction. This stance allows the teachers to support students while they are *applying* the skills and strategies they have been taught. When teachers use a student-supportive stance, they provide time for guided practice where they can gradually release the responsibility for the task to the students (Pearson & Gallagher, 1983). The teachers scaffold the instruction by increasing the demands of the task while decreasing the support provided until students can independently and flexibly apply the strategies that they have been taught. When teachers adopt a student-supportive stance, they also involve students in active engagement with authentic reading, writing, and speaking activities.

Research has not determined what the exact proportion of teacher-directed to student-supportive instruction should be in the elementary grades, but it has shown that when a teacher-directed stance is the primary form of instruction, there is a negative relationship between students' growth and achievement in reading (Taylor et al., 2003; Taylor & Peterson, 2006). This makes sense because if students are sitting and listening for the majority of the school day, they rarely have the opportunity to actually read, write, and talk about what they have read.

Research has also demonstrated that other related elements of instruction have an impact on students' learning (Pressley, Allington, Wharton-McDonald, Block, & Morrow, 2001; Taylor et al., 2003). These include opportunities for students to respond actively during instruction; an instructional purpose for a lesson or activity that is matched to the specific students' needs; and an appropriate pace of instruction, so that all students are challenged and motivated. Active responding occurs when every single student is reading, writing, or talking with a partner. In kindergarten or first grade, active responding might also take the form of manipulating materials (e.g., a sorting activity). Active responding contrasts with passive responding, in which students are required to listen or take turns reading or orally responding. The purpose and pacing of a specific lesson should be based on student assessment data and the teacher's knowledge of the individual students who will be completing the activity. The purpose should be clearly articulated to the students, so they know why they are doing the activity and how it will help them grow as readers and writers. The pacing should be reasonably rigorous, so that students are challenged, but not so demanding that they are overwhelmed or frustrated.

Using data on students' performance and adapting the instruction to meet their needs are major emphases of the *response-to-intervention* (RTI) *model*, which addresses differentiated and appropriate instruction for all students during classroom instruction or Tier 1 instruction (Fuchs, Fuchs, & Vaughn, 2008; Johnston, 2010; Mesmer & Mesmer, 2008–2009). The features of effective instruction described above emerged from previous research and from analyses of many years of classroom observations. The *cognitive engagement model* (Taylor et al., 2003) includes all of these features to help teachers focus and reflect on "how" they teach as well as on "what" they teach. Specifically, the cognitive engagement model includes the following:

1. Engaging students in *higher-level talk and writing about text*, in addition to lower-level questioning. (See Garas-York, Shanahan, & Almasi, Chapter 10, this volume, for more details.)
2. Teaching comprehension and word recognition as *strategies* and not just as skills. (See Stahl, Chapter 9, this volume, for more information about comprehension instruction.)
3. Teaching from a *student-supportive stance* (in which the teacher is modeling, coaching, listening, and giving feedback), as well as from a *teacher-directed stance* (in which the teacher is primarily telling students information or leading a question–answer session).
4. Engaging the students in *active responding* (where every child is reading, writing, talking with a partner, or manipulating materials), not simply passive responding (where students are listening or taking turns reading, writing, or orally responding).
5. Teaching with a clear *purpose* and appropriate *pacing* to meet the needs of the specific students involved.

SUMMARY OF BIG IDEAS FROM RESEARCH

These elements of effective instruction have been identified by other researchers who have studied elementary reading instruction. Pressley and his colleagues (2001; Pressley, 2006) studied accomplished first- and second-grade teachers and found that effective teachers coached students as they were reading and writing. The teachers also provided scaffolding in their instruction by adapting the learning tasks to the students' needs and increasing the demands of the tasks as students became more adept at the required skills and strategies. Allington and Johnston (2002) observed fourth-grade teachers and found that students benefited from teacher modeling and demonstration. Guthrie and colleagues (1996, 2004) found that students' reading improved when they were actively engaged in reading, writing, talking, researching, and experimenting around an integrated science concept. A report from the Center for Research on Education, Diversity, and Excellence (Genesee, Lindholm-Leary, Saunders, & Christian, 2006) reviewed research on effective instruction for students who were English language learners (ELLs). They stated, "The best recommendation to emerge from our review favors instruction that combines interactive and direct approaches" (p. 140). *Direct* approaches involve explicit or direct explanation of material by the teacher. *Interactive* approaches involve students in active responding, as in cooperative learning, instructional conversations, or student-led discussion groups. During interactive approaches, the teacher serves as a model, coach, or facilitator while students are engaged in literacy activities.

The elements of the cognitive engagement model have been shown to have a positive impact on diverse learners (Peterson & Taylor, 2012; Taylor et al., 2003, 2005; Taylor & Peterson, 2006; Taylor, Peterson, Marx, & Chein, 2007). These include students at various age and developmental levels (grades K–6), students who are ELLs, students receiving special education services, and struggling readers. These elements of effective instruction have also been found to be positively related to growth in reading for students that are reading at and above grade level. These big ideas and the research studies supporting each idea are listed in Table 4.1.

EXAMPLES OF EFFECTIVE PRACTICES

Examples of Teachers Using the Student-Supportive Stance

The following examples provide snapshots of how elementary teachers can scaffold their support according to students' needs. In Teaching Vignette 3, the teacher checks in with students as they are independently writing about what they have read. She asks questions to prompt students to elaborate on what they are writing and to help them make connections between their lives and the text. In Teaching Vignette 4, the teacher models how to use a decoding strategy during a teacher read-aloud. She then coaches the students to apply that decoding strategy in their guided reading group. Both examples demonstrate how teachers support students in actively applying what they have learned to their own reading and writing.

TABLE 4.1. Research Studies Examining Effective Classroom Instruction

Citation	Balance between teacher-directed and student-supportive instruction	Active student engagement	Clear purpose for instruction	Appropriate pacing and challenge of activities
Allington & Johnston (2002)	✕	✕		
Connor, Morrison, & Katch (2004)	✕			
Guthrie et al. (2004)		✕	✕	
McIntyre, Kyle, & Moore (2006)	✕	✕		
Paterson, Henry, O'Quin, Ceprano, & Blue (2003)	✕	✕		
Pressley et al. (2001)	✕		✕	✕
Pressley, Mohan, Raphael, & Fingeret (2007)		✕		✕
Taylor, Pearson, Clark, & Walpole (2000)	✕	✕		
Taylor, Pearson, Peterson, & Rodriguez (2003, 2005)	✕	✕	✕	✕
Taylor, Peterson, Marx, & Chein (2007)	✕	✕	✕	✕

Teaching Vignette 3

Mrs. Larson is circulating around her second-grade classroom, listening, watching, and giving feedback to her students as they write in their response journals. They are writing in response to a fictional story where animals and birds are playing a game. Students are supposed to write about which team they would like to play on and why they would choose that team.

Mrs. Larson stops at one student's desk and asks her to read what she has written so far. Then Mrs. Larson asks her, "You wrote that you would like to be on the animals' team because they learned a good lesson. What does that mean?" Mai Li replies, "They found out that you can't judge someone by their size." Mrs. Larson comments, "Good idea. Make sure you explain that in your response."

She goes on to another student. After he reads what he wrote to her, Mrs. Larson says, "You wrote that you didn't want to be on the animals' team because they were mean. What do you mean by that?" Javier responds, "They were not fair. Just because the bird was small doesn't mean he can't do stuff." Mrs. Larson asks, "Does that remind you of something from your own life?" Javier nods. "Yes, my brothers won't let me play with them because they say I am too little." Mrs. Larson comments, "You could add that connection from your own experiences to your response."

Teaching Vignette 4

Ms. Peterson, a first-grade teacher, has just read a book aloud to her whole class. After the class has talked about the meaning of the text, Ms. Peterson says, "First graders, I am going to show you what you can do when you come to a word that you don't know. Watch what I do, so that you will be able to use this strategy when you are reading. On this page of the book it says, 'Rosie the hen went for a walk . . . past the _____.' I don't know this word, but I do see a familiar chunk. I know *i-l-l* is *-ill* and the letter *m* is /m/. If I put those sounds together, /m/-/ill/, I can read the word. It is *mill*. Now I am going to reread to make sure the sentence makes sense."

Later that day, as she is working with a small guided reading group, Ms. Peterson asks the students to read with partners as she listens to one of the children read. Maxwell reads several sentences without stopping, but then he pauses on the word *strike*. Ms. Peterson asks, "Is there a familiar chunk that you recognize?" Maxwell says, "*I-k-e* as in *bike*." Ms. Peterson replies, "Good. Now put the beginning sounds with *ike*." Maxwell successfully sounds out the word. Ms. Peterson responds, "Good work on using your strategies to figure that out. Now reread the sentence to make sure it makes sense."

When teachers are coaching students, they often ask probing or prompting questions to help the students elaborate on their ideas. Here are some examples of prompts that might be helpful when coaching students as they talk and write about text:

"What in the text makes you think that?"

"Please tell me more about that."

"Does this remind you of anything from your own life?"

"Please explain that more."

"Why do you think that?"

"What do you mean? I want to make sure that I understand what you are thinking."

Here are some examples of prompts that might be helpful as teachers coach students to use their phonics knowledge and word recognition strategies:

"What sound does that letter make?"

"Do you see any familiar chunks or smaller words within the word?"

"What can you do to figure that word out?"

"Do the pictures give you any clues?"

"Now that you have sounded out the word, read the sentence again to see if it makes sense. Good readers always check to make sure they understand what they read."

Examples of Teachers Using Active Pupil Engagement

The next three teaching examples show how elementary teachers can involve their students in active responding, where every student is reading, writing, or sharing with a partner. Active responding gives students more practice in literacy, is more motivating and engaging than passive responding, and provides opportunities for students to actually use what they are learning in meaningful ways. (See Roehrig, Brinkerhoff, Rawls, & Pressley, Chapter 1, this volume, for more on motivation.)

Teaching Vignette 5

Mrs. Swenson's kindergarten students have each written their own pattern books, based on a text that she read aloud to the whole group. The little books that the students have written are four sentences long and repeat, "What do you have? I have a _____. What do you have? I have a _____." Students have copied the repeated words within each sentence, but have used their own invented spellings for the words that are unique to their sentences. Writing the sentences allows each student to practice letter formation, concepts of print (e.g., capital letters at the beginning of sentences, spaces between words, punctuation), and familiar sight words.

After students have written their four sentences, Mrs. Swenson asks them to read their stories to a partner. The kindergartners quickly select partners, sit on the floor around the room, and read their texts to their partners. Mrs. Swenson rotates from pair to pair, listening in and encouraging students to point to each word as they read.

Teaching Vignette 6

Mr. Owens is working with his third-grade class. They have been reading a narrative story from the basal anthology about a girl whose mother has a new baby. When the family goes to the hospital, the staff will not let the little girl visit her mom or the new baby. Mr. Owens asks the class, "How would you feel if you were Ramona? Think about that for a minute. Now turn to your partner and share."

Students then share their ideas with a peer. Peng says to his partner, "I would want to go see my mom, and I would be hurt that I couldn't go see her." Luis replies, "Yeah, I would feel terrible and sad because it would be sad that I couldn't see my baby brother and sad that I can't see my mom." Carmen tells her partner, "I would be confused. Why wouldn't they let me see my mom? I would want to obey the rules, but I would want to see my mom." Jesse replies, "I would be angry and hurt at the same time."

Teaching Vignette 7

Ms. Pearson is working with a small group of second-grade students who are ELLs. Together they chorally read from a picture book about an orchestra conductor. At one point in the story, Ms. Pearson stops and says, "I am starting to think about what is happening in the story. I am making some *inferences*. When we *infer*, we think about the story, and we make a connection to something we already know. What do we know from the story on this page?"

Luis responds, "People are bringing Arturo flowers." Ms. Pearson nods. "Yes, people are bringing him flowers. That is what we know. Let's write that in the first box on our response sheet." She hands out paper and pencils to each student. They all write on their sheets.

Ms. Pearson then says, "It doesn't tell us in the story why they do this, so we have to think. What do we know about why people give each other flowers? Think . . . now turn to your partner and share your ideas about why people give each other flowers."

The students share with each other. Ideas include "The people like the music," "People like to hear music," and "They really like Arturo."

Ms. Pearson smiles. "I heard many good ideas. If someone were to ask me that question, I would say that people give flowers to other people who are really good at something or are famous. So I think that people give Arturo flowers because they think he is a good conductor and they like his music. Now write your inference on your response sheet."

Students write their ideas on their sheets. The group continues reading to see whether they can find other evidence in the text to support their inferences.

Instructional tips to help teachers shift from passive to active pupil responding are provided in Table 4.2.

Examples of Teachers Identifying a Clear Purpose for the Lesson

Effective elementary teachers use the data they have gathered on their students to select the particular learning objectives and activities that will move their students forward in their reading achievement (Pressley, 2006; Taylor et al., 2000, 2003). (See Valencia & Hebard, Chapter 5, this volume, for more on using assessments to inform instruction.) Reflecting on the purpose of a lesson aids a teacher in focusing on what really matters in the lesson for the specific students involved. For example, if the purpose of a kindergarten lesson is to help students hear the sounds in spoken words and to write the letters that make the sounds in those words, than the teacher may decide not to focus on correct letter formation at this time. If the teacher's guide says to teach a phonics element to the whole class, but the progress-monitoring data show that the students already know and can use that phonics element, than the teacher may elect to focus on another aspect of the lesson. If the focus of the lesson is to help teach students to summarize informational material, than the teacher may not address all the detail-oriented questions a student may have about a topic at this time. Maintaining a focus on the purpose of a lesson helps a teacher prioritize among all the standards and objectives that could be selected for a particular lesson. Once these objectives are identified, the teacher can explicitly explain the purpose of the lesson to the students. This clarity of purpose helps students understand why they are doing a specific activity and how that activity will help them as readers today and in the future.

TABLE 4.2. Tips for Shifting from Passive to Active Responding in Daily Instruction

Passive responding	Active responding
• Taking turns reading, or "round-robin reading," with the whole class.	• Partner reading: Students alternate reading page by page with a partner. This provides more time when each student is reading, while also providing the support students need to decode the words successfully and understand the text. Students can be taught to "coach" one another instead of just telling their partners the word.
• Taking turns reading, or "round-robin reading," in a small group.	• Choral reading: All students read aloud together at the same time • "Whisper reading": Each student reads aloud in a quiet voice at his or her own pace. The teacher can listen in while individual students are reading and coach individuals in their word recognition strategies or comprehension while the other students continue their own reading. • Partner reading: While students in the small group are reading with a partner, the teacher can do a quick running record on one or two individual students or conduct an individual reading conference with a student.
• Taking turns orally responding in the whole class.	• Turn to a partner and share: Students can talk with a partner about the question that the teacher has asked. This gives everyone the opportunity to think of their own ideas and to practice their oral language. • Write and show the answer: Students can write their answers on individual whiteboards or journals and then show their answers when prompted by the teacher. The teacher can quickly scan the room to see who has answered the question correctly or who needs more coaching.
• Taking turns orally responding in a small group.	• Turn to a partner and share. • Write and show the answer.
• Taking turns writing on the board or watching the teacher do the writing.	• Give every student an individual whiteboard, response journal, clipboard and paper, etc., and ask every student to write the sentence or word along with the teacher.

In the following three examples, you will see how teachers at three different grade levels (kindergarten, first grade, and second grade) explain the purpose of the lesson to their students. Their explanations go beyond just telling students what they will be doing in the lesson; they tell the students why they are doing that activity and how it will help them become good readers.

Teaching Vignette 8

Mr. Lynell, a kindergarten teacher, begins a lesson this way: "In our story today, Geraldine anticipates a big snow. She is eager or excited for the snow to come. Our purpose for reading today is to understand what we read. It isn't enough to just read the words. We want to understand the story. We'll do that by stopping along the way to ask and answer questions about what we are reading. Good readers do that to make sure they understand what they read. We'll also make a connection to our own lives by thinking of times we have anticipated or been excited for something to happen."

Teaching Vignette 9

Mrs. Daniels, a second-grade teacher, is working with a small guided reading group. As she begins the lesson, she points to the chart where she has written the three purposes of their lesson for that day. She says, "Good morning! We're going to be reading a new book today. The reason that we are reading today is first of all to identify unfamiliar words. Words that we just don't know or understand. The second reason we are going to read today is to use strategies to figure out these words."

She then asks the students to list some of their favorite word recognition strategies. Students list strategies like using the base word and the prefix or suffix, using the picture clues and thinking about what makes sense, looking for smaller words within a larger word, or looking for rhyming parts that they already know.

Mrs. Daniels then says, "When you get your whiteboards, draw a line across the board. In the top half of your board, you will write down any unfamiliar words you find and how you figured them out. On the bottom half of your board, you will write a higher-order thinking question about the story because that is our third reason for reading today. We are going to talk and write about our story, using some of your questions and some of my questions."

Teaching Vignette 10

Mrs. Stevens is a first-grade teacher. At the beginning of a guided reading group, she introduces the purpose of the lesson in this way: "Our purpose today, first graders, is to practice our fluency by using partner reading. Good readers read fluently. What do readers do when they read fluently? Think about that, and when you have an idea, share it with your partner."

The students think for a moment, and then they begin to share. Mrs. Stevens listens to their conversations and asks clarifying questions.

BRANDON: They read as if they are having a conversation.
CHANTEL: They read with pace.
MRS. STEVENS: Does that mean they speed-read?
CHANTEL: No, they just keep the pace going.

This is the conversation from another pair of students:

GEORGE: They watch for end marks.
SANDRA: They reread if it doesn't make sense.

Once the students have shared their ideas with their partners, Mrs. Stevens calls the group back together. She says, "I heard many helpful ideas about what good readers do when they read fluently. I heard someone say that they read like they are having a conversation. When we read fluently, we understand the meaning of the story better, and we can think about the story because we aren't just focusing on sounding out the words."

LOOKING FORWARD

With the adoption of the Common Core State Standards by over 40 states, educators across the United States have a solid foundation for designing instruction and making decisions about what to teach at each grade level. These standards also provide a developmental progression of what needs to be taught in grades K–12 to prepare the students of today for college and career paths in the future. What the standards do not tell us, though, is *how* we should teach reading to our students. This is where the art of teaching enters in, and where the expertise and knowledge of individual teachers working with specific students take over. To meet the needs of an ever-increasing, more diverse student population, teachers are going to have to differentiate their instruction effectively. Differentiation goes beyond providing leveled, guided reading groups or appropriate reading interventions. The type of differentiation required involves complex diagnoses (based on research on best practices and student assessment data) of individual students' strengths and needs by expert and adaptable teachers, who then provide targeted instruction to students during the core reading program. This means knowing how much support an individual student needs to complete a specific challenging and rigorous task successfully; making decisions about how to engage all students effectively, so they have multiple opportunities to talk and write meaningfully about what they are reading; and offering appropriate, varied pacing of instruction for students who differ in their knowledge and skills. Certainly the emphasis today on meeting more rigorous state standards, on being guided by research-based curricula, and on systematically assessing students is helpful at all grade levels, but there is even more to effective instruction than all this.

Educational researchers, teacher educators, administrators, literacy coaches, and classroom teachers will be challenged to study and document the intricacies of differentiated instruction and its impact on student growth and achievement. Some questions to pursue might include the following:

- What is an appropriate balance between teacher-directed and student-supportive instruction for various grade levels? How does this balance vary for learners at different ability levels or from diverse cultural and linguistic backgrounds?
- How are schools providing time for teachers to analyze their students' assessment data and collaboratively plan differentiated instruction for students during core reading instruction, as well as during interventions or supplemental services? What impact does this collaboration across reading instruction have on diverse learners?
- How are effective teachers adjusting their pacing of instruction for various students within their classrooms, while still covering the grade-level material?
- How can teacher preparation programs train new teachers to work collaboratively with their grade-level or department colleagues, as well as the specialists within their schools, to provide differentiated and coherent instruction across the reading program?
- How can professional development equip inservice teachers to analyze assessment data, reflect on their own instructional practices, and make informed decisions about curricular and instructional issues?

QUESTIONS FOR REFLECTION •

1. To what extent do I engage in teacher-directed instruction, where I am telling students information or leading a question–answer session?

2. To what extent do I engage in a student-supportive stance, where I am coaching, modeling, listening and giving feedback while students are reading, writing, or working with a partner?

3. How is the balance of my instruction working with this group of students? What evidence am I collecting to help me make this determination?

4. How am I providing support and opportunities for guided practice to my students? How am I differentiating the level of support based on student need?

5. To what extent do I engage students in active responding, where every student is reading, writing, or talking with a partner?

6. How can I provide more opportunities for meaningful active engagement within my lessons?

7. How am I reflecting on the purpose of the lesson? How do I decide whether it is an appropriate purpose for these students?

8. How am I explaining the purpose of the lesson to my students? Do they know why they are doing specific activities? Do they know how these activities will help them grow as readers and writers? What evidence am I collecting to help me make this determination?

9. How am I adjusting the pacing of my instruction so that it is appropriately rigorous and challenging without being overwhelming for my students? What evidence am I collecting to help me make this determination?

SUGGESTIONS FOR ONGOING PROFESSIONAL LEARNING • • • • • • •

Learning and reflecting together with colleagues constitute a powerful way to refine your daily reading instruction. Study groups, professional learning communities (PLCs), grade-level meetings, or department team meetings can be effective venues for this collaborative professional learning. In Chapter 21 of this book, I give a variety of examples and tools that can be used to help you reflect on your instruction. Here are some additional suggestions for ongoing professional discussion about balanced, differentiated instruction:

Session 1

Discuss this chapter with a group of colleagues. How are you providing a balance between teacher-directed, explicit instruction and scaffolded support to your students in each lesson? What are you currently doing to differentiate the amount of support that is provided to students at various achievement levels within your class? How are you balancing the amount of time students are passively responding (i.e., listening, watching, taking turns reading and talking) with active engagement (i.e., every student is reading, writing, or talking with a partner)? Keep track of the time you spend on each activity in four or more lessons over the next 2 weeks. Note your observations of students when they are passively responding versus when they are actively engaged.

Session 2

Bring in your notes about the time spent in teacher-directed versus student-supportive instruction, and your observations of students during activities that require passive versus active responding. Talk with your colleagues about the things they are doing to increase the amount of coaching, modeling, listening, and giving feedback they are doing while students are actively reading, writing, or talking with a partner. Decide on two or three specific things that you will adapt or add to your instruction. Keep notes on the differences you observe in your students' behavior and attitudes as a result of these changes. Collect students' work to document their progress.

Session 3

Bring in your notes and the student work you have collected. Share these with your colleagues. What other questions or concerns have emerged for you as you have adjusted the balance within your instruction? Read an article from the *Research-Based Resources* list (see pp. 103–104) to give you further ideas. Continue to refine your instruction, document changes, and analyze student work. (See Chapter 21 for a sample protocol for analyzing student work.) One or two members of the group could also volunteer to bring in a 5- to 7-minute video clip of their instruction to share and discuss at the next meeting. (See Chapter 21 for suggestions for engaging in video sharing.)

Session 4

Bring in your notes, student work, and video clips of instruction. Discuss them, using a video-sharing protocol like the example in Chapter 21, or asking other discussion questions of your choosing. How has your instruction changed as a result of your professional conversations? How have the data you have collected (notes on instruction, observations of students, student work, video clips) helped inform your reflection? What are students doing differently as a result of the changes you have made? Discuss your progress and concerns, generate new ideas, and plan next steps for continued refinement of instruction. Set up a schedule so that members of the group can observe each other during reading instruction. Use the Observation Protocol in Figure 4.1 to help you collect observable evidence of the elements of balanced, differentiated instruction that you are all currently using.

Session 5

Bring in your notes from your peer observations. Talk about what you learned from watching your peers. Share suggestions for future lessons. Continue reading and discussing research articles, sharing videos, and analyzing student work.

ELEMENTS OF EFFECTIVE INSTRUCTION: OBSERVATION PROTOCOL

In the middle column, list evidence for each element of effective instruction. Jot down other comments as they apply. In the right-hand column, list one suggestion for a possible change in the lesson or a suggestion for a future lesson.

Element of Instruction	Evidence of the Element/ Other Comments	Possible Suggestions or Ideas for Change
High-level questioning (Did the students give higher-order responses?)		
Explicit instruction in strategies (Did the instruction explicitly state *why* the strategy is being used, *how* it will help students as readers, and *how* the strategy can be used in the future or in other subject areas?)		
Student-supportive stance (Is teacher modeling, coaching, listening/watching and giving feedback?) **vs. teacher-directed stance** (Is teacher telling or leading a question–answer session?)		

(continued)

FIGURE 4.1. Observation Protocol form. Adapted with permission from *Catching Schools: An Action Guide to Schoolwide Reading Improvement* by Barbara M. Taylor. Copyright © 2011 by Barbara M. Taylor. Published by Heinemann, Portsmouth, NH. All rights reserved.

Element of Instruction	Evidence of the Element/ Other Comments	Possible Suggestions or Ideas for Change
Active responding (Is every single child reading, writing, manipulating, or talking with a partner?)		
Purpose (Did the teacher explicitly tell students *why* they would be doing the activity?)		
Pacing (Is the instruction progressing at a pace that keeps students' attention?)		
What applications to your own classroom can you make?		

FIGURE 4.1. *(page 2 of 2)*

Session 6

Video-record the introduction of a lesson or activity. Note the time it took to give directions and to state the purpose of the lesson. Reflect on how clear, concise, and organized this instruction appeared. What could be done in the future to make the introduction more efficient, so that students can more quickly move into actual reading, writing, and talking with a partner or a small group rather than just listening? Did you clearly explain why the students were being asked to do the activity? Did they understand how the instruction would be applied to their own reading, writing, and speaking in the future? Bring your video clip and notes from your self-reflection to your PLC. Share with your group and generate ideas for the future. Take some time to write out a few examples of purpose statements that explicitly explain why the students are doing the task and how it will help them grow as readers and writers.

Session 7

Ask a colleague to come into your classroom and watch students during your instruction. The person who is observing can note how many students are on task at 2-minute intervals throughout your instruction. Analyze these notes to see whether the pacing of activities is too slow. If you see that 98% of students are on task during the first 10 minutes of the task, but that the percentage of on-task behavior begins to decrease at the 15-minute mark, then you may want to decrease the amount of time you allow in the future for similar tasks. Share your notes and analysis with your PLC. Share ideas on how to adjust the pacing of instruction to meet the needs of specific students. Continue to read research, share videos, analyze student work, and plan next steps for instruction.

RESEARCH-BASED RESOURCES

Duke, N. K., & Bennett-Armistead, V. S. (2003). *Reading and writing informational text in the primary grades: Research-based practices.* New York: Scholastic.

Duke, N. K., Purcell-Gates, V., Hall, L. A., & Tower, C. (2006/2007). Authentic literacy activities for developing comprehension and writing. *The Reading Teacher, 60*(4), 344–355.

Fisher, D., Frey, N., & Lapp, D. (2008). Shared readings, modeling comprehension, vocabulary, text structures, and text features for older readers. *The Reading Teacher, 61*(7), 548–556.

Heller, M. F. (2006–2007). Telling stories and talking facts: First graders' engagements in a nonfiction book club. *The Reading Teacher, 60*(4), 358–369.

Helman, L. (2009). Effective instructional practices for English learners. In L. Helman (Ed.), *Literacy development with English learners: Research-based instruction in grades K–6* (pp. 234–251). New York: Guilford Press.

Lane, H. B., & Allen, S. A. (2010). The vocabulary-rich classroom: Modeling sophisticated word use to promote word consciousness and vocabulary growth. *The Reading Teacher, 63*(5), 362–370.

McGee, L. M., & Ukrainetz, T. A. (2009). Using scaffolding to teach phonemic awareness in preschool and kindergarten. *The Reading Teacher, 62*(7), 599–603.

Parsons, S. (2008). Providing all students ACCESS to self-regulated literacy learning. *The Reading Teacher, 61*(8), 628–635.

Peterson, D. S., & Taylor, B. M. (2012). Using higher order questioning to accelerate students' growth in reading. *The Reading Teacher, 65*(5), 295–304.

Pressley, M., Dolezal, S. E., Raphael, L. M., Mohan, L., Roehrig, A. D., & Bogner, K. (2003). *Motivating primary-grade students.* New York: Guilford Press.

Ranker, J. (2009). Learning nonfiction in an ESL class: The interaction of situated practice and teacher scaffolding in a genre study. *The Reading Teacher, 62*(7), 580–589.

Taylor, B. M., Peterson, D. S., Pearson, P. D., & Rodriguez, M. C. (2002). Looking inside classrooms: Reflecting on the "how" as well as the "what" in effective reading instruction. *The Reading Teacher, 56*, 70–79.

Teale, W. H., & Gambrell, L. B. (2007). Raising urban students' literacy achievement by engaging in authentic, challenging work. *The Reading Teacher, 60*(8), 728–739.

REFERENCES

Allington, R. L., & Johnston, P. H. (2002). *Reading to learn: Lessons from exemplary fourth-grade classrooms.* New York: Guilford Press.

Connor, C. M., Morrison, F. J., & Katch, L. E. (2004). Beyond the reading wars: Exploring the effect of child–instruction interactions on growth in early reading. *Scientific Studies of Reading, 8*, 305–336.

Fuchs, D., Fuchs, L. S., & Vaughn, S. (Eds.). (2008). *Response to intervention: A framework for reading educators.* Newark, DE: International Reading Association.

Genesee, F., Lindholm-Leary, K., Saunders, W., & Christian, D. (2006). *Educating English language learners.* New York: Cambridge University Press.

Guthrie, J. T., Van Meter, P., McCann, A. D., Wigfield, A., Bennett, L., Poundstone, C. C., et al. (1996). Growth of literacy engagement: Changes in motivations and strategies during concept-oriented reading instruction. *Reading Research Quarterly, 31*, 306–332.

Guthrie, J. T., Wigfield, A., Barbosa, P., Perencevich, K. C., Taboada, A., Davis, M. H., et al. (2004). Increasing reading comprehension and engagement through Concept-Oriented Reading Instruction. *Journal of Educational Psychology, 96*, 403–423.

Johnston, P. H. (Ed.). (2010). *RTI in literacy: Responsive and comprehensive.* Newark, DE: International Reading Association.

McIntyre, E., Kyle, D. W., & Moore, G. H. (2006). A primary-grade teacher's guidance toward small-group dialogue. *Reading Research Quarterly, 41*(1), 36–66.

Mesmer, E. M., & Mesmer, A. E. (2008–2009). Response to intervention (RTI): What teachers of reading need to know. *The Reading Teacher, 62*(4), 280–290.

Paterson, W. A., Henry, J. J., O'Quin, K., Ceprano, M. A., & Blue, E. V. (2003). Investigating the effectiveness of an integrated learning system on early emergent readers. *Reading Research Quarterly, 38*(2), 172–207.

Pearson, P. D., & Gallagher, M. C. (1983). The instruction of reading comprehension. *Contemporary Educational Psychology, 8*, 317–344.

Peterson, D. S., & Taylor, B. M. (2012). Using higher order questioning to accelerate students' growth in reading. *The Reading Teacher, 65*(5), 295–304.

Pressley, M. (2006). *Reading instruction that works: The case for balanced teaching* (3rd ed.). New York: Guilford Press.

Pressley, M., Allington, R., Wharton-McDonald, R., Block, C., & Morrow, L. (2001). *Learning to read: Lessons from exemplary first-grade classrooms.* New York: Guilford Press.

Pressley, M., Mohan, L., Raphael, L. M., & Fingeret, L. (2007). How does Bennett Woods Elementary School produce such high reading and writing achievement? *Journal of Educational Psychology, 99*(2), 221–240.

Taylor, B. M. (2011). *Catching schools.* Portsmouth, NH: Heinemann.

Taylor, B. M., Pearson, P. D., Clark, K., & Walpole, S. (2000). Effective schools and accomplished teachers: Lessons about primary grade reading instruction in low-income schools. *Elementary School Journal, 101*, 121–165.

Taylor, B. M., Pearson, P. D., Peterson, D. S., & Rodriguez, M. C. (2003). Reading growth in high-poverty classrooms: The influence of teacher practices that encourage cognitive engagement in literacy learning. *Elementary School Journal, 104*, 3–28.

Taylor, B. M., Pearson, P. D., Peterson, D. S., & Rodriguez, M. C. (2005). The CIERA School Change Framework: An evidence-based approach to professional development and school reading improvement. *Reading Research Quarterly, 40*(1), 40–69.

Taylor, B. M., & Peterson, D. S. (2006). *The impact of the School Change Framework in twenty-three Minnesota REA schools* (Research Report No. 1). Minneapolis: University of Minnesota, Minnesota Center for Reading Research.

Taylor, B. M., Peterson, D. S., Marx, M., & Chein, M. (2007). Scaling up a reading reform in high-poverty elementary schools. In B. M. Taylor & J. E. Ysseldyke (Eds.), *Effective instruction for struggling readers, K–6* (pp. 216–234). New York: Teachers College Press.

CHAPTER 5

Classroom Literacy Assessment● ● ● ●
Strategies for Informing Instruction and Monitoring Student Progress

SHEILA W. VALENCIA
HEATHER HEBARD

Now, perhaps more than at any other time, the federal government and school systems are demanding testing and assessment of students. Data-driven decision making is the new mantra, yet some have suggested that educators are now "data-rich and information-poor" (Stringfield, Wayman, & Yakimowski-Srebnick, 2005, p. 137). Even with the enormous amount of data generated by state, district, and classroom assessments, educators may not have the kind of information they need to improve their teaching and students' learning. Most educators and measurement experts agree that understanding the purposes of assessment is essential for making good assessment decisions. In fact, it is this confusion over different purposes that has probably led to the sense that we are data-rich and information-poor; many educators and policymakers can't distinguish which information is useful for which purposes. Consequently, we begin with a review of research and theory on the purposes of assessment, as well as implications for effectively using classroom assessment to inform instruction and monitor student progress. Then we provide several approaches to classroom assessment that teachers can implement and adapt to assess reading and writing. Finally, we describe a professional development model for examining student work and assessments in professional learning communities (PLCs) that will help teachers build strong conceptual and practical tools for implementing and using classroom literacy assessment.

OVERVIEW OF RESEARCH

Background

At the dawn of the standards movement, the National Council on Education Standards and Testing (NCEST, 1992) issued a report calling for important changes in the way assessments were conceptualized. Assessments were to be derived from and aligned with content standards, rather than the other way around. In addition, NCEST called for a *system* of assessments that considered multiple purposes, types of measures, and levels of information. Equally important, NCEST argued that new assessments alone could not accomplish the goals of reform or assure improved teaching and learning. It called for professional development, curriculum frameworks, and attention to health and social barriers to learning that would need to accompany changes in assessment.

Since the release of the NCEST report, other reform efforts—such as No Child Left Behind (NCLB), Reading First, Race to the Top, and, most recently, the Common Core State Standards—have targeted standards and assessments. Nevertheless, the field has yet to clarify how various types of assessments might best be used to improve teaching and learning. As Herman noted in a National Research Council workshop, when one type of assessment is used to serve multiple purposes and audiences, it serves none very well (Beatty, 2010).

A Framework for Understanding Assessment

To address the perennial confusion about matching assessments with purposes and audiences, Perie, Marion, and Gong (2009) have reconceptualized and labeled three types or purposes of assessment as *summative, interim,* and *formative,* according to the frequency of administration, duration of testing cycle, and specificity of content (see Figure 5.1). In this triangle graphic, the *x*-axis shows increasing frequency of assessment, and the *y*-axis indicates increasing scope and duration of cycle. Although the primary audience or "consumer" of assessment information is not explicitly included in the graphic, it is implied, and ultimately determined, by the other defining variables.

Summative assessments are administered least frequently, have the longest time between administrations, and include test content at a broader scope or "grain size." Typically, they are end-of-year standardized or state tests administered to large groups of students and used for accountability purposes. In reading, summative tests for students at third grade and above typically include mostly multiple-choice items that assess literal and inferential comprehension, and sometimes vocabulary. They are unlikely to include assessment of self-monitoring, questioning, author's craft, or the like; nor do they include many open-ended items. Results are typically reported in broad categories according to preestablished standards, norms, or benchmark scores. Similarly, in writing, summative assessments typically require students to write on demand, in response to a prompt. The writing is usually scored holistically (i.e., producing a single score), and the results are reported according to a standard score. Although summative assessments may sometimes yield slightly more "fine-grained" scores (e.g., reading—main idea, evaluate; writing—ideas and content, organization), measurement experts caution against using these finer interpretations because summative tests are unlikely to have

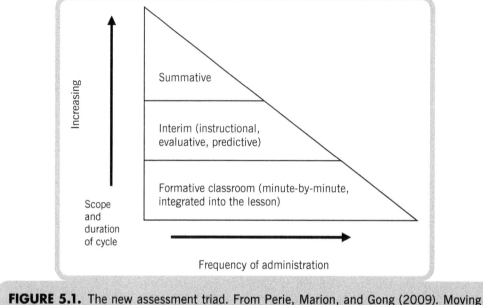

FIGURE 5.1. The new assessment triad. From Perie, Marion, and Gong (2009). Moving toward a comprehensive assessment system: A framework for considering interim assessments. *Educational Measurement: Issues and Practice, 28,* 5–13, p. 7. Used with permission.

a sufficient number of items in subcategories to make the results reliable for individual students (Popham, 2009). (For a more detailed discussion of limitations of using summative assessment results to make instructional decisions, see Valencia, 2011.)

At the other end of the continuum, *formative* assessment happens most frequently. This allows for a very short cycle between assessments (e.g., weekly, daily, minute-to-minute) and a finer-grained analysis of reading and writing skills and strategies. Formative assessment taps what students are learning in the classroom as part of instruction. It is particularly useful for enabling teachers and students to set goals and adjust instruction. Yet, as we elaborate below, new definitions of formative assessment include more than the typical classroom tasks, documentation, or even portfolios of student learning.

Between summative and formative assessment is *interim* assessment—also referred to as *benchmark* assessment. This type of medium-scale, medium-cycle assessment is usually administered three to five times a year and is typically designed to measure the same broad goals as summative assessment or to predict student performance on high-stakes summative assessments given at the end of the school year. In many ways, the format, frequency, audience, and use of interim assessments represent efforts to bridge the distance between formative and summative assessment. Administrators, recognizing that summative assessment cannot provide the type of information needed to improve classroom teaching and learning and concerned about high-stakes end-of-year tests, tend to use these assessments as ways to monitor student progress and to serve as "early-warning" indicators of students who may not be on track to meet end-of-year benchmarks. Teachers tend to use interim assessments in similar ways, and sometimes rely on them to check on their own formative assessment data and judgments about student performance. As we detail below, the purposes and uses of interim assessment are sometimes confused with those of formative assessment; this confusion makes it difficult for teachers to use interim assessment appropriately to inform instruction and monitor student progress.

Foundations for Classroom Reading and Writing Assessment

All three types of literacy assessments—summative, interim, and formative—must begin with an understanding of both the processes underlying competent reading and writing, and the products (i.e., outcomes) of student learning. Without such a firm grounding, assessment is more likely to target less important but easily tested standards, and assessment results are more likely to be interpreted simplistically, inaccurately, or incompletely.

An interactive model of reading and writing processes combines research on cognitive information processing and the sociocultural nature of literacy (Lipson & Wixson, 2009). It posits that reading and writing are processes of constructing meaning that result from the interaction of the reader/writer and the context of the reading/writing situation. Many variables within the reader/writer (e.g., prior knowledge, reading and writing skills, linguistic and cultural background, attitudes, motivation, etc.) interact with variables within the context (e.g., curriculum, instructional support, setting, materials, tasks, purposes, language, etc.) to influence an individual's reading/writing processes and performance. Furthermore, the interactions among these various factors are dynamic, changing as readers and writers engage in a range of meaning-making activities. So assessing reading and writing must include attention to the interactive nature and multiple factors that shape reading and writing processes and products.

To understand how an interactive model of reading and writing shapes assessment and interpretation of assessment information, it is helpful to think of some common classroom assessment situations that could be easily misinterpreted and might lead to incorrect conclusions about a student's strengths and needs. In reading, for example, an interactive model suggests that students who are struggling to comprehend grade-level material, even on a topic about which they know a good deal, may be experiencing difficulties with decoding, vocabulary, automaticity, inferential comprehension, or a combination of these and other abilities. It also affirms that in addition to understanding students' skills and strategies, it is equally important to assess how they engage in reading—how the students self-monitor, solve confusions, persist in the face of challenge, and make connections within and between texts. Similarly, in writing, writers must consider their purpose for writing and their intended audience, make judicious choices about genre and craft techniques, employ a number of process strategies to move from idea to written product, and adjust to the demands of the context in which they are writing. For example, a student's response to a writing prompt does not indicate how well he or she can choose an idea; consider possibilities of genre, structure, and technique; develop a writing project over time; or use feedback to revise the writing. Overall, when students are engaged in real reading and writing, their performance will be shaped by the interaction of many factors, and our interpretation of assessment results must consider these.

Formative Assessment of Reading and Writing

Characteristics of Formative Assessment

Interest in formative assessment gained momentum with the publication of several papers by Black and Wiliam (1998a, 1998b). The formative assessment model that has resulted from this work, and the one that we put forward here, is framed as a "new theory of formative assessment" (Wiliam, 2010, p. 18) because it brings together research from a range of fields—including sociocultural theories of learning and teaching, cognitive theories of teaching and learning, metacognition, motivation, and measurement—rather than drawing only on the work in measurement. Building on earlier reviews, Black and Wiliam's review of 250 studies found significant improvement in students' test scores when various aspects of formative assessment were implemented in classrooms. As the authors explain, their results would mean that an average student (i.e., a student scoring at the 50th percentile) participating in a classroom using formative assessment would end up with the same achievement as a student in the top 10–35% of those who did not participate in a formative assessment classroom. Equally important, Black and Wiliam found that effective formative assessment produced larger gains for low-achieving students than for other students; that is, the use of formative assessment appeared to close the achievement gap, while raising achievement overall.

What is essential to understand about this research is that the results were obtained by implementing specific features of formative assessment that are quite different from those typically associated with assessment (Black & Wiliam, 1998b; Educational Testing Service, 2009; Heritage, 2010). More specifically, the type of formative assessment that produced these positive results resembles teaching more than assessment! It is not a set of tests or even open-ended activities that students complete; formative assessment is an interaction between a teacher and a student. Thus formative assessment is defined as all activities used by teachers and by students themselves that provide information for adjusting teaching and learning activities. The evidence from the assessment *must actually be used* to modify teaching to meet students' needs. So it is not the frequency of the assessment, speed of results, location of implementation, specific assessment strategies, or even the purposes that make an assessment formative; it is the *use* of the information and the interaction between the teacher and student. Action must be taken to close the gap between a student's current learning and the desired instructional goals for that student. Consequently, formative assessment is a process rather than a measurement instrument (Heritage, 2010).

Four key features are associated with the kind of formative assessment that results in improved student achievement. First, the information teachers get from formative assessments must be used not only to make changes in teaching, but also to help students understand how they can improve their own learning. Teachers' feedback must be tied to specific tasks the students are asked to do, and it must provide specific suggestions or cues about how to improve (Black & Wiliam, 1998a; Hattie & Timperley, 2007). General statements about performance or praise (e.g., "Good job," "Can you think of another option?") are not considered feedback. Second, students must be engaged in self-assessment and peer assessment, so that they can understand the standards for good work, monitor their progress, set appropriate goals, develop needed skills and strategies, and develop a sense of ownership for their learning (Andrade, 2010; Black, Harrison, Lee, Marshall, & Wiliam, 2004). Third, formative assessment needs to be responsive to students' needs. Because assessment takes place both informally during instruction and more systematically as part of the curriculum, teachers must be skilled at using a variety of questioning strategies, tasks, observations, and interactions to help their students demonstrate learning and move it forward (Black & Wiliam, 2010; Wiliam, 2010). Formative assessment also must be appropriate for each student and responsive to his or her needs; therefore, not all students will experience the same assessment or the same feedback. As a consequence, teachers will need to differentiate assessment as well as instruction. Finally, because formative assessment clearly requires teachers to have strong pedagogical content knowledge as well as knowledge of the subject matter they are assessing, long-term, site-based professional development is a necessary part of its successful implementation (Heritage, 2010; Shepard, 2000; Wiliam, 2007–2008).

Teachers should use caution as they review classroom assessments that are marketed as "formative assessments." Many of these assessments include tests from item banks, computer-adapted tests, brief tests of oral reading, and curriculum-based measures (CBMs). Others examine students' skills in isolation or under contrived situations (e.g., finding the main idea of a 50-word paragraph; writing sentences that include specific vocabulary words; selecting the sentence with correct punctuation). These assessments do not reflect the complexity and interactive nature of real reading and writing (Johnston, 1997; Lipson & Wixson, 2009) and fail to meet the research-based criteria for formative assessment. They are mistakenly labeled as "formative" because the focus is on providing information to teachers quickly and consistently (i.e., more in line with interim assessment, as we discuss below)—not because they are implemented in ways that engage students and teachers in assessment as an opportunity for learning. In a review of assessments that were labeled "formative," assessment expert Lorrie Shepard (2009) warned, "Just because it's labeled formative assessment doesn't make it so" (p. 33).

Next, we provide examples of several "high-leverage" formative assessments—practices that are common in many classrooms and can provide a wealth of information to inform and improve teaching and learning. These high-leverage assessments permit insights into the interactive nature of students' reading and writing, as well as windows into literacy processes and products.

Classroom Examples: Formative Assessments of Reading and Writing

INDIVIDUAL READING EPISODES

Informal reading inventories (IRIs), running records (RRs), and leveled reading passages have great potential as formative assessments. They typically involve a student reading aloud, and sometimes silently (especially for a student reading at fourth-grade level or above), while the teacher annotates specific information about the student's reading behaviors. Although many teachers use these sorts of assessments, they are not always used as formative assessments, and in our view their potential may be lost. For example, some school districts and schools mandate that teachers administer these types of measures at the beginning and/or the end of the school year, tally the percentage of oral reading errors a student makes, and then simply report each student's reading level as a number or letter. In other situations, teachers are required to administer grade-level IRIs or passages to all students, regardless of their reading instructional level. Both of these examples fall short of the criteria for formative assessment. Alternatively, these types of assessments could offer opportunities for teachers to observe how comprehension, vocabulary, decoding, fluency, and language work in concert; to engage with students about their reading strategies and skills; to provide immediate, specific feedback to students; and to use the evidence to adjust instruction.

Recent research suggests that when IRIs, RRs, or leveled reading passages are conceptualized as formative assessments and used in that way, they are extremely powerful. An experimental study examining the reading achievement of third-grade students whose teachers implemented RRs in line with the interactive features of formative assessment found that the students significantly improved their reading and writing performance, and that they outperformed students in control schools (Ross, 2004). In this study, RRs were integrated with teaching, administered at students' instructional levels, and actively used by teachers to make instructional decisions. Teachers and their principals participated in PLCs aimed at building a deep understanding of reading assessment and instruction with a focus on using RRs to enhance their practice. This approach is in sharp contrast to others that focus on using the results to place students, rank them, or report to others for accountability.

A good example of how a teacher can use an individual reading episode as a formative assessment is captured by the following exchange between a fourth-grade student, Sacha, and her teacher, Ms. Lo (all names are pseudonyms). Ms. Lo reads individually with all the students in her class, although she assesses some students more frequently than others and selects different levels and types of material to use, depending on each student's performance. She administers at least two reading selections each time she works with a student because she knows a student's reading performance varies according to such factors as genre, topic, and student interest. She uses a form like the one in Figure 5.2 to record this information because it helps her consider important factors that may influence a student's performance and helps her analyze data to plan instruction.

Before beginning the brief assessment session, Ms. Lo reminds Sacha of the process they will use, telling her that she should be sure to read for understanding so they can talk about the passage after she reads. She begins with a third-grade passage because she is unsure of Sacha's familiarity with the topic. Sacha reads aloud while Ms. Lo records her miscues, using a simple strategy of writing mispronounced words, circling omissions, noting insertions, and recording reading time. She finds that Sacha's decoding accuracy, fluency, and comprehension are strong. Then she moves to the fourth-grade passage, deciding to have Sacha read the first half aloud (approximately 250 words) and the second half silently, so she can compare her comprehension in the two situations. Although both passages come with comprehension questions, Ms. Lo first prompts Sacha to retell each selection to gain insight into the quality, quantity, and organization of information Sacha has constructed during reading. Using an open-ended prompt she has developed to assure consistency and reliability across students and passages (Lipson & Wixson, 2009), Ms. Lo says, "Tell me what this reading passage is about. Tell me as much as you can about it." After reading the fourth-grade passage, Sacha retells:

> "I think it was mostly about how a girl named Krystal was waiting for her aunt to come home. And there was tornado, and she heard it on the radio, and she thought what she should do, and she went to the sealer [*sic*]. And she was worrying about

Name _Sacha_____   Teacher _Ms. Lo_____

Date _____

Reading mode: _X_ Oral   _____ Silent   _____Listening

Response mode: _X_ Oral   _____ Written

Passage level: _X_ Easy   _____ Average   _____Difficult

Type of passage: _X_ Narrative   _____ Informational   _____

Amt. teacher scaffolding: _____ Great   _____ Some   _X_ None

Describe:

_____

	Decoding	Fluency	Comprehension
Passage (level): L Hungry	98%	150 WCPM approx. (75%ile)	Retell = 3/4 Questions = 80%
	5 self-corrections on mispronounced words (reread).		Good literal and inferential comprehension; little personal response.

Reading mode: _X_ Oral   _X_ Silent   _____Listening

Response mode: _X_ Oral   _____ Written

Passage level: _____ Easy   _X_ Average   _____Difficult

Type of passage: _X_ Narrative   _____ Informational

Amt. teacher scaffolding: _____ Great   _X_ Some   _____None

Describe:

_____

	Decoding	Fluency	Comprehension
Passage (level): O Excitement	96%	144 WCPM approx. (75%ile)	Retell = 2/4 Questions = 60%
	Sealer = cellar Insised = insisted Smoothed = soothed. These words don't seem to be in listening vocabulary.	Few pauses even when text concepts became difficult. Fast but not expressive.	Good literal; difficulty with inference at all levels; should work on look-backs with her.

FIGURE 5.2. Formative reading assessment record.

her Aunt Ruth, and so she came and she got a flashlight, and she came and went into her arms."

Using a retelling rubric the fourth-grade team has developed, Ms. Lo assigns a score of 2 out of 4 to the retelling, and then scores the comprehension questions according to the answer key that comes with the passage. Rather than simply recording the scores on Sacha's decoding accuracy and retelling, Ms. Lo capitalizes on the opportunity to talk with Sacha about the content of the passage and her reading processes; she then analyzes the quantitative and qualitative information from the assessment to inform her instruction. For example, Ms. Lo finds that Sacha does a good job of capturing the literal problem of the story in her retelling, but misses the implicit idea of a summer that goes from not enough excitement to "too much excitement." She also notes that Sacha's responses to the five comprehension questions confirm this analysis: She does an excellent job of answering detail questions, yet she struggles with inferences at the paragraph and whole-passage level. Ms. Lo takes advantage of the assessment situation to talk with Sacha about vocabulary in the story that might be new to her (e.g., *cellar*, *soothing*) and how she might infer the meaning of these words from context. As she talks with Sacha, she helps her understand that monitoring her comprehension is more important than reading quickly—her words correct per minute (WCPM) rate is at the 75th percentile for fourth-grade students—and together they set self-monitoring as a goal.

THINK-ALOUDS

Think-alouds are another type of "high-leverage" comprehension assessment strategy that have great potential to be used formatively. Like the conversation between Sacha and her teacher, think-alouds provide both an assessment opportunity and an opportunity for students to learn how to engage in internal and external metacognitive conversations about their reading (Schoenbach, Greenleaf, Cziko, & Hurwitz, 1999). They are a way to uncover what is going on "inside the head" of a reader: They provide insights into students' reading strategies and skills, their goals and dispositions toward reading, their personal responses, and how they make sense of what they are reading as they work their way through a text (Afflerbach, 2000; Langer, 1990; Lipson & Wixson, 2009). In addition, the act of talking about these topics also seems to reveal considerable information about readers' motivation and prior knowledge. Think-alouds are particularly well suited to formative assessment because they provide genuine teacher–student interaction and because the think-aloud exchange is situated in authentic acts of reading, where complex thinking and flexible strategies are necessary to achieve understanding.

During a think-aloud assessment, readers are given a text of at least 200 words to read either orally or silently. They are asked to stop at various strategically selected points to talk about what they are thinking, what they are doing, or what is happening in the text; the choice of the prompt depends on what a teacher wants to learn about a reader and on a student's needs. The strategic stopping points selected by the teacher may correspond to places in the text that might be confusing (at the word, sentence, or paragraph level) or where readers might make connections or simply a logical transition in the text; again, the choice depends on the purpose of the think-aloud and on a student's needs. We have also encouraged students to self-select stopping places to talk with us about their thinking. Any type of text can be used (narratives, information, documents), although it is important to understand students' reading behaviors, and verbal reports may vary as the texts, tasks, and prompts are changed. Some teachers use texts that are part of the curriculum or students' independent reading, while others use a specially created "think-aloud passage" that is structured to elicit specific types of reader strategies or responses.

Think-alouds can be easily integrated into the type of informal reading episodes we describe above, or they can be added to a more formal assessment after the student has completed it according to required guidelines. It is important to understand, however, that thinking aloud may not come easily or naturally for all students. In fact, much of the research using think-alouds has been done with skilled readers, who are typically more verbal and more sophisticated strategy users (Afflerbach, 2000). Nevertheless, students can learn how to become more metacognitive and to engage in metacognitive conversations with their teachers and peers if they are provided with instruction and practice. Early efforts to use think-alouds for formative assessment will require more teacher prompting and scaffolding during the assessment. As time goes on, think-aloud assessments can become less teacher-directed and more student-directed.

An example of using think-alouds as formative assessment comes from a study we conducted with fourth- and fifth-grade intermediate-level English language learners (ELLs) (Valencia, Lucero, & Alvarez, 2010). Using released reading selections from a state assessment, our goal was to learn about these students' reading strategies, how they made sense of the text, and what they understood about the selection. After several opportunities for students to practice talking about "what is going on 'inside your head' while you read" and explaining "how you figured that out," the students and teachers engaged in metacognitive conversations about the texts.

We began the assessment by showing students a passage, including the title and accompanying illustrations. Then we talked with them to elicit a passage prediction and their prior knowledge about the topic. Students read a short section of the passage aloud (100–150 words), so that we could check on their decoding accuracy to be sure the passage was at an appropriate instructional level before we proceeded. If a student's accuracy was below 90%, we discussed the reading of this short segment and then moved to an easier passage because when decoding is in the frustration range, reading strategies break down, frustration sets in, and the data are not valid for instructional decision making (Kibby, 1979). If a student's accuracy was 90% or above, we continued with the passage. At the end of the first oral section and the subsequent "Stop and talk" points, we asked the following types of questions:

> "What's going on in this part? What do you think the author wanted you to understand here [to get at inferential comprehension]?"
> "What were you thinking [or what came to mind] as you were reading?"
> "Let's talk about the 'inside your head' part of reading."
>> "What did you do as you were reading this part?"
>> "What parts of this were difficult or tricky for you? It could be words, sentence, or whole parts. Point to that part. What did you do when you read that part?"
>> "What parts of this [words, sentence, or ideas] do you think other fourth graders might find difficult or tricky?"

The results of these interviews provided helpful insights into each student's processes and a finer-grained analysis of his or her strengths and needs. While reading a passage about whale migration, one of the students told us:

> STUDENT: I know a lot about whales because we studied them in third grade. So I know that they go back and forth from cold places to warm places, and it says here that they go from warm water in Baya [sic] California to the Artic. But I don't really get what it means about "cloudy water." Like, how can there be clouds in the water?
>
> TEACHER: That's good, Jorge, that you can identify what is confusing. Let's try to figure this part out together.
>
> [They go on to examine the context and clues that might make the phrase clear.]
>
> TEACHER: Tell me more about what happens while you are reading in your head.
>
> STUDENT: Sometimes I skip a line when I read.
>
> TEACHER: What happens then?
>
> STUDENT: Nothing, really. I keep on reading.

Although the think-aloud confirmed that Jorge had difficulty with comprehension, we learned that he was aware when he did not understand. Other students, however, were not as metacognitively aware, so we pressed them by asking specific questions at specific stopping points to see whether they were building understanding. We used these opportunities to introduce self-monitoring, teach the idea of fix-up strategies, and set goals for instruction. Overall, by using a combination of think-alouds and probing questions, we were able to gain fine-grained insights into students' reading and then work interactively with them to scaffold learning during the assessment.

WRITING CONFERENCES

The writing conference can be a powerful formative assessment tool when strong instruction, clear writing expectations, and plenty of time to write are also in place (Hillocks, 1984; Sadoski, Wilson, & Norton, 1997). We define *writing conferences* here as short meetings between a teacher and a student (or a group of students) that are centered on the current writing work of the student(s). Conferences embody the key characteristics of formative assessment; they are interactive, engage each student in self-assessment, and include feedback on how the student might improve. They provide an opportunity to assess and support students' writing processes, knowledge, and strategies.

It takes time and effort to develop a conference-based formative assessment system. Teachers must cultivate a classroom community that can function well while they are meeting with students. An efficient record-keeping system is also needed to document work with individuals and provide a resource for instructional planning. Fortunately, several books provide suggestions for creating this environment, getting started with conferences, and using conferences to drive instruction (see Anderson, 2000; Calkins, 1994; Ray, 2001). We limit our discussion here to key conference components as they relate to formative assessment and the challenges of conferring.

In a writing conference, a teacher and student(s) collaborate to expand and improve students' process and strategy repertoires. These meetings can take place at all points in the writing process (Sperling, 1990). A teacher often begins the conversation by asking a student to explain his or her current work and to identify an area in which the student would like support (Anderson, 2000; Calkins, 1994). Listening to the student's self-assessment and looking at the written work, the teacher must decide how to focus the conversation. The teacher must also consider his or her own assessment of the student's progress relative to the unit and year-long goals. Then the teacher provides instruction and talks with the student about the contexts in which the student might use the new learning. The teacher and student discuss next steps, and they may jot these down as a reminder. Finally, the teacher records notes to document their ongoing work; the notes also inform instruction for small-group conferences and whole-class lessons.

Teachers will need to vary their conferring strategies to respond to students' self-assessing abilities. Students who can articulate their writing goals and needs may only need the invitation, "How can I help you today?" to start the conversation. Other students may need more coaching. Teachers can respond to the writing as readers, noting their thoughts as they read. Or teachers can provide a question that writers ask, such as, "Does this make sense?" and ask the students to read and reflect on this question. After a brief discussion, teachers can teach a strategy that responds to the identified need (Glasswell, 2001).

Teachers can also provide support by explicitly teaching strategies for conference participation. Teachers should be flexible with roles and expectations, as students' communicative preferences will differ by culture and individual characteristics (Heath, 1983). These differences include norms for interacting that many teachers take for granted. For example, teacher expectations for eye contact may violate students' experiences for relating to adults, or expectations that students share deeply personal events and feelings through writing may be in conflict with students' cultural norms or need for privacy (Ball, 2002; Gay, 2010; McCarthy, 1994). Learning about a variety of cultural norms is a good starting point for developing greater communicative competence, but it is important to remember that students are individuals who shape and are shaped by the multiple contexts in which they participate (Gutierrez & Rogoff, 2003). The more teachers learn about students and their families and communities, the more they will be able to assess reliably and teach responsively.

Conferring can also be challenging for teachers. They must develop a mentoring stance and learn to provide responsive, immediate feedback. Teachers differ in their conferring styles, but those with effective styles share several characteristics. First, they resist the temptation to "take over" a student's writing. Instead, they teach writing processes and strategies for use in that moment and in similar writing situations in the future. Effective teachers also provide explicit feedback that teaches "the writer, and not the writing" (Calkins, 1994, p. 228). For example, imagine that a teacher directs a student to change the end of a story, providing a suggestion of what to write. Not only has the teacher taken over the writing, he or she has not explained why a revision of the ending might be needed, or taught revision processes or strategies (Freedman, 1987). Students need feedback about the *specific features* of their writing (Ferris, 2003; Sweeney, 1999). For example, a teacher might say, "I noticed that you directly addressed the reader in your lead. After I read that question, I wanted to learn more about snakes."

In the following classroom example, we show how the conference functions as a formative assessment. In Ms. Jones's fourth-grade class, the students are writing opinion pieces about a topic of interest. Jacob has written an article about the role schoolteachers and administrators play in preventing cyberbullying. Ms. Jones has read Jacob's piece the day before and, using the class-created rubric on opinion writing as a guide, has noted several ways in which she could help Jacob improve his piece: She could teach him a strategy to make his lead more compelling; she could teach him a strategy for researching counterarguments (which are not addressed in his article); or she could teach him a strategy for writing conclusions that compel the reader to action.

When Ms. Jones meets with Jacob, he explains that he is not satisfied with his lead because it does not "draw the reader in" (a characteristic of strong leads that has been emphasized in class). Ms. Jones decides to capitalize on Jacob's desire to improve this aspect of his article, and she revisits a lesson on lead techniques from the previous week. Jacob remembers the lesson, but he has had difficulty moving from the examples in the model texts to his own writing. Jacob and Ms. Jones look at some examples together, and she helps him draw parallels between the ways in which techniques are used in the examples and the ways in which he might use those in his article. The two decide on next steps: Jacob will write several leads, using two of the techniques they discussed. Jacob records his task on a sticky note, while Ms. Jones records a brief conference summary in her notebook. She tells him that she will check in tomorrow to see how his work on leads is going.

This example shows how the teacher's conference serves several purposes that parallel those highlighted in the formative assessment literature. She *assesses* Jacob's needs as a writer, grounding her decisions in her knowledge of Jacob as a writer and her objectives, which are made clear to Jacob through explicit teaching and co-constructed rubrics. She *teaches* in a way that is *specific to the task at hand*, and she confirms that Jacob understands how he might incorporate her feedback. She also reinforces the expectation of *self-assessment* as part of the writing process by engaging him in conversation. Finally, her work with Jacob involves writing process strategies—consulting mentor texts for ideas, envisioning and trying out multiple text possibilities, and eliciting and responding to feedback—in the context of a writing task with a clear, meaningful audience and purpose.

WRITTEN FEEDBACK

Teachers often collect samples of student writing as part of formative assessment. They look closely to determine the quality of the writing—focusing on the aspects of writing that they have been teaching, and noting areas of strength and need. They consider the challenge of the topic, genre, and purpose, as well as the level of scaffolding to provide as they craft written comments to encourage student reflection and revision. Providing useful written feedback is a deceptively straightforward task that, in fact, requires a great deal of skill; most teachers provide unhelpful written feedback, writing vague comments and focusing disproportionately on language conventions (Matsumura, Patthey-Chavez, Valdés, & Garnier, 2002; Straub, 1996). Fortunately, research suggests that when high-quality written feedback is implemented alongside other assessment methods and instruction, student self-assessment and learning are promoted (Hillocks, 1982).

If written feedback is intended to encourage students to self-assess and subse-quently take some action, the comments must be clear. Researchers have found that students who receive specific written feedback make significant gains over students who receive vague feedback (Hillocks, 1982; Sweeney, 1999). However, even well-crafted comments can be difficult for students to interpret (Sperling & Freedman, 1987), but teaching and consistent use of a shared language for writing can help. Students must also learn how to respond to teachers' feedback while maintaining ownership of their writing choices. Too often, students simply produce what they think their teachers want, without giving the changes much thought (Sperling & Freedman, 1987). Feedback that provides guidance, but leaves the thinking and writing work to the students, can mitigate this problem. Teachers can also model how to use their comments for reflection and revision by limiting feedback to one or two comments that are tailored to students' needs (Ferris, 2003). The two examples below describe how written feedback might be used in intermediate and primary grades.

Mr. Sanchez uses written feedback with his fifth and sixth graders at points in an argument writing unit that are likely to be challenging. He knows that the standards for argument writing reflect communication norms with which most of his students are not accustomed, and he recognizes that facility with this genre is imperative for aca-demic success. Mr. Sanchez teaches students how to make a claim and what "counts" as supporting reasons and evidence, and they have extended opportunities to hone these strategies through classroom activities. After students research an issue and sketch out their argument, Mr. Sanchez collects and analyzes their plans; documents students' strengths and needs in his writing assessment notebook; and provides written feedback to students on their positions, reasons, evidence, and organization. Students work in groups to discuss this feedback and plan their next steps as Mr. Sanchez circulates to provide additional support.

In contrast, Ms. Carroll, a first-grade teacher, tailors her written feedback to her emergent writers by writing one simple comment on a sticky note attached to each stu-dent's writing that reinforces a recent teaching point. She models how to read the note, reflect, and revise. Then, as students practice with their classmates, Ms. Carroll provides additional scaffolding and notes students' conversations and revisions. Although writ-ten feedback is no substitute for conferring—particularly for emergent literacy learn-ers—it serves a valuable function in a classroom filled with writing, talking, lessons, literature, and multiple modes of self-, peer, and teacher assessment (Hebard, 2010).

Interim Assessments of Reading and Writing

Characteristics of Interim Assessment

There has been a dramatic increase in the use of interim reading and writing assess-ments over the past 10 years (Olson, 2005; Perie et al., 2009). In 2005, just 4 years after NCLB was adopted, 70% of superintendents reported that they periodically gave dis-trictwide tests (usually three to five times per year), and another 10% said that they were planning to give them the next academic year (Olson, 2005). The burgeoning use of interim assessments is due in part to a growing understanding that summa-tive assessments cannot provide the detailed information needed to improve classroom teaching and learning, and in part to the high stakes associated with NCLB and Race to the Top. School districts want to be able to monitor student progress and intervene along the way, instead of waiting for the results of the summative assessment and possible sanctions.

The increase in interim assessment is also a result of confusion and misappropriation of the term *formative* by test publishers and others, in an effort to convince educators that interim assessments can contribute to improved student achievement (Goertz, Olah, & Riggan, 2009; Perie et al., 2009; Shepard, 2010). However, although measurement scholars generally agree that there is a strong research base for formative assessment, most "formative assessments" that are being marketed commercially or developed by districts are actually *interim* assessments, designed to be administered three to five times each year to monitor progress or predict performance on end-of-year tests. Furthermore, they do not satisfy the research-based criteria for formative assessment: Assessment is not integrated with daily instructional interactions; teachers and students do not receive immediate and specific feedback; and students are not involved in self-assessment.

To date, there has been only limited research on the effects of using interim assessments to improve teaching and learning. The available research suggests that the information can be useful in helping teachers broadly identify students who *may* need additional instruction; however, it does not help teachers identify what or how to teach (Goertz et al., 2009; Heritage, Kim, Vendlinski, & Herman, 2009; Olah, Lawrence, & Riggan, 2010). These results have led some experts to suggest that the vast resources being spent on interim assessments might be better spent helping teachers learn formative assessment techniques, including using the information to intervene with students (Perie et al., 2009; Shepard, 2009). Others suggest that if interim assessments are to be used to inform instruction, teachers must be supported by strong school leaders who help them focus on data-driven decisions in a "culture focused on strengthening instruction, professional learning, and collective responsibility for student success" (Blanc et al., 2010, p. 206). Without this support and the ability to identify students' specific needs, interim assessment has limited influence on teacher practice and student learning. With this level of knowledge and support, interim assessment may be a useful addition to teachers' assessment toolkits.

As educators consider how best to use data from district-required or teacher-developed interim assessments, it is important to understand some of the inherent limitations of assessments designed to be administered with a good deal of efficiency and economy to large groups of students. This is especially important because interim assessments have been granted the "authority" of accountability, and consequently have had a major impact on classroom practice.

One widely held concern is that efforts to minimize cost and maximize efficiency have led to overreliance on multiple-choice formats and assessments that can be quickly administered, scored, and aggregated (Perie et al., 2009). The associated risks are that interim test developers may focus on easily tested skills and lower-level learning (Olson, 2005), and that the results will lead to quick placement or instructional decisions. A related issue is that interim assessments, by their very nature and purpose, are too broad in scope and sample too limited a range of learning to provide useful data about specific student needs. As we have noted with formative assessments, issues such as genre, topic, interest, and the like will influence student performance. Formative assessments can compensate for these limitations by their frequency and flexibility (e.g., teachers can vary topics, genres, etc.), but interim assessments do not offer these options.

A second concern relates to the timing and alignment of interim assessments. If assessments are designed as mini-summative tests to be administered throughout the year (i.e., modeled after the format and content of the end-of-year high-stakes assessment), students may have not yet been instructed on the skills and strategies they need to do well on the assessment. In addition, if assessments are scored outside the classroom, there will be a lag time before results come back to teachers, and thus a lost opportunity for them to gain insights into their students' work. Furthermore, in some cases, these mini-summative assessments are not as closely aligned as they should be with the classroom curriculum, so "teaching to the test" (i.e., test preparation) may now occur several times a year rather than the typical once a year.

Finally, in contrast with mini-summative types of interim assessments, others use proxy measures that are highly correlated with a summative measure to predict which students may be at risk of failing. As our reading example highlights below, the concern here is that the proxy becomes the focus of instruction, rather than the actual reading or writing abilities that are the desired outcomes.

We conclude these cautions about using interim assessments with a compelling reason that teachers *should* consider the data they get from interim assessments. Several years ago, teachers in one urban school who had implemented formative leveled-reading assessments and small-group reading instruction were asked by their principal to administer grade-level interim comprehension assessments to all the students in their classrooms, regardless of their instructional reading levels. The teachers were concerned that the experience would be frustrating for some of their students, and they shared their concern with the principal and the reading coach. Together, they studied the formative reading data on each child and decided to (1) exclude students who were reading significantly (more than 2 years) below grade level from the grade-level interim assessment, and (2) use both formative and interim assessment data to inform their instructional interventions. To everyone's surprise, approximately 30% of the students who were placed in below-grade-level reading groups performed well on the grade-level assessment, and approximately 5% of those who were placed at grade level exhibited some difficulty. These data provided teachers with a good check on their formative assessment data and an opportunity to examine classroom expectations and instruction.

Classroom Examples: Interim Assessments of Reading and Writing

In reading, interim assessments have taken a number of different forms. At early reading levels, they represent a slightly different model from the mini-summative model because an end-of-year summative test is rarely given to students below third grade and because the nature of foundational reading skills is developmental. As a result, interim measures in grades K–2 typically focus on specific skills, such as phonemic awareness, decoding, and early text reading. The tests are often individually administered, providing opportunities for teachers to supplement the interim administration with "formative-like" interactions and data gathering with students. At third grade and above, the most common interim assessments are commercial or district-developed multiple-choice comprehension tests that are modeled after state assessments, or quick assessments of oral reading fluency (ORF) such as the Dynamic Indicators of Basic Early Literacy Skills (DIBELS) and AIMSweb, which are intended to identify students who may not be making adequate progress or who are at risk of not doing well on the end-of-year summative assessment. Because these tests of ORF are so quick, easy, and inexpensive to administer, they have become enormously popular as interim assessments (Olson, 2007).

ORF ASSESSMENTS

A brief history of ORF assessments provides insight into their current use as interim measures. These assessments were built on early work in CBM, the goal of which was to help teachers use technically sound but simple data to monitor student progress, modify instruction, and predict performance on an end-of-year summative test (Deno, 1985; Fuchs & Deno, 1994). It is important to understand that these oral reading assessments—1-minute measures of oral reading that produced WCPM scores—were originally designed to "produce reliable and valid indicators of student growth in reading proficiency broadly defined" (Deno & Marston, 2006, p. 180). Because WCPM scores are correlated with scores on summative assessments of comprehension, the rationale was that ORF measures could help identify students who might be at risk for failing the summative test or who were not making progress across the school year. As predictive measures, these oral reading CBMs were never intended to be direct measures of comprehension or to align with instruction; they simply correlated with comprehension. In addition, oral reading CBMs were not intended to measure fluency, nor were they originally labeled "oral reading fluency"; they were simply called "general outcome measurement," to indicate they were measuring overall reading ability. Thus measures of ORF most closely fit the predictive purpose of interim assessments and should not be used as an indication that increasing a student's WCPM score or more practice with fluency will lead to better end-of-year test performance.

Since the increased popularity of ORF measures as interim assessments, several studies have raised concerns about the correlation between ORF and reading comprehension. Early studies, conducted mostly with special education populations across multiple grade levels, found correlations between .63 and .90, which are relatively strong correlations. However, more recent research studies conducted with typical students have identified four concerns related to using ORF scores to identify students at risk: (1) considerably lower correlations than in earlier studies (.40–.50); (2) a concerning number of "false negatives" (i.e., students who have acceptable WCPM scores but low comprehension scores on standardized tests) when cutoff scores are used; (3) developmental differences suggesting that the relation between ORF and comprehension decreases at intermediate grades and above; and (4) the likelihood that ORF measures miscategorize a substantial number of ELLs (see Valencia, Smith, et al., 2010, for a review). Taken together, these data suggest that educators should exercise caution in using interim ORF measures to predict which students may be at risk or to monitor progress. At a minimum, we suggest that results from ORF interim assessments should be supplemented with comprehension assessment, formative classroom assessment data, and (if needed) more diagnostic data to guide identification and instructional decisions.

COMBINING MULTIPLE INTERIM READING ASSESSMENTS

In contrast to interim assessments that use ORF measures, many schools and districts have implemented a different approach that involves using more direct, multiple measures of reading abilities. For example, some districts administer a standardized reading comprehension test to students at grade 3 and above at the beginning of the school year. Then, using the results as a sort of "screening tool," they identify children scoring at the 35th percentile or below for additional assessment with a range of leveled reading assessments. Using this information, teams of teachers meet to identify appropriate instructional interventions for the children, and then these children are monitored three or four times a year with leveled reading selections. Other schools use these procedures to monitor all children, rather than just those who have been identified from an initial assessment. Another variation on this approach relies on administration of both instructional-level and grade-level comprehension assessments to monitor progress three or four times a year with either individual leveled reading assessments or whole-class written comprehension assessments. This approach allows teachers to compare student performance, using grade-level and instructional-level expectations; however, they interpret scores of students reading substantially below grade level with caution because of the possible floor effects of a test at a student's frustration level. Underlying all of these models is a commitment to use interim reading assessments as one of several indicators that students may not be making adequate progress, to follow up with more formative in-depth assessment to identify students' specific needs (as well as information about their motivation, interest, academic history, etc.); and to work as a school- or grade-level team to determine optimal instructional interventions to support student growth.

Similar approaches have been used in primary grades at several schools in Vermont (M. Y. Lipson, personal communication, August 13, 2011). Working as a PLC for more than 2 years, teachers have put into place a system for using several formative and interim assessments matched to students' development. For example, kindergarten teachers use assessments of phonemic awareness, sight word reading, letter names and sounds, sentence dictation, and so on four times a year to document students' progress on these essential skills. At first grade, teachers continue to use kindergarten assessments that students have not yet passed, and they add an assessment of text reading with leveled reading texts three times a year. At second grade, they add a fluency assessment to any first-grade measures on which students have not yet met the benchmark. Over the years these school-level teams have been working, referrals to special education have dramatically decreased, and the percentage of children who are meeting grade-level expectations has increased. All this is possible because they have worked together to identify and use multiple assessments (both interim and formative) to identify students' needs and to monitor progress, and they have used the results to implement appropriate instruction. (For more on deliberate, schoolwide use of pupil assessment data, see Taylor, Chapter 18, and Weber, Chapter 19, this volume.)

ON-DEMAND WRITING ASSESSMENTS

The majority of interim assessments in writing are designed as on-demand tasks in which students write to a prompt under standard conditions. They can be useful complements to formative assessments, such as conferring and written feedback, because teachers can easily track students' development as writers and identify class trends. Sometimes these assessments are designed, administered, and scored by classroom teachers, but in most cases they are designed and mandated by schools, districts, or states. Some teachers find mandated assessments timely and useful, while others bemoan the loss of instructional time, long delays in obtaining results, and scoring systems that are not transparent. Regardless of the origin of the writing assessment, it is important for teachers to think carefully about what aspects of writing are being assessed (e.g., genre, crafting techniques, process, conventions) and how they are measured. (For more on writing assessments, see Troia, Chapter 12, this volume.)

Genre. Most grade-level standards require that students write in a variety of forms and for a variety of purposes. The demands of these writing tasks are varied, and a student's performance from one genre to the next will vary as well (Quellmalz, Capell, & Chou, 1982). Thus assessors face a dilemma: In what genre should students be assessed?

One common approach is to assess students in the same genre throughout the year, providing an opportunity to track student growth over time. Yet this approach does not adequately assess students' writing proficiencies across genres and is likely to encourage teachers to focus disproportionately on the tested genre (Hillocks, 2002). Assessing a single genre over time may be a good option when it is identified as critical for a particular grade and is likely to occupy a major portion of instructional time. In contrast, interim writing assessments can include several genres, each at a different time in the year. When assessment and curricular calendars are coordinated, the results can be very useful for teachers. Trends in results can inform current instruction and future planning. Unfortunately, scores cannot be used to document student growth over the year; for example, we cannot compare a narrative written in September to a literature response written in April to draw conclusions about a student's growth as a writer. As these two approaches make clear, there may be no "best" way to organize for interim writing assessments, and decisions will depend on the purpose of the assessment. Regardless of approach, considerations in the design and interpretation of interim writing assessments must include the limitations and affordances inherent in decisions about genre. (For more on reading and writing in multiple genres, see Duke & Watanabe, Chapter 13, this volume.)

Prompts and Procedures. Writing prompts and procedures are also important considerations in the design and interpretation of interim writing assessments. The uniform nature of interim assessments may seem to provide a fair measure of student achievement; however, some students will struggle with the assessment context more than others, and thus the assessment could underestimate their writing performance under more typical circumstances. For example, most state assessments begin with a prompt that narrows the genre, topic, audience, and purpose. A student's motivation, knowledge of the subject (Langer, 1984), linguistic and cultural background (Basham & Kwachka, 1991), and task interpretation (Murphy, Carroll, Kinzer, & Robyns, 1982) all affect performance. Even topics that may appear neutral place some students at a disadvantage. For example, consider the descriptive writing prompt "Describe your bedroom in a way that shows what you are like." How might a student who shares a room with several family members feel about and respond to such a question? Teachers creating their own assessments might consider asking students to write about a shared experience at school, or a topic or issue the class has been studying (Calfee & Miller, 2007). When interpreting mandated prompts, teachers should consider how particular prompts and procedures may have influenced student performance.

Similarly, student performance can be influenced by the ways in which the assessment process does or does not reflect typical classroom routines and support. In order to learn the most about their students as writers, teachers designing their own assessments should allow students to use these tools and routines (Calfee & Miller, 2007). They should also provide ample time to complete the task, which will result in better scores that are more reflective of students' proficiencies; this is especially true for struggling writers and ELLs (Murphy & Yancey, 2010).

Such flexibility is usually not permissible in school-, district-, and statewide assessments. In these cases, the following questions should be considered in interpreting results: Is there support for students to prewrite, revise, or edit? How might the imposition of genre, topic, audience, and purpose influence students' willingness to engage in the task? Are students allowed to use the tools for writing typically available to them, such as editing checklists and rubrics? Does the time allotted mirror the timeline of typical classroom writing tasks?

A helpful example of interpreting interim writing assessment results is the case of Maria, a third-grade student who scored below the standard on a timed writing assessment. One explanation for her below-standard performance could be that she is learning English as a second language. Time to talk through ideas with a partner, along with additional time to write, might have significantly improved her score. Or perhaps Maria, along with several other classmates, struggled with the assessment because it was vastly different from their classroom context. Their weeks-long studies of genre included extended opportunities to develop ideas, envision text possibilities, and use feedback to revise. The possible explanations for Maria's score are numerous, which is why knowing each student as a writer is critical to interpreting any interim assessment. Maria's assessment should be considered alongside writing produced in typical classroom circumstances, as well as documentation of her writing process development. Teachers can document writing processes by aggregating formative assessment notes and distilling them into a descriptive summary, a quarterly checklist, or a rubric.

Measuring Writing Proficiency. The method for measuring students' writing performance will vary, depending on the audience and purpose for the interim assessment and on available resources. Rubrics are a popular choice because they provide descriptors of proficiency along a continuum. When accompanied by anchor papers that provide an example of proficiency at each level, rubrics can help teachers across a grade, school, or district develop shared expectations. Rubrics can be helpful for identifying class trends and tracking individual growth over time, and the descriptors at each level can also provide indicators for next instructional steps.

However, the use of a rubric does not guarantee useful information for teachers. Due to the cost and time required to score writing samples, many state and district interim assessments are typically given one holistic score without additional explanation (Hillocks, 2010). Unfortunately, these scores do not reveal much about students' strengths and needs; they only delineate how students score in relation to each other and to a benchmark score (if one has been set) on this particular assessment task. For example, two students could score a 4 out of 6 points for very different reasons. One response to this criticism has been to provide two scores—one for conventions and one for everything else. Although this parsing does not offer much more information, it is important because scorers tend to undervalue writing that violates conventions of neatness and Standard English.

When outside scorers provide a holistic score, teachers may find it helpful to work together as teams to assess the writing themselves. Students' papers may be copied before they are submitted, so that teachers can evaluate them immediately. In order to increase scoring validity, teachers should remove students' names and randomly order the papers (Graham, Harris, & Hebert, 2011). Using the same assessment rubric that is used by outside scorers, teachers can highlight each descriptor in the rubric that most closely represents each student's writing, clarifying areas of strength and need. This highlighting is likely to span two or more score levels, and the document becomes a useful tool for instructional planning. Next, teachers can decide on an overall score. If a student performs below the lowest category, the rubric for a lower grade should be used to accurately document the student's proficiency and to develop instructional goals. If teachers have questions about a student's performance, timely scoring will allow them to talk with the student before the assessment is long forgotten. Finally, teachers may find it useful to compare their scores with those from the outside scorers. It is not uncommon for teachers to find that they score more critically or more generously than others, and this can be a useful starting point for professional learning. The more teachers compare and discuss their evaluations of student writing, the better calibrated they will be in assessment, instruction, and communicating expectations to students.

Using a holistic rubric may be a good way to balance efficiency in scoring with providing useful information to teachers, particularly if teachers also use the same rubric and highlight each descriptor. However, for those who desire more detailed information that can be easily aggregated, an analytic approach may be a better option because it provides scores in several categories (e.g., ideas, organization). Although scoring with analytic rubrics can be time-consuming, the scores facilitate rapid identification of achievement trends by class, grade, school, and beyond once the process is complete.

Rubrics also vary considerably in their length, emphasis, and degree of inference required. For example, some rubrics are created for evaluating writing in a particular genre, providing descriptors and examples specific to that type of writing. Other rubrics are designed for use across genres and provide general descriptors. These tend to require more inference to identify how the descriptors might look within a particular genre.

To illustrate how rubric design influences how and what is assessed, Figure 5.3 shows one column of descriptors from two different rubrics. On the left is an excerpt from a 6+1 Trait rubric for grades K–3 (Education Northwest, n.d.). These are the descriptors for a score of 5 on a 6-point scale in the categories of ideas, organization, voice, word choice, and sentence fluency. (We have left out conventions and presentation because of space constraints.) This excerpt represents an analytic approach to scoring, emphasizing the importance of each of the traits. The rubric is designed to be used across genres and may require a fair amount of inference. On the right are descriptors for a score of 4 out of 5 from a second-grade procedural writing rubric. This excerpt represents a holistic approach to scoring and emphasizes the importance of genre-specific features

Excerpt from 6+1 Traits Rubric for K–3 Level 5 Out of 6: "Capable"	Excerpt from a Second-Grade Rubric for Procedural Writing Level 4 Out of 5: "Meets Standard"
Ideas • Big idea is clear, but general—a simple story or explanation • Details are telling, and sometimes specific to big idea • Experience with topic is supported by text • Pictures, if present, add descriptive details to topic **Organization** • Beginning, middle, and predictable ending are present • Transitions work in predictable fashion • Sequencing is sound • Pacing moves reader through piece • Title (if required) fits content • Structure matches purpose **Voice** • Individual expression is supported by text • Writing connects to audience • Voice supports writer's purpose • Risk taking uncovers individual perspective **Word choice** • Favorite words are used correctly • New and different words are used with some success • Vocabulary is expanding • Modifiers add to mix of words • Words clarify topic and convey meaning • Phrases, word groups create specific mental imagery **Sentence fluency** • Simple and compound sentences strengthen piece • Sentence structure varies; variety in beginnings and length exists • Connective words are more varied • Rhythm is more fluid than mechanical and is easy to read aloud	• Identifies the topic • Engages the reader (e.g., directly addresses the reader, conveys enthusiasm, or explains purpose/ significance of activity) • Provides step-by-step instructions in sufficient detail • Includes only relevant information • Uses specific verbs and nouns to clearly communicate ideas • Uses some transitions, sequencing words, or numbers to indicate steps • Illustrations, if present, are used to clarify or accurately portray procedures • Provides closure (e.g., revisits purpose, conveys enthusiasm, directly addresses the reader)

FIGURE 5.3. Comparison of "generic" rubric and genre-specific rubric.

of writing. The school that uses this rubric uses a separate rubric for conventions. Consider the ways in which each of these might be useful for assessing student work. Figure 5.4, a writing sample from Jenny, a second-grade student, provides a good example for thinking about the affordances of each rubric.

Jenny's text, "How to Make Root Beer Floats," was written in response to a prompt to write about a procedure (Hebard, 2010). Her teacher, Ms. Gonzales, hoped to use this on-demand writing to help her decide on the length and focus of an upcoming unit that would revisit this genre, which was first taught several months ago. Using each of the rubric excerpts to analyze Jenny's writing provides very different areas of focus, specificity, and information for Ms. Gonzales. It is helpful to ask: How do the rubrics compare in terms of efficiency, clarity, and usefulness? What information does each provide about the writing? What information is not provided by either rubric that Ms. Gonzales might need?

Although rubrics can be a useful tool to focus our assessment and instruction, they should not be the only lenses through which we view our students as writers. Rubrics can create a narrow definition for what counts as "good writing"—one that marginalizes students and limits opportunities for more sophisticated and expansive understandings of genres as malleable historical and cultural constructions (Bazerman, 2004). For example, there are many ways to tell a story, and narrative is one of the ways that we build identity, connect with others, build community, and make sense of our world. Unfortunately, researchers have found that teachers, as well as school curriculum, privilege mainstream structures for sharing and writing stories (Ball, 1992; Cazden, 2001;

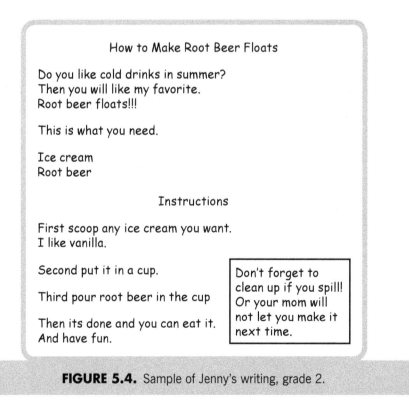

How to Make Root Beer Floats

Do you like cold drinks in summer?
Then you will like my favorite.
Root beer floats!!!

This is what you need.

Ice cream
Root beer

Instructions

First scoop any ice cream you want.
I like vanilla.

Second put it in a cup.

Third pour root beer in the cup

Then its done and you can eat it.
And have fun.

> Don't forget to clean up if you spill! Or your mom will not let you make it next time.

FIGURE 5.4. Sample of Jenny's writing, grade 2.

McCarthy, 1994; Michaels, 1981). A narrow view of what constitutes "good" storytelling may be reflected in a traditional narrative rubric, disregarding the narrative resources of students from nondominant cultures and closing the door on opportunities for more expansive teaching, learning, and assessment. Both teachers and students can develop as writers by exploring how writing varies across cultural contexts. Through this examination, students' rich communicative resources can be acknowledged and fostered, as they also learn the ways of writing that serve as gateways to success in traditional academic settings (Ball & Ellis, 2010; Michaels, 1981).

SUMMARY OF BIG IDEAS FROM RESEARCH

- There are different purposes for assessment. These purposes shape the format, focus, specificity, and nature of the assessment. Teachers' interpretation and use of assessment information must take these purposes into consideration.
- Assessment of students' reading and writing should always include multiple indicators of learning. Student performance varies as a result of genre, topic, assessment guidelines, etc., and these have implications for instructional decisions.
- Formative assessment that is linked to improved student learning requires teachers to engage actively with students around the assessment task and to use the information to adjust instruction.
- Interim (benchmark) assessments have different purposes and uses than formative assessments. To be useful for instructional planning, interim assessment should be supplemented with information from formative or diagnostic assessments.
- Professional development and PLCs are associated with improved classroom assessment and improved instruction.

LOOKING FORWARD

As we reflect on the past and look to the future of assessment, we are reminded of the overwhelming body of research indicating that assessment, by itself, will not improve teaching or learning. We offer these suggestions for future assessment efforts:

- Increase coordination to ensure that assessment is intimately tied to curriculum, instruction, professional knowledge, and systemic support for high-quality teaching and learning.
- Select, design, and use assessments with care. Just because something can be measured doesn't make it a valid assessment of the desired learning. Conversely, some literacy processes and products are difficult to measure but are highly valued.
- Guard against using any single measure to make placement or instructional decisions. Require multiple indicators collected across a reasonable time frame.
- Document classroom assessments in ways that can be shared with others to augment formal test results.
- Engage students in the assessment process, interpretation of results, and goal setting.

QUESTIONS FOR REFLECTION ●

1. How do I use formative assessment as part of my teaching?

2. In what ways can I enhance my formative assessment tools to align with the critical features that optimize their efficacy: specific feedback to students, student self-assessment, use for instructional decisions?

3. What interim assessments are used in my district, school, and classroom? What are they intended to assess, and how can I best interpret the results?

4. How can I adjust my classroom assessments tools to align with individual students' needs?

5. Which reading and writing standards am I (or is my district) adequately assessing, and which do I need to add or enhance?

6. How can I more actively engage my students in the assessment process?

7. How can I work with my colleagues to develop a shared understanding of assessment strategies and appropriate expectations for student learning?

SUGGESTIONS FOR ONGOING PROFESSIONAL LEARNING ● ● ● ● ● ●

We close this chapter by reaffirming the importance of professional development and collaboration as teachers take on new assessment strategies in their classrooms. Drawing on our work in schools and districts, we describe how examining student work collaboratively can contribute to a shared understanding of assessment and instruction, and to an articulated view of what students should know and be able to do across the grades. The strategy is designed to bring groups of teachers together to analyze and inquire into student work by using a structured protocol to guide professional conversations.

Looking at Student Work: The Collaborative Analysis Process

The four-step *collaborative analysis process* (CAP) we present here builds on existing models of examining student work used successfully with cross-grade and grade-level teams in a variety of schools and districts (Little, Gearhart, Curry, & Kafka, 2003; Valencia, 1998). In general, the four steps—*description, alignment, moderation,* and *evaluation*— build on one another, with description being the most general and evaluation, the most complex. The CAP requires teachers to share samples of student assessment work with a group of four to six colleagues. Both formative and interim assessment work can be used, as long as actual student work is shared (not simply scores). Although writing products are fairly easy to examine, evidence of writing processes and some aspects of reading are less so. The teachers with whom we have worked addressed this challenge in several ways: (1) sharing teacher checklists, anecdotal notes, and rubrics; (2) using audio recordings of a student reading or of think-alouds, so that colleagues can actually "hear" the work; (3) making copies of tests and oral reading records to share; and (4) using a small digital camera to record individual conferences with students. Teachers do not need to provide these types of data for all students; one or two will be sufficient to accomplish the goals of the CAP.

Moving through the four steps of the CAP takes time, with several weeks to several months spent on each step, depending on how often the teams meet (because these meetings are intended to build trust as well as shared knowledge). In the first step, *description*, teachers bring several different student samples from a specific assessment activity. The conversation is very general: Teachers describe what they notice about each student's reading and/or writing, based on the work. The activity is a productive and nonthreatening way for teachers to open their practice and their students' work to colleagues. We have found that although the conversation is supposed to focus on particular students, it often strays to questions about instruction such as these: "How do you get your third-grade students to write like this?" "Would you share the criteria for a research project with me?" "Would you tell me how you run your literature circles?" As teachers discuss the evidence of their own and their colleagues' students, it is natural to turn attention to teaching practice in specific and meaningful ways.

The next step, *alignment*, moves to matching student assessment work with district or state learning standards. This step generates conversations about standards, validity of assessments, and (once again) instruction. With copies of content standards in hand, the teachers discuss the standards that appear to be assessed in the student assessment work samples presented by each teacher. Here, what happens is that the intent of each standard and the evidence that would be needed to assess it become the focus of discussion. This is not as straightforward as it may seem. Standards such as "Describe how a narrator's or speaker's point of view influences how events are described"—a fifth-grade Common Core State Standard (National Governors Association Center for Best Practices & Council of Chief State School Officers, 2010)—require a good deal of unpacking and concrete examples for a group to develop shared understanding. Then, matching that understanding with students' assessment evidence adds another layer of analysis, with the aim of understanding what aspects of the standard are included in a particular assessment. The conversation can move in the opposite direction as well: Teachers might ask, "What standards are important to assess (and teach) that are not captured in this evidence? And how should this mismatch be addressed?" The value of this question is in guarding against emphasizing the "easy-to-measure" standards, to be sure that teachers are considering all standards that are worthy of teaching and assessing.

The validity issue arises as the group considers how well the assessment evidence represents the standards and objectives it is intended to assess. Our earlier example of using ORF scores to predict students who may be at risk of failure is relevant here. When teachers understand that some assessments are used as predictors and others are intended to assess the learning directly, the student work is interpreted and used differently. Similarly, when teachers discuss the difference between assessing writing conventions through a proofreading task and a writing sample, they are exploring issues of validity that will inform instruction.

The *moderation* step builds on *description* and *alignment*, with the added edge of encouraging various perspectives about next steps for assessment and instruction. Teachers again share assessment evidence from one or two of their students, but they do not participate in the discussion until the others have discussed the work. The group addresses four questions: (1) "What did you learn about this student from the assessment evidence?" (2) "What standards does this evidence help you assess?" (3) "What instructional targets or strategies might advance this student's learning?" and (4) "What additional information would you need to make sound instructional decisions?" After the group discusses these questions, the presenting teacher has an opportunity to comment on how the group's comments fit with his or her interpretation of the evidence. Although remaining quiet while a group discusses one of their own students is difficult for most teachers, who are eager to supplement the assessment evidence with personal anecdotes and insights, the process of considering colleagues' analyses provides a rare opportunity to consider multiple interpretations. And the new questions related to additional information and next steps for instruction help everyone in the group to think beyond their current practices.

The final step in this process is *evaluation*. More than assigning a score, the conversation in this step centers on performance expectations for students and criteria for good work. As we have discussed, using rubrics (e.g., writing, retelling, fluency) can be helpful for rating student performance; the process can be especially useful for comparing state and district rubric scores with collegial discussions and evaluation of formative classroom assessments. But the majority of formative assessments teachers engage in with students do not involve rubrics; they require teachers to have a firm understanding of students, standards, assessment, and instruction, all of which is built throughout the CAP. So the essence of this final step is simply asking, "How does this student's work fit with our expectations for all students at this particular grade, at this particular time of year, with respect to these particular standards?" And then, because teachers understand that students have individual needs, they ask the follow-up question: "How does this work fit with my expectations for this particular student, given what I know about him [or her]?" These questions help teachers gauge, and collaboratively create, high expectations for all students at the same time that they stay attuned to individual students' needs. Answering these questions wisely is the ultimate goal of sound classroom assessment and the road to improved teaching and learning.

RESEARCH-BASED RESOURCES

Anderson, C. (2000). *How's it going?: A practical guide to conferring with student writers.* Portsmouth, NH: Heinemann.

Caldwell, J. S., & Leslie, L. (2009). *Intervention strategies to follow informal reading inventory assessment: So what do I do now?* Boston: Pearson.

Glasswell, K., Parr, J., & McNaughton, S. (2003). Four ways to work against yourself when conferencing with struggling writers. *Language Arts, 80,* 291–298.

Joint Task Force on Assessment of the International Reading Association and the National Council of Teachers of English. (2010). *Standards for the assessment of reading and writing.* Newark, DE: International Reading Association.

Lipson, M. Y., & Wixson, K. K. (2009). *Assessment and instruction of reading and writing difficulties: An interactive approach.* Boston: Pearson.

Paratore, J. R., & McCormack, R. L. (Eds.). (2007). *Classroom literacy assessment: Making sense of what students know and do.* New York: Guilford Press.

Samway, K. D. (2006). *When English language learners write: Connecting research to practice, K–8* (pp. 79–100). Portsmouth, NH: Heinemann.

Spandel, V. (2004). *Creating writers through 6-trait writing assessment and instruction.* Upper Saddle River, NJ: Pearson Education.

Tompkins, G. E. (1992). Assessing the process students use as writers. *Journal of Reading, 36,* 244–246.

Valencia, S. W., & Riddle Buly, M. R. (2004). What struggling readers REALLY need. *The Reading Teacher, 57,* 520–533.

REFERENCES

Afflerbach, P. A. (2000). Verbal reports and protocol analysis. In M. Kamil, P. Mosenthal, P. Pearson, & R. Barr (Eds.), *Handbook of reading research* (Vol. 3, pp. 163–179). Mahwah, NJ: Erlbaum.

Anderson, C. (2000). *How's it going?: A practical guide to conferring with student writers.* Portsmouth, NH: Heinemann.

Andrade, H. L. (2010). Students as the definitive source of formative assessment: Academic self-assessment and the self-regulation of learning. In H. L. Andrade & G. J. Cizek (Eds.), *Handbook of formative assessment* (pp. 90–105). New York: Routledge.

Ball, A. (1992). Cultural preference and the expository writing of African American adolescents. *Written Communication, 9,* 501–532.

Ball, A. (2002). Three decades of research on classroom life: Illuminating the classroom communicative lives of America's at-risk students. In W. Secada (Ed.), *Review of research in education* (Vol. 26, pp. 71–111). Washington, DC: American Educational Research Association.

Ball, A., & Ellis, P. (2010). Identity and the writing of culturally and linguistically diverse students. In C. Bazerman (Ed.), *Handbook of research on writing* (pp. 225–248). New York: Routledge.

Basham, C. S., & Kwachka, P. E. (1991). Reading the world differently: A cross-cultural approach to writing assessment. In L. Hamp-Lyons (Ed.), *Assessing second language writing in academic contexts* (pp. 37–49). Norwood, NJ: Ablex.

Bazerman, C. (2004). Speech acts, genres, and activity systems: How texts organize activity and people. In C. Bazerman & P. Prior (Eds.), *What writing does and how it does it* (pp. 309–339). Mahwah, NJ: Erlbaum.

Beatty, A. (2010). *State assessment systems: Exploring best practices and innovation: Summary of two workshops.* Committee on Best Practices for State Assessment Systems: Improving assessment while revisiting standards. Washington, DC: National Academies Press.

Black, P. J., Harrison, C., Lee, C., Marshall, B., & Wiliam, D. (2004). Working inside the black box: Assessment for learning in the classroom. *Phi Delta Kappan, 86*(1), 8–21.

Black, P. J., & Wiliam, D. (1998a). Assessment and classroom learning. *Assessment in Education: Principles, Policy and Practice, 5*(1), 7–74.

Black, P. J., & Wiliam, D. (1998b). Inside the black box: Raising standards through classroom assessment. *Phi Delta Kappan, 80*(2), 139–148.

Black, P. J., & Wiliam, D. (2010). A pleasant surprise. *Phi Delta Kappan, 92*(1), 47–48.

Blanc, S., Christman, J. B., Liu, R., Mitchell, C., Travers, E., & Bulkley, K. E. (2010). Learning to learn from data: Benchmarks and instructional communities. *Peabody Journal of Education, 85*(2), 205–225.

Calfee, R. C., & Miller, R. G. (2007). Best practices in writing assessment. In S. Graham, C. MacArthur, & J. Fitzgerald (Eds.), *Best practices in writing instruction* (pp. 265–286). New York: Guilford Press.

Calkins, L. (1994). *The art of teaching writing.* Portsmouth, NH: Heinemann.

Cazden, C. (2001). *Classroom discourse: The language of teaching and learning* (2nd ed.). Portsmouth, NH: Heinemann.

Deno, S. L. (1985). Curriculum-based measurement: The emerging alternative. *Exceptional Children, 52,* 219–232.

Deno, S. L., & Marston, D. B. (2006). Curriculum-based measurement of oral reading: An indicator of growth in fluency. In S. J. Samuels & A. Farstrup (Eds.), *What research has to say about fluency instruction* (pp. 379–405). Newark, DE: International Reading Association.

Education Northwest. (n.d.). 6+1 Trait rubrics (aka scoring guides). Retrieved March 10, 2011, from *http://educationnorthwest.org/resource/464.*

Educational Testing Service. (2009). *Research rationale for the Keeping Learning on Track Program.* Princeton, NJ: Author.

Ferris, D. R. (2003). *Response to student writing: Implications for second language students.* Mahwah, NJ: Erlbaum.

Freedman, S. W. (1987). *Response to student writing* (NCTE Research Report No. 23). Urbana, IL: National Council of Teachers of English.

Fuchs, L. S., & Deno, S. L. (1994). Must instructionally useful performance assessment be based in the curriculum? *Exceptional Children, 16,* 15–24.

Gay, G. (2010). *Culturally responsive teaching: Theory, research, and practice.* New York: Teachers College Press.

Glasswell, K. (2001). Matthew effects in writing: The patterning of difference in classrooms K–8. *Reading Research Quarterly, 36,* 348–349.

Goertz, M. E., Olah, L. N., & Riggan, M. (2009). *Can interim assessments be used for instructional change?* Philadelphia: University of Pennsylvania, Consortium for Policy Research in Education.

Graham, S., Harris, K., & Hebert, M. A. (2011). *Informing writing: The benefits of formative assessment. A Carnegie Corporation Time to Act report.* Washington, DC: Alliance for Excellent Education.

Gutierrez, K. D., & Rogoff, B. (2003). Cultural ways of learning: Individual traits or repertoires of practice. *Educational Researcher, 32*(5), 19–25.

Hattie, J., & Timperley, H. (2007). The power of feedback. *Review of Educational Research, 77,* 81–112.

Heath, S. B. (1983). *Ways with words.* Cambridge, UK: Cambridge University Press.

Hebard, H. (2010). *Writing lessons: Case studies of beginning teachers.* Unpublished doctoral dissertation, Stanford University.

Heritage, M. (2010). *Formative assessment and next generation assessment systems: Are we losing an opportunity?* Los Angeles: National Center for Research on Evaluation, Standards and Student Testing.

Heritage, M., Kim, J., Vendlinski, T., & Herman, J. (2009). From evidence to action: A seamless process in formative assessment. *Educational Measurement: Issues and Practice, 28,* 24–31.

Hillocks, G., Jr. (1982). The interaction of instruction, teacher comment, and revision in teaching the composing process. *Research in the Teaching of English, 16,* 261–278.

Hillocks, G., Jr. (1984). What works well in teaching composition: A meta-analysis of experimental treatment studies. *American Journal of Education, 93,* 133–170.

Hillocks, G., Jr. (2002). *The testing trap: How state writing assessments control learning.* New York: Teachers College Press.

Hillocks, G., Jr. (2010). Writing in secondary schools. In C. Bazerman (Ed.), *Handbook of research on writing* (pp. 311–329). New York: Routledge.

Johnston, P. A. (1997). *Knowing literacy: Constructive literacy assessment.* York, ME: Stenhouse.

Kibby, M. W. (1979). Passage readability affects the oral reading strategies of disabled readers. *The Reading Teacher, 32,* 390–396.

Langer, J. A. (1984). The effects of available information on responses to school writing tasks. *Research in the Teaching of English, 18,* 27–44.

Langer, J. (1990). The process of understanding: Reading for literary and informative purposes. *Research in the Teaching of English, 24,* 229–260.

Lipson, M. Y., & Wixson, K. K. (2009). *Assessment and instruction of reading and writing difficulties: An interactive approach.* Boston: Pearson.

Little, J. W., Gearhart, M., Curry, M., & Kafka, J. (2003). Looking at student work for teacher learning, teacher community, and school reform. *Phi Delta Kappan, 85*(3), 185–192.

Matsumura, L. C., Patthey-Chavez, G., Valdés, R., & Garnier, H. (2002). Teacher feedback, writing assignment quality, and third-grade students' revision in lower- and higher-achieving urban schools. *Elementary School Journal, 103,* 3–25.

McCarthy, S. (1994). Authors, text, and talk: The internalization of dialogue from social interaction during writing. *Reading Research Quarterly, 29,* 200–231.

Michaels, S. A. (1981). "Sharing time": Children's narrative styles and differential access to literacy. *Language in Society, 10,* 423–442.

Murphy, S., Carroll, K., Kinzer, C., & Robyns, A. (1982). A study of the construction of the meaning of a writing prompt by its authors, the student writers, and the raters. In J. R. Gray & L. P. Ruth (Eds.), *Properties of writing tasks: A study of alternative procedures for holistic writing assessment* (pp. 386–468). Berkeley: University of California, Graduate School of Education, Bay Area Writing Project. (ERIC Document Reproduction Service No. ED230576)

Murphy, S., & Yancey, K. B. (2010). Construct and consequence: Validity in writing assessment. In C. Bazerman (Ed.), *Handbook of research on writing* (pp. 365–385). New York: Routledge.

National Council on Education Standards and Testing (NCEST). (1992). *Raising standards for American education.* Washington, DC: U.S. Government Printing Office.

National Governors Association Center for Best Practices & Council of Chief State School Officers. (2010). *Common Core State Standards for English language arts and literacy in history/social studies, science, and technical subjects.* Washington, DC: Authors. Retrieved from *www.corestandards.org/the-standards*

Olah, L. N., Lawrence, N. R., & Riggan, N. (2010). Learning to learn from benchmark assessment data: How teachers analyze results. *Peabody Journal of Education, 85*(2), 226–245.

Olson, L. (2005). Benchmark assessments offer regular achievement. *Education Week, 25*(13), 13–14.

Olson, L. (2007). Instant read on reading, in palms of their hands. *Education Week, 26*(35), 24–34.

Perie, M., Marion, S., & Gong, B. (2009). Moving toward a comprehension assessment system: A framework for considering interim assessments. *Educational Measurement: Issues and Practice, 28,* 5–13.

Popham, W. J. (2009). *Unlearned lessons: Six stumbling blocks to our schools' success.* Cambridge, MA: Harvard University Press.

Quellmalz, E., Capell, F., & Chou, C. (1982). Effects of discourse and response mode on the measurement of writing competence. *Journal of Education Measurement, 19*(4), 241–258.

Ray, K. W. (2001). *The writing workshop: Working through the hard parts (and they're all hard parts).* Urbana, IL: National Council of Teachers of English.

Ross, J. (2004). Effects of running records assessment on early literacy achievement. *Journal of Educational Research, 97,* 186–194.

Sadoski, M., Wilson, V., & Norton, D. (1997). The relative contributions of research-based composition activities to writing improvement in the lower and middle grades. *Research in the Teaching of English, 31,* 120–150.

Schoenbach, R., Greenleaf, C., Cziko, C., & Hurwitz, L. (1999). *Reading for understanding.* San Francisco: Jossey-Bass.

Shepard, L. (2000). The role of assessment in a learning culture. *Educational Researcher, 29,* 4–14.

Shepard, L. A. (2009). Commentary: Evaluating the validity of formative and interim assessment. *Educational Measurement: Issues and Practice, 28*(3), 32–37.

Shepard, L. A. (2010). What the marketplace has brought us: Item-by-item teaching with little instructional insight. *Peabody Journal of Education, 85,* 246–257.

Sperling, M. (1990). I want to talk to each of you: Collaboration and the teacher–student writing conference. *Research in the Teaching of English, 24,* 279–332.

Sperling, M., & Freedman, S. W. (1987). A good girl writes like a good girl: Written response and clues to the teaching/learning process. *Written Communication, 4,* 343–363.

Straub, R. (1996). The concept of control in teacher response: Defining the varieties of "directive" and "facilitative" commentary. *College Composition and Communication, 47,* 223–251.

Stringfield, S., Wayman, W. C., & Yakimowski-Srebnick, M. (2005). Scaling up data use in classrooms, schools, and districts. In C. Dede, J. Honan, & L. Peters (Eds.), *Scaling up success: Lessons learned from technology-based educational innovation* (pp. 133–152). San Francisco: Jossey-Bass.

Sweeney, M. (1999). Relating revision skills to teacher commentary. *Teaching in the Two-Year College, 27,* 213–218.

Valencia, S. W. (1998). *Literacy portfolios in action.* Fort Worth, TX: Harcourt Brace.

Valencia, S. W. (2011). Using assessment to improve teaching and learning. In S. J. Samuels & A. E. Farstrup (Eds.), *What research has to say about reading instruction* (4th ed., pp. 379–405). Newark, DE: International Reading Association.

Valencia, S. W., Lucero, A. M., & Alvarez, L. (2010). *Reading comprehension challenges of English language learners.* Paper presented at the annual conference of the Literacy Research Association, Fort Worth, TX.

Valencia, S. W., Smith, A., Reece, A. M., Li, M., Wixson, K. K., & Newman, H. (2010). Oral reading fluency assessment: Issues of construct, criterion, and consequential validity. *Reading Research Quarterly, 45,* 270–291.

Wiliam, D. (2007–2008). Changing classroom practice. *Educational Leadership, 65*(4), 36–42.

Wiliam, D. (2010). An integrative summary of the research literature and implications for a new theory of formative assessment. In H. L. Andrade & G. J. Cizek (Eds.), *Handbook of formative assessment* (pp. 18–40). New York: Routledge.

CHAPTER 6

Culturally Responsive Literacy Instruction • • • • • • • • • • • • •

ELLEN MCINTYRE
JENNIFER DANRIDGE TURNER

The population of children in today's U.S. classrooms is rich in ethnic and cultural diversity. To meet the needs of each child in their classrooms, teachers must adopt instructional perspectives, attitudes, and instructional strategies that attend specifically to their students' cultural and linguistic backgrounds in ways that build on the skills and understandings the students bring to school. Some teaching interactions do just that, while others fall short. First, consider this example of instruction.

> Carla is a first-grade teacher in a rural Appalachian school. The children in her classroom have knowledge of agriculture, although few of the children's families actually work on farms. One exception is Jason's family. Jason, a child who has struggled with literacy since arriving at school almost 2 years ago, loves books on tractors; he is 7 years old and just beginning to read the most basic books. The book he is reading today has a picture of a broken tractor, and the line of text says, "It will not go."
>   Jason correctly reads the sentence in his dialect, and his language sounds like "Hee-it wee-ill nat go."
>   Carla, his teacher, is bothered by Jason's pronunciation of the word *it* and says, "No, *it* will not go."
>   Jason repeats her, "Hee-it wee-ill nat go."
>   Carla says again, with emphasis, "That word is *it*."
>   Jason points to the words as he reads: "Hee-it wee-ill nat go."
>   Carla turns to the researcher in the room, shrugs, and says, "He can't get it."

Now consider another example of Carla's teaching:

Carla and her colleague prepare their primary-grade students for an annual event called Agricultural Field Day. The teachers capitalize on their students' rural backgrounds and knowledge of farming to help them develop deep concepts of agriculture and the environment, while also working on their reading, writing, and mathematics skills. They begin by reading aloud many books about farms and lead the children in discussions about the topics. The teachers guide the children in reading differently challenging books that are of interest and developmentally appropriate for various groups of children, and the teachers encourage the children to reread the books during independent time. In later lessons, the teachers instruct the students to sort and classify seeds, plant seeds and predict growth, and write about what they know about the plants, complete with drawings and labels. The teachers lead the children in estimating and graphing food needed for animals on the farm, estimating how much corn can be planted per acre, and even calculating how much money it takes to run a farm (a lot!) Throughout these lessons, the teachers repeatedly have the children read and write on related topics.

In the first example, Carla was not responsive to Jason's linguistic skills. Jason was able to read the sentence (the whole book, in fact!) perfectly well. His pronunciation was merely different from the dialect of his teacher, who saw Jason's language as incorrect and in need of remediation. The second example could be called *culturally responsive instruction* (CRI) because Carla and her colleague responded to the children's background interests and abilities by using books on topics familiar and interesting to the children. The teachers also allowed the children to work together in pairs and small groups to assist one another, and they allowed the children to work in their own dialects. They challenged the children with high-level questions and provided much support when children attempted to respond. These teaching actions are all components of culturally responsive instruction.

It may be surprising that both examples involve the same teacher. Carla was involved in a research project about CRI. She learned much about the principles of CRI, and gradually, over time, about implementing the practices of CRI. She did this by engaging in the following: carefully listening to and observing her students; trying out ideas, strategies, and topics; working with other teachers; and referring to many examples already published in books and articles for teachers. Like most teachers, Carla was not able to change her instruction all at once: At times her instruction looked culturally responsive (as in the second example), and at other times it showed a lack of understanding of her students' linguistic abilities. This is not uncommon. What is clear, however, is that when she followed particular principles for instruction, her students became more engaged in the academic work she designed for them (McIntyre & Stone, 1998). These principles are the focus of this chapter. First, though, we provide a comment about classroom environments that reflect good teaching for all children, and this point is an especially important idea about CRI. Then we summarize the research literature behind the big ideas of CRI.

If you observe in a classroom for a few hours or days, it becomes clear which classrooms have the potential for CRI. There is an atmosphere of care and respect for the children. Teachers in these classrooms rarely use harsh language, never publicly embarrass a child, do not allow putdowns of any kind, and work hard to help make each child successful. These teachers intentionally use materials that reflect the

backgrounds and identities of the students in the class. They also often ask questions of the students that illustrate their interest in the children's lives and minds, such as "How did you learn that?" "How did you spend your weekend?" "What sorts of texts would you like to read?" and "Are you doing OK?" The teachers maintain high standards for all children through rigorous activities and high-level questioning, and they have high expectations that all students will be able to accomplish the interesting and challenging work in their classrooms. (For related work on building positive relationships and community in the classroom, see Roehrig, Brinkerhoff, Rawls, & Pressley, Chapter 1, this volume.)

CRI also includes how teachers respond to the language patterns of the children. That is, teachers accept dialectal differences while also explicitly teaching students the "languages" of power. (We discuss this point in more detail later in the chapter.) Below we share the research literature on CRI and provide specific instructional principles that emanate from this body of research. Importantly, the research-based reading instruction described throughout this book is not at odds with CRI. When planning instruction, teachers must begin with instructional strategies shown in research studies to be effective for improving reading. However, teachers must also be aware that some research was conducted with populations of students that did not include representatives of the students they teach (e.g., English language learners or ELLs). This means that teachers must attempt to implement practices that honor the integrity of the strategies shown to "work," while also adapting these strategies to include and engage all students in their classrooms (McIntyre, Hulan, & Layne, 2011).

OVERVIEW OF RESEARCH

In the last several decades, as U.S. classrooms have become increasingly diverse, researchers have produced volumes on how nonwhite, immigrant, and poor children have become more disengaged in traditional-style classrooms designed for middle-class white children of European descent. Researchers have shown disconnections between the culture and communication of classrooms and the lives of the students outside of school (Banks, 2003, 2006; Heath, 1983; Tharp & Gallimore, 1988). Subsequently, many studies on classroom instruction in which teachers have attempted to bridge these differences have emerged (e.g., Dantas & Manyak, 2010; Gutiérrez, Baquedano-Lopez, & Alvarez, 2001; Lee, 1998; Moll & González, 2003; Tharp, Estrada, Dalton, & Yamauchi, 2000). These studies have been conducted on many different populations of children (e.g., nonwhites; ELLs; whites with distinct cultural backgrounds, such as Appalachians; and children of families living in poverty, both rural and urban).

Studies of Cultural Systems

In the 1980s, two seminal studies illustrated that when teachers attend closely to the cultural and linguistic patterns of students, achievement can improve remarkably. Heath (1983) studied rural whites in Appalachia, rural and small-town blacks, and small-town whites who were better off economically than the other two groups. She helped teachers see strengths in children and learn how to connect curriculum to the students' backgrounds and language patterns. Tharp and Gallimore (1988) did similar work with native Hawaiian children. When teachers learned to recognize and value the overlapping speech of native Hawaiians ("talk story"), they were able to see these language patterns as strengths rather than behavior problems and to base instruction on them. These studies were followed by many others showing that it was not the children who were the problem in classrooms characterized by low achievement, but the teaching. In another example, Gay (2000) details the story of Amy and Aaron, two poor, urban African American siblings who were intellectually curious learners outside school and who routinely scored poorly on school tests. Gay argues that if their teachers had consistently incorporated African American content and styles of learning into the curriculum, these children might have succeeded.

Indeed, in more recent decades, many scholars have shown that when teachers acknowledge the legitimacy of the cultural heritages of different ethnic groups, help students get to know and praise their own cultural heritages, and incorporate multicultural information, increased student engagement and learning occur (Banks, 2003, 2006; Gay, 2000; Irvine, 2006; Ladson-Billings, 1994). Gay (2000) suggests that teachers be deliberate about "incorporating specific aspects of the cultural systems of different groups into instruction" (p. 6). By *cultural systems*, these scholars mean the systems of social values, cognitive understandings, behavioral standards, worldviews, and beliefs we all use to give meaning to our lives (Delgado-Gaitan & Trueba, 1991). For example, how children respond to their teachers, how they show interest and engagement, how they stand up for themselves and their classmates, what they value for leisure activity, what they believe in, and what they know about are all part of their culture. These cultural systems are different for individuals, but there are some group (i.e., population) similarities as well. Importantly, the culture of European American middle-class people in the United States is so "deeply ingrained in the structures, ethos, programs, and etiquette of schools that it is considered simply the "normal" and "right" source for things to do (Gay, 2000, p. 9).

Cultural systems also include the bodies of knowledge groups of people know in order to work and thrive in communities. One body of work that has emerged on how teachers use students' cultural systems to build instruction and foster student success is called *funds-of-knowledge* work. It is championed by Moll and González (2003), who use families' knowledge to build school curricula. *Funds of knowledge* is a term coined by Vélez-Ibáñez and Greenburg (1992), and it refers to the various social and linguistic practices and knowledge that are essential to students' homes and communities. In some households, funds of knowledge might consist of candy making, car mechanics, or farming. In another, they might include the Bible, gardening, or even television. Teachers use a variety of ways to assess families' knowledge and build activities and curricular units around those topics. This sort of planning and teaching not only serves to motivate children and families; it contextualizes (Tharp et al., 2000) instruction in what the children already know, increasing the likelihood that the children will learn. Importantly, however, teachers may lower expectations and rigor if they implement a "funds-of-knowledge approach to teaching" without a simultaneous focus on research-based instruction (McIntyre, 2010a, 2010b; McIntyre, Kyle, & Rightmyer, 2005). (Again, for related work on building positive relationships and community in the classroom, see Roehrig et al., Chapter 1.)

Studies of Grouping and Collaborative Work

Studies of grouping patterns that provide opportunities for academic dialogue in classrooms also show more engaged students, especially students of color and those who might struggle with reading. In Chapter 3 of this book, Taylor has presented a summary of research on effective grouping practices. Taylor emphasizes that balance in grouping practices is essential to providing the necessary attention to individual and small groups of children. Varied grouping practices are especially important when classrooms are diverse in population. Sometimes teachers can and should group children by the language they speak, allowing children to work together in their first language (Soto-Hinman & Hetzel, 2009). Other groupings can be based on skill level, project focus, book topic, and even friendship. One idea behind grouping that is not emphasized in Chapter 3, but that is essential in diverse classrooms, is that students must have many opportunities to engage in dialogue for the purposes of learning content. This is important because children (and adults) talk *through* something to come to understand it (Goldenberg, 1993; Lemke, 1990; Luxford & Smart, 2009), not the other way around (Tharp & Gallimore, 1988; Wells & Wells, 1989). Students learn from one another and therefore should have multiple opportunities to work in pairs and small groups. Students must also have opportunities to practice academic talk in these group settings, with assistance from the teacher to clarify misconceptions or nudge students' thinking. (For more about discussion, see Garas-York, Shanahan, & Almasi, Chapter 10, this volume.)

Studies Concerning Rigor and High Expectations

Studies of classrooms characterized as providing CRI show that while teachers purposefully connect the curriculum to students' lives, they also maintain rigor and have high expectations (Irvine & Armento, 2001; Tharp et al., 2000). One unfortunate practice in the United States is that schools serving poor and working-class students often seem to adopt basic-skills instructional models and packaged programs for reading instruction more often than schools serving middle-class students (Dudley-Marling & Paugh, 2005; Valencia & Buly, 2004). These programs sometimes illustrate big gain scores on reading tests for struggling readers. Educators have made the case that "these kids" need this type of instruction. The argument is that if children lack "basic skills," then these programs are needed to raise those skill levels before the children can move on to more high-level skills. In one famous study (Anyon, 1997), a researcher compared elementary instruction in different schools that served four different income groups: working-class (i.e., children of unskilled workers), middle-class (e.g., children of teachers, firefighters), upper-middle-class (e.g., children of doctors, TV executives), and elite (e.g., children of corporate executives). The researcher found that the children in the lower-socioeconomic-status (lower-SES) schools received more rote-type instruction focused on basic skills, whereas those in the higher-SES schools received high-level thinking instruction. Children in the schools serving working-class and middle-class students were taught to follow rules, while those in professional and wealthy populations were taught to question authority, think beyond what is written in text, analyze data, and create new knowledge.

Yet a curriculum focused on basic skills arguably limits what students can learn by limiting access to high-quality instruction (Allington & McGill-Franzen, 2003; Dudley-Marling & Paugh, 2005; McGill-Franzen & Allington, 1993; McIntyre, 2011; Miller, 1995). This may be one of the factors contributing to school failure. It is important for teachers and school leaders to constantly ask the questions, "Who is getting instruction focused only on the most basic skills? Who is getting instruction focused on analytic and critical reading?" The question of who gets what kind of instruction is essential for working against these patterns. Reading programs focused on basic skills often work against some students by helping students learn a few skills temporarily, but never moving them toward the sort of analytic and critical thinking necessary for advanced reading (Allington & McGill-Franzen, 2003; McIntyre, 2011). (For a related discussion on the value of high-level thinking in the research on effective school reform, see Taylor, Chapter 18, this volume.)

Teachers' beliefs about and expectations of students also affect achievement. These beliefs and expectations may result in a self-fulfilling prophecy (Allington, 1977; Rist, 1970; Rothstein, 2004; Stanovich, 1986; Weinstein, 2002). Rist (1970) conducted one of the most important sociological studies of teachers' expectations and the self-fulfilling prophecy. He observed regularly in an urban school serving all black students. The children came from families of different SES, though, and more than half received public welfare funds. The kindergarten teacher received extensive information about each individual student before the start of the school year, including the child's zip code and whether he or she had attended preschool. The teacher grouped children at tables according to perceived similarities in expected performance. The children placed at the front table near the teacher were well dressed, were quite verbal, and spoke in Standard English. The children at the other tables were poor, spoke in dialect, and were less verbal; some had body odor. They were also darker in skin color than those at the front table. The teacher allowed those at the front table to lead the Pledge of Allegiance and help her in other ways. During lessons, she gave them more assistance, and she communicated to them that they were expected to do well. The teacher had low expectations for the other children and told the researcher that those children had no idea what was going on in the classroom. Eventually, the children behaved in the expected ways; they even began calling each other words like "dummy" and worse. The children at the front table also internalized the disdain their teacher had for the other children and began communicating their views to their classmates.

Although we may not observe such dramatically classist and disturbing practices today, many well-meaning teachers believe that students living in poverty and/or students from ethnic minority groups cannot achieve as capably as middle-class white students, largely due to their backgrounds, families, and life circumstances, and that they need to be taught remedial basic skills (Delpit, 1986, 1988; Ferguson, 1998; Weinstein, 2002). Some teachers believe that poor students are in dire need of being rescued from their communities, families, and cultures (Finn, 1999; Lee, 2008; Marx, 2006). Certainly racism has also played a major role in the low expectations some educators have of some students. Some Americans still believe in the innate cultural and intellectual inferiority of students of color. Even well-meaning whites who do not think they hold prejudices often do. Subtle feelings and behaviors are communicated to students, who act on them, and these actions affect the students' achievement (Ferguson, 1998; Weinsten, 2002). Weinstein (2002) describes an experiment in which she took a 10-year-old (a nonreader) out of the bottom reading group and re-placed him in the middle group, where she watched him learn to read, make friends, and become a confident student. She also reports on a few large-scale studies that claim similar results—particularly when they are conducted early in the school year, when teachers have little prior knowledge of students.

Studies of Discourse and Communicative Styles

One prevalent topic in the research literature on CRI concerns classroom discourse. Elements of discourse include who participates in communicative interactions, how they communicate, under what conditions, and why. How teachers use language—how they ask questions, respond to learners, look at children, display body language—affects what is learned and how engaged children are in the lessons. And it includes verbal and nonverbal communication cues, such as eye contact and shrugs.

Traditional classroom discourse looks familiar to most European American middle-class students and adults. The teacher does most of the talking, while the children sit quietly and listen. Once the teacher finishes presenting, she asks a question of the students (to which he or she already knows the answer), seeks a short response from an approved student (perhaps someone raising a hand to respond), and then either affirms the answer or not. This discourse pattern includes highly structured nonverbal cues and an expectation that students face the teacher, sit quietly with little movement, and maintain eye contact with the teacher (Cazden, 1988). (For more on teacher questioning related to texts students have read, see Garas-York et al., Chapter 10.)

But some cultural and ethnic groups in the United States have communication styles that contrast starkly with this conventional classroom discourse. Communication can vary according to participation structures, dialects, and body language. Teachers need to familiarize themselves with the *typical* characteristics of the communication modes of different ethnic groups. Importantly, though, teachers must not assume that because a child is a member of a cultural or ethnic group, the child automatically participates in the language patterns of that group. Therefore, we always use the word *some* when we refer to cultural and linguistic patterns of students in groups. For example, some African Americans, especially those who strongly identify with their ethnicity and cultural heritage, value personal assertiveness in interactions (Gay, 2000; Irvine & Armento, 2001) and work to "gain the floor" during discussions. Some children participate in "breaking in and talking over" others, and in "talking back" in defense of their views. Importantly, these participation structures are highly valued in some communities, and when children exhibit these patterns in classrooms, teachers can and should see the patterns as strengths (Gay, 2000; Lee, 1998). Some teachers have learned to incorporate patterns such as "call and response" into classroom exchanges (Foster & Peele, 2001; O'Gilvie, Turner, & Hughes, 2011); doing so engages African American students, as well as other children whose patterns of response tend to be choral and assertive.

Some Asian students have learned to defer to others, rarely speaking up in whole-class settings, but many may want to spend one-on-one time with their teacher. Some students of Asian descent also use "hedges" in their language, such as "I am not sure, but . . . " and "I may be wrong, but . . . ," when in fact they do know and are not wrong (Gay, 2000). Some students in many different groups, such as Native Americans, African Americans, and Asians, have particular nonverbal cues that can be misunderstood by European American teachers (Tharp, 1989). For instance, some children do not make eye contact with teachers because the children see it as inciting conflict. However, many teachers insist on eye contact and believe that children show them a lack of respect when they avoid eye contact.

Of course, all children, regardless of their background, number of years in the United States, or ancestry, are speakers of dialects. Dialects differ from one another in pronunciation of words, word usage (e.g., *soft drink*, *pop*, or *Coke*), and grammar. In the United States alone, language varies widely across different SES groups, cultural groups, and geographic regions. It differs in pronunciation, word usage, syntax or grammar, and in less obvious ways such as eye contact, gestures, and body language. For example, some children grow up in homes in which family members speak and react directly (e.g., "Shut the door!"), with gestures and body language that others may see as blunt, whereas others use less direct speech and body language (e.g., "What is the rule when we enter the house?"). No one style is better or worse than any other. They are merely different (Adger, Wolfram, & Christian, 2007; Dalton, 2007; Delpit, 2005).

How does a teacher manage to create a dialogic classroom community when a classroom is full of "language differences"? The first answer to this question is to recognize that we all have language differences, including individuals whose families have been in the United States for many years. There is no one "correct" way to speak. Even dialects that sound very different to some people (e.g., African American English, Appalachian English, or Chicano English) are not incorrect or improper ways of speaking. These dialects are sophisticated, rule-governed, and valued by the members of the groups who use them. The increasingly common English–Spanish combination of dialect is also a growing and rule-governed language form, not sloppy English. Linguists who study differences have found that *all* speakers are speakers of dialects, no matter how "standard" one person might sound compared to another.

Of course, there is a language of power (Delpit, 1995). In this country, that language is a certain form of English in which grammar constructions are commonly accepted forms spoken by an educated class. Why should we care that our students learn to speak like another class of individuals? Many scholars wrestle with this question. If we must teach them "Standard English," whatever that might mean (many linguists suggest that there is no one standard), then does that not communicate to the students the deficiencies of their own dialects? These are tough questions. Yet, because U.S. society does provide access to or membership in groups based on perceived education (and language differences are a marker), we must find ways to teach our students about these differences and the features of the language of power.

Studies of ELLs

Much of the research literature on the education of students whose first language is not English suggests that ELLs need "enhanced teaching of what is good for native-language speakers" (August & Shanahan, 2006, p. 16). This includes building on students' backgrounds, explicit and challenging discourse, active involvement of all students, scaffolded instruction, visual and graphic organizers, feedback to students, and opportunities for inquiry-based collaborative work. Indeed, in a review of research on elementary literacy instruction for ELLs, Amendum and Fitzgerald (2011) also suggest that what is good for native English speakers is generally good for ELLs. Certainly the explicit teaching of phonemic awareness, phonics, vocabulary, comprehension, and writing benefits ELLs as it does native English speakers (Goldenberg, 1994). Also, children's learning tends to mirror what they were taught (Fitzgerald & Noblit, 2000), and the developmental patterns of ELLs parallel the patterns of native English speakers' literacy learning patterns. Amendum and Fitzgerald's review suggests that phonological awareness and understandings about word recognition develop for ELLs and native English speakers in similar ways. These authors also report on studies (e.g., Gersten & Jiménez, 1994) in which teachers used culturally responsive techniques and strategies to engage learners in more traditional lessons.

ELLs, like all children, have varied experiences and skill levels with English. Many of these children have been born in the United States and speak fluent conversational English, but live in homes where adults speak something other than English. These lucky children who are growing up bilingual (or with multiple languages) are sometimes ironically and sadly viewed as deficient rather than as talented. Some teachers do not realize that the ability to speak multiple languages is an asset to be fostered rather than an obstacle to overcome. Indeed, students who have competence in multiple languages have higher metalinguistic awareness than monolingual students (Bialystok, 2007). However, as teachers, we must not assume that all such children understand all the English they hear, especially the discipline-based academic language of science, mathematics, and social studies. The majority of ELLs need extra time and support. Some recent immigrants get this support through special classes (ESL/ELL) with specially trained teachers. But most ELLs are in the regular classroom full time and must be provided with accommodations by the teacher. In literacy classrooms, it may be important to provide special materials or tasks for ELLs, depending on their needs. It may also mean that the teacher needs to spend a few extra minutes with these children to give them the chance to share their views in both their languages (August & Shanahan, 2006; McIntyre, 2010b; Soto-Hinman & Hetzel, 2009).

SUMMARY OF BIG IDEAS FROM RESEARCH

From the research literature on CRI reviewed above, we propose several instructional principles that can make literacy instruction culturally responsive. These principles are similar to those outlined elsewhere (Dalton, 2007; McIntyre et al., 2011; McIntyre, Rosebery, & González, 2002; Tharp et al., 2000). Although a common term for these principles is *culturally responsive instruction* (CRI), similar perspectives are referred to as *culturally relevant pedagogy, equity pedagogy, standards for effective pedagogy,* or *multicultural instruction* (Banks, 2003, 2006; Dalton, 2007; Irvine & Armento, 2001). The instructional principles synthesized from the studies described above include the following:

- *Connecting curriculum to students' backgrounds.* Find out what students know and are interested in, and use that knowledge to develop curriculum for new understandings.
- *Planning for collaborative work and dialogic instruction.* Provide many opportunities for students to engage in academic conversation with you and their peers in a variety of grouping patterns.
- *Maintaining a rigorous curriculum.* Never allow the curriculum to be watered down, but provide support so that all students can engage in high-level thinking and meaningful work.
- *Attending to classroom discourse.* Build on students' home languages or dialects while also teaching academic English, and attend to strategies such as wait time, turn taking, and questioning so that students are helped to be successful.
- *Being explicit about what you are teaching.* Show and tell children how to do what you want them to do, from manipulating phonemes to connecting information across multiple texts.

These principles also reflect the extensive research conducted by the Center for Research on Education, Diversity and Excellence (CREDE) at the University of California, Berkeley, and other universities. Researchers associated with the center have conducted studies of many different populations of students in U.S. schools and have discerned patterns of what works with all students. The CREDE standards are meant to be implemented within a classroom culture of respect, care, and high expectations (Tharp et al., 2000). Furthermore, these principles overlap. For instance, when teachers plan for collaborative work and dialogic instruction, they attend to classroom discourse to make the dialogue meaningful for all learners. Also, to maintain rigor, teachers also attend to classroom discourse because teachers focus on asking high-level questions and providing much support to individual students as they attempt to answer those questions.

EXAMPLES OF EFFECTIVE PRACTICES

Below we give practical suggestions for all teachers for implementing the culturally responsive principles we have just summarized from the research literature. Many of these practices will seem familiar. The important point is that teachers who make it a point to be responsive to their students' cultural and linguistic backgrounds conduct these activities with goals for students' engagement and achievement in mind.

Connecting Curriculum to Students' Backgrounds

To implement the first principle, purposely connect instruction with students' backgrounds while assisting them in developing fluency, comprehension, and vocabulary skills in reading and voice and craft in writing. To do this, the most important instructional strategy for connecting curriculum to your students' backgrounds is to get to know your students! Then you can find ways to connect their backgrounds to your literacy instruction. Here are a few ways to do this:

- Listen to your students—really listen—as they tell you about their lives. Keep a journal or record of the sorts of things you hear that illustrate what they and their families know about and are interested in. Soon you may find patterns in your classroom. If several children love baseball, have that group do a week of reading about nothing but baseball. Children will be motivated to read more sophisticated texts if the topic is extremely compelling to them.
- Plan a Family Night (Kyle, McIntyre, Miller, & Moore, 2006) in which you invite parents and guardians to the school to work on a curricular area with their children. First, read aloud several books on whatever the topic might be, and have students read texts in reading groups that relate to the Family Night topic. Get the families involved in the planning and presenting as much as possible. You will get to know the families' skills and knowledge in ways that will surprise you.
- Have students write (or draw, label, scrapbook, or video-record) their autobiographies (Gay, 2000). These provide excellent opportunities for reading and writing, enable you to help your students improve all communication skills, and give you a chance to get to know the students well at the same time.
- Take a walking field trip in the community where many of your students live. Have them show you the area, explaining where they play, shop, eat, and do other things. Then have the students return to class to write about their communities.
- Have newcomers (students who have recently arrived in the United States) conduct and lead research projects on their home countries, and then write "Then and Now" books (McIntyre, Kyle, Chen, Kraemer, & Parr, 2009) that illustrate and describe life in their home countries and life in the United States.

A further instructional strategy is to bring in popular culture texts that connect with students' lives and build bridges to reading and writing skills. Popular culture texts are generally characterized as print texts (e.g., comics) or nonprint texts (e.g., icons, images, and multimedia found on the Internet; in television shows, music, and music videos; in films; and in PlayStations, Game Boys, and video games) that children interact with and make meaning of outside of school (Xu, 2001). For example, hip-hop lyrics are popular culture texts that have been used in classrooms with African American students. In one urban fifth-grade classroom, an African American teacher used the lyrics from the hip-hop song "Hey Mama" by Kanye West (2005) to promote critical reading, writing, and thinking skills. By analyzing the lyrics to "Hey Mama," students learned that rappers have particular messages that they intend to impart to their audiences; this set the foundation for a later discussion about an author's purpose and message (O'Gilvie et al., 2011). Other teachers have used Spanish lyrics and compared them with hip-hop to have students practice comparing and contrasting texts (Xu, 2001); have used comic books to do interactive read-alouds with ELLs (Ranker, 2007); have video games to engage boys in literacy learning (Ranker, 2006); and have used trading cards, television shows, and movies as frames for reading and writing (Xu, Perkins, & Zunich, 2005).

Two considerations are important in using popular culture texts. First, carefully consider the texts and how they will be used in your lessons; they should be appropriate

for the grade level and/or developmental level of the students. Second, popular culture texts should not be taught as an end to themselves; rather, they should be taught as a "bridge" to the curriculum, so that all students ultimately acquire the academic conventions and literary skills that are so crucial to success in school and in the workplace.

Planning for Collaborative Work and Dialogic Instruction

Outdated whole-class instruction with the raise-your-hand-if-you-know-the-answer method can intimidate students and deter them from being active participants. Instead, opportunities to work in groups or activities such as Think–Pair–Share (Lyman, 1981) allow students time to think and respond in a safe environment, and encourage them to take risks. We add to Taylor's ideas about grouping in Chapter 3 by focusing on how you can get your students talking about the content of their reading in ways that support their literacy learning. We also add to Garas-York and colleagues' ideas in Chapter 10 about discussion.

- During small-group or whole-class discussion, practice Think–Pair–Share: Pose a high-level, open-ended question to the students and ask them to think first (30 seconds of silence!), then turn to a partner and share their responses (rehearsal). This allows students to formulate more articulate responses, and it can provide opportunities for more students to share with the whole class when there is an opportunity.
- Practice Talk Triangle (Luxford & Smart, 2009). One student takes the role of *speaker*, who will talk extensively about a topic. The second role is the *questioner*, whose role is to ask the kind of questions that keep the speaker going, adding detail and depth to the topic. The third role is the *observer*, who records the questions asked and assesses how well those questions brought out details from the speaker. Each student is given a role card that names the role and reminds him or her of what to do. A broad topic is then decided (e.g., "What was it probably like for an African American to live in the United States in the 1950s?") After the

conversation, the three assess the quality of the talk. The students then switch roles and (if they choose) begin with new questions.

- Make authentic texts the center of student interaction. Orchestrating paired activities (e.g., buddy reading), small-group activities (e.g., book clubs, literature circles) and other types of collaborative activities (e.g., jigsaw puzzles) not only encourages students to socialize, but also supports cross-cultural understanding and literacy learning, because students are grouped heterogeneously.
- Implement whole-class activities such as Character Chats, where students mingle with each other while talking about and/or acting like a character from a book they read.

Taken together, these collaborative and dialogic practices highlight the importance of *classroom literacy communities*. These communities are "dynamic classroom environments that are rich in social relationships, in partnerships, and in collaborations involving talking, reading, thinking, and writing" (Rousculp & Maring, 1992, p. 384). Classroom literacy communities provide the ideal social contexts for developing students' academic, social, and cross-cultural skills because they create openings for students to take intellectual risks, talk about their learning, and "take up" new literacy skills and strategies.

For example, Turner and Kim (2005) studied the classroom literacy community that Rita, a European American teacher, developed with her third graders. Her class was diverse, with 13 European American students, six African American students, one Latino student, and one Asian American student. Rita wanted to build a literacy community in her classroom that embraced the cultural backgrounds of her students, but also supported their literacy development. To build positive relationships within the literacy community, Rita designed what she called "trust-building activities" to help her students get to know one another. On the first day of school, community members created a beautiful display of paper dolls. Students initially created the dolls as self-portraits reflecting their own individual styles, personalities, and cultural backgrounds, but the spirit of community coalesced as Rita and her students introduced themselves by using their dolls, and began talking about their hopes and dreams for their time together. Throughout the year, Rita implemented the Ted E. Bear project: Each child had the opportunity to take Ted E., a stuffed teddy bear, home with him or her for the weekend, and to write about the bear's adventures in an adventure journal. Each Monday, the student who took Ted E. home would read his or her entry in the adventure journal, and students were encouraged to ask questions and make connections. The Ted E. Bear activity was particularly exciting for these third graders because they were learning to write (and read) for an authentic audience (Rita and their peers), and their texts held special personal meaning. Best of all, Rita made explicit comments about the similarities and differences in Ted E.'s adventures (e.g., "Isn't it cool that Ted has visited a church, a synagogue, and a mosque this year?"), and encouraged students to ask questions if they were curious about particular activities (e.g., one African American girl was asked about Ted's visit to a hair-braiding salon). In this way, the Ted E. Bear project not only made children's differences a "safe topic" to explore and talk about in the classroom, but it served as the common thread within their literacy community. Tamika, one of the African American students, summed up the spirit of their literacy community best: "We are all different, but that's what makes us all special!"

Maintaining a Rigorous Curriculum

How do you maintain rigor and have high expectations for all students while providing all students with support and skills, especially those children who struggle with reading? It is a challenge, but many teachers have been successful in meeting it. Below are some reminders.

- Offer choices for classroom work or texts to read as often as you can. Children often choose what is developmentally appropriate for them and gain motivation and ownership in work if they have had a part in choosing tasks and texts.
- Read aloud texts (or have another adult in the room do so) to students who cannot yet read those texts on their own, but then encourage the students to reread the texts during their independent time.
- When you are planning group research projects, be sure to have a wide variety of text levels available. Have children work in small groups on meaningful projects—but with much guidance, so that the students who struggle with reading are not merely doing all the artwork or talking, but add to the project through books they have read on their own.
- Create a text-rich classroom, and provide access to texts throughout the day. Classroom libraries should include as many genres in both fiction (e.g., historical fiction, fantasy, folktales, poetry) and nonfiction (e.g., encyclopedia entries, textbooks, nonfiction trade books) as possible. Multicultural literature—that is, texts that authentically represent cultural diversity (e.g., race, ethnicity, language, skin color, SES) and open possibilities for critique of social and historical issues—should also be incorporated into the classroom (Au, 2005). Other texts, such as newspaper articles, blogs, and articles in magazines like *Time for Kids*, are excellent sources for understanding issues of diversity and history.
- For children who do not have access to computers at home, provide opportunities for them to use technology whenever possible. Encourage online reading at sites like the International Children Digital Library (*http://en.childrenslibrary.org*), where students can read stories in Spanish, French, Farsi, Hebrew, Arabic, and 50 other languages; or National Geographic Kids (*http://kids.nationalgeographic.com/kids*), where students can deepen their content knowledge and literacy skills through informational texts.

Attending to Classroom Discourse

To assess the quality of your classroom discourse, ask yourself the following questions about your classroom (Luxford & Smart, 2009; McIntyre, Kyle, & Moore, 2006):

- Who does most of the talking?
- What kind of talk is it?
- Do the children respond to each other, or just to me?
- What types of questions do the students ask?
- What types of questions do I ask?
- What are the length and quality of children's responses?

An assessment of the quality of classroom talk can lead you toward improving the overall classroom discourse for all learners, even those who have usually contributed less to discussions. Other strategies to practice include the following:

- Ask high-level questions that do not have known answers to expected responses, but that get students to think, such as "Why do you think that?" "What do you think about . . . ?" "How do you know . . . ?" "What would you think if . . . ?" (For more on high-level questioning, see Garas-York et al., Chapter 10.)
- Practice increasing your wait time. To take advantage of the excellent, open-ended questions that require thinking, you must also increase the amount of time for student thinking. All children at all levels of language skill benefit from time to prepare or rehearse responses before sharing in a whole-class setting. Increasing wait time is not always easy and must be practiced. The idea is to teach children that this time is to be spent *thinking*.
- Be sure to include all students. Sometimes this is difficult to do if some students' discourse style is to "gain the floor" while others is to sit back and observe. Therefore, try to be deliberate about attending to which students are engaged and participating (in their own ways) and which ones have "checked out." When you monitor student involvement, rather than taking it for granted that all are engaged, you will often be surprised by what you find and seek ways to include more students in class discussions.
- Teach children how to listen to one another. Children must listen in order to learn, and therefore you must teach children explicitly how to listen. You can create a signal for listening that is something other than your voice, such as a bell, a special clap, or a song. Spend time early in the year teaching children to sit as still as possible and listen—to sounds they did not know existed. Encourage them to practice "active listening," which means not just listening, but thinking about what is being said and then discussing with others what they have heard. Reteach these skills as needed.
- Respond to children's responses with scaffolding that teaches, beyond just "Good!" "Right," or "Yes!" Responses such as these may sound positive, but they often simply confuse children. Instead, try to make more nonjudgmental responses that *encourage* rather than *praise*. Responses such as "OK . . . " or "Hmmm, what else?" encourage a learner to continue (McIntyre, Kyle, & Rightmyer, 2005).

Consider the following dialogue (McIntyre et al., 2011, p. 68) about a Chris Van Allsburg book between a teacher and student. (This is the gist of the conversation, not an exact transcript.)

TEACHER: What did you think of the book?
CHILD: It was good.
TEACHER: In what way?
CHILD: I like the story.
TEACHER: OK. (*Waits, looking at the child and nodding.*)

CHILD: (after a 3-second pause) Well, I liked how there was, like, a puzzle to the story, like a mystery. You didn't know how that boat got up there, and so that made it interesting.

TEACHER: OK, what else?

CHILD: Well, at the end when the old man was walking away with his hurt leg, it made me want to read the story all over again.

TEACHER: Why?

CHILD: Well, I started to think. That boy flew that boat a long time ago, and the story is the old man telling about the boy who flew the boat that crashed. So, the man is, maybe, the boy grown up. It's like what some writers do. They give you hints about what is going to happen.

TEACHER: Yes, many good writers do that. It is a writing technique called foreshadowing. . . .

In traditional classrooms, the teacher might have stopped with this child after the first, second, or even the third question. But it was her pushing with "What else?" and "Why?" that helped the child recognize, and the teacher make explicit, the literary technique of foreshadowing.

Being Explicit About What You Are Teaching

Many scholars who advocate for children of color or for others who are "not of the culture of power" (Delpit, 1988) recommend that teachers make explicit what they want children to do and how they are to do it. It is important to note that we use the term *explicit* to mean communicating clear expectations for behavior and work in the classroom. It does not refer to a skills-based approach or rote teaching that is directed entirely by a teacher, who merely tells children what to do. Rather, it means helping children understand what they need to do (e.g., to read a passage), how they should go about it, why they are doing it, and how it will help them be successful.

For example, Jane, a third-grade teacher at a multiracial school, provided access to her students by making the skills and strategies of good readers "transparent" through explicit instruction (Turner, 2005). She designed mini-lessons to be responsive to students' needs as readers. For example, one day during Drop Everything and Read, several African American students asked Jane to help them read unfamiliar words in their books. The next day, Jane organized a mini-lesson on the topic "What can you do if you get stuck on a word?" During the mini-lesson, the class generated several strategies (e.g., sound out the word, use context clues, substitute another word that makes sense), and Jane modeled these strategies by using several texts from the classroom library. Throughout the day, Jane reminded her students to practice using the strategies when they came across unfamiliar words in doing seatwork, reading independently, or working at centers. In addition, Jane organized individual conferences with students to review and reinforce reading skills and strategies introduced during mini-lessons. During these conferences, she assessed comprehension through retellings, coached students in the use of independent reading strategies, and monitored students' use of comprehension strategies. Through these explicit teaching moves, the teacher helped her students understand how to become skilled readers. As Kionna explained, "I finally get what I'm supposed to be *doing* when I read!" And that's exactly what the kind of readers we want our students to be—strategic, knowledgeable, and confident.

If teachers create classrooms characterized by care and practice a few specific strategies focused on helping their particular students become successful, they can find themselves on their way toward CRI. These strategies include connecting the curriculum to students' backgrounds through learning more about the students, and finding texts and pedagogies suited for those learners. They also include providing many opportunities for students to work collaboratively, so that they can learn through one another and through language. They include keeping the curriculum rigorous and maintaining high expectations for all learners. They also include attending to the classroom discourse to build on students' home languages or dialects, while also teaching academic English. Furthermore, teachers should attend to strategies such as wait time, turn taking, and questioning, so that students are helped to be successful. Finally, if teachers help make learning explicit by showing and explaining to children how to do what they want them to do, students will learn more. The principles of CRI are meant to be implemented within a classroom culture of respect, care, and high expectations (Tharp et al., 2000).

LOOKING FORWARD

The topic of CRI is not new, and it is likely to be with us forever. As U.S. classrooms continue to become diverse—and more interesting—so too will teachers' needs. These needs call for more research studies that focus on how teachers can successfully address the needs of all students:

- Studies taken up in diverse locations (such as urban, suburban, and rural schools) to enrich our understanding of how geographic context, as well as home–school–community factors, shape CRI in literacy.
- Studies that provide "thick description" (Geertz, 1973) of how children respond to particular texts, tasks, and interactions. Such studies help teachers decide what is best for their own students, and more studies of this sort are needed.
- Well-designed experimental studies of particular instructional actions or moves with particular groups of children, that can show the impact on student achievement in reading or writing.
- Studies (including teacher research/action research investigations) that illuminate how educators become more aware of students' diverse racial, ethnic, cultural, and linguistic backgrounds, and develop the capacity to teach literacy in culturally responsive ways.

QUESTIONS FOR REFLECTION ●

1. What do I know about my students? Can I name something about each of my students?

2. What do I truly think about my students of color? Do I believe that they can and will succeed like white students?

3. What do I think about my students who come from backgrounds of poverty? Do I truly believe that they can and will succeed as my middle-class students will?

4. How can I provide a curriculum that is linked to my students' backgrounds, while also covering the required curriculum?

5. How can I adapt instructional strategies to fit my students, while also ensuring that my practices remain research-based?

6. How can I make changes in the classroom environment (e.g., classroom library, technology) that will include more students more of the time?

7. How can I make changes in my classroom discourse (e.g., who is silent who talks) that will help students feel comfortable taking risks to read and write?

8. How can I foster more collaboration and dialogic instruction in my literacy block?

SUGGESTIONS FOR ONGOING PROFESSIONAL LEARNING ● ● ● ● ● ●

Becoming a culturally responsive literacy teacher is a lifelong process. An essential part of that process is helping teachers understand their own culture. Lazar (2011) contends:

> Many Whites do not believe they have a culture and that others who "have it" deviate from "the norm." Movement beyond these narrow conceptions is necessary for recognizing who we are in relation to the children we teach and for making important cultural connections with students. (p. 15)

To help you think more about your culture, try the *ABCs of cultural understanding and communication* model (Schmidt, Rodriguez, & Sandroni, 2011). The A represents *autobiography*, and this is the way you can explore your own culture. For example, what beliefs and values are important in your family/community? What family traditions do you celebrate? What language(s) do you speak at home? How did your family arrive in America? What role does religion play in your life and family, if any? What are significant milestones in your life? These are the kinds of questions that will help you understand your own cultural background. The B represents *biography*, and you can use the same questions listed above to learn more about the culture of one of your students. Finally, the C represents *cross-cultural analysis*; using a Venn diagram or other visual representation, you can examine the cultural similarities and differences between you and your student. Schmidt and colleagues' (2011) ABCs model is a wonderful way not only to begin learning more about your own culture, but also to recognize and appreciate others' cultures as well.

Thinking about new ways to transform your literacy instruction and make it more culturally responsive is also critical. One way to reflect upon your teaching, and to think of new possibilities for practice, is through a framework called *vision* (Turner, 2006, 2007). Vision is a tool that enables teachers to think about what they would like to see occurring in their classrooms, and to begin planning how they might make those "images and imaginings" a reality. Vision has five dimensions that teachers can use to consider the kinds of culturally responsive practices they would like to see in their classrooms:

1. *Classroom environment.* What are the sights and sounds of the classroom? What are students and teachers doing? How is the room organized? Is it student-centered, friendly, and accessible?

2. *Role of the teacher.* What roles is the teacher taking up in the classroom? How is he or she interacting with students and with other teachers?

3. *Role of students.* What are students' roles in the classroom and in the learning process? How do students interact with one another? How is student behavior managed and by whom? What do students like to read and write outside of school?

4. *Role of parents.* What are parents' roles in the classroom and in the learning process? How do teachers and parents interact? What cultural strengths and resources do parents possess, and how can they be used for literacy learning in school?

5. *Curriculum.* What are the major skills and concepts that need to be learned in reading and writing? Does the curriculum represent diverse peoples, languages, backgrounds, and abilities? If not, where are the gaps? What seems to be missing?

The concept of vision can help you to pull together the concepts, strategies, and practices of CRI presented in this chapter into a cohesive, comprehensive framework for teaching in diverse classrooms. Following these three key steps will help you develop and actualize your vision of CRI in literacy:

1. After reading the information in this chapter, use the "My Vision . . . " column of the Vision Worksheet (see Figure 6.1) to write about or draw your ideal culturally responsive classroom. Be sure to write brief descriptions to cover each of the five dimensions, so that your vision is complete. If you have photos or images that embody your culturally responsive classroom, include those as well.

2. Talk to colleagues in your grade level, or in your professional learning community, about your vision. Share your ideals and thoughts about culturally responsive literacy instruction, and discuss why they are important to you. Take time to consider other viewpoints, ideas, and perspectives about culturally responsive literacy instruction.

3. Complete the "Steps to Achieving My Vision" column of the Vision Worksheet. Make sure that your steps are realistic, are fairly simple, and can be achieved by a particular date. Work with other colleagues at your grade level, or in your professional learning community, to follow the steps you have outlined, to talk through setbacks, and to celebrate the successes!

My Vision of Culturally Responsive Literacy Instruction	Steps to Achieving My Vision
Classroom environment	Goal: Steps: Do it by _____ (date)
My role as teacher	Goal: Steps: Do it by _____ (date)
Role of my students	Goal: Steps: Do it by _____ (date)
Role of my students' families	Goal: Steps: Do it by _____ (date)
Literacy curriculum	Goal: Steps: Do it by _____ (date)

FIGURE 6.1. Vision Worksheet.

RESEARCH-BASED RESOURCES

The following books and websites are some of our favorite teacher resources, most of which have been cited in this chapter. Each is briefly summarized.

- For a delightful romp into understanding dialects in the United States, read *Dialects in Schools and Communities* (2007) by Adger, Wolfram, and Christian. This book will dispel myths about dialect and even help you understand your own.
- For an excellent "big-picture" view of CRI, read *Culturally Responsive Instruction: Theory, Research, and Practice* by Gay (2000). This text is widely cited by those summarizing the field.
- For an award-winning read about effective and responsive instruction for African American children, read *Change Is Gonna Come: Transforming Literacy Education for African American Students* by Edwards, McMillon, and Turner (2010). Written by three African American women literacy scholars, this book offers a highly nuanced look at African American children and their fight for literacy. Woven into the fabric of this book are rich personal stories from the authors and their families; these corroborate the findings of the research that anchors the books, as well as illuminate the challenges and promises of educating African American literacy learners in today's schools.
- For a quick and easy read on practices focused on one standard, connecting curriculum to students' backgrounds, read *Classroom Diversity: Connecting Curriculum to Students' Lives* by McIntyre, Rosebery, and González (2001). The examples come from many different cultural groups.
- For specific, practical lessons on adapting your instruction, read *Culturally Responsive Teaching: Lesson Planning for Elementary and Middle Grades* by Irvine and Armento (2001) or *The Literacy Gaps: Bridge-Building Strategies for English Language Learners and Standard English Learners* by Soto-Hinman and Hetzel (2009). Both books are excellent resources.
- For one of the classic books on the topic, focused on African American children, read *The Dreamkeepers: Successful Teachers of African American Children* by Ladson-Billings (1994). This beautifully written book is inspiring and transformational.
- For a book that describes how to adapt research-based reading instruction to make it more culturally responsive for diverse classrooms, read *Reading Instruction for Diverse Classrooms: Research-Based, Culturally Responsive Practice* by McIntyre, Hulan, and Layne (2011). This book covers reading instruction broadly and provides many classroom examples and resources.

REFERENCES

Adger, C. T., Wolfram, W., & Christian, D. (2007). *Dialects in schools and communities* (2nd ed.). Mahwah, NJ: Erlbaum.

Allington, R. C. (1977). If they don't read much, how they ever gonna get good? *The Reading Teacher, 36*, 556–561.

Allington, R. L., & McGill-Franzen, A. (2003). The impact of summer reading setback on the reading achievement gap. *Phi Delta Kappan, 85*, 68–75.

Amendum, S., & Fitzgerald, J. (2011). Reading instruction research for English-language learners in kindergarten through sixth grade: The last twenty years. In A. McGill-Franzen & R. Allington (Eds.), *Handbook of reading disabilities research* (pp. 373–391). New York: Routledge.

Anyon, J. (1997). *Ghetto schooling: A political economy of urban education reform.* New York: Teachers College Press.

Au, K. (2005). *Multicultural issues and literacy achievement*. Mahwah, NJ: Erlbaum.

August, D., & Shanahan, T. (2006). Introduction and methodology. In D. August & T. Shanahan (Eds.), *Developing literacy in second-language learners: Report of the National Literacy Panel on Language Minority Children and Youth* (pp. 1–42). Mahwah, NJ: Erlbaum.

Banks, J. A. (2003). Teaching literacy for social justice and global citizenship. *Language Arts, 81*(1), 18–19.

Banks, J. A. (2006). *Race, culture, and education*. London: Routledge.

Bialystok, E. (2007). Acquisition of literacy in bilingual children: A framework for research. *Language Learning, 57*, 45–77.

Cazden, C. (1988). *Classroom discourse: The language of teaching and learning*. Portsmouth, NH: Heinemann.

Dalton, S. (2007). *Five standards for effective teaching: How to succeed with all learners*. San Francisco: Jossey-Bass.

Dantas, M. L., & Manyak, P. C. (Eds.). (2010). *Home–school connections in a multicultural society: Learning from and with culturally and linguistically diverse families*. New York: Routledge.

Delgado-Gaitan, C., & Trueba, H. (1991). *Crossing cultural borders: Education for immigrant families in America*. New York: Falmer.

Delpit, L. D. (1986). Skills and dilemmas of a progressive black educator. *Harvard Educational Review, 56*, 379–385.

Delpit, L. D. (1988). The silenced dialogue: Power and pedagogy in educating other people's children. *Harvard Educational Review, 58*, 280–298.

Delpit, L. D. (1995). *Other people's children: Cultural conflict in the classroom*. New York: New Press.

Dudley-Marling, C., & Paugh, P. (2005). The rich get richer; the poor get direct instruction. In B. Altwerger (Ed.), *Reading for profit: How the bottom line leaves kids behind* (pp. 156–171). Portsmouth, NH: Heinemann.

Edwards, P. A., McMillon, G. T., & Turner, J. D. (2010). *Change is gonna come: Transforming literacy education for African American students*. New York: Teachers College Press.

Ferguson, R. F. (1998). Teachers' perceptions and expectations and the black–white test score gap. In C. Jencks & M. Phillips (Eds.), *The black–white test score gap* (pp. 273–317). Washington, DC: Brookings Institution Press.

Finn, P. J. (1999). *Literacy with an attitude: Educating working-class children in their own self-interest*. Albany: State University of New York Press.

Fitzgerald, J., & Noblit, G. (2000). Balance in the making: Learning to read in an ethnically diverse first grade classroom. *Journal of Educational Psychology, 92*, 3–22.

Foster, M., & Peele, T. (2001). Ring my bell: Contextualizing home and school in an African American community. In E. McIntyre, A. Rosebery, & N. González (Eds.), *Classroom diversity: Connecting curriculum to students' lives* (pp. 27–36). Portsmouth, NH: Heinemann.

Gay, G. (2000). *Culturally responsive instruction: Theory, research, and practice*. New York: Teachers College Press.

Geertz, C. (1973). Thick description: Toward an interpretive theory of culture. In C. Geertz, *The interpretation of cultures: Selected essays* (pp. 3–30). New York: Basic Books.

Gersten, R., & Jiménez, R. (1994). A delicate balance: Enhancing literature instruction for students of English as a second language. *The Reading Teacher, 47*, 438–439.

Goldenberg, C. (1993). Instructional conversations: Promoting comprehension through discussion. *The Reading Teacher, 46*, 316–326.

Goldenberg, C. (1994). Promoting early literacy development among Spanish speaking children: Lessons from two studies. In E. Hiebert & B. M. Taylor (Eds.), *Getting reading right from the start* (pp. 171–200). Boston: Allyn & Bacon.

Gutiérrez, K. D., Baquedano-Lopez, P., & Alvarez, H. H. (2001). Literacy as hybridity: Moving beyond bilingualism in urban classrooms. In M. D. L. L. Reyes & J. J. Halcon (Eds.), *The best for our children: Critical perspectives on literacy for Latino students* (pp. 122–141). New York: Teachers College Press.

Heath, S. B. (1983). *Ways with words: Language, life, and work in communities and classrooms.* New York: Cambridge University Press.

Irvine, J. J. (2006). *Educating teachers for diversity: Seeing with a cultural eye.* New York: Teachers College Press.

Irvine, J. J., & Armento, B. J. (2001). *Culturally responsive teaching: Lesson planning for elementary and middle grades.* Boston: McGraw-Hill.

Kyle, D. W., McIntyre, E., Miller, K. B., & Moore, G. H. (2006). *Bridging school and home through family nights: Ready-to-use plans for grades K–8.* Thousand Oaks, CA: Corwin Press.

Ladson-Billings, G. (1994). *The dreamkeepers: Successful teachers of African American children.* San Francisco: Jossey-Bass.

Lazar, A. M. (2011). Access to excellence: Serving today's students through culturally responsive literacy teaching. In P. R. Schmidt & A. M. Lazar (Eds.), *Practicing what we teach: How culturally responsive literacy classrooms make a difference* (pp. 3–26). New York: Teachers College Press.

Lee, C. D. (1998). Signifying in the zone of proximal development. In C. D. Lee & P. Smagorinsky (Eds.), *Vygotskian perspectives on literacy research: Constructing meaning through collaborative inquiry* (pp. 191–225). Cambridge, UK: Cambridge University Press.

Lee, C. D. (2008). The centrality of culture to the scientific study of learning and development: How an ecological framework in education research facilitates civic responsibility. *Educational Researcher, 37,* 267–270.

Lemke, J. L. (1990). *Talking science: Language, learning, and values.* Norwood, NJ: Ablex.

Luxford, H., & Smart, L. (2009). *Learning through talk: Developing learning dialogues in the primary classroom.* New York: Routledge.

Lyman, F. (1981). Think Pair Share: The responsive classroom instruction. In A. S. Anderson (Ed.), *Mainstreaming digest.* College Park: University of Maryland College of Education.

Marx, S. (2006). *Revealing the invisible: Confronting passive racism in teacher education.* New York: Routledge.

McGill-Franzen, A., & Allington, R. L. (1993). Flunk 'em or get them classified: The contamination of primary grade accountability data. *Educational Researcher, 22,* 19–22.

McIntyre, E. (2010a). Issues in funds of knowledge teaching and research: Key concepts from a study of Appalachian families and schooling. In M. L. Dantas & P. Manyak (Eds.), *Home–school connections in a multicultural society: Learning from and with culturally and linguistically diverse families* (pp. 201–217). New York: Routledge.

McIntyre, E. (2010b). Principles for teaching young ELLs in the mainstream classroom: Adapting best practices for all learners. In G. Li & P. A. Edwards (Eds.), *Best practices in ELL instruction* (pp. 61–83). New York: Guilford Press.

McIntyre, E. (2011b). Sociocultural perspectives on children with reading difficulties. In A. McGill-Franzen & R. Allington (Eds.), *Handbook of reading disability research* (pp. 45–56). New York: Routledge.

McIntyre, E., Hulan, N., & Layne, N. (2011). *Reading instruction for diverse classrooms: Research-based, culturally responsive practice.* New York: Guilford Press.

McIntyre, E., Kyle, D. W., Chen, C., Kraemer, J., & Parr, J. (2009). *Six principles for teaching English language learners in all classrooms.* Thousand Oaks, CA: Corwin Press.

McIntyre, E., Kyle, D. W., & Moore, G. (2006). A teacher's guidance toward small group dialogue in a low-SES primary grade classroom. *Reading Research Quarterly, 41*(1), 36–63.

McIntyre, E., Kyle, D. W., & Rightmyer, E. C. (2005). Families' funds of knowledge to mediate teaching in rural schools. *Cultura y Educación, 17*(2), 175–195.

McIntyre, E., Rosebery, A., & González, N. (2001). *Classroom diversity: Connecting curriculum to students' lives.* Portsmouth, NH: Heinemann.

McIntyre, E., & Stone, N. J. (1998). Culturally contextualized instruction in Appalachian descent and African American classrooms. In T. Shanahan & F. V. Rodriguez-Brown (Eds.), *47th yearbook of the National Reading Conference* (pp. 209–220). Chicago: National Reading Conference.

Miller, L. S. (1995). *An American imperative: Accelerating minority educational advancement.* Cambridge, UK: Cambridge University Press.

Moll, L. C., & Gonzalez, N. (2003). Engaging life: A funds-of-knowledge approach to multicultural education. In J. A. Banks & C. A. Banks (Eds.), *Handbook of research on multicultural education* (pp. 299–314). San Francisco: Jossey-Bass.

O'Gilvie, H. O., Turner, J. D., & Hughes, H. L. (2011). Teaching through language: Using multilingual tools to promote literacy achievement among African American elementary students. In P. R. Schmidt & A. M. Lazar (Eds.), *Practicing what we teach: How culturally responsive literacy classrooms make a difference* (pp. 141–155). New York: Teachers College Press.

Ranker, J. (2006). "There's fire magic, electric magic, ice magic, or poison magic": The world of video games and Adrian's compositions about Gauntlet Legends. *Language Arts, 84,* 21–33.

Ranker, J. (2007). Using comic books as read-alouds: Insights on reading instruction from an English as a second language classroom. *The Reading Teacher, 61*(4), 296–305.

Rist, R. C. (1970). Student social class and teacher expectations: The self-fulfilling prophecy in ghetto education. *Harvard Educational Review, 40,* 411–451.

Rothstein, R. (2004). *Class and schools: Using social, economic, and educational reform to close the black–white achievement gap.* New York: Teachers College Press.

Rousculp, E. E., & Maring, G. H. (1992). Portfolios for a community of learners. *Journal of Reading, 35,* 378–385.

Schmidt, P. R., Rodriguez, F., & Sandroni, L. (2011). Encountering the ABCs and meeting the challenges. In P. R. Schmidt & A. M. Lazar (Eds.), *Practicing what we teach: How culturally responsive literacy classrooms make a difference* (pp. 199–217). New York: Teachers College Press.

Soto-Hinman, I., & Hetzel, J. (2009). *The literacy gaps: Bridge-building strategies for English language learners and standard English learners.* Thousand Oaks, CA: Corwin Press.

Stanovich, K. E. (1986). Matthew effects in reading: Some consequences of individual differences in the acquisition of literacy. *Reading Research Quarterly, 21,* 360–406.

Tharp, R. G. (1989). Psychocultural variables and constants: Effects on teaching and learning in schools. *American Psychologist, 44,* 349–59.

Tharp, R. G., Estrada, P., Dalton, S. S., & Yamauchi, L. (2000). *Teaching transformed: Achieving excellence, fairness, inclusion, and harmony.* Boulder, CO: Westview Press.

Tharp, R. G., & Gallimore, R. (1988). *Rousing minds to life: Teaching, learning, and schooling in social context.* Cambridge, UK: Cambridge University Press.

Turner, J. D. (2005). Orchestrating success for African American readers: The case of an effective third-grade teacher. *Reading Research and Instruction, 44,* 27–48.

Turner, J. D. (2006). "I want to meet my students where they are!": Preservice teachers' visions of culturally responsive reading instruction. In J. V. Hoffman, D. L. Schallert, C. M. Fairbanks, J. Worthy, & B. Maloch (Eds.), *55th yearbook of the National Reading Conference* (pp. 309–323). Oak Creek, WI: National Reading Conference.

Turner, J. D. (2007). Beyond cultural awareness: Prospective teachers' "visions" of culturally responsive literacy teaching. *Action in Teacher Education, 29,* 12–24.

Turner, J. D., & Kim, Y. (2005). Learning about building literacy communities in multicultural and multilingual communities from effective elementary teachers. *Literacy Teaching and Learning, 10*, 21–42.

Valencia, S. W., & Buly, M. R. (2004). Behind test scores: What struggling readers *really* need. *The Reading Teacher, 57*, 520–531.

Vélez-Ibáñez, C., & Greenburg, J. (1992). Formation and transformation of funds of knowledge among U.S. households. *Anthropology and Education Quarterly, 23*, 313–335.

Weinstein, R. (2002). *Reaching higher: The power of expectations in schooling.* Cambridge, MA: Harvard University Press.

Wells, G., & Wells, J. (1989). Learning to talk and talking to learn. *Theory into Practice, 23*, 190–196.

West, K. (2005). Hey Mama. On *Late registration* [CD]. New York: Roc-A-Fella, Def Jam.

Xu, S. H. (2001, July–August). Exploring diversity issues in teacher education. *Reading Online, 5*(1). Retrieved from *www.readingonline.org/newliteracies/lit_index.asp?HREF=action/xu/index.html.*

Xu, S. H., Perkins, R. S., & Zunich, L. O. (2005). *Trading cards to comic strips: Popular culture texts and literacy learning in grades K–8.* Newark, DE: International Reading Association.

CHAPTER 7

Digital Literacy ● ● ● ● ● ● ● ● ● ● ● ● ● ● ●

SUSAN WATTS TAFFE
LAURIE B. BAUER

Technology has always had a strong influence on teaching and learning, as it has influenced all other aspects of our lives and world. The technology of graphite pencils, the printing press, the mimeograph machine, and the overhead projector all changed the way we approached literacy teaching and learning. After all, each of these is an example of technology at work—and, in its time, each was a new technology at that. Today, the new technologies most strongly influencing teaching and learning are the Internet and related information and communication technologies (ICTs), including weblogs (or blogs), wikis, podcasts, discussion boards, and streaming video. However, Leu and his colleagues contend that today's new technologies are very different from those of the past. They are so different that they are changing the very nature of what it means to be literate and, by extension, the very nature of what it means to be a literacy teacher (Leu, Kinzer, Coiro, & Cammack, 2004). According to Coiro, Knobel, Lanskhear, and Leu (2008a):

> The Internet . . . has brought unprecedented dimensions to both the speed and the scale of change in the technologies for literacy, forcing us to directly confront the issue of new literacies. No previous technology for literacy has been adopted by so many, in so many different places, in such a short period, and with such profound consequences. (p. 3)

In this chapter, we address digital learning as it relates to the skills and strategies associated with traditional print text as well as newer digital texts. Learning in the digital realm can support the development of skills and strategies we are already teaching; equally important, however, are the ways in which digital learning requires us to teach new skills and strategies. In this chapter, we look at digital learning from both of these perspectives.

OVERVIEW OF RESEARCH

The impact of the digital age on literacy learning is the subject of an ever-growing body of research, much of which is reported in the *Handbook of Research on New Literacies* (Coiro, Knobel, Lankshear, & Leu, 2008b), a volume over 1,300 pages in length. The editors of this handbook argue that literacy as we have known it for the past 500 years has changed significantly, and they identify the following as central characteristics of digital technologies:

- They are critical to full participation in our 21st-century world.
- They are *deictic*, meaning that they are rapidly and continuously changing.
- They are multiple, multimodal, and multifaceted, and therefore require not literacy as a singular entity, but *multiple literacies.*
- For effective use, they require new and different skills, strategies, and dispositions, which are termed *new literacies*.

Anstey and Bull (2006) suggest that a literate person in the 21st century

- Is able to read both traditional texts and new digital texts, and to use these to communicate.
- Has at his or her disposal a large repertoire of literacy skills and strategies.
- Is flexible enough to respond to the ever-changing landscape of new literacies.

In this section, we present an overview of research related to the prevalence of digital technologies, the nature of digital texts and digital literacies, teacher practice with respect to digital technologies, and implications of digital learning for central constructs addressed in this book.

The Prevalence of Digital Technologies in Today's World

We teach in a world very different from the one we grew up in, and this is especially true for those of us over the age of 30. Tools such as cell phones, laptop computers, MP3 players, and iPads; social networking sites such as Facebook and Twitter; and video-sharing sites such as YouTube are not only "firmly embedded in youth culture," as Merchant (2010) remarks, but in adult culture as well. It has been reported that the average student ages 8–18 spends over 7 hours a day participating in various technologies (Rideout, Foehr, & Roberts, 2010). In a study of U.S. children ages 6 and under, Vandewater and her colleagues (2007) found that on a typical day when they used technology, such as video games and computers, they did so for an average of 50–55 minutes. In a study of 37 children in grades K–2, Dodge, Husain, and Duke (2011) found that 84% reported using the Internet outside of school. These figures align with those showing a fast-paced increase in Internet use among students ages 12–17, 93% of whom reported using the Internet in 2008 (Pew Internet Group, 2009).

Older students are producing more text than ever before in their out-of-school lives. Whether they are writing an e-mail, sending a text message, or updating their status on Facebook, today's students are constantly composing, and we have the recent advances in technology to thank (or, in some cases, blame) for these changes. In fact, digital technologies have been shown to pique the interest of even reluctant writers (Quenneville, 2001). One reason for this is that digital technologies allow students to become producers of text rather than merely consumers (Dezuanni, 2010). Richardson (2010) reports that even elementary school children are creating content, producing information, and interacting with others via the Internet. Researchers have identified the following ways in which digital tools both motivate students and change the nature of written expression:

- *Freedom.* As producers of text outside of school, students are not restricted to guidelines set by a teacher, a district, or the state. Yet even without a rubric, they are successful in navigating within and among determined requirements.
- *Choice.* Students are drawn to the variety of technologies and the abundant choices available for all ages and achievement levels.
- *Accessibility.* The term *being mobile* has taken on new meanings. Even our youngest students are taking advantage of being able to be connected "on the go." Furthermore, keyboards, spelling assistance, and the availability of multiple media make text production, communication, and authorship possible even for students who experience difficulty with traditional print-based writing.
- *Identity and voice.* By expanding the range of what's possible in the arena of written expression, ICTs give students greater capacity for identity construction and personal voice. This comes through in rich connections with home culture and language (Witte, 2007).
- *Authenticity.* One of the most powerful dimensions of many digital tools is the capacity they provide for writing to real audiences, beyond the classroom. This source of motivation, along with the others above, holds great instructional potential (Warschauer & Ware, 2008).

The fact that daily literacy practices now include interactions with texts presented through multiple modes presents a challenge to traditional views of literacy and learning (Kress, 2000). Prensky (2001) refers to students growing up today as "digital natives," a term that highlights their frequent and natural interactions with digital technologies. As more and more students are "born digital" (Palfrey & Gasser, 2008), they will enter the classroom with new experiences, proficiencies, and needs.

Despite the prevalence of new digital technologies in the lives of our students, the digital divide still separates the "haves" from the "have-nots" both in home access and in access and appropriate use in school. In October 2005, reports from the U.S. Census Bureau indicated that over 85% of households with an annual income of $75,000 or more had a household computer with Internet access, compared to just 30% of households with an annual income below $25,000. This wide margin of difference in home access and use is compounded by differences in school access and use. Leu and colleagues (2009) highlight the fact that the poorest U.S. school districts are the least likely to integrate the Internet into the curriculum because they are the hardest pressed to raise students' scores on tests that do not include measures of new literacies. They make the strong statement that "Our failure to understand the Internet as a reading comprehension issue has produced policies that actually work to perpetuate the achievement gaps among poor and diverse students" (p. 173). Thus, adequate accessibility is not the only issue students and their teachers face. In order for low-income students to catch up to their often more technologically advanced peers, opportunities to use computers strategically—that is, beyond basic skill practice—are necessary (Celano & Neuman, 2010). Therefore, providing opportunities for in-school assignments that utilize technology to its full potential will benefit all students and help bridge the gap between the "haves" and the "have-nots."

The Nature of Digital Texts

Differences between print and digital texts have important implications for reading and writing. Coiro and Dobler (2007) point to key features of digital text that require different types of comprehension than traditional print text: *nonlinear hypertext, inclusion of multiple media,* and *interactive design.* The hyperlinks embedded in most digital text allow the reader to move quickly, either from one part of the text to another or from one text to a related but entirely different text. Moreover, *text* includes a variety of media, such as symbols, animation, photographs, audio, and video. Several of these features are apparent on author/illustrator Eric Carle's rich and informative blog (which is one of several hyperlinks on the website *www.eric-carle.com*), including a short "Dear Friends" letter, hyperlinks to previous posts in a column to the right of the letter, artwork, photos of exhibitions and books signings, a hyperlink to video about a recent book, and a link to the *Eric Carle Museum of Picture Book Art* website, which itself includes possibilities for a virtual tour, news about traveling exhibits, and a link to the museum store. In addition to nonlinear hypertext and multimedia text, digital texts are often interactive. Visit the *United Nations Cyberschoolbus: Global Teaching and Learning Project* website (*http://cyberschoolbus.un.org*) to find interactive games focused on the availability of safe food and water worldwide, and on responses to natural disasters, for example. Other interactive sites offer opportunities for students to post responses to text using their own words, pictures, or art, in order to question, expand upon, engage in dialogue about, or offer an alternative perspective to the information presented. In addition, digital technologies offer opportunities to go public with writing in the form of personal webpages and digital storytelling, as well as to make connections with others worldwide, in the forms of pen-pal correspondence and online literature discussion groups (e.g., Castek, Bevans-Mangelson, & Goldstone, 2006; Grisham & Wolsey, 2006; Larson, 2009; Sylvester & Greenidge, 2009).

The Nature of Digital Literacies

As stated earlier, digital technologies have generated the need for new types of literacy or new literacies. As we consider the role of the literacy teacher with respect to digital learning, it is helpful to consider several informed perspectives. First, we find the following definition of new literacies associated with the Internet and other digital technologies helpful.

> The new literacies of the Internet include the skills, strategies, and dispositions necessary to successfully use and adapt to rapidly changing information and communication technologies and contexts that continuously emerge in our world and influence all areas of our personal and professional lives. These new literacies allow us to use the Internet and other ICTs to identify important questions, navigate to locate information,

critically evaluate the usefulness of that information, synthesize information to solve problems, and communicate the solutions to others. (Leu, Leu, & Coiro, 2004, p. 421)

Second, we consider the International Society of Technology in Education (ISTE, 2007) National Educational Technology Standards for Students, which include the following:

- Students demonstrate creative thinking, construct knowledge, and develop innovative products and processes using technology. (*Creativity and Innovation*)
- Students apply digital tools to gather, evaluate, and use information. (*Research and Information Fluency*)
- Students use critical thinking skills to plan and conduct research, manage projects, solve problems, and make informed decisions using appropriate digital tools and resources. (*Critical Thinking, Problem Solving, and Decision Making*)

Third, the International Reading Association's (2009) position statement *New Literacies and 21st-Century Technologies* states that students have the right to many things, among them:

- Teachers who use ICTs skillfully for teaching and learning effectively.
- A literacy curriculum that offers opportunities to read, share, and create content collaboratively with peers from around the world.
- Literacy instruction that embeds critical and culturally sensitive thinking into print and digital literacy practices.
- State reading and writing standards that include new literacies.
- Equal access to ICTs for all classrooms and all students.

Fourth, digital literacies are embedded in the Common Core State Standards for English Language Arts and Literacy in History/Social Studies, Science, and Technical Subjects (CCSS; National Governors Association Center for Best Practices & Council of Chief State School Officers, 2010). As early as grade 2, the CCSS reference digital text within the Reading and Writing Standards. By grade 5, students are expected to do the following:

- Analyze how visual and multimedia elements contribute to the meaning, tone, or beauty of a text (e.g., graphic novel, multimedia presentation of fiction, folktale, myth, poem). (Reading Standards, p. 12)
- Use technology, including the Internet [with support from adults], to produce and publish writing as well as to interact and collaborate with others. (Writing Standards, p. 21)
- Include multimedia components and visual displays (e.g., graphics, sound) in presentations when appropriate to enhance the development of main ideas or themes. (Speaking and Listening Standards, p. 24)

As indicated in the introduction to the CCSS, preparation for life in the 21st century requires the ability to "analyze and create a high volume and extensive range of print and nonprint texts in media forms old and new" (National Governors Association Center for Best Practices & Council of Chief State School Officers, 2010, p. 4).

Finally, much has been written about the importance of connecting in-school experiences to students' out-of-school experiences (Tatum, 2011). Today, such connections necessarily include digital connections aligned with characteristics of the 21st-century learner. Students bring new expectations into the classrooms that connect to their personal, out-of-school experiences with digital learning and literacy. Table 7.1 highlights the unique experiences and expectations of many 21st-century learners, along with the instructional needs of all such learners.

Teacher Practice with Respect to Digital Technologies

Just as the ISTE has issued national standards for students (see above), it has issued standards for teachers. The National Educational Technology Standards for Teachers (ISTE, 2008) highlight the importance of designing technology-rich learning environments that include authentic instructional and assessment experiences, coupled with teaching and modeling of the knowledge and work processes required in a global and digital society. However, the road toward achieving these standards has been difficult for teachers.

In 2009, only 40% of teachers reported that they or their students *often* used computers in the classroom during instructional time (U.S. Department of Education, National Center for Educational Statistics, 2010). With respect to quality of use, Cuban, Kirkpatrick, and Peck (2001) found that even when teachers had access to exceptional technology, they used it infrequently, and that when they did, it was to sustain current

TABLE 7.1. Digital Learning Experiences, Expectations, and Needs of 21st-Century Learners

Experiences	Expectations	Needs
• Active participation in out-of-school digital literacy practices (e.g., blogs, video games) • Familiarity with a variety of text formats (e.g., traditional print, online, images, videos, audio) • Participation in multimodal text production (e.g., drawing software, narrated video) • Ability to learn features of new technologies quickly through exploration and experimentation	• High-interest academic materials • Hands-on learning experiences • Multifaceted, collaborative learning experiences • Freedom for exploration and individual choice	• Focus on higher-order critical thinking skills • Understanding that students are often unaware of the quality of information online and often assign greater value to this information than to information from traditional print-based texts (e.g., Schacter, Chung, & Dorr, 1998) • Explicit instruction aimed at improving students' website evaluation skills (Zhang & Duke, 2011) • Opportunities for creative thinking and innovation • Proficient movement between and among multiple modalities • Explicit instruction, demonstration, and guided practice in attainment of 21st-century skills and strategies

instructional practices (e.g., reviewing homework) rather than to create new learning experiences. The lack of sustained professional development opportunities, and the focus on traditional reading and writing in most statewide tests, are contributing factors. Other issues—such as feeling overwhelmed with trying to learn and keep up with new technologies, frustration when technology fails, and fear of the unknown—have been discussed as reasons why teachers are hesitant to incorporate technology into their classrooms (Hayes, 2007).

There is a direct correlation between effective classroom implementation of new technologies and teachers' personal beliefs about and use of these technologies. Teachers who are frequent users of new technologies often have higher comfort levels with them and are more likely to create successful opportunities for integration (Mueller, Wood, Willoughby, Ross, & Specht, 2008). In addition, teachers' interaction with their students during technology engagement has lead to more constructive academic experiences and opportunities for active learning (Hsu, 2011). An overall increase in technology use, by both teachers and students, has had a positive influence on how technology is viewed for instructional purposes (Baylor & Richie, 2002) and is a constant reminder of how changes in society affect and drive learning experiences. Reports of teacher engagement in digital teaching and learning indicate great variation, and almost all teacher self-reports refer to the process as an ever-unfolding journey (Karchmer, Mallette, Kara-Soteriou, & Leu, 2005) in which the teachers are perpetual learners. This disposition may feel uncomfortable for teachers who associate effective practice with the mastery of instructional tools, and it is also a challenge for teachers who are uncomfortable with the idea that they are co-learners with their students, as opposed to "the experts." Finally, with the preponderance of options available, it is important for teachers to engage students in "meaningful, purpose-driven literacy technology integration" (Watts-Taffe & Gwinn, 2007, p. 31), rather than the use of digital tools for their own sake. Just as students can be attracted to the newest, flashiest tools, teachers too can be tempted to incorporate tools without a firm grasp on the ways in which their use is aligned with appropriate instructional goals and objectives. Although we believe that literacy learning in the 21st century requires an expansion of traditional competencies, effective instruction is determined not by whether traditional materials/methods or methods/materials associated with new technologies are used. Effective instruction is determined by the degree to which the selected methods/materials reflect the current strengths and limitations each student brings to the wide array of literacy learning goals encountered in school.

Up to this point, we have emphasized that new technologies have implications for instruction that promotes independence, critical thinking, and collaboration. Here we want to make four points clear. First, it is possible to integrate new technologies into literacy instruction without fundamentally altering approaches to instruction or goals for literacy learning. For example, many teachers make effective use of software to build traditional literacy competencies such as phonological awareness, fluency, vocabulary, and comprehension. Second, the use of new technologies does not ensure the implementation of best practices with respect to literacy teaching. It is up to each teacher to incorporate new technologies in ways that reflect research-based characteristics of effective instruction. Too often, "new" digital tools coexist with outdated instructional practices, serving as nothing more than electronic worksheets or flashcards, where the goal is rote memorization rather than in-depth understanding and independent application.

Third, in classrooms where very little technology is available, teachers can nonetheless address skills and strategies for new literacies. For example, using multiple print sources on the same topic, and teaching students how to synthesize information across these sources, are two of the most important comprehension strategies associated with the Internet. Finally, while digital technologies afford new opportunities for student choice, text accessibility, and personal connection in reading and writing, research indicates that students require teacher direction, scaffolding, and specific strategy instruction, just as they do when reading traditional print texts, in order to maximize these opportunities (Dalton & Proctor, 2008; McKenna, Labbo, Conradi, & Baxter, 2011).

The remainder of this chapter aims to illustrate some of the ways in which digital learning can be a daily part of literacy instruction, and to show how it can be used to further student success and achievement in meaningful, purpose-driven ways. Previous chapters of this book have addressed some central elements in literacy teaching and learning. In Table 7.2, we highlight the role of digital technologies with respect to these elements.

Meeting the Needs of All Learners

New technologies, coupled with the central instructional elements discussed above, greatly expand the range of possibilities for meeting the individual needs of all students. In addition to common features of digital learning environments, such as hyperlinks to word pronunciations, embedded spelling and word meaning resources, and visual displays of information, numerous software applications have been designed specifically to increase the literacy development of struggling readers and writers. For example, the software program Thinking Reader has been used successfully to promote comprehension (Dalton & Strangman, 2006). In addition, research highlights the promise of software programs for increasing reading comprehension and English language competency among English language learners (McKenna et al., 2011). Liaw (1997), for example, found that using computerized books increased verbal interaction between and among students and helped foster language development. Recent research focused on gifted learners points to the power of new technologies in providing access to above-grade-level text and content, as well as forums for learning and expressing knowledge in multiple ways and engaging in learning communities outside the classroom (Thomson, 2010). Finally, new technologies can support teachers through websites offering multiple and varied texts and text recommendations (e.g., *www.starfall.com, www.storylineonline.net, www.storycart.com*), language translation applications (*translate.google.com*), and communities of practice (e.g., *www.readwritethink.org; www.thinkfinity.org*).

SUMMARY OF BIG IDEAS FROM RESEARCH

- Digital technology use outside of school is prevalent among school-age children, but the "digital divide" still exists and is too often perpetuated in classrooms.
- Differences between digital and print texts are significant enough to warrant instruction in the new literacies associated with digital texts and related technology.
- New technologies can be used to support learning of traditional literacy skills and strategies, as well as skills and strategies for new literacies.

TABLE 7.2. Impact and Implications of Digital Technologies on Central Instructional Elements

Instructional element	Impact and implications of digital technologies
Motivation and engagement	Through quick, easy connections to current information, presented in a variety of ways, students see relevance to their daily lives, in both *what* and *how* they are learning. Digital technologies can be used to heighten student interest, expand student choice, increase student collaboration, and broaden thematic connections in learning, all of which are linked to increased motivation (Guthrie, 2011).
Classroom environment	Digital technologies can change the ways students interact with classroom space, materials, ideas, and each other. Collaboration becomes more robust, and collaborators can include students and teachers in other schools, states, or countries. A print-rich environment includes words, as well as images and symbols, captured on bulletin boards, chart paper, easels, screens, journals, blogs, and slideshows (Barone & Wright, 2008). The teacher can be more of a facilitator than ever before; provision of explicit models is as vital as ever before; thematic instruction is more accessible than ever before; and the learning community can be more collaborative than ever before.
Balanced, differentiated instruction	Digital technologies offer new possibilities for the processes and products of teaching and learning. Teachers have more options for customizing instruction, both with respect to how students engage in learning and how they demonstrate what they have learned. Anderson-Inman and Horney (2007) suggest that technologies' malleability and their capacity to change and adapt texts bring direct advantages to readers, especially those with reading difficulties. For example, the text-to-speech feature of many digital texts and software programs can assist students who struggle to decode grade-level texts, while hyperlinks to word meanings, multimedia representations, and virtual tours can provide "just-in-time" support in building text-specific vocabulary and prior knowledge (Dalton & Proctor, 2008). Research also indicates that strong readers of traditional print text may struggle with the multimodal elements of digital text, whereas strong online navigational skills, ability to "control" the text, and the assistance of multimedia features may compensate for limitations, such as lack of prior knowledge, among other readers (Bilal, 2001; Castek, Zawilinski, McVerry, O'Byrne, & Leu, 2011; Coiro, 2011). Furthermore, various software programs and Web-based applications (e.g., TELE-Web) have effectively supported the writing performance of students with learning disabilities (Englert, Wu, & Zhao, 2005). Thus digital technologies can change the dynamics of difficulty.
Ongoing assessment and progress monitoring	Digital technologies offer tremendous possibilities for collecting, storing, analyzing, and sharing data related to student achievement and ongoing progress, such as audio recordings of oral reading and retellings, writing samples, and videos of response to various types of instruction. Such samples can be stored individually or collectively in electronic portfolios, and can be shared with colleagues, parents, and students themselves for purposes of collaborative decision making (Fahey, Lawrence, & Paratore, 2007). Teachers can also observe each other more readily by using video-sharing software and collaborative problem solving (Taylor, 2011). The other side is the need to assess reading and writing in multiple formats, especially those related to the Internet (Afflerbach, Kim, Crassas, & Cho, 2011).

(continued)

TABLE 7.2. *(continued)*

Instructional element	Impact and implications of digital technologies
Culturally responsive instruction	Digital technologies offer students and teachers opportunities to "step outside of personal experience within a particular linguistic, ethnic, and cultural group to experience others," a fundamental component of the 2010 International Reading Association Standards for Reading Professionals as described by Tatum (2011, p. 437). Furthermore, culturally responsive instruction is supported by an expansion of what counts as reading and writing, greater diversity in texts and text types, the affordance of a wider array of learning response options (including those that integrate out-of-school literacies and popular culture with in-school literacies), and language translation capabilities (Alvermann, 2011; Morrell & Duncan-Andrade, 2002).

- Skills and strategies for new literacies include website navigation, critical evaluation of information, synthesis of information from multiple texts and across multiple text types, communication, and collaboration. Students require a great deal of teacher support and direction to develop these competencies.
- Effective use of new technologies in the classroom requires careful decision making on the part of teachers, as well as the ability to assume the role of facilitators and co-learners in the classroom.

In the next section of this chapter, we discuss classroom applications of digital technologies and instruction in new literacies.

EXAMPLES OF EFFECTIVE PRACTICES

Focus on Word Recognition and Vocabulary

Digital Language Experience Approach

Kevin Ray (all names in this section are pseudonyms) has incorporated the *digital language experience approach* (D-LEA; Labbo, Eakle, & Montero, 2002) into the weekly routine of his first-grade class at Franklin Elementary School. Using the school's digital camera, each Monday he photographs an event or events related to the life of his classroom. He then loads the digital photos onto the classroom computer for collaborative writing the next day. On Tuesday, he projects the photos onto a whiteboard and engages his students in conversation about each photo. He then assigns each photo to a pair or triad who come up with a sentence to describe what is depicted in the photo. As these sentences are dictated, Kevin types them as photo captions (see Figure 7.1). After he types each caption, the class reads it aloud. These photos and captions become repeated reading experiences for the remainder of the week and are routinely used to highlight a word recognition or spelling strategy Kevin wants to introduce or review. Saving these texts in digital format allows for multiple review opportunities. He can load them onto individual computers for students to return to them independently or to incorporate them into center activities; he can also save them in a folder on the desktop to

This is the Writing Center.

We can look at books we've read to get ideas for words to use when we write.

FIGURE 7.1. Two photographs in first-grade digital story, with captions dictated by the class.

return to them over time as an illustration of his class's growth in the conventions of text (sequence of events, main idea and details, etc.). In addition, they become a model for storytelling his students will do in small groups as the year unfolds, using presentation software such as KidPix.

At the beginning of the year, Kevin uses these photos to tie his students' language to the articulation and understanding of classroom routines—the order in which things happen, as well as various classroom procedures (e.g., getting lunch in the cafeteria, selecting a book at the library, and using the computer stations). As new routines are introduced, such as writing workshop, he uses this to reinforce them and encourage his students to use their growing academic vocabularies to describe them. He also photographs events related to topics of study, such as safety, communities, and habitats. The language experience approach (Stauffer, 1970), on which the D-LEA is based, is an established means of reinforcing the connection between oral and written language; it also provides students with easier access to word recognition and the act of reading, via familiar, self-generated text.

Kevin has extended this approach to focus on his students' use of academic language and appropriation of conventional text grammars, as well as exploration into the new text grammars of the digital world. He also considers this an ideal time to be intentional in his own vocabulary choices—explaining what he's doing by using the vocabulary of digital texts, such as *digital photos, desktop, folder, save, caption*, and *move the captions into a word-processing document*. Furthermore, he has found the D-LEA to support differentiation of instruction. While all of his students benefit from the production of meaningful text within mutually understood contexts and supported by photo images, collaboration with peers, and reinforcement and practice over the week, he has seen tremendous benefit for his students with special educational needs related to language processing. (For more about teaching word recognition, see Johnson & Kuhn, Chapter 8, this volume.)

Vocabulary Images

Susanna Montero and her third graders use images in the public domain—for example, ones found in Google Images and Flickr (*www.flikr.com*)—to learn new vocabulary. In her school, the majority of students are English language learners; vocabulary has been identified as a buildingwide focus, and all teachers are encouraged to devote in-depth instruction to new vocabulary found in read-alouds and reading selections used for instruction. Digital images allow Susanna's students to "see" the meanings of words such as *persistent, gnarled,* and *canopy.* She transports these images to PowerPoint slides that can be shown on "the big screen" during whole-class lessons, viewed on "the small screen" during independent work, and printed as handouts to take home. She also gives her students chances to locate their own images from a set Susanna has compiled, and to create individual slides to pair with written definitions and to practice throughout the week. (For more about vocabulary instruction, see Kucan, Chapter 11, this volume.)

Focus on Comprehension

Fostering Comprehension of Print-Based, Linear Text by Using Digital Concept Maps

Successful readers of all ages and academic levels connect preexisting knowledge to new ideas founds in texts. In addition, it is important to support students as they make connections between texts, and between a text and the world in which the text was written and is usually meant to reflect in some way.

Kristan Jacobs, a fifth-grade teacher at Summit Elementary, uses electronic graphic organizers to help her students make connections as they read (see Figure 7.2). When students have completed an independent novel, one theme from the novel becomes the main topic for each concept map. Students are encouraged to illustrate relationships between the theme/topic in the novel and similar themes found in other novels. Finally, they are encouraged to relate the novel to experiences in the world, beyond their personal experiences, by relating the theme to outside sources (including images, videos, and audio clips). Relationships are shown through the use of linking words, and further explanation of the relationships is included in written text. Having used paper–pencil concept maps in the past, Kristan has learned that using them along with electronic maps can provide learning support. She recognizes the advantages of electronic concept-mapping software (e.g., Kidspiration, Inspiration) and websites (e.g., *www.bubbl.us*), including the unique way information is presented, the multiple opportunities to highlight intertextuality among all types of texts, and the capability for students to include imagery as demonstration (and construction) of their understanding.

Concept maps and other digital presentation tools, such as Prezi (*http://prezi.com*) and iMovie, are increasingly used in lieu of more traditional book reports as a means of assessing reading comprehension and reader response. These multimodal tools provide excellent forums for assessing higher-level comprehension and/or engaging students in collaborative learning opportunities. This is the case in Jeannette Wu's sixth-grade class,

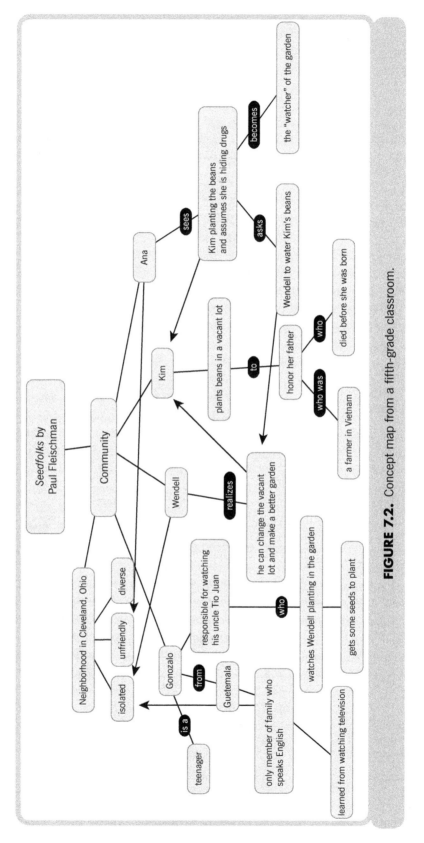

FIGURE 7.2. Concept map from a fifth-grade classroom.

where students create multimodal presentations to demonstrate their understanding of *The Watsons Go to Birmingham—1963* by Christopher Paul Curtis (1995). Working in groups, they explore the capabilities of presentation software such as KidPix and Power-Point, as well as free Web-based tools such as Prezi and Camtasia (Screencast-O-Matic). Inspired by examples Jeannette found on websites such as YouTube, TeacherTube, and Prezi, her students use these tools to go beyond the limitations of a traditional book report to represent with depth and individuality what the Curtis book meant to them. Furthermore, Jeannette finds that her students reading above grade level are challenged and remain engaged.

Fostering Comprehension of Digital Text

Digital technologies provide us with different ways to achieve existing learning objectives, and often to deepen students' learning. But it is clear that digital technologies also call for different learning objectives. As noted earlier, the nature of digital texts calls for different comprehension skills and strategies from those associated with print-based text. As Tapscott (1998) stated, "It's not point and click. It's point, read, think, click." Recent research to determine the specific types of reading and thinking required (Coiro & Dobler, 2007; Henry, 2006; Leu et al., 2008) point to the use of coordinated higher-order comprehension strategies, including students' ability to do the following:

- Identify important questions.
- Navigate to locate information.
- Critically evaluate the credibility and usefulness of information.
- Synthesize to solve problems.

Think-alouds, modeling, learning guides, and independent practice are effective in teaching the higher-order strategies of digital comprehension. As early as second grade, Jenna Martin teaches her students how to navigate among hypertext links. Visiting the Eric Carle website together, Jenna begins by asking her students what they see on the site. Using her interactive whiteboard, she makes a list of what they say. She then slowly scrolls down the page and asks what else they see. One student calls out, "I want to see his studio!" and another suggests, "Let's watch the video." These comments are tied to Jenna's next step, which is to ask her students where they should go next. After hearing several different responses, she asks, "How should we decide which hyperlink to click on?" This brings a pause, and Jenna continues by explaining that a reader's purpose determines his or her navigation strategy. Here Jenna's goal is to help her students understand the thought processes behind navigational moves. She reminds her students that they have been studying the role of nature in Eric Carle's illustrations. Using this information, she asks again which sites they should visit. She then allows them to work in pairs, using a learning guide to direct their decision making. After this period of guided practice, the students come back together as a whole class and discuss the various approaches that pairs took and what they learned.

During pair work, Jenna circulates among her students to observe their decision making and provide support as needed. Knowing that this task requires different competencies than other reading comprehension tasks her students have engaged in, Jenna has paired students with complementary print-based literacy strengths. For example,

Joey, who is a very strong decoder with developing comprehension strategies, has been paired with Lucia, who uses comprehension strategies well. Marianne, who is a strong reader all around, has been paired with Dani, who is a beginning reader with strong visual and design abilities. As she is able, Jenna takes notes on what she is observing. Using these notes and the students' completed learning guides, Jenna later assesses not only how well students completed the task, but also what she has learned about students' strengths and needs within this new literacy domain of navigating a website. Later that month, Jenna brings some of these work samples and her reflections to her professional learning community (PLC) as a contribution to her and others' ongoing professional development. (For more on PLCs, see Peterson, Chapter 21, this volume.)

Meanwhile, back in Jeannette's sixth-grade classroom, students are learning how to critically evaluate information on the Internet. During the process of making connections between *The Watsons Go to Birmingham—1963* and the real-world events of the 1960s, particularly the civil rights movement, Jeannette conducts a lesson on website evaluation, using the site *www.martinlutherking.org.* Although the URL for this site seems reasonable, and the homepage speaks directly to students, the site is in fact hosted by a white pride organization and is aimed at disseminating misinformation and encouraging hate. Due to the nature of the site, Jeannette obtains parents' permission before teaching this lesson; it could also be taught with other sites, including "hoax sites" designed specifically to fool the reader and promote more critical reading among students. (See, e.g., *www.zapatopi.net/treeoctopus*, a site devoted to saving the "endangered Pacific Northwest Tree Octopus.") Jeannette's interest in using a real site, and one so disconcerting, is both to underscore the dangers of consuming online information without thinking critically and to make a powerful connection between the tragic 1963 bombing of a Birmingham church (depicted in the Curtis book) and the present-day existence of hate among some individuals and groups. This approach to one dimension of *The Watsons Go to Birmingham—1963* includes a look at nationwide and worldwide organizations that work toward peace and the elimination of violence based on hate. Instruction such as this reflects a critical stance and is aligned with powerful teaching and learning in our diverse society. (For more about comprehension instruction, see Stahl, Chapter 9, and Garas-York, Shanahan, & Almasi, Chapter 10, this volume.)

Focus on Written Expression

Fostering Digital Communication

After completing an author study on Grace Lin, students in Chris Leezer's third-grade class are interested in getting to know Lin even more as an author. Lin's website (*www.gracelin.com*) provides some of the information students are interested in knowing, as well as new information about her work and her life as a writer. However, they still have questions. Drawing on the interest of the students, Chris suggests that they contact Lin directly. Her website provides several ways to get in touch with the author, and after much discussion, the students decide that as a class they will send a written letter and post a comment on her blog. This decision is informed by a mini-lesson comparing and contrasting letters, e-mail messages, and blog posts. Since students want to reach out quickly in an informal message to convey their appreciation of Lin's books, the blog seems like the perfect avenue to complete this task. To ask some of their more personal questions, and to discuss specific connections they've made with Lin's work, the students choose a letter to the author as the most appropriate vehicle. Through these activities, Chris's students practice writing across genres, as well as decision making with respect to available genres. Since many of Chris's students have never created a blog post, this is an entirely new genre with new conventions to learn. Once learned, students can appropriate it by creating a class blog to keep parents and community members apprised of school events.

Responding to Reading

After a reading of *When You Reach Me* by Rebecca Stead (2009), Lucy Garcia has her fourth-grade participants in a gifted languages arts program complete a book review by using VoiceThread (*www.voicethread.com*), a collaborative, multimedia site that encourages group conversation. Throughout this interactive project, students are expected to discuss information about the text and their reading experience by using voice, images, and videos. After students have uploaded their final VoiceThread book report, they have the opportunity to view and comment on their classmates' work. Comments can be recorded by using a computer microphone, by making a telephone call, or by uploading an audio file. In addition, students can leave typed comments or video comments via a webcam. This innovative project takes the standard book report to a new level and provides students with the opportunity to become producers not only of their own work, but of their own learning. This lesson encourages students to socialize and situate themselves in a social environment while creating meaning in response to a text. Learning opportunities such as these build upon the social and oral traditions of meaning making that are prevalent in many students' homes and communities. (For more about developing students' written expression, see Troia, Chapter 12, this volume.)

Focus on the Disciplines

Historically, content-area literacy has involved instruction intended to help students better comprehend material as presented in textbooks (Lesley & Matthews, 2009). More recently, researchers have illustrated that disciplinary literacy "requires an understanding of how knowledges are constructed and organized in the content area, an understanding of what counts as warrant or evidence for a claim, and an understanding of the conventions of communicating that knowledge" (Moje et al., 2004, p. 45). In this respect, digital technologies offer amazing opportunities for students to step into the worlds of scientists, mathematicians, historians, artists, and other. This type of meaningful participation, engagement, and reading *in* the disciplines provides learning opportunities far beyond those afforded by reading *about* the disciplines (Bean, 2010).

Virtual Field Trips

Virtual field trips provide students and teachers with a wealth of resources that are visually appealing, interactive and provide accurate, current information tied to content-area standards. The Smithsonian National Museum of Natural History, for example, currently offers The Ocean Portal (*http://ocean.si.edu*), an expansive website designed for marine exploration. This website includes a section entitled "For Educators," offering lesson plans and activities, as well as a number of additional resources for building background information or for further reading. Providing students with the opportunity to navigate and experience this website before a required reading helps situate their learning and has the potential to lead to autonomous problem solving and increase overall understanding. Such activities, however, are not limited to science and social studies; a quick browse through different websites will show the expansive and diverse resources available. For example, the San Francisco Museum of Modern Art (*www.sfmoma.org*) and the Exploratorium's The Science of Music (*www.exploratorium. edu/music*) provide online exhibits, movies, podcasts and interviews that appeal to students and encourage active exploration and learning. See Table 7.3 for a list of museum websites that offer interactive exhibits for teachers and students to visit without leaving the classroom. (For more about teaching literacy in the disciplines, see Cervetti, Chapter 14; Halvorsen, Alleman, & Brugar, Chapter 15; Fogelberg, Satz, & Skalinder, Chapter 16; and Fisher, McDonald, & Frey, Chapter 17, this volume.)

The Evolution of Effective Classroom Practices

Much of what we know about effective practice with respect to digital texts and new literacies is emerging. This is true both for the field at large and for individual teachers who are learning from their experiences each day. The rapidly changing nature of digital technologies requires a high degree of teacher observation and reflection, in order to gain insights into what and how to teach most effectively. Watts-Taffe and Gwinn (2007)

TABLE 7.3. Museum Websites and Interactive Museum Exhibits

- Benjamin Franklin Tercentenary
  www.benfranklin300.org
- Colonial Williamsburg
  www.history.org
- Exploratorium's The Science of Music
  www.exploratorium.edu/music
- Field Museum
  http://fieldmuseum.org
- John F. Kennedy Presidential Library and Museum
  www.jfklibrary.org
- Louvre
  www.louvre.fr/llv/commun/home.jsp
- Monticello Classroom
  http://classroom.monticello.org
- Museum of Modern Art
  www.moma.org
- NASA
  www.nasa.gov

- San Francisco Museum of Modern Art
  www.sfmoma.org
- Smithsonian National Air and Space Museum
  www.nasm.si.edu
- Smithsonian National Museum of African Art
  http://africa.si.edu
- Smithsonian National Museum of American History
  www.americanhistory.si.edu
- Smithsonian National Museum of Natural History
  www.mnh.si.edu
- Smithsonian National Postal Museum
  http://postalmuseum.si.edu
- Smithsonian National Zoological Park
  http://nationalzoo.si.edu
- Sterling and Francine Clark Art Institute
  www.clarkart.edu
- Victoria and Albert Museum
  www.vam.ac.uk

highlight the importance of planning for literacy–technology integration; implementing meaningful, purpose-driven instruction; assessing student learning; and assessing and reflecting on instruction. They have found that when teachers work through this cycle together, within school buildings, districts, or even virtual PLCs, their efforts are greatly enhanced.

Guidelines for Incorporating Technology into Literacy Instruction

- Encourage students to become critically aware of what is written and read on the Internet.
- Allow students to be creators and producers of text.
- Don't be afraid to learn from your students and show interest in their technology discoveries.
- Engage in the cycle of planning, implementation, assessment, and reflection, based on the instructional needs of your students.
- Include activities that highlight imagination, curiosity, and innovation.
- Focus on audience awareness and purpose when selecting digital tools.
- Remember that the flexibility and adaptation you model when things don't go as planned, and as you continue to learn new things, is vital to your students. The world they are growing up in is a world in which adaptation is key.

LOOKING FORWARD

Research on digital learning with respect to literacy acquisition and development is still in the early stages. Having established that digital texts are in fact different from print texts, requiring different and new literacies, research and development for the future is likely to include the following:

- A focus on instructional strategies that work best to address the new literacies' requirements in the areas of asking important questions, searching for information, critically evaluating information, and synthesizing information. Questions will focus on the degree to which current effective practices (such as reciprocal teaching) can be successfully modified for online environments, as well as on the construction of very new instructional approaches (see Castek & Langham, 2005, for teaching resources on Internet reciprocal reaching).
- Attention to students who are experiencing difficulty learning to read—and, specifically, how they can attain "basic literacy skills" as well as the higher-order skills required for digital reading and writing.
- Concern for equity issues related to digital learning, to ensure that students living in poverty or students whose language or culture does not match that of the school have equal access to high-quality digital learning experiences.
- A focus on teacher professional development related to digital learning, with concern for how to support teachers as they support their students in obtaining the knowledge, skills, strategies, and dispositions needed for success in the 21st century.

QUESTIONS FOR REFLECTION •

1. Before reading this chapter, how much did I know about the new literacies associated with digital technologies? What ideas presented in this chapter are resonating with me as I consider my own teaching practice?

2. What are my personal dispositions toward digital technologies? Am I an eager explorer with respect to new digital tools, or am I more wary of new tools? How do I see my personal disposition playing itself out in my instruction? In what ways does my disposition support effective instruction, and in what ways is it holding me back?

3. Whether I am personally using digital technologies often or not, what opportunities do I provide for students to "learn to learn"? In what ways do I foster exploration and inquiry among my students? How can I enhance my practice in this area?

4. In a typical day, how often do I incorporate digital technologies into my instruction?

5. In a typical day, how often do I provide instruction in some aspect of new literacies?

6. In a typical week, do all of my students have similar access (in terms of quantity of time, quality of time, and attention to higher-order skills and strategies) to digital tools and instruction in new literacies? If not, what changes can I make to equalize access?

7. In what ways do I link assessment with instruction in dimensions of new literacies?

8. What are my existing resources to support effective integration of digital tools into my instruction? (These resources may be online.) How can I be strategic about using these resources to improve my practice?

SUGGESTIONS FOR ONGOING PROFESSIONAL LEARNING • • • • • • •

As discussed throughout this book, PLCs are powerful forums for professional learning and instructional improvement. They are particularly important in building teachers' capacity to address new literacies in digital learning environments. Whereas reflective practice is the hallmark of all powerful instruction, it is vital in the ever-changing landscape of digital learning, where teachers cannot learn to use "one tool, once and for all." Rather, like their students, teachers are learning how to learn. Given the vast range of individual teachers' dispositions, knowledge, and available contextual resources (i.e., what is available in the school or district), it is important that collaborative inquiry occur within PLCs of shared trust and mutual support, regardless of where individuals are on the spectrum of digital teaching and learning. It is also important that PLC meetings be as "hands-on" as possible. So PLC members should make the necessary arrangements to meet in the school computer lab or to bring laptop computers to the meetings. This way, instead of talking about what they might do, they can concentrate on doing the things that they will continue to do. Another possibility to consider is the option of "distance PLCs." Tools such as Skype and Adobe Connect make it possible to widen the scope of a PLC beyond the parameters of a single school or district.

Exploration

One of the challenges of digital teaching and learning is finding the time to keep up with the ever-expanding array of tools available. Teachers who use digital tools effectively spend a great deal of time exploring, experimenting, and reflecting on the ways in which various tools can support student learning. Simultaneously, they are discovering firsthand the skills and strategies associated with new literacies, and thinking about how they can address these skills and strategies in the classroom.

Session 1

Discuss this chapter with members of your PLC. Describe your current practice with respect to (a) integrating digital tools into your instruction, and (b) addressing new-literacies skills and strategies in your instruction. Share one idea gleaned from the chapter that you would like to follow up on by doing some personal exploration. This might be a website, an application such as iMovie, or a professional development streaming video. Your focus may be on the digital tool itself or on a new-literacies strategy associated with the tool. Make a commitment over the next 2 weeks to this exploration. Prepare the following to share at your next PLC meeting:

Digital tool or new-literacies strategy	What it is and how it works	What I have discovered	Possibilities for integration into my practice	Questions I have

Session 2

Report the results of your exploration to your PLC. If possible, provide an informal demonstration of or quick look at the tool/strategy. Talk with other members of your PLC to process each tool/strategy shared as a group. What experiences have others had with the tool or new-literacies strategy? What might one of you know that can help another better understanding each tool or strategy? What ideas do others have for ways to integrate the tool into practice? What questions might be answered, or further exploration undertaken in the moment, as a part of the PLC meeting? At the end of this meeting, make a commitment to explore the same tool/strategy further or to explore a new one during the next 2 weeks.

Session 3

Once again, provide a report of your exploration to your PLC. This time, do some thinking in advance and share a brief demonstration of the tool or strategy, with specific thoughts about how it fits with your current literacy instruction. As a group, brainstorm considerations for planning instruction around this tool or strategy. What complications can you foresee? What links can be made with students' prior knowledge and/or prior instruction? What types of grouping arrangements might work best for this instruction? What will be needed in terms of hardware and learning supports (e.g., hard-copy learning guides)? For the next meeting, take the ideas from your PLC conversation and design a lesson or series of lessons around this new-tool or new literacies strategy.

Session 4

Share your lesson with your PLC. Be prepared to discuss your learning objectives and how they align with your students' learning needs. Describe the lesson, then walk your colleagues through a portion, just as you would with your students. (In other words, practice.) Provide time for your colleagues to share constructive feedback.

Implementation

Session 1

Working with your PLC, engage in "interactive planning" for a lesson series (two or more sequential and related lessons) you will teach within the next 2 weeks. Together, determine an appropriate instructional focus, learning objectives, and general lesson design. As you plan, be mindful of ways to differentiate your instruction for the variety of literacy learners in your classroom. Select at least two students, with very different literacy-learning strengths and needs, as focal students. After teaching the lessons, make brief reflective notes related to the lessons in general, as well as to your observations of the two focal students' responses to instruction.

Session 2

Share your reflective notes and work samples from the lesson series with your PLC. Collaboratively, think about what you can learn from each set of reflections and work samples. What do these data say about possibilities for improving instruction? What do they say about the strengths and needs of the students, especially the two focal learners? In the next 2 weeks, teach another lesson series, and continue to monitor the progress of your two focal students. Video-record a segment of your instruction to share at your next PLC meeting.

Session 3

Share instructional video clips with your colleagues. What do you notice about each other's instruction? What are you learning about the digital tools employed? What are you learning about the new-literacies strategies being taught? How can you further support one another in your continuing efforts?

Session 4

Along with members of your PLC, determine a plan for continuing your professional development with respect to digital technologies and new literacies. What resources can you utilize? What time-saving strategies can you share with one another? What changes, if any, are required at the school or district level in order to support your continued professional development? How can you actively work to bring about the needed changes?

RESEARCH-BASED RESOURCES

Barone, D., & Wright, T. (2008). Literacy instruction with digital and media technologies. *The Reading Teacher, 62*(4), 292–302.

Besnoy, K. D., & Clarke, L. W. (Eds.). (2010). *High-tech teaching success!: A step-by-step guide to using innovative technology in your classroom*. Waco, TX: Prufrock Press.

Coiro, J. (2003). Reading comprehension on the Internet: Expanding our understanding of reading comprehension to encompass new literacies. *The Reading Teacher, 56*(5), 458–464.

Handsfield, L. J., Dean, T. R., & Cielocha, K. M. (2009). Becoming critical consumers and producers of text: Teaching literacy with Web 1.0 and Web 2.0. *The Reading Teacher, 63*, 40–50.

Henry, L. A. (2006). SEARCHing for an answer: The critical role of new literacies while reading on the Internet. *The Reading Teacher, 59*, 614–627.

Karchmer, R. A., Mallette, M. H., Kara-Soteriou, J., & Leu, D. J. (2005). *Innovative approaches to literacy education: Using the Internet to support new literacies*. Newark, DE: International Reading Association.

Labbo, L. D., Eakle, A. J., & Montero, K. M. (2002, May). Digital language experience approach: Using digital photographs and creativity software as a language experience approach innovation. *Reading Online, 5*(8). Retrieved from *www.readingonline.org/electronic/elec_index.asp?HREF=labbo2/index.html*.

Leu, D. J., Coiro, J., Castek, J., Hartman, D. K., Henry, L. A., & Reinking, D. (2008). Research on instruction and assessment in the new literacies of online reading comprehension. In C. C. Block & S. Parris (Eds.), *Comprehension instruction: Research-based best practices* (2nd ed., pp. 321–346). New York: Guilford Press.

Leu, D. J., Leu, D. D., & Coiro, J. (2004). *Teaching with the Internet K–12: New literacies for new times* (4th ed.). Norwood, MA: Christopher Gordon.

McKenna, M. C., Labbo, L. D., Conradi, K., & Baxter, J. (2011). Effective uses of technology in literacy instruction. In L. M. Morrow & L. B. Gambrell (Eds.), *Best practices in literacy instruction* (4th ed., pp. 361–394). New York: Guilford Press.

Prensku, M. (2010). *Teaching digital natives: Partnering for real learning*. Thousand Oaks, CA: Corwin Press.

Richardson, W. (2010). *Blogs, wikis, podcasts and other powerful Web tools for classrooms* (3rd ed.). Thousand Oaks, CA: Corwin Press.

Sylvester, R., & Greenidge, W. (2010). Digital storytelling: Extending the potential for struggling writers. *The Reading Teacher, 63*, 284–295.

Watts-Taffe, S., & Gwinn, C. G. (2007). *Integrating literacy and technology: Effective practice for grades K–6*. New York: Guilford Press.

ofessional Development

sites offer downloadable research reports, policy updates, books for pur-
al development webinars, and conference opportunities. They are spon-
ing professional organizations focused on literacy learning.

www. *N*ational Council of Teachers of English)
www.reading.c..g (International Reading Association)

The following website offers free, downloadable research reports, lesson plans and related materials, and video clips of lessons in action. It is sponsored by a research team leading efforts to further understand new literacies and how to address them in the classroom.

www.newliteracies.uconn

The following website, cosponsored by the International Reading Association and the National Council of Teachers of English, offers free downloadable lesson plans organized by theme and grade level, as well as parent and after-school program resources.

www.readwritethink.org

Digital Tools to Support Teaching and Learning

Wordle—word cloud generated by written text (*www.wordle.net*)
Toondoo—comic strip generator (*www.toondoo.com*)
Glogster—generator for interactive posters (*www.glogster.com*)
Aviary—image and audio editor (*www.aviary.com*)
CoolText—graphic generator (*http://cooltext.com*)
Avidemux—free video editor (*http://avidemux.sourceforge.net*)
Diigo—personal information management system allowing students to highlight text on a webpage, attach sticky notes, and discuss via threaded discussion (*www.diigo.com*)
Idroo—online educational whiteboard (*www.idroo.com*)
Bubbl.us—mindmap creator (*https://bubbl.us*)
PhotoPeach—slideshow creator (*http://photopeach.com/about*)
Prezi—cloud-based presentation software (*http://prezi.com*)

REFERENCES

Afflerbach, P., Kim, J.-Y., Crassas, M. E., & Cho, B-Y. (2011). Best practices in literacy assessment. In L. M. Morrow & L. B. Gambrell (Eds.), *Best practices in literacy instruction* (4th ed., pp. 319–340). New York: Guilford Press.

Alvermann, D. E. (2011). Popular culture and literacy practices. In M. L. Kamil, P. D. Pearson, E. B. Moje, & P. P. Afflerbach (Eds.), *Handbook of reading research* (Vol. 4, pp. 541–560). New York: Routledge.

Anderson-Inman, L., & Horney, M. A. (2007). Assistive technology through text transformations. *Reading Research Quarterly, 42,* 153–160.

Anstey, M., & Bull, G. (2006). *Teaching and learning multiliteracies: Changing times, changing literacies.* Newark, DE: International Reading Association.

Barone, D., & Wright, T. (2008). Literacy instruction with digital and media technologies. *The Reading Teacher, 62*(4), 292–302.

Baylor, A., & Richie, B. (2002). What factors facilitate teacher skill, teacher morale, and perceived student learning in technology-using classrooms? *Computers and Education,* *39,* 395–414.

Bean, T. (2010). *Multimodal learning for the 21st century adolescent.* Huntington Beach, CA: Shell Education.

Bilal, D. (2001). Children's use of the Yahooligans! Web search engine: II. Cognitive and physical behaviors on research tasks. *Journal of the American Society for Information Science and Technology, 52*(2), 118–136.

Castek, J., Bevans-Mangelson, J., & Goldstone, B. (2006). Children's books: Reading adventures online: Five ways to introduce the new literacies of the Internet through children's literature. *The Reading Teacher, 59*(7), 714–728.

Castek, J., & Langham, K. (2005, May). *Enhancing Internet comprehension using reciprocal teaching.* Paper presented at the conference of the International Reading Association, San Antonio, TX. Retrieved from *http://ctell1.uconn.edu/IRA/InternetRT.htm.*

Castek, J., Zawilinski, L., McVerry, G., O'Byrne, I., & Leu, D. J. (2011). The new literacies of online reading comprehension: New opportunities and challenges for students with learning difficulties. In C. Wyatt-Smith, J. Elkins, & S. Gunn (Eds.), *Multiple perspectives on difficulties in learning literacy and numeracy* (pp. 91–110). New York: Springer.

Celano, D., & Neuman, S. B. (2010). Roadblocks on the information highway. *Educational Leadership, 68,* 50–53.

Coiro, J. (2011). Predicting reading comprehension on the Internet: Contributions of offline reading skills, online reading skills, and prior knowledge. *Journal of Literacy Research, 43*(4), 352–392.

Coiro, J., & Dobler, E. (2007). Exploring the online reading comprehension strategies used by sixth-grade skilled readers to search for and locate information on the Internet. *Reading Research Quarterly, 42,* 214–257.

Coiro, J., Knobel, M., Lankshear, C., & Leu, D. J. (2008a). Central issues in new literacies and new literacies research. In J. Coiro, M. Knobel, C. Lankshear, & D. J. Leu (Eds.), *Handbook of research on new literacies* (pp. 1–21). New York: Erlbaum.

Coiro, J., Knobel, M., Lankshear, C., & Leu, D. J. (Eds.). (2008b). *Handbook of research on new literacies.* New York: Erlbaum/Taylor & Francis.

Cuban, L., Kirkpatrick, H., & Peck, C. (2001). High access and low use of technologies in high school classrooms: Explaining an apparent paradox. *American Educational Research Journal, 38,* 813–834.

Curtis, C. P. (1995). *The Watsons go to Birmingham—1963.* New York: Random House.

Dalton, B., & Proctor, C. P. (2008). The changing landscape of text and comprehension in the age of new literacies. In J. Coiro, M. Knobel, C. Lankshear, & D. J. Leu (Eds.), *Handbook of research on new literacies* (pp. 297–324). New York: Erlbaum/Taylor & Francis.

Dalton, B., & Strangman, N. (2006). Improving struggling readers' comprehension through scaffolded hypertexts and other computer-based literacy programs. In D. Reinking, M. C. McKenna, L. D. Labbo, & R. D. Keiffer (Eds.), *Handbook of literacy and technology* (2nd ed.). Mahwah, NJ: Erlbaum.

Dezuanni, M. L. (2010). Digital media literacy: Connecting young people's identities, creative production and learning about video games. In D. Alvermann (Ed.), *Adolescents' online literacies: Connecting classrooms, digital media, and popular culture* (125–143). New York: Peter Lang.

Dodge, A. M., Husain, N., & Duke, N. K. (2011). Connected kids?: K–2 children's use and understanding of the Internet. *Language Arts, 89*(2), 86–98.

Englert, C. S., Wu, X., & Zhao, Y. (2005). Cognitive tools for writing: Scaffolding the performance of students through technology. *Learning Disabilities Research and Practice, 20*(3), 184–198.

Fahey, K., Lawrence, J., & Paratore, J. (2007). Using electronic portfolios to make learning public. *Journal of Adolescent and Adult Literacy, 50*(6), 460–471.

Grisham, D. L., & Wolsey, T. D. (2006). Recentering the middle school classroom as a vibrant learning community: Students, literacy, and technology intersect. *Journal of Adolescent and Adult Literacy, 49*(8), 648–660.

Guthrie, J. (2011). Best practices in motivating students to read. In L. M. Morrow & L. B. Gambrell (Eds.), *Best practices in literacy instruction* (4th ed., pp. 177–198). New York: Guilford Press.

Hayes, D. (2007). ICT and learning: Lessons from Australian classrooms. *Computers and Education, 49,* 385–395.

Henry, L. A. (2006). SEARCHing for an answer: The critical role of new literacies while reading on the Internet. *The Reading Teacher, 59,* 614–627.

Hsu, S. (2011). Who assigns the most ICT activities?: Examining the relationship between teacher and student usage. *Computers and Education, 56,* 847–855.

International Reading Association. (2009). *New literacies and 21st-century technologies: A position statement of the International Reading Association.* Newark, DE: Author.

International Society for Technology in Education. (2007). *National educational technology standards for students.* Washington, DC. Author. Retrieved November 15, 2012, from *www.iste.org/standards/nets-for-students.*

International Society for Technology in Education. (2008). *National educational technology standards for teachers.* Washington, DC. Author. Retrieved November 15, 2012, from *www.iste.org/standards/nets-for-teachers.*

Karchmer R. A., Mallette, M. H., Kara-Soteriou, J., & Leu, D. J. (2005). *Innovative approaches to literacy education: Using the Internet to support new literacies.* Newark, DE: International Reading Association.

Kress, G. (2000). Multimodality. In B. Cope & M. Kalantzis (Eds.), *Multiliteracies: Literacy learning and the design of the social features* (pp. 1–16). Chicago: National Reading Conference.

Labbo, L. D., Eakle, A. J., & Montero, K. M. (2002, May). Digital language experience approach: Using digital photographs and creativity software as a language experience approach innovation. *Reading Online, 5*(8). Retrieved from *www.readingonline.org/electronic/elec_index.asp?HREF=labbo2/index.html.*

Larson, L. C. (2009). Reader response meets new literacies: Empowering readers in online learning communities. *The Reading Teacher, 62*(8), 638–648.

Lesley, M., & Matthews, M. (2009). Place-based essay writing and content area literacy instruction for preservice secondary teachers. *Journal of Adolescent and Adult Literacy, 52,* 523–533.

Leu, D. J., Coiro, J., Castek, J., Hartman, D. K., Henry, L. A., & Reinking, D. (2008). Research on instruction and assessment in the new literacies of online reading comprehension. In C. C. Block & S. Parris (Eds.), *Comprehension instruction: Research-based best practices* (2nd ed., pp. 321–346). New York: Guilford Press.

Leu, D. J., Kinzer, C. K., Coiro, J. L., & Cammack, D. W. (2004). Toward a theory of new literacies emerging from the Internet and other information and communication technologies. In R. R. Ruddell & N. J. Unrauh (Eds.), *Theoretical models and processes of reading* (5th ed., pp. 1570–1613). Newark, DE: International Reading Association.

Leu, D. J., Leu, D. D., & Coiro, J. (2004). *Teaching with the Internet K–12: New literacies for new times* (4th ed.). Norwood, MA: Christopher-Gordon.

Leu, D. J., McVerry, G., O'Byrne, W. I., Zawalinski, L., Castek, J., & Hartman, D. K. (2009). The new literacies of online reading comprehension and the irony of No Child Left Behind: Students who require our assistance the most actually receive it the least. In

L. M. Morrow, R. Rueda, & D. Lapp (Eds.), *Handbook of research on literacy and diversity* (pp. 173–194). New York: Guilford Press.

Liaw, M. L. (1997). An analysis of ESL children's verbal interaction during computer book reading. *Computers in the Schools, 13*(3/4), 55–73.

McKenna, M. C., Labbo, L. D., Conradi, K., & Baxter, J. (2011). Effective uses of technology in literacy instruction. In L. M. Morrow & L. B. Gambrell (Eds.), *Best practices in literacy instruction* (4th ed., pp. 361–394). New York: Guilford Press.

Merchant, G. (2010). View my profile(s). In D. Alvermann (Ed.), *Adolescents' online literacies: Connecting classrooms, digital media, and popular culture* (pp. 51–69). New York: Peter Lang.

Moje, E. B., Ciechanowski, K. M., Kramer, K., Ellis, L., Carrillo, R., & Collazo, T. (2004). Working toward third space in content area literacy: An examination of everyday funds of knowledge and discourse. *Reading Research Quarterly, 39,* 38–70.

Morrell, E., & Duncan-Andrade, J. M. R. (2002). Promoting academic literacy with urban youth through engaging hip-hop culture. *English Journal, 91*(6), 88–94.

Mueller, J., Wood, E., Willoughby, T., Ross, C., & Specht, J. (2008). Identifying discriminating variables between teachers who fully integrate computers and teachers with limited integration. *Computers and Education, 51,* 1523–1537.

National Governors Association Center for Best Practices & Council of Chief State School Officers. (2010). *Common Core State Standards for English language arts and literacy in history/social studies, science, and technical subjects.* Washington, DC: Authors. Retrieved from *www.corestandards.org/the-standards.*

Palfrey, J., & Gasser, U. (2008). *Born digital: Understanding the first generation of digital natives.* New York: Basic Books.

Pew Internet Group. (2009). Generations online in 2009. Retrieved from *www.pewinternet.org/Reports/2009/Generations-Online-in-2009.aspx.*

Prensky, M. (2001). Digital natives, digital immigrants. *On the Horizon, 9,* 1–6.

Quenneville, J. (2001). Tech tools for students with learning disabilities: Infusion into inclusive classrooms. *Preventing School Failure, 45*(4), 167–170.

Richardson, W. (2010). *Blogs, Wikis, podcasts and other powerful Web tools for classrooms.* Thousand Oaks, CA: Corwin Press.

Rideout, V. J., Foehr, U., G., & Roberts, D. F. (2010). *Generation M²: Media in the lives of 8–18 year-olds.* Menlo Park, CA: Kaiser Family Foundation. Retrieved from *www.kff.org/entmedia/upload/8010.pdf.*

Schacter, J., Chung, G., & Dorr, A. (1998). Children's Internet searching on complex problems: Performance and process analysis. *Journal of the American Society for Information Science, 49,* 840–849.

Stauffer, R. G. (1970). *The language experience approach to the teaching of reading.* New York: Harper & Row.

Stead, R. (2009). *When you reach me.* New York: Random House.

Sylvester, R., & Greenidge, W. L. (2009). Digital storytelling: Extending the potential for struggling writers. *The Reading Teacher, 63*(4), 284–295.

Tapscott, D. (1998). *Growing up digital: The rise of the Net generation.* New York: McGraw-Hill.

Tatum, A. W. (2011). Diversity and literacy. In S. J. Samuels & A. E. Farstrup (Eds.), *What research has to say about reading instruction* (4th ed., pp. 425–447). Newark, DE: International Reading Association.

Taylor, B. M. (2011). *Catching schools: An action guide to schoolwide reading improvement.* Portsmouth, NH: Heinemann.

Thomson, D. L. (2010). Beyond the classroom walls: Teachers' and students' perspectives on how online learning can meet the needs of gifted students. *Journal of Advanced Academics, 4,* 662–712.

U.S. Department of Education, National Center for Education Statistics. (2010). *Teachers' use of educational technology in U.S. public schools: 2009* (NCES 2010-040). Washington, DC: Author.

Vandewater, E., Rideout, V., Wartella, E., Huang, X., Lee, J., & Shim, M. (2007). Digital childhood: Electronic media and technology use among infants, toddlers, and preschoolers. *Pediatrics, 119,* e1006–e1015.

Warschauer, M., & Ware, P. (2008). Learning, change, and power: Competing frames of technology and literacy. In J. Coiro, M. Knobel, C. Lankshear, & D. J. Leu (Eds.), *Handbook of research on new literacies* (pp. 215–240). New York: Erlbaum.

Watts-Taffe, S., & Gwinn, C. G. (2007). *Integrating literacy and technology: Effective practice for grades K–6.* New York: Guilford Press.

Witte, S. (2007). "That's online writing, not boring school writing": Writing with blogs and the Talkback Project. *Journal of Adolescent and Adult Literacy, 51,* 92–96.

Zhang, S., & Duke, N. K. (2011). The impact of instruction in the WWWDOT framework on students' disposition and ability to evaluate web sites as sources of information. *Elementary School Journal, 112*(1), 132–154.

PART II

Effective Teaching and Assessment to Develop Essential Literacy Abilities in Students

CHAPTER 8

Automaticity versus Fluency • • • • • •
Developing Essential Literacy Abilities with Print

SUSAN DOUGHERTY JOHNSON
MELANIE R. KUHN

OVERVIEW OF RESEARCH

When we think about the reading development of young learners, it is clear that students have a multifaceted task in front of them (see, e.g., National Reading Panel, 2000). They need to bring their knowledge of oral language to print while developing a series of skills that are unique to reading, from phonemic awareness to the alphabetic principle to fluency. Of course, vocabulary and comprehension are intricately woven into effective literacy instruction from the outset, and underlie our contextualized instruction, but those are dealt with deftly (and more directly) in other chapters in this volume. Instead, we concentrate on the processes that take learners from emergent to fluent readers.

Constrained versus Unconstrained Skills

According to Paris (2005, 2009), reading consists of two categories of skills, *constrained* and *unconstrained*. Constrained skills, which are the focus of this chapter, include phonological awareness, letter recognition, and decoding, whereas unconstrained skills encompass vocabulary and comprehension. And, depending on how it is defined, fluency can be considered somewhat constrained. Although all of these skills are important, they develop in different ways. Constrained skills, such as letter recognition, are limited and develop over a relatively brief period of time. They can also be taught directly and assessed relatively easily and accurately. Alternatively, unconstrained skills, such as vocabulary, incorporate an extensive knowledge base that is developed over a lifetime. Furthermore, they benefit from both direct and indirect instruction and are difficult to assess fully. Finally, for the vast majority of students, constrained skills are an important focus in the primary grades. Unconstrained skills, on the other hand, need to be part of the instructional focus throughout a learner's school career, and they continue to be expanded beyond formal schooling.

Although both types of skills are critical to literacy development, we would argue that certain misunderstandings have emerged about the role of constrained skills and the ways they can best be developed (e.g., Kuhn, Schwanenflugel, & Meisinger, 2010). Because these skills can be assessed in a manner that is uncomplicated, is inexpensive, and shows significant growth over short periods of time, they have come to dominate the literacy curriculum in many schools. In fact, mastering these skills has become the litmus test for reading success in many places. In addition, we would argue that the concepts of fluency and automaticity have been confounded, and that this muddles, rather than clarifies, each of these understandings. Finally, although most students benefit from direct instruction of constrained skills, these skills should not be taught in a rote manner. Instead, they should be taught in a manner that makes clear their importance in the process of reading for meaning. They can also be taught in conjunction with unconstrained skills through a more holistic literacy curriculum that includes a focus on rich literature and oral language development. We address each of these issues in greater detail, with the bulk of the chapter dedicated to effective instructional approaches that should engage learners while helping them to see themselves as budding—and successful—readers.

Automaticity versus Fluency

Both the National Reading Panel (2000), and the Reading First legislation that followed, focused on five areas of reading (phonemic awareness, phonics, fluency, vocabulary, and comprehension) as critical to skilled-reading development. However, there has been a particular emphasis on phonological awareness, the alphabetic principle, and oral reading fluency as the "big ideas" (Good, Kaminski, Simmons, & Kame'enui, 2001, p. 7) of beginning reading. To a large extent, this focus on constrained skills has gained dominance in many elementary schools because they are seen as fundamental to later reading success (e.g., Fletcher, Lyon, Fuchs, & Barnes, 2007; Kame'enui, Simmons, Good, & Harn, 2001). That is, if we are to prevent later reading difficulties, it is critical to identify students experiencing problems with these skills early, and to provide intensive instruction to ensure proficiency (Good et al., 2001). Although this is absolutely true, it is not the full story. An emphasis on oral language, motivation, extensive opportunities to read and interact with connected text, and a range of other factors that contribute to vocabulary and comprehension development must also be included as part of a balanced reading curriculum (Bredekamp & Pikulski, 2008; Pikulski, 2005; Schwanenflugel et al., in press; Shanahan, 2005). Furthermore, the ways in which these skills have been conceptualized, taught, and assessed have led to a skewed understanding of how best to develop not only constrained skills, but literacy in general.

For example, tests such as the Dynamic Indicators of Basic Early Literacy Skills (DIBELS) and AIMSweb measure a range of skills (initial sounds, letter naming, phoneme segmentation, nonsense words, oral reading fluency) through speed of recognition or so-called "fluency." However, the use of the term *fluency* in this context equates to automaticity "in the component skills and lower-level processes" (Kame'enui et al., 2001, p. 308). This definition is in fact significantly different from the more common definition of *fluency*—that of proficient word recognition in the reading of connected text (e.g., Kuhn et al., 2010). Furthermore, we would argue that the equation of fluency with automaticity actually narrows the concept; as Hudson and her colleagues note, "the concept of automaticity actually implies more about a response than does the concept of fluency" (Hudson, Pullen, Lane, & Torgesen, 2009, p. 9). Indeed, these authors choose to use the term *automaticity*, rather than *fluency*, to describe a response, such as rapid letter recognition, that "requires few processing resources, is obligatory, and outside of conscious control." Although we agree that automaticity is a critical piece in successful early literacy, we also contend that it does not, in and of itself, provide an adequate explanation of the complexities of beginning reading.

Unfortunately, this confounding of automaticity and fluency has led to some concrete difficulties in the classroom in terms of how instruction and assessments should be implemented. So, for example, in the case of oral reading fluency, the emphasis on automaticity has created a privileging of rapid word recognition in oral reading instruction (Applegate, Applegate, & Modla, 2009; Pressley et al., 2006). In addition, the importance placed on assessments that measure reading rate, coupled with their repeated use across the elementary years, has intensified this emphasis (Paris, 2005, 2009). Unfortunately, an excessive focus on rate can lead to rapid, choppy reading and is likely to interfere with, rather than promote, comprehension (Applegate et al., 2009; Samuels, 2007). To counter this, it is important for oral reading instruction to develop appropriate pacing and intonation, rather than excessive rate, as part of effective fluency instruction.

Similar arguments can be made for the instruction of other constrained skills. Rather than simply trying to ensure students develop automaticity in terms of phonemic awareness, alphabet knowledge, or word recognition exclusively in isolation, students' knowledge of these skills needs to be developed in a contextualized manner that allows them to see the connection to their overall reading development (e.g., Kuhn et al., 2010; Paris, 2005, 2009). This can involve instruction embedded within a holistic literacy curriculum and should incorporate extensive experiences with connected text. This chapter provides examples of such instruction while maintaining a focus on the development of constrained skills. We believe that such an integration will better help students develop into skilled readers who are willing to engage with text.

Developing Phonological Awareness, including Phonemic Awareness: Research and Practice

In order to learn to read and write, children first need to gain an important insight into spoken language. They need to recognize that oral language can be broken down into various-sized components of sound. These insights are described using the term *phonological awareness*. The most basic insight is the identification of individual words among the many words that occur in speech (Adams, 1990; Anthony, Lonigan, Driscoll, Phillips, & Burgess, 2003; Goswami & Bryant, 1990; Stanovich, 1992). While children are going about the task of learning language, they begin to be able to recognize particular words from among other, unrecognized words and sounds (Walley, Metsala, & Garlock, 2003). Consider a scenario in which an adult asks a very young child, Amanda, "Where is your ball?" After multiple exposures to the word *ball* within meaningful conversations, Amanda becomes able to identify that word from the stream of words spoken to her; this allows her to recognize that the speaker is referring to a familiar object: a ball. As Amanda learns more and more words, she becomes able to parse spoken sentences into words and use them in her own speech. Some of the speaking errors made by young children result from the inability to parse sentences correctly. Consider the delightful renditions of "The Star-Spangled Banner" by young children. Youngsters who sing "by donzer's lee light" are attempting to divide the oral speech stream into recognizable word components, but their unfamiliarity with the word *dawn* results in an error.

Eventually, with increasing exposure to new words and word play involving rhyme, alliteration, and the like, children begin to notice smaller aspects of words (Dickinson, McCabe, Anastasopoulos, Peisner-Feinberg, & Poe, 2003.) They begin to notice syllables; onsets and rimes (i.e., components of syllables); and individual phonemes (Adams, 1990; Anthony et al., 2003; Goswami & Bryant, 1990; Stanovich, 1992). A preschool child who is asked, "Would you like some juice?" might respond, "Juice, goose, loose." This child demonstrates an awareness of a smaller segment of sound than the word; this child recognizes the rime. The onset is the initial consonant or consonants within a syllable, and the rime consists of the vowel and any consonants that follow it. The child who chants, "Juice, goose, loose," is able to remove the onset (the initial *j*) and replace it with new consonants, keeping the rime consistent.

A *phoneme* is "a unit of sound in a language that cannot be analyzed into smaller linear units and that can distinguish one word from another" (*OED Online*, 2011). So, for example, the sounds /m/ and /n/ are the phonemes at the beginning of the words *map* and *nap*. Likewise, the sounds /p/ and /t/ are the phonemes at the ends of the words *map* and *mat*. Each of the words in the "Juice, loose, goose" example contains three phonemes: a consonant, a vowel, and another consonant. When a child becomes aware of the individual phonemes in a word, we say that the child has become "phonemically aware." Thus phonemic awareness is one type of phonological awareness. Children who are phonemically aware can attend to and manipulate the individual sounds in words (Stanovich, Cunningham, & Freeman, 1984). A child who can count the sounds in a word is showing evidence of phonemic awareness. Continuing with our example above, the phonemically aware child would recognize that there are three sounds in the word *juice* (/j/ /oo/ /s/). Importantly, these three sounds are represented by five letters—a distinction we discuss in depth later in the chapter.

Research has indicated that phonemic awareness makes an essential contribution to early reading success (Hulme et al., 2002; Share, Jorm, Maclean, & Matthews, 1984). Children must be able to segment and blend individual sounds in words, in order to make sense of phonics instruction and apply sound–symbol relationships in the attempt to read unknown words (Ehri & Roberts, 2006).

The different levels of phonological awareness, including phonemic awareness, are often acquired through exposure to playful language use and to certain types of texts (see Figure 8.1 for examples of such texts). For example, exposure to nursery rhymes and rhyming books prompts young children to notice the sound qualities of words (Griffith & Olson, 1992; Yopp & Yopp, 2000). Playful oral activities, such as songs, word chants, and sound games, also help children to acquire phonological awareness (Adams & Bruck, 1995; Beck & Juel, 1995; Bryant, Bradley, MacLean, & Crossland, 1989; Mattingly, 1984; Yopp & Yopp, 2000). Teachers can engage children in the singing of songs

Read-Aloud Books That Play with Language

Books in English

Altoona Baboona, by J. Bynum. 1999. San Diego: Harcourt.

Altoona Up North, by J. Bynum. 2001. San Diego: Harcourt.

Bearsie Bear and the Suprise Sleepover Party, by B. Waber. 1997. New York: Houghton Mifflin.

Chugga Chugga Choo Choo, by K. Lewis. 1999. New York: Hyperion.

Cock-a-doodle-Moo! by B. Most. 1996. San Diego, CA: Harcourt.

The Happy Hippopotami, by B. Martin Jr. 1970. San Diego: Voyager.

Here's a Little Poem: A Very First Book of Poetry, by J. Yolen. 2007. Cambridge, MA: Candlewick.

The Hungry Thing, by J. A. Slepian & A. Seidler. 1967. New York: Scholastic.

Jamberry, by B. Degen. 2000. 25th ann. ed. New York: HarperCollins.

Llama llama Mad at Mama, by A. Dewdney. 2007. New York: Viking.

Llama llama Red Pajama, by A. Dewdney. 2005. New York: Viking.

The Piggy in the Puddle, by C. Pomerantz. 1974. New York: Simon & Schuster.

Runny Babbit, by S. Silverstein. 2005. New York: HarperCollins.

Tanka Tanka Skunk, by S. Webb. 2004. New York: Orchard.

There's a Wocket in My Pocket, by Dr. Seuss. 1974. New York: Random House.

What Will You Wear, Jenny Jenkins? by J. Garcia & D. Grisman. 2000. New York: HarperCollins.

Books in Spanish

Albertina anda arriba: El abecedario, by N. M. G. Tabor. 1992. Watertown, MA: Charlesbridge.

Arroró mi niño: Latino Lullabies and Gentle Games, by L. Delacre. 2004. New York: Lee & Low.

Aserrín, Aserrán: Las canciones de la abuela (Grandmother's songs), by A. Longo. 2004. New York: Scholastic.

Destrabalenguerías para trabalengueros, by H. G. Delgado. 2002. Bogotá, Columbia: Intermedio.

¡Hay un molillo en mi bolsillo! by Dr. Seuss. Tran. Y. Canetti. 2007. New York: Lectorum.

La mansión misteriosa, by C. Gil. 2007. Barcelona: Combel.

Mother Goose on the Rio Grande, by F. Alexander. 1997. Lincolnwood, IL: Passport.

Las nanas de abuelita: Canciones de cuna, trabalenguas y adivinanzas de Suramérica, by N. P. Jaramillo. 1994. New York: Henry Holt.

Los niños alfabeticos, by L. Ayala & M. Isona-Rodriguez. 1995. Watertown, MA: Charlesbridge.

Números tragaldabas, by M. Robleda. 2003. Mexico: Ediciones Destino.

¡Pío Peep! Rimas tradicionales en español. Edición especial, by A. F. Ada & F. I. Campoy. 2003. New York: HarperCollins.

Los pollitos dicen: Juegos, rimas y canciones infantiles de paises de habla hispana, by N. A. Hall & J. Syverson-Stork. 1999. Boston: Little, Brown.

El sapo distraido, by J. Rondon. 1988. Caracaz, Venezuela: Ediciones Ekare.

Los sonidos a mi alrededor, P. Showers. 1996. New York: HarperCollins.

El toro pinto and Other Songs in Spanish, by A. Rockwell. 1995. New York: Aladdin.

Tortillas para Mama, by M. C. Griego, B. L. Bucks, S. S. Gilbert, & L. H. Kimball. 1981. New York: Henry Holt.

FIGURE 8.1. Books that play with sounds. From Yopp and Yopp (2009, p. 5). Reprinted with permission from the National Association for the Education of Young Children. Copyright © 2009 by NAEYC.

A Family Example

Kai's parents have been reading Mem Fox's *Time for Bed* (1993) to him at bedtime several nights a week since he was a tiny baby. The story is made up of rhyming couplets, each featuring a different creature and its mother's admonition to go to sleep. The book begins with the words, "It's time for bed, little mouse, little mouse, darkness is falling all over the house." A few pages later, the text reads, "It's time for bed, little fish, little fish, so hold your breath and make a wish." When Kai was about 4 years old, he started to request that his mother or father use one of the couplets when they told him it was time for bed. He would say, "Which one am I?", and soon this became a family game. Kai's mother or father would say, "It's time for bed, Kai." He would reply, "Which one am I?", and they would reply with one of the couplets. Before long, Kai wanted to be an animal that was not in the book. Each night he would request a new animal, and his parents were challenged to come up with a new rhyming couplet. Sometimes, when they could not readily come up with a rhyme, his mother or father would end the couplet with a word that did not rhyme. Kai delighted in exclaiming, "No!" when such a response was given.

    Through repeated exposures to rhyming books like *Time for Bed*, Kai has become aware of rhyme. He has not been explicitly taught what rhyming is, but he knows what it sounds like.

---

that involve switching one sound in a particular word. For example, the song "Willoughby Wallaby Woo" involves changing the first letter of a child's name in each line of the song. The lyrics, as sung by Raffi (1975), begin:

> Willoughby wallaby wee, an elephant sat on me,
> Willoughby wallaby woo, an elephant sat on you,
> Willoughby wallaby Wustin, an elephant sat on Justin,
> Willoughby wallaby Wania, an elephant sat on Tania.

Classroom Examples

Preschool and kindergarten teachers can also engage children daily in oral language activities that encourage the development of phonological awareness. Each morning, Mrs. Gamble, a preschool teacher who works with 4-year-olds, engages her students in playing games that involve clapping the syllables in their names or counting the phonemes in the names of book characters. One day, for example, after singing "Old MacDonald Had a Farm," she led the children in counting out the number of phonemes in each of the types of animals they included in the song. Together, they sorted pictures of the animals into three-sound and four-sound categories. Mrs. Gamble also leads the children in singing songs that emphasize alliteration and rhyme, such as "The Ants Go Marching." They sing other songs that involve changing the initial sounds of words, such

---

**Songs and Rhymes
That Call Attention to Sound**

- "Willoughby Wallaby Woo"
- "Teddy Bear Song"
- "Apples and Bananas"
- "Miss Mary Mack"
- "Pease Porridge Hot"
- "The Ants Go Marching"

as "Willoughby Wallaby Woo." Mrs. Gamble also joins small groups of children during snacktime and lunchtime and playfully helps them segment the names of food items contained in their lunches. Through these short, daily sessions, the children become increasingly aware of segments of sound in words, including syllables and individual phonemes. Parents of children in Mrs. Gamble's class report that their children have sometimes engaged the whole family in segmenting activities at the dinner table and that they have a good time trying to counting the syllables in words like *spaghetti* and *tortilla*.

Meeting All Students' Needs in Developing Phonological Awareness

Most often, children who do not acquire these insights in natural contexts can be taught to pay attention to syllables, onsets/rimes, and individual phonemes through short, explicit lessons. However, these training sessions should not take the place of other literacy experiences—such as listening to stories being read aloud, opportunities to explore writing materials and to attempt to write, and opportunities to "read" familiar books by narrating the illustrations—which build other essential early literacy skills.

In fact, research studies that examined the usefulness of explicit training programs found that a rather small number of short sessions led to significant results. The National Reading Panel (2000) reported that phonemic awareness training sessions totaling between 5 and 18 hours produced greater effects than those with shorter or longer durations. Most often, the training sessions reported in these studies ranged between 15 and 20 minutes in duration and occurred each day for several weeks. The lesson here is that explicit training in phonemic awareness can be done in a rather short period of time; in other words, any program that requires many more hours of instruction than 18 is unlikely to be the best use of instructional time for children. In fact, such instruction may have a negative effect on the other aspects of literacy development that are neglected as a result.

Blachman, Ball, Black, and Tangel (1994) demonstrated the effectiveness of a short-term phonemic awareness training program with kindergartners who had low levels of literacy skill knowledge upon entry to school. Children in the treatment group received between 11 and 13 hours of training in total, spread across 11 weeks. The children worked in small groups with a teacher or classroom assistant for between 15 and 20 minutes, four times a week, on three phonemic awareness activities. The first activity, called *say-it-and-move-it*, involved sliding a disk into a two-dimensional box drawn on paper to represent each of the phonemes in a one-, two-, or three-phoneme word. As the program progressed, actual letters were written on some of the disks. The purpose of the say-it-and-move-it activity was to teach children to segment words into phonemes. Each lesson also involved another segmentation-related activity, which sometimes required segmenting words into phonemes, but might also have involved identifying words beginning with the same sound or recognizing rhyming words. The final part of each lesson involved instruction in letter names and letter sounds. Each of the eight letters taught over the course of the 11 weeks was represented with an illustrated letter–sound card. The children played games such as bingo to practice the names and associated sounds of the letters. At the conclusion of the study, children in the treatment group outperformed children in the control group on measures of phonemic awareness and letter–sound knowledge, in their ability to read phonemically regular real words and nonsense words, and in their ability to represent sounds through invented spelling. This study demonstrates that through short, manipulative-based activities, children who enter school with low levels of literacy knowledge can acquire phonemic awareness and other essential foundational skills (e.g., beginning phonics instruction).

Teachers can use informal classroom assessments to identify children who have not yet acquired phonemic awareness. One such assessment, the Yopp–Singer Test of Phoneme Segmentation (Yopp, 1995), comprises 22 one-syllable words that are pronounced orally by the test administrator. The child responds to each item by segmenting it into its component phonemes. An item is scored as correct if the child can fully segment the word. The child's performance on the assessment allows the teacher to determine whether the child has already acquired phonemic awareness to a level that should support the learning of phonics, and therefore does not require much practice with segmenting or blending tasks. Likewise, the assessment allows the teacher to identify those children who would benefit from instruction that supports the development of phonemic awareness.

Developing Alphabet Recognition: Research and Classroom Examples

Learning to recognize and name the letters of the alphabet is perhaps the most familiar early literacy skill; it is also an important foundation for learning to read. The National Early Literacy Panel (2008) found a strong relationship (.50) between alphabet knowledge and decoding skills across 52 studies that involved 7,570 children. Although learning the letters of the alphabet is certainly a constrained skill—there are 26 letters, each with an upper- and lowercase version—it is by no means an easy task for a young child. In order to identify the letters of the alphabet, children must notice the visual characteristics of different letters (Adams, 1990; Ehri, 1998; Gibson & Levin, 1975). Letters in the English alphabet are composed of a variety of straight lines and curves. Some letters (e.g., uppercase *E* and uppercase *F*) differ in rather slight ways. Importantly, while children learn early to ignore characteristics related to orientation and direction when identifying other visual stimuli (e.g., a chair is a chair whether it is upright or tipped over), these qualities are important with regard to alphabet letters and cannot be ignored (Schickedanz, 1998; Schickedanz, Schickedanz, & Forsyth, 1982). When we think about letter recognition in this way, it is not hard to understand why even first graders and second graders sometimes confuse letters like lowercase *b* and *d*, which differ only in terms of orientation.

When adults read storybooks to children, they tend to focus on meaning; therefore, not much attention is paid to learning letters and letter names (Yaden, Smolkin, & Conlon, 1989). Shared experiences with ABC books, on the other

---

Recommended Alphabet Books

- *Alphabet Adventure*
  by Audrey and Bruce Wood
- *The Alphabet Book*
  by P. D. Eastman
- *Eating the Alphabet*
  by Lois Ehlert
- *WILD Alphabet: An A to Zoo Pop-Up Book*
  by Dan Green and Julia Frohlich
- *Eric Carle's ABC*
  by Eric Carle
- *A to Z*
  by Sandra Boynton
- *LMNO Peas*
  by Keith Baker
- *Gone Wild*
  by David McLimans

hand, do tend to result in attention to letter names, shapes, and corresponding sounds (Bus & van IJzendoorn, 1988). We recommend, therefore, that preschool and kindergarten teachers purposefully integrate alphabet books into their read-aloud repertoires.

Meeting All Students' Needs in Developing Alphabet Recognition

In situations in which children arrive in school with weak knowledge of letter names, teachers can incorporate explicit print referencing as they read and discuss storybooks. Justice, Kaderavek, Fan, Sofka, and Hunt (2009) trained kindergarten teachers to engage in print referencing as they read aloud storybooks. The teachers called the children's attention to the print by asking questions about the print, by commenting on the print, and by tracking the print with their fingers as they read (p. 68). They encouraged the children to interact with the print when they said things such as "Where should I start reading on this page?" and "Do you see the uppercase S on this page?" The children in these classrooms made larger gains on measures of print knowledge than children in the control classrooms, whose teachers read aloud but maintained the more common focus on meaning during the study. Because the focus on meaning during shared storybook reading yields growth in other essential areas of literacy (e.g., vocabulary development), we recommend that teachers—particularly those whose students demonstrate weak letter knowledge—incorporate explicit print referencing comments and questions *into* their meaning-based discussions. In other words, it is not necessary to stop talking about the story, the characters, or interesting vocabulary in order to make specific references to print as well!

Developing Concepts about Print: Research and Classroom Examples

In addition to gaining important insights about the sounds of language and developing the ability to identify the letters of the alphabet, very young children must also acquire understandings about how print works before they can themselves begin to read. These concepts include book conventions such as turning pages from front to back, holding the book right side up (not upside down), and knowing the front and the back of the book. They also include concepts related to the English print system, including the recognition that lines of text on a page are read from top to bottom, that each line is read from left to right, and that the beginning of a sentence is marked with a capital letter and the end with a punctuation mark (Clay, 1989).

In a meta-analysis of studies evaluating the relationships between early literacy skills and later success in learning to read and write, the National Early Literacy Panel (2008) found that "knowledge of print conventions (e.g., left–right, front–back) and concepts (book cover, author, text)" assessed with either a measure developed by an investigator or using an established measure, such as Clay's (2000) Concepts about Print Test, when children were in preschool or kindergarten, had a significant relationship with literacy skills measured in first grade and beyond (p. 42). The relationship between concepts of print and comprehension was strong (.54) across three studies. The relationship between concepts of print and decoding and concepts of print and spelling were moderate (.34 across 12 studies and .43 across four studies). However, it is important to note that concepts of print were not always predictive of literacy outcomes once phonemic awareness and alphabet knowledge were controlled for.

One way that teachers can help children learn concepts about print is through the reading of *Big Books*. A Big Book is simply an oversized version of a picture book that can be propped on an easel. Because the book is oversized, the children can observe the teacher as he or she points to particular features of the print. For example, the teacher might highlight the use of a question mark at the end of a sentence or show the students that a person begins reading at the top of the page.

Another essential insight acquired by young children is that the print on the page is what tells the story or provides the information to be read. Very young children attend primarily to the illustrations or photographs in books, and the realization that print exists apart from the visual features of the page and encodes the "message" is a notable milestone. Young children gradually acquire this understanding through read-aloud experiences. They begin to notice that the reader looks at the text as he or she speaks and that the page is not turned until the reader has completed scanning the print (Sulzby, 1985).

Connected to the realization that print encodes the story is the recognition that particular letters are used to represent specific sounds. This insight is referred to as the *alphabetic principle*. The written messages of children who have print awareness, and therefore understand that print is used to convey a message, but who have not yet acquired the alphabetic principle, are quite remarkable. At this stage, children simply use familiar letters (or letter-like shapes) with no regard to sound–symbol connections. In Figure 8.2, Adam (a child described by Schickedanz, 1990) used the letters from his name and a few other letters that he knew how to form to write a list of words.

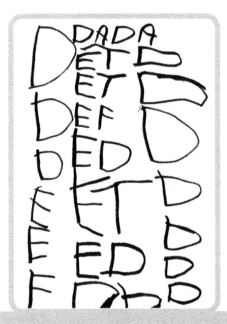

FIGURE 8.2. Adam's (age 3 years, 7 months) list of words. From Schickedanz (1990). Copyright 1990 by Judith A. Schickedanz. Reprinted by permission.

Developing Word Recognition: Research and Classroom Examples

Ehri (1991, 1994, 1995) has identified five phases that learners pass through on their way to mature word recognition ability. In the first phase, called the *prealphabetic* stage, children rely on visual cues because they have not yet acquired an understanding of the sound–symbol relationships that define an alphabetic language like English. Instead, children at this stage "read" words by relying on visual contexts. For example, they may be able to read the word *stop* in the context of a red hexagon, or the word *fish* posted on a classroom fish tank or on a classroom job chart accompanied by a drawing of a fish. A tell-tale sign that these children rely on the visual context to recognize these words is the inability to read these words when they are taken out of context (e.g., *stop* written on a piece of paper without the red hexagon as a clue). Children in this stage may also rely on particular visual aspects of the word itself as a cue to recognition. Ehri and McCormick (1998) provide the example of a child using the "eyes" or double *o*'s in the word *look* as a cue to recognizing the word. However, this strategy has limited usefulness because it does not help a child differentiate *look* from *pool* or *moon*.

In the second phase, which Ehri (1991, 1994, 1995) calls the *partial-alphabetic* stage, children begin to apply knowledge of letter–sound relationships to aid in the recognition of words. Children frequently use first letters and the context to "guess" at words. Ehri and McCormick (1998) provide the example of the child who encounters the word *barn* accompanied with an illustration of a farm in a storybook. The child uses the first consonant and the illustration to determine that the initially unrecognized word is *barn*. Because children in this stage are only able to use a limited amount of information about sound and symbols, they are likely to mistake words with similar spellings, reading *house* for *home* and *book* for *block*.

Children move next into the *full-alphabetic* stage (Ehri, 1991, 1994, 1995). At this stage children have acquired knowledge of most common sound–symbol relationships, including vowels. This stage is characterized by slow, laborious decoding of unfamiliar words, in which child may decode by analogy or using a known word (e.g., *beak*) to recognize an unknown word (e.g., *peak*) or by segmenting and blending the sounds—a process commonly referred to as "sounding out." As children progress through this stage, they are able to apply their knowledge of sound–symbol relationships more rapidly and they recognize more and more words automatically, or "by sight."

In the *consolidated-alphabetic* stage (Ehri, 1991, 1994, 1995), children begin to utilize common sequences of letters in their decoding efforts. According to Ehri and McCormick (1998), among the first sequences to become consolidated are morphemic suffixes such as *-ed* and *-ing*, and high-frequency rime patterns such as *-at*, *-in*, and *-all*. Because the number of units requiring attention is reduced in comparison to the full-alphabetic stage, decoding of words of similar length is often reduced. In addition, children begin to engage in hierarchical as well as sequential decoding. They are able to utilize visual information present later in a written word, rather than proceeding strictly from left to right. A hierarchical approach to decoding is required, for example, by words ending in a silent *e*, in order to assign a long sound to the medial vowel. Due to their successful efforts to decode unknown words and repeated exposure to written words in connected text, the size of children's sight vocabulary continues to grow in this stage.

In the final phase, the *automatic* phase, word recognition is predominantly rapid and seemingly effortless. Most of the words a reader encounters are sight words, and unfamiliar words are typically identified quickly through the facile use of a variety of strategies. At this stage, much of the reader's mental effort is freed to focus on the meaning of the text.

Learning Phonics

Once children recognize that particular letters represent particular sounds (or, to use Ehri's terminology, are entering the partial-alphabetic stage), they are ready to begin learning about these relationships formally. Although it is possible, and all too common, to isolate this instruction—labeled *phonics*—from authentic reading and writing experiences, we see doing so as a grave mistake. It is clear that the best types of phonics instruction are explicit and systematic (Stahl, Duffy-Hester, & Stahl, 1998), but this does not mean that phonics instruction cannot (or should not) be conducted within the context of wonderful stories or interesting nonfiction texts. In fact, we argue, as have others (e.g., Trachtenberg, 1990; Tunmer & Nicholson, 2011; Wharton-McDonald, Pressley, & Hampston, 1998), that by connecting explicit, systematic phonics instruction to meaningful texts, we help children to see how their newly acquired decoding skills can be used in the context of real reading. Too many children who are taught phonics skills in isolation do not transfer their knowledge of letters and sounds to the task of reading real texts. By embedding phonics instruction within reading experiences, teachers help children recognize how and when they might use this information to assist in their reading attempts.

A straightforward way to combine phonics instruction with meaningful reading experiences is to use children's books to introduce phonics lessons (e.g., Trachtenberg, 1990). For example, a first-grade teacher introducing short-*a* rime patterns to her students might begin by reading *The Magic Hat* by Mem Fox (2002). After the reading and a discussion that focuses on comprehension, the teacher could draw the children's attention to the word *hat* in the story and begin to teach them explicitly about the -*at* rime pattern and the use of the letter *a* to represent the short-*a* vowel sound. The lesson would then move to the use of manipulatives such as magnetic letters and whiteboards to allow for the manipulation of the -*at* rime pattern and various initial consonants. A second short-*a* rime pattern could also be introduced for the purpose of providing contrast and encouraging the students to notice the importance of each letter. Following this practice with short-*a* patterns separate from the context of the book, the teacher could again draw the students' attention to the book *The Magic Hat* and talk about how they could use this new information about letters and sounds to help them decode the word *hat*. In the days that follow, additional children's books such as *Splat the Cat* (Scotton, 2008) would be used to reinforce the -*at* rime pattern, and others, such as *Caps for Sale* (Slobodkina, 1987) and *Bread and Jam for Frances* (Hoban, 1964), could be used to introduce new short-*a* rime patterns. In addition, because the use of sophisticated vocabulary and complex sentence structures in these books may prevent students from reading these books independently, leveled texts that contain the target pattern but also match the children's reading level should be used as a part of these lessons (Adams, 1990; Pressley, 2006). For example, *Shut the Gate* (Wignell, 2004), a leveled reader that is part of Scholastic's Alphakids series, could offer early readers the opportunity to practice decoding words containing the -*ut* rime pattern through their own reading.

As stated above, for phonics instruction to be effective, it needs to be systematic and explicit. Children should be taken through a sequence that logically begins with the most basic letter–sound relationships and works toward the more difficult patterns. For most children, the most obvious letter–sound connection occurs with their first names (Treiman & Broderick, 1998). Next, children are likely to learn those consonants with letter names that contain the phoneme that they are most commonly used to represent (Treiman, Weatherston, & Berch, 1994). For example, when the letter name *b* is spoken, the /b/ phoneme is the first sound uttered. These types of letter–sound pairs are typically the easiest for children to learn. Whereas the /b/ sound occurs right at the beginning of the letter name, other letter names contain the phoneme they are used to represent at the end. The letter *m*, for example, contains the /m/ phoneme at the end of the letter name. Lastly, children can be introduced to the consonants whose names do not contain the phoneme that they are commonly used to represent (e.g., *h, w, g*). Fortunately, there are only a few such letters. The match between vowels and what is commonly referred to as the long sound, or the vowel's "name," is also fairly straightforward; in other words, the letter name is a perfect match with the sound (e.g., *o* as in the word *open*).

Soon after learning the pairings of single consonants and the phonemes they most commonly represent, children can be taught short vowel sounds. And because vowel sounds are most stable within clusters of letters, it is beneficial to begin to teach children the most common rime patterns at this time (Wylie & Durrell, 1970). The *rime* is the part of a syllable that contains the vowel and any consonants that follow it. So in a one-syllable word, like *hat*, the rime is *-at*. Children benefit greatly from learning the most commonly used rime patterns. Note that beginning to utilize larger-size graphophonic units, such as rime patterns, is a defining feature of Ehri's consolidated-alphabetic stage. Wylie and Durrell (1970) identified 37 rimes that are used in over 500 words commonly found in texts meant for young children. Typically, the two-letter short-vowel rime patterns are learned first. Later, usually sometime in first grade, children are taught the most common long-vowel rime patterns, which are created by adding a silent *e* in the final position (e.g., *-ake, -ide, -ope*). See Figure 8.3 for the 37 rimes arranged in a recommended instructional sequence.

Short-Vowel Patterns						
at	ap	aw	an	ack	ash	ank
it	ip	in	ill	ick	ing	ink
op	ock	ug	uck	ump	unk	ell
est						
Long-Vowel Patterns						
ay	ate	ake	ame	ale	ide	ine
ice	oke	ore	or	ail	ain	eat
ight						

FIGURE 8.3. Thirty-seven rimes that occur in nearly 500 primary-level words. Based on Wylie and Durrell (1970).

A Suggested Sequence of Phonics Instruction

Kindergarten

Consonant sounds:
> Begin with letters whose names contain the sound (*b, f, l, m*).
> Move on to letters whose names do not contain the sound (*g, h, c*).

Vowel sounds:
> Begin with long-vowel sounds.
> Introduce short-vowel sounds.

First Grade

Begin teaching rime patterns.
> Begin with simple vowel–consonant patterns.
>> Begin with short-*a* patterns (-*at, -ap, -an, -ack*).
>> Then move to short-*i* patterns (-*it, -ip, -in, -ick*).
>> Follow with short-*o*, short-*u*, and short-*e* patterns.

Teach consonant blends and consonant digraphs.
> Digraphs—two letters used to represent one sound (*sh, ch, th, wh, ph*).
> Blends—two or three consonants blended together; each letter maintains
>   its original sound (*bl, st, fl, gr, sm, str*).

Teach vowel–consonant–*e* rime patterns.
> The function of the silent *e* in the final position in these patterns is to indicate
>   that the previous vowel should be pronounced with its long sound (-*ake,
>   -ade, -ave, -ike, -ide, -ice, -ole, -oke, -ope*).

Second Grade

Continue teaching long-vowel patterns.
> Review vowel–consonant–*e* patterns and contrast with vowel–consonant
>   patterns (e.g., *mane* vs. *man, kite* vs. *kit, take* vs. *tack*).

Introduce long-vowel digraphs: *ai* (-*ain, -ail*), *ee* (-*een, -eep*), *oa* (-*oat, -oan*).

Work with final-consonant blends: -*nk* (-*ink, -ank*), -*rp* (-*arp, -urp*), -*ng* (-*ong, -ang*).

Introduce diphthongs: -*oi* (-*oil, -oin*), -*ow* (*cow, brow*).

Introduce other common rime patterns (e.g., -*ight, -ought*).

As students learn common rime patterns and begin to pair them with the consonants learned previously in the onset position or the sound(s) preceding the vowel (e.g., *h* plus *at* = *hat*), children should also be introduced to consonant clusters. There are two main types of consonant clusters: consonant *digraphs* and consonant *blends*. In a digraph, two letters are used to represent one unique sound. For example, in the consonant digraph *sh*, the *s* and the *h* are partnered together to represent a sound /sh/. In contrast, in consonant blends, which also contain two or three letters, the sounds of the individual letters are heard, but are blended or glided together. Children should be taught to recognize consonant digraphs in the initial position (e.g., *sh, ch, th, wh, ph*) and to combine them with rime patterns as they attempt to decode unknown words. They should also be taught to use consonant blends (e.g., *fr, st, gl, sn*) in their attempts to read new words.

Once children can successfully decode words containing short-vowel patterns (e.g., *-at, -et, -id, -op, -un*) and various types of onsets, they are ready to be introduced to long-vowel patterns. Typically, instruction about long-vowel patterns begins with the common vowel, consonant, and silent-*e* pattern (e.g., *-ake, -ite, -ope*). Children then learn about other long-vowel patterns, including those containing vowel digraphs (e.g., *-oat, -ain, -eep*). See the box on the previous page for a suggested sequence of phonics instruction in the early elementary grades.

Meeting All Learners' Needs in Word Recognition Development

In their review of research that supports a balanced approach to word recognition instruction, Tunmer and Nicholson (2011) note that it is becoming increasingly clear that children with different levels of knowledge about letter–sound relationships benefit from different types of instruction. Children in the early phases of word recognition (i.e., those in Ehri's pre- and partial-alphabetic phases) are more *environment-dependent* and seem to benefit most from intensive, explicit instruction in phonemic awareness and the use of letter–sound relationships. Children who have successfully acquired knowledge of the basic letter–sound relationships, and who have therefore entered the full-alphabetic phase, seem to be more *learner-dependent*; that is, they benefit most from opportunities to apply their knowledge of letter–sound relationships in the reading of texts. For example, in a study of four first-grade teachers who used different approaches to reading instruction, Juel and Minden-Cupp (2000) found that children who entered first grade with low levels of alphabetic knowledge benefited most from an instructional approach that incorporated high levels of explicit, systematic phonics instruction. In contrast, children who entered first grade with some knowledge of sound–symbol relationships benefited most from an instructional approach that emphasized reading of trade books and opportunities to write. In light of this study and others, Tunmer and Nicholson make the recommendation that beginning readers should receive explicit, systematic instruction in phonics, and that once knowledge of the basic sound–symbol relationships has been acquired, greater emphasis should be placed on opportunities to practice reading and using this information in connected text. That said, Tunmer and Nicholson make it clear that even during the period requiring phonics instruction, children benefit from instruction that addresses how to use sound–symbol relationships during reading. They state, "Although beginning readers should receive explicit instruction in letter–sound patterns outside the context of reading connected text, they also should be taught how and when to use this information during text reading through demonstration, modeling, direct explanation, and guided practice" (p. 419).

Teachers can use informal assessment measures to help them determine which children have already acquired a solid foundation in sound–symbol relationships. The Informal Phonics Survey (McKenna & Stahl, 2009) can be used to estimate children's knowledge of consonants, consonant digraphs, consonant blends, short-vowel sounds, words ending in a silent *e*, vowel digraphs, vowel diphthongs, and *r*-controlled vowels. By administering this short screening tool early in the school year, first-grade teachers in particular will be able to identify those students who would benefit most from instruction on these basic phonics elements and those who probably have enough foundational knowledge to benefit from a greater focus on reading appropriately challenging texts that will allow them to practice using these elements.

Learning to Apply Word-Reading Strategies

As discussed by Tunmer and Nicholson (2001), effective elementary-grade teachers also spend time teaching children strategies for reading words that they do not automatically recognize. In a study involving 14 schools serving large numbers of low-income students, Taylor, Pearson, Clark, and Walpole (2000) found that first- and second-grade teachers in the most effective schools spent considerable time "coaching" students in the use of strategies that would support the students' recognition of words. These teachers coached learners as they listened to them individually read aloud. In the most effective schools, teachers of third-grade struggling readers continued to coach them explicitly on the use of word recognition strategies as well.

Tompkins (2010) identifies four word identification strategies: *phonic analysis, decoding by analogy, syllabic analysis*, and *morphemic analysis*. When children use phonic analysis to decode a word, they apply what they know about letter–sound correspondences, vowel patterns, and onsets and rimes in their attempts. For example, upon encountering the word *slit*, a child might first identify the familiar rime pattern *-it* and then connect the consonant blend *sl-* to this ending to decode the word successfully. Teachers can coach children to use the phonics patterns and generalizations that they have been taught by offering cues that prompt specific actions, such as "What does *spr* say?" or "Do you see one of our word families here?" (Clark, 2004).

Decoding by analogy involves comparing a known word to the initially unrecognized word. For example, a child who encounters the word *fright* might make a comparison to the word *light*. The Word ID program, which was developed at the Benchmark School in Media, Pennsylvania, to assist children struggling with word identification, relies on such decoding by analogy (Gaskins, Gaskins, & Gaskins, 1991, 1992). Students are taught keywords that contain the most common rime patterns, and they learn to rely on these keywords as an aid in their decoding of new words. For example, the word *king* is used as a keyword for any word or syllable containing *-ing*. A child who initially struggles to identify the word *swing* will be encouraged to think of the keyword *king* in his attempt to decode *swing*. Decoding by analogy can also be encouraged through teacher coaching during one-on-one reading sessions (Clark, 2004).

A third type of word-reading strategy is syllabic analysis (Tompkins, 2010). This strategy becomes necessary as readers encounter multisyllabic words that they are unlikely to recognize automatically, such as *situation, difficulty,* and *rescue.* Teachers often encourage children to "look for a part you know" or to "chunk the word." These types of cues are intended to help the children break the word into sections as an aid to decoding it. Readers can also be taught explicit rules for breaking words into syllables. This may be helpful for some children, especially because the vowel sounds become more predictable within the context of a syllable. For example, the vowel sound in a syllable that follows a consonant–vowel–consonant pattern will typically be short, whereas the vowel sound in a syllable that follows the consonant–vowel pattern is typically long. Eventually students can be taught to combine syllabic analysis with morphemic analysis, which entails attending to affixes and root words as an aid to decoding the word and determining its meaning. For example, recognizing the prefix *in-* and the suffix *-ible* within the word *inflexible* helps the reader to divide the word effectively into its three syllables and pronounce each syllable correctly. Morphemic awareness also can be used as a support in determining a word's meaning.

Putting It All Together: Becoming Fluent Readers

Fluent reading incorporates several elements: It is smooth, effortless, and expressive (e.g., Rasinski, Reutzel, Chard, & Linan-Thompson, 2011). In terms of mechanics, fluent readers' word recognition is automatic and accurate, and they incorporate appropriate phrasing and intonation into their reading. The integration of these elements indicates a level of comfort with the material being read. However, fluent reading goes beyond such surface-level elements, acting as a "bridge" between decoding and comprehension in two important ways (e.g., Pikulski & Chard, 2005). The first involves accurate, automatic word recognition, while the second builds upon the appropriate use of prosodic features such as stress, pitch, or suitable phrasing. As such, it serves as a critical role in the development of skilled reading (National Reading Panel, 2000).

Research on the Role of Automaticity in Text Comprehension

In order to make sense of what is read, it is necessary that readers be able to accurately identify the vast majority of words they encounter in text quickly and effortlessly (e.g., Chall, 1996; National Reading Panel, 2000). As we have discussed above, this process involves accurate identification of words through the use of various word recognition strategies. However, when students first begin reading, they often appear to be overly focused on this process; the result is reading that sounds stilted and uneven. Furthermore, the attention such word recognition requires actually impedes their comprehension. In order for learners to attend to the meaning of a text, it is critical that learners develop their automaticity as well.

The importance of automaticity can best be explained through *automaticity theory* (e.g., LaBerge & Samuels, 1974; Logan, 1997), which is based on the understanding that individuals have a limited amount of attention available for any complex task. When they encounter activities that consist of multiple components, it is difficult for them to focus fully on each aspect. Instead, attention is directed to various components sequentially. In order to deal with multiple components simultaneously, it is necessary for some of these to become effortless or automatic. In the case of reading, higher-order processes such as comprehension are underpinned by the need to correctly identify what is written. In other words, in order to focus on meaning, word recognition needs to be automatic.

The question remains: How do learners develop automatic word recognition? The answer lies in practice. When individuals are learning a new skill, from sports to an instrument, the move from novice to expert status occurs through practice (Samuels, 2004). In regard to reading, this means ensuring that learners have extensive exposure to print; such exposure develops comfort with the spelling patterns, or orthography, that constitute written English. In other words, learners need to spend significant amounts of time reading to develop automatic word recognition. And, although word study is an essential component of such practice, it is critical that students have opportunities to apply their knowledge to the reading of connected text if they are to become fluent readers (e.g., Kuhn et al., 2010). It is only with such practice that what students learn about word recognition will transfer to reading; on the other hand, when learners are given plentiful opportunities to read (with appropriate support where necessary), the likelihood that they will develop automaticity increases significantly.

Research on the Role of Prosody in Text Comprehension

In addition to automaticity, *prosody* makes a critical contribution to both fluency and readers' ability to comprehend text. Prosody incorporates those aspects of oral reading that allow it to sound expressive, including pitch or intonation, stress or emphasis, tempo or rate, and the rhythmic patterns of language (e.g., Erekson, 2003; Kuhn & Stahl, 2003). Although these elements can be represented in written text by punctuation, many of the attributes that appear in oral language, such as the fluctuation of a speaker's voice or the correct phrasing, do not translate directly to print. For example, while phrase units can sometimes be identified through the use of commas, this is not always the case, as can be seen from the opening sentence of *Absalom, Absalom!* (Faulkner, 1936/1993):

> From a little after two o'clock until almost sundown of the long still hot weary dead September afternoon they sat in what Miss Coldfield still called the office because her father had called it that—a dim hot airless room with the blinds all closed and fastened for forty-three summers because when she was a girl someone had believed that light and moving air carried heat and that dark was always cooler, and which (as the sun shone fuller and fuller on that side of the house) became latticed with yellow slashes full of dust motes which Quentin thought of as being flecks of the dead old dried paint itself blown inward from the scaling blinds as wind might have blown them. (p. 1)

This is important because inappropriate breaks in a sentence can interfere with a learner's understanding of the text. Similar difficulties occur with incorrect emphasis and intonation. Fortunately, a series of studies (e.g., Casteel, 1988; Cromer, 1970; Weiss, 1983) indicate that comprehension improves when students learn to apply prosodic elements to text. Given this, the argument can be made not only that fluency is comprised of automaticity and prosody, but that both contribute to readers' ability to construct meaning from text.

Developing Fluency through Reading: Research and Classroom Examples

Importantly, fluency can be developed in two ways: either through repeated reading (e.g., Chomsky, 1976; Samuels, 1979) or through wide reading (Kuhn, 2004/2005). In repeated readings, a text is read a number of times until a certain level of competency is established. Rereading a selection multiple times makes it possible for learners to increase rate, determine appropriate prosody, and improve comprehension (e.g., Rasinski et al., 2011). Wide reading, on the other hand, allows learners to develop these factors through the reading of a range of texts, often with support. There is research indicating not only that words are learned more easily when presented in multiple contexts (e.g., *blue* sky, *blue* car, *blue* dress; Mostow & Beck, 2005), but that fluency and comprehension are also more likely to improve under these circumstances (Kuhn, 2004/2005).

It is also important to see how fundamentally different approaches to instruction can result from the two definitions of fluency discussed at the beginning of the chapter. When the emphasis is simply on developing automatic word recognition, or increasing reading rate, the instructional approach that makes the most sense is the use of repeated readings of short passages. On the other hand, when the focus is broader—emphasizing appropriate pacing and intonation, along with accuracy and automaticity—the instruction becomes more holistic. In this scenario, fluency instruction should occur primarily in context, through strategies such as echo, choral, and partner reading. Although there is room for repetition of short passages in this more contextualized approach, it should not be the primary instructional format for most learners (e.g., Kuhn & Schwanenflugel, 2008).

In fact, several approaches can be highly effective in assisting learners as they become fluent readers in the broadest sense of the word. Which approach is selected should depend upon the learners' needs, the difficulty of the text, and the amount of support or scaffolding that can be provided. Although we cannot present the full range of approaches designed to improve reading fluency, we present two methods that we feel are particularly effective for two varied classroom situations. The first, *cross-age reading* (Labbo & Teale, 1990), is designed for individual learners who are experiencing difficulty with their reading development. The second is a pair of strategies called *fluency-oriented reading instruction* (FORI) and *wide fluency–oriented reading instruction* (Wide FORI) (Kuhn et al., 2006); these are meant for groups of learners (whole classes or large groups) who are often at multiple reading levels.

Cross-Age Reading

It is often the case that older struggling readers do not want to be seen reading texts they feel are "childish," even though material written for young readers is somewhat challenging for them. Linda Labbo and Bill Teale (1990) developed an effective solution to this dilemma when they created the cross-age reading strategy. This approach provides readers with an alternative reason for reading texts written for younger learners. In their initial study, the authors asked struggling fifth graders to read aloud to kindergartners, using books that were likely to appeal to the younger students. This allowed the older learners to practice reading with relatively easy books, without appearing as if the goal was to improve their own reading. Rather, their goal was to perform eloquently for a younger audience.

Preparation for the read-alouds involved three steps: selecting texts that their audience would enjoy; practicing reading their selection aloud until their rendition was smooth and expressive; and learning how to engage the kindergartners in discussions of the books. Not only did the older students become more confident readers; they also became more competent readers (Labbo & Teale, 1990). The procedure had the added benefit of proving enjoyable for both the readers and those students listening to the story. And if it is not feasible for older students to work directly with younger learners, the older students could create recordings of books that could be placed in listening centers instead.

LESSON SNAPSHOT

The student or students participating in a cross-age reading project need to follow a three-step procedure:

1. Students should try to select texts that younger learners (i.e., students in grades K–2) will enjoy. At the same time, the books need to be challenging, but not too challenging, for the older readers. This is likely to require teacher guidance, at least initially. And, depending on the current reading levels of the older readers, these selections could be a relatively simple chapter book, such as *Porcupine's Pajama Party* (Harshman, 1988), or a more complex picture book, such as *Make Way for Ducklings* (McCloskey, 1941/1999).

2. Next, students practice reading the book until they are able to read it aloud fluently—that is, smoothly and with expression. In order to achieve this, the classroom teacher must determine when the students are ready for their performance. If the students are practicing the text primarily on their own, they should work with a selection that has approximately 90–95% accuracy on the initial reading. It they are reading in a supported manner (e.g., through echo reading of the selection), the initial accuracy level can be lower (85–90% accuracy). Of course, this will vary, depending on the readers' success with and motivation toward a given selection. And, importantly, as students' reading ability continues to improve, they should select increasingly challenging texts for their read-alouds.

3. Finally, it is critical that the readers learn to interact with their audience to ensure that there is a focus on comprehension. They can do this by asking a range of questions, from fact-based to inferential, that will require the listeners to think about and engage with the readings. This is also likely to require scaffolding from teachers, at least initially; such scaffolding may consist of simply showing readers how to pick appropriate stopping places for making predictions or asking why a character might have taken a certain action. By integrating this procedure, the readers will be developing a comprehension strategy as well as their fluency. And, should the integration of questions transfer to their own reading, it is likely to benefit their reading of other texts as well.

Fluency-Oriented Reading Instruction/Wide Fluency–Oriented Reading Instruction

In order to develop their fluency, students need to spend extensive time reading connected text. One way to ensure that this happens is to create whole-class instruction that focuses on integrating such reading into the literacy curriculum. FORI and Wide FORI (Kuhn et al., 2006) are just such strategies. They are designed to use the shared weekly text that is the backbone of many classrooms' literacy curriculum, whether that text is from a basal reader, a literature anthology, or a stand-alone trade book. Since such texts are often at the upper end of many students' instructional level, or even at a challenging level for some learners, these approaches integrate significant amounts of scaffolding. In fact, they were designed specifically to provide students with the support necessary to handle grade-level material that would otherwise be too difficult for them.

The strategies are designed to be both easy to implement and to incorporate significant amounts of scaffolded practice in one of two ways. FORI ensures that students have multiple opportunities to read a single selection over the course of the week, while Wide FORI involves the reading of several texts over the same period. Furthermore, because of the support provided, the texts used need to be challenging; we have found grade-level texts for striving readers and above-grade-level texts for more successful readers to be very effective. Next, it is essential that students spend at least 20–30 minutes per day reading connected text. This means that although poems and other short selections are an essential part of any literacy curriculum, they are too brief to be used for these approaches.

In fact, because these approaches can be implemented so easily, it is easy for them to be treated casually. However, unless attention is paid to text length, time on task, and purposeful implementation of the procedures, the approaches are less effective than they might otherwise be. That being said, when FORI and Wide FORI are implemented purposefully and with adequate attention to details, they have been shown to be more effective than alternatives such as round-robin reading or readers' workshop. And while some teachers find the regularity of these strategies a bit tedious, the vast majority of the students themselves very much enjoy them. The approaches have the additional benefit of providing students access to material that would be too difficult for them to read on their own, and thereby exposing them to richer vocabulary and a broader range of concepts than they would otherwise be able to access.

LESSON SNAPSHOT: FORI

Generally, the FORI procedure follows a 5-day lesson plan that allows one story per week to be covered.

Day 1
- Each week's selection should be introduced through prereading activities (e.g., discussing key vocabulary words, making predictions, developing the students' background knowledge).
- The text should then be read aloud while students follow along in their own copies. (Circulating around the room to ensure that students are following along, or asking some students to track the print, may be necessary at first to ensure that students are focusing on the text as it is read.)
- Students should then engage in a discussion of the story, in order to bring comprehension to the forefront of the week's lessons.

Day 2

- An echo reading of the text should take place. As students become increasingly familiar with the process of echo reading, the amount of text read before echoing back should become longer; this ensures that students are not relying on verbal memory to echo back the text.
- Throughout the reading of the text, it is important to integrate a focus on meaning rather than exclusively on word recognition. This can be done by integrating questions at appropriate pausing points, by summarizing sections of texts in pairs, by having students create questions that they want to ask about the story, or by using a number of additional comprehension strategies (Stahl, 2008).
- Students should read the selection at home for additional practice.

Day 3

- The third day consists of a choral or unison reading of the selection, with special attention paid to those students experiencing difficulty in keeping pace with their peers. These students should be asked to practice the text again independently at home or elsewhere.

Day 4

- A partner reading of the selection should occur on the fourth day. Initially, this should involve having partners alternate paragraphs, but the amount of text should increase until they are reading approximately a page of text at a time. If time permits, an additional reading of the text with learners reading alternate sections should occur. Again, circulating among partners provides room for evaluation, and assistance keeps students on task. Any student still reading dysfluently should be asked to read the text again independently at home.

Day 5

- The final day of the lesson should consist of extension activities designed to develop a richer understanding of the text (e.g., student-led discussions, written responses to the text, an artistic response to the selection, or any other effective postreading comprehension strategy).
- Students should read a self-selected book for homework.

WIDE FORI AND FORI: DIFFERENCES AND SIMILARITIES

The Wide FORI approach is similar to FORI, in that it is a heavily scaffolded instructional plan; however, it differs from FORI in that it involves the reading of three texts over the course of a week. As a result, it may require some creativity to ensure that enough reading material is available. In the original study (Kuhn et al., 2006), the school's basal reader or literature anthology was used as the first text, and grade-level trade books were provided for the second and third selections. Teachers might also consider older versions of basals, student magazines with substantive articles such as *My Weekly Reader* or *National Geographic Kids*, or material downloaded from the Internet (e.g., NASA's site for students) as sources of texts to be used in Wide FORI lessons.

Furthermore, multiple copies from several classrooms and the school library can often be combined for a class set of a given trade book. Any of these could be resources for the second and third texts.

In terms of similarities, both the FORI and Wide FORI approaches are 5-day programs that are relatively easy to implement as part of a shared reading program. Next, comprehension is in the forefront of both methods. Third, they both require students to spend a minimum of 20–30 minutes per day reading connected text to ensure substantial growth; therefore, it is critical that selected texts be substantive enough to deserve the focus of such a daily reading lesson. Finally, classroom-based research has shown both FORI and Wide FORI to be successful (Kuhn et al., 2006). In fact, the students using both approaches made significantly greater growth on standardized measures of comprehension and word recognition in isolation than did their peers who used a range of alternative reading methods. However, the students using the Wide FORI approach also did better in terms of correct words read per minute. As a result, we feel the evidence indicates that Wide FORI is the preferable choice.

LESSON SNAPSHOT: WIDE FORI

Again, the Wide FORI procedure focuses on three texts over a 5-day period. The first text incorporates a limited amount of repetition, whereas the second and third texts typically involve a single reading.

Day 1
- The text that is to be the week's primary focus is introduced on Day 1 in a manner that parallels the FORI approach. This involves prereading activities such as building background knowledge, making predictions, and preteaching important terms that the students will encounter as they read the text.
- Next, the text is read aloud while students follow along in their own copies. (Again, circulating around the room to ensure that students are following along, or asking some students to track the print, may be necessary at first to ensure that students are focusing on the text as it is read.)
- Finally, students should participate in a discussion of the selection, in order to ensure that comprehension is brought to the fore.

Day 2
- Day 2 consists of an echo reading of the week's primary text. As mentioned earlier, this process should begin with a paragraph or two—or even a sentence or two— until students become familiar with the procedure. This can be expanded—up to a page or two, depending upon the amount of text per page—to ensure that students are not relying on verbal memory.
- In addition to giving students the opportunity to develop their word recognition, it is important to work on expanding readers' comprehension of the selection on Day 2. As we have discussed for FORI, this can be done by integrating questions at appropriate pausing points, by summarizing sections of texts in pairs, by having students create questions that they want to ask about the story, or by using a number of additional comprehension strategies (Stahl, 2008).

- If time allows, students can partner-read the text at this point as well.
- Students should take home the selection for additional reading practice.

Day 3

- On Day 3, the Wide FORI lesson plan begins to diverge from its FORI counterpart. At this point, the focus shifts to postreading and extension activities to further students' comprehension (e.g., student-led discussions, written responses to the text, an artistic response to the selection, or any other effective postreading comprehension strategy).
- If students need additional practice, they should reread the primary text again for homework. On the other hand, if they are fairly fluent with this selection, they should choose another text that they want to read.

Days 4 and 5

- A second text is echo-read on Day 4, and a third text is echo-read on Day 5. Since these texts may only be read once as a class, it is important that comprehension be integrated into the lesson either through a structured activity (such as a directed reading–thinking activity) or through informal questioning and discussion.
- If there is sufficient time available, a second reading should be conducted (e.g., an additional echo, choral, or partner reading).
- Students should also read each of these texts for homework to receive additional practice.

SUMMARY OF BIG IDEAS FROM RESEARCH

- Phonemic awareness makes an essential contribution to early reading success (Ehri & Roberts, 2006; Hulme et al., 2002; Share et al., 1984).
- The ability to discriminate between letter forms and assign the correct names to each letter supports early decoding success (National Early Literacy Panel, 2008).
- Knowledge of concepts of print is associated with early success in decoding and spelling and with comprehension (National Early Literacy Panel, 2008).
- Both explicit/systematic instruction on basic phonics skills and opportunities to practice transferring new phonics knowledge to the reading of connected text support young readers in the early phases of word recognition (Tunmer & Nicholson, 2011).
- Effective teachers coach children as they read texts by providing cues that encourage them to use sound–symbol relationships and meaning when they encounter words that are not recognized initially (Taylor et al., 2000).
- Fluency acts as a bridge between decoding and comprehension by incorporating accurate and automatic word recognition with attending to prosodic elements of language such as stress, pitch, and phrasing (Casteel, 1988; Cromer, 1970; Pikulski & Chard, 2005; Weiss, 1983).
- Fluent reading develops through rereading of familiar texts or wide reading across a range of texts (Chomsky, 1976; Kuhn, 2004/2005; Samuels, 1979).

LOOKING FORWARD

The myriad instructional approaches for constrained skills described in this chapter serve as indicators of the strength of literacy instruction available to teachers of young learners. We firmly believe not only that it is possible to create contextualized literacy instruction of constrained skills for young learners, but that this instruction is more effective because it clearly relates to the reading of connected text. (For more on a print-rich environment, see Sailors, Kumar, Blady, & Willson, Chapter 2, this volume.) Furthermore, we feel that such instruction not only better helps students as they gain comfort with the mechanics of print, but provides them with a broader base for their development of unconstrained skills. Ultimately, by creating such instruction, we are helping students not only to develop automaticity in their responses to certain components of the reading process, but to become skilled, engaged readers as well.

We hope that this chapter (along with the work of others we have cited throughout) encourages teachers to reflect upon their instruction of the skills related to word recognition and fluency, and to consider whether these skills are taught in connection with real reading and writing tasks. Because so many of the skills that support accurate and automatic word recognition are constrained skills (Paris, 2005, 2009), we also call for teachers to differentiate their teaching of these skills as much as possible. Once children have acquired phonemic awareness or the basic phonics skills, they should not spend considerable periods of time working with these skills. Instead, they should be engaged in new, more challenging activities that bring them closer to skillful, fluent reading. For example, in the case of phonics instruction, research has demonstrated that providing opportunities to read connected texts is the most beneficial activity after the basics have been acquired (Tunmer & Nicholson, 2011). We also encourage teachers to begin paying attention to the ways in which they coach young readers who are making attempts to use various strategies for reading initially unrecognized words. Finally, we hope that this chapter clarifies both the meaning of and the role of fluent reading. Fluency is an important link between decoding and comprehension; it is more than accurate and automatic recognition of words (Pikulski & Chard, 2005). By offering students opportunities to practice attending to the prosodic features of language (stress, pitch, and phrasing) when reading, we support their ability to comprehend texts.

QUESTIONS FOR REFLECTION ⊕ ⊕ ⊕ ⊕ ⊕ ⊕ ⊕ ⊕ ⊕ ⊕ ⊕ ⊕ ⊕ ⊕ ⊕ ⊕ ⊕ ⊕

1. Do I use informal classroom-based assessments to determine whether each of my students has acquired the constrained skills that support word recognition (phonological awareness, phonemic awareness, phonics skills)?

2. Do I provide systematic, explicit instruction to students who have not yet acquired these foundational skills?

3. Do I shift the focus of instruction to the reading of texts for children who demonstrate knowledge of the basic phonics skills?

4. Do I provide all students (including those still acquiring foundational skills, such as knowledge of phonics) with opportunities to practice using these skills in the reading and writing of connected text?

5. Do I provide coaching to children as they attempt to read unfamiliar words in connected text?

6. Do I engage students in instructional routines that foster fluency, or reading that is both accurate and automatic with regard to word recognition, but also attends to prosodic elements such as stress, pitch, and phrasing?

SUGGESTIONS FOR ONGOING PROFESSIONAL LEARNING • • • • • •

Below we outline two potential inquiry projects. The first project is focused on word recognition instruction, and the second is focused on fluency instruction.

Word Recognition Inquiry Project

With a group of grade-level colleagues (if possible), examine your instructional practices around word recognition. At your first meeting, you might consider these questions:

1. Do we have a systematic curriculum in place for helping children develop phonological and phonemic awareness and alphabet knowledge (preschool and kindergarten) or phonics (kindergarten through second grade)?
2. Do we use informal assessments to determine which students have already acquired the target skills?
3. Do we connect the teaching of these word-level skills to authentic children's literature?
4. Do we coach children in the use of their newly acquired word recognition skills as they read?

Select one or more of the questions above to serve as a focus of your inquiry. Agree to review curricula, gather student work, or record observations related to the question you select before your second meeting. For example, if you decide to examine the use of informal assessments to determine students' current skill levels, you might collect the informal assessments that you currently use (and search for additional ones) and administer the assessments to some or all of your students.

At a second meeting, share the assessments that you use (or found) and the results of administering them. Discuss how these results match with your observations of these students and the instruction you are currently providing. To continue with the example above, if you administered the Informal Phonics Survey (McKenna & Stahl, 2009) and found that a group of your students are able to utilize the phonics elements currently being taught and some elements that you have not yet formally addressed, consider how you might differentiate instruction for these students.

Fluency Inquiry Project

With a group of grade-level colleagues (if possible), examine your instructional practices around fluency. At your first meeting, you might consider these questions:

1. What instructional methods do you use to help students attend to the prosodic aspects of fluency (stress, pitch, and phrasing)?
2. Do you provide opportunities for students to practice these features in the context of reading authentic texts?
3. Do you use either of the approaches to developing fluency described in this chapter: cross-age reading or FORI/Wide FORI?

Select one or more of the questions above to serve as a focus of your inquiry. Agree to review curricula, gather student work, or record observations related to the question you select before your second meeting. For example, if you decide to try out Wide FORI, you might select appropriate materials and implement a 1-week cycle of Wide FORI with either a group of students or the entire class. At the end of the week, you would listen to the students (or select students) read a new passage and evaluate their progress with regard to fluency.

At a second meeting, you would share your findings with regard to fluency instruction in your classroom and discuss plans for modifying or strengthening that instruction. To continue with the example above, you would discuss the implementation of Wide FORI in each classroom and share observations regarding its effect on fluency. Then you would work together to plan changes to the implementation, or to gather new materials to support implementation for an additional period of time. Finally, you would agree to meet again after a second implementation trial to discuss the effectiveness of the approach for your students.

RESEARCH-BASED RESOURCES

Adams, M. J. (1990). *Beginning to read: Thinking and learning about print.* Cambridge, MA: MIT Press.

Bear, D. R., Invernizzi, M., Templeton, S., & Johnston, F. R. (2012). *Words their way: Word study for phonics, vocabulary, and spelling instruction* (5th ed.). Boston: Pearson/Allyn & Bacon.

Beck, I. L. (2006). *Making sense of phonics: The hows and whys.* New York: Guilford Press.

Clay, M. M. (2000). *Concepts about print: What have children learned about the way we print language?* Portsmouth, NH: Heinemann.

Cunningham, P. M. (2009). *Phonics they use: Words for reading and writing* (5th ed.). Boston: Pearson/Allyn & Bacon.

Johns, J. L., & Berglund, R. L. (2010). *Fluency: Differentiated interventions and process-monitoring assessments* (4th ed.). Dubuque, IA/Newark, DE: Kendall Hunt/International Reading Association.

Kuhn, M. R. (2009). *The hows and whys of fluency instruction.* Boston: Pearson/Allyn & Bacon.

Kuhn, M. R., & Schwanenflugel, P. J. (2008). *Fluency in the classroom.* New York: Guilford Press.

McKenna, M. C., & Stahl, K. A. D. (2009). *Assessment for reading instruction* (2nd ed.). New York: Guilford Press.

Pressley, M. (2006). *Reading instruction that works: The case for balanced teaching* (3rd ed.). New York: Guilford Press.

Rasinski, T., Blachowicz, C., & Lems, K. (2006). *Fluency instruction: Research-based best practices.* New York: Guilford Press.

Walpole, S., McKenna, M. C., & Philippakos, Z. A. (2011). *Differentiated reading instruction in grades 4 and 5: Strategies and resources.* New York: Guilford Press.

REFERENCES

Adams, M. J. (1990). *Beginning to read: Thinking and learning about print.* Cambridge, MA: MIT Press.

Adams, M. J., & Bruck, M. (1995). Resolving the "great debate." *American Educator, 8,* 7–20.

Anthony, J. L., Lonigan, C. J., Driscoll, K., Phillips, B. M., & Burgess, S. R. (2003). Phonological sensitivity: A quasi-parallel progression of word structure units and cognitive operations. *Reading Research Quarterly, 38,* 470–487.

Applegate, M. D., Applegate, A. J., & Modla, V. B. (2009). "She's my best reader; she just can't comprehend": Studying the relationship between fluency and comprehension. *The Reading Teacher, 62,* 512–521.

Beck, I., & Juel, C. (1995). The role of decoding in learning to read. *American Educator, 8,* 21–25, 39–42.

Blachman, B. A., Ball, E. W., Black, R. S., & Tangel, D. M. (1994). Kindergarten teachers develop phoneme awareness in low-income, inner-city classrooms: Does it make a difference? *Reading and Writing: An Interdisciplinary Journal, 6,* 1–18.

Bredekamp, S., & Pikulski, J. (2008, May). *Preventing reading difficulties in young children: Cognitive factors.* Keynote presented at the International Reading Association Preconference Institute #8, Atlanta, GA.

Bryant, P. E., Bradley, L., MacLean, M., & Crossland, J. (1989). Nursery rhymes, phonological skills and reading. *Journal of Child Language, 16,* 407–428.

Bus, A. J., & van IJzendoorn, M. H. (1988). Mother–child interactions, attachment, and emergent literacy: A cross-sectional study. *Child Development, 59,* 1262–1272.

Casteel, C. A. (1988). Effects of chunked reading among learning disabled students: An experimental comparison of computer and traditional chunked passages. *Journal of Educational Technology Systems, 17,* 115–121.

Chall, J. S. (1996). *Stages of reading development* (2nd ed.). Fort Worth, TX: Harcourt, Brace.

Chomsky, C. (1976). After decoding: What? *Language Arts, 53*(3), 288–296, 314.

Clark, K. F. (2004). What can I say besides "sound it out"?: Coaching word recognition in beginning reading. *The Reading Teacher, 57*(5), 440–450.

Clay, M. M. (1989). Concepts about print in English and other languages. *The Reading Teacher, 42*(4), 268–276.

Clay, M. M. (2000). *Concepts about print: What have children learned about the way we print language?* Portsmouth, NH: Heinemann.

Cromer, W. (1970). The difference model: A new explanation for some reading difficulties. *Journal of Educational Psychology, 61,* 471–483.

Dickinson, D. K., McCabe, A., Anastasopoulos, L., Peisner-Feinberg, E., & Poe, M. (2003). The comprehensive language approach to early literacy: The interrelationships among vocabulary, phonological sensitivity, and print knowledge among preschool-aged children. *Journal of Educational Psychology, 95,* 465–481.

Ehri, L. (1991). Development of the ability to read words. In R. Barr, M. Kamil, P. Mosenthal, & P. Pearson (Eds.), *Handbook of reading research* (Vol. 2, pp. 383–417). New York: Longman.

Ehri, L. (1994). Development of the ability to read words: Update. In R. Ruddell, M. Ruddell,

& H. Singer (Eds.), *Theoretical models and processes of reading* (4th ed., pp. 323–358). Newark, DE: International Reading Association.

Ehri, L. (1995). Phases of development in learning to recognize words by sight. *Journal of Research in Reading, 18*, 116–125.

Ehri, L. (1998). Grapheme–phoneme knowledge is essential for learning to read words in English. In J. Metsala & L. Ehri (Eds.), *Word recognition in beginning literacy* (pp. 3–40). Mahwah, NJ: Erlbaum.

Ehri, L., & McCormick, S. (1998). Phases of word learning: Implications for instruction with delayed and disabled readers. *Reading and Writing Quarterly: Overcoming Learning Difficulties, 14*(2), 135–163.

Ehri, L. C., & Roberts, T. (2006). The roots of learning to read and write: Acquisition of letters and phonemic awareness. In D. K. Dickinson & S. B. Neuman (Eds.), *Handbook of early literacy research* (Vol. 2, pp. 113–131). New York: Guilford Press.

Erekson, J. (2003, May). *Prosody: The problem of expression in fluency.* Paper presented at the annual meeting of the International Reading Association, Orlando, FL.

Faulkner, W. (1993). *Absalom, Absalom!* New York: Modern Library. (Original work published 1936)

Fletcher, J. M., Lyon, G. R., Fuchs, L. S., & Barnes, M. A. (2007). *Learning disabilities: From identification to intervention.* New York: Guilford Press.

Fox, M. (1993). *Time for bed.* San Diego, CA: Harcourt Brace Jovanovich.

Fox, M. (2002) *The magic hat.* San Diego, CA: Harcourt.

Gaskins, R. W., Gaskins, J. C., & Gaskins, I. W. (1991). A decoding program for poor readers—and the rest of the class, too! *Language Arts, 68*, 213–225.

Gaskins, R. W., Gaskins, J. C., & Gaskins, I. W. (1992). Using what you know to figure out what you don't know: An analogy approach to decoding. *Reading and Writing Quarterly, 8*, 197–221.

Gibson, E. J., & Levin, H. (1975). *The psychology of reading.* Cambridge, MA: MIT Press.

Good, R. H. III, Kaminski, R. A., Simmons, D., & Kame'enui, E. J. (2001). Using Dynamic Indicators of Basic Early Literacy Skills (DIBELS) in an outcomes-driven model: Steps to reading outcomes. *Oregon School Study Council, 44*, 6–24.

Goswami, U., & Bryant, P. E. (1990). *Phonological skills and learning to read.* Hillsdale, NJ: Erlbaum.

Griffith, P. L., & Olson, M. W. (1992). Phonemic awareness helps beginning readers break the code. *The Reading Teacher, 45*(7), 516–523.

Harshman, T. W. (1988). *Porcupine's pajama party.* New York: HarperTrophy.

Hoban, R. (1964). *Bread and jam for Frances.* New York: HarperCollins.

Hudson, R. F., Pullen, P. C., Lane, H. B., & Torgesen, J. K. (2009). The complex nature of reading fluency: A multidimensional view. *Reading and Writing Quarterly, 25*(1), 4–32.

Hulme, C., Hatcher, P. J., Nation, K., Brown, A., Adams, J., & Stuart, G. (2002). Phoneme awareness is a better predictor of early reading than onset-rime awareness. *Journal of Experimental Child Psychology, 82*(1), 2–28.

Juel, C., & Minden-Cupp, C. (2000). Learning to read words: Linguistic units and instructional strategies. *Reading Research Quarterly, 35*(4), 458–492.

Justice, L. M., Kaderavek, J. N., Fan, X., Sofka, A., & Hunt, A. (2009). Accelerating preschoolers' early literacy development through classroom-based teacher-child storybook reading and explicit print referencing. *Language, Speech, and Hearing Services in Schools, 40*(1), 67–85.

Kame'enui, E. J., Simmons, D. C., Good, R. H. III, & Harn, B. A. (2001). The use of fluency-based measures in early identification and evaluation of intervention efficacy in schools. In M. Wolf (Ed.), *Dyslexia, fluency, and the brain* (pp. 307–331). Timonium, MD: York Press.

Kuhn, M. R. (2004/2005). Helping students become accurate, expressive readers: Fluency instruction for small groups. *The Reading Teacher, 58,* 338–344.

Kuhn, M. R., & Schwanenflugel, P. J. (Eds.). (2008). *Fluency in the classroom.* New York: Guilford Press.

Kuhn, M. R., Schwanenflugel, P. J., & Meisinger, E. B. (2010). Aligning theory and assessment of reading fluency: Automaticity, prosody, and definitions of fluency. Invited review of the literature. *Reading Research Quarterly, 45,* 232–253.

Kuhn, M. R., Schwanenflugel, P. J., Morris, R. D., Morrow, L. M., Woo, D., Meisinger, B., et al. (2006). Teaching children to become fluent and automatic readers. *Journal of Literacy Research, 38,* 357–387.

Kuhn, M. R., & Stahl, S. (2003). Fluency: A review of developmental and remedial practices. *Journal of Educational Psychology, 95,* 3–21.

Labbo, L. D., & Teale, W. H. (1990). Cross age reading: A strategy for helping poor readers. *The Reading Teacher, 43,* 363–369.

LaBerge, D., & Samuels, S. J. (1974). Toward a theory of automatic information processing in reading. *Cognitive Psychology, 6*(2), 293–323.

Logan, G. D. (1997). Automaticity and reading: Perspectives from the instance theory of automatization. *Reading and Writing Quarterly, 13*(2), 123–146.

Mattingly, I. (1984). Reading, linguistic awareness, and language acquisition. In J. Downing & R. Valtin (Eds.), *Language awareness and learning to read* (pp. 9–25). New York: Springer-Verlag.

McCloskey, R. (1999). *Make way for ducklings.* New York: Puffin. (Original work published 1941)

McKenna, M. C., & Stahl, K. A. D. (2009). *Assessment for reading instruction* (2nd ed.). New York: Guilford Press.

Mostow, J., & Beck, J. (2005, June). *Micro-analysis of fluency gains in a reading tutor that listens.* Paper presented at the annual meeting of the Society for the Scientific Study of Reading, Toronto.

National Early Literacy Panel. (2008). *Developing early literacy: Report of the National Early Literacy Panel.* Washington, DC: National Institute for Literacy.

National Reading Panel. (2000). *Report of the National Reading Panel. Teaching children to read: An evidence-based assessment of the scientific research literature on reading and its implications for reading instruction* (NIH Publication No. 00-4769). Washington, DC: National Institute of Child Health and Human Development.

National Reading Panel. (2000). *Report of the National Reading Panel: Teaching children to read. Report of the subgroups.* Washington, DC: U.S. Department of Health and Human Services, National Institutes of Health.

OED Online. (2011). Phoneme. Retrieved from *www.oed.com/view/Entry/142626?redirectedFrom=phoneme.*

Paris, S. G. (2005). Reinterpreting the development of reading skills. *Reading Research Quarterly, 40*(2), 184–202.

Paris, S. G. (2009, December). *Constrained skills—so what?* Oscar Causey Address presented at the National Reading Conference, Orlando, FL.

Pikulski, J. (2005, May). *The critical nature of building vocabulary in early literacy.* Keynote presented at the International Reading Association Preconference Institute #8, San Antonio, TX.

Pikulski, J. J., & Chard, D. J. (2005). Fluency: Bridge between decoding and reading comprehension. *The Reading Teacher, 58,* 510–519.

Pressley, M. (2006). *Reading instruction that works: The case for balanced teaching* (3rd ed.). New York: Guilford Press.

Raffi. (1975). Willoughby Wallaby Woo. On *Singable songs for the very young* [CD]. Burlington, MA: Rounder Records.

Rasinski, T. V., Reutzel, C. R., Chard, D., & Linan-Thompson, S. (2011). Reading fluency. In M. L. Kamil, P. D. Pearson, E. B. Moje, & P. Afflerbach (Eds.), *Handbook of reading research* (Vol. 4, pp. 286–319). New York: Routledge.

Samuels, S. J. (1979). The method of repeated readings. *The Reading Teacher, 32*, 403–408.

Samuels, S. J. (2004). Toward a theory of automatic information processing in reading, revisited. In R. B. Ruddell & N. J. Unrau (Eds.), *Theoretical models and processes* (pp. 1127–1148). Newark, DE: International Reading Association.

Samuels, S. J. (2007). The DIBELS tests: Is speed of barking at print what we mean by reading fluency? *Reading Research Quarterly, 42*, 563–566.

Schickedanz, J. A. (1998). What is developmentally appropriate practice in early literacy: Considering the alphabet. In S. B. Neuman & K. A. Roskos (Eds.), *Children achieving: Best practices in early literacy* (pp. 20–37). Newark, DE: International Reading Association.

Schickedanz, J. A. (1990). *Adam's righting revolutions: One child's literacy development from infancy through grade one.* Portsmouth, NH: Heinemann.

Schickedanz, J. A., Schickedanz, D. I., & Forsyth, P. D. (1982). *Toward understanding children.* Boston: Little, Brown.

Schwanenflugel, P. J., Hamilton, C. E., Neuharth-Pritchett, S., Restrepo, M. A., Bradley, B. A., & Webb, M.-Y. (in press). PAVEd for Success: An evaluation of a comprehensive literacy program for 4-year-old children. *Journal of Literacy Research.*

Scotton, R. (2008). *Splat the cat.* New York: HarperCollins.

Shanahan, T. (2005, May). *Improving instruction for young children: Making sense of the National Literacy Panel.* Paper presented at the International Reading Association Preconference Institute #8, San Antonio, TX.

Share, D. L., Jorm, A. F., Maclean, R., & Matthews, R. (1984). Sources of individual differences in reading acquisition. *Journal of Educational Psychology, 76*(6), 1309–1324.

Slobodkina, E. (1987). *Caps for sale: A tale of a peddler, some monkeys and their monkey business.* New York: HarperCollins.

Stahl, K. A. D. (2008). Creating opportunities for comprehension within fluency-oriented reading. In M. R. Kuhn & P. J. Schwanenflugel (Eds.), *Fluency in the classroom* (pp. 55–74). New York: Guilford Press.

Stahl, S. A., Duffy-Hester, A. M., & Stahl, K. A. D. (1998). Everything you wanted to know about phonics (but were afraid to ask). *Reading Research Quarterly, 33*, 338–355.

Stanovich, K. E. (1992). Speculations on the causes and consequences of individual differences in early reading acquisition. In P. Gough, L. Ehri, & R. Trieman (Eds.), *Reading acquisition* (pp. 307–342). Hillsdale, NJ: Erlbaum.

Stanovich, K. E., Cunningham, A. E., & Freeman, D.]. (1984). Intelligence, cognitive skills and early reading progress. *Reading Research Quarterly, 14*, 278–303.

Sulzby, E. (1985). Children's emergent reading of favorite storybooks: A developmental study. *Reading Research Quarterly, 20*, 458–481.

Taylor, B. M., Pearson, P. D., Clark, K., & Walpole, S. (2000). Effective schools and accomplished teachers: Lessons about primary-grade reading instruction in low-income schools. *Elementary School Journal, 101*, 121–165.

Tompkins, G. E. (2010). *Literacy in the middle grades: Teaching reading and writing to fourth through eighth graders* (2nd ed.). Boston: Pearson.

Trachtenberg, P. (1990). Using children's literature to enhance phonics instruction. *The Reading Teacher, 45*, 648–653.

Treiman, R., & Broderick, V. (1998). What's in a name: Children's knowledge about the letters in their own names. *Journal of Experimental Child Psychology, 70*, 97–116.

Treiman, R., Weatherston, S., & Berch, D. (1994). The role of letter names in children's learning of phoneme–grapheme relations. *Applied Psycholinguistics, 15*(1), 97–122.

Tunmer, W. E., & Nicholson, T. (2011). The development and teaching of word recognition skill. In M. L. Kamil, P. D. Pearson, E. Birr Moje, & P. P. Afflerbach (Eds.), *Handbook of reading research* (pp. 405–431). New York: Routledge.

Walley, A. C., Metsala, J. L., & Garlock, V. M. (2003). Spoken vocabulary growth: Its role in the development of phoneme awareness and early reading ability. *Reading and Writing: An Interdisciplinary Journal, 16*, 5–20.

Weiss, D. S. (1983). The effects of text segmentation on children's reading comprehension. *Discourse Processes, 6*, 77–89.

Wharton-McDonald, R., Pressley, M., & Hampston, J. M. (1998). Outstanding literacy instruction in first grade: Teacher practices and student achievement. *Elementary School Journal, 99*, 101–128.

Wignell, E. (2004). *Shut the gate.* South Yarra, Victoria, Australia: Eleanor Curtain Publishing.

Wylie, R. E., & Durrell, D. D. (1970). Teaching vowels through phonograms. *Elementary English, 47*, 787–791.

Yaden, D., Smolkin, L., & Conlon, A. (1989). Preschoolers' questions about pictures, print conventions, and story text during reading aloud at home. *Reading Research Quarterly, 24*, 188–214.

Yopp, H. K. (1995). A test for assessing phonemic awareness in young children. *The Reading Teacher, 49*(1), 20–29.

Yopp, H. K., & Yopp, R. H. (2000). Supporting phonemic awareness development in the classroom. *The Reading Teacher, 54*(2), 130–143.

Yopp, H. K., & Yopp, R. H. (2009, January). Phonological awareness is child's play! *Beyond the Journal: Young Children in the Web.* Retrieved from *www.naeyc.org/files/yc/files/200901/BTJPhonologicalAwareness.pdf.*

CHAPTER 9

Today's Comprehension Strategy Instruction • • • • • • • • • • • • • •
"Not Your Father's Oldsmobile"

KATHERINE A. DOUGHERTY STAHL

Success in school depends on the ability to make sense of a range of different types of texts. In Kintsch's (1998) words, reading comprehension is a "paradigm for cognition." The RAND Reading Study Group (2002) defines comprehension as "the process of simultaneously extracting and constructing meaning through interaction and involvement with written language" (p. 11). Whether one is reading for enjoyment, for a deep literary experience, or for new information, comprehension is the key.

The foundational skills described by Johnson and Kuhn in Chapter 8 act in service to the successful acquisition of reading comprehension. They are necessary but not sufficient for children to become proficient at making sense of the texts they read. As we begin our discussion of comprehension, *constrained-skills theory* (Paris, 2005) can help us understand and address some of the ways that comprehension instruction and assessment are more complex than the instruction and assessment of the constrained skills of phonemic awareness, phonics, and fluency (see Stahl, 2011). As an unconstrained skill, comprehension is different from the constrained skills that are learned to mastery levels within a short time period. Comprehension is learned across a lifetime. It is never fully mastered because proficiency varies by text difficulty, genre, task, and instructional context. Both instruction and assessment must be considerate of these dimensions of comprehension.

Therefore, although we certainly want to be thorough, explicit, and systematic in teaching the constrained skills in the primary grades, recent research has demonstrated that we also want to be intentional and assertive in our attention to comprehension instruction as early as preschool and throughout the primary grades (Dooley, 2010; Shanahan et al., 2010; Solari & Gerber, 2008; Stahl, 2008b, 2009). Providing opportunities for children to be accountable for making sense of a wide range of texts for a range of purposes should span the entire school experience.

The present chapter through Chapter 17 of this volume provide research on and examples of some effective ways for teachers to address the multiple dimensions of the comprehension process (see Figure 9.1). In this chapter, I focus on effective comprehension strategy instruction, one aspect of the comprehension curriculum that is supported by a robust research base. In addition to the classic studies that are the foundation for strategy instruction, I focus on the instructional implications of recent research that changes the face of traditional strategy instruction in important ways.

First, I provide a brief review of research on effective strategy instruction and discuss considerations for linguistically or academically diverse learners. Next is a description of three models of comprehension strategy instruction in action in real classrooms. Finally, I describe some ways that teachers can engage in professional development to enhance comprehension strategy instruction in their own classrooms.

OVERVIEW OF RESEARCH

Any discussion of comprehension strategies must begin with a definition. The National Reading Panel (2000) report, like some other documents, was a bit confusing because it addressed cognitive strategies and teaching strategies collectively in its section on comprehension. Also misleading is the set of skills that might be listed in a core reading program or the item analysis for a standardized test. *Strategies are intentional cognitive actions undertaken by readers in the initial stages of learning a new skill or at the point of reading difficulty* (Afflerbach, Pearson, & Paris, 2008). Paris, Lipson, and Wixson

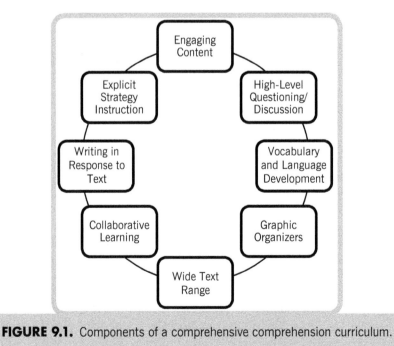

FIGURE 9.1. Components of a comprehensive comprehension curriculum.

(1983) describe reading strategies as "skills under consideration," to indicate that the same action might be a skill or a strategy, depending on the reader's intention and control of the reading task. Simply put, *skills* tend to be automatic, fluid, and effortless, but cognitive *strategies* are deliberate mental efforts by a reader to help remember or gain a deeper understanding of the text. To avoid confusion when referring to what teachers do, I use the term *technique*.

What Strategies Should Be Taught?

Deciding what strategies to teach does not have to be confusing, even though a few research syntheses have recommended slightly different strategies depending on the criteria being used for inclusion in the synthesis (National Reading Panel, 2000; Shanahan et al., 2010; Stahl, 2004). Most of the comprehension studies that were included in the National Reading Panel report were conducted in grades 3–6. The Shanahan and colleagues (2010) and Stahl (2004) reviews looked exclusively at studies conducted in grades K–3. However, in general, the converging research supports from strong to moderate levels the instruction of the strategies in Table 9.1.

How to Teach Strategies

Although it is important to explicitly teach each strategy individually, strategies need to be viewed as a repertoire (Brown, Pressley, Van Meter, & Schuder, 1996; Palincsar & Brown, 1984; Schuder, 1993). You might consider teaching comprehension strategies as being analogous to planning a meal. In planning a dinner party, you would be mindful of the total menu and how the foods will work together, but you would look up the individual recipes. In preparing the meal, you might have a few dishes cooking simultaneously, but you always have an eye on the preparation of each dish as a separate entity. The actual meal incorporates all of the dishes, some individually and others simultaneously. The beverage, like monitoring, is there from start to finish.

Research indicates that an explicit approach to teaching the individual strategies is useful (Baumann & Schmitt, 1986; Duffy, 1993a; Paris et al., 1983). The direct instructional model should include *declarative, procedural,* and *conditional* knowledge. First, teachers share an explicit description of the strategy with the students (declarative knowledge). In addition, they describe a procedure for applying the strategy or how to do it. Conditional knowledge includes a discussion of why the strategy is useful, when it is useful, and when it is not likely to be useful as an aid to comprehension. See the box on page 227 for an example of how one teacher explicitly taught purposeful predictions.

Because of the complexity of teaching comprehension strategies, most experts recommend applying a *gradual release of responsibility* (Baumann & Schmitt, 1986; Brown & Coy-Ogan, 1993; Pearson & -Gallagher, 1983; Pressley et al., 1992). The gradual release of responsibility begins with explicit instruction by the teacher, who over time releases more responsibility to the students for assuming ownership of strategy application (see Figure 9.2). Typically, after the direct instruction of the strategy, a teacher might model the strategy, followed by students modeling the application of the strategy. Before the children are asked to be responsible for engaging in the activity independently, there would be a series of scaffolded experiences moving from highly supported contexts to

TABLE 9.1. Comprehension Strategies Supported by Research

Strategy	Description	Instructional implications and supportive teaching techniques
Targeted activation of prior knowledge and purposeful predictions	Students activate their existing, relevant knowledge and integrate it with text-based information to hypothesize what will happen in the text, followed by verification and taking stock.	In a targeted way, support students to make connections between their existing knowledge and what is likely to be in the text. Use DL/R-TA; RT.
Text structure: Narrative and expository	Students are able to use the organizational structure of narrative and informational texts to enhance meaning making and recall.	Explicitly teach both narrative and expository text structures, using the visual support of graphic organizers (including story maps).
Visualizing	Students create a mental image or representation of text.	Display a concrete object, then conceal; ask students to describe their mental image of the object. Gradually make the transition to sentences and shorter pieces of text, modeling the text cues that help us create mental images.
Questions: Answering high-level questions and generating questions	Students can both answer and ask important questions about the text.	Answering questions: Students are taught question–answer relationships or the source of the answers to teacher-generated questions. Use Right There, Think and Search, Author and Me, In My Head (Raphael, 1986). Asking questions: Common question stems are taught, practiced, and posted. Question stems might be common words like *when*, *why*, and *how*, or stems related to common text elements (e.g., "The character said _____; what does that tell you about him?"). Use RT.
Taking stock/ summarizing/ retelling	Either orally or in writing, students can identify and report the key elements of a text.	During reading, stop periodically to ask children to describe the text events or information in their own words. Teach summary writing by physically limiting the number of words permitted to describe the key elements of increasingly longer pieces of text.
Generating inferences	Students retrieve information related to the text that is not explicitly stated, and they are able to generate new ideas based on text concepts (deductive reasoning).	Engage students in high-level questioning that focuses attention on causal lines in stories. Include both teacher and student think-alouds during the reading of complex texts. Include attention to critical analysis of the texts.

(continued)

TABLE 9.1. *(continued)*

Strategy	Description	Instructional implications and supportive teaching techniques
Monitoring and applying fix-up strategies	Students are aware of the need to make sense of text in an ongoing way, to identify any point at which they do not understand either the vocabulary or ideas in a text, and to decide what they might do to overcome comprehension hurdles.	Using a collection of very short text selections with a wide complexity band, students may be taught to decide whether their reading is "clicking" or "clunking." Fix-up strategies including decoding strategies, rereading, leveling the degree of confusion, and peer collaboration may be taught and posted.

Explicitly Teaching Purposeful Predictions: An Example

Declarative Knowledge: Making a purposeful prediction means thinking about what might happen next or what we are likely to learn about in an informational text, based on our experience and other clues found in the book. A purposeful prediction is *not* a wild guess about what we think is going to happen. We must use evidence. We must use clues.

Conditional Knowledge: We use purposeful predictions to help us stay focused as we read, to help us connect new information with what we already know, and to help us remember the story or important information.

Procedural Knowledge: We can make purposeful predictions for stories and informational texts *that we have never read before.* We can make them before we begin reading a book or story, and we make them at certain stopping points while we are reading for the next section or chapter, or even within a chapter. During reading, as we stop to take stock, we can check to see whether our prediction was on target (verifying). Then we can make a purposeful prediction to help us get ready to read the next bit. To make a prediction, we look at the title and think about what we know about the topic or what the story might be likely to be about. If it's an informational book, we can look at the table of contents and, based on what we know, predict what information the author might be telling us in each chapter. As we get inside the book, we can also use the pictures. Finally, we know that stories and books work in certain predictable ways. We know that stories usually have some problem that the character is trying to solve, so we can use that knowledge to anticipate what might happen next. In informational books, we know that headings can provide good clues about what the page or text section will be about. Good readers use all of these tools to make powerful and purposeful predictions.

Teaching Tip: Create a personal script like this for each strategy in Table 9.1.

Task	Share of Responsibility for the Task				
Explicit Strategy Instruction					
Modeling					
Collaborative Use					
Guided Practice					
Independent Application					

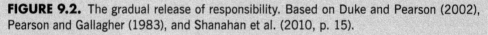 Students   ☐ Teachers

FIGURE 9.2. The gradual release of responsibility. Based on Duke and Pearson (2002), Pearson and Gallagher (1983), and Shanahan et al. (2010, p. 15).

less supportive contexts. Children might engage in a sequence of collaborative activities likely to include Think–Pair–Share within a whole-class discussion, a teacher-led small group, a student-led small group, or partner activity before the students ever assume independent responsibility for an accountable product (such as a summary or story map). The grouping practices described by Taylor in Chapter 3 allow for collaborative application and guided practice in using the strategy in isolation, or combinations of multiple strategies, to enhance the meaning-making process. In addition, posters, bookmarks, and other physical scaffolds may help students move from external to internal application of the strategies.

Instructional Protocols for Strategy Instruction

Several instructional protocols are effective ways to introduce and apply strategies before, during, and after text reading. In addition to supporting students, the application of these approaches can provide scaffolding for teachers who want to begin using strategy instruction in their classrooms. Although research shows that instruction in a single strategy can improve comprehension (e.g., Gambrell & Jawitz, 1993; Morrow, 1985; Rosenshine, Meister, & Chapman, 1996), evidence seems to indicate that efficacious readers use multiple strategies in flexible ways (Cartwright, 2009; Kintsch, 1998; Paris & Hamilton, 2009; Pressley & Afflerbach, 1995). As a result, several researchers have developed instructional protocols that incorporate multiple strategies and hold students accountable for orchestrating them as needed during the reading process (Gaskins, Anderson, Pressley, Cunicelli, & Satlow, 1993; Klingner, Vaughn, Arguelles, Hughes, & Leftwich, 2004; Klingner, Vaughn, Hughes, Schumm, & Elbaum, 1998; Palincsar & Brown, 1984; Paris et al., 1983; Schuder, 1993). These protocols are intended to

Definiton of scaffold (handwritten annotation)

be temporary scaffolds or ways to make visible the internal cognitive processing. It is also important to note that the following three protocols integrate strategy and discussion, so it is difficult to separate the contribution of each (Palincsar, 1986).

Directed Reading/Listening–Thinking Activity

The *Directed Reading/Listening–Thinking Activity* (DR/L-TA) is an instructional framework that engages children in thinking and talking about texts that they have listened to or read. The simplicity of the procedure and its robust research base enable it to serve as a good introduction to strategies for children and teachers alike (Baumann, Seifert-Kessell, & Jones, 1992; Davidson & Wilkerson, 1988; Stahl, 2008b; Stauffer, 1969). The teacher's role is to select an instructional-level text, divide the text into meaningful sections, and facilitate the discussion of each section. Students are responsible for establishing their own purposes for reading, generating predictions, justifying those predictions, independently reading the text, and verifying or revising predictions based on evaluations of information in the text during the teacher-led discussion of each section of text. Stauffer (1969) has recommended the use of the DR/L-TA with narrative or non-narrative text at all grade levels.

Reciprocal Teaching

Reciprocal teaching (RT; Palincsar & Brown, 1984) is an instructional activity that takes place during reading with the purpose of gaining meaning from text and self-monitoring. The teacher and students engage in a discussion about a segment of text structured by four strategies: summarizing, questioning, clarifying, and predicting (Palincsar & Brown, 1984). Initially, the teacher teaches each of these strategies individually for the students. After the strategies have been taught, the students take turns leading the discussion about each segment of text. Each student leader facilitates a dialogue that focuses on the four strategies. Typically, the students read a segment of text. Then a student discussion leader asks a question about the important information in the text; the other students answer the question and may suggest others. The student leader leads the group in clarifying any impediments to comprehension. Then he or she summarizes the text and predicts what is likely to come next, encouraging additional input from the group. The process is repeated as the children read each section of text, followed by a different student leading the discussion. RT has effectively been implemented in all grade levels, with both good and poor readers and with a range of text types.

Transactional Strategy Instruction

Transactional strategy instruction (TSI) is a term used to describe a body of practices that are transactional in three senses: (1) Readers link the text to prior knowledge; (2) meaning construction reflects the group and differs from personal interpretations; and (3) the dynamics of the group determine the responses of all members, including the teacher. These practices were designed to systematize strategy instruction while allowing for flexible use of multiple strategies to prompt reader engagement (Brown & Coy-Ogan, 1993; Brown et al., 1996; Gaskins et al., 1993; Schuder, 1993). Each strategy is taught explicitly, but the text discussions incorporate all of the strategies in organic ways. TSI is long term, and the strategies act as the vehicle for text discussions. TSI also applies a gradual-release-of-responsibility instructional model (Pearson & Gallagher, 1983), with the goal being to transform students into independent, self-regulating readers. Although the original research studies applied TSI predominantly with narrative texts, Reutzel, Smith, and Fawson (2005) demonstrated that the protocol was effective in supporting students in their recall and elaborations of the content in informational texts.

Concerns and Cautions Regarding Strategy Protocols

There do seem to be some issues surrounding comprehension repertoire protocols, and teachers need to attend to these as they implement strategy instruction. It is important for teachers and school administrators to remember that the purpose of strategy instruction is to enhance meaning making, not to require perfect strategy application. The goal is for children to use the strategies in flexible, responsive ways that help them overcome comprehension hurdles. Teachers need to guard against protocols becoming so rote that mental engagement is compromised. A protocol should only serve as a temporary scaffold until children can apply the strategies flexibly as needed. Ideally, the strategies become internalized, but the protocols may be revisited and applied as new genres or more difficult texts are encountered.

What's New in Strategy Research?

Much of the research on strategy instruction was conducted in the late 1980s or early 1990s. However, new research about the role of strategy instruction in a comprehensive literacy program is ongoing. Recently, there has been an increased emphasis on conducting strategy instruction with children in the primary grades during teacher read-alouds and as they read a wide range of text genres (Dooley, 2010; Garcia, Pearson, Taylor, Bauer, & Stahl, 2011; Stahl, 2008b, 2009; Williams et al., 2002). In addition, there is evidence to indicate that comprehension is not restricted to a single medium (print, video, audio) (Coiro & Dobler, 2007; Kendeou et al., 2006), and that comprehension instruction of young children can be fortified with videos (Goldman, Varma, Sharp, & Cognition and Technology Group at Vanderbilt, 1999; Kendeou, Bohn-Gettler, White, & van den Broek, 2008; Kendeou et al., 2006). These studies did not engage children in "strategy instruction," but the researchers discussed and held children accountable for predicting, retelling, and making inferences, indicating that we can provide children with developmentally appropriate contexts for thinking about narratives and informational resources in ways that will support them on the road to becoming successful, thoughtful readers.

Finally, there is still ambivalence regarding whether the strategies themselves or the deep thinking that occurs during strategy application actually causes improvements in reading comprehension (Rosenshine & Meister, 1994; Rosenshine et al., 1996; Taylor, Pearson, Garcia, Stahl, & Bauer, 2006). At its best, strategy instruction teaches children how to mentally process a wide range of texts in dynamic, flexible ways in order to make meaning. However, engagement is compromised when strategies are taught in a formulaic fashion, without the students assuming increasing responsibility for selecting and applying the most useful strategies. When strategies are taught in rigid, routinized ways, the very thinking that yields text comprehension is absent (Hacker & Tenant, 2002). When approached in this manner, strategy instruction is likely to be less effective than other instructional approaches (McKeown, Beck, & Blake, 2009).

In brief, the research seems to indicate that a good comprehension program does not rely on strategy instruction alone, but includes many other elements, including deliberate opportunities for high-level conversation and writing in response to or related to reading (see Figure 9.1). More in-depth information on discussions, conversations, vocabulary, concept learning, and writing in response to text can be found in Chapters 10 through 17 of this book.

Meeting All Students' Needs

Classroom teachers can take comfort in knowing that good strategy instruction is also effective in meeting the needs of children with diverse academic needs and children who come to school with diverse linguistic needs. The only difference is that these populations actually rely more heavily than the general population on thorough and explicit instruction of strategies in intentional ways.

Diverse Academic Needs

Reviews of comprehension interventions applied with students who had learning disabilities determined that explicit strategy instruction and a few other instructional enhancements yielded strong positive results (Berkeley, Scruggs, & Mastropieri, 2010; Gersten, Fuchs, Williams, & Baker, 2001). Text enhancements, including things like graphic organizers and question placement within the text, seem to encourage thinking during reading. Berkeley and colleagues (2010) determined that many additional characteristics, such as peer mediation and training in self-regulation, could be useful. For children who have encountered repeated failure in reading, self-regulation, and attribution assume increasing importance. *Attribution means the degree to which a child associates his or her own actions with success or failure.* Often struggling readers possess a "can't do" attitude, or they assume other children are successful because they are "smarter" or "good readers." Teaching children how to regulate their own reading by setting goals, monitoring, and applying strategies can be empowering. It makes explicit what was previously unseen and mysterious. RT (Klingner & Vaughn, 1996; Palincsar & Brown, 1984), *collaborative strategic reading* (CST; Klingner et al., 1998, 2004; Klingner & Vaughn, 1999), and *peer-assisted learning strategies* (PALS; Fuchs, Fuchs, Mathes, & Simmons, 1997) are all examples of strategy repertoire protocols that engage students in working collaboratively with peers to make sense of text. All engage children in using a few basic strategies, including predicting, summarizing, questioning, and monitoring. Research studies have demonstrated the effectiveness of these protocols for children with reading difficulties.

Diverse Linguistic Needs

Because of the dynamic, unconstrained nature of comprehension, the instruction of students who are English language learners (ELLs) assumes increasing importance because there are so many things that can hinder the meaning-making process. Background knowledge, vocabulary, and figurative language are all potential comprehension traps for ELLs who are reading a text written in U.S. English. Therefore, strategy application assumes an increasingly important role (Jiménez, García, & Pearson, 1996; Langer, Bartolomé, Vasquez, & Lucas, 1990).

The Center for Research on Education, Diversity and Excellence (CREDE) has promoted a great deal of research involving children who are linguistically diverse (*http://crede.berkeley.edu*). Their standards for effective pedagogy include the application of language and literacy across the curriculum, teaching complex thinking, teaching through conversation, and relating student experiences to curriculum. A series of studies in comprehension involved the use of theme-based instruction, explicit instruction in strategies, and instructional conversations (Saunders & Goldenberg, 1999). These studies found that the integration of strategy instruction, response writing, and small-group discussion around engaging themes increased the likelihood that students who were ELLs could overcome comprehension hurdles.

SUMMARY OF BIG IDEAS FROM RESEARCH

- Teach comprehension strategies across the grade levels, beginning with the youngest students, and using a range of genres and complexity bands of texts (Dooley, 2010; Garcia et al., 2011; Shanahan et al., 2010; Stahl, 2008b, 2009; Williams et al., 2002).
- Teach strategies explicitly, applying a gradual release of responsibility (National Reading Panel, 2000; Pearson & Gallagher, 1983; Shanahan et al., 2010).
- Hold students accountable for orchestrating multiple strategies in responsive ways to make sense of texts and to expand their knowledge about the world (Brown & Coy-Ogan, 1993; Brown et al., 1996; Gaskins et al., 1993; Schuder, 1993).
- Expand strategy instruction to include text enhancements, graphic organizers, and methods of self-regulation when students have learning difficulties (Klingner et al., 1998, 2004; Klingner & Vaughn, 1999).
- Be deliberate in integrating strategy instruction with small-group discussion and response writing around rich disciplinary (literature, science, social studies) content when students are ELLs (*http://crede.berkeley.edu*; Jiménez et al., 1996; Langer et al., 1990; Saunders & Goldenberg, 1999).

EXAMPLES OF EFFECTIVE PRACTICES

Much of the research about comprehension instruction is based on studies of expert readers. Researchers determined the behaviors that good readers used to attain high levels of comprehension, and then the researchers developed instructional practices that would enable teachers to foster these behaviors in their students. Because of the multidimensional quality of comprehension, it is hard teaching. A classic study by Durkin (1976) determined that most teachers asked their students questions about texts or gave assignments about texts, but that very little instruction on *how* to comprehend a text was provided. In essence, as teachers, we have tended to assess rather than to instruct comprehension. In today's classrooms, teachers may confront two additional and equally challenging dilemmas hindering the kind of sustained instruction that characterizes the most effective comprehension instruction. On one hand, increased pressure to raise standardized test scores may limit comprehension instruction in some schools to teaching children to answer literal to low-level inference questions found on standardized tests. At the other extreme, well-intentioned teachers may allocate large blocks of time to independent, self-selected student reading that is only discussed briefly and superficially in a conference. Missing in both approaches is the opportunity to expand thinking to the new perspectives and cognitive frontiers described as the goal in Kintsch's (1998) comprehension model.

In this section of the chapter, I provide some real classroom examples of how teachers incorporated strategy instruction into a comprehensive literacy program. The following three examples move from the most discreet use of strategy instruction to a model that is content-driven and strategy-embedded. All three models are research-based. Teachers can feel confident that applying any one of the three models is likely to be effective in improving student comprehension. However, novice teachers may feel more comfortable starting with the structures provided in Model 1, Synthesized Comprehension Instruction, and over time moving gradually toward the more integrative Models 2 and 3, Modified Transactional Strategies Instruction and Concept-Oriented Reading Instruction. In essence, what is provided below could serve as a gradual release of responsibility for teachers.

Model 1: Synthesized Comprehension Instruction

Engagement seems to be a crucial component in reading comprehension. Both open-ended discussions and strategy instruction are means to get students to engage with texts in ways that result in high levels of comprehension. In addition, prior knowledge and vocabulary strongly influence the meaning-making process. *Synthesized comprehension instruction* (SCI) brings together cognitive strategy instruction (purposeful prediction, visualizing, taking stock/summarizing, questioning, and monitoring), responsive engagement (instructional conversations, theme identification, personal connections), and vocabulary instruction to form a comprehensive model of comprehension instruction (Garcia et al., 2011; Stahl, 2009; Stahl, Garcia, Bauer, Pearson, & Taylor, 2006; Taylor et al., 2006). Teachers in grades 2–5 applied SCI three times a week for 30–45 minutes, using their existing curriculum materials.

Typically, the instruction was carried out during the shared reading of grade-level texts. Teachers discovered that for strategy instruction, provocative conversations, and even rich vocabulary development, it was important to use *heavy texts* (Stahl, 2008a). Heavy narrative texts have well-developed plots, sophisticated vocabulary, and compelling themes. Informational texts are considered heavy texts if they introduce new concepts and present open-ended or controversial issues. Little books, particularly in the lower grades, did not have the content or vocabulary needed to stimulate rich instruction and discussion. Therefore, teachers tended to use stories found in their grade-level basal readers or other authentic literature, especially award-winning books that addressed multicultural and contemporary issues. Rather than applying a protocol, the teachers adhered to a set of principles that incorporated explicit strategy instruction, responsive engagement, and elaborated vocabulary instruction. Based on monthly observations and the teachers' lesson plans, the lessons tended to include all of the components but to emphasize certain components at particular points of the lesson (see Table 9.2).

TABLE 9.2. Synthesized Comprehension Instruction

	Vocabulary	Strategy	Responsive engagement
Before reading	Essential	Activation of prior knowledge Purposeful predictions	Targeted connections
During reading	Point of contact	**All as needed**	Connections Critique
After reading	Elaborated	Clarification Summarizing	**Themes** **Connections** **Critique**

Note. **Boldfaced** areas receive emphasis at that point of instruction.

Early in the year, the children had whole-class lessons on each of the strategies individually; ways to generate "juicy," higher-order, open-ended questions; and conversational conventions. Using think-alouds, the teachers modeled their own use of strategies, question generation, theme identification, and recognition of personal connections. While still operating in the whole-class setting, teachers conducted Think–Pair–Share conversations to model the components further. Next, teachers led small-group instruction that incorporated the components. Often these groups were conducted with instructional-level texts, particularly when strategies such as summarization or question generation were being practiced. This was followed by teachers sitting "on the side" as students assumed responsibility for leading the small-group conversations. These small-group conversations might take the form of RT (during reading) or instructional conversations (after reading). During the instructional conversations, the children might discuss themes, make personal connections, or share their response journal comments related to a compelling prompt such as "Describe a time when you should not tell the truth," or "Which energy alternative described in the book do you support and why?" This phase of instruction also included the occasional "fishbowl" conversation: One group carried on its discussion in the middle of the room as the other students observed from outside the "fishbowl." This was immediately followed by the observers participating in a teacher-led discussion about things that went well inside the "fishbowl" and what might have been done to improve the conversation.

This instruction was simply mapped onto the existing literacy curriculum in each research site. By beginning with whole-class instruction and introduction to individual strategies, it gave both the children and the teachers the time to gain expertise before moving into small group application of multiple strategies. Beginning with the RT format provided a structure for both the small-group interaction and concentrated practice in using the four strategies before moving to more flexible and responsive application. The small group provided a safe context for diverse learners to practice the strategies and share personal connections by using academic discourse associated with conversations about books.

Model 2: Modified Transactional Strategy Instruction

As a second-grade teacher, I was strongly influenced by the studies of TSI that had been conducted in other second-grade classrooms (Brown & Coy-Ogan, 1993; Schuder,

1993). My school's literacy curriculum was built around a basal literature anthology, with additional time allocated for small-group reading with instructional-level texts. In this high-poverty school, a majority of the children entered second grade reading below level. I spent the first semester teaching the individual strategies explicitly, using the gradual-release-of-responsibility model in Figure 9.2. Explicit instruction, modeling, and collaborative practice with communal feedback occurred during read-alouds and shared reading of authentic literature and content materials. Much as in the cooking metaphor used earlier, I would focus on one or two particular strategies during each themed basal unit, but our discussions were transactional; *all* strategies were applied in flexible, responsive ways. I selected strategies that seemed most likely to support the meaning making of particular kinds of texts that were prevalent in the units (see Table 9.3). For example, our first themed unit— Families, Friends, and Neighbors—consisted of narratives. So my emphasis was on teaching the children to activate prior knowledge and to generate purposeful predictions. Since purposeful predictions had been taught in first grade, I felt comfortable moving on quickly to visualizing. Visualizing also was

TABLE 9.3. Sample Curriculum Calendar

Unit title	Content	Strategy focus
Family, Friends, and Neighbors (Narrative)	Social studies: Communities	Activating prior knowledge Purposeful predictions Visualizing
Nature (Informational)	Science: Animals and their habitats	Text structure: Description Summarizing
Native Americans (Informational and narrative)	Social Studies: Native Americans and resources	Monitoring Inferring Critical literacy intro
Our Nation: A Melting Pot (Narrative, informational, and procedural)	Social studies: Culture and traditions	Monitoring Answering questions: Question–answer relationships Creating products by following directions
Folktales	Social studies: Culture and map skills	Narrative story structure Retelling/summarizing stories
Biographies	Social studies: Civil and women's rights	Asking good questions
Family Narratives	Social studies: Heritage	Asking good questions
Poetry	Literature: Poetry	Visualizing Inferring
Prehistoric Life and Earth Changes (Informational)	Science: Our changing earth	Asking inquiry questions

emphasized as we moved into our Nature unit with the text *Nature Spy* (Kreisler & Rotner, 1992). The Nature unit relied heavily on informational texts, which presented a need to explore the descriptive text structure and summarization to enhance communication processes. In my class, strategy instruction did not exist in a bubble. It was in service to reading, writing, and talking about texts and the ideas presented in those texts.

During the first half of the year, most strategy instruction occurred during read-alouds, shared reading, and small-group guided reading. Posters describing before, during and after reading behaviors served as reminders about how and when each of the strategies might be applied. By the end of January, most of the strategies had been explicitly taught and practiced in teacher-led guided reading groups. In February, the children self-selected partners and a wide range of biographies. Using the posters as reminders, children applied the strategies intermittently as needed except for taking stock and questioning, which occurred every two to four pages as they read their books with their partners. In March and April, the children applied the strategies as they read independently, but checked in through their participation in self-selected book clubs. In May, they conducted individual inquiry projects. These projects required them to ask a question with an answer unknown to anyone in our class (including me). Each student conducted independent research and then presented an exhibit to share the findings, incorporating spoken, written, and visual explanations.

By treating my curriculum as a collective, I was able to expand the blocks of time in which reading and writing were taught with authentic materials for real-life purposes, such as taking action to protect local threatened and endangered species during our "Animals and Their Habitats" unit (Purcell-Gates, Duke, & Martineau, 2007). The experiences that were part of our content instruction supported the knowledge and vocabulary called for when the students were reading, writing, and talking about the engaging topics. Repeated exposures to vocabulary occurred in discussions, reading, and writing. This supported vocabulary development for all students, but especially for ELLs. The application of the strategies became transparent and functional for the students.

Model 3: Concept-Oriented Reading Instruction

Concept-Oriented Reading Instruction (CORI) is an instructional framework for integrating science and literacy instruction that has been extensively tested in grades 3–5 but is likely to have wider applicability (Guthrie et al., 2004). Unlike the modified TSI that I implemented, CORI consists of more expansive science units that engage children in a series of learning phases: (1) observe and personalize, (2) search and retrieve, (3) comprehend and integrate, and (4) communicate to others. Each science inquiry unit spans 6–12 weeks. Instruction of comprehension strategies is embedded within this framework. CORI applies the gradual-release-of-responsibility model for developing the activation of prior knowledge, questioning, summarizing, the use of graphic organizers, and searching for information. Students use the strategies to help them learn content to address

their own questions and to present/share with others. Curriculum guides, while not scripted, provide a scope and sequence for instruction. Additional teacher resources are provided in the form of books, modules, videos, and summer institutes (Swan, 2003). To see CORI in action, go to *www.cori.umd.edu/what-is-cori/classroom-videos.php.*

LOOKING FORWARD

Throughout the years, there has been a great deal of converging evidence regarding strategy instruction. Teachers can feel confident in making some shifts that seem likely to increase their effectiveness and improve their students' text comprehension.

- Select a few key strategies and teach them well, using a gradual release of responsibility (National Reading Panel, 2000; Pearson & Gallagher, 1983; Shanahan et al., 2010).
- Be planful in incorporating a range of texts, including variations in genre, media, and degree of challenge (Adams, 2010–2011; Coiro & Dobler, 2007; Kendeou et al., 2008; Purcell-Gates et al., 2007).
- Address comprehension strategies across the curriculum and integrate whenever possible (Cervetti, Pearson, Bravo, & Barber, 2006; Guthrie et al., 2004; Klingner & Vaughn, 1999; Klingner et al., 2004; Reutzel et al., 2005) .
- Incorporate teacher mediation, peer mediation, and posters as forms of scaffolding (Palincsar & Brown, 1984; Paris et al., 1983; Stahl, 2008b, 2009).
- Avoid rote strategy sequences, which discourage students' ownership of flexible strategy application in response to personal meaning-making hurdles (Hacker & Tenant, 2002; McKeown et al., 2009).
- Use a wide range of assessments to capture the multidimensional characteristics of reading comprehension (Afflerbach et al., 2008; McKenna & Stahl, 2009; Paris, 2005).

QUESTIONS FOR REFLECTION •

1. Is my tendency to teach the declarative, procedural, and conditional knowledge associated with each strategy explicitly, or simply to mention and model each strategy before holding students accountable for application of the strategies?

2. To what extent do I apply a gradual release of responsibility, being mindful of (a) moving from more to less support from others, as well as (b) moving from more to less supportive media forms (e.g., experiential, video, picture books, hypertext, text only)?

3. To what extent do I weave strategy instruction across grouping configurations and curriculum areas?

4. Am I deliberate in matching my strategy emphasis with particular genres and curricular units, so that there is cohesion in my instruction in a way that is useful and makes sense to my students? For example, if my class science unit on plants includes many texts with sequential text structures, do I teach that text structure and facilitate a range of reading, writing, and discussion experiences that allow for application?

5. Do I engage in sustained strategy work, or is my tendency to teach a strategy once, twice, or intermittently?

6. Do I use opportunities with multimedia to engage my students with strategy application?

7. Are peer mediation and collaborative activities part of my own instructional repertoire? What do I need to do to prepare my students to maximize the effectiveness of peer mediation techniques (e.g., RT, CSR, PALS) in my classroom?

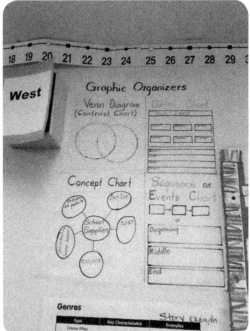

8. Do I take advantage of posters, bookmarks, and other "cheat sheets" as physical scaffolds to support my students on their way to independent, flexible strategy application?

9. To what extent does my instructional repertoire encourage my students' application of strategies in flexible, responsive ways, as opposed to boring, mindless routines and scripts? How might I stretch my own instructional repertoire?

10. To what extent do I use a wide range of assessments that reflect the multidimensional aspects of reading comprehension, so that I can adjust and differentiate instruction?

SUGGESTIONS FOR ONGOING PROFESSIONAL LEARNING •

Teaching comprehension strategies well is a juggling act. Unlike instruction in the constrained abilities, comprehension is neither linear nor taught to mastery. Comprehension varies by text, depending on prior knowledge, conceptual vocabulary, text decodability, text complexity, genre, and instructional context. When teaching comprehension strategies, teachers must balance those factors with their knowledge of their students. The complexity of the process makes it somewhat difficult to negotiate in a classroom (El-Dinary & Schuder, 1993; Gaskins et al., 1993). Some evidence indicates that more experienced teachers may be able to balance process–content instruction more efficaciously than novice teachers (Gaskins et al., 1993). Evidence also indicates that a staff development model devoted to the implementation of a multiple-strategy program must be long term. The cognitive flexibility and adaptability required of teachers in these programs seem to be processes that develop over time. Because the instruction is transactional, it takes time and reflection to adjust these programs to the teachers, the texts being used, the students, and the classroom routines. Teachers in research projects report that their programs evolve over the course of 2–3 years, with continual minor modifications for improvement (Brown & Coy-Ogan, 1993; Duffy, 1993a, 1993b; Garcia et al., 2011; Gaskins et al., 1993; Stahl, 2009). Involvement in a professional learning community (PLC) can provide ongoing support and encouragement.

Duffy (1993b) proposes a recursive nine-point continuum of teachers' progress and attitudes as they become expert teachers of strategies. On his continuum, teachers start out confused about which strategies to teach, the order of instruction, and integration with materials. They move to a midpoint in which they are more informed about the individual strategies, but have not yet learned how to implement strategy instruction within the traditional school curriculum and how to maintain a smooth classroom activity flow. At Duffy's later points, the teachers have become more fluid, flexible, and responsive to student needs in their strategy instruction, selection of materials, and choice of tasks.

Fine-Tuning Strategy Instruction

Session 1

- *PLC reflection.* Discuss this chapter with members of your PLC. In addition, discuss your answers to the *Questions for Reflection* (see pp. 237–238). What aspects of strategy instruction do you currently do well? What aspects of strategy instruction do you find challenging?
- *Moving forward.* Select two comprehension strategies and use Figure 9.3 to record your instructional decisions related for each of these two strategies for the next 2 weeks. Select strategies that are a good match for your upcoming curriculum in literacy and the content areas.

Session 2

- *PLC reflection.* Bring Figure 9.3 to the meeting. How did a deliberate focus on two strategies change your teaching? How did a deliberate focus on the gradual release of responsibility change your teaching? What differences did you notice in your students? How comfortable were you and your students with using the strategies throughout the day in multiple contexts?
- *Moving forward.* Based on a discussion with your PLC, what might you try next to enhance your instruction of one or two additional strategies? Continue polishing and taking notes on your instruction of the strategies, using a gradual release of responsibility in a range of student contexts. Record what is working well for you and what is going well for your students. Record elements that you find challenging and the elements that are challenging for your students.

Session 3

- *PLC reflection.* Discuss the successes and challenges of your instruction since the last session. How well do you think your students are able to apply the selected strategies in a supportive setting? Next, consider using a strategy repertoire protocol. Have you ever used such a protocol with your students? What do you need to do to get your students ready to apply a peer-mediated repertoire protocol for continuing practice of the set of strategies? What steps can you take to prepare your students for peer-mediated

Using a Gradual Release of Responsibility to Teach _____

(Strategy)

Week of _____

Date					
Text					
Grouping configuration					

Select and briefly describe the degree of shared responsibility that best describes each lesson. A lesson may incorporate more than one form of interaction.

Explicit strategy instruction					
Modeling					
Collaborative use					
Guided practice					
Independent application					

FIGURE 9.3. Gradual-release-of-responsibility planning form.

reading activities? Discuss releasing responsibility to them, and decide how you will scaffold the process and determine that they are functioning at high levels as you let go. With your PLC, discuss the external structures that you can put into place to make the gradual release of responsibility a smooth one. Consider temporarily using the DR/L-TA or RT to scaffold the small-group setting protocol. How might you use posters, bookmarks, discussion rubrics, fishbowl demonstrations, and video-recording of small-group work to facilitate the process?

- *Moving forward.* Before the next PLC session, begin the transition to peer-mediated collaborative groups. Your actions will depend on how comfortable you and your students currently are with working in small-group collaboratives. At a minimum, it is likely that your students are now ready to participate in small-group applications of the repertoire of instructed strategies, with you modeling the discourse. Classrooms that have been engaged in small-group collaboratives may be ready to shift to student-led groups with a teacher listening in "on the side."

Session 4

- *PLC reflection.* Share your notes that describe your transition. Record accommodations that struggling readers, ELLs, and children with behavior issues may need to participate in a way that makes them shine as valued participants in the collaborative groups.
- *Moving forward.* Before the next PLC session, facilitate each peer-mediated discussion group from the beginning to the end of their discussion "from the side." Scaffold gently only as needed to prompt strategy use in ways that would enhance meaning making or to clarify the protocol that you established. Take notes to inform your next instructional moves.

Session 5

- *PLC reflection.* Discuss the successes and challenges that your students are encountering in their small-group and independent reading. How flexibly are they applying the strategies? Are the strategies being applied to help them remember and comprehend at deeper levels, or in a rote fashion? How well are they transferring the strategies to their nonstructured and independent reading? What evidence do you have?
- *Moving forward.* Review your notes. Discuss experiences with your PLC. Is more work needed on particular strategies or in transferring students' knowledge of strategies to more complex texts? Are more whole-class lessons called for on the more difficult strategies, such as asking high-level questions or monitoring for conceptual confusions beyond hard vocabulary? How are your diverse learners functioning in the small groups? Discuss next steps with your PLC.

RESEARCH-BASED RESOURCES

Almasi, J. F. (2003). *Teaching strategic processes in reading.* New York: Guilford Press.
Blachowicz, C., & Ogle, D. (2008). *Reading comprehension: Strategies for independent learners* (2nd ed.). New York: Guilford Press.

Block, C. C., Gambrell, L. B., & Pressley, M. (Eds.). (2002). *Improving comprehension instruction: Rethinking research, theory, and classroom practice.* San Francisco: Jossey-Bass.

Duffy, G. G. (2009). *Explaining reading: A resource for teaching concepts, skills, and strategies* (2nd ed.). New York: Guilford Press.

Duke, N. K., Caughlan, S., Juzwik, M. M., & Martin, N. M. (2012). *Reading and writing genre with purpose in K–8 classrooms.* Portsmouth, NH: Heinemann.

Hiebert, E. H., & Pearson, P. D. (2010). *An examination of current text difficulty indices with early reading texts.* San Francisco: TextProject.

Oczkus, L. D. (2010). *Reciprocal teaching at work: Powerful strategies and lessons for improving reading comprehension* (2nd ed.). Newark, DE: International Reading Association.

Owocki, G. (2003). *Comprehension: Strategic instruction for K–3 students.* Portsmouth, NH: Heinemann.

Palincsar, A. S., David, Y., & Brown, A. L. (1992). *Using reciprocal teaching in the classroom: A guide for teachers.* Ann Arbor: University of Michigan.

Pressley, M., & Woloshyn, V. (1995). *Cognitive strategy instruction that really improves children's academic performance.* Cambridge, MA: Brookline Press.

Raphael, T. (1986). Teaching question–answer relationships, revisited. *The Reading Teacher, 39,* 516–522.

Swan, E. A. (2003). *Concept-oriented reading instruction: Engaging classrooms, lifelong learners.* New York: Guilford Press.

Zinny, J. M. (2008). *Using picture books to teach comprehension strategies.* New York: Scholastic Teaching Resources.

REFERENCES

Adams, M. J. (2010–2011). Advancing our students' language and literacy: The challenge of complex texts. *American Educator, 34*(4), 3–12.

Afflerbach, P., Pearson, P. D., & Paris, S. G. (2008). Clarifying differences between reading skills and reading strategies. *The Reading Teacher, 61,* 364–373.

Baumann, J. F., & Schmitt, M. C. (1986). The what, why, how, and when of comprehension instruction. *The Reading Teacher, 39*(7), 640–646.

Baumann, J. F., Seifert-Kessell, N., & Jones, L. A. (1992). Effect of think-aloud instruction on elementary students' comprehension monitoring abilities. *Journal of Reading Behavior, 24,* 143–172.

Berkeley, S., Scruggs, T. E., & Mastropieri, M. A. (2010). Reading comprehension instruction for students with learning disabilities, 1995–2006: A meta-analysis. *Remedial and Special Education, 31,* 423–436.

Brown, R., & Coy-Ogan, L. (1993). The evolution of transactional strategies instruction in one teacher's classroom. *Elementary School Journal, 94,* 221–233.

Brown, R., Pressley, M., Van Meter, P., & Schuder, T. (1996). A quasi-experimental validation of transactional strategies instruction with low-achieving second grade readers. *Journal of Educational Psychology, 88,* 18–37.

Cartwright, K. B. (2009). The role of cognitive flexibility in reading comprehension: Past, present, and future. In S. E. Israel & G. G. Duffy (Eds.), *Handbook of research on reading comprehension* (pp. 115–139). New York: Routledge.

Cervetti, G., Pearson, P. D., Bravo, M., & Barber, J. (2006) Reading and writing in the service of inquiry-based science. In R. Douglas, M. P. Klentschy, & K. Worth (Eds.), *Linking science and literacy in the K–8 classroom* (pp. 221–244). Arlington, VA: National Science Teachers Association Press.

Coiro, J., & Dobler, E. (2007). Exploring the online reading comprehension strategies used by sixth-grade skilled readers to search for and locate information on the Internet. *Reading Research Quarterly, 42,* 214–257.

Davidson, J. L., & Wilkerson, B. C. (1988). *Directed Reading–Thinking activities.* Monroe, NY: Trillium Press.

Dooley, C. M. (2010). Young children's approaches to books: The emergence of comprehension. *The Reading Teacher, 64,* 120–131.

Duffy, G. (1993a). Rethinking strategy instruction: Four teachers' development and their low achievers' understanding. *Elementary School Journal, 93,* 231–247.

Duffy, G. (1993b). Teachers' progress toward becoming expert strategy teachers. *Elementary School Journal, 94,* 109–120.

Duke, N. K., & Pearson, P. (2002). Effective practices for developing reading comprehension. In A. E. Farstrup & S. Samuels (Eds.), *What research has to say about reading instruction* (pp. 205–242). Newark, DE: International Reading Association.

Durkin, D. (1979). What classroom observations reveal about reading comprehension. *Reading Research Quarterly, 14,* 518–544.

El-Dinary, P. B., & Schuder, T. (1993). Seven teachers' acceptance of transactional strategies instruction during their first year using it. *Elementary School Journal, 94,* 207–219.

Fuchs, D., Fuchs, L. S., Mathes, P. G., & Simmons, D. C. (1997). Peer-Assisted Learning Strategies: Making classrooms more responsive to diversity. *American Educational Research Journal, 34,* 174–206.

Gambrell, L. B., & Jawitz, P. B. (1993). Mental imagery, text illustrations, and children's story comprehension and recall. *Reading Research Quarterly, 28,* 265–273.

Garcia, G. E., Pearson, P. D., Taylor, B. M., Bauer, E. B., & Stahl, K. A. D. (2011). Socioconstructivist and political views on the implementation of two types of reading comprehension approaches in low-income schools. *Theory into Practice, 50*(2), 149–156.

Gaskins, I. W., Anderson, R. C., Pressley, M., Cunicelli, E., & Satlow, E. (1993). Six teachers' dialogue during cognitive process instruction. *Elementary School Journal, 93,* 277–304.

Gersten, R., Fuchs, L. S., Williams, J. P., & Baker, S. (2001) Teaching reading comprehension strategies to students with learning disabilities: A review of the research. *Review of Educational Research, 71,* 279–321.

Goldman, S. R., Varma, K. O., Sharp, D., & Cognition and Technology Group at Vanderbilt. (1999). Children's understanding of complex stories: Issues of representation and assessment. In S. R. Goldman, A. C. Graesser, & P. van den Broek (Eds.), *Narrative comprehension, causality, and coherence: Essays in honor of Tom Trabaso.* Mahwah, NJ: Erlbaum.

Guthrie, J. T., Wigfield, A., Barbosa, P., Perencevich, K. C., Taboada, A., Davis, M. H., et al. (2004). Increasing reading comprehension and engagement through Concept-Oriented Reading Instruction. *Journal of Educational Psychology, 96,* 403–423.

Hacker, D., & Tenant, A. (2002). Implementing reciprocal teaching in the classroom: Overcoming obstacles and making modifications. *Journal of Educational Psychology, 94,* 699–718.

Jiménez, R. T., García, E. G., & Pearson, P. D. (1996). The reading strategies of bilingual Latina/o students who are successful English readers: Opportunities and obstacles. *Reading Research Quarterly, 31,* 90–112.

Kendeou, P., Bohn-Gettler, C., White, M. J., & van den Broek, P. (2008). Children's inference generation across different media. *Journal of Research in Reading, 31*(3), 259–272.

Kendeou, P., Lynch, J. S., van den Broek, P., Espin, C. A., White, M. J., & Kremer, K. E. (2006). Developing successful readers: Building early comprehension skills through television viewing and listening. *Early Childhood Education Journal, 33*(2), 91–98.

Kintsch, W. (1998). *Comprehension: A paradigm for cognition.* Cambridge, UK: Cambridge University Press.

Klingner, J. K., & Vaughn, S. (1996). Reciprocal teaching of reading comprehension strategies for students with learning disabilities who use English as a second language. *Elementary School Journal, 96,* 275–293.

Klingner, J. K., & Vaughn, S. (1999). Promoting reading comprehension, content learning and English acquisition through collaborative strategic reading. *The Reading Teacher, 52,* 738–747.

Klingner, J. K., Vaughn, S., Arguelles, M. E., Hughes, T. J., & Leftwich, S. A. (2004). Collaborative strategic reading: 'Real-world' lessons from classroom teachers. *Remedial and Special Education, 25*(5), 291–302.

Klingner, J. K., Vaughn, S., Hughes, M. T., Schumm, J. S., & Elbaum, B. (1998). Outcomes for students with and without learning disabilities in inclusive classrooms. *Learning Disabilities Research and Practice, 13*(3), 153–161.

Kreisler, K., & Rotner, S. (1992). *Nature spy.* New York: Atheneum.

Langer, J. A., Bartolomé, L., Vasquez, O., & Lucas, T. (1990). Meaning construction in school literacy tasks: A study of bilingual students. *American Educational Research Journal, 27,* 427–471.

McKenna, M. C., & Stahl, K. A. D. (2009). *Assessment for reading instruction* (2nd ed.). New York: Guilford Press.

McKeown, M. G., Beck, I. L., & Blake, R. G. K. (2009). Rethinking reading comprehension instruction: A comparison of instruction for strategies and content approaches. *Reading Research Quarterly, 44*(3), 218–253.

Morrow, L. M. (1985). Retelling stories: A strategy for improving young children's comprehension concept of story structure, and oral language complexity. *Elementary School Journal, 85,* 646–660.

National Reading Panel. (2000). *Report of the National Reading Panel. Teaching children to read: An evidence-based assessment of the scientific research literature on reading and its implications for reading instruction* (NIH Publication No. 00-4769). Washington, DC: National Institute of Child Health and Human Development. Retrieved from *www.nationalreadingpanel.org.*

Palincsar, A. S. (1986). The role of dialogue in providing scaffolded instruction. *Educational Psychologist, 21,* 73–98.

Palincsar, A. S., & Brown, A. L. (1984). Reciprocal teaching of comprehension-fostering and comprehension-monitoring activities. *Cognition and Instruction, 2,* 117–175.

Paris, S. G. (2005). Re-interpreting the development of reading skills. *Reading Research Quarterly, 40,* 184–202.

Paris, S. G., & Hamilton, E. E. (2009). The development of children's reading comprehension. In S. E. Israel & G. G. Duffy (Eds.), *Handbook of research on reading comprehension* (pp. 32–53). New York: Routledge.

Paris, S. G., Lipson, M. Y., & Wixson, K. K. (1983). Becoming a strategic reader. *Contemporary Educational Psychology, 8,* 293–316.

Pearson, P. D., & Gallagher, M. C. (1983). The instruction of reading comprehension. *Contemporary Educational Psychology, 8,* 317–344.

Pressley, M., & Afflerbach, P. (1995). *Verbal protocols of reading: The nature of constructively responsive reading.* Mahwah, NJ: Erlbaum.

Pressley, M., El-Dinary, P. B., Gaskins, I., Schuder, T., Bergman, J. L., Almasi, J., et al. (1992). Beyond direct explanation: Transactional instruction of reading comprehension strategies. *Elementary School Journal, 92,* 513–555.

Purcell-Gates, V., Duke, N. K., & Martineau, J. A. (2007). Learning to read and write genre-specific text: Roles of authentic experience and explicit teaching. *Reading Research Quarterly, 42,* 8–45.

RAND Reading Study Group. (2002). *Reading for understanding: Toward an R & D program in reading comprehension.* Santa Monica, CA: RAND Corporation.

Raphael, T. (1986). Teaching question–answer relationships, revisited. *The Reading Teacher, 39,* 516–522.

Reutzel, D. R., Smith, J. A., & Fawson, P. C. (2005). An evaluation of two approaches for teaching comprehension strategies in the primary years using science information texts. *Early Childhood Research Quarterly, 20,* 276–305.

Rosenshine, B., & Meister, C. (1994). Reciprocal teaching: A review of the research. *Review of Educational Research, 64,* 479–530.

Rosenshine, B., Meister, C., & Chapman, S. (1996). Teaching students to generate questions: A review of the intervention studies. *Review of Educational Research, 66,* 181–221.

Saunders, W. M., & Goldenberg, C. (1999). Effects of instructional conversations and literature logs on limited- and fluent-English-proficient students' story comprehension and thematic understanding. *Elementary School Journal, 99,* 279–301.

Schuder, T. (1993). The genesis of transactional strategies instruction in a reading program for at-risk students. *Elementary School Journal, 94,* 183–200.

Shanahan, T., Callison, K., Carriere, C., Duke, N. K., Pearson, P. D., Schatschneider, C., et al. (2010). *Improving reading comprehension in kindergarten through 3rd grade: A practice guide* (NCEE Publication No. 2010-4038). Washington, DC: National Center for Education Evaluation and Regional Assistance, Institute of Education Sciences, U.S. Department of Education. Retrieved from *http://whatworks.ed.gov/publications/practiceguides.*

Solari, E. J., & Gerber, M. M. (2008). Comprehension instruction for Spanish-speaking English language learners: Teaching text level reading skills while maintaining effects on word level skills. *Learning Disabilities Research and Practice, 23,* 155–168.

Stahl, K. A. D. (2004). Proof, practice and promise: Comprehension strategy instruction in the primary grades. *The Reading Teacher, 57,* 598–609.

Stahl, K. A. D. (2008a). Creating opportunities for comprehension instruction with fluency-oriented reading. In M. R. Kuhn & P. J. Schwanenflugel (Eds.), *Fluency in the classroom* (pp. 55–74). New York: Guilford Press.

Stahl, K. A. D. (2008b). The effects of three instructional methods on the reading comprehension and content acquisition of novice readers. *Journal of Literacy Research, 40,* 359–393.

Stahl, K. A. D. (2009). Comprehensive synthesized comprehension instruction in primary classrooms: A story of successes and challenges. *Reading and Writing Quarterly, 25,* 334–355.

Stahl, K. A. D. (2011). Applying new visions of reading development in today's classrooms. *The Reading Teacher, 65,* 52–56.

Stahl, K. A. D., Garcia, G. E., Bauer, E. B., Pearson, P. D., & Taylor, B. M. (2006). Making the invisible visible: The development of a comprehension assessment system. In K. A. D. Stahl & M. C. McKenna (Eds.), *Reading research at work: Foundations of effective practice* (pp. 425–436). New York: Guilford Press.

Stauffer, R. G. (1969). *Directing reading maturity as a cognitive process.* New York: Harper & Row.

Swan, E. A. (2003). *Concept-oriented reading instruction: Engaging classrooms, lifelong learners.* New York: Guilford Press.

Taylor, B. M., Pearson, P. D., Garcia, G. E., Stahl, K. A. D., & Bauer, E. B. (2006). Improving students' reading comprehension. In K. A. D. Stahl & M. C. McKenna (Eds.), *Reading research at work: Foundations of effective practice* (pp. 303–315). New York: Guilford Press.

Williams, J. P., Lauer, K. D., Hall, K. M., Lord, K. M., Gugga, S., Bak, S. J., et al. (2002). Teaching elementary school students to identify story themes. *Journal of Educational Psychology, 94,* 235–248.

CHAPTER 10

Comprehension • • • • • • • • • • • • • • •
High-Level Talk and Writing about Texts

KELI GARAS-YORK
LYNN E. SHANAHAN
JANICE F. ALMASI

OVERVIEW OF RESEARCH
• •

Oral Response

Discussion-based instructional activities, when coupled with high academic demands, foster higher levels of literacy performance. Specifically, they improve students' ability to write analytically and compose elaborate descriptions, regardless of the students' grade level, academic ability, socioeconomic status, race, or gender (Applebee, Langer, Nystrand, & Gamoran, 2003). As well, discussion-based approaches facilitate literal understanding of text (Fall, Webb, & Chudowsky, 2000; van den Branden, 2000) and inferential comprehension for students at all levels of language proficiency (van den Branden, 2000).

For the purposes of this chapter, we define *discussions* as classroom events in which students and teachers are cognitively, socially, and affectively engaged in collaboratively constructing meaning or considering alternative interpretations of texts to arrive at new understandings (Almasi, 2002). Hadjioannou (2007) explained that these types of "authentic discussions" have "no one preordained conclusion to be reached. Rather, they are motivated by authentically dialogic purposes, and the objective is to reach new and more sophisticated understandings" (p. 371). Nystrand's (2006) review of research found that this type of classroom discourse is characterized by three features: (1) It is a dynamic process of negotiation; (2) it is co-constructed by participants in the moment; and (3) it is structured reciprocally by participants, based on their emergent dialogue.

These three features capture the essence of what it means to have a "discussion" of text. The talk, or discourse, evolves and emerges depending on the participants and how they respond to one another. That is, there is no predetermined "end" or "place" where the discussion is intended to go. Applebee and colleagues (2003) noted that participants in these "open" discussions work as partners to co-construct meaning collaboratively. Any questions that are asked are authentic and open-ended, in that there are no particular or preordained "answers." The questions that are asked are truly meant to bring meaning to the text or construct an understanding—not to assess or evaluate participants' understanding or recall. Participants are free to agree or disagree with one another.

This type of discussion contrasts with what have been referred to as "teacher-led discussions" (e.g., Almasi, 1995) or "recitations" (e.g., Mehan, 1979), in which the teacher initiates the topic(s) of the discussion, most commonly by asking questions and calling on students to respond. Then the teacher evaluates students' responses—either explicitly by stating, "Yes," "Uh-huh," or "Not quite," or implicitly by nodding in agreement or disagreement. Cazden (1986) and Mehan (1979) characterized the patterns of discourse in these classroom events as having an "initiate, respond, evaluate" (I-R-E) participant structure. The types of questions asked during these more controlled teacher-led discussions of text tend to be literal and factual (Alpert, 1987; Skidmore, Perez-Parent, & Arnfield, 2003). Traditional teacher-led discussions also often consist of the teacher asking questions with known answers—leaving little to discuss because it is assumed that there is a single, correct interpretation of text (Almasi, 2002). Thus teacher-led discussions take on an evaluative tone in which there are correct answers that lead to one interpretation of the text, with the teacher controlling who talks, when, and for how long. When the focus of discussion is on such questions and answers, students focus on literal readings of texts rather than critical, higher-level, or interpretive readings. This kind of questioning in teacher-led discussions reduces students' cognitive, affective, and expressive responses; stalls and interrupts student discussion; and leads to decreased motivation, cognitive disengagement, and passivity (Alpert, 1987; Dillon, 1985).

In contrast to the notion of a single correct interpretation of text typically found in teacher-led discussions, the definition of *discussion* used above suggests that multiple and conflicting interpretations of text can coexist (Rosenblatt, 1938/1976, 1978). This kind of discussion requires the type of critical and evaluative thinking that is essential to achieving higher levels of comprehension. It requires that participants have a questioning attitude, engage in logical analysis, make inferences, make evaluations, and make judgments about the texts they read and the ideas and interpretations of others (Almasi, 2007). Discussions that rely on a more student-centered approach to discussion that moves beyond traditional, I-R-E participant formats lead to significant growth in comprehension (Murphy, Wilkinson, Soter, Hennessey, & Alexander, 2009; Peterson & Taylor, 2012; Taylor, Pearson, Peterson, & Rodriguez, 2003; Wilkinson & Hye Son, 2011). These findings are consistent across the research and suggest that there is far less value in traditional teacher-led discussions than in more student-centered discussions.

In the 1990s, many studies of classroom discussion were published (Murphy et al., 2009). Peer discussion, book clubs, and students' responses to literature enjoyed widespread interest among educators during this era. Commeyras and DeGroff's (1998) survey of literacy professionals during that time found that nearly all teachers valued reading and talking about books in a book club–like atmosphere, but only 33% reported that peer discussion was a regular part of their curriculum. Although classroom discussion and peer discussion of text was valued among educators, it was a rare classroom event decades ago, and it remains a rarity in classrooms today (Applebee et al., 2003; Barr & Dreeben, 1991; Commeyras & DeGroff, 1998; Nystrand, 2006).

With the advent of the Common Core State Standards (National Governors Association Center for Best Practices & Council of Chief State School Officers, 2010), the absence of discussion in classrooms may be nearing an end. An important focus of the Speaking and Listening Standards is discussion in one-on-one, small-group, and whole-class settings. The standards note that "formal presentations are one important way such talk occurs, but so is the more informal discussion that takes place as students collaborate to answer questions, build understanding, and solve problems" (p. 23). For example, students as young as kindergartners are expected to "participate in collaborative conversations with diverse partners about kindergarten topics and texts with peers and adults in small and larger groups" (p. 23). As well, students of all ages are expected to "follow agreed-upon rules for discussions" (e.g., listening to others, taking turns speaking about the topics and texts under discussion, gaining the floor in respectful ways), and they are expected to "build on others' talk in conversations by linking their comments to the remarks of others" (National Association of Governors Center for Best Practices & Council of Chief State School Officers, 2010, p. 23). These standards, adopted by 48 states and territories of the United States, suggest that discussion may yet become prevalent within classrooms.

In addition to the Common Core State Standards, the U.S. Department of Education's Institute of Education Sciences has issued practice guides for children in grades K–3 (Shanahan et al., 2010) and adolescents (Kamil et al., 2008). Both documents recommend that discussion be used to foster comprehension. The K–3 practice guide recommends

> that teachers lead their students through focused, high-quality discussions in order to help them develop a deeper understanding of what they read. Such discussions among students or between the students and the teacher go beyond simply asking and answering surface-level questions to a more thoughtful exploration of the text. Through this type of exploration, students learn how to argue for or against points raised in the discussion, resolve ambiguities in the text, and draw conclusions or inferences about the text. (Shanahan et al., 2010, p. 23)

Although the K–3 panel of scholars found "minimal evidence" to support this recommendation, they believe that discussion is critical in helping very young students comprehend text. Because there are more studies focused on discussion in middle and high schools, the adolescent panel (Kamil et al., 2008) found "moderate evidence" to support its recommendation. Like the K–3 scholars, the adolescent scholars recommend that teachers provide opportunities for students to engage in "high-quality discussions of the meaning and interpretation of texts in content areas" (p. 21). They likewise recommend that discussions focus on building a deeper, more complex understanding of text that critically analyzes or challenges the author's meaning, rather than focusing on superficial or literal details.

Thus the consensus from federal sources (e.g., the Common Core State Standards, the U.S. Department of Education's Institute of Education Sciences) is that authentic, dialogic discussion that includes high-quality talk is a valuable instructional activity and should be a staple of every classroom from kindergarten through high school.

How Learning Occurs in Discussions

Sociocultural perspectives on learning maintain that learners actively construct knowledge through interactions with others (Vygotsky, 1978). Children learn the intellectual rules, procedural rules, and social conventions of discussion by observing and participating in them (Vygotsky, 1978). Social learning environments, such as peer discussions, allow learners to observe and interact with more knowledgeable others as they engage in thought processes they may not be able to engage in on their own. Learning in these social environments may occur incidentally as learners observe the thought processes and social processes of their peers, or learning may be more direct when teachers or peers function as more knowledgeable others to scaffold or support learning. Through scaffolding, learners become capable of achieving more than they could have on their own (Rogoff, 1990; Vygotsky, 1978). As a result of incidental learning or scaffolded instruction, learners gradually internalize higher cognitive functions, such as interpreting literature or monitoring comprehension. Peer discussions provide a social environment in which students can observe the thought processes and social processes of their peers, and can begin to practice and use the strategies they observe for interpreting literature and interacting with one another. The discussion environment can be beneficial in developing both social understandings and text interpretation among diverse populations, such as middle school students with special needs and English language learners (ELLs) (Blum, Lipsett, & Yocum, 2002; Morocco & Hindin, 2002).

One promising peer scaffold that Staarman (2003) implemented in her online discussion study was having one group of sixth-grade students work in dyads during the online discussion, while another group worked individually. Students responding online in dyads could talk with one another before responding, unlike those in the control group, who worked alone. The students in dyads wrote almost twice as many responses as those who worked independently. In addition, students in dyads demonstrated more awareness of the task and the strategies needed. Both of these findings point to the importance of socially constructing knowledge, whether this occurs in face-to-face or online discussions.

Types of Scaffolding That Support Learning during Discussions

There are two kinds of scaffolding that can occur during discussions: *short-term* and *long-term* scaffolding (Almasi & Garas-York, 2009; Liang & Dole, 2006). Short-term scaffolding occurs when the teacher provides specific support to enhance students' understanding of a particular text. Liang and Dole (2006) explained that the ultimate goal of such scaffolding is to enable the students to understand the content of a given text. They further explained that this type of scaffolding often features a high level of teacher involvement. Teachers in discussions that feature short-term scaffolding ask more open-ended questions, queries, and probes designed to help students think and comprehend at deeper levels. As we describe below, teachers may also assign roles during discussion as a means of scaffolding the interaction. Thus discussions that feature short-term scaffolding will differ from those that feature long-term scaffolding.

In our review of research related to comprehension and discussion of text, Almasi and Garas-York (2009) noted that one way teachers provide short-term scaffolding to students during discussions is to assign roles. Bond (2001) and Morocco and Hindin (2002) found that role assignment during discussion enhanced comprehension. In contrast, Almasi and Russell (1998, 1999) found teacher assignment of static roles during peer discussion of expository text to be limiting. Although the teachers' instructional moves (i.e., assigning roles, assigning a discussion task) were intended to scaffold student learning and comprehension, they led to power struggles among students and created fewer opportunities to construct meaning. Teachers are thus encouraged to assess the needs of the students in discussion groups and scaffold accordingly.

Second, Almasi and Garas-York (2009) noted that teachers also utilize short-term scaffolding that includes open-ended questions, queries, and probes to help students to understand a particular text. Overall, the studies found that such short-term scaffolding during discussions had a positive impact on students' comprehension. In particular, such scaffolding enhanced the quality of student talk and led to discussions with a more academic focus (Wolf, Crosson, & Resnick, 2005); led to significant gains in comprehension, recall, and ability to monitor comprehension (Beck, McKeown, Sandora, Kucan, & Worthy, 1996; Sandora, Beck, & McKeown, 1999); led to significantly higher scores on literal and inferential comprehension (McElvain, 2010) and understanding of theme (Saunders & Goldenberg, 1999); and led to more complex conceptual understanding of the texts and the development of a repertoire of strategies for making sense of text (Many, 2002).

The research on long-term scaffolding illustrates some different benefits. During long-term scaffolding, the teacher's goal is not to help students toward immediate understanding of a text, but to foster the students' abilities to interpret text and learn to sustain conversations about text across time (Almasi & Garas-York, 2009). This type of scaffolding requires that rather than guiding and scaffolding students' interpretations to deeper levels immediately, teachers foster long-term cognitive and social development. This type of fostering is more readily accomplished through discussions that have less teacher involvement, such as peer discussion. Almasi (2002) described peer discussion as an event in which

> students gather to talk about, critique, and understand texts with minimal teacher assistance. Students determine their own topics of conversation and negotiate the procedural rules and social conventions that govern their discussion. Discourse is lively and focuses on personal reactions, responses, and interpretations of what has been read. Students also use a variety of strategic reading behaviors (e.g., comprehension monitoring, imagery, prediction, summarization) and higher levels of abstract and critical thinking (e.g., making intertextual connections, critiquing author's craft) to participate meaningfully in discussions. (p. 420)

Overall, studies of long-term scaffolding have found a positive impact on students' comprehension, but a different type of impact from that of short-term scaffolding. Rather than general improvements on broad measures of literal and inferential comprehension, these studies showed the impact of peer discussion on specific aspects of comprehension and interpretation of text. Both students whose primary language was English and ELL students were able to use background knowledge available to them because of cultural differences (Goatley, Brock, & Raphael, 1995; Martinez-Roldán, 2005) and sociocultural differences (i.e., socioeconomic status and race) (Martinez-Roldán, 2005; Martinez-Roldán & López-Robertson, 2000; Rice, 2005) to make sense of and interpret text. Students in peer discussions were also able to internalize the ability to recognize and resolve conflicts significantly better than students in teacher-led discussions (Almasi, 1995). As well, these studies showed that students were capable of learning how to engage in conversations about text on their own (McMahon & Goatley, 1995), even as early as kindergarten and first grade (Almasi et al., 2005). Students were also able to learn to think critically, retrieve argument-relevant information, construct and repair arguments, and anticipate flaws in arguments when they learn the principles of argumentative reasoning and enact them in peer discussions (Anderson et al., 2001; Reznitskaya et al., 2001). Finally, studies of peer discussion of text have shown that students show significant social and affective growth and development when compared to their peers in teacher-led contexts (Almasi, Palmer, et al., 2004).

Teachers who provide long-term scaffolding teach students about interpretive strategies and ways to interact in a peer discussion *before* and *after* such a discussion, rather than *during* the discussion (see Figure 10.1). These notions are similar to the Speaking and Listening Standards discussed earlier as part of the Common Core State Standards. During long-term scaffolding, teachers scaffold in ways that help students learn to recognize features of the task (e.g., "What went well in your discussion today? What might we work on to make the discussion better? What might we do to help one another understand the text better?"). As well, they scaffold to help students learn to resolve issues on their own (e.g., "You said that during your discussion some people tend to dominate, making it difficult for others to join in the conversation. What can we do next time so this is not a problem?"). O'Flahavan (1995) developed a discussion process whereby teachers can engage in long-term scaffolding before and after students' peer discussions. O'Flahavan's format, the *conversational discussion group* (CDG), uses long-term scaffolding prior to discussion during a 5-minute introduction, and after discussion during a 5-minute debriefing. Figure 10.2 depicts the process teachers and students use during CDGs. Almasi and her colleagues (e.g., Almasi, 1995; Almasi, O'Flahavan, & Arya, 2001; Almasi, Palmer, et al., 2004) used the CDG format in our studies of peer discussion in grades K–4. Figure 10.1 depicts a sample anchor chart that first graders used to help them learn how to function as a group.

Discussion Reminders

1. You don't have to raise your hands to speak.
2. Call each other by your names.
3. Take turns speaking.
4. Don't interrupt each other.
5. Use your inside voice, but talk loud enough so everyone in the group can hear you.
6. Don't use bad words or talk mean.
7. If someone is doing something they shouldn't be doing, ask them to stop.

FIGURE 10.1. Sample first-grade anchor chart indicating the discussion reminders related to interacting with one another.

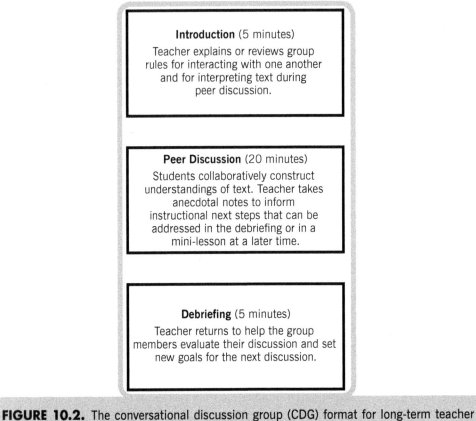

Introduction (5 minutes)

Teacher explains or reviews group rules for interacting with one another and for interpreting text during peer discussion.

Peer Discussion (20 minutes)

Students collaboratively construct understandings of text. Teacher takes anecdotal notes to inform instructional next steps that can be addressed in the debriefing or in a mini-lesson at a later time.

Debriefing (5 minutes)

Teacher returns to help the group members evaluate their discussion and set new goals for the next discussion.

FIGURE 10.2. The conversational discussion group (CDG) format for long-term teacher scaffolding during peer discussion.

Scaffolding for ELL students needs to be carefully considered and monitored. Farris, Nelson, and L'Allier (2007) pointed to the benefits of using peer discussion with ELL students; however, they warned, "Too few directions and too little modeling by the classroom teacher often leave ELL students bewildered" (p. 39). In bilingual classrooms, teachers and students should decide which language(s) to use. Such decisions can either empower or limit students' participation (DeNicolo, 2010; Martinez-Roldán, 2005). If bilingual and ELL students use both their primary language and English, doing so can be regarded as an intellectual resource that increases participation, engagement, and motivation (DeNicolo, 2010; Martinez-Roldán, 2005; McElvain, 2010).

Overall findings on the two types of scaffolding suggest that each type fosters distinct areas of growth. Discussions featuring short-term scaffolding that uses open-ended teacher questions, queries, and probes foster general overall comprehension of the content of texts. Peer discussions featuring long-term scaffolding over time tend to foster the development of comprehension and interpretive processes. This suggests that teachers should use both types of discussion; however, their use should be well planned and deliberate. Teachers should not default to one particular type of scaffolding over the other. Instead, it will be helpful to assess the quality of student discussions and use such assessment to design a developmentally appropriate plan for long-term scaffolding, so students learn how to use interpretive and comprehension strategies to make sense of text, as well as how to interact with one another in a way that fosters respect, tolerance, and acceptance of others and of diverse perspectives. Along the way, other types of discussions should periodically have more teacher involvement by way of short-term scaffolding (e.g., using open-ended questions, queries, and probes, along with nonevaluative feedback) to teach students how to understand the content of particular texts. All scaffolding should be conducted as a joint, collaborative effort among teachers and students, in which the teachers provide temporary support and then gradually releases responsibility for the task to students (Meyer, 1993). After either short-term or long-term scaffolding occurs, teachers will need to evaluate the processes and products as students negotiate interpretations and understandings of text through discussion.

Discussion in Online Environments

The increasing presence of technology within the classroom has made it possible for students to engage in online discussions or online book clubs. (For more on the use of technology in literacy instruction, see Watts Taffe & Bauer, Chapter 7, this volume.) This presence may also lead to greater use of discussion in classrooms. Using the Internet and software tools, such as Moodle, Blackboard, or First Class, students can engage in two different types of online discussions: *asynchronous* and *synchronous*. In asynchronous discussions, students are not online at the same time; as a result, the discussion accumulates over time. Some researchers claim that engaging in asynchronous discussions provides time for students to reflect on other group members' discussion points before responding (Veerman, Andriessen, & Kanselaar, 2000; Wolsey, 2004). Emerging research on asynchronous online discussions at the middle school level indicates that students think more deeply about their responses than in written-response journals or face-to-face discussions (Grisham & Wolsey, 2006). Another interesting parallel between face-to-face discussion and asynchronous online discussion is that once students use certain patterns of talk to make an argument, those patterns increase in frequency throughout the discussion, just as they would in a face-to-face discussion. Unlike asynchronous online discussions, in synchronous online discussions all discussion group members are online at the same time. The communication that occurs in a synchronous online discussion mirrors the type of communication that occurs in instant messaging (Staarman, 2003). Unlike asynchronous and face-to-face discussion, synchronous discussions occur at a rapid pace, and students do not have to wait to take a turn (Day & Kroon, 2010). In both types of online discussions, the quality of students' discussion is contingent on the discussion task, features of the learning environment, and the students' prior knowledge, as well as teacher scaffolding (Day & Kroon, 2010; Staarman, 2003).

Research focused on online discussion environment found that quieter students who were less apt to participate in face-to-face discussions were more comfortable in the online context (Day & Kroon, 2010). Furthermore, students who were apprehensive about speaking out in class did not have to utilize attention-getting and conversational skills in an online context (Staarman, 2003). As well, the types of group process *metatalk* (i.e., talk related to how the group functions) that characterized less proficient peer discussions in Almasi and colleagues' (2001) comparative study of more and less proficient peer discussions were missing from online discourse (Kim, Anderson, Nguyen-Jahiel, & Archodidou, 2007). Kim and colleagues (2007) found that comments such as "Let

[name] talk!" simply did not exist in online discussions. Findings such as these are important for teachers to keep in mind when deciding on the discussion environment.

Written Response

Written response, in addition to response to literature through oral discussions, can lead to higher-level comprehension. Various types of written responses, such as literature response journals, response logs, or dialogue journals, can serve as tools for students to construct meaning, elaborate on personal reactions, and reflect on ideas (Martinez & Roser, 2003). Given that reading and writing are reciprocal processes (Langer, 1986; Sweet, 1993) it stands to reason that students can use written responses to articulate their perspective about issues contained in the text; make discussion points; and remind them of specific connections, questions, predictions, or feelings toward the text when engaging in discussion. Writing for these purposes is also linked to the Writing Standards in the Common Core State Standards, which emphasize that "the ability to write logical arguments based on substantive claims, sound reasoning, and relevant evidence is a cornerstone of the writing standards, with opinion writing—a basic form of argument—extending down into the earliest grades" (National Association of Governors Center for Best Practices & Council of Chief State School Officers, 2010, *www. corestandards.org/about-the-standards/key-points-in-english-language-arts*).

Research indicates that engaging students in both reading and writing experiences around texts leads to higher-level thinking (Sweet, 1993). Furthermore, when students are afforded the opportunity to share their ideas with a group of peers, they develop cognitive self-awareness (Palincsar & Brown, 1984), as well as an awareness of others' perspectives (Harste, Woodward, & Burke, 1984; Wollman-Bonilla & Werchadlo, 1999). Sharing written responses in a discussion context is a natural context for peers to scaffold and challenge one another's thinking and to reveal alternative perspectives (Cazden, 1986; Reznitskaya et al., 2001; Wollman-Bonilla & Werchadlo, 1999). Using written responses to prepare for the rich discussion context requires students to anticipate their audience's needs in order to communicate their ideas effectively.

A *dialogue journal* is a specific form of written response that involves a regular written conversation between a teacher and a student. Wollman-Bonilla (1989) used dialogue journals with the idea that this type of conversation would increase the amount of effort or energy the student put into the response. In addition, Barone (1990) examined the patterns of response in dialogue journals and found that students engaged in retelling, personal subjective responses, and questions around their understandings of the text. Taken together, these studies suggest that students' responses move beyond summary and also establish a private personal conversation between the teacher and students. When utilizing dialogue journals with middle school students, Werderich (2006) found that teachers needed to facilitate their students carefully, so that the students responded freely but maintained a specific response quality. Asking too many questions and focusing on the level of writing could deter students from responding to text.

Students' written responses to text have been found to vary across grade levels and to be influenced by teacher scaffolding. In one study, emerging readers and primary-grade students focused their responses on the story world instead of overarching themes or messages (Hancock, 1993; Martinez, Roser, & Dooley, 2003). In another study, the findings indicated that just giving the primary students the chance to engage in written response was not effective enough. Instead, findings pointed to the importance of teacher scaffolding to achieve both reading and writing growth (Wollman-Bonilla & Werchadlo, 1999).

Interestingly, not only does written response support literature discussion, but so too does visual response. Students in one study were asked to draw a favorite part of a story or to draw what was going on in their minds as they read or listened to the story (Hubbard, Winerbourne, & Ostrow, 1996). Findings demonstrated that students used the visual representations to facilitate their literature discussion and to make personal connections to the story. Although using visual representation to respond may be especially beneficial for students who have difficulty writing, Hubbard and colleagues' (1996) findings suggest that representing ideas through visual response is not just for those who cannot write fluently. These authors claim that creating such a response is another mode of communication that also results in meaning making.

Interrelationships between Written and Oral Responses

Over time, researchers have developed category systems to describe types of both written and oral responses. Raphael, Pardo, Highfield, and McMahon (1997) have identified three categories of response: *personal, creative,* and *critical.* Personal response involves the reader's emotional reaction to text and the inclusion of any personal experiences that the text brings to mind. Creative response involves the reader engaging with the text in creative ways (e.g., putting one's self in a situation or imagining one's self as author). Critical response includes the analysis of the author's literary techniques. Similarly, Hancock (1993) has identified three major areas of response as *personal meaning making, character and plot involvement,* and *literary evaluation.* Both Hancock (1993) and Raphael and colleagues (1997) point to the importance of sharing written responses within a discussion context in order to deepen and extend comprehension.

Not only writing can prepare students for deeper participation in discussions; classroom interactions such as *collaborative reasoning* or CR (Clark et al., 2003), in which students listen to each other think out loud as they participate in reasoned argumentation, can also do so. In CR, students use both personal experiences and evidence from the stories read to prepare for writing reasoned arguments. There is widespread belief that social interactions occurring in the context of discussion provide a rich context for developing individual reasoning (e.g., Reznitskaya et al., 2001). Within the discussion context, students make their own ideas public and are exposed to alternative perspectives that challenge their own ideas. Students have the opportunity to develop argumentative discourse, which can later be used to develop persuasive essays proposing alternative theories. Reznitskaya and colleagues (2001) found that "students who participated in CR discussions wrote essays that contained a significantly greater number of arguments, counterarguments, rebuttals, uses of formal argument devices, and references to text information than the essays of similar students who did not experience CR" (p. 171).

ELLs' writing is also influenced by the use of peer discussion in their classrooms. ELL students placed in an English-only environment demonstrated improved writing skill development, as well as increased engagement in motivation to read and participate in whole-class discussions, after being involved in instruction that combined the use of discussion and strategy instruction (McElvain, 2010). The considerable gains made in writing on an English proficiency test (i.e., 30 points, compared to 12.4 in the control group) suggest that an equal amount of instructional time spent on reading, writing, and discussion may benefit ELLs.

The classroom teacher plays a pivotal role in mediating students' written responses throughout the school year. Research analyzing students' written responses in the areas of content, format, and ideas found that their writing developed over time (Raphael, Boyd, & Rittenhouse, 1993) and was influenced by both the teacher and peers (Wollman-Bonilla & Werchadlo, 1999). Pedagogical recommendations include modeling, scaffolding or adjusting support, providing mini-lessons, and sharing/group feedback (Raphael et al., 1997; Werderich, 2006; Wollman-Bonilla & Werchadlo, 1999). Modeling how to respond to text in varied ways after reading aloud is an effective instructional strategy. Hancock (1993) notes in regard to her three broad response areas or types of written response (personal meaning making, character and plot involvement, and literary criticism) that scaffolding students' responses requires teachers to know how students already respond to text, so that they can move students' writing from one type of response to another. For example, if a student's written responses always involve personal meaning making, the teacher can model how to compare and contrast different characters, to move the type of response to character and plot involvement. Using mini-lessons where the teacher reviews and critiques different response types or expectations of a response type with students is also an effective instructional strategy. In a mini-lesson, the teacher may have the students view a sample response and then ask the group to critique the strengths and area of development for the response. Using instructional strategies such as these assists in making clear the expectations for the contents of a written response.

Kelly and Farnan (1991) found that the use of teacher prompts influenced the way students responded to text. When an open prompt was used, such as "Tell me about the book," readers' written responses were less critical and analytic. Conversely, when prompts focused the readers on personal interpretations of the text, their responses showed more analytic thinking.

In sum, due to the interrelationships between oral and written responses, students benefit from engaging in both activities together (Wollman-Bonilla & Werchadlo, 1999). Students draw on written ideas during literature discussion, and discussion has an impact on their writing (Raphael et al., 1993; Reznitskaya et al., 2001). Researchers have documented that if students across the grade levels engage in both types of response experiences (i.e., writing and oral discussion) with modeling, scaffolding, and purposeful selection of prompts from their teacher, students increase their comprehension, connection to text, and development of metacognitive skills. Furthermore, ELLs demonstrate a significant increase in writing skill development when peer discussion and strategy instruction are combined (McElvain, 2010). (For more on the impact of instruction that engages students in complex thinking through high-level talk and writing about texts, see Taylor, Chapter 18, this volume.)

Assessing the Quality of Discussion and Comprehension

Research has also been conducted on the quality of peer discussions (Almasi et al., 2001; Chinn & Anderson, 1998; Keefer, Zeitz, & Resnick, 2000; Roller & Beed, 1994). Paradis, Chatton, Boswell, Smith, and Yovich (1991) described various systems used by teachers to assess comprehension during literature discussions. They provided examples of a group comprehension matrix, a group record form, an individual record form, and a final form that documented comprehension strategies and their application in a discussion group. Overall, the authors found that a teacher could not implement an accountability procedure developed by someone else. Each teacher had to develop a procedure or system that worked for his or her students and classroom across time.

SUMMARY OF BIG IDEAS FROM RESEARCH

- Teacher-led recitations versus peer discussions:
  - Discussions that rely on more student-centered or dialogic approaches—that is, discussions that move beyond traditional, I-R-E participant formats—lead to significant growth in comprehension and comprehension-related constructs. These findings are consistent across the research and suggest that there is little value in traditional teacher-led discussions focused on recitation and low-level responses, compared with more student-centered dialogic discussions.
- Learning through social interactions:
  - Social learning environments, such as those in which peer discussions occur, allow learners to observe and interact with more knowledgeable others as they engage in thought processes they may not be able to engage in on their own.
  - Learning in these social environments may occur incidentally as learners observe the thought processes and social processes of their peers, or learning may be more direct when teachers or peers function as more knowledgeable others to scaffold or support learning.
- Short-term and long-term scaffolding:
  - Short-term scaffolding occurs when a teacher provides specific support to enhance student understanding of a particular text.
    - This type of scaffolding often features a high level of teacher involvement.
    - Teachers in discussions that feature short-term scaffolding ask more open-ended questions, queries, and probes designed to help students think and comprehend at deeper levels.
  - During long-term scaffolding, a teacher's goal is not helping students toward immediate understanding of a text, but fostering the students' abilities to interpret text and to sustain conversations about text across time.
    - With this type of scaffolding, rather than guiding and scaffolding students' interpretations to deeper levels immediately, teachers foster long-term cognitive and social development.
    - Long-term cognitive and social development is fostered through discussions that have less teacher involvement, such as peer discussion.
- Accountability:
  - Each teacher should develop a procedure or system that works for his or her students and classroom across time, to show comprehension growth and group interactions.

EXAMPLES OF EFFECTIVE PRACTICES

This section provides practical examples of effective discussion practices. We begin by providing an overview of various approaches to discussion and examining the characteristics that distinguish effective approaches. Then we examine two classroom teachers' practices to see how they meet diverse students' needs through discussion, how they form groups of students for discussion, and how texts are selected.

Meeting All Students' Needs through Effective Discussion Practices

Approaches to Discussion

Discussion can be used as a means to interpret and understand texts, as well as to foster comprehension strategy use for all students. The strengths, needs, and interests of all students should be considered when teachers select texts, form groups, and make decisions about the type of scaffolding that will be employed.

Chinn, Anderson, and Waggoner (2001) examined four factors that characterized different approaches to discussion, to see how they influenced discourse. The four factors included (1) literary stance toward text, (2) interpretive authority, (3) control of turns, and (4) control of topics. We use these characteristics to help depict various approaches to discussion in Table 10.1. Table 10.1 also provides an overview of each approach to discussion in terms of the type of scaffolding used, and the success of each approach in regard to literal comprehension, inferential comprehension, and comprehension processes such as metacognition.

Literary stance stems from Rosenblatt's (1978) transactional theory. *Stance* refers to what the reader (or discussant) focuses attention on and what is ignored. It is important to consider stance when deciding which type of discussion to use in the classroom because the purpose or goal of the discussion determines the stance discussants will assume. Readers or discussants taking a primarily *efferent* stance focus their attention on the meaning that is retained *after* reading. Such discussions may focus on what they can recall, paraphrase, or analyze from the text (Rosenblatt, 1985). Readers taking a primarily *aesthetic* stance focus attention on their personal affective experiences *during* the reading event (Rosenblatt, 1985). Conversation from an aesthetic stance may focus on readers' thoughts, feelings, or emotions about the text, characters, characters' actions, or events. Chinn and colleagues (2001) added the *critical/analytic* stance, which refers to talk that critically evaluates or analyzes problems characters face or characters' motives.

Interpretive authority refers to who frames the questions and issues that are discussed (i.e., who asks the question or opens the topic), who develops those questions and issues (i.e., who responds to those questions or invitations), and who evaluates the interpretation that emerges (i.e., who affirms, disputes, or contradicts the interpretation) (Mayer, 2009). Responsibility can rest entirely with the teacher, as in a traditional teacher-led discussion or recitation, or responsibility can rest entirely with students, as in more student-centered discussions (Chinn et al., 2001). Both the teacher and the students can also share responsibility for interpretive authority.

The third factor, *control of turns*, refers to who decides who may talk, when they may talk, and how frequently they may talk. This factor has implications in terms of power and authority. If an individual manages turn taking, that individual, in essence, holds the power to decide whose voice is allowed into the conversation and whose voice is silenced. The ability to learn how to negotiate turn taking is one of the Speaking and Listening Standards in the Common Core State Standards.

TABLE 10.1. Characteristics of Varied Approaches to Discussion of Text

Approach to discussion	Description of approach	Interpretive focus/ stance	Interpretive authority	Control of topic	Control of turns	Amount of talk	Type of scaffolding	Comprehension findings
Recitation	Primary goal is to make certain that students know and recall text content	Primarily efferent	Primarily controlled by teacher	Almost entirely by teacher via questions	Almost entirely by teacher	Primarily by teacher (about 67%)	Short-term	Literal, factual, and known-answer questioning reduced students' cognitive, affective, and expressive responses; stalled student discussion; and led to decreased motivation, cognitive disengagement, and passivity (Alpert, 1987; Dillon, 1985)
Book club (Goatley, Brock, & Raphael, 1995; Raphael & McMahon, 1994; Raphael, Pardo, Highfield, & McMahon, 1997)	Consists of four parts that support student-led discussion of text: (1) reading, (2) writing, (3) community share, (4) instruction	Primarily aesthetic, partly efferent	Primarily by students	Primarily by students	Primarily by students	Primarily by students	Short-term and long-term	Students used background knowledge available because of cultural differences (Goatley, Brock, & Raphael, 1995); increased use of metacognitive strategies (Kong & Fitch, 2002–2003)

(continued)

TABLE 10.1. (continued)

Approach to discussion	Description of approach	Interpretive focus/stance	Interpretive authority	Control of topic	Control of turns	Amount of talk	Type of scaffolding	Comprehension findings
Collaborative reasoning (CR) (Chinn, Anderson, & Waggoner, 2001; Waggoner, Chinn, Yi, & Anderson, 1995)	Students in small groups discuss positions about a central question; students present reasons for and against the positions	Primarily critical/analytic, partly expressive	Students are completely responsible for their own judgments about which positions and arguments are stronger	Shared by teacher and students	Students may talk whenever they wish, but teachers may retain control for purposes of scaffolding	Primarily by students	Long-term	Students provided more arguments, reasons, varied perspectives, and story details (Reznitskaya et al., 2001)
Conversational discussion group (CDG) (Almasi, 1995; Almasi, O'Flahavan, & Arya, 2001; Almasi et al., 2005; O'Flahavan, 1995; Wiencek & O'Flahavan, 1994)	Groups of 5–6 students read texts, prepare individual responses to the texts, and discuss them; groups establish rules for interacting and interpreting texts; teacher scaffolding occurs before and after the discussion	Partly aesthetic, partly efferent, partly critical/analytic	Primarily by students	Almost entirely by students	Almost entirely by students	Primarily students (ranges from 69% in kindergarten to 94% in fourth grade)	Short-term and long-term	Students' in peer discussions showed greater ability to recognize and resolve conflict than students in teacher-led discussions (Almasi, 1995); students in peer discussions demonstrated use of a range of interpretive strategies (Almasi et al., 2005)
Grand conversations (Eeds & Wells, 1989; Peterson & Eeds, 2007)	Small groups of 4–8 students, with a teacher, construct meaning about texts they have selected to read	Primarily expressive, partly efferent, partly evaluative	Shared by students and teacher	Shared by students and teacher	Shared by students and teacher	Primarily students (55%)	Short-term and long-term	Students constructed meaning of text at a basic level, made personal connections to the stories, and made and verified predictions (McGee, 1992)

Approach	Description						Outcomes
Instructional conversations (Goldenberg, 1993; Tharp & Gallimore, 1988)	Small-group discussions aimed at developing analysis, reflection, and critical thinking about text	Primarily efferent	Shared by teacher and students	Shared by students and teachers, but teachers may provide scaffolding to help students attain deeper insights	Shared by students and teacher	Primarily teacher	Short-term	Teachers and peers supported students with limited English proficiency to access prior knowledge and construct meaning (Olezza, 1999)
Literature circles (Daniels, 2002; Short & Pierce, 1998)	Small-group discussions aimed at collaboratively constructing meaning and sharing responses to text	Primarily expressive	Primarily by students	Primarily by students	Primarily by students	Primarily student	Short-term and long-term	Students' abilities to use questioning and predicting strategies improved (Martin, 1998)
Questioning the author (Beck, McKeown, Hamilton, & Kucan, 1997; Beck, McKeown, Sandora, Kucan, & Worthy, 1996)	Students grapple with and reflect on what author is trying to say in text to build a representation from text	Primarily efferent, with some critical/analytic	Shared by teacher and students; students are expected to take primary responsibility	Generally shared by students and teachers, but teachers exert a fair amount of control by posing questions and queries	Generally by teacher	Ranges between 50–60% teacher talk and 40–50% student talk	Short-term and long-term	Students' questions became less literal, more inferential (Flynn, 2002); students gave longer and more in-depth story retellings (Sandora, Beck, & McKeown, 1999)

Note. From Chinn, Anderson, and Waggoner (2001). Copyright 2001 by the International Reading Association. Adapted by permission.

Control of topic was the fourth factor Chinn and colleagues (2001) used to characterize different approaches to discussion. They noted that topic control has both local and global features. At a local level, topic control means "who decides what topic the group will discuss at this moment." At a global level, topic control refers to the boundaries set around topic selection for the discussion as a whole. In classroom discussions of text, an example of a global topic boundary would be "to discuss the text we have read" or "to stay on topic once a topic is established."

Keys to Effective Dialogic Discussion

Some teachers find student-centered, dialogic discussions intimidating. Christoph and Nystrand (2001) found that three elements were key to making the transition from teacher-led to more dialogic discussions for high school teachers: (1) creating an atmosphere of involvement and respect in the classroom; (2) using scaffolding and questioning in ways that encouraged extended student–student conversation; and (3) making space for students' interpersonal relationships. For elementary teachers, Maloch (2002, 2004) found that it was essential for the teachers to help students learn how to develop response topics and questions for discussion, as well as how to interact with one another. There are always some growing pains, but researchers have documented that teachers and students even as young as kindergartners are able to meet with success in classrooms in the United States (e.g., Almasi et al., 2001, 2005; Certo, Moxley, Reffitt, & Miller, 2010; Maloch, 2002) and in China and Korea (e.g., Dong, Anderson, Kim, & Li, 2008), when appropriate efforts are made.

A Classroom Example of Dialogic Discussion in First Grade

Mrs. Dillon's first-grade classroom in a suburban school (all names are pseudonyms) is an example of one in which shifts to student-centered, dialogic discussions were managed successfully. In our research (e.g., Almasi et al., 2005), we used the CDG format described earlier in this chapter for peer discussions (Wiencek & O'Flahavan, 1994). Mrs. Dillon began the year by establishing three groups for response to and discussion of text (CDGs) and three different groups for small-group reading instruction. Following Wiencek and O'Flahavan's (1994) advice, Mrs. Dillon rated all of the students in her class on three dimensions before forming the groups: (1) social ability, (2) comprehension/interpretive ability, and (3) reading/decoding ability. Figure 10.3 is a form that can be used to rate students on each dimension. After students were rated, Mrs. Dillon formed heterogeneous groups of four to eight students.

Week 1, Day 1

During a week at the beginning of the school year, Mrs. Dillon spent 20–30 minutes each day preparing students. She set the stage by explaining that the goal of a discussion was to work together to co-construct an understanding of the text. She noted that the roles students and teachers take in a CDG are different from those in other class activities. Students take responsibility for deciding what topics are discussed, managing the discussion, and respectfully challenging and critiquing one another's ideas. The first day, she taught students how to think about topics for discussion and ask authentic

Social

1 = Student who is very quiet in group discussions.

2 = Student who willingly shares his or her ideas in group discussions most of the time.

3 = Student who willingly participates in group discussions and often assumes the role of leader.

Interpretive

1 = Student has considerable difficulty comprehending text independently and is unable to share the basic story ideas with peers.

2 = Student usually is able to comprehend most text independently and shares understanding with peers.

3 = Student comprehends text independently using prior knowledge and textual clues to create meaning and is able to justify the meanings he or she has created.

Reading Ability

1 = Student who is unable to read/decode text independently.

2 = Student who is able to read/decode most text independently with little difficulty.

3 = Student who is able to read/decode a variety of texts independently.

FIGURE 10.3. Rating students' social, interpretive, and reading ability to form discussion groups.

questions. She used a read-aloud of a Big Book to model and demonstrate how to generate authentic questions. As she read the book aloud, she stopped at various points to model how to generate questions. She used stems such as "I wonder . . . ," "I wish . . . ," "I worry . . . ," and "I don't understand . . . ." to focus on thinking critically about characters' actions, the events in the story, and whether the text made sense. As she generated a question, she asked students to turn and talk to a partner about any questions they had at that point in the read-aloud.

Week 1, Day 2

The second day, Mrs. Dillon explained the importance of coming to CDGs prepared to discuss. She noted, "Creating sticky notes and writing in a journal are two ways to record your thoughts and questions as you read, and these thoughts can become topics for discussion." During the read-aloud that day, Mrs. Dillon asked students to draw or write the questions and thoughts that came to mind as she read. After reading a page or two, she stopped and asked students to think about what they were wondering about, worrying about, or wishing, or what they didn't understand. A sample of a first-grade student's response to the read aloud of *Charlie Anderson* by Barbara Abercrombie (1990) is provided in Figure 10.4. For students who struggled somewhat to write, Mrs. Dillon encouraged them to draw their responses. For others who struggled even more, she used previously made sticky notes with smiley faces, frowney faces, and question marks on them. As the read-aloud progressed, those students who struggled the most to write placed smiley faces in places that they enjoyed, frowney faces in places that they did not enjoy, and question marks in places where they had a question. After students wrote, they turned and talked to a partner about what they wrote.

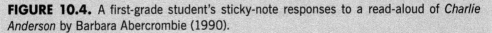

FIGURE 10.4. A first-grade student's sticky-note responses to a read-aloud of *Charlie Anderson* by Barbara Abercrombie (1990).

Week 1, Day 3

After learning how to think about text as it is read and how to write responses, students were ready to begin learning how to discuss by the third day. Mrs. Dillon reminded them that they were responsible for deciding which topics to discuss and for managing the discussion. She described her own role as that of a "coach" who would help them before and after the discussion and would only step into the actual discussion if the group got stuck. Mrs. Dillon then showed the class a video of a CDG from a previous year. As her current students watched, she asked them to focus on what the students were doing during the discussion and to jot down or draw what they noticed. After watching for several minutes, Mrs. Dillon paused the video to give her students time to jot down what they noticed and share with a partner. They noticed things such as "They are talking to each other," and "They are using their sticky notes." Mrs. Dillon recorded their ideas on chart paper and developed them a bit further by asking students to notice how the students knew when they could speak, or how they knew what to talk about, or how the students talked with one another. Then the class watched 2 or 3 more minutes of the video and repeated the process of recording and sharing what they noticed.

Week 1, Day 4

The next day, Mrs. Dillon used the chart paper to remind students of what they noticed in the video. She organized the class into the three heterogeneous CDGs she had created by using the form in Figure 10.3. She explained that each group would meet to create two sets of rules to follow during discussions: (1) one set of rules for interacting with one another, and (2) another set of rules for what interpretive strategies the group members might use in discussions (Wiencek & O'Flahavan, 1994). An interaction chart that one of Mrs. Dillon's groups created has been presented earlier in this chapter in Figure 10.1. We recommend that each group develop and revise its own rules, rather than having one set of rules for the whole class.

While Mrs. Dillon met with one group to identify, discuss, and record its rules, the other groups were either rereading and responding to the text, or they were watching a video of another CDG to notice how the students interacted and interpreted a different text.

Week 1, Day 5

On the fifth day, Mrs. Dillon's students were ready to try their first discussions using the CDG format (see Figure 10.2). Each group began with a 5-minute introduction in which Mrs. Dillon reviewed the rules developed the previous day. After the introduction, she encouraged the group members to begin their discussion. Ideally the discussion portion is intended to be 20 minutes long, but Mrs. Dillon found that at the beginning of the year her first graders were only able to engage in sustained discussion for about 6 minutes. The first discussions were far from perfect. Although each student shared the sticky notes he or she had written, there was little to no dialogic conversation about the text or to one another, and there did not seem to be any attempt to construct meaning. This is the point at which some teachers get discouraged. Sometimes teachers want to see immediate results; however, some types of learning take longer than others. It is important to view discussion in terms of long-term scaffolding that leads to sustained learning. This means identifying long-term goals and step-by step ways to help students attain those goals over time. As each group of students discussed, Mrs. Dillon sat near the group and took anecdotal notes related to aspects of interaction and interpretation that went well and aspects that needed improvement. These notes became the start of her long-term scaffolding, which began immediately after the discussion as she facilitated each group's first debriefing. The chart in Figure 10.5 is one way in which teachers might identify the long-term goals for students, record their observations from each discussion, and evaluate students' progress toward the long-term goal. Note that each long-term goal is linked to the relevant Common Core State Standards for Speaking and Listening in first grade.

Debriefing

Mrs. Dillon noticed that one group of first graders had difficulty with the third long-term goal in Figure 10.5 ("Build on others' talk by responding to one another's comments through multiple exchanges"). She also noticed that the group managed turn taking by going around the circle one by one to share responses, rather than responding

Long-Term Goal*	Date	Observation	Progress toward Long-Term Goal	Next Steps	Date	Observation	Progress toward Long-Term Goal	Next Steps	Date	Observation	Progress toward Long-Term Goal	Next Steps
1. Listen to others with care												
2. Speak one at a time about topics and texts under discussion												
3. Build on others' talk by responding to one another's comments through multiple exchanges												
4. Ask questions to clear up any confusion about topics and texts under discussion												

*Long-term goals for interaction are taken from the Grade 1 Speaking and Listening Standards (K–5) of the Common Core State Standards (Standards 1a, 1b, 1c).

FIGURE 10.5. Long-term scaffolding plan for interaction.

naturally to one another's ideas; this suggested to her that maybe the group was also having difficulty with the first long-term goal in Figure 10.5 ("Listen to others with care"). With each goal, she explained to students what she had noticed, and she offered several suggestions for ways in which the group might enhance the next discussion. Figure 10.6 depicts the group during the following debriefing.

Week 2

The next week, Mrs. Dillon provided an opportunity for students to reflect further on their first discussion. She reviewed the discussion reminder chart related to interaction and reiterated her observations from the debriefing. Then she asked students to re-view a video of their discussion. As they viewed, students were encouraged to watch only their own performance. After the video, she asked them to evaluate their individual performance and set personal goals for the next discussion, using a self-evaluation form (see Figure 10.7) to rate their performance on the four long-term goals, write about one thing they did very well, indicate one thing they would like to improve, and set one goal for the next discussion. Self-evaluations and re-viewing videos of past discussions are valuable for helping students to focus on their own learning, as well as to begin learning how to reflect critically on their performance (Silvers, 2001).

Discussion 3 Months Later

After patiently scaffolding students' interaction and interpretation for 3 months, Mrs. Dillon observed that her first graders were beginning to internalize some aspects of dialogic conversation. They still had some difficulty managing turns, but they were beginning to respond to one another's comments, and they were beginning to engage in extended conversation aimed at constructing meaning. They understood that one purpose for discussion was to help each other construct meaning. As well, they understood that the concept of *discussion* required responding to one another and building an extended conversation around a topic. Although there was room to grow, the group members had clearly made progress, due to Mrs. Dillon's patient long-term scaffolding.

FIGURE 10.6. First-grade teacher engaged in long-term scaffolding during a debriefing with students following their peer discussion of Barbara Abercrombie's *Charlie Anderson* (1990).

1. I listened carefully to what others said.	A lot like me	Somewhat like me	A little like me	Not at all like me
2. I did not interrupt others when I spoke.	A lot like me	Somewhat like me	A little like me	Not at all like me
3. I added to what others said.	A lot like me	Somewhat like me	A little like me	Not at all like me
4. I asked questions to help me understand the text better.	A lot like me	Somewhat like me	A little like me	Not at all like me

5. I think I _____ really well in the discussion.

6. Next time we have a discussion, I would like to improve _____ .

7. Next time we discuss, my goal is to _____ .

FIGURE 10.7. Student self-evaluation after discussion.

Mrs. Dillon's next step in long-term scaffolding included helping students learn to build on one another's comments to arrive at deeper understanding.

Discussion at End of School Year

By May of that year, the groups had progressed to the point where members were able to speculate about events in ways that took them beyond a literal interpretation of the text. In the excerpt that follows, a group is discussing the book *How Smudge Came* by Nan Gregory (1997). In the book Cindy, a young woman with Down syndrome, finds a puppy to love but is unable to keep it at the home where she lives. Ashley tried to imagine how the dog arrived and how Cindy was able to keep the dog hidden from others. The group members worked together to consider various explanations:

> ASHLEY: I wonder where the dog came from. Like when she was just sitting there.
>
> DJ: I think it ran away from its owner.
>
> ASHLEY: I wonder if she [the main character, Cindy] found it and she just wanted to take it home?
>
> ROSE: Maybe it was just, like, there. Maybe the puppy ran away from its home. Or maybe it ran away from its mother 'cause maybe it got lost from its mother when they were taking a walk.
>
> CYNTHIA: Maybe its mother died.
>
> ASHLEY: That happened before.
>
> ROSE: Maybe the mother died when she was having the babies.
>
> TRINITY: Maybe the dog was born over there.
>
> ASHLEY: Oh yeah, true, 'cause it's just a puppy. I think I got it, but I didn't really understand why she was, like, . . .
>
> ROSE: How she hid it all the time?
>
> ASHLEY: Yeah, like, wouldn't like it be hungry? Like, wouldn't it be thirsty and start whining?
>
> CYNTHIA: Or have to go to the bathroom?
>
> ASHLEY: Yeah.
>
> ROSE: Well, she would just, like, go in her room and go downstairs and get a broom and say, "I got to go sweep up my room. I got to go upstairs" [and then go take care of the puppy].

This example shows how far this group of first graders came in one year—not only in their ability to manage a discussion, but also in their ability to think at deeper levels about the text and jointly construct meaning. The group members might work on learning how to take their speculations and link them to evidence from the text to evaluate each other's ideas in terms of plausibility, but those would be long-term goals for the next year. Although there might have been days in the beginning of the year where Mrs. Dillon wondered whether the CDGs would make it, by the end of the year they had attained her four long-term goals: These first graders were clearly able to listen carefully to one another, speak one at a time, respond to topics with multiple exchanges, and ask questions to clarify confusions.

A Classroom Example of Dialogic Discussion in Third Grade

Ms. Kincaid taught third grade in an urban elementary school. Her students' reading levels ranged from preprimer to fourth grade. She saw the potential benefits of having her students engage in peer discussion of the texts they were reading and was eager to get started. She jumped right into grouping her students and selecting texts that were readily available. Much to her chagrin, the discussion groups didn't work well. She found it difficult to manage the groups and appropriately scaffold her students' ideas about the texts. She gave up on the discussion groups for a short time while she did some reading about the different aspects and benefits of peer discussion. She wondered whether the discussion groups were worth it, but she knew that, as with anything else she decided to do with her class, it would take careful planning and time to facilitate peer discussion and reap the benefits. Ms. Kincaid had admittedly jumped into peer discussion with her students without much thought or planning and was disappointed with the results.

She slowly returned to implementing the discussion groups in her classroom later that year. Ms. Kincaid carefully grouped her students and strategically selected texts that lent themselves to more interesting discussions. This time, she developed charts with the students to help guide their discussions, instead of just expecting them to talk (as she had done when first attempting peer discussion). Ms. Kincaid and the student groups came up with rules for their discussions, as well as lists of things the groups could discuss. In addition, she assigned the students to bring a drawing or something they had written about their reading to each group session, to help get the discussions going. This seemed to Ms. Kincaid to make the groups more manageable and productive. She also took time after the discussions to talk to the students about how their discussions had gone and what they had learned from one another.

For the remainder of the school year, Ms. Kincaid worked to select engaging yet appropriate texts and to come up with ways to scaffold students' understandings of the texts through discussion. She reflected that she was able to see how peer discussion helped her students to understand texts better, but she sought to make improvements with future classes by improving her scaffolding and developing a way to assess her students' discussions.

Suggestions for Moving from Teacher-Led to Student-Led Discussions

Ms. Kincaid's experiences with peer discussion are not uncommon. Wiencek and O'Flahavan (1994) have provided a variety of suggestions for teachers on how to move from teacher-led to peer-led discussions about texts. They suggest that teachers select the highest-quality literature possible to allow for more engaging discussions. This may take some effort, instead of just choosing books that a classroom has multiple copies of. Teachers should consider requesting multiple copies of texts from district or public libraries. As well, they can borrow copies of texts from colleagues in the building, or use bonus points from book orders to purchase multiple copies of appropriate books for future peer discussions.

Engaging texts are not always texts that can be read (decoded) by all of the students in a group or class. Teachers can read texts aloud, encourage buddy reading, record books for students to listen to, use electronic books (with a "Read to me" function), or send texts home for parental assistance. It is important for students, especially those who struggle to decode texts, to be part of peer discussion groups because this enables students from a variety of ability levels to come together to make sense of what they read or was read to them (Wiencek & O'Flahavan, 1994). Students' reading abilities and a variety of other factors should be considered as teachers are forming peer discussion groups.

LOOKING FORWARD

Research has suggested that both oral discussion and written response enhance students' comprehension of text. As schools in the United States become more familiar with the Common Core State Standards, it is likely that teachers will turn to peer discussion to assist in preparing their students for the future. It is also likely that technology will continue to alter our notions of peer discussion. It is important for educators to carefully examine and assess which discussion formats are most effective in meeting the needs of all their students.

QUESTIONS FOR REFLECTION ● ● ● ● ● ● ● ● ● ● ● ● ● ● ● ● ● ●

1. To what extent do I, or teachers I have observed, model and scaffold the social norms for face-to-face and online discussion?

2. To what extent do I, or teachers I have observed, model high-quality responses?

3. To what extent do I, or teachers I have observed, model various response types?

4. To what extent do I, or teachers I have observed, vary response types to include students' making personal interpretations so that they think on analytic and critical levels?

5. To what extent do I, or teachers I have observed, guide or scaffold students to a deeper thinking around the text? For example, am I providing additional information so that students can extend or expand on their ideas?

6. To what extent do I, or teachers I have observed, ask authentic questions and share genuine comments?

7. In what ways can I combine the use of face-to-face discussion, online discussions, and written response to facilitate comprehension and reasoning skills?

8. In what ways am I monitoring students' social interactions to maintain positive group dynamics?

SUGGESTIONS FOR ONGOING PROFESSIONAL LEARNING • • • • • •

Teaming with others is an effective way to learn about and try different instructional techniques. Colleagues can use the resources provided in this chapter to facilitate study groups about peer discussion. Finding time to meet before, during, or after school for multiple months with colleagues who are interested in peer discussion can provide teachers with numerous ideas about how to provide the most beneficial discussion experiences for their students. Teachers can share their successes and challenges, and can be encouraged and supported by colleagues. They can share text ideas, scaffolding techniques, and means by which to assess the discussions. Visiting classrooms or watching recordings of actual discussions can also be a helpful way to reflect on and improve peer discussion in the classroom. Teachers can even have their students participate in a "fishbowl"-style peer discussion, so that other students and teachers can observe and learn from their discussion.

Almasi and colleagues (2005) used many of the aforementioned techniques with teachers while conducting research on peer discussions of texts in K–3 classrooms. They held week-long institutes for teachers to read about and discuss research on peer discussion. During these institutes, teachers from urban, rural, and suburban schools came together to discuss their experiences and concerns with peer discussions. They were able to review recordings of various peer discussions, and to study and discuss scaffolding techniques, text selections, grouping formations, and so forth with the participating teachers. Throughout the year, each group of teachers also participated in monthly study group meetings in which they shared issues or problems they faced in implementing peer discussion, read articles related to implementing peer discussion, viewed and critiqued video excerpts from each other's classrooms, and shared resources. This form of job-embedded professional development was critical in providing initial and ongoing support for teachers as they made the transition from teacher-led to peer discussion.

Monroe-Bailargeon and Shema (2010) examined a school's attempt to provide professional development on using literature circles, and found that educators were able to reap all of the benefits their students gleaned from literature circles. The participants in their study enjoyed interacting in a heterogeneous group (colleagues from different grade levels and different building assignments). The participants also felt that discussing a similar text and sharing ideas helped reinforce a lot of the exciting things they were doing, but it also opened them up to new ideas and perspectives. The format of the literature circle for the teachers themselves allowed them to feel more like a community of learners.

RESEARCH-BASED RESOURCES

Boyd, M., & Galda, L. (2011). *Real talk in elementary classrooms: Effective oral language practice.* New York: Guilford Press.

Cavanaugh, T. W. (2006). *Literature circles through technology.* Santa Barbara, CA: Linworth Books.

Daniels, H. (2002). *Literature circles: Voice and choice in book clubs and reading groups.* Portland, ME: Stenhouse.

Day, J. P., Spiegel, D. L., McLellan, J., & Brown, V. B. (2002). *Moving forward with literature circles: How to plan, manage, and evaluate literature circles to deepen understanding and foster a love of reading.* New York: Scholastic.

Raphael, T. E., Florio-Ruane, S., George, M., Hasty, N., & Highfield, K. (2004). *Book club plus!: A literacy framework for the primary grades.* Lawrence, MA: Small Planet Communications.

REFERENCES

Abercrombie, B. (1990). *Charlie Anderson.* New York: McElderry Books.

Almasi, J. F. (1995). The nature of fourth graders' sociocognitive conflicts in peer-led and teacher-led discussions of literature. *Reading Research Quarterly, 30*(3), 314–351.

Almasi, J. F. (2002). Peer discussion. In B. Guzzetti (Ed.), *Literacy in America: An encyclopedia* (Vol. 2, pp. 420–424). New York: ABC.

Almasi, J. F. (2007). Using questioning strategies to promote students' active comprehension of content area material. In D. Lapp & J. Flood (Eds.), *Content area reading instruction* (5th ed., pp. 487–513). Mahwah, NJ: Erlbaum.

Almasi, J. F., Garas, K., Cho, H., Ma, W., Shanahan, L., Augustino, A., et al. (2005, November). *A longitudinal study of development: Comprehension, interpretive strategy use, and language use among children in grades K–3.* Paper presented at the 55th Annual Meeting of the National Reading Conference, Miami, FL.

Almasi, J. F., & Garas-York, K. (2009). Comprehension and discussion of text. In S. Israel & G. Duffy (Eds.), *Handbook of research on reading comprehension* (pp. 470–493). New York: Routledge.

Almasi, J. F., O'Flahavan, J. F., & Arya, P. (2001). A comparative analysis of student and teacher development in more proficient and less proficient peer discussions of literature. *Reading Research Quarterly, 36*(2), 96–120.

Almasi, J. F., Palmer, B. M., Garas, K., Cho, H., Ma, W., Shanahan, L., et al. (2004). *A longitudinal investigation of peer discussion of text on reading development in grades K–3.* Final report submitted to the Institute of Education Sciences.

Almasi, J. F., & Russell, W. (1998, December). *Scaffold to nowhere?: Appropriated voice, metatalk, and personal narrative in third graders' peer discussions of information text.* Paper presented at the 48th Annual Meeting of the National Reading Conference, Austin, TX.

Almasi, J. F., & Russell, W. (1999, December). An ecology of communication: Peer discussions as semiotic systems. In L. Galda (Chair), *Classroom talk about literature: The social dimensions of a solitary act.* Symposium conducted at the 49th Annual Meeting of the National Reading Conference, Orlando, FL.

Alpert, B. R. (1987). Active, silent, and controlled discussions: Explaining variations in classroom conversation. *Teaching and Teacher Education, 3*(1), 29–40.

Anderson, R. C., Nguyen-Jahiel, K., McNurlen, B., Archodidou, A., Kim, S., Reznitskaya, A., et al. (2001). The snowball phenomenon: Spread of ways of talking and ways of thinking across groups of children. *Cognition and Instruction, 19*(1), 1—46.

Applebee, A. N., Langer, J. A., Nystrand, M., & Gamoran, A. (2003). Discussion-based approaches to developing understanding: Classroom instruction and student performance in middle and high school English. *American Educational Research Journal, 40*(3), 685–730.

Barone, D. (1990). The written responses of young children: Beyond comprehension to story understanding. *The New Advocate, 3,* 49–56.

Barr, R., & Dreeben, R. (1991). Grouping students for reading instruction. In R. Barr, M.

L. Kamil, P. B. Mosenthal, & P. D. Pearson (Eds.), *Handbook of reading research* (Vol. 2, pp. 885–910). New York: Longman.

Beck, I. L., McKeown, M. G., Hamilton, R. L., & Kucan, L. (1997). *Questioning the author: An approach for enhancing student engagement with text*. Newark, DE: International Reading Association.

Beck, I. L., McKeown, M. G., Sandora, C., Kucan, L., & Worthy, J. (1996). Questioning the author: A yearlong classroom implementation to engage students with text. *Elementary School Journal, 96*(4), 385–414.

Blum, H. T., Lipsett, L. R., & Yocum, D. J. (2002). Literature circles: A tool for self-determination in one middle school inclusive classroom. *Remedial and Special Education, 23*(2), 99–108.

Bond, T. F. (2001). Giving them free rein: Connections in student-led book groups. *The Reading Teacher, 54*(6), 574–584.

Cazden, C. B. (1986). Classroom discourse. In M. C. Wittrock (Ed.), *Handbook of research on teaching* (3rd ed., pp. 432–463). New York: Macmillan.

Certo, J., Moxley, K., Reffitt, K., & Miller, J. A. (2010). I learned how to talk about a book: Children's perceptions of literature circles across grade and ability levels. *Literacy Research and Instruction, 49*, 243–263.

Chinn, C. A., & Anderson, R. C. (1998). The structure of discussions that promote reasoning. *Teachers College Record, 100*, 315–368.

Chinn, C. A., Anderson, R. C., & Waggoner, M. A. (2001). Patterns of discourse in two kinds of literature discussion. *Reading Research Quarterly, 36*(4), 378–411.

Christoph, J. N., & Nystrand, M. (2001). Taking risks, negotiating relationships: One teacher's transition toward a dialogic classroom. *Research in the Teaching of English, 36*(2), 249–286.

Clark, A. M., Anderson, R. C., Kuo, L. J., Kim, I. H., Archodidou, A., & Nguyen-Jahiel, K. (2003). Collaborative reasoning: Expanding ways for children to talk and think in school. *Educational Psychology Review, 15*, 181–198.

Commeyras, M., & DeGroff, L. (1998). Literacy professionals' perspectives on professional development and pedagogy: A national survey. *Reading Research Quarterly, 33*(4), 434–472.

Daniels, H. (2002). *Literature circles: Voice and choice in book clubs and reading groups* (2nd ed.). Portland, ME: Stenhouse.

Day, D., & Kroon, S. (2010, November). "Online literature circles rock!": Organizing online literature circles in a middle school classroom. *Middle School Journal, 42*(2), 18–28.

DeNicolo, C. P. (2010). What language counts in literature discussion?: Exploring linguistic mediation in an English language arts classroom. *Bilingual Research Journal, 33*, 220–240.

Dillon, J. T. (1985). Using questions to foil discussion. *Teaching and Teacher Education, 1*, 109–121.

Dong, T., Anderson, R. C., Kim, I., & Li, Y. (2008). Collaborative reasoning in China and Korea. *Reading Research Quarterly, 43*(4), 400–424.

Eeds, M., & Wells, D. (1989). Grand conversations: An exploration of meaning construction in literature study groups. *Research in the Teaching of English, 23*(1), 4–29.

Fall, R., Webb, N., & Chudowsky, N. (2000). Group discussion and large-scale language arts assessment: Effects on students' comprehension. *American Educational Research Journal, 37*(4), 911–941.

Farris, P. J., Nelson, P. A., & L'Allier, S. (2007, March). Using literature circles with English language learners at the middle level. *Middle School Journal, 38*(4), 38–42.

Flynn, P. A. M. (2002). *Dialogic approaches toward developing third graders' comprehension using questioning the author and its influence on teacher change*. Unpublished doctoral dissertation, Fordham University.

Goatley, V. J., Brock, C. H., & Raphael, T. E. (1995). Diverse learners participating in regular education "book clubs." *Reading Research Quarterly, 30*, 352–380.

Goldenberg, C. (1993). Instructional conversations: Promoting comprehension through discussion. *The Reading Teacher, 46*(4), 316–326.

Gregory, N. (1997). *How Smudge came.* New York: Walker.

Grisham, D. L., & Wolsey, T. D. (2006). Recentering the middle school classroom as a vibrant learning community: Students, literacy, and technology intersect. *Journal of Adolescent and Adult Literacy, 49*(8), 648–660.

Hadjioannou, X. (2007). Bringing the background to the foreground: What do classroom environments that support authentic discussions look like? *American Educational Research Journal, 44*(2), 370–399.

Hancock, M. R. (1993). Exploring and extending personal response through literature journals. *The Reading Teacher, 46*(6), 466–474.

Harste, J. C., Woodward, V. A., & Burke, C. L. (1984). *Language stories and literacies lessons.* Portsmouth, NH: Heinemann.

Hubbard, R. S., Winerbourne, N., & Ostrow, J. (1996). Visual responses to literature: Imagination through images. *The New Advocate, 9,* 309–323.

Kamil, M. L., Borman, G. D., Dole, J., Kral, C. C., Salinger, T., & Torgesen, J. (2008). *Improving adolescent literacy: Effective classroom and intervention practices: A practice guide* (NCEE Publication No. 2008-4027). Washington, DC: National Center for Education Evaluation and Regional Assistance, Institute of Education Sciences, U.S. Department of Education. Retrieved from *http://ies.ed.gov/ncee/wwc.*

Keefer, M. W., Zeitz, C. M., & Resnick, L. B. (2000). Judging the quality of peer-led student dialogues. *Cognition and Instruction, 18*(1), 53–81.

Kelly, P. R., & Farnan, N. (1991). Promoting critical thinking through response logs: A reader response approach with fourth graders. In J. Zutell & S. McCormick (Eds.), *Learner factors/teacher factors: Issues in literary research and instruction. 40th yearbook of the National Reading Conference* (pp. 277–284). Chicago: National Reading Conference.

Kim, I. H., Anderson, R. C., Nguyen-Jahiel, K., & Archodidou, A. (2007). Discourse patterns during children's collaborative online discussions. *Journal of the Learning Sciences, 16*(3), 333–370.

Kong, A., & Fitch, E. (2002–2003). Using book club to engage culturally and linguistically diverse learners in reading, writing, and talking about books. *The Reading Teacher, 56,* 352–362.

Langer, J. A. (1986). Reading, writing, and understanding: An analysis of the construction of meaning. *Written Communication, 3*(2), 219–267.

Lewis, C. (1997). The social drama of literature discussions in a fifth/sixth grade classroom. *Research in the Teaching of English, 31*(2), 163–204.

Liang, L. A., & Dole, J. A. (2006). Help with teaching reading comprehension: Comprehension instructional frameworks. *The Reading Teacher, 59*(8), 742–753.

Maloch, B. (2002). Scaffolding student talk: One teacher's role in literature discussion groups. *Reading Research Quarterly, 37*(1), 94–112.

Maloch, B. (2004). On the road to literature discussion groups: Teacher scaffolding during preparatory experiences. *Reading Research and Instruction, 44*(2), 1–20.

Mandura, S. (1995). The line and texture of aesthetic response: Primary children study authors and illustrators. *The Reading Teacher, 49,* 110–118.

Many, J. E. (2002). An exhibition and analysis of verbal tapestries: Understanding how scaffolding is woven into the fabric of instructional conversations. *Reading Research Quarterly, 37*(4), 376–407.

Martin, J. (1998). Literature circles. *Thresholds in Education, 24,* 15–19.

Martinez, M., & Roser, N. L. (2003). Children's responses to literature. In J. Flood, D. Lapp, J. R. Squire, & J. Jensen (Eds.), *Handbook of research on teaching the English language arts* (Vol. 42, pp. 271–278). Chicago: National Reading Conference.

Martinez, M., Roser, N. L., & Dooley, C. (2003). Young children's literary meaning making. In N. Hall, J. Larson, & J. Marsh (Eds.), *Handbook of early childhood literacy* (pp. 222–234). London: Sage.

Martinez-Roldán, C. M. (2005). The inquiry acts of bilingual children in literature discussion. *Language Arts, 83*(1), 22–32.

Martinez-Roldán, C. M., & López-Robertson, J. M. (2000). Initiating literature circles in a first-grade bilingual classroom. *The Reading Teacher, 53*(4), 270–281.

Mayer, S. J. (2009). Conceptualizing interpretive authority in practical terms. *Language and Education, 23*(3), 199–216.

McElvain, C. M. (2010). Transactional literature circles and the reading comprehension of English learners in the mainstream classroom. *Journal of Research in Reading, 33*(2), 178–205.

McGee, L. (1992). An exploration of meaning construction in first graders' grand conversations. In C. K. Kinzer & D. J. Leu (Eds.), *Literacy research, theory, and practice: Views from many perspectives. 41st yearbook of the National Reading Conference* (pp. 177–186). Chicago: National Reading Conference.

McMahon, S. I., & Goatley, V. J. (1995). Fifth graders helping peers discuss texts in student-led groups. *Journal of Educational Research, 89*(1), 23–34.

Mehan, H. (1979). *Learning lessons.* Cambridge, MA: Harvard University Press.

Meyer, D. K. (1993). What is scaffolded instruction?: Definitions, distinguishing features, and misnomers. In D. J. Leu & C. K. Kinzer (Eds.), *Examining central issues in literacy research, theory, and practice: 42nd yearbook of the National Reading Conference* (pp. 41–53). Chicago, IL: National Reading Conference.

Monroe-Bailargeon, A., & Shema, A. L. (2010). Time to talk: An urban school's use of literature circles to create a professional learning community. *Education and Urban Society, 42*(6), 651–673.

Morocco, C. C., & Hindin, A. (2002). The role of conversation in a thematic understanding of literature. *Learning Disabilities Research and Practice, 17*(3), 144–159.

Murphy, P. K., Wilkinson, I. A. G., Soter, A. O., Hennessey, M. N., & Alexander, J. F. (2009). Examining the effects of classroom discussion on students' comprehension of text: A meta-analysis. *Journal of Educational Psychology, 101*(3), 740–764.

National Governors Association Center for Best Practices & Council of Chief State School Officers. (2010, June). *Common Core State Standards for English language arts and literacy in history/social studies, science, and technical subjects.* Washington, DC: Authors. Retrieved from *www.corestandards.org/the-standards.*

Nystrand, M. (2006). Research on the role of classroom discourse as it affects reading comprehension. *Research in the Teaching of English, 40*(4), 392–412.

O'Flahavan, J. F. (1995). Teacher role options in peer discussions about literature. *The Reading Teacher, 48*(4), 354–356.

Olezza, A. M. (1999). *An examination of effective instructional and social interactions to learn English as a second language in a bilingual setting.* Unpublished doctoral dissertation. University of Connecticut.

Palincsar, A. S., & Brown, A. L. (1984). Reciprocal teaching of comprehension-fostering and comprehension-monitoring activities. *Cognition and Instruction, 1,* 117–175.

Paradis, E. E., Chatton, B., Boswell, A., Smith, M., & Yovich, S. (1991). Accountability: Assessing comprehension during literature discussion. *The Reading Teacher, 45*(1), 8–17.

Peterson, D. S., & Taylor, B. M. (2012). Using higher order questioning to accelerate students' growth in reading. *The Reading Teacher, 65*(5), 295–304.

Peterson, R., & Eeds, M. (2007). *Grand conversations: Literature groups in action.* New York: Scholastic.

Raphael, T. E., Boyd, F. B., & Rittenhouse, P. S. (1993, April). *Reading logs in the book club program: Using writing to support understanding and interpretation of text.* Paper presented at the annual meeting of the American Educational Research Association, Atlanta, GA.

Raphael, T. E., & McMahon, S. I. (1994). Book club: An alternative framework for reading instruction. *The Reading Teacher, 48,* 102–116.

Raphael, T. E., Pardo, L., Highfield, K., & McMahon, S. (1997). *Book club: A literature-based curriculum.* Littleton, MA: Small Planet Communications.

Reznitskaya, A., Anderson, R. C., McNurlen, B., Nguyen-Jahiel, K., Archodidou, A., & Kim, S. (2001). Influence of oral discussion on written argument. *Discourse Processes, 32*(2–3), 155–175.

Rice, P. S. (2005). It "ain't" always so: Sixth graders' interpretations of Hispanic-American stories with universal terms. *Children's Literature in Education, 36*(4), 343–362.

Rogoff, B. (1990). *Apprenticeship in thinking: Cognitive development in social context.* New York: Oxford University Press.

Roller, C., & Beed, P. (1994). Sometimes the conversations were grand and sometimes . . . *Language Arts, 71,* 509–515.

Rosenblatt, L. M. (1976). *Literature as exploration.* New York: Modern Language Association. (Original work published 1938)

Rosenblatt, L. M. (1978). *The reader, the text, the poem: The transactional theory of the literary work.* Carbondale: Southern Illinois University Press.

Rosenblatt, L. M. (1985). Viewpoints: Transaction versus interaction—A terminological rescue operation. *Research in the Teaching of English, 19*(1), 96–107.

Sandora, C., Beck, I., & McKeown, M. (1999). A comparison of two discussion strategies on students' comprehension and interpretation of complex literature. *Journal of Reading Psychology, 20,* 177–212.

Saunders, W. M., & Goldenberg, C. (1999). Effects of instructional conversations and literature logs on limited- and fluent-English-proficient students' story comprehension and thematic understanding. *Elementary School Journal, 99*(4), 277–301.

Shanahan, T., Callison, K., Carriere, C., Duke, N. K., Pearson, P. D., Schatschneider, C., et al. (2010). *Improving reading comprehension in kindergarten through 3rd grade: A practice guide* (NCEE Publication No. 2010-4038). Washington, DC: National Center for Education Evaluation and Regional Assistance, Institute of Education Sciences, U.S. Department of Education. Retrieved from *whatworks.ed.gov/publications/practiceguides.*

Short, K. G., & Pierce, K. M. (Eds.). (1998). *Talking about books: Literature discussion groups in K–8 classrooms.* Portsmouth, NH: Heinemann.

Silvers, P. (2001). Critical reflection in the elementary grades: A new dimension in literature discussions. *Language Arts, 78*(6), 556–563.

Skidmore, D., Perez-Parent, M., & Arnfield, S. (2003). Teacher–pupil dialogue in the guided reading session. *Reading: Literacy and Language, 37*(2), 47–53.

Staarman, J. K. (2003, July). Face-to-face talk to support computer-mediated discussion in a primary school literacy practice. *Reading: Literacy and Language, 37*(2), 73–80.

Sweet, A. P. (1993, November). *State of the art: Transforming ideas for teaching and learning to read.* Washington, DC: U.S. Department of Education, Office of Educational Research and Improvement.

Taylor, B. M., Pearson, P. D., Peterson, D. S., & Rodriguez, M. C. (2003). Reading growth in high-poverty classrooms: The influence of teacher practices that encourage cognitive engagement in literacy learning. *Elementary School Journal, 104,* 3–28.

Tharp, R. G., & Gallimore, R. (1988). *Rousing minds to life: Teaching, learning, and schooling in social context.* Cambridge, UK: Cambridge University Press.

van den Branden, K. (2000). Does negotiation of meaning promote reading comprehension?: A study of multilingual primary school classes. *Reading Research Quarterly, 35*(3), 426–443.

Veerman, A. L., Andriessen, J. E. B., & Kanselaar, G. (2000). Learning through synchronous electronic discussion. *Computers in Education, 34*, 269–290.

Vygotsky, L. S. (1978). *Mind in society: The development of higher psychological processes.* Cambridge, MA: Harvard University Press.

Waggoner, M., Chinn, C. A., Yi, H., & Anderson, R. C. (1995). Collaborative reasoning about stories. *Language Arts, 72*(8), 582–589.

Werderich, D. E. (2006). The teacher's response process in dialogue journals. *Reading Horizons, 47*(1), 47–73.

Wiencek, J., & O'Flahavan, J. F. (1994). From teacher-led to peer discussions about literature: Suggestions for making the shift. *Language Arts, 71*(7), 488–498.

Wilkinson, I. A. G., & Hye Son, E. (2011). A dialogic turn in research on learning and teaching to comprehend. In M. L. Kamil, P. D. Pearson, E. Moje, & P. Afflerbach (Eds.), *Handbook of reading research* (Vol. 4, pp. 358–387). New York: Routledge.

Wolf, M. K., Crosson, A. C., & Resnick, L. B. (2005). Classroom talk for rigorous reading comprehension instruction. *Reading Psychology, 26*, 27–53.

Wollman-Bonilla, J. E. (1989). Reading journals: Invitations to participate in literature. *The Reading Teacher, 43*, 112–120.

Wollman-Bonilla, J. E., & Werchadlo, B. (1999). Teacher and peer roles in scaffolding first graders' responses to literature. *The Reading Teacher, 52*(6), 598–608.

Wolsey, T. D. (2004, January–February). Literature discussions in cyberspace: Young adolescent using threaded discussion groups to talk about books. *Reading Online, 7*(4). Retrieved September 2011 from *www.readingonline.org/articles/art_index.asp?HREF=wolsey/index.html.*

CHAPTER 11

Vocabulary Instruction ● ● ● ● ● ● ● ● ● ● ●

LINDA KUCAN

Attention to vocabulary instruction has never been greater, and researchers are providing robust resources for enacting that instruction with students across grade levels, disciplines, and languages. The resources range from books and articles to websites and television programs. For example, although older PBS children's programs such as *Sesame Street* and *Between the Lions* have always highlighted vocabulary, two recent programs—*Martha Speaks* and *Word Girl*—place vocabulary at center stage. *Martha Speaks* is targeted for preschoolers and children in kindergarten and the primary grades. Martha is a dog who can speak if she eats alphabet soup, and when she talks she uses precise vocabulary such as *persuade, evidence, unique,* and *specialize.* Word Girl is a fifth grader, and the target audience for her show is upper elementary students. Word Girl is a super-hero with a versatile vocabulary that she uses in expert fashion. Both programs introduce sophisticated words by providing friendly explanations of word meanings and demonstrating how the words can be used in diverse settings to explain or describe various characters, events, ideas, or situations. Research has demonstrated that all of those elements are key to vocabulary learning.

The Word Generation online program (*http://wordgeneration.org*) is another example of how research-based principles are informing vocabulary instruction presented in multimedia resources. Whereas *Martha Speaks* and *Word Girl* target students in preschool through the upper elementary grades, Word Generation focuses on students in middle school. The Word Generation resources emphasize academic vocabulary across English language arts, science, social studies, and math, and provide specific activities for teachers to use. In a school that has adopted Word Generation, as students move from one class to another, they are provided with reading and writing opportunities to learn about and use the same set of words in discipline-specific contexts.

Professional development related to vocabulary instruction begins with building an understanding of how vocabulary research informs such principled instructional approaches.

OVERVIEW OF RESEARCH

This selective overview of vocabulary research addresses these topics:

- Vocabulary acquisition
- Knowledge of word features
- Instructional approaches that support vocabulary acquisition

Vocabulary Acquisition

The initial vocabulary acquisition context for children is the verbal environment of the home. In that context, the number of different words that children hear and the kinds of interactions around those words in which children are engaged have profound consequences. In their landmark study, Hart and Risley (1995, 2003) documented the vocabulary acquisition of children ages 7–9 months to 3 years from welfare, working-class, and professional families. They found that, on average, children in welfare families were exposed to about half as many words per hour as children in working-class families, and fewer than a third as many words as children in professional families. As a result, "The three year old children from families on welfare not only had smaller vocabularies [on average] than did children of the same age in professional families, but they were also adding words more slowly" (2003, p. 7).

This finding makes sense, according to research by Nagy and Scott (2000), who emphasized the *incrementality* and *interrelatedness* of word learning. That is, children need multiple exposures to words and how those words can be used in different ways in order to learn the words (incrementality), and learning the meaning of one word can scaffold the learning of words with related meanings (interrelatedness). For example, knowing the meaning of *confusion* can support children in building an understanding of synonyms such as *chaos*, as well as antonyms such as *clarity*.

Because of diversity in their initial language experiences, children come to school with vast differences in the depth and breadth of their vocabulary knowledge, and the disparity only increases over time (Biemiller & Slonim, 2001; Cunningham & Stanovich, 1997; Graves, Brunetti, & Slater, 1982; Smith, 1941; White, Graves, & Slater, 1990). Once children are in school, there is a dramatic shift in the nature of their vocabulary acquisition. Whereas language in the home is most often focused on concrete events, situations, and objects, and on familiar people and pets, the language in school relates to "ideas that are beyond the here and now" (Beck & McKeown, 2001, p. 10). In order to gain access to those ideas, children need to be engaged in conversations that enlarge the focus and range of their experiences. Toward that end, reading trade books aloud and engaging children in interacting with the ideas and words in those books is an approach that has been shown to provide encouraging results (Beck & McKeown, 2001; Coyne, Simmons, Kame'enui, & Stoolmiller, 2004; Dickinson & Smith, 1994; Silverman, 2007; Teale, 2003). Specifically, classroom discourse around books that encourages children to focus on text content in interpretive and reflective ways, and to attend to the interesting and precise language authors use to present that content, provides a robust context for learning. Literary language—words such as *heroic* and *devious, forlorn* and *exuberant*—is the kind of language that most children do not have access to in everyday conversations. Information books for young children also offer opportunities for vocabulary learning with words such as *erode, nocturnal,* and *arid.* Such words are sophisticated and precise, surprising and interesting. And, as described below in the section on instructional approaches, young children can learn these words and enjoy using them.

Rich verbal interaction around read-alouds is an important feature of the energized verbal environment that characterizes classrooms in which vocabulary acquisition is supported (Kucan, 2012). In such classrooms, words are noticed and discussed. Teachers choose their words with care and invite students to do the same. Lane and Allen (2010) concur and assert that "it is time to elevate our instructional language to enhance our students' vocabularies" (p. 368). They suggest, for example, that teachers use words such as *accomplished, exemplary, masterful,* and *superior* to respond to student comments, instead of repeating overused phrases such as "Good job" or "OK." Such mindfulness can create the kind of rich verbal environment that is not available to many students outside school.

The importance of the oral verbal environment in which students are immersed cannot be underestimated; however, as children progress through the grades, reading rather than listening becomes the primary context for vocabulary acquisition, and the range of kinds of vocabulary expands. Specifically, students are exposed to more *academic vocabulary,* or the discourse of school found in textbooks and novels, and the instruction related to those resources. Baumann and Graves (2010) have defined academic vocabulary "(1) as *domain-specific academic vocabulary,* or the content-specific words used in disciplines like biology, geometry, civics, and geography; or (2) as *general academic vocabulary,* or the broad, all-purpose terms that appear across content areas but that may vary in meaning because of the discipline itself" (p. 6). Examples of domain-specific academic vocabulary include words like *diameter, butte,* and *ecosystem.* Such words represent well the importance of the interrelatedness of word learning (Nagy & Scott, 2000). Knowing what a *butte* is can support students in learning about other landforms, such as *tables, plateaus,* and *mesas.* Examples of general academic vocabulary include words like *table, conduct,* and *period.* Such words with multiple meanings, or

polysemy (Nagy & Scott, 2000), demonstrate the increasing complexity of word knowledge.

In addition to discipline-specific and general academic vocabulary, Baumann and Graves (2010) include the rich literary vocabulary that authors use to describe characters, settings, and plot developments as another category within academic vocabulary. Students encounter words such as *sinister, humble, admire,* and *coincidence* in novels and stories, as well as other genres such as editorials and informational texts.

As students discover the rich array of academic vocabulary, they also have opportunities to attend to the features of those words, which are described in the next section.

Knowledge of Word Features

English is a *morphophonemic* language; that is, "the spelling system is based on both representations of sound (phonemes) and units of meaning (morphemes)" (Carlisle & Stone, 2005, p. 428). As such, specific spelling or orthographic patterns provide cues for phonology, or pronouncing words. For example, the consonant–vowel–consonant spelling pattern usually indicates that the vowel between two consonants will represent a short-vowel sound, as in *ran, pep, sit, job,* and *tub.* Likewise, specific spelling or orthographic patterns provide cues to word meanings. For example, the morpheme spelled *-er* added to the end of a base word can mean "more than," as in *bigger,* or "one who," as in *bookbinder* or *singer.*

According to Carlisle and Stone (2005), *derived* words (i.e., forms or words created by adding affixes or inflectional endings) can exhibit *phonological transparency,* or consistency in pronunciation, as in *growth (grow)* and *odd (oddity);* or a lack of such

Word Features	
Word feature and explanation	**Example**
Base word: Word to which affixes or inflectional endings can be added	*Health* is a base word to which the suffix *-ful* can be added to form the derived word *healthful. Strong* is a base word to which the inflectional endings *-er* and *-est* can be added to form the derived words *stronger* and *strongest.*
Word root: Greek or Latin element to which affixes are attached and which cannot usually stand alone	*Derm* (skin) is a Greek word root that appears in the words *epidermis, dermatology,* and *hypodermic. Spect* (to look) is a Latin word root that appears in the words *spectator, inspect, prospect, suspect,* and *spectacle.*
Affix: A prefix or suffix added to a base word or word root	Words with prefixes include <u>in</u>correct, <u>un</u>usual, and <u>pre</u>judge. Words with suffixes include *correct<u>ion</u>, usual<u>ly</u>,* and *judg<u>ment</u>.*
Inflectional endings: Endings added to words to indicate changes in: • Tense • Number (singular and plural) • Degree	Examples of words with inflectional endings include: • *jump–jumped* (tense) • *book–books* (number) • *simple–simpler–simplest* (degree)

transparency, as in *health* (*heal*) and *decision* (*decide*). Awareness that pronunciation can act as a cue to meaning can assist readers in accessing the meanings of words. Words that do not exhibit phonological transparency can provide meaning clues through orthographic transparency, or consistency in spelling, as in *muscular* (*muscle*) and *signature* (*sign*). Research summarized by Carlisle and Stone (2005) reveals that "Students who are learning to read derived words are likely to make use of morphemes that are transparent in sound and spelling, whereas for older readers, orthographic transparency aids in recognition of morphemes in derived words that lack phonological transparency" (p. 432). Thus learning to read involves not only developing skill in decoding (letters–sounds) but also in increasing attention to and use of morphemes (units of meaning). An example from one student is shown in Figure 11.1.

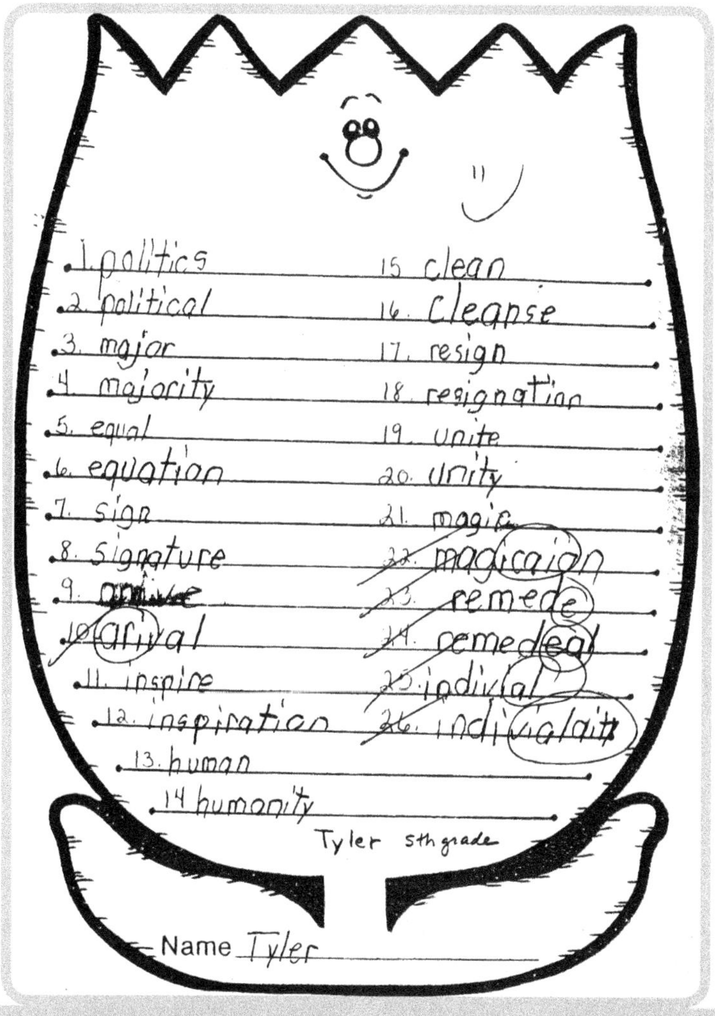

FIGURE 11.1. Tyler's spelling list includes pairs of words demonstrating orthographic transparency but lacking in phonological transparency. That is, the word pairs are consistent in spelling but not in pronunciation, such as *clean*–*cleanse* and *sign*–*signature*.

For Perfetti (2007), a high-quality mental representation of a word includes "well-specified and partly redundant representations of form (orthography and phonology) and flexible representations of meaning, allowing for rapid and reliable meaning retrieval" (p. 357). *Lexical quality*, or the quality of a word's representation in a person's mental *lexicon* (or dictionary), is influenced by knowledge of the word's pronunciation, spelling, internal units of meaning, and syntax, as well as by the ability to coordinate those constituent elements quickly and accurately. So, for example, a reader with a high-quality lexical representation for the word *sensational* would know what the word means, how to say the word, and how to spell it; would recognize that the suffixes *-ation* and *-al* have been added to the base word *sense*; and would use that knowledge to understand how the word functions as an adjective in a sentence. In addition, the reader would also have access to multiple forms of the word, such as *sense, sensation, sensible,* and *sensitive,* and would recognize these as related in meaning. A student example is shown in Figure 11.2.

For Nagy and Scott (2000), key word features also include *polysemy* and *interrelatedness*. Readers develop an awareness of the *polysemy*, or multiple meanings, of words. Thus readers would come to know that the word *sensation* can refer to a physical feeling related to a sense, such as the sensation of heat or cold; or to an emotional feeling, such as a sensation of well-being; or to a person or event that elicits great excitement and interest, such as a singer or actor who is described as an "overnight sensation."

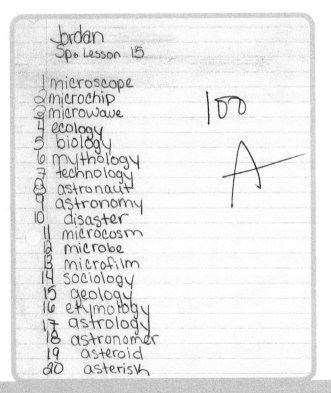

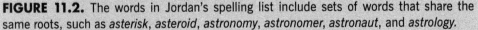

FIGURE 11.2. The words in Jordan's spelling list include sets of words that share the same roots, such as *asterisk, asteroid, astronomy, astronomer, astronaut,* and *astrology.*

Interrelatedness is another aspect of words that readers develop over time. For example, an understanding of the word *sensible* becomes connected to other words and phrases, such as *common sense* and *reasonable*. Reading about an overly sensitive person can evoke such words as *moody* and *emotional*.

Interrelatedness and polysemy emphasize the richness and complexity of the mental networks that capture word meanings, and contrast with notions that word meanings are stored in narrow slots or entries like dictionary definitions.

Given the vast range of vocabulary demands in terms of the kinds of words and the features of words that students need to learn, a logical question is this: What kinds of vocabulary instruction can support such learning?

Instructional Approaches That Support Vocabulary Acquisition

Vocabulary Instruction for Young Children

A fundamental principle for effective vocabulary instruction was articulated by Beck and McKeown (1991) in their chapter on conditions of vocabulary acquisition, which appeared in the second volume of the *Handbook of Reading Research*. (Interestingly, there was no chapter about vocabulary in the first volume of the *Handbook*.) According to Beck and McKeown's review of research, active processing of word meanings is the key to effective instruction. Active processing is elicited by instruction that includes "frequent encounters with each word, instructional strategies that entail elaboration and discussion of word meaning, and opportunities to use the taught words outside of the classroom" (p. 806). Such instruction supports students in building multiple and varied connections that facilitate access to word meanings (e.g., Beck, McKeown, & Omanson, 1987; Beck, Perfetti, & McKeown, 1982).

Beck and McKeown (2001) described what that vocabulary instruction would look like in an article that introduced an approach called Text Talk. Although Text Talk mainly focuses on prompting children to engage with important ideas and themes in read-aloud contexts, it also includes suggestions for maximizing children's opportunities to learn sophisticated literary vocabulary through explicit activities focusing on introducing word meanings anchored in the context of the story, and subsequently using the words in situations not directly related to the story. For example, after children learned the meaning of *reluctant* and used the word to identify how a character in a story felt, they were provided with different scenarios and asked whether they would feel reluctant—for example, riding a roller coaster. Then children were asked to complete sentence stems such as "I might be reluctant to _____." Over the course of a week, children interacted with the word in a variety of ways, identifying examples and generating their own examples and comparing and contrasting feelings related to *reluctant*, such as *enthusiastic* and *eager*. The goal of such instruction is to support students in developing rich and elaborated representations of word meanings, both through encouraging attention and curiosity about words, and through implementing a specific instructional sequence.

Beck and McKeown (2007) implemented the rich vocabulary instruction described in their 2001 article in two studies with kindergarten and first-grade children. Participants in the first study were four classes of kindergartners and four classes of first graders. These children were African American students in a small urban school that was a candidate for state takeover if student achievement did not improve. More than 80% of the students in the school were eligible for free or reduced lunch.

Two classes at each grade level were assigned to the instructional group (52 children) and two to the comparison group (46 children). Children were pretested on the words targeted for instruction, and there were no differences between groups in vocabulary knowledge. Children in the comparison group participated in read-aloud sessions with trade books that included rich literary language, but the meanings of the words were not specifically taught. Children in the instructional group also participated in read-aloud sessions with a set of trade books, but they were introduced to the meanings of sophisticated words from each of the books and, across 3 days, were engaged in using the words in a variety of activities such as those described above. Sample target words included *cautiously, dazzling, envious,* and *forlorn* (for kindergarten) and *leisurely, panic, exquisite,* and *dignified* (for first grade). On the posttests, children in the instructional groups for kindergarten and first grade learned more of the target words than those in the comparison groups. The mean gain for kindergartners was 5.58 words and for first graders was 3.64 words. Beck and McKeown wondered why children hadn't learned more of the 22 target words. They hypothesized that the duration of the instruction might be an important factor.

In Study 2, the time spent on vocabulary instruction was a key variable. Participants in this study were three kindergarten and three first-grade classes (76 children). These children were from the same small urban school district described above. All children were introduced to six words from each of seven books. The instructional sequence consisted of reading the book on Day 1, introducing the six vocabulary words on Day 2, and participating in vocabulary activities on Day 3. On Days 4 and 5, children focused their attention on only three of the six words they were learning. The words selected each week for more rich instruction were also featured in two review cycles. Across the study, children spent 6.6 minutes on words selected for instruction, and 27.6 minutes on words selected for more rich instruction. On the posttests, kindergartners and first graders demonstrated gains about twice as large for words targeted for more rich instruction. Figure 11.3 illustrates kindergartners' improved understanding of some of the words they learned through rich instruction.

ASSESSMENT

The assessments that Beck and McKeown (2007) developed to test children's depth of vocabulary knowledge are a noteworthy aspect of these studies. Children responded to picture and verbal prompts for each word. The pictures required children to analyze four different scenes and consider which one could be described by using the target vocabulary word. For example, children considered the following scenes in order to select the one that could showed people being *dignified*: a couple dressed in elegant clothes, children in Halloween costumes, two men looking around as if they were hiding, and two children pulling on the arms of a teddy bear. For the verbal items, children responded to prompts such as these for the word *evaded*: "If a dog jumped in the air, would that be *evading*? Does *evade* mean to avoid or get away without doing something? If you steered your bike away from a big hole, would that be *evading*? Does *evade* mean to have a bad dream?" Beck and McKeown's research demonstrates that even on rigorous measures of vocabulary knowledge, young children can—with the right kind of

FIGURE 11.3. These sentences and drawings by kindergartners reveal their understanding of the sophisticated words *reluctant*, *comforting*, and *vain*, which they learned through rich instruction. From Beck, McKeown, and Kucan (2008). Copyright 2008 by The Guilford Press. Reprinted by permission.

instructional support—demonstrate their learning of the sophisticated vocabulary they will need as they progress through school.

Vocabulary Instruction for Linguistically Diverse Students

Lesaux, Kieffer, Faller, and Kelley (2010) focused their vocabulary research on linguistically diverse students in middle schools. Lesaux and her colleagues developed an instructional sequence they called *academic language instruction for all students* (ALIAS). The instruction took place with sixth graders during 45-minute sessions across an 8-day cycle for 18 weeks, and was supported by a strong professional development component. A total of 476 students participated in the study, only 130 of whom were native English speakers. There were 12 teachers and 296 students in the treatment group, and 7 teachers and 180 students in the control group.

ALIAS provided students with opportunities to learn the meanings of 72 high-utility academic words, such as *establish, distinctions, anticipate,* and *generate;* to learn about morphological features of derived forms of the words, such as *establishment, distinct, anticipation,* and *generative;* and to use the words in speaking, listening, reading, and writing activities. Students participated in whole-class, small-group, and individual settings.

Each set of 8–9 words was introduced in the context of a high-interest article, which was the focus of a discussion and the initial context for encountering the target words and their definitions. On subsequent days, students answered questions about the text that required the use of the vocabulary words and made sketches representing the word meanings. Later, they used the target words in different contexts, such as role plays and responses to questions and scenarios. Students were also introduced to multiple meanings of the target words and were shown how those meanings could be cued by context.

Morphology was an important focus of activities that drew students' attention to derived forms of the words. These activities involved learning about suffixes and inflectional endings and discovering how those morphemes change a word's part of speech, or function in a sentence. Using the target words in writing was also an integral part of the instructional sequence. Students participated in carefully scaffolded writing activities from prewriting to final drafts of paragraphs. Review units were interspersed within the instructional cycles for sets of words. These review units included game-like activities to reinforce word meanings as well as reteaching activities that addressed words and word features that students had difficulty with on assessments.

ASSESSMENT

To assess the depth of students' vocabulary knowledge, Lesaux and colleagues (2010) developed multiple measures. The Target Word Mastery assessment asked students to select an appropriate synonym for a target word. The Word Association assessment presented students with a target word in the center of a box surrounded by six other words. Students were asked to select the three words that "always go with the target word" (p. 208). For example, for the target word *effect,* the six word choices were *cause, consequence, result, negative, policy,* and *people.* The correct choices were *cause, consequence,* and *result.*

The Morphological Awareness measure presented students with a derived word and asked them to extract the base word in order to complete a sentence. For example, for the derived word *complexity*, students were asked to complete this sentence: "The problem is [complex]." The Word-Meanings-in-Context assessment required students to read a passage and respond to multiple-choice questions about the main idea, as well as the meanings of target words as used in the text. Distracters included choices for the meaning of a target word that was a correct meaning, but not the meaning of the word as it was used in the text.

Analysis of student performance on posttests indicated that those who participated in ALIAS demonstrated positive and statistically significant effects on the Target Word Mastery, Morphological Decomposition, and Word-Meanings-in-Context measures. The analysis also revealed marginally significant effects on the Word Association measure and a norm-referenced comprehension assessment. These results were comparable for native speakers of English and for English language learners (ELLs).

The research of Lesaux and colleagues (2010) demonstrates the positive impact of vocabulary instruction that addresses both word meanings and word features. Like the instructional sequence developed by Beck and McKeown (2007) for young children, the sequence developed by Lesaux and her colleagues provided multiple exposures to target words in different contexts across a series of days so that students had enough time to interact with and use the words. The study also foregrounds the positive impact of instruction about word features.

SUMMARY OF BIG IDEAS FROM RESEARCH

- The verbal environment of the home has a significant impact on children's vocabulary acquisition (Hart & Risley, 1995, 2003).
- Children come to school with vast differences in vocabulary knowledge, and the disparity increases over time (Biemiller & Slonim, 2001; Cunningham & Stanovich, 1997; Graves, Brunetti, & Slater, 1982; Smith, 1941; White et al., 1990).
- Word learning can be enhanced in school settings through attention to word choices during classroom activities, as well as through rich verbal interactions around well-written trade books in read-aloud contexts (Beck & McKeown, 2001; Coyne et al., 2004; Dickinson & Smith, 1994; Silverman, 2007; Teale, 2003).
- Informal encounters with sophisticated vocabulary are not sufficient to support students' vocabulary acquisition, particularly acquisition of the academic vocabulary that students need to succeed in school. Thoughtfully designed instructional sequences that engage students in active processing of word meanings through multiple encounters and interactions with words are required to support students' deep knowledge of word meanings (Baumann & Graves, 2010; Beck & McKeown, 1991, 2001, 2007; Beck et al., 1982, 1987; Lesaux et al., 2010).
- Word learning is incremental and interrelated; that is, learning words takes time and involves connecting known words and new words (Nagy & Scott, 2000).
- Developing an understanding of word meanings is enhanced through instruction related to morphology, or meaningful word parts (Carlisle & Stone, 2005; Lesaux et al., 2010).
- A high-quality mental representation of a word includes knowledge of a word's meaning, pronunciation, spelling, internal units of meaning, and syntax, as well as the ability to coordinate these elements quickly and accurately (Perfetti, 2007).

EXAMPLES OF EFFECTIVE PRACTICES

The examples of instructional approaches that follow emphasize the critical role of teacher scaffolding in developing instructional activities for vocabulary development and the importance of social interaction around vocabulary learning.

Thoughtful Word Selection for Focusing Attention on Cognates

Carlo, August, and Snow (2005) developed a vocabulary improvement program (VIP) that targets students whose first language is Spanish. The program includes a curriculum for vocabulary instruction—including a rationale for selecting words and emphasizing specific word features—and instructional strategies for implementing the curriculum. An important feature of VIP is focusing students' attention on *cognates*, or Spanish and English words that share the same root and have similar meanings—for example, the words *composition* in English and *composición* in Spanish. In selecting words to teach, Carlo and colleagues paid attention to English–Spanish cognates such as *contained–contener* and *journey–jornada*. They also selected target English words for which there were Spanish cognates for sophisticated synonyms—for example, *sprouted–germinar* (*germinate*); *likely–probable* (*probable*); and *glowing–candente* (*candescent*) (p. 142). An explicit part of the instructional sequence for the target words was having Spanish-speaking students act as resources for identifying cognates. Bravo, Hiebert, and Pearson (2007) suggested that "Spanish–English cognates can also be regarded as a 'fund of knowledge' that can be used to bridge community with classroom ways of knowing" (p. 147). The VIP approach specifically encourages students who are Spanish speakers to share their knowledge of cognates; this not only supports their vocabulary learning, but also draws attention to the interrelatedness of languages for all students.

Supporting Students' Understanding of Derived Words

Kieffer and Lesaux (2010) designed an 18-week instructional sequence to focus middle school students' attention on suffixes and the derived words that they create when added to a base word (e.g., *nation–national*, *discuss–discussion*). First, they developed a list of suffixes that they would teach, selecting those that are used most frequently. Then, they developed a spiraling curriculum that involved revisiting suffixes in more complex words over time. For example, the introduction to the suffixes *-al* and *-ical* focused on words that were familiar to students, such as *accidental, magical*, and *musical*. In subsequent lessons, the suffixes were identified in less familiar words, such as *cultural, optional, methodical*, and *periodical*.

Students were introduced to the idea of suffixes and how they function to create derived words by being presented with the following chart and the prompts by the teacher included below (Kieffer & Lesaux, 2010, p. 51):

invent	invention
invite	invitation
celebrate	celebration
imagine	imagination

TEACHER: . . . Today, we are going to talk about one way you can learn new words on your own—by breaking them down into parts that you already know. Look at the four sets of words I have on the board. Turn to your partners and tell them what you think the words in each column have in common. Think about both their forms and their meanings.

FIRST STUDENT: My partner said that the ones on the left are things you do.

TEACHER: Good thinking. The words on the left are all action words for things that you do. . . . We call that type of word a *verb*. How about the ones on the right? . . . What did you notice about the meaning of those words? How are their meanings different from the words on the left?

SECOND STUDENT: My partner said that all the words on the right have "-tion."

TEACHER: Great. What did you notice about the meaning of those words? How are their meanings different from the words on the left?

THIRD STUDENT: I'm not sure, but an invention is a thing . . . it's something that you invent.

TEACHER: You're right. When you add "-tion" to *invent*, you change it from an action into an object, the thing that someone invents. It's the same with these other words— adding "-tion" changes them from verbs to nouns.

As this exchange demonstrates, the instruction around the meaning of suffixes included learning about how suffixes change a word's part of speech. To reinforce this notion, Kieffer and Lesaux (2010) also posted cumulative word form charts such as the one below, so that students could add to them as they learned more suffixes (p. 54):

verbs (actions)	nouns (person, place, thing, or idea)	adjectives (words to describe nouns)	adverbs (words to describe actions)
contribute	contribution		
	culture	cultural	culturally
	method	methodical	methodically

By organizing words in a chart, students could see how suffixes created derived words and how those words would function in sentences.

Engaging Students in Developing Word Consciousness

Scott and Nagy (2004) reported on a program called The Gift of Words. The program addressed students' *word consciousness*, or their awareness of how authors select words and craft phrases to convey their ideas in memorable ways. The program engages students in noticing the interesting and precise language used by authors, and in attempting the same kind of careful language choice in their own writing. The underlying rationale for the program is that "Emerging writers need to study master writers, just as emerging musicians and artists study the masters in their fields" (p. 208).

Teachers who used the program read books and poems to students, and worked with students to collect "phrases the author used to paint a particularly vivid picture or a descriptive phrase that added texture and tone to the writing" (p. 209). These phrases were posted in the classroom and analyzed through discussion. Phrases were grouped so that students could see how authors craft comparisons or enhance descriptions of characters or settings. And students were encouraged to incorporate phrases that they selected in their own writing.

Students were also taught how to make use of how phrases were structured so that they could use similar structures in their own writing. "For example, the phrase 'There are more thieves than trees in a place like this,' from *The Half-a-Moon Inn* (Fleischman, 1980), became 'There is more filth than clean air in a dump like this' in one student's writing. Another changed 'She was a great potato of a woman' (from *Tuck Everlasting* by Natalie Babbitt, 1975) to 'He was a long string bean of a man'" (p. 210).

The consistent attention to authors' word choices and structuring of phrases in high-quality literature is one way to support students' developing word consciousness; it also provides a context for connecting vocabulary development and writing.

LOOKING FORWARD

Current research suggests the following:

- Children in kindergarten and first grade can learn sophisticated vocabulary through the use of instructional sequences that promote active engagement with word meanings (Beck & McKeown, 2007; Silverman, 2007).
- Students in middle school—including ELLs—can acquire the kind of academic vocabulary they need to succeed in school through the implementation of instructional sequences that focus students' attention on word meanings and word features in authentic contexts and opportunities to interact with the words in reading, writing, listening, and speaking activities (Lesaux et al., 2010).
- Attention to vocabulary development can be provided across a typical school day in activities that specifically address vocabulary development, but also during lessons focusing on phonics, spelling, grammar, and word study (Kucan, 2012).

Future research is needed to investigate these issues:

- The potentially positive relationship between students' vocabulary development and the quality of the word choices that they make for expressing their ideas in writing (Beck, McKeown, & Kucan, 2008).
- How linguistic knowledge of cognates can be drawn upon by ELLs to support their vocabulary acquisition (Bravo et al., 2007).
- The potential impact of accessible resources for vocabulary instruction on the classroom practices of teachers, and on the efforts of teacher educators, literacy coaches, and professional developers.

QUESTIONS FOR REFLECTION •

1. What kinds of vocabulary do students in your classroom encounter during the course of a day? What opportunities for enhancing the verbal environment do you create? Brainstorm lists of words related to classroom routines that you might use as contexts for carefully chosen word choices. For example, what kinds of comments might you write on student papers to offer specific suggestions for improvement, or to express your assessment and appreciation of their accomplishments? How might you model and encourage students to use precise words in offering comments, suggestions, or ideas, and also in responding to what other students share during a discussion?

2. How do you encourage students to notice words and to observe how words are used in unusual ways? What kinds of books or other resources are available for students to consult when they want to find out more about words that have piqued their interest?

3. Given the tremendous impact of the language children hear and are encouraged to use in their homes, how do you support and engage parents in scaffolding their children's vocabulary development?

SUGGESTIONS FOR ONGOING PROFESSIONAL LEARNING • • • • • • •

Analyzing Current Vocabulary Instructional Sequences and Assessments

Session 1

- Discuss this chapter with colleagues in a professional learning community (PLC). Specifically, articulate the key features of instructional approaches that support students' vocabulary development.
- Refer to your current teachers' guides or curriculum guides for reading/language arts (including spelling), science, social studies, and mathematics. List the vocabulary words that are suggested for a weekly unit of study in each subject—all the words that students would be required to learn across subject areas in a typical week.
  - ◆ What kinds of words are students expected to learn? What are useful categories for sorting the words?
  - ◆ What are the most important words for them to learn? Why?
  - ◆ How are the words introduced and explained to students?

Session 2

- Analyze the vocabulary activities and assessments suggested in the teachers' guides or curriculum guides that you use.
  - ◆ Do the activities support students in building high-quality mental representations of word meanings and word features?
  - ◆ Do the assessments provide information about students' depth of knowledge about words?
  - ◆ Provide specific examples to support your conclusions.

Developing Vocabulary Instructional Sequences and Assessments

Session 1: Preparation

- Invite colleagues in your PLC to secure copies of the books and articles listed under *Research-Based Resources* at the end of this chapter. Ask for volunteers to use the resources to prepare reports on the topics listed below, and then to lead a working session to address the questions related to the topic.

Session 2: Selecting Words to Teach

- What principles should guide word selection for vocabulary instruction?
- Do these principles apply to the words identified in the teachers' guides and curriculum guides that you use?
- Develop a plan for selecting the words that you will target for rich, or in-depth, vocabulary instruction each week.

Session 3: Providing Student-Friendly Definitions

- What are important features of definitions or explanations that provide students with the kind of information that will allow them to build an understanding of word meaning?
- Are these features present in the definitions and explanations in the resources that you use?
- What resources can you consult to support your efforts to craft student-friendly definitions? For example, the *Collins COBUILD Student's Dictionary* (Sinclair et al., 2005) provides models of very useful definitions. The entry for *skeptical* is "Someone who is skeptical about something has a lot of doubts about it" (p. 618).
- Select a set of words that you have identified for vocabulary instruction, and develop definitions for the words. Include instructional sentences that provide examples of how the words are used—for example, "She was skeptical about the success of the team because the players had practiced together for only a very short time."

Session 4: Designing Activities That Engage Students in Using Words Orally and in Writing

- What kinds of activities engage students in using words that they are learning in meaningful ways?
- Are these kinds of activities included in the resources that you use?
- Create a menu of instructional activities with examples that you can refer to as you develop vocabulary lessons (see, e.g., Appendix A in Beck et al., 2008).

Session 5: Developing Students' Knowledge of Word Features

- What are the important word features that students need to know?
- What kinds of activities support students in developing an understanding of those features?

- Are these kinds of activities included in the resources that you use?
- Create a bank of examples of the kinds of activities that draw students' attention to word features such as spelling patterns, roots, affixes, and inflectional endings (see, e.g., Bear, Invernizzi, Templeton, & Johnston, 2012; Ganske, 2000, 2008; Kieffer & Lesaux, 2007, 2010).

Session 6: Assessing Vocabulary Knowledge

- What kinds of assessments reveal the depth of students' vocabulary knowledge?
- Are these kinds of assessments included in the resources that you use?
- Develop assessments for a set of words that you will be teaching. Create multiple items for each word. (Descriptions of assessments can be found in this chapter in the section entitled *Instructional Approaches That Support Vocabulary Acquisition*).

RESEARCH-BASED RESOURCES

Bear, D. R., Invernizzi, M., Templeton, S., & Johnston, F. (2012). *Words their way: Word study for phonics, vocabulary, and spelling instruction* (5th ed.). Boston: Pearson/Allyn & Bacon.

Beck, I. L., & McKeown, M. G. (2001). Text talk: Capturing the benefits of read-aloud experiences for young children. *The Reading Teacher, 55*(1), 10–20.

Beck, I. L., McKeown, M. G., & Kucan, L. (2002). *Bringing words to life: Robust vocabulary instruction.* New York: Guilford Press.

Beck, I. L., McKeown, M. G., & Kucan, L. (2008). *Creating robust vocabulary: Frequently asked questions and extended examples.* New York: Guilford Press.

Blachowicz, C., & Fisher, P. J. (2010). *Teaching vocabulary in all classrooms* (4th ed.). Boston: Pearson/Allyn & Bacon.

Collins COBUILD student's dictionary plus grammar. (2005). New York: HarperCollins.

Farstrup, A. E., & Samuels, S. J. (Eds.). (2008). *What research has to say about vocabulary instruction.* Newark, DE: International Reading Association.

Ganske, K. (2000). *Word journeys: Assessment-guided phonics, spelling, and vocabulary instruction.* New York: Guilford Press.

Ganske, K. (2008). *Mindful of words: Spelling and vocabulary explorations 4–8.* New York: Guilford Press.

Graves, M. F. (2006). *The vocabulary book: Learning and instruction.* New York: Teachers College Press.

Hiebert, E. H., & Kamil, M. L. (Eds.). (2005). *Teaching and learning vocabulary: Bringing research to practice.* Mahwah, NJ: Erlbaum.

Lubliner, S., & Scott, J. A. (2008). *Nourishing vocabulary: Balancing words and learning.* Thousand Oaks, CA: Corwin Press.

Marzano, R. J., & Pickering, D. J. (2005). *Building academic vocabulary: Teacher's manual.* Alexandria, VA: Association for Supervision and Curriculum Development.

Nation, I. S. P. (2008). *Teaching vocabulary: Strategies and techniques.* Boston: Heinle.

Scott, J. A., Skobel, B. J., & Wells, J. (2008). *The word-conscious classroom: Building vocabulary readers and writers need.* New York: Scholastic.

Strategic Education Research Partnership. (2011). Word Generation: A middle school academic language program. Retrieved from *http://wordgeneration.org.*

REFERENCES

Babbitt, N. (1975). *Tuck everlasting.* New York: Farrar, Straus, Giroux.

Baumann, J. F., & Graves, M. F. (2010). What is academic vocabulary? *Journal of Adolescent and Adult Literacy, 54*(1), 4–12.

Bear, D. R., Invernizzi, M., Templeton, S., & Johnston, F. (2012). *Words their way: Word study for phonics, vocabulary, and spelling instruction* (5th ed.). Boston: Pearson/Allyn & Bacon.

Beck, I. L., & McKeown, M. G. (1991). Conditions of vocabulary acquisition. In R. Barr, M. L. Kamil, P. Mosenthal, & P. D. Pearson (Eds.), *Handbook of reading research* (Vol. II, pp. 789–814). New York: Longman.

Beck, I. L., & McKeown, M. G. (2001). Text talk: Capturing the benefits of read-aloud experiences for young children. *The Reading Teacher, 55*(1), 10–20.

Beck, I. L., & McKeown, M. G. (2007). Increasing young low-income children's oral vocabulary repertoires through rich and focused instruction. *Elementary School Journal, 107*(3), 251–271.

Beck, I. L., McKeown, M. G., & Kucan, L. (2008). *Creating robust vocabulary: Frequently asked questions and extended examples.* New York: Guilford Press.

Beck, I. L., McKeown, M. G., & Omanson, R. C. (1987). The effects and uses of diverse vocabulary instructional techniques. In M. G. McKeown & M. E. Curtis (Eds.), *The nature of vocabulary acquisition* (pp. 147–163). Hillsdale, NJ: Erlbaum.

Beck, I. L., Perfetti, C. A., & McKeown, M. G. (1982). Effects of long-term vocabulary instruction on lexical access and reading comprehension. *Journal of Educational Psychology, 74,* 506–521.

Biemiller, A., & Slonim, N. (2001). Estimating root word vocabulary growth in normative and advantaged populations. *Journal of Educational Psychology, 98*(1), 44–62.

Bravo, M. A., Hiebert, E. H., & Pearson, P. D. (2007). Tapping the linguistic resources of Spanish–English bilinguals. In R. K. Wagner, A. E. Muse, & K. R. Tannenbaum (Eds.), *Vocabulary acquisition: Implications for reading comprehension* (pp. 140–156). New York: Guilford Press.

Carlisle, J. F., & Stone, A. C. (2005). Exploring the role of morphemes in word reading. *Reading Research Quarterly, 40*(4), 428–449.

Carlo, M. S., August, E., & Snow, C. E. (2005). Sustained vocabulary-learning strategy instruction for English-language learners. In E. H. Hiebert & M. L. Kamil (Eds.), *Teaching and learning vocabulary: Bringing research to practice* (pp. 137–153). Mahwah, NJ: Erlbaum.

Collins COBUILD student's dictionary plus grammar. (2005). New York: HarperCollins.

Coyne, M. D., Simmons, D. C., Kame'enui, E. J., & Stoolmiller, M. (2004). Teaching vocabulary during shared storybook reading: An examination of differential effects. *Exceptionality, 12*(3), 145–162.

Cunningham, A. E., & Stanovich, K. (1997). Early reading acquisition and its relation to reading experience and ability 10 years later. *Developmental Psychology, 33,* 934–945.

Dickinson, D., & Smith, M. K. (1994). Long-term effects of preschool teachers' book reading on low-income children's vocabulary and story comprehension. *Reading Research Quarterly, 29*(2), 104–122.

Fleischman, P. (1980). *The Half-a-Moon Inn.* New York: Harper & Row.

Ganske, K. (2000). *Word journeys: Assessment-guided phonics, spelling, and vocabulary instruction.* New York: Guilford Press.

Ganske, K. (2008). *Mindful of words: Spelling and vocabulary explorations 4–8.* New York: Guilford Press.

Graves, M. F., Brunetti, G. J., & Slater, W. H. (1982). The reading vocabularies of primary-grade children of varying geographic and social backgrounds. In J. A. Harris & L. A.

Harris (Eds.), *New inquiries in reading research and instruction* (pp. 99–104). Rochester, NY: National Reading Conference.

Hart, B., & Risley, T. R. (1995). *Meaningful differences in the everyday experience of young American children.* Baltimore: Brookes.

Hart, B., & Risley, T. R. (2003). The early catastrophe: The 30 million word gap by age 4. *American Educator, 27*(1), 4–9.

Kieffer, M. J., & Lesaux, N. K. (2007). Breaking down words to build meaning: Morphology, vocabulary, and reading comprehension in the urban classroom. *The Reading Teacher, 61*(2), 134–144.

Kieffer, M. J., & Lesaux, N. K. (2010). Morphing into adolescents: Active word learning for English-language learners and their classmates in middle school. *Journal of Adolescent and Adult Literacy, 54*(1), 47–56.

Kucan, L. (2012). What is most important to know about vocabulary? *The Reading Teacher, 65*(6), 360–366.

Lane, H. B., & Allen, S. A. (2010). The vocabulary-rich classroom: Modeling sophisticated word use to promote word consciousness and vocabulary growth. *The Reading Teacher, 63*(5), 362–370.

Lesaux, N. K., Kieffer, M. J., Faller, S. E., & Kelley, J. G. (2010). The effectiveness and ease of implementation of an academic vocabulary intervention for linguistically diverse students in urban middle schools. *Reading Research Quarterly, 45*(2), 196–228.

Nagy, W. E., & Scott, J. A. (2000). Vocabulary processes. In M. L. Kamil, P. B. Mosenthal, P. D. Pearson, & R. Barr (Eds.), *Handbook of reading research* (Vol. 3, pp. 269–284). Mahwah, NJ: Erlbaum.

Perfetti, C. A. (2007). Reading ability: Lexical quality to comprehension. *Scientific Studies of Reading, 11*(4), 357–383.

Scott, J. A., & Nagy, W. E. (2004). Developing word consciousness. In J. F. Baumann & E. J. Kame'enui (Eds.), *Vocabulary instruction: Research to practice* (pp. 201–217). New York: Guilford Press.

Silverman, R. (2007). A comparison of three methods of vocabulary instruction during read-alouds in kindergarten. *Elementary School Journal, 108*(2), 97–113.

Smith, M. K. (1941). Measurements of the size of general English vocabulary through the elementary grades and high school. *Genetic Psychology Monographs, 24*, 311–345.

Teale, W. H. (2003). Reading aloud to young children as a classroom instructional activity: Insights from research and practice. In A. van Kleeck, S. A. Stahl, & E. B. Bauer (Eds.), *On reading books to children* (pp. 114–139). Mahwah, NJ: Erlbaum.

White, T. G., Graves, M. F., & Slater, W. H. (1990). Growth of reading vocabulary in diverse elementary schools: Decoding and word meaning. *Journal of Educational Psychology, 82*, 281–290.

CHAPTER 12

Effective Writing Instruction in the 21st Century ● ● ● ● ● ● ● ● ● ● ● ● ●

GARY A. TROIA

Writing purposeful, comprehensible, and engaging texts clearly is one of the most challenging tasks we ask of our students. Composing text is a complex and difficult undertaking because it requires the mindful deployment and coordination of multiple affective, cognitive, linguistic, and physical operations to accomplish goals associated with genre- and task-specific conventions, audience needs, and an author's communicative purposes. Even prolific authors find writing high-quality texts to be demanding. For instance, celebrated author, editor, and journalist Gene Fowler quipped, "Writing is easy; all you do is sit staring at a blank sheet of paper until the drops of blood form on your forehead!" George Orwell, whose works include the acclaimed dystopian novels *Nineteen Eighty-Four* and *Animal Farm*, noted, "Writing a book is a horrible, exhausting struggle, like a long bout of some painful illness. One would never undertake such a thing if one was not driven on by some demon whom one can neither resist nor understand." Mary Higgins Clark (whose daughter and daughter-in-law also are prolific novelists), the writer of dozens of popular suspense novels, said of one of her first efforts, "The first four months of writing the book, my mental image is scratching with my hands through granite. My other image is pushing a train up a mountain, and it's icy, and I'm in bare feet." If accomplished writers express such consternation regarding writing, it is little wonder that students are often not up for the challenge.

OVERVIEW OF RESEARCH

Findings from the National Assessment of Educational Progress reinforce the notion that students generally struggle with this academic area: Nearly three-quarters of children and youth are not able to produce texts that are judged to meet grade-level expectations fully (Persky, Daane, & Jin, 2003; Salahu-Din, Persky, & Miller, 2008). At least four instructional factors may be related to this widespread difficulty with writing among America's school-age population: (1) too little time devoted to teaching writing (Cutler & Graham, 2008); (2) differences in how teachers define and implement a process approach to writing instruction, which is often the "default" approach to teaching written expression (Lipson, Mosenthal, Daniels, & Woodside-Jiron, 2000; Troia, Lin, Cohen, & Monroe, 2011); (3) mismatches between what teachers communicate is important during instruction and their actual written feedback to students and comments during writing conferences (Clare, Valdez, & Patthey-Chavez, 2000); and (4) systemic barriers to effective teaching, such as limited professional development, vague standards, and unsupportive curriculum materials (Troia & Maddox, 2004).

Of course, student variables also contribute to the weak writing performance we observe in our schools. Students from impoverished neighborhoods and from culturally and linguistically diverse families, as well as children and youth with special needs who are educated most of the time in the general education classroom, are likely to have language and literacy backgrounds that are a poor match for classroom performance expectations in this age of rigorous standards and increased accountability. Therefore, many of today's students struggle with writing. As I have summarized elsewhere (Troia, 2006), struggling writers typically compose papers that are shorter, more poorly organized, and weaker in overall quality than those written by their peers. In addition, these students' compositions typically contain more irrelevant information and more mechanical and grammatical errors that render their texts less readable. The problems experienced by struggling writers are attributable to weaknesses in their knowledge about, skills in, and motivation for writing (e.g., Graham & Harris, 2000; Graham, Harris, & Troia, 1998; Troia, 2002; Troia & Graham, 2003; Troia, Shankland, & Wolbers, 2012). For instance, struggling writers often have underdeveloped knowledge of word and sentence structures, of topic-related content, and of what constitute high-quality writing and good writing behaviors. They also frequently have limited ability to self-regulate their thoughts, feelings, and actions throughout the writing process. They may display poor attention and concentration, and even weak visual–motor integration and fine motor control. Of course, many struggling writers lack sufficient skill with the conventions of written language. In the area of motivation, struggling writers often (1) fail to balance performance goals, which relate to documenting performance and achieving success, with mastery goals, which relate to acquiring competence; (2) exhibit maladaptive attributions by attributing academic success to external and uncontrollable factors, such as task ease or teacher assistance, but academic failure to internal yet uncontrollable factors, such as limited aptitude; (3) have negative self-efficacy (competence) beliefs; and (4) lack persistence. We must keep in mind that individuals struggle with writing for diverse reasons, and so differentiated instruction should place greater emphasis on strengthening students' limitations in knowledge, skills, and/or motivation, while also drawing on their natural talents and abilities (e.g., areas of interest or extensive topic knowledge).

In order for teachers to support writing development for all students, especially those who struggle with writing, certain qualities must be present in the writing classroom. Ten core attributes of effective writing instruction constitute the foundation of any good writing program; these are presented in Figure 12.1. All of these basic attributes must be thoughtfully coordinated to form a comprehensive writing program for students. These characteristics of exemplary writing instruction are equally relevant for elementary and secondary teachers—regardless of content-area focus—and their young writers. If students are expected to become competent writers, then writing instruction must be approached in highly orchestrated ways by all teachers who expect writing performance in their classrooms, and must be sustained across the grades to support students as they gradually become accomplished writers (e.g., Taylor, Pearson, Clark, & Walpole, 2000). Writing workshop is a prevalent instructional model in which the process of writing is emphasized more than the written product, and in which students' interests and autonomy are highly valued. Because so many teachers use some variation of writing workshop as the fundamental structure for their writing program, the attributes of an exemplary workshop regarding student work, instructional approach, and routines are described in Figure 12.2. Some of the most important attributes include

- Meaningful writing experiences and authentic writing tasks that promote personal and collective expression, reflection, inquiry, discovery, and social change.
- Predictable routines that permit students to become comfortable with the writing process and move through the process over a sustained period of time at their own rate.
- Lessons to help students master craft elements (e.g., text structure, character development), writing skills (e.g., spelling, punctuation), and process strategies (e.g., planning and revising tactics).
- A common language for shared expectations and feedback regarding writing quality, which might include the use of traits (e.g., organization, ideas, sentence fluency, word choice, voice, conventions, and presentation).
- Procedural supports such as conferences, planning forms and charts, checklists for revision/editing, and computer tools for removing transcription barriers.
- A sense of community in which risks are supported, children and teachers are viewed as writers, personal ownership is expected, and collaboration is a cornerstone of the program.
- Integration of writing instruction with reading instruction and content-area instruction (e.g., use of touchstone texts to guide genre study, use of common themes across the curriculum, maintaining learning notebooks in math and science classes).
- A cadre of trained volunteers who respond to, encourage, coach, and celebrate children's writing, and who help classroom teachers give more feedback and potentially individualize their instruction.
- Resident writers and guest authors who share their expertise, struggles, and successes, so that children and teachers have positive role models and develop a broader sense of writing as craft.
- Opportunities for teachers to upgrade and expand their own conceptions of writing, the writing process, and how children learn to write—primarily through professional development activities, but also through being active members of a writing community (e.g., the National Writing Project).

FIGURE 12.1. Ten core attributes of a top-notch classroom writing program (see Atwell, 1998; Calkins, 1994; Culham, 2003; Elbow, 1998a, 1998b; Graves, 1994; Spandel, 2001; Troia & Graham, 2003).

Student Work

- There are frequent opportunities for students to regulate their writing behaviors, the writing environment, and the use of resources.
- Daily writing occurs at school and at home, with students working on a wide range of composing tasks for multiple authentic audiences and purposes.
- Students select their own writing topics or may modify teacher assignments that are compatible with students' interests.
- Students work through the writing process at their own paces.
- Students present work in progress, as well as completed papers, to other students in and out of the classroom to receive praise and feedback.
- Students' written work is prominently displayed in the classroom and throughout the school.

Instructional Approach

- Teachers intentionally adjust their instructional emphasis on meaning, form, and process to meet individual students' needs.
- Instruction covers a broad range of knowledge, skills, and strategies, including writing conventions, sentence and text structure, the functions and forms of writing, and planning and revising.
- Teachers overtly model the writing process, writing strategies and skills, and positive attitudes toward writing during teacher-directed mini-lessons.
- Follow-up instruction is provided to ensure mastery of target knowledge, skills, and strategies.

Routines

- A predictable routine typically entails a mini-lesson, an individual progress check, independent writing and conferencing, and finally group sharing.
- Regular student–teacher conferences are scheduled to discuss progress, establish writing goals and self-evaluation criteria, and provide individualized feedback, all in the context of high expectations.
- Cooperative arrangements are established where students help one another to plan, draft, revise, edit, and publish their written work.
- Teachers arrange for periodic conferences and frequent communication with families to discuss the writing program and students' progress.

FIGURE 12.2. Specific characteristics of an exemplary writers' workshop.

explicit modeling, regular conferencing with students and families, high expectations, encouragement, flexibility, cooperative learning arrangements, and ample opportunities for self-regulation (e.g., Cutler & Graham, 2008; Gersten & Baker, 2001; Graham & Perin, 2007; Knapp & Associates, 1995; Rogers & Graham, 2008; Wharton-McDonald, Pressley, & Hampston, 1998).

Establishing Routines

A major step in implementing strong writing instruction is establishing routines (e.g., Wharton-McDonald et al., 1998) for (1) daily writing instruction, (2) covering the whole writing curriculum, and (3) examining the valued qualities of good writing. A typical writing lesson will have at least four parts, plus an occasional fifth:

- *Mini-lesson* (15 minutes). Teacher-directed lesson on writing skills, composition strategies, and crafting elements (e.g., traits of high-quality writing, character development, dialogue, leads for exposition, literary devices), which are demonstrated and practiced through direct modeling of the teacher's writing or others' work (e.g., shared writing, literature, student papers); initially, mini-lessons will need to focus on establishing routines and expectations.
- *Check-in* (5 minutes). Students indicate where they are in the writing process (i.e., planning, drafting, revising, editing, publishing). The teacher asks students to identify how they plan to use what was taught during the mini-lesson in their writing activities for that day.
- *Independent writing and conferring* (30 minutes). Students are expected to be writing or revising/editing, consulting with a peer, and/or conferencing with the teacher during this time.
- *Sharing* (10 minutes). Students identify how they used what was taught during the mini-lesson in their own writing and what challenges arose. The teacher may discuss impressions from conferring with students; students share their writing (it does not have to be a complete paper and may, in fact, only be initial ideas for writing) with the group or a partner, while others provide praise and constructive feedback. Students discuss next steps in the writing assignment.
- *Publishing celebration* (occasionally). Students need a variety of outlets for their writing to make it purposeful and enjoyable, such as a class anthology of stories or poems, a grade-level newspaper or school magazine, a public reading in or out of school, a website for student writing, a pen pal, the library, and dramatizations.

Several tools can help the teacher maintain the integrity of this lesson structure. First, each student should have a writing notebook for (1) recording "seed" ideas for writing, such as memories, wishes, observations, quotations, questions, illustrations, and artifacts (e.g., a letter or recipe); (2) performing planning activities; (3) drafting written compositions; and (4) logging writing activities and reflections (see Fletcher, 1996). Second, writing folders in which students keep their papers should be located in boxes that are labeled for different phases of the writing process. These folders will help organize different versions of a piece of writing students generate, as well as the various writing projects students work on at a given time. Of course, such a filing system can easily be created by using laptop or desktop computers and cloud computing that affords easy file sharing, collaboration, and revision (e.g., Dropbox).

Third, some means for visually displaying check-in status will help students and the teacher monitor individual and class progress in writing. Each student might, for example, put a card in the appropriate slot of a class pocket chart labeled with the stages of the writing process. Or the student might display the appropriate side of a personalized cube that represents the different writing stages (the sixth side might simply be labeled "Help" and would be used when teacher assistance is required). Fourth, a personal journal that may or may not be shared with the teacher or other students helps the teacher encourage writing outside the writing period (e.g., content-area instruction, independent activity, writing homework) and may be used later to provide material for student writing. If a journal is intended to be shared, the teacher should help students use a dialogue format that yields productive interactions between the author and readers (e.g., a double-column entry journal for another's remarks in response to the writer's entry) and to give thought to how the journal is to be evaluated, if at all.

A carefully orchestrated routine should also guide coverage of the writing curriculum. One type of routine includes genre study. In genre study, each instructional cycle focuses on a single genre (e.g., poetry) and one or two particular forms of that genre (e.g., cinquain and haiku). To develop a strong sense of the genre, a genre study cycle should typically last about one marking period. For primary-grade students, it is advisable to begin genre study with a highly familiar genre, such as personal narrative, so that students have an opportunity to become accustomed to the activities associated with genre study. However, an exclusive focus on narrative, even for young learners, is ill advised; genre study should encompass a broad set of authentic writing purposes. For any genre of instructional focus, teachers need to do the following:

- Develop students' explicit understanding of the genre structure, perhaps using a graphic aid or mnemonic device.
- Share "touchstone" texts that exemplify the structure and valued genre traits, and that represent high-quality writing (perhaps solicit suggestions from students).
- Establish a compelling purpose and audience for composing texts that use the genre structure.
- Give students time to explore potential ideas for writing through reflection, discussion, and research (writing notebooks are helpful for this).
- Identify and teach key vocabulary/phrases and leads that will help students create texts that "sound" like those written by authors.
- Provide students with graphic aids for planning their texts.
- Have students quickly write (*flash-draft*) parts of their papers, to diminish their reluctance to revise.
- Allow enough time for students to proceed through multiple iterations of revising and editing before publishing the finished product.

One way of thinking about the organization of genre study is to relate it to the process of growing a prize-winning begonia for entry into a garden show. The first step is to *plant the seed* for writing by helping students comprehend the purpose of the genre as a communicative tool, immersing students in *touchstone* texts (i.e., exemplary models) of the genre targeted for instruction, and discussing the key qualities of those examples to illustrate the structure and function of the genre. The next step is to *grow the seed* idea through careful planning and small increments of drafting (much like giving a seed just the right amount of sunlight, water, and fertilizer to help it grow). Then, as any accomplished gardener will tell you, once a plant begins to grow, it is often necessary to *prune back dead branches and leaves, add structural supports, and perhaps even graft new plants*. Likewise, once a draft has been produced, it requires multiple trimmings of unworkable portions or irrelevant information; expansions through the addition of details, examples, and even new portions of text; and attention to writing conventions for ultimate publication. Displaying one's writing in some public forum to gain valuable feedback and accolades, much like a prized begonia, is the culmination of all the hard work invested in the writing process and the written product.

Even when a top-notch writing program is firmly established in the classroom, some students will require additional assistance in mastering the skills and strategies of effective writing. Such assistance can be provided through adaptations, which include accommodations in the learning environment, instructional materials, and teaching strategies, as well as more significant modifications to task demands and actual writing tasks. A list of such adaptations is provided in Figure 12.3.

Teaching Spelling and Handwriting

Of course, elementary school teachers must explicitly teach spelling and handwriting to their students (this is not to say that secondary educators do not address these skills, but they do so to a much lesser extent) as one means of accommodating the needs of a diverse group of students, some of whom will probably not be adept at spelling and/or handwriting for a variety of reasons. Research-based suggestions for teaching spelling and handwriting to students with and without writing difficulties are summarized in Figures 12.4 and 12.5, respectively. For students with disabilities and for other struggling writers, more extensive practice and review of spelling, vocabulary, and letter forms, as well as the thoughtful application of other adaptations (e.g., individualized and abbreviated spelling lists, special writing paper) by the teacher, will be required. In the teaching of either spelling or handwriting, certain curriculum considerations should be addressed, including the following:

- Sequencing skills or grouping elements (words or letters) in developmentally and instructionally appropriate ways, based on careful observation of students' writing behaviors and performance.
- Providing students with opportunities to generalize spelling and handwriting skills to text composition.
- Using activities that promote independence.
- Establishing weekly routines (see Figures 12.4 and 12.5 for suggestions).
- Providing spelling or handwriting instruction for 15 minutes per day.
- Selecting instructional targets (i.e., spelling words and letters) for groups of students within the classroom, based on assessment data, so that instruction is differentiated for the range of student ability present.
- Introducing the elements at the beginning of the week.
- Modeling how to spell the words or write the letters correctly.
- Highlighting patterns and pointing out distinctive attributes (or having students "discover" these).
- Giving students ample opportunity to practice, with immediate corrective feedback.

Students can spend time practicing their spelling and/or handwriting and self-evaluating their performance, with the teacher frequently checking their work (error correction is critical). Depending on how well the students do, the teacher may teach additional lessons. The students might also work with each other to study/practice and evaluate each other's work. Finally, at the end of the week, the teacher should assess how well the students have learned the elements taught.

Accommodations in the Learning Environment

- Increase instructional time for writing.
- Provide quiet and comfortable spaces for students to work.
- Provide unimpeded access to writing tools.
- Let students identify and select meaningful reinforcements for achieving writing goals (e.g., a reinforcement menu).
- Consult with an occupational therapist to identify specialized adaptations (e.g., chair and desk height).

Accommodations in Instructional Materials

- Simplify language of writing prompts.
- Highlight (e.g., color-code) key words and phrases.
- Make a gradual transition from simple to more elaborate graphic organizers and procedural checklists.
- Post strategies, graphic organizers, and checklists in the classroom, and give students personal copies.
- Develop individualized spelling lists.
- Have students keep a personal dictionary of "demon" words and frequently used spelling vocabulary.
- Provide paper-positioning marks on students' desks.
- Provide pencil grips for students.
- Provide raised- or colored-lined paper.
- Provide students with personal copies of alphabet strips.

Accommodations in Teaching Strategies

- Devote more instructional time to writing mechanics.
- Provide physical assistance during handwriting practice.
- Reteach writing skills and strategies as needed.
- Expect and support mastery learning of skills and strategies (e.g., memorization of strategy steps).
- Use cross-age peer tutors to reinforce skills and strategies.
- Assign homework designed to reinforce writing instruction.
- Help students set specific and challenging yet attainable goals for the writing process (e.g., completing a planning sheet before beginning to draft) and written products (e.g., a quantity goal of including 10 descriptive words in a story, which is perhaps linked to a quality goal of improving word choice by 2 points on an analytic quality scale).
- Help students develop self-instructions (e.g., "I can handle this if I go slow") and self-questions (e.g., "Am I following my plan?") that focus on positive attributions for success and task progress.
- Teach students to evaluate and adjust their writing behaviors and writing strategy use to improve their writing productivity and performance.
- Promote maintenance and generalization of writing strategies by doing the following:
  - Modeling and discussing how strategies may be used in multiple contexts.
  - Relating writing performance to strategy use.
  - Having students teach others how to use strategies.
  - Having students keep a strategy notebook that they can consult at any time.
  - Ensuring that all staff members and caregivers are familiar with and prompt the use of the strategies.
  - Reviewing strategies often.

(continued)

FIGURE 12.3. Adaptations for struggling writers. These accommodations and modifications possess face validity, but many of them have not been empirically validated for struggling writers.

Modifications to Task Demands

- Increase the amount of time allotted for completing written assignments.
- Decrease the length and/or complexity of written assignments.
- Have students complete text frames (i.e., partially finished texts).
- Reduce or eliminate copying demands (e.g., teach students abbreviations for note taking, supply worksheets with math problems from textbook).
- Allow students to use temporary/invented spelling.
- Preteach spelling vocabulary for assignments.
- Evaluate spelling by using correct letter sequences (e.g., *hopping* has eight possible correct letter sequences) rather than number of words spelled correctly, to measure and reward incremental progress attributable to partial correct spelling.
- Permit students to dictate written work to a scribe.
- If students have adequately developed keyboarding skills, permit them to write papers with a word processor,
- Permit students to use outlining and semantic mapping software to facilitate planning.
- Permit students to use voice recognition technology to facilitate text transcription.
- Permit students to use integrated spell checker and/or word prediction software to facilitate correct spelling.
- Permit students to use speech synthesis technology to facilitate revising and editing.
- Selectively weight grading for content, organization, style, and conventions.
- Grade assignments based on the amount of improvement rather than absolute performance.
- Assign letter grades for body of work collected over time (i.e., portfolio assessment) rather than for each paper.
- Provide feedback on content, organization, style, and conventions for some rather than all assignments (which may reduce students' anxiety about writing).
- Provide feedback on targeted aspects of writing rather than all aspects, to avoid overwhelming students.

Modifications to Learning Tasks

- Permit students to dramatize or orally present a written assignment, either in lieu of writing or in preparation for writing.
- Assign students suitable roles (e.g., brainstorm manager) for the creation of a group-generated paper.

FIGURE 12.3. *(continued)*

To facilitate the establishment of weekly routines in spelling (which is usually a focus of instruction across elementary grades), the reader is encouraged to review the spelling handouts and activities presented in Figure 12.6 (see Graham, 1983). Specifically, to help students develop strategic competence and independence, they can use the *Spelling Study Plan* to summarize how well they performed on their pretest and how they plan to study their missed words, and, at the end of the week, to identify how effective their study plan was and what tactics they might employ to do better next time. When students study their spelling words during the remainder of the week, they can use the *Spelling Study Strategies* handout to remind them of the steps for multisensory rehearsal and mnemonics for remembering how to spell long words. Spelling study should not always be a solitary activity, so the *Partner Study Games* handout provides students with step-by-step instructions for two games that facilitate efficient

Curriculum Considerations

- Spelling vocabulary includes words drawn from children's reading materials, children's writing, self-selected words, high-frequency word lists (Graham, Harris, & Loynachan, 1993, 1994), and pattern words.
- Students are typically taught phonemic awareness and phoneme–grapheme associations (with the least consistent mappings, such as consonants /k/ and /z/ and long vowels, reserved for last) in kindergarten and first grade. Common spelling patterns (e.g., phonograms or rime families; Bear, Invernizzi, Templeton, & Johnston, 2012; Carnine, Silbert, & Kame'enui, 1997; Cunningham, 2000) are taught in first and second grades. Morphological structures (i.e., roots and affixes; Bear et al., 2012; Carnine et al., 1997; Cunningham, 2000; Harris & Sipay, 1985) and helpful spelling rules (e.g., add -*es* to make words ending in -*s*, -*z*, -*x*, -*ch*, or -*sh* plural) are taught in second grade and beyond.
- Students are taught systematic and effective strategies for studying new spelling words (e.g., mnemonic spelling links, multisensory strategies).
- Previously taught spelling words are periodically reviewed to promote retention.
- Correct use of spelling vocabulary in students' written work is monitored and reinforced.
- Students are taught and encouraged to use dictionaries, spell checkers, and other resources to determine the spelling of unknown words.
- Spelling "demons" and other difficult words are posted on wall charts.

Weekly Routines

- A minimum of 60–75 minutes per week is allocated for spelling instruction.
- Students take a Monday pretest to determine which words they need to study during subsequent activities and to set spelling performance goals.
- After studying new spelling words, students take a Friday posttest to determine which words were mastered.
- Immediately after taking a spelling test, students correct their misspellings.
- The teacher conducts word sorts and guided spelling activities to explicitly teach spelling patterns and rules at the beginning of the week.
- Daily opportunities are provided for cumulative study and testing of new spelling words (e.g., through computer-assisted instruction).
- Students work together each day to learn new spelling words.
- While studying, students monitor their on-task behavior or the number of times they correctly spell a target word, to promote active learning.

FIGURE 12.4. Tips for teaching spelling. Although the research base for these recommendations is limited (as compared to, for instance, the research base for instructional recommendations in reading), study findings are generally consistent (see Bourassa & Treiman, 2001; Graham, 1999, 2000; Templeton & Morris, 1999; Troia & Graham, 2003).

spelling study. Of course, all of these materials will require an introduction and initial guidance from the teacher. Directions for conducting word sorts and guided spelling are summarized in *Teacher-Directed Spelling Activities*. These activities are basic lesson formats, but the content for an actual lesson is derived from the spelling patterns (either orthographic or morphemic) targeted for instruction. These teacher-directed activities are used to provide more explicit spelling instruction, as student self-study or partner activities are insufficient for many students (especially those who struggle with spelling) to learn spelling patterns and rules.

Curriculum Considerations

- The initial use of one type of script (e.g., printing vs. cursive or different versions of printing) does not appear to affect handwriting performance.
- Special emphasis is placed on difficult-to-form letters and those that are frequently reversed.
- Lowercase letters are introduced before uppercase letters, unless they are formed by using similar strokes (e.g., *C, c*).
- Letters that share common strokes are grouped together (e.g., *o, c, d, a*).
- The introduction of easily confused letters (e.g., *b, d, p, q*) is staggered.
- The formation of individual upper- and lowercase letters and, for cursive, difficult letter transitions (e.g., *roam*) are modeled.
- Visual cues, such as numbered dots and arrows, and verbal descriptions are used to guide letter formation.
- Activities to reinforce letter recognition and naming are combined with handwriting practice.
- Students practice using a comfortable and efficient tripod pencil grasp.
- Students are shown and expected to use appropriate posture and paper positioning for their handedness.
- Handwriting fluency is developed through frequent writing and speed trials, with an emphasis on maintaining legibility.
- Opportunities are provided for distributed practice and judicious review of individual letters and letter sequences.
- Students are permitted to develop their own handwriting style and to choose which script (printing, cursive, or even a blend) they prefer to use after mastering handwriting (printing tends to be more legible than cursive and can be written just as quickly if it is given equal emphasis).
- Students are prompted to identify when a high degree of legibility is and is not necessary.

Weekly Routines

- In the primary grades, a minimum of 60–75 minutes per week is allocated for handwriting instruction.
- Students are encouraged to compare letters to discover patterns and to highlight their similarities and differences.
- Students are given opportunities to reinforce target letters by tracing them (a dashed or faded model), copying them, and writing them from memory.
- Students' handwriting is monitored and immediately reinforced for correct letter formation, spacing, alignment, size, slant, and line quality.
- Students are asked to self-evaluate their handwriting and to set goals for improving specific aspects of their handwriting each day.
- Students are encouraged to correct poorly formed letters and to rewrite illegible work.

FIGURE 12.5. Tips for teaching handwriting. Although the research base for these recommendations is limited (as compared to, e.g., the research base for instructional recommendations in reading), study findings are generally consistent (see Graham, 1999; Graham & Weintraub, 1996; Troia & Graham, 2003).

Spelling Study Plan

This handout can be used to help students summarize their performance on their pretest, so they can develop strategies for studying the words they missed.

1. I missed _____ words on my Monday test.
2. My goal is to learn to spell _____ words correctly.
3. I will use the following to help me study my spelling words:

    _____ Three-step study strategy

    _____ Word sorts

    _____ Making words

    _____ Partner study

    _____ Memory links

    _____ Finger spelling

    _____ Computer games

4. I correctly spelled _____ words on my Friday test.
5. I _____ did _____ did not meet my goal.
6. I _____ did _____ did not use my study plan.
7. To improve my spelling, next time I will . . . _____.

Spelling Study Strategies

This handout can be used to remind students of (1) the steps for multisensory rehearsal and (2) mnemonics for remembering how to spell long words.

Three-Step Study Strategy

Step 1: Look & Say
1. Look at the word you want to learn.
2. Say the word out loud.
3. Spell the word out loud.

Step 2: Cover & See
1. Cover the word.
2. See the word in your mind.
3. Trace the letters in the air.
4. Spell the word out loud and trace again.

Step 3: Write & Check
1. Cover the word.
2. Write the word.
3. Check the spelling.
4. Write the word two more times if your spelling is correct; if not, go back to Step 1.

Memory Links for Studying Long Words

Built-In Word Link
Example: Business is a sin.
Example: Clothes are made from cloth.

(continued)

FIGURE 12.6. Spelling handouts and activities.

Story Sentence Link
Example: When I go past a cemetery, I go "e e e!"
Example: My principal is my pal, but he has lots of rules or principles for us to follow.

Pronunciation Link
Example: Wed-nes-day
Example: tom-or-row

Partner Study Games

This handout can be used to provide students with instructions for games that facilitate efficient spelling study.

Circle Dot
1. Your partner says a word on your spelling list.
2. You write the word.
3. Your partner spells the word one letter at a time.
4. As your partner spells, draw a dot under each correct letter and a circle under each incorrect or omitted letter on your paper.
5. Study the parts of the word with circles.
6. Write the word again and check again.

Capture
1. Make five rows of dots with five dots in each row.
2. Decide who will go first.
3. Your partner should say a word on your list, and you should spell it out loud.
4. If you are correct, you get to connect two dots that are side by side; if not, your partner gets a turn (you get another turn when your partner misses a word).
5. Each time a player connects four dots to make a square, the player writes his or her initial in it so the square is "captured."
6. The player who has the most initialed squares at the end wins the game.

Teacher-Directed Spelling Activities

These activities are used to provide explicit spelling instruction in spelling patterns and rules.

Word Sorts
1. Students sort words, printed on index cards, containing a novel orthographic (e.g., *plight, frightening, mightily*) or graphomorphemic (e.g., *assignment, designate, signify, resignation*) pattern in order to discover the pattern.
2. The novel pattern is discussed and the representative words are added to a word wall, grouped together under an easily recognized anchor word for the pattern (e.g., *light, sign*).
3. Students search reading materials and their own writing samples for other examples of the new pattern, and they add these to the word wall.

Guided Spelling (Making Words)
1. Students are given single-letter or multi-letter tiles to combine into as many different real words as possible. These tiles represent the orthographic or graphomorphemic units in a "mystery" word that can be derived when all of the tiles are combined.
2. The words are recorded and verified with a dictionary or other spelling guide.
3. If a word is acceptable, it is written in a sentence to demonstrate understanding of its meaning.
4. Students are encouraged to spell other "transfer" words that contain some of the targeted letters or units.
5. Students read texts that contain the relevant spelling patterns and monitor their ability to recognize and define the words.

FIGURE 12.6. *(continued)*

Teaching Composing Strategies

Students who struggle with writing, as well as those who are more accomplished writers, typically require explicit and systematic instruction in specific composing strategies. The most emphasis should be placed on strategies that support the planning and revising aspects of the writing process, which trouble struggling writers the most. Fortunately, there have been numerous studies examining the effectiveness of various planning and revising strategies for students with and without writing difficulties in multiple educational contexts (i.e., whole classrooms, small-group instruction, individualized tutoring). Two excellent resources that describe this research and give advice on how to teach the many available strategies are *Writing Better: Effective Strategies for Teaching Students with Learning Difficulties* (Graham & Harris, 2005) and *Making the Writing Process Work: Strategies for Composition and Self-Regulation* (Harris & Graham, 1996). In this chapter, only a few research-based strategies are presented in depth, to give teachers an idea of how to implement composing strategies in their particular setting.

Self-Regulation of Writing

Before introducing these strategies, teachers need to consider the role of self-regulation in writing, as successful writers are highly aware of themselves as writers, of factors that influence their writing performance, and of how to use diverse strategies to manage these factors effectively. Self-regulation in writing includes at least four coordinated components (Graham, MacArthur, Schwartz, & Page-Voth, 1992): (1) goal setting, (2) self-talk, (3) self-evaluation, and (4) self-reinforcement. Generally speaking, the incorporation of self-regulation components in writing instruction has been shown to have a strong positive effect on both strong and weak writers' composing abilities (e.g., Gersten & Baker, 2001; Graham & Harris, 1989a, 1989b; Graham, Harris, & Mason, 2005; Graham & Perin, 2007; Sawyer, Graham, & Harris, 1992).

Setting goals enhances attention, motivation, and effort and facilitates strategic behavior (e.g., planning in advance of writing) through the valuation of goal attainment. In other words, if a goal is sufficiently important, a student will do all that is necessary to attain it. Research has demonstrated that goal setting improves writing skills in struggling writers (De La Paz, 2007; Graham & MacArthur, 1988; Graham, MacArthur, & Schwartz, 1995; Graham et al., 1992; Page-Voth & Graham, 1999; Schunk & Swartz, 1993a, 1993b). For goals to have the most beneficial impact on writing behavior and performance and to encourage the student to marshal sufficient effort, they should be challenging (i.e., just beyond the student's current level of writing skill), proximal (i.e., attainable within a short period of time), concrete, and self-selected or collaboratively established (because real or perceived control boosts achievement motivation). Goals can focus on a writing process or an aspect of the product. For writing product goals, quality and quantity goals can be established and explicitly linked. Examples of process goals might include the following:

1. Complete a planning sheet/graphic organizer, using words or short phrases, before writing. The use of single words or phrases to note planning ideas helps students feel less wedded to their initial plans because these plans do not become first drafts of whole texts.

2. Revise at least three times—once with a checklist, once with a peer, and once during a conference with the teacher before turning in the paper. Setting up multiple "passes" at a composition with different tools and individuals helps establish an expectation that meaningful changes to one's goals, plans, and text will be made.

3. Use the spell checker on the computer plus backward read-aloud to correct spelling mistakes, followed by use of a peer editor. Spell checkers catch a fairly limited number of spelling errors made by struggling writers, so rereading the text aloud (backward reading decouples orthographic recognition from linguistic processing, which tends to filter information and make mistakes harder to detect) and asking a peer to check for mistakes can facilitate editing.

Examples of product goals (a quality goal linked with a quantity goal aimed to make the quality goal more concrete) might include these:

1. Increase organization score by 1 point → include an initiating event, a character goal, then two actions to achieve the goal, and finally a consequence.
2. Increase content score by 2 points → include five main ideas in an informational text with at least two supporting details for each main idea.
3. Increase word choice score by 2 points → include at least 15 action helpers, descriptive words, or transition words per page.
4. Increase conventions score by 1 point → have no more than three errors per page on the final copy.

Self-talk (instructions, questions, affirmations, or exhortations directed to oneself) helps orient attention to relevant information, organize thoughts, plan actions, and execute behaviors. In addition, self-talk helps one cope with anxiety, frustration, self-doubt, and impulsivity, which tend to plague struggling writers and even those who are more accomplished writers. Self-talk has been widely investigated for several decades by researchers in many areas of psychology—sports, counseling, psychotherapeutic, and educational—with promising results: Adaptive self-talk is a powerful mediator of human performance (e.g., Dobson, 2010; Hamilton, Scott, & MacDougall, 2007; Manning & Payne, 1996). With respect to teaching struggling writers to use self-talk, it is most effective when (1) the content is tailored to the demands of the task and the individual's needs; (2) it is rehearsed aloud to automaticity and then used as a form of "inner speech" to control thoughts, feelings, and actions; and (3) it is monitored for fidelity of use by the teacher. Examples of self-talk include "Have I used my revising checklist to check my work?," "This is hard, but I can do it if I try my best," "I'm good at coming up with ideas, so I'll turn in a good paper," and "Keep concentrating so you don't get distracted!"

Self-evaluation consists of both self-monitoring and self-recording of behavior, and can be used to assess attention, strategy use, and task performance. Frequently, self-evaluation is accomplished through the graphic representation of a target behavior's occurrence in relation to a goal (thus these two aspects of self-regulation are functionally interdependent). For instance, students might quantify their use of story grammar elements in fictional narratives produced over time on a chart that has the maximum score at the top (the goal). Likewise, students can track how many words they have written per time interval, with the goal of increasing their productivity by 25% over baseline. Self-evaluation has been found to produce positive effects on behavior and academic performance in students with language and learning problems (e.g., Harris, 1986; Lloyd, Bateman, Landrum, & Hallahan, 1989; Maag, Reid, & DiGangi, 1993). Self-evaluation helps students establish worthwhile goals because the concrete data collected during this process provide feedback on their status relative to an external benchmark or a personal goal.

Finally, self-reinforcement can be enacted when students attain a performance criterion while self-evaluating their work. This component of self-management is just as powerful as external inducements to motivate behavior (e.g., Rosenbaum & Drabman, 1979) and can boost the efficacy of self-evaluation in writing (e.g., Ballard & Glynn, 1975). Reinforcement might take the form of self-congratulatory remarks, the procurement of tangible rewards, or participation in a preferred activity. Students with language and learning challenges are likely to require guidance in forming accurate judgments about their performance, adhering to stringent guidelines for the application of contingencies, and selecting acceptable reinforcements.

Following are three planning strategies (one each for narrative, persuasive, and expository genres) and three revising/editing strategies. For all of these, the teacher should first model how to use the strategy, then give students an opportunity to cooperatively apply the strategy while producing group papers, and finally let students practice using the strategy while writing individual papers. Throughout these stages of instruction, the teacher should provide extensive feedback and encouragement, discuss how to apply the strategy in diverse contexts, solicit students' suggestions for improvement, and directly link strategy use to writing performance. All of the strategies presented here use acronyms that encapsulate the multiple steps of the strategies. Furthermore, each strategy has an accompanying watermark illustration that serves to cue the acronym. These features help reduce memory and retrieval demands for students, particularly those with learning problems.

Planning Strategies

SPACE LAUNCH

SPACE LAUNCH is a narrative planning strategy (personal or fictional) that incorporates the basic structure of narrative (i.e., SPACE) and the steps for planning and writing a good story (i.e., LAUNCH). A prompt sheet (Figure 12.7) identifies the strategy steps and can be copied for each student or reproduced for a poster display. A planning sheet (Figure 12.8) allows students to record their story ideas, writing goals, and self-talk statements. First, the student should establish and record personalized writing goals: a quality goal and a related quantity goal. For example, a student struggling with word choice might identify a goal to increase quality rating from a 3 to a 5 on a 6-point scale. A related quantity goal to help the student reach this level of quality in word choice might be to include a minimum of 10 vivid descriptive words in the story. Next, the student should generate ideas for a story and record single words or short phrases that capture these ideas (it is important to discourage students from writing complete

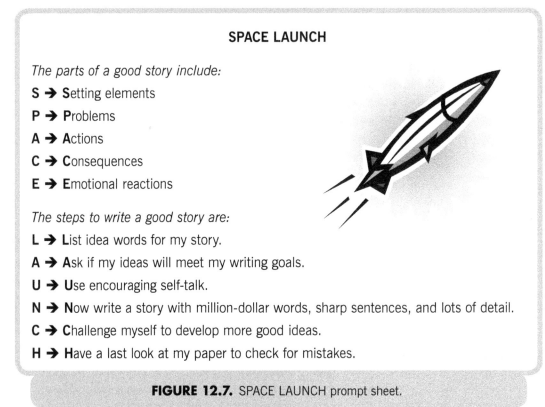

SPACE LAUNCH

The parts of a good story include:

S ➔ **S**etting elements

P ➔ **P**roblems

A ➔ **A**ctions

C ➔ **C**onsequences

E ➔ **E**motional reactions

The steps to write a good story are:

L ➔ **L**ist idea words for my story.

A ➔ **A**sk if my ideas will meet my writing goals.

U ➔ **U**se encouraging self-talk.

N ➔ **N**ow write a story with million-dollar words, sharp sentences, and lots of detail.

C ➔ **C**hallenge myself to develop more good ideas.

H ➔ **H**ave a last look at my paper to check for mistakes.

FIGURE 12.7. SPACE LAUNCH prompt sheet.

sentences on a planning sheet, as this will restrain flexibility in planning and yield a rough draft rather than a true plan). Note that space is provided for multiple ideas for each basic part of a story; students should be encouraged to explore several possibilities for setting and plot elements to foster creativity and to permit evaluation of each idea's merit. Finally, the student should record self-talk statements to be spoken aloud (initially) or subvocalized (once memorized) while planning and writing. For example, a student who believes that writing is hard might record, "This is a challenge, but I like challenges and I have my strategy to help me do well." The last sheet (Figure 12.9) is a scorecard, which is used by a peer to evaluate the student's writing performance. The evaluation criteria are closely linked to the valued qualities embedded in the strategy itself (i.e., million-dollar words, sharp sentences, and lots of detail), the basic structure of a narrative, and writing mechanics. Of course, these criteria could be modified to align more with particular writing traits, and the rating scale could be adjusted to match the scale used by the teacher. At the bottom of the scorecard, the writer tallies the points, determines any improvement (this implies progress monitoring, a critical aspect of strategy instruction that helps students see how their efforts impact their writing), and sets goals for the next story.

SPACE LAUNCH

Story Planning Sheet

Author: _____   Date: _____

My quality goal for this story is: _____

My quantity goal for this story is: _____

Generate idea words for . . .

Setting elements: _____   _____

    _____   _____

    _____   _____

    _____   _____

Problems: _____   _____

    _____   _____

    _____   _____

Actions: _____   _____

    _____   _____

    _____   _____

Consequences: _____   _____

    _____   _____

    _____   _____

Emotions: _____   _____

    _____   _____

    _____   _____

Self-talk statements: _____

_____

_____

FIGURE 12.8. SPACE LAUNCH planning sheet.

From *Handbook of Effective Literacy Instruction: Research-Based Practice K–8,* edited by Barbara M. Taylor and Nell K. Duke. Copyright 2013 by The Guilford Press. Permission to photocopy this figure is granted to purchasers of this book for personal use only (see copyright page for details). Purchasers may download a larger version of this figure from *www.guilford.com/p/taylor3.*

SPACE LAUNCH

Scorecard for Story

Author: _____   Partner: _____

Points

1 = Needs a lot more work.

2 = Could be a little better.

3 = Pretty good the way it is.

4 = Terrific! Other kids should see this.

Questions for Your Partner

After reading and marking the author's story, answer the following:

1. Does the writer use lots of descriptive words?	1	2	3	4
2. Does the writer use different kinds of sentences that are clear?	1	2	3	4
3. Is the story creative and enjoyable to read?	1	2	3	4
4. Does the story have a beginning, middle, and end?	1	2	3	4
5. Does the writer include the five parts of a good story (SPACE)?	1	2	3	4
6. Is the paper free of errors (such as in spelling and punctuation)?	1	2	3	4

Author Goals

My total score this time was _____.

My score _____ did _____ did not go up from last time.

The quality goal for my next story is _____ points.

Next time I will try to improve my score most for question number   1 2 3 4 5 6.

I also have set a quantity goal for my next story of _____.

FIGURE 12.9. SPACE LAUNCH scorecard.

DARE TO DEFEND

The DARE to DEFEND strategy for planning persuasive papers incorporates the structure of persuasion (i.e., DARE) and the steps for planning and writing a good opinion paper (i.e., DEFEND). The materials for this strategy are very similar to those provided for SPACE LAUNCH; there is a prompt sheet, a planning sheet, and a scorecard (see Figures 12.10–12.12). Note that the student is required to identify and record ideas that support the position and ideas that counter the position. In the process of doing this, the student may decide to alter the position after evaluating the importance and relevance of each idea. The student can place an asterisk next to those ideas to elaborate upon or to provide concrete supporting evidence for, which encourages further planning.

TREE BRANCH

The TREE BRANCH strategy for planning expository papers incorporates the structure of common expository essays (i.e., TREE) and the steps for planning and writing a high-quality piece of exposition (i.e., BRANCH). The materials are similar to those provided for SPACE LAUNCH and DARE to DEFEND (see Figures 12.13–12.15). In essence, these

DARE to DEFEND

The parts of a good opinion paper include:

D ➜ **D**evelop a position statement.

A ➜ **A**dd supporting arguments.

R ➜ **R**eport and refute counterarguments.

E ➜ **E**nd with a strong conclusion.

The steps to write a good opinion paper are:

D ➜ **D**evelop a list of idea words for my essay.

E ➜ **E**valuate their importance.

F ➜ **F**ind even more ways to convince my readers.

E ➜ **E**ncourage myself through self-talk.

N ➜ **N**ow write an essay with clear ideas, sharp sentences, and great impact.

D ➜ **D**ecide if I met my writing goals.

FIGURE 12.10. DARE to DEFEND prompt sheet.

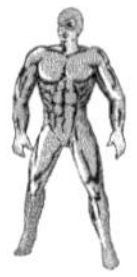

DARE to DEFEND

Opinion Paper Planning Sheet

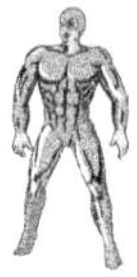

Author: ______________________________ Date: ______________

My quality goal for this essay is: ______________________________

My quantity goal for this essay is: ______________________________

Generate idea words to build arguments . . .

For my position	***Against*** my position
____________________	____________________
____________________	____________________
____________________	____________________
____________________	____________________
____________________	____________________
____________________	____________________
____________________	____________________
____________________	____________________
____________________	____________________
____________________	____________________
____________________	____________________
____________________	____________________
____________________	____________________
____________________	____________________
____________________	____________________
____________________	____________________

Self-talk statements: ______________________________

____

____

____

____

FIGURE 12.11. DARE to DEFEND planning sheet.

DARE to DEFEND

Score Card for Opinion Paper

Author: _____   Partner: _____

Points

1 = Needs a lot more work.
2 = Could be a little better.
3 = Pretty good the way it is.
4 = Terrific! Other kids should see this.

Questions for Your Partner

After reading and marking the author's essay, answer the following:

1. Does the writer use lots of descriptive words?	1	2	3	4
2. Does the writer use different kinds of sentences that are clear?	1	2	3	4
3. Is the essay convincing?	1	2	3	4
4. Does the essay include logical supporting ideas?	1	2	3	4
5. Does the writer include and logically refute counterarguments?	1	2	3	4
6. Is the paper free of errors (such as in spelling and punctuation)?	1	2	3	4

Author Goals

My total score this time was _____.

My score _____ did _____ did not go up from last time.

The quality goal for my next essay is _____ points.

Next time I will try to improve my score most for question number   1 2 3 4 5 6.

I also have set a quantity goal for my next essay of _____.

FIGURE 12.12. DARE to DEFEND scorecard.

three planning strategies represent a coherent strand with a common set of features to target the most common forms of academic writing assigned to students.

Revision and Revising Strategies

Compared with planning, revision places perhaps an even greater premium on self-regulation and *metacognition* (reflection upon and evaluation of one's thinking, including the visible products of thinking such as written text). Revising involves "re-seeing" goals, ideas, and text; it is iterative (i.e., it occurs repeatedly) and recursive (i.e., revision affects further planning, transcription, and revision, and these affect revision). Research suggests that when revision occurs varies for some writers under some circumstances: Sometimes the bulk of revision occurs after a draft is produced, and sometimes it is dispersed throughout text generation (e.g., Fitzgerald, 1987). According to Fitzgerald (1987), revision is deemed necessary when a writer detects dissonance between his or her intentions and beliefs, the existing text, and the reader's needs and goals. The act of revising serves to address this dissonance, which can occur at

---

TREE BRANCH

The parts of a good report include:

T ➔ **T**ell what your topic is and why it's important with a good lead.

R ➔ **R**elate important and interesting facts about your topic.

E ➔ **E**laborate on the facts with supporting data.

E ➔ **E**nd with a summary that makes the reader want to find out more.

The steps to write a good report are:

B ➔ **B**rainstorm idea words for my plan.

R ➔ **R**ecite my self-talk to keep me going strong.

A ➔ **A**sk myself if my ideas will meet my writing goals.

N ➔ **N**ow write a report with good organization, powerful words, and accurate information.

C ➔ **C**hallenge myself to come up with more good ideas.

H ➔ **H**ave a close look at my paper for mistakes.

FIGURE 12.13. TREE BRANCH prompt sheet.

TREE BRANCH

Expository Paper Planning Sheet

Author: _____   Date: _____

My quality goal for this report is: _____

My quantity goal for this report is: _____

Generate idea words for: _____

Topic leads: _____   _____

                     _____   _____

                     _____   _____

Relevant facts: _____   _____

                     _____   _____

                     _____   _____

Elaborate details: _____   _____

                     _____   _____

                     _____   _____

Ending summary: _____   _____

                     _____   _____

                     _____   _____

Self-talk statements: _____

_____

_____

_____

_____

FIGURE 12.14. TREE BRANCH planning sheet.

TREE BRANCH

Scorecard for Expository Paper

Author: _____ Partner: _____

Points

1 = Needs a lot more work.
2 = Could be a little better.
3 = Pretty good the way it is.
4 = Terrific! Other kids should see this.

Questions for Your Partner

After reading and marking the author's essay, answer the following:

1. Does the writer use lots of descriptive words?	1	2	3	4
2. Does the writer use different kinds of sentences that are clear?	1	2	3	4
3. Is the paper informative?	1	2	3	4
4. Does the paper include accurate supporting data?	1	2	3	4
5. Does the writer include details to make the topic interesting?	1	2	3	4
6. Is the paper free of errors (such as in spelling and punctuation)?	1	2	3	4

Author Goals

My total score this time was _____.

My score _____ did _____ did not go up from last time.

The quality goal for my next essay is _____ points.

Next time I will try to improve my score most for question number   1 2 3 4 5 6.

I also have set a quantity goal for my next essay of _____.

FIGURE 12.15. TREE BRANCH scorecard.

microstructural and macrostructural levels and can involve form, content, or both. All of this can overwhelm the writer. In general, revision efforts increase with age and writing competence, as does the effectiveness of those efforts (e.g., Hayes, Flower, Schriver, Stratman, & Carey, 1987). Revising is difficult, especially for struggling writers, for at least five reasons:

1. Students often make inaccurate presuppositions regarding shared understandings between themselves and their audience, which leads to generally egocentric texts that require the reader to infer far too much from too few details (Bereiter & Scardamalia, 1987; Sperling, 1996).
2. When students do revise, they tend to focus on localized and superficial issues rather than discourse-level concerns, and thus make changes that have little impact on the quality of their papers (Bereiter & Scardamalia, 1987; Graham, 1997; MacArthur & Graham, 1987; McCutchen, 1995).
3. Students frequently miss inaccuracies and confusing spots in their texts (i.e., dissonance location) and/or do not know how to make an adequate change when a problem is detected (i.e., dissonance resolution).
4. Poor writers in particular feel too wedded to their written text because so much effort was invested in creating what exists.
5. Many children and adolescents have difficulty managing revising along with the other cognitive, linguistic, physical, and motivational operations involved with composing text.

Several practices based on empirical research and informed professional practice can help teachers to foster effective revising by students (see Graham & Perin, 2007). The examination of touchstone or mentor texts for attributes that students can mimic in their own writing (e.g., a strong lead for a feature article, the use of dialogue to advance the plot in a story, applying onomatopoeia to create vivid sensory details, the use of punctuation and capitalization to mark and build cadence in a poem) helps them internalize a mental model for the written product and identify rhetorical goals, and thus gives students a focus for their revision efforts. Use of mentor texts is enhanced when strong models of particular aspects of writing are contrasted with weak examples. A related instructional practice involves activities to develop genre and topic knowledge. Again, such knowledge can help students acquire internal frames of reference or performance benchmarks for making meaningful revisions to their writing. In many cases, knowledge about a genre is appropriated through immersion in texts that exemplify the canonical genre traits (e.g., story grammar) and discussion of (1) how the genre reflects a unique way of communicating ideas within specific contexts (its purposes and functions) and (2) how the genre is embodied in the structure of the text (its form). Explicit and systematic instruction in genre structure, coupled with authentic purposes for reading and writing in that genre, does have a positive impact on the quality of students' writing within a genre (e.g., Fitzgerald & Teasley, 1983; Purcell-Gates, Duke, & Martineau, 2007).

Word processing often results in more text revisions, but these tend to address superficial and localized issues and thus have little impact on the overall quality of text (e.g., Daiute, 1986; MacArthur, 2006; MacArthur, Ferretti, Okolo, & Cavalier, 2001; MacArthur & Graham, 1987). However, incorporating strong revising instruction with the use of a word processor can yield notable improvements in students' texts. More-over, the addition of other computer tools (e.g., speech recognition, speech synthesis, and word prediction capabilities) enhances students' ability to detect and correct errors and instances of dissonance (MacArthur, 2006; Raskind & Higgins, 1995, 1999), as does software that prompts revising activity (e.g., Daedalus Group; *www.daedalus.com*). For such aids to be maximally beneficial, however, students must be fluent in keyboard-ing skills, and word processing must be integrated throughout the composing process rather than treated as an add-on for the final copy.

Peer and teacher conferencing (e.g., Neubert & McNelis, 1986)—whether one-on-one or in small groups, or whether live or virtual—is frequently used in writing work-shop to engineer better student papers (Beach & Friedrich, 2006). Research has demon-strated that peer feedback regarding text clarity can facilitate changes in the revising behavior of poor writers (MacArthur, Schwartz, & Graham, 1991; Stoddard & MacAr-thur, 1993). However, conferencing between students and teachers often has the "fla-vor" of typical instructional discourse (teacher-controlled and centered on assignment requirements and teacher expectations) rather than egalitarian conversations regard-ing writing craft and composition content, especially when the teacher is clearly more knowledgeable about the writing topic (e.g., Nickel, 2001; Ulichny & Watson-Gegeo, 1989). Moreover, peer respondents often provide vague and unhelpful comments and suggestions to authors unless they are very well trained to give meaningful feedback (e.g., Fitzgerald & Stamm, 1990). Thus the positive impact of conference feedback on the quality of poor writers' papers noted above is most likely due to the fact that these writers benefit from attention to even the most global aspects of composition, such as text structure and form, and notably improve their texts with even limited revision because they are so qualitatively inferior in the first place (Fitzgerald & Stamm, 1990). To maximize the effectiveness of writing conferences, an instructor should aim to do the following (see Martin & Certo, 2008):

- Establish a conversational stance to understand a student's goals and ideas before discussing specific textual issues.
- Provide frequent and varied opportunities for conferencing about pieces of writ-ing.
- Encourage *flash drafting*, a technique in which smaller segments of text (e.g., the climax of a story) are drafted, examined (through conferencing), and revised, to help the student feel less invested in a completed draft of the whole paper.
- Collaboratively establish concrete goals for revision.
- Give weaker writers more conference time that also is of high quality.

Checklists and questionnaires that encapsulate prompts for revising and editing are staples in many classrooms, though of course a checklist does not guarantee that students will use it to make the requisite changes or even dependably to evaluate their papers. Nevertheless, checklists are meant to be flexible procedural facilitators that scaf-fold revising behaviors, and as such should (1) reflect students' increasing competence by including more items over time and (2) contain at least some items suited for the individual needs of each writer. Two such checklists and an alternative strategy are presented below.

COLA

COLA is a comprehensive checklist developed by Singer and Bashir (1999) and suitable for older students or more advanced writers, though items can be removed or reworded to make the checklist more useful to beginning writers. The form presented in Figure 12.16 is used for exposition and persuasion rather than narration, but the items on the checklist can be modified to make it appropriate for narratives.

SEARCH

The SEARCH revising/editing strategy (Ellis & Friend, 1991) employs a checklist (see Figure 12.17) but it does have two unique aspects. First, the student is expected to set writing goals before even beginning to write—and, when finished revising and editing a paper, to determine whether the goals were met. Second, the student is expected to work with a peer to double-check editing. As with any checklist, the teacher can add more items once the student attains mastery of those listed.

CDO

As an alternative to a checklist, the CDO strategy for individual revising (De La Paz, Swanson, & Graham, 1998; Graham, 1997) involves a greater degree of self-regulation on the part of the writer than checklists and is considerably more powerful; consequently, it is very helpful for students with writing difficulties. The prompt sheet (Figure 12.18) lists the three steps for strategy deployment: *compare* (identifying discrepancies between written text and intended meaning), *diagnose* (selecting a specific reason for the mismatch), and *operate* (fixing the problem and evaluating the effectiveness of the change). These strategy steps occur first while a student attends to each sentence in the paper, and then, during a second "cycle," while the student attends to each paragraph in the paper. A third cycle, focusing on the whole text, could be added. A minimum of two cycles is necessary to help the student attend to local as well as more global problems in the text. The diagnostic options for making meaningful revisions vary depending on the level of text to which the student is attending. The teacher will need to develop sets of diagnostic cards, color-coded for each cycle, from which the student selects. The diagnostic cards serve both to focus the student's efforts and to limit the variables in play (which, in greater numbers, could easily frustrate a struggling writer). Obviously, using CDO requires quite a bit of explanation, modeling, and guided practice because it is complex. It necessitates lengthy interactions with text because the procedure is enacted for each sentence before a student moves on to identifying and correcting problems in larger units of text. Given this, it may be advantageous to use CDO for relatively short texts until students have internalized and automatized the procedure. CDO facilitates self-regulation in revising because it provides a structured approach for self-monitoring writing problems and using self-talk to manage the process; certainly other components of self-regulation could easily be added. For instance, a student might determine that a reduction in the number of times he or she selects "lacks details" as a diagnostic option is warranted as a goal, and then the student records relevant data while using CDO to monitor progress in reaching that goal.

COLA

Content:

☐ Does my introduction establish the purpose and topic?

☐ Does the paper have a definite beginning, middle, and end?

☐ Do all of the ideas relate to the topic?

☐ Does the title capture the topic and main ideas?

☐ Will any part of my paper be confusing or unclear to a reader?

☐ Does my ending leave the reader with something interesting to think about?

Organization:

☐ Do the ideas follow each other in a logical order?

☐ Do all paragraphs have a main idea sentence and at least two supporting details?

☐ Are transitions between paragraphs and ideas clear?

☐ Is there enough information to support my main ideas?

Language:

☐ Does each sentence sound right when I read it out loud?

☐ Does each sentence say what I mean?

☐ Do I use unusual words that make my writing interesting?

Appearance:

☐ Does each sentence start with a capital letter and end with correct punctuation?

☐ Did I capitalize names, specific places, and titles?

☐ Are all words spelled correctly when I check by reading out loud backwards?

☐ Have I carefully examined my demon words and used a spelling guide?

☐ Is the overall appearance of the paper neat and clean?

FIGURE 12.16. COLA checklist.

SEARCH

Set goals:

☐ I've thought about who is the audience and the impression I want to give them; I want them to think . . . (e.g., my story is scary).

☐ My quality goal is . . . (e.g., a score of 5 on a scale of 1–6 in word choice).

☐ My quantity goal is . . . (e.g., at least 10 different descriptive words).

Examine paper to see if it makes sense:

☐ I've read my paper out loud.

☐ Each sentence and the whole paper make sense.

☐ No words have been omitted.

☐ I've combined sentences that are too short and broken up ones that are too long.

Ask if you said what you meant:

☐ My ideas are clear and related to the topic.

☐ The order of my ideas is logical.

Reveal picky errors:

☐ I've corrected all errors in spelling, capitalization, and punctuation that I found.

☐ Someone else has double-checked my work.

Copy over neatly.

Have a last look for errors:

☐ I made sure my final copy doesn't have any new or remaining errors in it.

☐ Someone else has checked my work one last time.

☐ I did/did not meet my goals.

FIGURE 12.17. SEARCH checklist.

Compare:

☐ *First Cycle*: Ask myself, "Does my sentence match what I really wanted to say?"

☐ *Second Cycle*: Ask myself, "Does my paragraph match the main idea I wanted to express?"

Diagnose:

☐ *First Cycle*: Pick a diagnostic card (e.g., words are too vague, forgot some words, sentence lacks detail, sentence is too long or short, words are in the wrong order).

☐ *Second Cycle*: Pick a diagnostic card (e.g., forgot a topic or main idea sentence, lacks a transition, paragraph is too long or short, sentences are in the wrong order, need more details about the main idea).

Operate:

☐ *First Cycle*: Make the change and evaluate the impact by asking, "Was the change effective?"

☐ *Second Cycle*: Make the change and evaluate the impact by asking, "Was the change effective?"

FIGURE 12.18. CDO strategy.

From *Handbook of Effective Literacy Instruction: Research-Based Practice K–8*, edited by Barbara M. Taylor and Nell K. Duke. Copyright 2013 by The Guilford Press. Permission to photocopy this figure is granted to purchasers of this book for personal use only (see copyright page for details). Purchasers may download a larger version of this figure from *www.guilford.com/p/taylor3*.

Integrating Writing Instruction with Content-Area Learning

Teachers often feel that devoting ample time to writing instruction is problematic, given the voluminous content-area information that must be covered in the typical curriculum (Troia & Maddox, 2004). Simultaneously, they sometimes struggle to identify relevant and stimulating writing topics and assignments that will help students develop their expertise as writers. One way to resolve these dilemmas is to integrate writing instruction with content-area learning.

One important aspect of content-area learning is developing communicative competence for interacting with others who have shared knowledge about a discipline or area of study. Individuals within a discipline—such as literary critics, historians, economists, biologists, physicists, and mathematicians—possess a unique way of talking and writing about the theories, principles, concepts, facts, methods of inquiry, and so forth connected with that discipline. Thus a common goal of content-area instruction and writing instruction is to help students acquire proficiency in disciplinary writing. This does not mean, however, that less content-driven writing exercises are undesirable or unnecessary; the inclusion of disciplinary writing is simply one part of a strong writing program. If teachers have students write regularly in content-area classes and use content-area materials as stimuli for writing workshop, it is more likely that students will develop the capacity to communicate effectively in varied disciplinary discourse communities and will write for more educationally and personally germane purposes.

There are a number of very simple ways to encourage content-relevant writing on a frequent basis in a social studies, science, or mathematics class. Following are some examples:

- The teacher can ask students to produce a 1-minute closing paper (on an index card) at the end of each lesson, in which they pose a genuine question about the topic studied that day, identify the key point from the content materials reviewed, summarize a discussion, or develop a question that might be used for a class test.
- Journaling is another vehicle for writing across the curriculum. In science class, for example, students can be asked to describe what was done, why it was done, what happened, and why it happened. In math, students might record which specific problem-solving procedures they employed for the problems assigned, why these were effective or ineffective, and what advice they would offer to other students faced with the same math problems. In social studies, students can use their accumulating knowledge of a historical character to write a first-person fictionalized account of the individual's life.
- The *story impressions* method (McGinley & Denner, 1987), similar to *exchange–compare* writing (Wood, 1986), utilizes a cooperative learning framework. Students are assigned to a group and given roles (researcher, scribe, content editor, proofreader, and reporter) for writing a brief summary that predicts the content of a lesson or unit text, based on key vocabulary provided by the teacher. Once the group members have read the text, they rewrite their summary to reflect the actual content of the text and their improved understanding of the material, and discuss this revised version with the rest of the class.
- A *jigsaw* content-learning group (Aronson & Patnoe, 1997) is another cooperative learning strategy for writing in the content areas. It can be coupled with double-entry journals (Cox, 1996) for an effective and efficient means of learning from multiple source materials on a topic. The steps for these activities are as follows:
  1. Students are assigned to *home* groups, and each person in a group is given a different source text (e.g., a magazine article about exercise and cardiovascular health, a newspaper clipping about new medical procedures and drugs that can help reduce the risk of heart attacks, a consumer brochure outlining healthy eating tips for promoting cardiac health, and a textbook chapter about the human circulatory system) to read.
  2. Then each student completes a double-entry journal while reading the assigned source text. This is a journal in which the student records some important piece of information from the source text on the left side of the journal page (with an accompanying page number) and a response, question, or evaluative comment on the right side. After completing their double-entry journals, students disperse to an *expert* group—a group where everyone else has read the same source text. Members of the expert group share their journal entries and summarize the material, using a graphic organizer.
  3. Finally, students return to their home groups to teach the other members

about the content information they learned from their text and discuss how this information relates to that covered by the other texts. The double-entry journal could be expanded to a triple-entry journal by having students within the home groups respond to each others' responses, questions, or evaluations in a third column.

- The K-W-L-H+ strategy (Carr & Ogle, 1987; Ogle, 1986) is a time-honored method for activating background knowledge about a topic (Know), setting learning goals (Wonder), summarizing learning from text (Learned), and promoting continued investigation (How to Find Out More). The plus (+) portion of the method is a written summary of what was learned and what additional things students would like to learn. This method can be used as a teacher-led pre- and postreading class exercise or as a small-group activity. Below is an example of how this activity can work for a unit on geometry:

  1. In math, a class might be about to embark on a unit of study related to geometry. The teacher asks students to brainstorm all that they know about geometry and list these under the *Know* column. This student-generated information should be organized into categories either by the teacher or by the students with teacher guidance (e.g., shapes, angles, spatial orientation, and measurement) that will facilitate text comprehension.

  2. Then the teacher lists under the *Wonder* column those things students would like to discover about geometry (which helps motivate them to read the text). After reading, the teacher records under the *Learned* column what the students learned through the text, with particular attention paid to information that confirmed their prior knowledge, information that was inconsistent with what was anticipated, or new information. If appropriate, new categories are added.

  3. Next, students write their summary paragraph based on the information listed in the *Learned* column.

  4. Finally, students identify how they would locate missing information in the *How to Find Out More* column (e.g., use a Web browser to search for documents related to geometry), which can help motivate additional learning.

(For more ideas about teaching reading and writing in the content areas, see Chapters 14–17, this volume.)

All of these methods are helpful for students who struggle with writing because they activate prior knowledge about the topic of study, require text summarization, and/or encourage discussion through which students are exposed to multiple perspectives. Of course, students who have writing problems sometimes have reading problems, so adaptations may be needed to help these students read the texts assigned. Some appropriate adaptations might include (1) having the text on CD or in electronic file format for computer readout; (2) having the struggling reader/writer work with a partner who is a better reader; or (3) providing the student with a modified version of the text that is written with the same essential content but at a lower grade level. Likewise, students who struggle with writing may have difficulty working in cooperative learning arrangements. Here are three proactive measures teachers can take:

1. Carefully consider with whom students are most likely to work well in a group, and place them in groups accordingly.
2. Assign roles that are well suited for students' particular strengths (e.g., assign a student who is an accomplished speaker but a struggling writer the role of reporter).
3. Seek professional development opportunities that focus on cooperative and peer-mediated learning.

Assessing Writing in the Classroom

The assessment of writing is a frequently vexing issue for teachers. Good writing is simply hard to define, and even more difficult to measure accurately. Although a number of assessment methods applicable to the classroom context (i.e., other than high-stakes or norm-referenced tests) exist, no single one appears adequate for the goals of reliably judging student writing performance and monitoring student progress in written expression in response to instruction. These methods include the following:

1. Direct or on-demand writing assessment, where students are asked to respond to a prompt to construct a written composition, and the product is evaluated by using some form of a rubric (see Benson & Campbell, 2009; Olinghouse & Santangelo, 2010).
2. Indirect writing assessment, where the students respond to multiple-choice, true–false, or error correction items to demonstrate their writing knowledge (see Benson & Campbell, 2009).
3. Portfolios, in which students gradually accumulate a varied collection of authentic writing process and product artifacts (these may include actual compositions in various stages of completion with or without peer/teacher comments, planning notes, completed revising and editing checklists, personal reflections and self-evaluations, responses to questionnaires, teacher and parent observations, etc.), and the artifacts are evaluated according to externally established criteria, usually collaboratively developed with each student (see Gearhart, 2009; Nolet, 1992).
4. Curriculum-based measurement of writing, where students copy or produce a text in a brief period of time under standardized conditions, and the product is evaluated by using one or more measures that are generally predictive of overall writing quality. Samples of writing are taken at regular intervals, and the results are compared to track student growth (see Benson & Campbell, 2009; McMaster & Espin, 2007).

Each of these assessment methods has benefits and constraints, and these are summarized in Table 12.1.

TABLE 12.1. Assessment of Writing

Assessment method	Benefits	Constraints
Portfolios	Provide opportunities for assessment conversations to consider readers' interpretations.	Judgments of writing performance too often based on highest-quality pieces rather than entire body of work.
	Focus on authentic writing tasks rather than writing in response to assessment-driven prompts.	Samples written and selected under diverse conditions and levels of support, rendering judgments difficult to interpret.
	Accommodate evaluation of writing knowledge, skills, and processes, as well as writing outcomes.	Wide array of portfolio models can obfuscate alignment among portfolio design, data collection and analysis, and assessment purposes.
	Can represent a balanced view of communicative competence because oral and visual performances can be included.	Tensions between assessment and learning functions of portfolios can have a negative impact on reliability and validity of evidence.
Indirect	Measurement reliability is enhanced through ease of scoring and high degree of consistency across test items.	Lacks content and face validity because tasks do not evaluate application of writing knowledge, skills, or processes.
	Permits large-scale assessment in a single session.	Does not reflect real-world writing demands.
Direct/ On-demand	Assessment conditions and writing measures can be standardized.	Measurement error is introduced through poorly written prompts; presentation effects (e.g., legibility, spelling mistakes) and writer identity can lead to scoring bias.
	Holistic, analytic trait, and primary trait rubrics are robust for evaluating multiple aspects of written composition in multiple forms for multiple purposes.	Rubrics tend not to be sensitive to small increments of change and are difficult to use reliably.
Curriculum-based measurement	Brief, repeated sampling of timed on-demand writing (for young writers, copying of text is acceptable) performance is standardized, as are scoring procedures.	Brevity of writing sample influences validity of inferences regarding writing performance—older students need longer sampling periods.
	Several writing measures can be applied to a given sample, including total words written, words spelled correctly, correct letter sequences, and correct word sequences.	No single measure is sufficiently reliable and valid for all students at all grades; more complex measures appear to be better predictors of writing competence.
	Progress monitoring of individual students for evaluating responsiveness to intervention is permitted.	Though long-term gains are found, research has yet to identify how frequently samples should be collected, the rates of growth that can be expected, or how these measures are affected by instruction.

SUMMARY OF BIG IDEAS FROM RESEARCH

Several "take-home" messages can be deduced from the extant research on writing instruction discussed in this chapter. These include the following:

- The majority of U.S. students do not perform adequately on high-stakes assessments of writing proficiency for a variety of reasons, some of which are related to individual characteristics and others to environment.
- High-quality writing instruction incorporates firmly established but adaptive instructional routines in which the relative emphases on the meanings, forms, and processes of writing, as well as on the development of writing-specific knowledge, topic knowledge, writing skills, and motivation for writing, are tailored to match students' needs.
- Comprehensive, systematic, and sustained instruction in text transcription skills (e.g., spelling and handwriting) is fundamental to writing success, especially for elementary-age students, and must be connected to students' text-composing efforts.
- Educators should thoughtfully deploy a wide array of adaptations to their classroom environment, instructional materials, teaching strategies, task demands, and writing tasks to meet the needs of struggling writers. They should select the least intensive changes first (e.g., adaptations to the environment), apply them with fidelity and close monitoring of student outcomes, and try again (perhaps selecting a more intensive adaptation) when a student's writing performance is not successfully improved.
- Within the scope of process writing instruction, there should be an explicit focus on instructional practices and specific strategies that scaffold the major aspects of the writing process—planning, drafting, revising, and editing. It is not enough to tell students to create an outline or a web of ideas for their writing, or simply to ask them to check their writing for errors, because these requests do not foster self-regulation of the thoughts, feelings, and actions that accompany good writing performance and are far too vague.
- For students to become accomplished writers, they need to be comfortable with composing texts that evidence disciplinary conventions for content, form, and function. At a minimum, providing regular time for writing during content-area instruction and using instructional techniques to connect comprehension of expository texts with written expression should be staples at every grade.

LOOKING FORWARD

We have much to learn about precisely how various aspects of writing should be taught and in what sequence. Some potential points to investigate in future work include these:

- What does a comprehensive model of the dynamic relationships between writing and reading look like? Although there is ample evidence that writing and reading are indeed related, they are far from being similar enough for us to predict readily how development in one domain affects development in the other, or how to leverage instruction to foster knowledge, skill, and strategy transference between them (see Fitzgerald & Shanahan, 2000). Of course, any research that examines relationships between writing and reading must reconcile findings with the instructional context, which serves to confound these relationships (Smagorinsky, 1987).

- The extant research has not yet fully evaluated potential explanatory factors for individual responsiveness to writing instruction. Studies are needed to ascertain the relative contributions of oral language ability, reading ability, topic and genre knowledge, information-processing skills (e.g., attention, perception, and memory), transcription capabilities, strategic behavior, and motivation to predicting achievement gains and long-term outcomes in writing, as well as to predicting each other. This kind of information will be particularly helpful in developing specialized interventions for struggling writers who receive strong writing instruction in their general education classrooms, students who are English language learners, and older students who continue to struggle with basic writing skills.

- Identifying instructional adaptations that are valid and readily integrated into practice will go far in helping teachers, special educators, and other education professionals maximize the writing potential of grade school children and youth. Graham, Harris, Fink, and MacArthur's (2003) research suggests that most classroom teachers implement few if any adaptations, so it is imperative to understand more fully why teachers fail to adapt to meet the needs of struggling writers, how they can effectively incorporate meaningful adaptations, and which adaptations are likely to be parsimonious with process writing instruction and still reap the greatest benefits for students.

- The explosion of technology in recent years has already influenced and continues to influence the composing behaviors of 21st-century students. How should teachers address the native writing tools (e.g., hand-held devices, speech-to-text software, multimedia authoring tools) and authoring platforms (social media websites, blogging, texting) their students use outside school in the classroom? This is no trivial matter, as students are likely to perceive "old-school" writing tasks and tools as outdated and irrelevant to their writing selves, and to disengage from writing instruction that relies on them.

- With the advent of multi-tiered instructional models (i.e., response to intervention, or RTI), deciding what constitutes core versus supplemental writing instruction and which students should receive higher tiers of instructional support have become central issues in educational practice. Supplemental instruction would be likely to involve a lower student–teacher ratio; the use of more intensive adaptations; a tighter instructional focus on specific writing skills and strategies to address individual weaknesses; and a slower pace of instruction to accommodate more modeling, guided practice, and opportunities for independent practice with critical feedback. However, we do not know whether this kind of supplemental instruction will be sufficient for closing the achievement gap between struggling writers and their peers. As for determining who should receive supplemental instruction, no single assessment approach appears to be able to yield reliable and valid data with sufficient sensitivity and specificity to make such decisions.

- As most states have adopted the Common Core State Standards, alignment among these standards, writing curriculum materials, and classroom writing instruction and assessment practices is a matter of concern. Researchers and practitioners will need to work together to ensure that there is in fact a high degree of alignment, and that where gaps do exist, there is a commitment to address these through developmentally and culturally responsive instruction. Some of the gaps evident in the Common Core State Standards include the following:
  - The full diversity of writing purposes/genres in which students should be instructed is not represented.
  - The standards do not address writing motivation or the application of strategies for composing.
  - Collaborative interactions such as sharing and obtaining feedback are not addressed.
  - There is no clear specification of writing conventions and formatting features to be taught beyond grade 2.
  - The standards do not evenly attend to the development of a broad knowledge base in writing.

QUESTIONS FOR REFLECTION •

1. To what extent do I provide motivating (i.e., authentic and personally relevant), intellectually stimulating, and varied (e.g., in purpose, form, and length) writing tasks to move my students forward in their writing development, and to help them display, acquire, and transform their understanding of themselves, others, and the world around them?

2. To what extent do I differentiate writing tasks, my instructional foci, and the supports I provide to accommodate individual students' writing needs?

3. How do I incorporate a variety of assessment data from multiple sources—including curriculum-based measures, writing portfolios, on-demand writing performances, and indirect assessments of writing knowledge—to monitor my students' progress regularly, to differentiate instruction, and to select appropriate tasks and materials?

4. How well do the writing curriculum and associated materials I use address the development of my students' writing knowledge, skills, strategies, and motivation, as well as reflect research-based practices?

5. To what degree do I explicitly model, support, and reinforce self-regulation through goal setting, self-talk, self-evaluation, and self-reinforcement, to help my students become more independent and contemplative writers?

6. How often and how well do I connect writing with other areas of the school curriculum, so that my students view good writing as essential for communicating with others about subject matter ideas in conventional (and sometimes less conventional) ways that are accepted by a particular discourse community?

7. In what ways do I weave technology into my writing lessons, so that my instruction is cutting-edge—not simply for the sake of being engaging with "bells and whistles," but to use the possibilities of technology to advance my teaching and learning goals?

8. What efforts do I take to develop my own writing perspectives and capabilities, so that I can serve as an effective mentor for my students?

SUGGESTIONS FOR ONGOING PROFESSIONAL LEARNING • • • • • •

Teaching writing well is a daunting task. Many teachers feel ill prepared to tackle it because they themselves do not write much, are not comfortable with composing complex texts across a multitude of genres and forms covered in the curriculum, and/or are poor writers. Professional development that addresses not only teachers' content and pedagogical knowledge about writing development, instruction, and assessment, but also their perspectives on and proficiencies with writing, is critical. Such professional development, provided through participation in intensive summer institutes offered through local affiliates of the National Writing Project (NWP) and follow-up consulting projects designed and implemented by institute participants in their schools (i.e., a replication model for teacher training), has shown great promise. In the NWP model, participants spend about a month at a summer institute; during this time, they write, share their work in peer response groups, publish their work, read scholarly papers about writing instruction, discuss teaching and learning issues, and create demonstration lessons for their later use at school. They subsequently become teacher consultants, using their newfound expertise to collaborate with local school colleagues as they examine and modify their writing instructional practices. Pritchard's work (e.g., Pritchard & Honeycutt, 2006) indicates that the NWP model (and variations thereof) has a positive effect on teachers' views of themselves as writers and teachers of writing and on their attitudes about writing instruction, with concomitant changes in their reported practices and their students' writing achievement.

Other professional development approaches, especially those in which the teacher is integral to program design and implementation and in which teacher inquiry and self-examination are cornerstones, also appear to be valuable mechanisms for upgrading professional practice (e.g., Loucks-Horsley & Matsumoto, 1999; Stokes, 2001; Sykes, 1999). One such approach involves *lesson study*—a Japanese model of professional development that has been adopted in some U.S. schools and districts with success (Fernandez & Chokshi, 2002; Lewis, 2002; Lewis & Tsuchida, 1998). Lesson study is a process for developing, refining, and altering curriculum and instruction that is rooted in challenging goals and that places teachers in the role of researcher. That is, during lesson study, teachers (1) pose critical questions regarding their students' learning and their instruction; (2) study available units/lessons/materials and solicit external assistance to help them discover gaps in their understanding; (3) design lessons to answer their questions; (4) observe and collect data; and (5) use these data to inform their future practice. The sequence of a lesson study cycle typically includes the following steps:

- A team of four to six teachers collaboratively plans a research lesson to address identified student goals. The lesson is not intended to be idealized or necessarily novel. Teachers design the research lesson with the following general questions in mind:
  - What do students currently know about writing, and what writing skills and strategies do they posses?
  - What do I want them to learn and be able to display in their written texts?
  - What are the activities/experiences/supports I will provide and questions I will pose to aid their learning and writing performance?
  - How do I expect students to respond to my writing instruction?
  - How will I use students' misconceptions to deepen their understanding of writing content, form, function, and process?
  - What kinds of writing assignments and opportunities will make this motivating and meaningful?
  - What evidence should be collected to make judgments about students' writing performance and writing knowledge?
- One member of the lesson study team teaches the research lesson (the lesson plan is provided in advance to all members), while the others gather evidence about students' learning, using the general questions above (a question or two might be assigned a priori to each member observing) and possibly additional questions related to such issues as these:
  - Student socialization and engagement (e.g., motivation to write).
  - Classroom procedures (e.g., partnering for student writing conferences).
  - Particular instructional approaches (e.g., writing strategy instruction).
  - Technological enhancements (e.g., word prediction).
- The team convenes shortly after the research lesson to discuss the evidence gathered (assigning group roles and outlining normative standards for discussion can be beneficial). Although the lesson belongs to the team, the teacher who taught it begins the debriefing and may discuss the lesson plan, the lesson activities, impressions of student understanding, and the problems that arose. Video recordings and student artifacts are likely to be used to center the discussion.
- The lesson, unit, and instruction are redesigned with feedback from the team, and an improved version of the lesson is perhaps taught by another member of the team in another cycle of lesson study.
- The lesson study team meets about once a month to collaborate on a few research lessons each year, and the results of these collaborative efforts are published in some form; there might be grade-level teams, subject matter teams, cross-grade teams, or even district teams that meet to conduct their research.

Lesson study spreads instructional innovation quickly through the use of observation, publications, artifacts (such as video recordings), and the exchange of ideas. Ultimately, lesson study is believed to improve educational practice and student achievement, to establish and strengthen a community of practitioners, to resolve educational problems, and to advance curriculum design. For a concrete example of lesson study in writing, see Troia, Shankland, and Wolbers (2010).

RESEARCH-BASED RESOURCES

Bright, R. (1995). *Writing instruction in the intermediate grades: What is said, what is done, what is understood.* Newark, DE: International Reading Association.

Fearn, L., & Farnan, N. (1998). *Writing effectively: Helping children master the conventions of writing.* Needham Heights, MA: Allyn & Bacon.

Graham, S., & Harris, K. R. (2005). *Writing better: Effective strategies for teaching students with learning difficulties.* Baltimore: Brookes.

Indrisano, R., & Squire, J. R. (Eds.). (2000). *Perspectives on writing: Research, theory, and practice.* Newark, DE: International Reading Association.

Nelson, N. W., Bahr, C. B., & Van Meter, A. M. (2004). *The writing lab approach to language instruction and intervention.* Baltimore: Brookes.

Ray, K. W. (1999). *Wondrous words: Writers and writing in the elementary classroom.* Urbana, IL: National Council of Teachers of English.

Ray, K. W., & Laminack, L. (2001). *Writing workshop: Working through the hard parts (and they're all hard).* Urbana, IL: National Council of Teachers of English.

Somers, A. B. (1999). *Teaching poetry in high school.* Urbana, IL: National Council of Teachers of English.

Troia, G. A. (Ed.). (2009). *Instruction and assessment for struggling writers: Evidence-based practices.* New York: Guilford Press.

Troia, G. A., Shankland, R. K., & Heintz, A. (Eds.). (2010). *Putting writing research into practice: Applications for teacher professional development.* New York: Guilford Press.

Venezky, R. L. (1999). *The American way of spelling: The structure and origins of American English orthography.* New York: Guilford Press.

Wood, K. D., & Harmon, J. M. (2001). *Strategies for integrating reading and writing in middle and high school classrooms.* Westerville, OH: National Middle School Association.

Young, A. (2002). *Teaching writing across the curriculum* (3rd ed.). Upper Saddle River, NJ: Prentice Hall.

Web-Based Resources for Teaching Writing

Daedalus Group
www.daedalus.com
　　Interactive software for facilitating the writing process and student interaction in an online environment.

Don Johnston Incorporated
www.donjohnston.com/products/writing/index.html
　　Suite of software tools such as Co:Writer to help struggling writers.

FCPS Curriculum and Instruction
http://teach.fcps.net/currmap/literacy-con-la.htm
　　Lists of touchstone texts such as trade books to help teach different writing aspects, and other texts related to specific content-area topics.

Graphic Organizer
www.graphic.org/index.html
　　Examples of and online tools for making various graphic organizers, such as concept maps and Venn diagrams.

Interactive Six Trait Writing Process
www.literatelearner.com/6traits/page_template6t.php?f=main
   Explanations, rubrics, and scored samples for the six traits.

KidPub
www.kidpub.com
   Stories submitted by children; online submission and discussion forum.

Kim's Korner 4 Teacher Talk
www.kimskorner4teachertalk.com/writing/menu.html
   Guidelines for teaching the writing process and six traits.

National Council of Teachers of English
www.ncte.org
   Standards for literacy instruction; summaries of research on writing; resources for teaching writing and professional development.

National Writing Project
www.nwp.org
   Resources for professional development, and links to affiliates in every state.

PIZZAZ
http://pages.uoregon.edu/leslieob/pizzaz.html
   Directions and examples for writing various types of poems and stories, such as diamante poems and chain stories; online submission forum.

Poetry.Com
www.poetry.com
   Resources for writing poems, including examples of famous poems and a rhyming dictionary; online submission forum.

Poetry for Kids
www.poetry4kids.com
   Directions and resources for writing poems, including a rhyming dictionary and links to other sites; online submission and discussion forum.

Poetry 180
www.loc.gov/poetry/180
   A poem a day for high school students.

ReadWriteThink
www.readwritethink.org
   Resources for teaching writing, including lesson plans and links to other sites; directions and online tools for writing various genres; standards for literacy instruction.

Six Traits
www.edina.k12.mn.us/concord/teacherlinks/sixtraits/sixtraits.html
   Explanations, rubrics, posters, and scored samples for the six traits.

Stone Soup
www.stonesoup.com
Book reviews, stories, and poems submitted by children and youth, with audio files of authors' oral readings; online submission forum.

Teach Writing
http://teacher.scholastic.com/professional/teachwriting
Resources for teaching writing, including lesson plans, writing prompts, student worksheets, and links to online articles.

Writing.Com
www.writing.com/main/writing.php
Suite of online tools for teaching and supporting writing, including electronic portfolios, user surveys, online discussion forums, chain stories, sample papers, and links to other sites.

ACKNOWLEDGMENT

Portions of this chapter are adapted from The Access Center (2005). Teaching writing to diverse student populations. Retrieved from *www.k8accesscenter.org/writing/knowledgebank. asp.*

REFERENCES

Aronson, E., & Patnoe, S. (1997). *The jigsaw classroom: Building cooperation in the classroom* (2nd ed.). New York: Addison Wesley Longman.

Atwell, N. (1998). *In the middle: New understandings about writing, reading, and learning.* Portsmouth, NH: Boynton/Cook.

Ballard, K. D., & Glynn, T. (1975). Behavioral self-management in story writing with elementary school children. *Journal of Applied Behavior Analysis, 8,* 387–398.

Beach, R., & Friedrich, T. (2006). Response to writing. In C. A. MacArthur, S. Graham, & J. Fitzgerald (Eds.), *Handbook of writing research* (pp. 222–234). New York: Guilford Press.

Bear, D. R., Invernizzi, M., Templeton, S., & Johnston, F. (2012). *Words their way: Word study for phonics, vocabulary, and spelling instruction* (5th ed.). Boston: Pearson/Allyn & Bacon.

Benson, B. J., & Campbell, H. M. (2009). Assessment of student writing with curriculum-based measurement. In G. A. Troia (Ed.), *Instruction and assessment for struggling writers: Evidence-based practices* (pp. 337–357). New York: Guilford Press.

Bereiter, C., & Scardamalia, M. (1987). *The psychology of written expression.* Hillsdale, NJ: Erlbaum.

Bourassa, D. C., & Treiman, R. (2001). Spelling development and disability: The importance of linguistic factors. *Language, Speech, and Hearing Services in Schools, 32,* 172–181.

Calkins, L. M. (1994). *The art of teaching writing.* Portsmouth, NH: Heinemann.

Carnine, D. W., Silbert, J., & Kame'enui, E. J. (1997). *Direct instruction reading.* Upper Saddle River, NJ: Merrill.

Carr, E., & Ogle, D. M. (1987). K-W-L plus: A strategy for comprehension and summarization. *Journal of Reading, 30,* 626–631.

Clare, L., Valdes, R., & Patthey-Chavez, G. G. (2000). *Learning to write in urban elementary and middle schools: An investigation of teachers' written feedback on student compositions* (Center for the Study of Evaluation Technical Report No. 526). Los Angeles: National Center for Research on Evaluation, Standards, and Student Testing.

Cox, C. (1996). *Teaching language arts: A student and response centered classroom.* Boston: Allyn & Bacon.

Culham, R. (2003). *6 + 1 traits of writing: The complete guide grades 3 and up.* New York: Scholastic.

Cunningham, P. M. (2000). *Phonics they use: Words for reading and writing* (3rd ed.). New York: Addison Wesley Longman.

Cutler, L., & Graham, S. (2008). Primary grade writing instruction: A national survey. *Journal of Educational Psychology, 100,* 907–919.

Daiute, C. (1986). Physical and cognitive factors in revising: Insights from studies with computers. *Research in the Teaching of English, 20,* 141–159.

De La Paz, S. (2007). Managing cognitive demands for writing: Comparing the effects of instructional components in strategy instruction. *Reading and Writing Quarterly: Overcoming Learning Difficulties, 23,* 249–266.

De La Paz, S., Swanson, P. N., & Graham, S. (1998). The contribution of executive control to the revising by students with writing and learning difficulties. *Journal of Educational Psychology, 90,* 448–460.

Dobson, K. S. (Ed.). (2010). *Handbook of cognitive-behavioral therapies* (3rd ed.). New York: Guilford Press.

Elbow, P. (1998a). *Writing with power: Techniques for mastering the writing process* (2nd ed.). New York: Oxford University Press.

Elbow, P. (1998b). *Writing without teachers* (2nd ed.). New York: Oxford University Press.

Ellis, E. S., & Friend, P. (1991). Adolescents with learning disabilities. In B. Y. L. Wong (Ed.), *Learning about learning disabilities* (pp. 505–561). San Diego, CA: Academic Press.

Fernandez, C., & Chokshi, S. (2002). A practical guide to translating lesson study for a U.S. setting. *Phi Delta Kappan, 84*(2), 128–134.

Fitzgerald, J. (1987). Research on revision in writing. *Review of Educational Research, 57,* 481–506.

Fitzgerald, J., & Shanahan, T. (2000). Reading and writing relations and their development. *Educational Psychologist, 35*(1), 39–51.

Fitzgerald, J., & Stamm, C. (1990). Effects of group conferences on first graders' revision in writing. *Written Communication, 7,* 96–135.

Fitzgerald, J., & Teasley, A. B. (1983, November). *Effects of instruction in narrative structure on children's writing.* Paper presented at the annual meeting of the National Reading Conference, Austin, TX.

Fletcher, R. J. (1996). *Breathing in, breathing out: Keeping a writer's notebook.* Portsmouth, NH: Heinemann.

Gearhart, M. (2009). Classroom portfolio assessment for writing. In G. A. Troia (Ed.), *Instruction and assessment for struggling writers: Evidence-based practices* (pp. 311–336). New York: Guilford Press.

Gersten, R., & Baker, S. (2001). Teaching expressive writing to students with learning disabilities: A meta-analysis. *Elementary School Journal, 101,* 251–272.

Graham, S. (1983). Effective spelling instruction. *Elementary School Journal, 83,* 560–567.

Graham, S. (1997). Executive control in the revising of students with learning and writing difficulties. *Journal of Educational Psychology, 89,* 223–234.

Graham, S. (1999). Handwriting and spelling instruction for students with learning disabilities: A review. *Learning Disability Quarterly, 22,* 78–98.

Graham, S. (2000). Should the natural learning approach replace spelling instruction? *Journal of Educational Psychology, 92,* 235–247.

Graham, S., & Harris, K. R. (1989a). Components analysis of cognitive strategy instruction: Effects on learning disabled students' compositions and self-efficacy. *Journal of Educational Psychology, 81,* 353–361.

Graham, S., & Harris, K. R. (1989b). Improving learning disabled students' skills at composing essays: Self-instructional strategy training. *Exceptional Children, 56,* 201–214.

Graham, S., & Harris, K. R. (2000). The role of self-regulation and transcription skills in writing and writing development. *Educational Psychologist, 35,* 3–12.

Graham, S., & Harris, K. R. (2005). *Writing better: Effective strategies for teaching students with learning difficulties.* Baltimore: Brookes.

Graham, S., Harris, K. R., Fink, B., & MacArthur, C. A. (2003). Primary grade teachers' instructional adaptations for struggling writers: A national survey. *Journal of Educational Psychology, 95,* 279–292.

Graham, S., Harris, K. R., & Loynachan, C. (1993). The basic spelling vocabulary list. *Journal of Educational Research, 86,* 363–368.

Graham, S., Harris, K. R., & Loynachan, C. (1994). The spelling for writing list. *Journal of Learning Disabilities, 27,* 210–214.

Graham, S., Harris, K. R., & Mason, L. (2005). Improving the writing performance, knowledge, and self-efficacy of struggling young writers: The effects of self-regulated strategy development. *Contemporary Educational Psychology, 30,* 207–241.

Graham, S., Harris, K. R., & Troia, G. A. (1998). Writing and self-regulation: Cases from the self-regulated strategy development model. In D. H. Schunk & B. J. Zimmerman (Eds.), *Developing self-regulated learners: From teaching to self-reflective practice* (pp. 20–41). New York: Guilford Press.

Graham, S., & MacArthur, C. A. (1988). Improving learning disabled students' skills at revising essays produced on a word processor: Self-instructional strategy training. *Journal of Special Education, 22,* 133–152.

Graham, S., MacArthur, C. A., & Schwartz, S. S. (1995). Effects of goal setting and procedural facilitation on the revising behavior and writing performance of students with writing and learning problems. *Journal of Educational Psychology, 87,* 230–240.

Graham, S., MacArthur, C. A., Schwartz, S. S., & Page-Voth, V. (1992). Improving the compositions of students with learning disabilities using a strategy involving product and process goal setting. *Exceptional Children, 58,* 322–334.

Graham, S., & Perin, D. (2007). *Writing next: Effective strategies to improve writing of adolescents in middle and high schools—A report to Carnegie Corporation of New York.* Washington, DC: Alliance for Excellent Education.

Graham, S., & Weintraub, N. (1996). A review of handwriting research: Progress and prospects from 1980 to 1994. *Educational Psychology Review, 8,* 7–87.

Graves, D. H. (1994). *A fresh look at writing.* Portsmouth, NH: Heinemann.

Hamilton, R. A., Scott, D., & MacDougall, M. P. (2007). Assessing the effectiveness of self-talk interventions on endurance performance. *Journal of Applied Sport Psychology, 19,* 226–239.

Harris, A. J., & Sipay, E. R. (1985). *How to increase reading ability: A guide to developmental and remedial methods.* New York: Longman.

Harris, K. R. (1986). Self-monitoring of attentional behavior versus self-monitoring of productivity: Effects on on-task behavior and academic response rate among learning disabled children. *Journal of Applied Behavior Analysis, 19,* 417–423.

Harris, K. R., & Graham, S. (1996). *Making the writing process work: Strategies for composition and self-regulation.* Cambridge, MA: Brookline Books.

Hayes, J. R., Flower, L. S., Schriver, K., Stratman, J., & Carey, L. (1987). Cognitive processes in revision. In S. Rosenberg (Ed.), *Reading, writing, and language learning: Advances in applied psycholinguistics* (Vol. 2, pp. 176–240). Cambridge, UK: Cambridge University Press.

Knapp, M. S., & Associates. (Ed.). (1995). *Teaching for meaning in high-poverty classrooms.* New York: Teachers College Press.

Lewis, C. C. (2002). *Lesson study: A handbook of teacher-led instructional change.* Philadelphia: Research for Better Schools.

Lewis, C. C., & Tsuchida, I. (1998). A lesson is like a swiftly flowing river: Research lessons and the improvement of Japanese education. *American Educator, 51,* 14–17, 50–52.

Lipson, M. Y., Mosenthal, J., Daniels, P., & Woodside-Jiron, H. (2000). Process writing in the classrooms of eleven fifth-grade teachers with different orientations to teaching and learning. *Elementary School Journal, 101,* 209–231.

Lloyd, J. W., Bateman, D. F., Landrum, T. J., & Hallahan, D. P. (1989). Self-recording of attention versus productivity. *Journal of Applied Behavior Analysis, 22,* 315–323.

Loucks-Horsley, S., & Matsumoto, C. (1999). Research on professional development for teachers of mathematics and science: The state of the scene. *School Science and Mathematics, 99,* 258–271.

Maag, J. W., Reid, R., & DiGangi, S. A. (1993). Differential effects of self-monitoring attention, accuracy, and productivity. *Journal of Applied Behavior Analysis, 26,* 329–344.

MacArthur, C. A. (2006). The effects of new technologies on writing and writing processes. In C. A. MacArthur, S. Graham, & J. Fitzgerald (Eds.), *Handbook of writing research* (pp. 248–262). New York: Guilford Press.

MacArthur, C. A., Ferretti, R. P., Okolo, C. M., & Cavalier, A. R. (2001). Technology applications for students with literacy problems: A critical review. *Elementary School Journal, 101,* 273–301.

MacArthur, C. A., & Graham, S. (1987). Learning disabled students' composing with three methods: Handwriting, dictation, and word processing. *Journal of Special Education, 21,* 22–42.

MacArthur, C. A., Schwartz, S. S., & Graham, S. (1991). Effects of a reciprocal peer revision strategy in special education classrooms. *Learning Disabilities Research and Practice, 6,* 201–210.

Manning, B. H., & Payne, B. D. (1996). *Self-talk for teachers and students: Metacognitive strategies for personal and classroom use.* Boston: Allyn & Bacon.

Martin, N. M., & Certo, J. L. (2008, February). *Truth or tale?: The efficacy of teacher–student writing conferences.* Paper presented at the Third Writing Research across Borders Conference, Santa Barbara, CA.

McCutchen, D. (1995). Cognitive processes in children's writing: Developmental and individual differences. *Issues in Education: Contributions from Educational Psychology, 1,* 123–160.

McGinley, W. J., & Denner, P. R. (1987). Story impressions: A pre-reading/writing activity. *Journal of Reading, 31,* 248–253.

McMaster, K., & Espin, C. (2007). Technical features of curriculum-based measurement in writing: A literature review. *Journal of Special Education, 41,* 68–84.

Neubert, G. A., & McNelis, S. J. (1986). Improving writing in the disciplines. *Educational Leadership, 43*(7), 54–58.

Nickel, J. (2001). When writing conferences don't work: Students' retreat from teacher agenda. *Language Arts, 79*(2), 136–147.

Nolet, V. (1992). Classroom-based measurement and portfolio assessment. *Diagnostique, 18,* 5–26.

Ogle, D. M. (1986). K-W-L: A teaching model that develops active reading of expository text. *The Reading Teacher, 39,* 564–570.

Olinghouse, N. G., & Santangelo, T. (2010). Assessing the writing of struggling learners. *Focus on Exceptional Children, 43*(4), 1–27.

Page-Voth, V., & Graham, S. (1999). Effects of goal setting and strategy use on the writing performance and self-efficacy of students with writing and learning problems. *Journal of Educational Psychology, 91,* 230–240.

Persky, H. R., Daane, M. C., & Jin, Y. (2003). *The nation's report card: Writing 2002.* Washington, DC: National Center for Education Statistics, U.S. Department of Education.

Pritchard, R. J., & Honeycutt, R. L. (2006). The process approach to writing instruction: Examining its effectiveness. In C. A. MacArthur, S. Graham, & J. Fitzgerald (Eds.), *Handbook of writing research* (pp. 275–290). New York: Guilford Press.

Purcell-Gates, V., Duke, N. K., & Martineau, J. A. (2007). Learning to read and write genre-specific texts: Roles of authentic experience and explicit teaching. *Reading Research Quarterly, 42,* 8–45.

Raskind, M. H., & Higgins, E. L. (1995). Effects of speech synthesis on the proofreading efficiency of postsecondary students with learning disabilities. *Learning Disability Quarterly, 18,* 141–158.

Raskind, M. H., & Higgins, E. L. (1999). Speaking to read: The effects of speech recognition technology on the reading and spelling performance of children with learning disabilities. *Annals of Dyslexia National Center for Education Statistics, 49,* 251–281.

Rogers, L. A., & Graham, S. (2008). A meta-analysis of single subject design writing intervention research. *Journal of Educational Psychology, 100,* 879–906.

Rosenbaum, M. S., & Drabman, R. S. (1979). Self-control training in the classroom: A review and critique. *Journal of Applied Behavioral Analysis, 12,* 467–485.

Salahu-Din, D., Persky, H., & Miller, J. (2008). *The nation's report card: Writing 2007* (NCES Publication No. 2008-468). Washington, DC: National Center for Education Statistics, Institute of Education Sciences, U.S. Department of Education.

Sawyer, R. J., Graham, S., & Harris, K. R. (1992). Direct teaching, strategy instruction, and strategy instruction with explicit self-regulation: Effects on the composition skills and self-efficacy of students with learning disabilities. *Journal of Educational Psychology, 84,* 340–352.

Schunk, D. H., & Swartz, C. W. (1993a). Goals and progress feedback: Effects on self-efficacy and writing achievement. *Contemporary Educational Psychology, 18,* 337–354.

Schunk, D. H., & Swartz, C. W. (1993b). Writing strategy instruction with gifted students: Effects of goals and feedback on self-efficacy and skills. *Roeper Review, 15,* 225–230.

Singer, B. D., & Bashir, A. S. (1999). What are executive functions and self-regulation and what do they have to do with language-learning disorders? *Language, Speech, and Hearing Services in Schools, 30,* 265–273.

Smagorinsky, P. (1987). Graves revisited: A look at the methods and conclusions of the New Hampshire study. *Written Communication, 9,* 331–342.

Spandel, V. (2001). *Creating writers through 6-trait writing assessment and instruction* (3rd ed.). New York: Addison Wesley Longman.

Sperling, M. (1996). Revisiting the writing-speaking connection: Challenges for research on writing and writing instruction. *Review of Educational Research, 66,* 53–86.

Stoddard, B., & MacArthur, C. A. (1993). A peer editor strategy: Guiding learning-disabled students in response and revision. *Research in the Teaching of English, 27,* 76–103.

Stokes, L. (2001). Lessons from an inquiring school: Forms of inquiry and conditions for teacher learning. In A. Lieberman (Ed.), *Teachers caught in the action: Professional development that matters* (pp. 141–158). New York: Teachers College Press.

Sykes, G. (1999). Teacher and student learning: Strengthening their connections. In L. Darling-Hammond & G. Sykes (Eds.), *Teaching as the learning profession: Handbook of policy and practice* (pp. 151–179). San Francisco: Jossey-Bass.

Taylor, B. M., Pearson, P. D., Clark, K., & Walpole, S. (2000). Effective schools and accomplished teachers: Lessons about primary-grade reading instruction in low-income schools. *Elementary School Journal, 101,* 121–165.

Templeton, S., & Morris, D. (1999). Questions teachers ask about spelling. *Reading Research Quarterly, 34,* 102–112.

Troia, G. A. (2002). Teaching writing strategies to children with disabilities: Setting generalization as the goal. *Exceptionality, 10,* 249–269.

Troia, G. A. (2006). Writing instruction for students with learning disabilities. In C. A. MacArthur, S. Graham, & J. Fitzgerald (Eds.), *Handbook of writing research* (pp. 324–336). New York: Guilford Press.

Troia, G. A., & Graham, S. (2003). Effective writing instruction across the grades: What every educational consultant should know. *Journal of Educational and Psychological Consultation, 14,* 75–89.

Troia, G. A., Lin, S. C., Cohen, S., & Monroe, B. W. (2011). A year in the writing workshop: Linking writing instruction practices and teachers' epistemologies and beliefs about writing instruction. *Elementary School Journal, 112,* 155–182.

Troia, G. A., & Maddox, M. E. (2004). Writing instruction in middle schools: Special and general education teachers share their views and voice their concerns. *Exceptionality, 12,* 19–37.

Troia, G. A., Shankland, R. K., & Wolbers, K. A. (2010). Reluctant writers and their teachers: Changing self-efficacy beliefs through lesson study. In G. A. Troia, R. K. Shankland, & A. Heintz (Eds.), *Putting writing research into practice: Applications for teacher professional development* (pp. 70–90). New York: Guilford Press.

Troia, G. A., Shankland, R. K., & Wolbers, K. A. (2012). Motivation research in writing: Theoretical and empirical considerations. *Reading and Writing Quarterly: Overcoming Learning Difficulties, 28,* 5–28.

Ulichny, P., & Watson-Gegeo, K. A. (1989). Interactions and authority: The dominant interpretive framework in writing conferences. *Discourse Processes, 12,* 309–328.

Wharton-McDonald, R., Pressley, M., & Hampston, J. M. (1998). Literacy instruction in nine first-grade classrooms: Teacher characteristics and student achievement. *Elementary School Journal, 99,* 101–128.

Wood, K. D. (1986). How to smuggle writing into the classroom. *Middle School Journal, 17*(3), 5–6.

CHAPTER 13

Reading and Writing Specific Genres ● ● ● ● ● ● ● ● ● ● ● ● ● ●

NELL K. DUKE
LYNNE M. WATANABE

Imagine yourself sitting in an airport. Imagine the types of print that might be around you. There are the screens listing departing flights and their status; signs directing travelers to specific gates, the restrooms, and baggage claim; a menu at the nearby eatery; price tags on merchandise in the souvenir shop; the romance novel being read by a traveler sitting to the left; the news magazine being read by a traveler to your right; text messages flying back and forth on the phones of a cluster of teenagers across the way. All these different kinds of text are *genres*: They have particular purposes and use language and graphics in particular ways to accomplish those purposes. The flights are listed in alphabetical order by the name of each destination, so that travelers can easily locate their particular flights; the menu lists items and prices because that is the information consumers want to know; and so on.

Over the years, you have learned what to expect from each of these genres. You know how to adjust your reading for each of these different types of text. For example, you scan the entire menu to ascertain the range of foods available, but you selectively read the list of flights, reading only the status of the flight you are taking. Similarly, you adjust your writing for different text types. For example, although you would probably make little effort to be terse in writing a romance novel, you certainly would in composing a text message. Your reading and writing processes are, to a significant degree, genre-specific (Duke, Caughlan, Juzwik, & Martin, 2012; Duke & Roberts, 2010). Not surprisingly, then, your learning of them has also been genre-specific. All the experience in the world learning how to read a menu did not enable you to read a list of flights efficiently; you needed to learn the specific conventions and appropriate practices required for that particular type of text.

Part of the mission of schooling is to teach children what to expect from, how to read, and how to write the specific genres of text that are valued in school settings. We have to teach each genre—each specific set of conventions and practices—because proficiency with one does not automatically mean proficiency with another. This chapter is about how to teach students to read and write specific genres. It does not focus on learning skills that are largely the same across texts (such as decoding the words or grappling with the vocabulary), but rather focuses on developing knowledge and skills that apply to some texts and not others—for example, knowing how to use an index in an informational text versus learning attend to the setting of a narrative text.

We believe that typical instruction in U.S. classrooms does not sufficiently attend to genre. Many classrooms do not provide students the opportunity to encounter and experience a variety of genres, even genres that students need to be successful in school. Schools sometimes expect students to read and write in genres to which they have had only limited exposure (e.g., Jeong, Gaffney, & Choi, 2010; Pentimonti, Zucker, Justice, & Kaderavek, 2010). Students are not explicitly taught what the purposes and features of different genres are, or how to adjust their reading and writing processes to what they are reading or writing. Assessments often do not provide information related to the reading and writing of particular kinds of text. This chapter focuses on how we can begin better tailoring our instruction to particular genres of text.

OVERVIEW OF RESEARCH

In this section, we begin with an explanation of the term *genre*. We then discuss research on development of genre knowledge, followed by research on how to foster that development through teaching. Finally, we discuss which genres are and, according to the Common Core State Standards (CCSS; National Governors Association Center for Best Practices & Council of Chief State School Officers, 2010), should be a focus of instruction in U.S. classrooms.

Defining Genre

The word *genre* comes from the Latin word *genus*, meaning "kind." It has been seen as an important component of literacy learning, but a specific, agreed-upon definition of the term has been hard to come by (Dubrow, 1982). Genre was initially seen as something that described types of music, literature, or language. It was categorical, did not change, and included specific regularities in content and structure (Chapman, 1999). However, modern views of genre emphasize that they arise to serve specific purposes in a social context (Bakhtin, 1986). Genre is seen as resulting from a dynamic interplay of various situated factors, including purpose, audience, form, content, and social context (Chapman, 1999). Certain situations require and produce regularities in forms of communication. For example, if your students are writing an invitation for their families to the class play, the factors of purpose (to invite), audience (the family members), form (a letter/invitation), content (the necessary logistical information), and social context (relationships, roles, and norms of the family members, classroom, community, etc.) can all help to shape what they write and how they write it.

Duke and colleagues (2012) define genre as "recurring and recognizable communication with particular communicative purposes and particular features to accomplish those purposes" (p. 6). Paré and Smart (1994, p. 147) note that a given genre involves a "profile of regularities across four dimensions": (1) the text (including text forms and features), (2) the composition process of the text, (3) the practices used to read the text, and (4) the roles of the readers and writers. Texts within a particular genre share these four dimensions. Readers and writers must recognize these regularities and draw on them to read and write effectively. Genres are "cultural resources on which writers draw in the process of writing for particular purposes and in specific situations" (Chapman, 1999, p. 469).

Developing Genre Knowledge

One of us (Nell Duke) has a daughter who, as a young preschooler, pretended to read the fortune inside a cookie at a favorite Chinese restaurant. She said, "Truth is love." At this tender age, she had already developed some sense of this particular genre. Indeed, research suggests that genre knowledge begins to develop long before children are able to conventionally read and write (e.g., Donovan & Smolkin, 2006; Harste, Woodward, & Burke, 1994). Of course, children need to be exposed to a particular genre in order to acquire it (e.g., Kamberelis, 1999). Nell's daughter had developed some knowledge of the fortune cookie genre through many meals at a local Chinese eatery that concluded with fortune cookies.

Unfortunately, research suggests that elementary-age children have not been provided with substantial exposure to some of the genres they are expected to learn to read and write, most notably informational genres (e.g., Duke, 2000; Jeong et al., 2010). Narrative genres have dominated writing and reading instruction. Although this is good for narrative development, this is not sufficient to develop strong informational reading and writing skills because (as noted earlier) reading is largely genre-specific (Duke & Roberts, 2010); knowledge of one genre does not render one an effective reader and writer of another genre. Notably, if children are exposed to and engaged in reading and writing informational genres, research suggests that they begin to develop stronger knowledge of these genres (e.g., Chapman, 1999; Duke & Kays, 1998; Pappas, 1991).

Teaching Genre

Most research on reading and writing instruction has not focused on genre. However, we can draw some preliminary conclusions from the research that has been conducted. First, children develop stronger genre knowledge in classrooms where teachers engage them in reading and writing texts that are more like texts found outside a schooling context, for the purposes for which those genres are read and written outside a schooling context (Purcell-Gates, Duke, & Martineau, 2007). For example, engaging students in gathering information they need for an informational brochure they are writing to display at a local nature center would be predicted to result in stronger informational reading and writing development than would assigning students to write the answers to the questions in the back of a science textbook. This finding is derived from a study of second- and third-grade children reading and writing informational and procedural genres in science, but similar findings have emerged in research with other genres and with adults (Purcell-Gates, Degener, Jacobsen, & Soler, 2002), suggesting that this may be a general principle of genre learning.

Second, it appears that some genre features are acquired more easily, or at least earlier, than others (e.g., Donovan & Smolkin, 2002, 2006; Martin, 2011), suggesting that it may be important to target certain genre features for instruction. Certainly it appears that teaching children text structures specific to specific genres—story elements or structure for narrative genres, compare/contrast and other text structures for expository genres—supports reading comprehension and writing development (e.g., Graham & Perin, 2007; Shanahan et al., 2010).

Third, some instructional strategies that are tailored to specific genres can be effective at developing reading and writing skill. For example, *collaborative strategic reading*, which has been developed to foster comprehension of informational text genres, has a considerable research base demonstrating effectiveness (e.g., Vaughn et al., 2011). In this approach, teachers teach students a set of strategies—such as predicting what the text might teach them and reflecting on what they have learned from the text (Klingner, Vaughn, & Schumm, 1998)—that are not particularly appropriate to reading many other types of text, such as poetry or narrative genres. (For more about teaching comprehension, see Stahl, Chapter 9, and Garas-York, Shanahan, & Almasi, Chapter 10, this volume.) Similarly, research has demonstrated that an approach specific to teaching persuasive writing, known as *STOP* and *DARE*, is effective in improving the writing of students with learning disabilities (De La Paz & Graham, 1997a, 1997b). (For more about teaching writing, see Troia, Chapter 12, this volume.) In STOP, students:

Suspend judgment.
Take a side.
Organize ideas.
Plan more as you write.

They use a graphic organizer, with a column for ideas for and against a particular position, to support their planning and decision making. Cue cards help students remember the specific steps within STOP. For example, within the "Organize ideas" step, students are cued to star the ideas they want to use and those they want to dispute, as well as to number their ideas in the order they want to use them. Then, in the DARE phase, they ensure that their writing includes the following steps:

Develop a topic sentence.
Add supporting ideas.
Reject arguments for the other side.
End with a conclusion.

We cannot imagine applying this approach to narrative genres, poetry, drama, or even informational texts such as books about animals or geographic regions. Rather, this strategy is specific to a particular set of genres we would call *persuasive* or *argumentative*. As explained at the outset of this chapter, readers and writers use somewhat different processes with different emphases when reading and writing different kinds of text, so it makes sense that reading and writing instruction for different genres would be somewhat different as well.

Which Genres?

Research shows that children encounter some genres at home that they are unlikely to encounter at school, and vice versa (Duke & Purcell-Gates, 2003). Some genres, such as lists, descriptive texts, instructions, messages, labels, and signs, occur with some regularity in both contexts and thus might be particularly fruitful for helping students use their existing home-based knowledge to learn new school-based knowledge. With so many different genres in the world, and new genres emerging all the time (e.g., consider the Tweet, the unit of communication on Twitter.com), schools do have to make instructional decisions about which genres to prioritize. The CCSS (National Governors Association Center for Best Practices & Council of Chief State School Officers, 2010) is perhaps the most influential document currently available for identifying genres for instruction. In terms of broad categories for grades K–5, the CCSS document calls for the texts students read across the school day to be 50% informational and 50% literary, and for the writing they engage in to be 30% persuasive writing, 35% explanatory writing, and 35% writing to convey experience. More specifically, for K–5 it specifies the following range of text types (p. 31):

> Literature
> > Stories
> > > Includes children's adventure stories, folktales, legends, fables, fantasy, realistic fiction, and myth
> > Dramas
> > > Includes staged dialogue and brief familiar scenes
> > Poetry
> > > Includes nursery rhymes and the subgenres of the narrative poem, limerick, and free verse poem
> Informational
> > Literary Nonfiction and Historical, Scientific, and Technical Texts
> > > Includes biographies and autobiographies; books about history, social studies, science, and the arts; technical texts, including directions [what we would call *how-to* or *procedural texts*], forms, and information displayed in graphs, charts, or maps; and digital sources on a range of topics

In addition, while the CCSS document does not list persuasive genres, such as editorials, in range of text types, it does include standards that focus on persuasive writing—for example, at kindergarten:

> Use a combination of drawing, dictating, and writing to compose opinion pieces in which they tell a reader the topic or the name of the book they are writing about and state an opinion or preference about the topic or book (e.g., My favorite book is . . .). (p. 19)

And at grade 5:

Write opinion pieces on topics or texts, supporting a point of view with reasons and information.

a. Introduce a topic or text clearly, state an opinion, and create an organizational structure in which ideas are logically grouped to support the writer's purpose.
b. Provide logically ordered reasons that are supported by facts and details.
c. Link opinion and reasons using words, phrases, and clauses (e.g., consequently, specifically).
d. Provide a concluding statement or section related to the opinion presented.

After the summary of research that follows, we describe classroom efforts to meet these and other CCSS related to genre.

SUMMARY OF BIG IDEAS FROM RESEARCH

- Genres are recurring, recognizable forms of communication that serve specific communicative purposes in specific social contexts.
- Genre knowledge begins developing very early in life.
- Children must be exposed to the specific genres we want them to learn to read and write; the ability to read and write one genre will not transfer entirely to the ability to read and write another genre.
- Even young children should be exposed to a variety of school-valued genres, including informational text genres. The CCSS and other standards documents identify specific genres with which students should develop proficiency.
- Some genres are prevalent in both homes and schools, providing a possible bridge between home and school literacies.
- The development of students' ability to read and write specific genres is enhanced when students read and write those genres for the same reasons people read and write them outside a schooling context, using texts the same as or very much like those found outside a schooling context.
- Some genre features are acquired more easily than others. This suggests the need for teachers to engage in deliberate teaching of those features that are not as readily acquired as others.
- Use of instructional strategies specific to particular genres can be effective in improving students' reading and writing of specific genres. In general, reading and writing instruction should be sensitive to the genre being read or written.

EXAMPLES OF EFFECTIVE PRACTICES

We begin this section by discussing how teachers can create a genre-rich classroom environment. We then turn to examples of how teachers have engaged students in reading and writing various genres for compelling purposes. Next, we describe classroom practices that involve teaching genre-specific features and strategies; this section is organized by several different genre categories. Finally, we provide examples of practices that address specific standards related to genre.

Creating a Genre-Rich Classroom Environment

The classroom environment provides important and relatively easy ways to provide exposure to and experiences with a variety of genres. Teachers can develop a genre-rich environment by applying a genre-oriented perspective—by thinking about the reading and writing purposes and texts within the classroom. Many areas of the classroom environment can be "tweaked" to provide richer exposure to a wider array of genres.

One of the best places to begin is in the classroom library or book nook. This should be an area that promotes reading by providing books to read, a space to read them, and the opportunities to read. Classroom libraries should display a lot of different books, and these books should be from a variety of genres. Many teachers use book bins or baskets that include books of the same genre (e.g., poetry, information books, fairy tales). However, bins can also be organized by topic and therefore include a variety of genres about the same topic. For example, a bin of animal books might have animal stories, information books about animals, poetry about animals, and how-to books about animal craft projects. Writing can also be included in the book nook. Students can create charts and graphs on their favorite books or genres. They can post reviews of their favorite books, providing a summary as well as a few sentences to persuade others to read a particular book. This peer feedback can be used to connect others with familiar or new genres. Students can also post recommendations for books specific classmates might enjoy. The classroom library is an important component of any classroom and particularly a genre-rich classroom.

Classroom walls and surfaces can also be used to promote a genre-rich classroom environment. The walls and surfaces should exhibit student work and incorporate a variety of genres in various places. For example, how-to or procedural texts can explain procedures for how to line up for lunch, how to do work at a center, or how to wash hands. Explanatory informational text exposure can come from a "Did you know . . . ?" board, where students can post interesting facts they've learned from texts they're reading. A Poem-of-the-Day spot can feature a different student's or published poet's work each day. A binder placed near a waiting spot might include reviews students have written of storybooks or novels they do and do not recommend to others. Several of these strategies incorporate both reading and writing, and, again, help promote use of a variety of genres within the classroom environment. (For more about the classroom print environment, see Sailors, Kumar, Blady, & Willson, Chapter 2, this volume.)

Engaging Students in Reading and Writing Genres for Compelling Purposes

Students tend to be more motivated and engaged when there is a purpose for reading and writing beyond simply completing an assignment or satisfying the teacher. Table 13.1 provides the names and purposes of five common genre categories. Reading and writing genres for these purposes—and, in the case of writing, for actual audiences—is likely to be more compelling for students than writing solely for the teacher to satisfy an assignment. For example, if a student named Lucas is writing a persuasive text to his parents on why he deserves the amazing bike that he has been eyeing for months, his text is likely to be more engaging than the typical persuasive essay written for a hypothetical audience and/or the teacher. Lucas has a vested interest in communicating effectively to his audience (his parents) for his purpose (to convince them he needs the bike).

TABLE 13.1. Genre Purposes

Genre category	Primary purpose, briefly stated
Dramatic genres	• Gather and interact as a community (onstage and with an audience)
Explanatory informational genres	• To convey information about the natural or social world
Narrative genres	• To share and interpret past or present experience
Persuasive genres	• To influence the target audience's ideas or behaviors
Procedural genres	• To teach someone how to do something

Note. Purposes are based on Duke, Caughlan, Juzwik, and Martin (2012).

A real communicative purpose and an actual audience for a text are likely to make an important difference not only in the engagement of the students, but also in the literacy outcomes associated with the task. When a real purpose is emphasized along with the intended audience, students are more likely to develop and call upon their genre knowledge to read and write as effectively as possible, and this in turn may lead to improved literacy outcomes (see *Overview of Research*, above). For example, in one kindergarten classroom, students wanted to write individual thank-you letters to their fourth-grade "reading buddies" who read to them each week. Students researched how to write a simple letter by reading trade books, looking at actual mail, and seeing first-hand how mail systems work. They identified the purposes, audience, and features of letters in general and of thank-you letters specifically. They created a classroom postal system that included procedures for writing thank-you notes/letters and compliment letters. Students participated in modeled, shared, and independent letter-writing activities. They wrote the letters to the fourth graders and delivered them during one of their reading sessions at the end of the school year. The kindergartners wanted to thank the fourth graders, and they were interested in finding out how to do so through thank-you letters. Writing to the fourth graders, whom they saw as peers and mentors, fostered greater motivation for letter writing and led to greater concern with writing really good letters than might otherwise have been the case. The kindergartners gleaned more through the process of writing for a real purpose and audience than from a traditional how-to-write-a-letter lesson.

Audiences outside the school community can also be compelling, and the CCSS document does call for students to "learn to appreciate that a key purpose of writing is to communicate clearly to an external, sometimes unfamiliar audience" (p. 18). One of our favorite examples of this comes from the Michael J. Perkins Elementary School in South Boston (Duke et al., 2012). Each year, students get March 17 off from school not for St. Patrick's Day but for Evacuation Day; yet many Bostonians, and certainly people elsewhere in the United States, do not know what Evacuation Day is. So Principal Barney Brawer led students in researching and writing an historical account of Evacuation

FIGURE 13.1. Cover of *Why Do We Celebrate Evacuation Day?*, written by students from the Michael J. Perkins School in Boston, Massachusetts.

Day, called *Why Do We Celebrate Evacuation Day?* (see Figure 13.1), which is for sale on Amazon.com or directly through the Michael J. Perkins School (*perkins@boston.k12. ma.us*).

Reading and writing for compelling purposes and audiences need not involve extensive projects like those just described. Explanatory informational texts can be written on topics a class is already very familiar with (e.g., topics that have been the focus of science or social studies units) to be shared with other classes in the school. Short readers' theatre scripts can be obtained or written and performed for local audiences (e.g., Martinez, Roser, & Strecker, 1998–1999). Children can write narratives that do not require a lot of research, such as fifth graders writing about a special experience with grandparents or other family members, to be shared with those individuals. Procedural texts can be written to help new students learn how to do a particular procedure (e.g., how to get ready for lunch) or to share tips for an upcoming class about how to have a great year in that grade level. Students can look online for particular pieces of information, such as the weather forecast or the classification of a particular animal. Students can read poetry and narratives by authors they admire. There are many enriching possibilities when teachers consider purposes for reading and writing beyond just learning to read and write.

Teaching Genre-Specific Features and Strategies

When his class is reading information books on the solar system, Mr. Bates builds upon students' knowledge of the primary purpose of information books (to inform about the natural and social world) by calling attention to specific characteristics such as headings, captions, and descriptions. He also helps students understand how specific strategies can help them comprehend and use the information for the intended purpose (to learn information of interest to them about the solar system). As emphasized above, specific genres have specific features and call for the use of specific strategies in order for students to perform successfully in reading and writing.

If students do not understand the features of a specific genre, they cannot successfully navigate through that genre and use its features to accomplish the communicative purposes intended. It is beyond the scope of this chapter to describe the specific features of each genre employed in school settings. Features of texts in five broad genre categories (narrative, informational, procedural, persuasive, and dramatic), as well as information helpful to teaching students about these characteristics can be found in the Duke and colleagues (2012) book. Below, we focus on specific genres and refer to subsets of features of some common genres.

In addition to teaching students the features of a particular genre, teachers need to teach the specific strategies that are needed to read and write that genre successfully. For instance, a teacher cannot just give his or her students a copy of a play and expect those students to perform a reading of the text. Students must be taught such reading strategies as looking for the names of the characters they are portraying in the play margins, and reading lines aloud but blocking/stage directions silently. Similarly, students are likely to need help with identifying writing strategies appropriate to particular genres. For example, when they are writing narrative text, important questions to ask themselves during revision typically include "Do I provide a clear picture of the setting of this story?" and "Do I convey how the character is feeling?" On the other hand, when students are writing explanatory informational text, good questions to ask themselves during revision typically include "Does the text help readers find the information they want or need to know?" and "Does each graphic help readers learn and understand?" If writers are attempting to accomplish the communicative purpose of a genre (see Table 13.1), written texts need to be planned, created, and revised while considering purpose and audience.

Some examples of genre-specific reading strategies are given in Table 13.2, and some examples of genre-specific writing strategies are found in Table 13.3. As with teaching any strategy, instruction in genre-specific reading and writing strategies should include explicit modeling and teaching about the strategy followed by opportunities for students to practice the strategy with others and independently (see Stahl, Chapter 9, and Troia, Chapter 12). The following paragraphs discuss the teaching of reading and writing strategies specifically needed for engagement with narrative, explanatory informational, persuasive, and procedural genres.

Narrative Genres

Narrative genres are primarily used to share and interpret past or present experiences (real or imagined) the author has lived, has researched, or knows about (Duke et al., 2012). Due to this purpose, narrative genres lend themselves to the use of particular strategies for successful reading comprehension and writing. Two of the major influences on narrative genres are the presence of story elements (such as characters, setting, plot, and theme) and the use of particular kinds of language.

TABLE 13.2. Examples of Reading Strategies for Narrative, Explanatory Informational, Persuasive, and Procedural Genres

Narrative genres	Explanatory informational genres	Persuasive genres	Procedural genres
• Previewing the narrative and activating background knowledge	• Previewing with attention to text structure	• Assessing the author's credibility and purposes	• Previewing the text
• Visualizing the setting, characters, and events	• Skimming and scanning	• Determining the author's central argument	• Ensuring that you have the materials or ingredients needed
• Building "envisionments" (deeply interacting with story content) (Langer, 1995)	• Searching	• Identifying and evaluating the quality of reasons and evidence provided to support the argument	• Reading steps in order from beginning to end
• Reviewing the story after reading	• Activating topical background knowledge	• Identifying inconsistencies	• Pausing after each step before moving on to the next one
• Evaluating the significance of the reading	• Predicting (what the author will *tell* about next, not what will happen)	• Considering counterarguments	• Using the illustrations to learn how to complete a step
	• Visualizing		• Rereading as needed to complete a step
	• Visually representing (visualizing, using graphic organizers)		
	• Summarizing		

Note. Based on Duke, Caughlan, Juzwik, and Martin (2012).

TABLE 13.3. Examples of Writing Strategies for Narrative, Explanatory Informational, Persuasive, and Procedural Genres

Narrative genres	Explanatory informational genres	Persuasive genres	Procedural genres
• Planning using story elements as a framework • Conducting research to ensure accuracy (for nonfiction narrative) • Drafting with a focus on language that will convey experience and evaluation of it • Revising, including a focus on building the reader's envisionment	• Planning by thinking about who wants or needs the information and what information would be most useful • Researching (hands-on investigation, printed and digital sources, interviews, etc., transforming the information by synthesis or reframing) • Revising with an eye toward the reader's ability to navigate the text and understand the information	• Learning about target audience, including how its members may feel about the issue • Researching arguments, counterarguments, and evidence • Drafting the argument, including establishing credibility, giving reasons, providing evidence • Strengthening your argument by considering mode of presentation and opposing points of view	• Conducting the procedure while taking notes on the process • Developing graphics to depict each step when appropriate • Revising looking for specificity in description of materials and steps • Having someone representing your target audience try to carry out the procedure using your text (and then revising accordingly)

Note. Based on Duke, Caughlan, Juzwik, and Martin (2012).

One of us (Lynne Watanabe) taught story elements to develop her kindergarten students' reading and writing of narrative genres. During narrative read-alouds, she led students in identifying and defining the simple story elements of characters, setting, problem, and solution. The students applied these elements to the personal narratives they composed themselves (e.g., "Who are my characters?"). Lynne worked with students to use language that helped them identify and describe the story elements (e.g., "When I was at my grandma's house [setting], we couldn't find her dog [problem]"). The story elements served as cues for the students in reading and writing, and encouraged the use of appropriate language.

Explanatory Informational Genres

A major purpose for writing informational text is to convey information about the natural or social world. To comprehend informational texts, one must be able to glean information, and to compose these texts, one must be able to organize and present the information so that it is coherent.

One important focus of instruction is how to find information within informational text in cases in which reading the entire text is not necessary or advisable. This is important with many print-based information books, particularly reference books, and essential to Web-based texts. One second-grade teacher taught her students about the table of contents and headings in printed text and tabs and headings in digital text (e.g., *http://kids.nationalgeographic.com/kids/?source=NavKidsHome*) as important tools for locating information. Using a think-aloud, she modeled how to use these features and characteristics to find the information students needed for informational books they were writing for the classroom library and for buddy reading with another class in the school. Students participated in shared and independent writing experiences to compose their informational texts, and used some of these features. This process also involved genre-specific revision, as students examined their texts for how well they enabled readers to find information.

Persuasive Genres

Persuasive genres differ from informational and narrative genres, particularly in the way that persuasive texts are developed. The primary purpose of persuasive genres is to influence the target audience's ideas or behaviors. As suggested in Table 13.3, writing a persuasive text involves identifying (and in some cases researching) the target audience. It often entails researching the issue that will be the focus of the text, contemplating support for and evidence against this position, taking a position on the issue, and considering how the audience might react to any claims and evidence presented, all before actually writing the piece itself.

Model texts can be very helpful in developing the art of persuasion. For example, students can look at effective advertisements as models for writing their own advertisements. One upper elementary classroom participated in a project in which students formed teams that acted as ad agencies. Each team read and researched a book to promote in another classroom in the same grade. Students read book reviews as well as advertisements, and discussed the elements contained within them. Then they wrote promotional texts—containing elements of advertisements and book reviews, as book promotions often do—which they gave to the other class, along with a copy of each book. If, as students hoped, the class members were convinced by their promotions that a book was worth reading, they had a copy readily available to read.

The disciplinary context of persuasive writing should also be considered. For example, De La Paz (2005) developed an intervention for middle school students that involved them in particular ways of reading persuasive text in history. Examples of questions for students to consider include:

- Are people and events described differently in different sources?
- "What was the author's purpose?"
- "Do you find evidence of bias?"
- "What is missing from the author's argument?" (p. 145)

Procedural Genres

The purpose of procedural texts is to provide an explanation of and/or information on how to do something. This genre requires some strategies that are quite different from those in other genres because the reader is actually expected to do what the text directs. Indeed, Martin (2011) found that even elementary-age students use different strategies when reading procedural text than when reading biographical and persuasive text. Research on teaching reading and writing strategies for procedural text is scarce (Duke et al., 2012). However, observation provides some strategies that seem appropriate for instruction in reading these texts (see Table 13.2).

For writing procedural text, Duke and colleagues (2012, pp. 73–74) and teachers with whom they have worked identified five strategies that can be used in engaging students in writing procedural text (once a compelling purpose and audience for writing are established):

1. Have students conduct the procedure, taking notes or drafting their text in the process.
2. Provide a template or outline for students, particularly younger students, to help signal the information needed and where it might be placed.
3. Provide a rubric or list of characteristics of an effective procedural text, preferably derived from the students' study of some effective and ineffective procedural texts.
4. Engage students in several rounds of revision focused on different aspects of procedural text (e.g., graphics, layout, mechanics).
5. Have representatives of the target audience try out the procedure and provide feedback.

Notably, even young children benefit from the reading and writing of procedural texts. For example, preschoolers in one class created procedural texts on how to play a simple game for another preschool class. They learned how to play the game and make the necessary equipment. Then they participated in interactive writing to compose a text on how to make the equipment. The students gave the texts and the materials needed to make the equipment to the other classroom. Writing these how-to texts was an appropriate and enjoyable experience both for these preschoolers and for the class to which they gave the game.

Addressing Specific Standards Related to Genre

Lessons about genre should be informed in part by the specific standards teachers are trying to address. In this section, we provide three examples of standards related to genre and how teachers might address them in instruction.

- *Example 1: CCSS for kindergarten: "Recognize common types of texts (e.g., storybooks, poems)" (p. 11).* To address this standard, many teachers engage children in discussions about genre in the context of a read-aloud. Teachers name the genre or broader category of the text and explicitly explain why they view it as such. For example, a teacher might say, "I think this is a story because it has characters and events that happen." Children can be engaged in a discussion of genre through key questions such as "How do we know that this is a story?" and "Why do you think the author wrote this book?" At first, it may be most useful to engage in these conversations with prototypical examples of the genre, but it is not necessary to avoid less prototypical examples entirely. It is important to acknowledge the "fuzziness" of genre. For example, some poems are also stories (e.g., a number of Shel Silverstein poems have these dual identities). It is also important to challenge misconceptions about genre, such as that all stories are make-believe. Kindergarten teacher Patricia Zeichman teaches children that poems need not rhyme—a common misconception children hold (Certo, 2004). The poem in Figure 13.2, from one of Mrs. Zeichman's students, demonstrates an understanding that poems can be free verse.

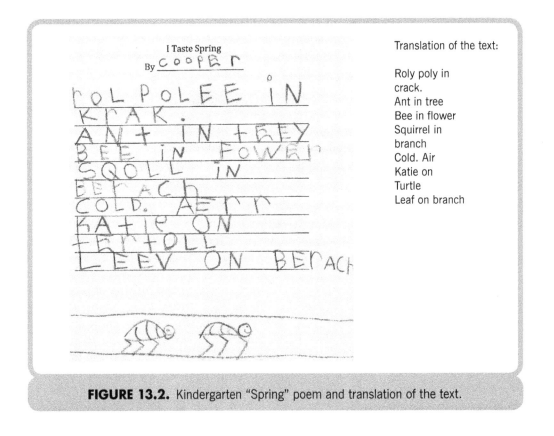

FIGURE 13.2. Kindergarten "Spring" poem and translation of the text.

• *Example 2: CCSS for second grade:* "Know and use various text features (e.g., headings, tables of contents, glossaries, electronic menus, icons) to locate key facts or information in a text" (p. 13). The *improve-a-text strategy* (Duke, Halladay, & Roberts, in press) is an authentic and engaging way for children to use reading, writing, and genre knowledge together to meet this standard. In this strategy, the teacher selects a book, and students create an addition to the text to improve upon it. This technique can be applied to a number of genres, but it was created specifically for expository informational texts. For example, when reading a book about different animals, the teacher might "think aloud" his or her wonderings about what a specific word means. The class might realize that there is no clear explanation of the word in the text and no glossary to refer to. Students might then put in a self-stick note or correction tape with an explanation of the word into the book, and/or they might create an entire glossary for the text through interactive writing or independently. Figure 13.3 shows a table of contents written by a student to improve a text titled *Space Mysteries* (Kenah, 2004).

• *Example 3: CCSS for fifth grade:* "Determine the meaning of general academic and domain-specific words and phrases in a[n informational] text relevant to a grade 5 topic or subject area" (p. 14). Information about strategies for addressing this standard is provided by Kucan in Chapter 11 of this book. Here we focus on genre knowledge that will aid students in meeting this standard. Vocabulary in informational text is different in important ways from vocabulary in other kinds of text. In many informational texts, such as a book about the human body, some important vocabulary is likely to be repeated several times (e.g., the word *system* as in *the digestive system, the circulatory system*, etc.). By contrast, in many other kinds of text, an important word—such as an adjective describing a character in a story or a noun identifying the geographic region where the story takes place—may appear only once. Furthermore, in an informational text, there are likely to be more clues to word meaning either in the running text (e.g., "Canines, commonly known as dogs . . . "), in graphic devices such as diagrams, or in an actual glossary. Morphological analysis may also be especially useful with the academic vocabulary in informational text, which is often of Latin and Greek origin (e.g.,

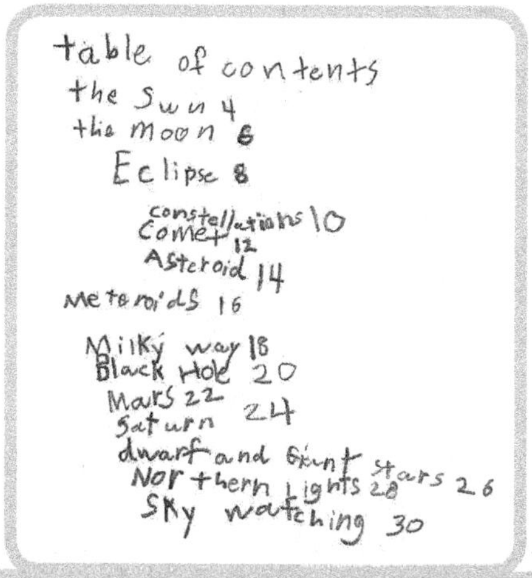

FIGURE 13.3. Table of contents created with the improve-a-text strategy.

Baumann et al., 2002). These characteristics of vocabulary in informational text suggest that lessons to address this standard might include teaching students to ascertain word meaning by using these strategies:

- Looking for other instances in which the word is used.
- Using diagrams and other graphical devices for information about word meaning.
- Drawing on any explanations or glosses provided in the running text or glossary.
- Examining the roots and affixes of the word.

We see here again an example of how genre-sensitive literacy instruction can support developing readers and writers.

Meeting All Students' Needs

We cannot assume that every student will have the same or similar genre knowledge as his or her classmates will have. Students' exposure and experience with various genres may differ a great deal, due to differences in cultural practices in their homes and communities, past schooling experiences, reading and writing ability, and even students' own personal preferences (e.g., some students may strongly prefer some genres over others, leading to more experience with some genres than others). For groups of students for whom many genres of schooling (or genres found in schools) are unfamiliar, it may be especially important to bring in familiar genres from their homes and communities and to discuss how they are similar to and different from genres that are the targets of instruction in school (Purcell-Gates, n.d.). (For more about culturally responsive teaching, see McIntyre & Turner, Chapter 6, this volume.)

Struggling readers and writers may have particular issues with reading and writing specific genres for a variety of reasons, including that their history of difficulties may have led to less engaged experience with some genres; that their focus on more basic aspects of the reading and writing process may have meant less attention to genre; and that some genre characteristics teachers and other students assume to be "common knowledge" may not be known or apparent to them. Extra opportunities to talk about and apply genre knowledge may be needed. Model texts, with encouragement to imitate and innovate on those texts, may be helpful. A compelling purpose for reading and writing specific genres may be particularly important, as these students may have to expend more effort than others in reading and writing. More intensive explicit teaching of reading and writing practices for specific genres is likely to be helpful. The STOP and DARE strategy described earlier, for example, has been shown to be effective for students with learning disabilities.

Variation in students' genre knowledge should be taken into account as we organize instruction. For example, rather than always grouping students by general reading level, it may sometimes make sense to group students according to their profiles of genre knowledge. Perhaps students who are better at reading literary genres (Park, 2008) could be grouped together to work on informational reading, while another group of students better at reading informational genres could be grouped for work on literary reading. Or perhaps students who are more naturally mindful of audience when they write could be paired with students who tend not to consider audience as much when they compose. In sum, just as we differentiate instruction in word recognition, spelling, and other foundational areas of literacy, so too should we differentiate instruction in genre.

LOOKING FORWARD

There is much work for researchers and practitioners to do to improve the teaching of specific genres in elementary classrooms. We look forward to future research and development addressing the following questions:

- Within the broad categories *informational* and *literary*, which genres should we prioritize? Which do we most want students to be able to read and write effectively, and at what ages?
- Should every important genre be the subject of instruction every year, or should some genres (e.g., biography) be a focus of instruction in some years and not others?
- How can we develop curricula that more often engage students in reading and writing genres for the real purposes for which they were developed?
- Which features of genres are worth teaching, and which are likely to be acquired naturally? How does this differ by student?
- What new instructional strategies can help us more effectively teach reading and writing processes appropriate for specific genres? What strategies are most effective in developing reading and writing skill with specific digital genres?
- How can preservice and inservice teacher education adjust to better develop knowledge of text and the teaching of text genre?

QUESTIONS FOR REFLECTION ● ● ● ● ● ● ● ● ● ● ● ● ● ● ● ● ● ● ●

1. To what extent do I, or teachers I have observed, provide exposure to (in the classroom library, on classroom walls, and on other surfaces), experience with (in classroom activities and home reading programs), and instruction in each of the types of text identified in the standards documents to which we are accountable? (See the *Overview of Research* section for a list from the CCSS.)

2. Is involvement with different types of text appropriately balanced? For example, if I am accountable to the CCSS at the elementary level, do I provide reading of 50% informational and 50% literary texts, and do I engage students in approximately 30% persuasive writing, 35% explanatory writing, and 35% writing to convey experience?

3. Do I incorporate genres important to children from their home environments, building bridges between them and genres emphasized in a schooling context?

4. To what extent do I engage students in reading and writing genres for the actual purposes for which those genres are read and written outside a schooling context? Are students reading and writing because I told them to, or because they want or need to for some compelling purpose? Do they have an audience for much of their writing beyond just me, their classmates, and their parents?

5. Am I carefully examining students' reading and writing not only for general characteristics, such as basic comprehension and mechanics, but for their effectiveness within that genre? For example, can they carry out a procedure based on a procedural text? Can they write an engaging play?

6. Am I teaching specific strategies students can use to be more effective readers or writers of a particular genre? Am I teaching students about genre features that may help them read and write more effectively?

7. Am I always careful to place my emphasis on what a particular strategy or feature does for the reader or writer, rather than teaching strategies or features as ends unto themselves?

8. Do I encourage students to make choices about, innovate on, and play with a genre, rather than just to reproduce it formulaically?

SUGGESTIONS FOR ONGOING PROFESSIONAL LEARNING • • • • • •

Most elementary teacher preparation programs and inservice teacher professional development initiatives provide little information about genre, development of genre knowledge and skill, or genre-sensitive instruction. This makes genre ripe as a focus for a professional learning community (PLC). Spending time with colleagues in a PLC provides regular, ongoing support and guidance, as well as opportunities to discuss and examine issues of practice, learning, and assessment. A PLC on reading and writing specific genres can be an effective and influential way to learn about text, students' learning, and your role as a teacher. This section includes suggestions for two series of sessions on genre for a PLC.

Strengthening Instruction for One or More Neglected Genres

Session 1

Discuss this chapter and the concept of genre with your PLC. What does the term *genre* mean? Make a list of all the different genres you have read or written since you got up this morning. What do you notice about them (their purposes, audience, form, features, etc.)? Did these genres resemble one another? How many different genres are represented in your list? Over the course of the next week or two, study the genres represented in your classroom libraries, on your classroom walls and other surfaces, and in your assessment and instruction.

Session 2

Share your lists of the various genres from your classroom with one another. Do you see any similarities in your lists? Differences? Create a group list of the items on your lists that you would label as being of the same genre (remember to pay particular attention to text purpose rather than text features). Is this an easy task? Why or why not? How would each of you categorize the types of genres taught, learned, and assessed in your classrooms? What do you think students know about these different types of text? What don't they know? For the next session, be prepared to talk about the genres represented in the standards documents you are accountable to and in any curricula or assessments used at your grade level.

Session 3

Share the genres that are represented in the standards, curricula, and assessments for your teaching situation. Do you see similarities and differences? Where are there discrepancies? Are there any genres you are not teaching at all, or as thoroughly as you should? Select one or more genres to which you would like to give more attention in instruction. Investigate instructional practices that are effective for teaching this genre or these genres. Discuss any resources or help you may need in making your instruction more effective. After the session, begin to implement changes in your classroom. As much as possible, draw on research and professional resources relevant to the genre or genres you are targeting. Collect samples of student work (recordings of their reading and discussions of text and/or pieces of their writing) to bring to the next session.

Session 4

Examine the samples of student work you have collected. Based on these, what lessons might be helpful to students? What reading or writing strategies might help them read and write that particular genre more effectively? What genre features would be helpful for them to understand better? How does this vary by student? Are there logical ways to group students for instruction tailored to their particular needs? Before the next session, work to provide some of the needed instruction and monitor the results.

Session 5

Discuss the reading and/or writing purposes and the specific lessons you have been implementing in your classroom. Talk about the experience of the process (e.g., strengths, challenges, resources used, strategies) and what modifications you can make to improve the implementation further. What do you suggest for others enacting this process? What do you plan to do next, and what resources do you need to make that happen? "Divide and conquer" the work of attaining reviews of research and professional resources to help you teach specific genre(s) more effectively.

Strengthening Attention to Genre in Specific Parts of the School Day

Session 1

Again, discuss this chapter and the concept of genre with your PLC. What does the term *genre* mean? Make a list of all the different genres you have read or written since you got up this morning. What do you notice about them (their purposes, audience, form, features, etc.)? Did these genres resemble one another? How many different genres are represented in your list? Over the course of the next week or two, study the genres represented in each part of your school day, such as during read-aloud time, during writers' workshop, and during science instruction. Think about the degree to which you adjust instruction based on the genre being read or written.

Session 2

Share your lists of the genres represented in each part of your school day with one another. Do you see any similarities in your lists? Differences? Discuss whether and how each member of the PLC adjusts (or doesn't adjust) instruction, depending on the genre being read or written. For example, do you provide students with different kinds of feedback, depending on the genre in which students are writing? Do you read aloud different genres of text differently? Do your mini-lessons on comprehension strategies explain how these strategies are applied similarly and differently, depending upon the genre? Continue to think about these questions as you prepare for the next session.

Session 3

Select a portion of your day in which you would like to be more attentive to genre (this might be the same portion for all group members, or different portions for different group members). Begin by brainstorming with colleagues how you could engage students in reading and writing specific genres in that portion of the day for the same reasons people read and write those genres outside a schooling context. For example, during guided reading, how could you create compelling purposes for students to be reading stories, and (different) compelling purposes for students to be reading expository, informational texts? Or during writers' workshop, how could you establish real audiences and purposes for students to write their own plays, and then to write their own procedural texts? Following the session, begin implementing these reading and/or writing purposes in your classroom.

Session 4

Debrief with colleagues about each person's efforts to provide more genre-sensitive instruction in the portion(s) of the school day you selected. Consider sharing lesson plans and/or arranging to view or video-record one another's lessons. "Divide and conquer" the work of attaining reviews of research and professional resources to help you learn more about teaching specific genre(s) during this portion of the day more effectively. Repeat Sessions 4 and 5 as you refine your instruction; then expand to another portion of the school day.

RESEARCH-BASED RESOURCES

Duke, N. K., & Bennett-Armistead, V. S., with Huxley, A., Johnson, M., McLurkin, D., Roberts, E., et al. (2003). *Reading and writing informational text in the primary grades: Research-based practices.* New York: Scholastic.

Duke, N. K., Caughlan, S., Juzwik, M. M., & Martin, N. M. (2012). *Reading and writing genre with purpose in K–8 classrooms.* Portsmouth, NH: Heinemann.

Eagleton, M. B., & Dobler, E. (2007). *Reading the Web: Strategies for Internet inquiry.* New York: Guilford Press.

Hartley, J., & McWilliam, K. (Eds.). (2009). *Story circle: Digital storytelling around the world.* Malden, MA: Wiley-Blackwell.

Hillocks, G. (2006). *Narrative writing: Learning a new model for teaching.* Portsmouth, NH: Boynton/Cook.

Hillocks, G. (2011). *Teaching argument writing, grades 6–12: Supporting claims with relevant evidence and clear reasoning.* Portsmouth, NH: Boynton/Cook.
Knapp, P., & Watkins, M. (2005). *Genre, text, and grammar: Technologies for teaching and assessing writing.* Sydney: University of New South Wales Press.
Schleppegrell, M. J. (2004). *The language of school: A functional linguistics perspective.* Mahwah, NJ: Erlbaum.

REFERENCES

Bakhtin, M. M. (1986). The problem of speech genres. In C. Emerson & M. Holquist (Eds.), *Speech genres and other late essays* (pp. 60–102). Austin: University of Texas Press.
Baumann, J. F., Edwards, E. C., Font, G., Tereshinski, C. A., Kame'enui, E. J., & Olejnik, S. (2002). Teaching morphemic and contextual analysis to fifth-grade students. *Reading Research Quarterly, 37,* 150–176.
Certo, J. L. (2004). Cold plums and the old men in the water: Let children read and write great poetry. *The Reading Teacher, 58*(3), 266–271.
Chapman, M. (1999). Situated, social, active: Rewriting genre in the elementary classroom. *Written Communication, 16,* 469–490.
De La Paz, S. (2005). Effects of historical reasoning instruction and writing strategy mastery in culturally and academically diverse middle school classrooms. *Journal of Educational Psychology, 97,* 139–156.
De La Paz, S., & Graham, S. (1997a). The effects of dictation and advanced planning instruction on the composing of students with writing and learning problems. *Journal of Educational Psychology, 89*(2), 203–222.
De La Paz, S., & Graham, S. (1997b). Strategy instruction in planning: Effects on the writing performance and behavior of students with learning difficulties. *Exceptional Children, 63,* 167–181.
Donovan, C. A., & Smolkin, L. B. (2002). Children's genre knowledge: An examination of K–5 students' performance on multiple tasks providing different levels of scaffolding. *Reading Research Quarterly, 37,* 428–465.
Donovan, C. A., & Smolkin, L. B. (2006). Children's understanding of genre and writing development. In C. A. MacArthur, S. Graham, & J. Fitzgerald (Eds.), *Handbook of writing research* (pp. 131–143). New York: Guilford Press.
Dubrow, H. (1982). *Genre.* London: Methuen.
Duke, N. K. (2000). 3.6 minutes per day: The scarcity of informational texts in first grade. *Reading Research Quarterly, 35,* 202–224.
Duke, N. K., Caughlan, S., Juzwik, M. M., & Martin, N. M. (2012). *Reading and writing genre with purpose in K–8 classrooms.* Portsmouth, NH: Heinemann.
Duke, N. K., Halladay, J. L., & Roberts, K. L. (2013). Reading standards for informational text. In L. M. Morrow, T. Shanahan, & K. K. Wixson (Eds.), *Teaching with the Common Core Standards for English language arts, PreK–2* (pp. 46–66). New York: Guilford Press.
Duke, N. K., & Kays, J. (1998). "Can I say 'once upon a time'?": Kindergarten children developing knowledge of information book language. *Early Childhood Research Quarterly, 13,* 295–318.
Duke, N. K., & Purcell-Gates, V. (2003). Genres at home and at school: Bridging the known to the new. *The Reading Teacher, 57,* 30–37.
Duke, N. K., & Roberts, K. L. (2010). The genre-specific nature of reading comprehension. In D. Wyse, R. Andrews, & J. Hoffman (Eds.), *The Routledge international handbook of English, language and literacy teaching* (pp. 74–86). London: Routledge.

Graham, S., & Perin, D. (2007). A meta-analysis of writing instruction for adolescent students. *Journal of Educational Psychology, 99*, 445–476.

Harste, J. C., Woodward, V. A., & Burke, C. (1994). Children's language and world: Initial encounters with print. In R. B. Ruddell, M. R. Ruddell, & H. Singer (Eds.), *Theoretical models and processes of reading* (4th ed., pp.48–69). Newark, DE: International Reading Association.

Jeong, J., Gaffney, J. S., & Choi, J.-O. (2010). Availability and use of informational texts in second-, third-, and fourth-grade classrooms. *Research in the Teaching of English, 44*, 435–456.

Kamberelis, G. (1999). Genre development and learning: Children writing stories, science reports, and poems. *Research in the Teaching of English, 33*, 403–460.

Kenah, K. (2004). *Space mysteries.* Columbus, OH: McGraw-Hill Children's Publishing.

Klingner, J. K., Vaughn, S., & Schumm, J. S. (1998). Collaborative strategic reading during social studies in heterogeneous fourth-grade classrooms. *Elementary School Journal, 99,* 3–22.

Langer, J. A. (1995). *Envisioning literature: Literary understanding and literature instruction.* New York: Teachers College Press.

Martin, N. M. (2011). *Exploring informational text comprehension: Reading biography, persuasive text, and procedural text in the elementary grades.* Unpublished doctoral dissertation, Michigan State University.

Martinez, M., Roser, N. L., & Strecker, S. (1998–1999). "I never thought I could be a star": A reader's theatre ticket to fluency. *The Reading Teacher, 52,* 326–334.

National Governors Association Center for Best Practices & Council of Chief State School Officers. (2010). *Common Core State Standards for English language arts and literacy in history/social studies, science, and technical subjects.* Washington, DC: Authors. Retrieved from *www.corestandards.org/the-standards/english-language-arts-standards.*

Pappas, C. C. (1991). Fostering full access to literacy by including information books. *Language Arts, 68,* 449–462.

Paré, A., & Smart, G. (1994). Observing genres in action: Towards a research methodology. In A. Freedman & P. Medway (Eds.), *Genre and the new rhetoric* (pp. 122–129). London: Taylor & Francis.

Park, Y. (2008). *Patterns in and predictors of elementary students' reading performance: Evidence from the data of the Progress in International Reading Literacy Study (PIRLS).* Unpublished doctoral dissertation, Michigan State University.

Pentimonti, J. M., Zucker, T. A., Justice, L. M., & Kaderavek, J. N. (2010). Informational text use in preschool classroom read-alouds. *The Reading Teacher, 63*(8), 656–665.

Purcell-Gates, V. (n.d.). *Real-life literacy instruction, K–3: A handbook for teachers.* Vancouver: University of British Columbia. Retrieved from *www.authenticliteracyinstruction.com/img/HandbookK3.pdf.*

Purcell-Gates, V., Degener, S., Jacobsen, E., & Soler M. (2002). Impact of authentic literacy instruction on adult literacy practices. *Reading Research Quarterly, 37,* 70–92.

Purcell-Gates, V., Duke, N. K., & Martineau, J. A. (2007). Learning to read and write genre-specific text: Roles of authentic experience and explicit teaching. *Reading Research Quarterly, 42,* 8–45.

Shanahan, T., Callison, K., Carriere, C., Duke, N. K., Pearson, P. D., Schatschneider, C., et al. (2010). *Improving reading comprehension in kindergarten through 3rd grade: A practice guide* (NCEE Publication No. 2010-4038). Washington, DC: National Center for Education Evaluation and Regional Assistance, Institute of Education Sciences, U.S. Department of Education. Retrieved from *whatworks.ed.gov/publications/practiceguides.*

Vaughn, S., Klingner, J. K., Swanson, E. A., Boardman, A. G., Roberts, G., Mohammed, S. S., et al. (2011). Efficacy of collaborative strategic reading with middle school students. *American Educational Research Journal, 48,* 938–964.

PART III

Effective Integration of Literacy with Instruction in Content Areas

CHAPTER 14

Integration of Literacy and Science ● ● ● ● ● ● ● ● ● ● ● ● ● ● ● ● ●

GINA CERVETTI

OVERVIEW OF RESEARCH

The ability to engage effectively with texts across content areas is increasingly viewed as central to advanced literacy in the 21st century (National Governors Association Center for Best Practices & Council of Chief State School Officers, 2010). As is becoming more widely recognized, reading, writing, and talk are shaped in part by the texts and contexts in which they are situated, such that reading in the scientific disciplines calls for different sets of skills and stances than, for example, reading literary texts does. Moreover, whereas science educators traditionally regarded reading and writing as separate from learning and participation in science, literacy is increasingly viewed as authentic and integral to science learning.

A growing body of instructional research provides insight into the characteristics of effective approaches to literacy and science integration. In particular, this research supports the efficacy of approaches that help students acquire strategies to understand and write science texts and tie the literacy practices of science to science inquiry. The approaches to literacy–science integration described in this chapter have demonstrated wide-ranging benefits for students' learning in science and literacy, and for students' engagement and motivation in both domains.

Helping Students Acquire Strategies to Understand and Write Science Texts

For many decades, reading was widely viewed as a set of general skills that could be applied to nearly any text and nearly any purpose. The underlying assumption was that students who were taught to read on literary texts would later simply transfer their reading skills to content-area texts (Shanahan & Shanahan, 2008). This view has been challenged recently by evidence that a focus on "basic" reading skills has failed to pre-pare adolescents for the demands of content-area reading. In addition, many educators now recognize that reading differs in important ways, depending on the nature of texts and the disciplinary practices in which reading is situated. (For more about helping students learn to read and write specific genres of text, see Duke & Watanabe, Chapter 13, this volume.)

Several recent reports on reading and adolescent literacy have called for attention to text- and discipline-specific reading and writing instruction (e.g., Alliance for Excellent Education, 2010; Heller & Greenleaf, 2007; RAND Reading Study Group, 2002). These reports emphasize that literacy instruction should continue beyond the elementary years and support students in developing the kinds of literacy skills that foster involve-ment in disciplinary learning and participation (Alliance for Excellent Education, 2010; Heller & Greenleaf, 2007). The reports emphasize that each discipline involves differ-ent kinds of texts, different approaches to reading, and different purposes for reading (Heller & Greenleaf, 2007).

The authors of some key adolescent literacy reports express concern that the emphasis on generic reading skills and strategies might lead students to believe that they can approach every text in the same way, when the texts that students encounter in history are different from those they encounter in chemistry (Carnegie Council on Advancing Adolescent Literacy, 2009; Heller & Greenleaf, 2007). For example, although texts differ across different disciplines in science, students are more likely to encounter reports, procedural texts, and explanations in the sciences than in other content areas (Fang, 2012), and each of these text genres is associated with different features. Lee and Spratley (2010) note that scientific reports often include features such as abstracts, headings, and diagrams, which can support understanding if students are taught to use them. Experts in adolescent literacy note that students can be supported in navigating the complexities of the texts they will encounter in science by being taught to use these features and to do the following:

- Make sense of technical vocabulary and complicated syntax, such as long noun phrases.
- Make sense of visual elements, such as diagrams, drawings, photographs, and maps.
- Use textual structures, such as cause-and-effect and sequential structures, to understand text.
- Search text to find information related to their purpose for reading.
- Read key parts of texts with exactitude—for example, noting even small differ-ences in research results (England, Huber, Nesbit, Rogers, & Webb, 2007; Fang, 2012; Heller & Greenleaf, 2007; Lee & Spratley, 2010).

Although the most obvious difference in reading as students move into differ-ent disciplinary contexts concerns the nature of the texts, reading in the disciplines involves the use of more sophisticated and specialized skills. Shanahan and Shana-han (2008) examined the reading processes of disciplinary experts as they read and thought about texts in their areas. The researchers found that the experts in each dis-cipline approached texts differently and leveraged a different set of reading strategies. For example, whereas historians attended to possible sources of bias, mathematicians engaged in close examination and rereading to ensure that they understood the contribution of each word to the meaning. Shanahan and Shanahan suggested that differences in the reading practices of disciplinary experts are related to the values, norms, and methods of scholarship within each discipline. That is because historical scholarship involves arguments about the interpretation of source documents and historical events, and because such scholarship risks selective analysis and biased interpretation, historians read for authors' perspectives. Readers of history must evaluate the arguments being made by the authors and the authors' interpretations of sources that underlie the arguments. Because chemists use experimentation to develop knowledge in their field, they read the reports of others' experiments with a careful eye to the quality of the instruments, data collection procedures, and analyses that produced the particular results. The recent adolescent literacy reports have also pointed out strategies and stances that scientists take toward texts. For example, Lee and Spratley (2010) point out that in the context of reading scientific reports, students need to be able to pose questions about these aspects:

- The functions of investigations.
- The appropriateness of the data collection and its analysis in relation to the questions and conclusions.
- The tradeoffs of the research design in terms of what we can learn from the research.
- The links between and among data, findings, previous research, and existing theory.
- Potential sources of bias that might have influenced the findings.

Moreover, students of science need to be able to look across texts in order to make sense of conflicting claims and in order to synthesize knowledge (McMahon & McCormack, 1998).

Several research studies have demonstrated the power of teaching students strategies to help them read and write science texts. One effective, research-based approach is that of the Reading Apprenticeship (RA) program (e.g., Greenleaf et al., 2011). The RA model is focused around the *metacognitive conversation*, in which teachers model and discuss how to read science texts, why people read science texts in these ways, and the content of the texts. Although teachers use well-known comprehension routines in RA, such as reciprocal teaching (Palincsar & Brown, 1984) and ReQuest (Manzo, 1969), they also use the metacognitive conversations to model and guide students explicitly in using an array of comprehension tools to understand and reason about science texts. For example, teachers might talk about how they pull apart difficult sentences, where they find information about unknown words, and how they take notes from a content-area text. In metacognitive conversations, teachers provide explicit support for science reading by making visible the processes of reading and comprehending complex texts.

Research on RA has demonstrated many positive outcomes for students. In one recent study, high school students in RA classrooms made greater gains on the state standardized test scores in English language arts, reading comprehension, and biology than students in comparable classrooms (Greenleaf et al., 2011). In addition, students in RA classrooms reported that that they were receiving more support for reading in science.

The Science Writing Heuristic (SWH) is an approach to engaging students in written and oral argumentation in order to support their learning from laboratory experiences in science (Hand & Keys, 1999). The SWH includes a student writing form that student use over the course of their laboratory experiences. The form, which is designed to scaffold students' writing and reasoning about their inquiries, includes the following questions (Hand, 2008, p. 6):

> Questions: What are my questions?
> Test and Collect Data/Observation: What did I do? What did I see?
> Claims: What can I claim?
> Evidence: How do I know? Why am I making these claims?
> Reading: How do my ideas compare with others?
> Reflection: How have my ideas changed?

The SWH also includes a template for teachers to use in designing laboratory activities and facilitating group discussions. The template lays out a series of instructional steps, including pre- and postassessments using concept mapping, prelaboratory activities (such as posing questions and brainstorming), laboratory activities, and several phases of negotiating understandings through writing and discussion.

In two separate studies (Hand, Wallace, & Yang, 2004; Hohenshell & Hand, 2006), SWH researchers found that 7th-, 9th-, and 10th-grade biology students using the SWH made greater gains in their conceptual understanding of cell biology than students in a control group who participated in traditional to laboratory activities across 7–8 weeks of instruction. In addition, 5th-, 7th-, and 10th-grade students using the SWH improved in their ability to make written arguments regarding their biology lab experiences over time.

Integrating literacy and science with a focus on reading and writing strategies has been shown to support literacy development for English language learners (ELLs). Lee, Mahotiere, Salinas, Penfield, and Maerten-Rivera (2009) worked with third-grade teachers to improve their students' science writing, with a particular focus on supporting the ELL students in their classrooms. In the professional development, teachers learned to use science instruction to teach literacy strategies, such as activation of prior knowledge, comprehension of science texts, and language functions in science, with a special focus on science writing. Teachers also learned to support ELL students' learning in science through the use of linguistic scaffolds (e.g., pacing, repetition, and rephrasing), the use of students' home language to provide access to science terms and concepts, and the incorporation of students' cultural experiences into science instruction. The teachers were provided with curriculum units that included language supports for ELLs in science, such as hands-on investigations and use of *realia* (i.e., visual images and artifacts, such as photographs and objects). In each of three years, the intervention had positive impacts on ELL students' writing gains. It is particularly notable that the ELL students made gains comparable to those of non-ELL students. In a related study, Lee, Maerten-Rivera, Penfield, LeRoy, and Secada (2008) reported that third-grade students whose teachers participated in the professional development intervention improved their science achievement scores. Importantly, the growth scores for students identified as ELLs were not different from those of students who had exited ELL status or had never been ELLs.

Tying the Literacy Practices of Science to Science Inquiry

Although there are many ways to define *inquiry* as it relates to science teaching and learning (Anderson, 2007; Minner, Levy, & Century, 2010; National Research Council [NRC], 2011), the defining characteristics of science inquiry for the purposes of this discussion of science and literacy learning are that students (1) actively engage in exploring scientifically oriented questions, (2) gather evidence in the interest of answering those questions, and (3) engage in firsthand or hands-on activities that allow them more concrete experiences with scientific phenomena (or models) and allow them to gather evidence in a firsthand way. Reading and writing are important tools of science inquiry, but they are too often used in place of students' involvement in firsthand investigations. There is a long history of division between textbook-based approaches to science learning and inquiry-based approaches to science learning, but research has increasingly demonstrated that a combined approach not only better supports students' science learning, but also supports students' reading and writing of science texts.

The most obvious reason to tie students' reading and writing to science inquiry is that combining these activities is a more accurate representation of science as a discipline and more supportive of students' learning in science. However, there is also substantial evidence that linking reading about science with doing science is powerful for children's literacy development. There are several possible explanations for these effects.

First, reading in the interest of answering compelling scientific questions—particularly when combined with hand-on experiences—offers the kind of reason for reading that has been shown to promote more active engagement with texts. Firsthand experiences and ongoing investigations can make the difficult task of pulling apart content-area texts more purposeful (Romance & Vitale, 1992). In the context of ongoing investigations, the goal of reading is not just getting from the beginning to the end of a particular text; the goal is understanding something that is connected to students' experiences in the classroom and the world. Science investigations offer opportunities to engage students in reading with the goal of understanding the material well enough to use it for other purposes, such as making an argument or applying a concept in some way. As such, when students are engaged in ongoing investigations, teachers and students tend to focus on deep understanding, rather than on the details of a particular text, and it turns out that a focus on deep understanding supports students' growth in reading comprehension (Knapp, 1995; Purcell-Gates, Duke, & Martineau, 2007; Taylor, Pearson, Peterson, & Rodriguez, 2003; Taylor, Peterson, Pearson, & Rodriguez, 2002). Purcell-Gates and colleagues (2007) examined the impact of authenticity of literacy activities involving the reading and writing of science text genres on second- and third-grade students' growth in reading and writing the genres. Purcell-Gates and colleagues defined *authentic activity* in the study as reading and writing the science text genres for purposes other than learning to read and write them (e.g., reading for information or writing to communicate information to someone who wants it). The researchers found that authenticity was strongly related to growth in students' abilities to read and write the text genres. Guthrie and colleagues (2004) provide one possible explanation for the impact of authenticity (or application) on comprehension: They note that the goal of understanding a conceptual theme provides a purpose for using comprehensions strategies, thus building students' skill with the strategies.

Relatedly, firsthand experiences in science support motivation to read. Reading motivation is an important outcome of reading instruction and a mediator of growth in reading comprehension (e.g., Wigfield et al., 2008). Several studies have demonstrated that hands-on experiences in science support sustained motivation and gains in reading comprehension. For example, Guthrie, Wigfield, and colleagues (2006) found that the number of stimulating (hands-on) activities that teachers used related to reading in science predicted third-grade students' growth in reading comprehension through the mechanism of motivation; that is, the stimulating tasks increased students' motivation to read, and motivation to read supported students' growth in reading comprehension. In a related study, Guthrie, Hoa, Wigfield, Tonks, and Perencevich (2006) studied the results of involving third-grade students in a reading program designed to increase their situated interest in reading (i.e., their enjoyment of reading particular texts in particular situations) by involving the students in observational and hands-on activities in science and then providing an abundance of related, interesting texts for students to choose to read. The researchers found that students who participated in the program not only increased their situated interest, but also increased their general motivation to read over 3 months.

Finally, firsthand experiences can build the knowledge that supports students' comprehension of text—both immediately and in the future. We have known for decades that having knowledge about a topic supports reading comprehension (Alexander, Kulikowich, & Schulze, 1994; McNamara, Kintsch, Songer, & Kintsch, 1996; Tierney & Cunningham, 1984). Readers who have more knowledge can more easily assimilate new information and can better distinguish between important and peripheral information (Stahl, Hare, Sinatra, & Gregory, 1991). As such, building a wide base of knowledge about the natural world is likely to support students' reading development as they move through school and beyond. It also appears that a developing bank of knowledge supports students in learning and use of reading strategies and in overall reading comprehension (Guthrie & Ozgungor, 2002; Taboada, Tonke, Wigfield, & Guthrie, 2009).

Several programs of instructional research have demonstrated the efficacy of approaches that bind reading and writing to inquiry experiences in science. Romance and Vitale (1992, 2001) have designed an integrated science–literacy program at the elementary level that involves students in hands-on science activities, reading comprehension instruction, concept mapping, and writing with the goal of supporting students' deep conceptual understanding in science. The program, In-Depth Expanded Applications of Science (IDEAS), involves teachers in developing concept maps of key science concepts and then planning a range of science and literacy experiences to engage students in different aspects of the concepts.

The reading comprehension program includes three components:

1. Text analysis, in which students are taught to use their prior knowledge for reading and to build new knowledge while reading.
2. Concept mapping, in which teachers guide students to pull apart and map ideas encountered during reading.
3. Writing summaries based on the concept maps.

These three activities not only help students make sense of the science concepts in the texts they read, but also help them to understand how these texts are organized.

In addition, because reading is linked to students' involvement in multiple hands-on inquiry experiences, students learn to bridge text and experiences in ways that are authentic to science. In a series of research studies, this approach has resulted in wide-ranging positive impacts for the students. Notably, students in grades 1–5 in classrooms that used this approach demonstrated greater gains on the Iowa Tests of Basic Skills Reading and Science subtests than students in classrooms that did not use this approach (Romance & Vitale, 1992, 2001; Vitale & Romance, 2010).

Concept-Oriented Reading Instruction (CORI) is an integrated science–literacy program based on a model of reading engagement that includes the following five practices (e.g., Guthrie et al., 2004):

1. Using content goals for reading instruction.
2. Affording choices and control to students.
3. Providing hands-on activities.
4. Using interesting texts for instruction.
5. Organizing collaboration for learning from text.

The program also involves students in assembling portfolios that include records of questions and reading inferences, summaries of text passages, illustrations, charts, and even physical models (Guthrie, McRae, & Klauda, 2007; Swan, 2003). Student use the portfolios to write books related to the themes of the units.

In the Guthrie and colleagues (2004) study, third-grade students in CORI classrooms were taught reading comprehension strategies, such as activating background knowledge, questioning, searching for information and summarizing, as they learned about a conceptual science theme (ecology). The students read texts of various genres related to the theme, and they participated in firsthand experiences, including observations of different habitats and an experiment with aquatic insects. The teachers made explicit connections between the texts and students' firsthand experiences. For example, the students took a habitat walk in their school yard and then compared their walk with a nature walk described in a trade book. Embedding strategy instruction in a knowledge-rich context full of firsthand experiences had a powerful influence on students' acquisition of the strategies. These students showed greater growth on a composite assessment of reading strategy use than did students who received more traditional strategy instruction.

The same framework has been implemented with students at other grade levels, with similar results. In a study of fourth-grade students, CORI was compared with cognitive strategies instruction and traditional instruction. Following 12 weeks of instruction, students in the CORI classrooms outperformed students in the other classrooms on measures of reading engagement, reading comprehension, multiple-text comprehension, and use of reading strategies. Guthrie and colleagues (2009) found positive results for fifth graders involved in CORI on measures of word recognition speed, reading comprehension, and ecology knowledge. Moreover, they found that the CORI instruction was equally effective for lower- and higher-achieving readers.

Seeds of Science/Roots of Reading (Seeds/Roots) is a curriculum-based integrated science–literacy program. Seeds/Roots is premised on the idea that both science and literacy development benefit from integration that focuses on shared and complementary skills, but that leads with science conceptual development and involvement in inquiry.

The curriculum units engage students in reading, writing, discussing, and using first-hand experiences to develop understandings about science concepts, the nature of science, and the process of inquiry. One of the main principles underlying the Seeds/Roots model is that texts can and should be used in various roles to support students' inquiries. To this end, students read texts that model the inquiry processes that they will use in their own investigations; they search handbooks for information that they can leverage as they investigate; and they read books that situate their classroom-based inquiries in the wider natural world. Students are instructed in issues related to science text genres and science reading and writing strategies as they use literacy to support their involvement in ongoing investigations.

In a study of second- and third-grade students learning about the shoreline ecosystem and the forest floor ecosystem, students who used the integrated Seeds/Roots units made greater gains in science understanding, science vocabulary, and science reading comprehension (in one of the two units) than did students who participated in an inquiry-based science unit involving firsthand experiences, but little reading and writing (Wang & Herman, 2005). In a study of third- and fourth-grade students studying light energy and light interactions, students using the Seeds/Roots integrated unit outperformed students in classes using their regular science materials (also on the topic of light) and literacy materials on measures of science writing, science understanding, and science vocabulary (Cervetti, Barber, Dorph, Pearson, & Goldschmidt, 2012).

SUMMARY OF BIG IDEAS FROM RESEARCH

The research on literacy–science integration is summarized in Table 14.1. This research supports the following big ideas:

- Effective teachers provide instruction that supports students' use of science literacy practices.
- Effective teachers help students develop the range of distinctive reading processes and stances toward text in science that characterize reading in the disciplines of science.
- Effective teachers tie the literacy practices of science to science inquiry.

EXAMPLES OF EFFECTIVE PRACTICES

Helping Secondary Students Acquire Strategies to Understand and Write Science Texts

High school science teacher Will Brown is working to apprentice his ethnically and linguistically diverse urban students into the literacy practices of science (Greenleaf, Brown, & Litman, 2004; Litman & Greenleaf, 2008). Will has been part of the RA project for several years and has learned to use metacognitive conversations to help his students make sense of science texts. In addition to engaging students in many firsthand investigations in chemistry, Will routinely gathers his chemistry students together to discuss their thinking, problem solving, and challenges as they make sense of their reading. In these conversations and in his in-the-moment interactions with students, Will thinks

TABLE 14.1. Positive Outcomes in Experimental and Quasi-Experimental Research Studies of Science and Literacy Integration

Citation	Grade(s)	Reading and vocabulary	Writing	Science knowledge	Motivation/ engagement
Cervetti, Barber, Dorph, Pearson, & Goldschmidt (2012)	4	Vocabulary	Writing (use of evidence, introduction, clarity, science content, and use of science vocabulary)	Science understanding	
Fang & Wei (2010)	6–8	Reading vocabulary and comprehension		Science knowledge Science grade	
Greenleaf et al. (2011)	8–10	English language arts Reading comprehension		Biology knowledge	
Guthrie, Anderson, Alao, & Rinehart (1999)	3, 5	Strategy use in a text search activity (grade 3) Comprehension of narrative texts Conceptual learning from text			
Guthrie et al. (2004)	3	Passage-reading comprehension Reading strategy use (a composite of activating background knowledge, searching for information to answer questions, and organizing information) Multiple-text reading comprehension Reading comprehension			Intrinsic motivation to read Extrinsic motivation to read Reading motivation

(continued)

TABLE 14.1. *(continued)*

Citation	Grade(s)	Reading and vocabulary	Writing	Science knowledge	Motivation/ engagement
Guthrie et al. (2009)	5	Reading comprehension Word recognition speed		Knowledge of ecology	
Guzzetti & Bang (2011)	11–12			Chemistry knowledge and scientific skills	Attitudes toward science
Hand, Wallace, & Yang (2004)	7			Science conceptual understanding	
Hohenshell & Hand (2006)	9–10			Science conceptual understanding	
Lee, Mahotiere, Salinas, Penfield, & Maerten-Rivera (2009)	3		Ability to explain science concepts in writing English proficiency in writing		
Lee, Maerten-Rivera, Penfield, LeRoy, & Secada (2008)	3			Science concepts and science inquiry	
Romance & Vitale (1992)	4	Reading		Science achievement	Attitudes toward learning science and reading Self-confidence in science
Romance & Vitale (2001)	2–5	Reading		Science achievement	Attitudes toward learning science and reading Self-confidence in science and reading

(continued)

TABLE 14.1. *(continued)*

Citation	Grade(s)	Reading and vocabulary	Writing	Science knowledge	Motivation/engagement
Vitale & Romance (2010)	1–2	Reading		Science achievement	
Wang & Herman (2005)	2–3	Science reading comprehension Science vocabulary		Science understanding	
Wigfield et al. (2008)	4	Reading strategy use (a composite of activating background knowledge and posing questions) Multiple-text reading comprehension Reading comprehension Reading engagement			

aloud about his own comprehension processes, making visible often-hidden problem-solving processes. Will invites students to see what it means to comprehend the texts, and helps them to acquire the strategies that proficient readers use to deal with the comprehension challenges encountered in complex science texts.

During one class period, the students watch Will think through a difficult passage and discuss the comprehension strategies that help him overcome the difficulty. Students listen as Will describes how first figuring out the meaning of boldfaced words in the science textbook can help them make sense of a difficult sentence or paragraph. He explains his strategy:

> "It can still be hard even when they give you the definitions of the key words. The words around the key words can be words you don't know. . . . Start with the word in bold or italics and the sentence it is in. Try to understand that one sentence, work very hard on it, and then look around it in the paragraph. Put most of your energy into understanding the boldfaced words."

Because words are often stumbling blocks for students in understanding school texts, including the science textbook, Will often focuses his metacognitive conversations on building students' knowledge about and interest in words. Will occasionally starts a class period by asking students to talk about "interesting" words they have learned recently. Sometimes this leads to a group problem-solving session, as it does one morning when Veronica shares the word *substantially*—explaining that she encountered it while reading the science textbook on the previous day, but does not know what it means. Veronica's classmates first try the strategy of looking for a familiar word in the unfamiliar word, but this leads them to *substance*, which does not seem to help. Will guides the students in using other strategies for figuring out the word, such as using the context to substitute a synonym. Veronica suggests *partially* as a synonym, and Will rereads the passage aloud, substituting the *partially* for *substantially*, to see whether it makes sense in context: "A fundamental property of acids and bases is that an acid and a base always react to 'neutralize' one another. That is, the products of the reaction do not have acidic or basic properties (or they are *partially* reduced compared to the reactant acid and base)." Will asks students whether they think *partially* and *substantially* mean similar things, but the class is divided. Will calls the students' attention to the phrase *that is*, and asks, "What does *that is* mean to you? What is it telling you?" Will asks Darren to reread the sentence, but stops Darren after the phrase *do not have*. Will asks, "How much is *do not have*? How does *partially reduced* compare to *do not have*?" Will points out the parentheses following *do not have acidic or basic properties*, and helps students see that *substantially reduced* must have a similar meaning to *do not have*. Karen suggests that *completely reduced* would fit.

Will's students gradually come to see that replicable strategies and determination are the keys of science comprehension. And they become more comfortable in sharing their own reading processes. Students discuss what's easy for them in texts and what's confusing, and they share their own strategies for overcoming comprehension challenges. Metacognitive conversations make individual reading and thinking processes part of the community of Will's classroom.

Will has worked hard to establish the kind of environment in which these kinds of conversations can take place. He has talked to his students since the beginning of the year about the purpose of the conversations, and he has guided students to explore their current ideas and feelings about reading in science. Throughout, Will has communicated excitement about figuring things out through firsthand inquiry and reading. Will has found that metacognitive conversations invite greater engagement in his classes and help students take on more productive roles as readers and learners.

Helping Elementary Students Acquire Strategies to Understand and Write Science Texts in Service of Inquiry

Lorna Ratliff is planning a science unit for her class around the second-grade standards related to changes in matter. Lorna has participated in the Science IDEAS professional development workshop over the last few years, and is using the IDEAS model to develop the unit.

Lorna begins by selecting a core concept to serve as an entry point into the unit. Lorna selects the concept of evaporation because she knows that many of her students will have had everyday experiences with this concept, such as watching when water is heated in a pot on the stove and disappears into the air as it turns into an invisible gas (water vapor), or noticing how water in a cup slowly disappears if it is left open for a day or two.

Following the IDEAS model, Lorna selects the concept of evaporation from the "Changes in Matter" concept map that the professional development facilitators provided in the IDEAS workshop (see Figure 14.1). Lorna learned in the IDEAS workshop that it is important to begin planning with a concept map of the key ideas, so that unit development is coherent, is guided by the structure of the concepts in the discipline (Romance & Vitale, 2010), and aligns with the NRC's new K–12 science framework (NRC, 2011).

Lorna uses sticky notes to add to or replace some ideas from the concept map, based on her objectives and her students' existing knowledge of changes in matter. Lorna knows that she will rebuild this concept map with her students as they move through the unit, and she will have students use the map as the basis for written explanations of evaporation.

Once she has a concept map that represents the core ideas in the unit, Lorna begins to plan instructional experiences. She decides that she will begin with a demonstration to invite students to puzzle about evaporation. At the beginning of the school day, she will introduce the unit and ask students to discuss what they already know

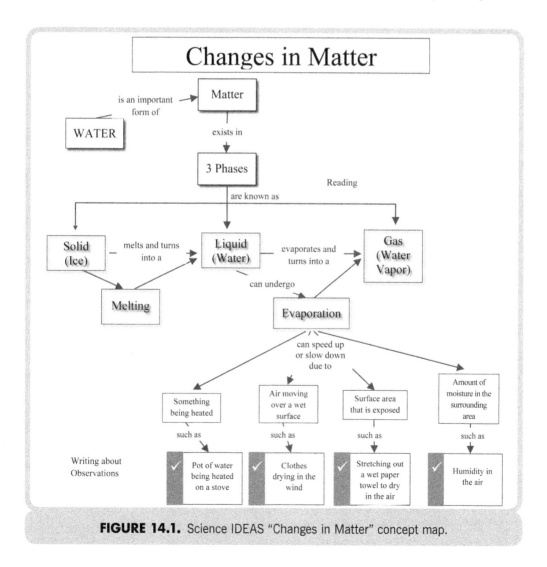

FIGURE 14.1. Science IDEAS "Changes in Matter" concept map.

about phases of matter. She knows that they are familiar with solids, liquids, and gases, but she doesn't think they understand a lot about how matter changes between these phases. Following the discussion, Lorna will dampen a thin rag and place it outside. She will ask students to make predictions about what will happen. Later in the day, they will revisit the rag and set up two additional firsthand experiences with evaporation.

As Lorna proceeds in planning the unit, she refers often to her concept map, annotating it with references to activities that address each concept cluster on the map. She includes reading experiences, which she can also use to reinforce students' understandings of informational text features. She also includes writing experiences to help students record their observations and make sense of the key ideas in the unit.

Lorna's objective is to ensure that the students understand that water changes phases because of specific factors, such as heat and surface area. She carefully lays out a series of science and literacy experiences that together form a journey to help students grasp these important concepts. She also makes preliminary plans to use students' experiences with reading and writing in the unit to help them acquire strategies for comprehending and writing science texts. She also knows that she can use the concept map as a blueprint to guide expository writing.

Tying the Literacy Practices of Science to Science Inquiry

Over the last 2 weeks, the students in Michael Medina's third-grade class have been engaged in an ongoing inquiry about soil as a habitat for plants and animals. They started the inquiry by building and observing two tabletop terrariums (see Figure 14.2). They built the terrariums in clear plastic containers by adding soil and other earth materials. Then they planted alfalfa seeds and observed the first sprouts. Michael told the students that the terrariums are models of a forest floor habitat. The students have been learning about habitats and know that they are preparing to add earthworms to the terrariums.

The students are excited on the day that Michael brings the earthworms. They observe the earthworms' body parts and how the earthworms move. They write their observations and make drawings of the worms. Michael asks them to write predictions about what will happen when they add the earthworms to the terrariums. What will the earthworms do? Some students think that the earthworms will eat the leaves in the terrariums and grow bigger. Others think that the earthworms will go underground. Finally, the students add earthworms to the terrariums.

The next day, the students observe the terrariums again, but the earthworms have disappeared. They look for evidence about where the earthworms might be. One student notices holes in the soil and suggests that the earthworms are under the soil. The other students agree that this must be the case. Michael asks how the earthworms can survive underground. He wonders aloud what the earthworms do down there. What do they eat? How do they move? The students join in with questions and wonderings about the activities of the earthworms underground.

Michael tells the students that he has a book about different forest floor animals that might help them answer their questions about the earthworms. The students join their reading partners and begin to read. Michael knows that the students can read this book with their partners, because they possess a powerful combination of curiosity and

FIGURE 14.2. A student's observation of her group's desktop terrarium.

relevant knowledge from their work in the habitat unit so far. They have encountered almost all of the challenging vocabulary in the book already, and they know how to use the glossary to look up words they don't recognize. In addition, Michael has been teaching students strategies for reading informational texts since they entered his classroom. Students use the reading to answer their observation-driven questions about the behavior of earthworms. Later they will pose questions about different aspects of life on and under the soil, answering the questions through firsthand investigations and reading (see Figure 14.3).

Planning for Integration of Literacy and Science

All of the teachers just described foreground science learning in their integration of literacy and science; they use both literacy activities and inquiry as the tools of conceptual development. Pratt and Pratt (2004) suggest that "the commonality between the science and reading comprehension goals should be obvious; both place the understanding of subject matter content as the ultimate outcome" (p. 396). The good news is that literacy benefits from this authentic supporting role, particularly when teachers provide explicit guidance about strategies and purposes of science reading and writing.

Directions. Write the question that you will write about in the space labeled "My Question." Then write about your question. Illustrate about your writing in the space provided.

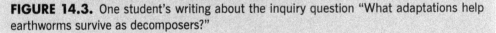

Eathworms dig underground.

My Question: What adaptatoins help eathworms survive as dea decomposers?

Eathworms have adaptation to help them survive as decomposers. Eathworms dig underground. They have a mouth to eat dead things also it puts nutrients in the soil. Intestines that help them poop out nnutrients.

Seeds of Science/Roots of Reading *Terrarium Investigations* © 2004 by The Regents of the University of California

FIGURE 14.3. One student's writing about the inquiry question "What adaptations help earthworms survive as decomposers?"

Perhaps the easiest way to begin enacting science–literacy integration is to use existing curriculum materials. Increasingly, there are curriculum materials available through publishers and online that support the integration of literacy and science instruction. However, it is also possible to design these experiences in your classroom. You might begin with a science unit that uses mainly firsthand experiences and look for authentic opportunities to infuse reading and writing. You might gather a set of thematically related science trade texts, or even a science textbook, and imagine where firsthand experiences could be used to support students' understandings of the science concepts. Or you might engage in the ambitious work of developing a fully fleshed out, integrated unit of instruction.

- Map out the science goals and the literacy goals that you are setting for students. The science goals should include attention to science concepts, science inquiry skills, and understandings about the nature of science. The literacy skills might include using the structural features of informational text genres (e.g., headings, glossaries); making sense of the visual features that often appear in these texts; reading for information across different texts; recording observations and taking notes; or using comprehension strategies that support students' comprehension of science text, such as goal setting, summarizing, and questioning.

● Gather sets of books that relate to your science goals. These may include everything from books about the science concepts you want to address to books about the lives of scientists to news articles that connect the science to everyday life. Try to select texts that provide the kinds of information and experiences that would be difficult to recreate in the classroom, such as experiences in distant places (under the ocean, in space) and experiences with things that are difficult to observe (molecules, internal body systems).

● Develop firsthand experiences that invite students to explore the concepts you are studying and to develop their inquiry skills.

Guzzetti (2009) describes an example of this approach: a chemistry teacher's implementation of a forensics unit she implemented with her high school class. While the teacher, Sharon, wanted to capitalize on the students' interests in forensics and to support their development of important science concepts (such as the difference between physical and chemical evidence), her main goals related to students' development of inquiry skills, such as the ability to evaluate evidence and to draw conclusions from this evidence. Sharon also wanted them to develop science literacy skills, including the ability to read a range of science texts for evidence and to communicate scientifically. Across the 3-week unit, the students read from a wide range of texts that Sharon had gathered. The students read about crime scene evidence in teacher-constructed cases. They also read forensics procedures and reference documents, news articles, (fictional) police reports, and sections from forensics textbooks. These readings supported the students' ability to solve the crime scene cases. In addition, the students used a variety of forensic processes, such as fingerprinting, blood spatter analysis, chromatography, and chemical analysis, to explore physical and chemical evidence "found" at the fictional crime scenes.

LOOKING FORWARD

Although the programs of research discussed in this chapter provide strong evidence for the efficacy of instructional approaches that integrate literacy and science, the following efforts will be needed in order to make instruction in disciplinary literacies a reality in U.S. classrooms:

● Broader development of materials and approaches that provide opportunity for students' authentic engagement in reading and writing (Purcell-Gates, Duke, & Martineau, 2007), particularly as part of inquiry-oriented content-area instruction (RAND Reading Study Group, 2002).

● Improvements in the quality and accessibility of content-rich texts across the K–12 spectrum (Pearson, Moje, & Greenleaf, 2010). Although science texts for young readers are changing, typical science textbooks are dense and disengaging (Lee & Spratley, 2010; Schleppegrell, 2004), and teachers still struggle to find good text for inexperienced science readers (Eisner, 1987; Lee & Spratley, 2010; NRC, 1990; Schleppegrell, 2004). In addition, most science texts present facts, but fail to help students understand the nature and processes of scientific inquiry (Cervetti & Barber, 2008).

- Changes in the structure of the elementary school day to allow more time for rich engagement with content-area learning. Undoubtedly, the biggest obstacle to the adoption of integrated approaches to science and literacy is the general status of science teaching at the elementary level. Surveys of elementary teachers over the last decade have indicated that the pressures of standards and testing have driven many teachers to forgo science instruction entirely, and that those who do teach science tend to devote only 1–2 hours per week to its instruction (Dorph et al., 2007; Fulp, 2002; McMurrer, 2008).

- The development of assessments to help us track students' progress in applying literacy skills in the interest of inquiring and learning in the content areas. As long as multiple-choice tests constitute the primary metric for measuring student learning in science and literacy, it will be difficult to advocate for the approaches described in this chapter.

- Professional development opportunities and changes in initial teacher preparation to soften the boundaries between literacy instruction and content-area instruction (Pearson et al., 2010).

- Research to help us better understand and capitalize upon complementarities between science and literacy at different points in students' development, including better understanding of how literacy skills are similar and different across the disciplines of science, and the relationship of these myriad skills to our goals for students' science and literacy development across the K–12 spectrum.

- Research to help us better understand the nature of the relationships among inquiry, knowledge development, reading motivation, and reading comprehension skill.

QUESTIONS FOR REFLECTION •

1. To what extent do I support students in understanding that science texts call for different approaches to reading than literary texts do? How do I ensure that students have strategies to make sense of challenging, content-rich informational texts?

2. To what extent do I make explicit for students the differences among the texts that we read across different content areas?

3. To what extent do I help students make sense of the visual elements of science texts, such as diagrams, tables, and graphs?

4. To what extent do I help my students develop the understanding that science involves reading, writing, talking, and doing—all in the interest of reaching a better understanding of the natural world?

5. To what extent do I invite students to read a wide range of books in and about science—from news articles to books that describe science concepts to books and articles about the lived experiences of practicing scientists?

6. To what extent do I use firsthand experiences in science to deepen students' understandings of the science concepts we are studying *and* to provide an insider's view of the practices that scientists use to inquire about the natural world and develop scientific knowledge?

7. To what extent do I invite students to use the results of their investigations to challenge or extend the understandings gained from reading?

8. To what extent do my students use writing throughout their science investigations—to plan their investigations, to record observations of natural phenomena, to record information gained through reading and firsthand inquiry, to reflect on and summarize their learning, and to communicate their learning to others?

9. To what extent do I use select and use texts that deepen students' involvement in firsthand investigations, rather than replacing them?

SUGGESTIONS FOR ONGOING PROFESSIONAL LEARNING • • • • • • •

- Ask your students about interests they have related to science. Do they watch science fiction films, read crime novels, and/or watch crime shows on television? Do they have questions about how something works the natural world? Work with your professional learning community (PLC) to review your science program and your grade-level science standards, to identify places where you can form connections between students' out-of-school interests and in-school science learning.
- Work with your PLC to ensure that students are reading a range of texts throughout the school day, starting in kindergarten. Work with your PLC to create lists (or sets) of thematically related science books for students at different grade levels. Develop approaches to text discussions and comprehension activities that foreground understanding of science concepts when students read about science.
- In your PLC, practice having metacognitive conversations over challenging texts. Keep a record of your efforts to make the literacy practices of science visible to students. Consider audio- or video-recording a metacognitive conversation with your students and sharing it with your PLC. Discuss challenges and successes in your PLC.
- Work with your PLC colleagues to review your science program for opportunities for integration—whether the program is mainly textbook-based or mainly a series of hands-on experiences. Look through your English language arts standards for learning goals that might be supported through your work in the textbook- or inquiry-based program. For example, the fourth-grade English Language Arts Standards from the Common Core State Standards include the following goals that can be well supported through integration with science:
  - RI.4.9. Integrate information from two texts on the same topic in order to write or speak about the subject knowledgeably.
  - RI.4.5. Describe the overall structure (e.g., chronology, comparison, cause/effect, problem/solution) of events, ideas, concepts, or information in a text or part of a text.

- ◆ W.4.2. Write informative/explanatory texts to examine a topic and convey ideas and information clearly.
- ◆ W.4.7. Conduct short research projects that build knowledge through investigation of different aspects of a topic.
- ◆ W.4.8. Recall relevant information from experiences or gather relevant information from print and digital sources; take notes and categorize information, and provide a list of sources.
- ◆ W.4.9. Draw evidence from literary or informational texts to support analysis, reflection, and research.
- Review your grade-level standards in science and in literacy to identify complementary learning goals.
- Work with members of your PLC to develop integrated units. If you have an inquiry-based science program, consider using it as the basis of integration. Identify texts, writing experiences, and literacy goals that could fit well within the existing science program.
- Discuss this chapter with members of your PLC, using the *Questions for Reflection* (see above) as a starting point for developing ways to integrate science and literacy.

RESEARCH-BASED RESOURCES

Freeman, G., & Taylor, V. (2006). *Integrating science and literacy instruction: A framework for bridging the gap.* Lanham, MD: Rowman & Littlefield.

Grant, M. C., & Fisher, D. B. (Eds.). (2009). *Reading and writing science: Tools to develop disciplinary literacy.* Thousand Oaks, CA: Corwin Press.

McKee, J. A., & Ogle, D. (2005). *Integrating instruction: Literacy and science.* New York: Guilford Press.

Wellington, J., & Osborne, J. (2001). *Language and literacy in science education.* Buckingham, UK: Open University Press.

Worth, K., Winokur, J., Crissman, S., Heller-Winokur, M., & Davis, M. (2009). *The essentials of science and literacy: A guide for teachers.* Portsmouth, NH: Heinemann.

ACKNOWLEDGMENTS

I would like to thank Jacquey Barber, Cyndy Greenleaf, and Nancy Romance for their invaluable help in developing and illustrating the classroom vignettes.

REFERENCES

Alexander, P. A., Kulikowich, J. M., & Schulze, S. K. (1994). How subject-matter knowledge affects recall and interest. *American Educational Research Journal, 31*(2), 313–337.

Alliance for Excellent Education. (2010). *Policy brief: The federal role in confronting the crisis in adolescent literacy.* Washington, DC: Author. Retrieved February 14, 2011, from *www. all4ed.org/files/FedRoleConfrontingAdolLit.pdf.*

Anderson, R. (2007). Inquiry as an organizing theme for science curricula. In S. Abell & N. Lederman (Eds.), *Handbook of research on science education* (pp. 807–830). Mahwah, NJ: Erlbaum.

Carnegie Council on Advancing Adolescent Literacy. (2010). *Time to act: An agenda for advancing adolescent literacy for college and career success.* New York: Carnegie Corporation of New York.

Cervetti, G. N., & Barber, J. (2008). Text in hands-on science. In E. H. Hiebert & M. Sailors (Eds.), *Finding the right texts: What works for beginning and struggling readers* (pp. 89–108). New York: Guilford Press.

Cervetti, G. N., Barber, J., Dorph, R., Pearson, P. D., & Goldschmidt, P. (2012). The impact of an integrated approach to science and literacy in elementary school classrooms. *Journal of Research in Science Teaching, 49*(5), 631–658.

Dorph, R., Goldstein, D., Lee, S., Lepori, K., Schneider, S., & Venkatesan, S. (2007). *The status of science education in the Bay Area.* Berkeley: Lawrence Hall of Science, University of California.

Eisner, E. W. (1987). Why the textbook influences curriculum. *Curriculum Review, 26*(3), 11–13.

England, V., Huber, R., Nesbit, C., Rogers, C., & Webb, P. (2007). *Scientific literacy: A new synthesis.* Port Elizabeth, South Africa: Bay Books.

Fang, Z. (2012). The challenges of reading disciplinary texts. In T. L. Jetton & C. Shanahan (Eds.), *Adolescent literacy in the academic disciplines: General principles and practical strategies* (pp. 34–68). New York: Guilford Press.

Fang, Z., & Wei, Y. (2010). Improving middle school students' science literacy through reading infusion. *Journal of Educational Research, 103*(4), 262–273.

Fulp, S. L. (2002). *2000 National Survey of Science and Mathematics Education: Status of elementary school science teaching.* Chapel Hill, NC: Horizon Research.

Greenleaf, C., Brown, W., & Litman, C. (2004). Apprenticing urban youth to science literacy. In D. S. Strickland & D. E. Alvermann (Eds.), *Bridging the literacy achievement gap grades 4–12* (pp. 200–226). New York: Teachers College Press.

Greenleaf, C. L., Litman, C., Handon, T. L., Rosen, R., Boscardin, C. K., Herman, J., et al. (2011). Integrating literacy and science in biology: Teaching and learning impacts of Reading Apprenticeship professional development. *American Educational Research Journal, 48*(3), 647–717.

Guthrie, J. T., Anderson, E., Alao, S., & Rinehart, J. (1999). Influences of concept-oriented reading instruction on strategy use and conceptual learning from text. *Elementary School Journal, 99*(4), 343–366.

Guthrie, J. T., Hoa, L. W., Wigfield, A., Tonks, S. M., & Perencevich, K. (2006). From spark to fire: Can situational reading interest lead to long-term reading motivation? *Reading Research and Instruction, 45*(2), 91–117.

Guthrie, J. T., McRae, A., Coddington, C. S., Klauda, S. L., Wigfield, A., & Barbosa, P. (2009). Impacts of comprehensive reading instruction on diverse outcomes of low- and high-achieving readers. *Journal of Learning Disabilities, 42*(3), 195–214.

Guthrie, J. T., McRae, A., & Klauda, S. L. (2007). Contributions of Concept-Oriented Reading Instruction to knowledge about interventions for motivations in reading. *Educational Psychologist, 42*(4), 237–250.

Guthrie, J. T., & Ozgungor, S. (2002). Instructional contexts for reading engagement. In C. C. Block & M. Pressley (Eds.), *Comprehension instruction: Research-based best practices* (pp. 275–288). New York: Guilford Press.

Guthrie, J. T., Wigfield, A., Barbosa, P., Perencevich, K. C., Taboada, A., David, M. H., et al. (2004). Increasing reading comprehension and engagement through Concept-Oriented Reading Instruction. *Journal of Educational Psychology, 96*(3), 403–423.

Guthrie, J. T., Wigfield, A., Humenick, N. M., Perencevich, K. C., Taboada, A., & Barbosa, P. (2006). Influences of stimulating tasks on reading motivation and comprehension. *Journal of Educational Research, 99*(4), 232–245.

Guzzetti, B. (2009). Thinking like a forensic scientist: Learning with academic and everyday texts. *Journal of Adolescent and Adult Literacy, 53*(3), 192–203.

Guzzetti, B., & Bang, E. (2011). The influence of literacy-based science instruction on adolescents' interest, participation, and achievement in science. *Literacy Research and Instruction, 50*, 46–67.

Hand, B. (2008). Introducing the science writing heuristic approach. In B. Hand (Ed.), *Science inquiry, argument and language: A case for the science writing heuristic* (pp. 1–12). Rotterdam, The Netherlands: Sense.

Hand, B., & Keys, C. (1999). Inquiry investigation: A new approach to laboratory reports. *The Science Teacher, 66*(4), 27–29.

Hand, B., Wallace, C., & Yang, E.-M. (2004). Using a science writing heuristic to enhance learning outcomes from laboratory activities in seventh-grade science: Quantitative and qualitative aspects. *International Journal of Science Education, 26*(2), 131–149.

Heller, R., & Greenleaf, C. L. (2007). *Literacy instruction in the content areas: Getting to the core of middle and high school improvement.* Washington, DC: Alliance for Excellent Education.

Hohenshell, L. M., & Hand, B. (2006). Writing-to-learn strategies in secondary school cell biology. *International Journal of Science Education, 28*(2–3), 261–189.

Knapp, M. S. (1995). *Teaching for meaning in high-poverty classrooms.* New York: Teachers College Press.

Lee, C. D., & Spratley, A. (2010). *Reading in the disciplines: The challenges of adolescent literacy.* New York: Carnegie Corporation.

Lee, O., Maerten-Rivera, J., Penfield, R. D., LeRoy, K., & Secada, W. G. (2008). Science achievement of English language learners in urban elementary schools: Results of a first-year professional development intervention. *Journal of Research in Science Teaching, 45*(1), 31–52.

Lee, O., Mahotiere, M., Salinas, A., Penfield, R. D., & Maerten-Rivera, J. (2009). Science writing achievement among English language learners: Results of three-year intervention in urban elementary schools. *Bilingual Research Journal, 32*(2), 153–167.

Litman, C., & Greenleaf, C. (2008). Traveling together over difficult ground: Negotiating success with a profoundly inexperienced reader in an introduction to chemistry class. In K. S. Hinchman & H. K. Sheridan-Thomas (Eds.), *Best practices in adolescent literacy instruction* (pp. 275–296). New York: Guilford Press.

Manzo, A. V. (1969). The ReQuest procedure. *Journal of Reading, 13*(2), 123–126.

McMahon, M. M., & McCormack, B. B. (1998). To think and act like a scientist: Learning disciplinary knowledge. In C. Hynd (Ed.), *Learning from text across conceptual domains* (pp. 227–22). Mahwah, NJ: Erlbaum.

McMurrer, J. (2008). *Instructional time in elementary schools: A closer look at changes for specific subjects.* Washington, DC: Center for Education Policy. Retrieved from *www.cep-dc.org/index.cfm?fuseaction=document.showDocumentByID&nodeID=1&DocumentID=234.*

McNamara, D. S., Kintsch, E., Songer, N., & Kintsch, W. (1996). Are good texts always better?: Interactions of text coherence, background knowledge, and levels of understanding in learning from text. *Cognition and Instruction, 14*(1), 1–43.

Minner, D. D., Levy, A. J., & Century, J. (2010). Inquiry-based science instruction—What is it and does it matter?: Results from a research synthesis years 1984 to 2002. *Journal of Research in Science Teaching, 47*(4), 474–496.

National Governors Association Center for Best Practices & Council of Chief State School Officers. (2010). *Common Core State Standards for English language arts and literacy in history/social studies, science, and technical subjects.* Washington, DC: Authors. Retrieved from *www.corestandards.org/the-standards.*

National Research Council (NRC). (2011). *A framework for K–12 science education: Practices, crosscutting concepts, and core ideas.* Washington, DC: National Academies Press.

Palincsar, A. S., & Brown, A. L. (1984). Reciprocal teaching of comprehension-fostering and monitoring activities. *Cognition and Instruction, 1*(2), 117–175.

Pearson, P. D., Moje, E. B., & Greenleaf, C. (2010). Literacy and science: Each in the service of the other. *Science, 328,* 459–463.

Pratt, H., & Pratt, N. (2004). Integrating science and literacy instruction with a common goal of learning science content. In W. E. Saul (Ed.), *Crossing borders in literacy and science instruction* (pp. 395–405). Arlington, VA: National Science Teachers Association Press.

Purcell-Gates, V., Duke, N. K., & Martineau, J. A. (2007). Learning to read and write genre-specific text: Roles of authentic experience and explicit teaching. *Reading Research Quarterly, 42*(1), 8–45.

RAND Reading Study Group. (2002). *Reading for understanding.* Santa Monica, CA: RAND Corporation.

Romance, N. R., & Vitale, M. R. (1992). A curriculum strategy that expands time for in-depth elementary science instruction by using science-based reading strategies: Effects of a year-long study in grade four. *Journal of Research in Science Teaching, 29*(6), 545–554.

Romance, N. R., & Vitale, M. R. (2001). Implementing an in-depth expanded science model in elementary schools: Multi-year findings, research issues, and policy implications. *International Journal of Science Education, 23*(4), 272–304.

Schleppegrell, M. J. (2004). *The language of schooling: A functional linguistics perspective.* Mahwah, NJ: Erlbaum.

Shanahan, T., & Shanahan, C. (2008). Teaching disciplinary literacy to adolescents: Rethinking content-area literacy. *Harvard Educational Review, 78*(1), 40–59.

Stahl, S. A., Hare, V. C., Sinatra, R., & Gregory, J. F. (1991). Defining the role of prior knowledge and vocabulary in reading comprehension: The retiring of number 41. *Journal of Reading Behavior, 23*(4), 487–508.

Swan, E. A. (2003). *Concept-Oriented Reading Instruction: Engaging classrooms, lifelong learners.* New York: Guilford Press.

Taboada, A., Tonke, S. M., Wigfield, A., & Guthrie, J. T. (2009). The effects of motivational and cognitive variables on reading comprehension. *Reading and Writing: An Interdisciplinary Journal, 22,* 85–106.

Taylor, B. M., Pearson, P. D., Peterson, D. S., & Rodriguez, M. C. (2003). Reading growth in high-poverty classrooms: The influence of teacher practices that encourage cognitive engagement in literacy learning. *Elementary School Journal, 104*(1), 3–28.

Taylor, B. M., Peterson, D. S., Pearson, P. D., & Rodriguez, M. C. (2002). Looking inside classrooms: Reflecting on the "how" as well as the "what" in effective reading instruction. *The Reading Teacher, 56*(3), 270–279.

Tierney, R. J., & Cunningham, J. W. (1984). Research on teaching reading comprehension. In P. D. Pearson, R. Barr, M. L. Kamil, & P. Mosenthal (Eds.), *Handbook of reading research* (pp. 609–655). New York: Longman.

Vitale, M. R., & Romance, N. R. (2010). *Effects of an integrated instructional model for accelerating student achievement in science and reading comprehension in grades 1–2.* Paper presented at the annual meeting of the American Educational Research Association, Denver, CO.

Wang, J., & Herman, J. (2005). *Evaluation of Seeds of Science/Roots of Reading project: Shoreline science and terrarium investigations.* Los Angeles: National Center for Research on Evaluation, Standards, & Student Testing.

Wigfield, A., Guthrie, J. T., Perencevich, K. C., Taboada, A., Klauda, S. L., McRae, A., et al. (2008). Role of reading engagement in mediating effects of reading comprehension instruction on reading outcomes. *Psychology in the Schools, 45,* 432–445.

CHAPTER 15

Integration of Literacy and Social Studies • • • • • • • • • • • • •

ANNE-LISE HALVORSEN
JANET ALLEMAN
KRISTY BRUGAR

The integration of literacy and social studies has the potential to lead to powerful and effective instruction. The two subjects are a natural pairing: Reading, writing, listening, and speaking skills need to be taught and used in content-area learning, and social studies teaching relies on students' abilities to read, write, listen, and speak effectively (Brophy, Alleman, & Knighton, 2010; Duke & Bennett-Armistead, 2003; Parker, 2011). However, effectively integrating these subjects requires thoughtful planning and consideration of the major goals and skills for each subject area being integrated. This chapter describes the research base in the integration of literacy and social studies, principles of effective integration, challenges to effective integration, student achievement and integration, and the relationship of engagement and motivation with integration. It also addresses ways to meet the needs of diverse learners through integration, provides examples from practice of effective literacy–social studies integration at various grade levels, and offers examples of professional development activities in this area.

OVERVIEW OF RESEARCH

Relationship between Social Studies and Literacy

Integration is an inherent part of social studies education. Social studies is a broad subject area that comprises the disciplines of history, geography, anthropology, sociology, economics, political science, and other social sciences. Good social studies teaching often blurs the boundaries among the disciplines when focusing on topics encountered in the world beyond school, such as human–environment interactions, political elections, and social movements. Social studies also integrates content and skills from other areas, such as the arts, mathematics, and sciences, as well as from current events and technology (National Council for the Social Studies [NCSS], 2008, 2010). However, literacy is particularly well suited for integration, due to the way the two subjects complement each other in content and skill acquisition. Reading is necessary for and adaptable to texts from a range of disciplines, such as history, mathematics, and science; however, experts in these disciplinary fields read differently (Shanahan & Shanahan, 2008).

In social studies, students engage in reading, writing, listening, and speaking skills to perform such tasks as interpreting historical and political documents; constructing timelines; creating and interpreting maps; and engaging in discussions of public issues (e.g., Barton & Levstik, 2004; Brophy & VanSledright, 1997; Hess, 2009; Levstik & Barton, 2005; Monte-Sano, 2008; Parker, 2011). The teaching of social studies can also involve reading instruction, such as comprehension strategy and text structure instruction (Klingner, Vaughn, & Schumm, 1998; VanSledright, 2002; Williams et al., 2007). In fact, because social studies and other content areas share many of the same skills and processes, the authors of the Common Core State Standards framed the English Language Arts Standards as the *Common Core State Standards for English Language Arts and Literacy in History/Social Studies, Science, and Technical Subjects*. These standards are not meant to replace standards in the content areas, but to supplement them (National Governors Association Center for Best Practices & Council of Chief State School Officers, 2010).

Effective Integration

Integration can be accomplished in varied ways, and given that social studies is often featured in the curriculum through integration in other subjects, it is important to distinguish desirable from undesirable integration (Alleman & Brophy, 1993, 2010). Integration should lead to the development of new understandings, knowledge, and skills. It should make content and skills more meaningful to the learner (i.e., the learner should see the authenticity and possibilities for application of the content and skills) (Beane, 1997). Integration should occur as a result of a natural necessity, rather than simply for its own sake. Very often integration is executed through instructional activities, and teaching social studies offers numerous opportunities to do so in meaningful ways. Alleman and Brophy (1993, p. 291) offer five guidelines for determining whether an instructional activity is appropriate for integrative teaching with social studies (these guidelines are equally applicable for integrating content from other subject areas into social studies units and lessons):

1. Each integration activity must be a useful means of accomplishing a worthwhile social studies goal.
2. The activity must represent social education content appropriately and not distort the integrity of the subject matter.
3. The activity's benefits to social education must justify its costs (for both teacher and students) in time and trouble.
4. The activity must be geared to the appropriate level of difficulty.
5. The activity must be feasible for implementation within the constraints under which the teacher must work (e.g., space and equipment, time, and types of students).

A curriculum that follows these guidelines does not downplay content in either of the integrated domains and presents material in an accessible and worthwhile manner. It can be done effectively: Sosniak and Stodolsky (1993) studied classrooms in which teachers using the Open Court reading series integrated social studies content, and Levstik (1993) found that students could learn reading and writing skills in the context of studying science and social studies. Unfortunately, however, this is not easy work.

Challenges of Effective Integration

Numerous obstacles exist to effective curriculum integration with social studies. First, integration can often come in the form of teaching two subjects concurrently, but not coherently. That is, an integrated literacy–social studies thematic unit may feature the teaching of literacy skills separate from the teaching of social studies content, leading to a "piecemeal approach void of networks of connected ideas that enhance meaningfulness" (Brophy et al., 2010, p. 53). Other challenges include cost-effectiveness problems (i.e., the learning activity eats up valuable class time without contributing to the acquisition of knowledge or skills); content distortion (i.e., the content from each subject being integrated is not aligned, or, worse, in conflict); tasks that are too difficult; and feasibility problems (Alleman & Brophy, 1993). Yet another challenge of integrating literacy and social studies is that social studies is often relegated to a supporting role and that integration is not systematic (Boyle-Baise, Hsu, Johnson, Serriere, & Stewart, 2008; Sunal & Sunal, 2007–2008). Unfortunately, integration is often an end unto itself, rather than a means for furthering student knowledge and skills in a meaningful way. To avoid these pitfalls, we recommend establishing goal relevance, whereby there are one or two goals that are clearly articulated and supported by both subjects being integrated.

Student Achievement and Integration

Unfortunately, few studies to date have investigated the relationship of integration of social studies and literacy to elementary students' achievement. However, there is evidence that curriculum integration, broadly speaking, benefits student learning. In his extensive review of research on good teaching practices, Brophy (1999) identified 12 principles; one of these is *curricular alignment*, which speaks to the value of integration. An aligned curriculum is one that integrates content from various areas meaningfully. Students are more likely to meet goals if all components of a curriculum are aligned, and their understanding of content is likely to be retained if such content is taught in a way that makes sense and has application to life. We do know that integrating literacy and science improves achievement in both areas, as early as kindergarten (e.g., Anderson & Guthrie, 1999; Anderson, West, Beck, MacDonnell, & Frisbie, 1997; Romance & Vitale, 2001; Wang & Herman, 2005). (For more on the integration of science and literacy, see Cervetti, Chapter 14, this volume.) We have reason to believe that the integration of social studies and literacy would confer similar benefits (Halvorsen et al., 2012).

The Relationship of Engagement and Motivation with Integration

There are also few studies investigating the relationship between social studies–literacy integration and motivation. However, we do know that students are motivated when they see value (e.g., meaningfulness or relevancy) in a task. Brophy (2010) describes motivation as being organized into an expectancy × value model, whereby people's effort toward a task depends on not only their expectations of success, but the value they place on the task itself and the rewards earned by successfully accomplishing the task. With regard to the "value" part of the model, when academic learning is grounded in students' everyday lives, students demonstrate more interest in such learning, and consequently tend to apply themselves more readily to it (Alleman & Brophy, 1998; Bennett, 2007; Brophy, 2010). An integrated curriculum can be presented in ways in which students see the real-world relevancy of the content (e.g., if the integrated curriculum focuses on problems or issues). Moreover, Alleman and Brophy (1993) found that students tended to have positive recollections of social studies when it was taught through thematic units—an approach that often integrates content and skills from two or more curricular areas. Thus an integrated curriculum has the potential to motivate students.

SUMMARY OF BIG IDEAS FROM RESEARCH

In the list below, we highlight the big ideas from research on integration in general and integration of social studies and literacy in particular.

- Myriad challenges to effective integration exist, such as a piecemeal approach, cost-effectiveness problems, difficulty levels, and the use of integration as an end rather than a means.
- Integration as a strategy can positively influence student learning, although research is needed to understand the benefits of social studies and literacy integration for student learning.
- Integration has the potential to increase student engagement and motivation.
- Social studies, by definition, is an integrative field, comprising history and the social sciences.
- Social studies and literacy share common skills, such as reading, writing, listening, and speaking.
- Social studies can be used to teach comprehension strategies and text structure.

In addition, researchers in this area recommend the following: Integration should lead to the development of new understandings, knowledge, and skills; integration should make content and skills more meaningful to the learner; and integration should occur as a result of a natural necessity rather than merely for its own sake.

EXAMPLES OF EFFECTIVE PRACTICES

Meeting All Students' Needs

Students will be more motivated to learn and better able to concentrate in a classroom learning community when the climate is collaborative and supportive than when it is competitive and judgmental. The process of building the community provides an authentic space for social studies and literacy to come together as students learn to work in groups; engage in conversations about their goals, hopes, and dreams for the year; co-construct guidelines for their behavior; share their personal histories; discuss their needs and wants; formulate the norms and expectations for the class; and so forth—the informal social studies.

The challenge of meeting all students' needs, even when a solid learning community is intact, seems daunting. We encourage you to begin with student, family, and community assets. Moll, Amanti, Neff, and Gonzalez (2001) have referred to these assets as "funds of knowledge." This concept rests on the principle that recognition of the strengths, gifts, and talents of individuals and communities is more likely to inspire positive action than an exclusive focus on needs and problems. The goal is to end the negative cycle of self-fulfilling prophecies that drive deficit-oriented thinking, and instead to increase students' self-efficacy and motivation.

A social studies unit on childhood, for example, can provide natural, instructional space for addressing students' assets, as well as an authentic segue into substantive social studies drawing heavily from the social science disciplines in pandisciplinary ways, and aligning with several NCSS content strands. A childhood unit can focus on how children's lives around the world are both similar and different; they differ according to culture, geographic conditions, economic resources, personal choices, and so on. This kind of unit has the potential to deepen students' understanding and appreciation of all members of their classroom community, and to integrate literacy skills with social studies in meaningful ways. During the childhood unit, students could also have the opportunity to address each student's specialness or uniqueness (e.g., unique fingerprints, footprints, voice, cells in the body, face; the way he or she looks, thinks, and feels; specific learning needs and talents; etc.). Conversations about diversity and respect will deepen students' thinking about these matters in natural ways and pave the way for introducing students to a host of tools to help them learn. While the literature often suggests strategies or tools for specific kinds of learners, we encourage you not to "pigeonhole" and instead make these available to all learners. We also suggest that you make the strategies explicit to the students. Provide reasons why a particular student might need a tool, and explain how the strategy is used. Matter-of-fact language does wonders in a classroom for engaging respect and truly appreciating diversity. In the following subsections, we describe the particular challenges students from various groups may encounter, and we offer classroom examples of integrating literacy and social studies to work effectively with those challenges.

Students from Different Cultural Groups

Often students from cultural backgrounds differing from those of most students in the classroom perceive themselves as out of the mainstream, especially if they have just arrived from another part of the world and are from a minority group. They also frequently are used to other teaching styles. To exacerbate the challenge, the curricular content is typically unfamiliar and at first glance does not relate to their world. We suggest the following:

1. Make your classroom come alive with visual literacy by using pictures from different parts of the world, showing the different ethnic, racial, and cultural groups represented by your students.

2. Capitalize on the funds of knowledge represented by the cultural groups of students in your class. For example, when the class is studying a region of the United States, have students bring in information that describes how the land is organized in their countries of origin (provinces, territories, etc.). Provide narratives laced with visuals.

3. Adapt the curricula to feature the cultures represented by the students. Modifications might include a different literature selection and/or several selections in order to illustrate multiple perspectives, rather than a single selection implying one interpretation.

4. Expose students to multimedia content that features models from cultural groups represented in your classroom. Portray the models not as stereotypes, but as examples of academic achievement (Baker, 1988; Delpit, 1992; Tucker et al., 2002; Walker, 1992).

5. Establish a pen pal e-mail exchange with classes in countries from which children in your classroom (or their families) have come. One thing pen pals do is share family stories (see Figure 15.1).

6. Invite all children in your classroom to share favorite traditions or customs with their classmates.

7. Most children around the world celebrate birthdays. Designate one or more class sessions to sharing and celebrating birthdays, drawing on the games, foods, and customs of the cultures represented in your classroom. For examples, children in Australia often celebrate their birthdays by making and eating "fairy bread"; children in Mexico often celebrate their birthdays with piñatas (see Figure 15.2).

8. People everywhere celebrate major happenings in their lives. Give the students in your classroom a flavor of what "coming of age" means for various cultural groups, keeping in mind that not all families within a given group celebrate these occasions. Encourage students to bring visuals to illustrate these events. Conduct a gallery walk for sharing.

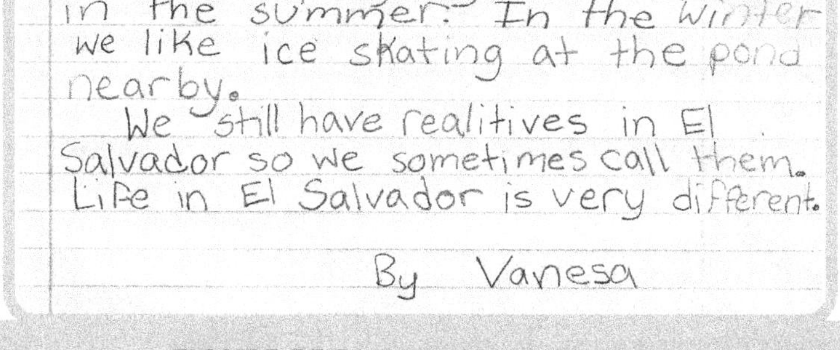

MY FAMILY STORY

Me and my family came to america when I was 3. We came from El Salvador.

We love playing at the park in the summer. In the winter we like ice skating at the pond nearby.

We still have realitives in El Salvador so we sometimes call them. Life in El Salvador is very different.

By Vanesa

FIGURE 15.1. A student's family story.

FIGURE 15.2. Childhood celebrations: Australian "fairy bread" and Mexican piñatas.

Students Who Are English Language Learners

Students' prior educational experiences affect their expectations about and performance in U.S. schools. Students who are English language learners (ELLs), not unlike other students, will vary in their ability to adjust—and even if they have never attended school in their native countries, their families have culturally based opinions regarding the value of education and attitudes about the various approaches to teaching and learning. For example, sharing work and helping classmates during tests are acceptable in some cultures, while often U.S. teachers might view this as cheating. There are cultures that view rote memorization as the primary means of learning; therefore, when U.S. teachers organize students in cooperative groups to solve a problem, students who are ELLs and their families may view this as fluff rather than academic work.

ELLs bring rich yet different experiences and knowledge from those of their U.S.-born peers to the classroom, and their lack of English proficiency often masks their intelligence and learning potential. We suggest the following:

1. Since background knowledge provides a distinct advantage in mastering content as well as learning the related English vocabulary, it behooves you as the teacher to figure out what schemas these students need to make meaning.
2. Avoid exclusive or heavy reliance on text, which is traditionally the norm in social studies. Incorporate many different media, such as firsthand experiences, dramatic play, role play, multimedia presentations, *realia* (objects and artifacts from real life), and so forth.
3. Use culturally sensitive pedagogy (Cruz & Thornton, 2009), which involves selecting topics that are relevant to students' lives beyond school.
4. Draw on students' personal stories and experiences.
5. Use a variety of visual cues.
6. Set up listening centers for revisiting recorded class discussions.
7. Select important words in the ELLs' home languages associated with learning community and social studies content, and teach them to the class.

8. Avoid teaching new literacy skills and new social studies content at the same time.
9. Provide ELLs with extra support in understanding directions for both in school and homework activities. In class, you should model the directions and use the skills needed to complete the assignment. Provide nonlinguistic examples (e.g., visual organizers, photographs, role plays, and demonstrations) that can help to explain or clarify the content, goals, and objectives of the assignment.
10. Allow ELLs to get started on their homework in class so that they have the opportunity to ask clarifying questions. Scaffold long-term assignments for ELLs by breaking the assignments into smaller, manageable tasks and frequently checking on their progress (Alleman et al., 2010).
11. Use community resources or free online tools to translate school material for ELL families to encourage their understanding of and involvement with school activities.

Students Who Are Struggling Readers/Writers

Often students who struggle with reading and writing are singled out early and experience major challenges associated with self-concept and self-esteem. We suggest remaining aware of this and determining ways to address these challenges as you build your learning community; these efforts can go a long way in helping all students realize that individuals have different assets, may learn in different ways, and often need special tools to assist them in their learning.

All too frequently, struggling learners are asked to do mundane tasks first and are not allowed, for example, to experience the library books that appeal to their interests or the "out-of-the-box" activities that would motivate them. We hope that you will rethink this reality and embrace their assets and interests early as you plan instruction. We suggest the following:

1. Maintain high expectations for all students, including those with special needs, but be willing to make short-term accommodations when students appear to need them (e.g., requiring them to write one paragraph instead of two, providing just enough scaffolding so that the students can be successful). A similar strategy can be used for reading.
2. During a class discussion, determine what individual students need. For example, establish the expectation that they will be called on in class, but if they do not have a ready response, give them more time to think and return to them. If you determine that they need more help, ask them to refer to some of the resources posted in the room (calendar, number line, word wall, list of books read, historical timeline, etc.). After they have consulted the sources and had time to think, raise the question again.
3. Prior to independent reading and writing, provide opportunities for Think–Pair–Share or Table Talk activities, so that these students acquire context for reading and ideas for writing.
4. Use modified word walls that focus on the lesson at hand. Using these prior

to the assigned reading and writing can set the stage for the task, provide "hooks," and serve as useful tools for building both competence and confidence (see Figure 15.3).

5. When students have limited vocabulary or tend to struggle in trying to convey their thoughts, attempt to determine what they mean and put the meaning in more understandable language.

6. During discussions, call on struggling students late in a sequence of ideas, after peers have modeled acceptable answers; provide extra wait time when necessary; and provide both meaning-based and sound clues to help them process and respond to questions.

7. Elicit ideas from family members, as well as from reluctant readers and writers themselves, regarding the kind of support needed. The clues they provide can be of immense value to you.

8. Model directions by providing lots of examples (e.g., visual organizers, photographs, role plays, and demonstrations) to help explain or clarify the content, goals, and objectives of the instruction and to follow up assignments intended as application.

9. Design learning centers that provide opportunities for students to practice the skills they are currently learning, paying particular attention to contextualizing

FIGURE 15.3. Modified word wall.

them within the social studies content. Keep the center materials current, and make sure you frequently remind students what materials are available and the exciting tasks they can accomplish.

10. With peer mentors, have students dictate their own stories related to the social studies content they are learning. Encourage them to draw on the modified word wall for prompts.

Students Performing at or above Grade Level, and Other Potentially Disengaged Students

Some students have so much background knowledge and skills related to the content at hand that they struggle to stay engaged in a social studies lesson or turn in assigned work because they do not view the content as particularly interesting or because they do not see the task as challenging or personally meaningful. Most of the strategies we recommend are suitable for all learners, but often it is a matter of degree. When you differentiate your social studies and literacy instruction for learners who are performing above grade level, we encourage you to have an eye toward the social studies topic being addressed, with the goal of embellishing the content—adding a new dimension or perspective that allows all class members to benefit. In a study by Cooper and McIntyre (1994) focusing on effective teaching, students generally preferred methods that produced high levels of imaginative and practical involvement. Among them were storytelling, which they found cognitively engaging; drama and role play; and visual stimuli such as photographs and videos. It is also important to vary grouping and consider whole-class, small-group, and individual learning opportunities. Game-like features that match the lesson goals can add challenge and promote interest (Brophy, 2010). We suggest the following:

1. Provide learning activities that produce high levels of imagination. For example, have students imagine that they could meet a historical figure, visit a geographical site, interact with a cultural group during a special celebration, and so forth. This can do wonders in adding interest to a reading or writing assignment.
2. Provide activities that incorporate visual stimuli, higher-order thinking, and multiple perspectives.
3. Assign learning tasks that incorporate "test yourself" challenges. For example, encourage students to formulate mental hypotheses about the content they are about to read, and then to decide after reading whether the hypotheses are correct.
4. Use instructional materials that provide sets of clues, such as multiple historical accounts of a single event. Provide data that can be rearranged to tell a story, or use game-like activities that involve suspense and simulations. Again, these add interest and promote higher-order thinking.
5. Make sure homework is optimally challenging instead of tedious. Assignments should stretch students' thinking with enough structure so they will feel confident and be successful.
6. Provide integrated learning opportunities for homework that are authentic and apply what has been learned in school. Leverage TV, the family assets, the neighborhood, and the community, making sure you use the students' oral and written responses in upcoming lessons.

7. Provide integrated learning opportunities that incorporate choices—with an eye always on the goals and big ideas. Be mindful of opportunities that use reading, writing, speaking, and listening.

8. Elicit ideas from students for integrated activities (that match the social studies goals) they would like to engage in that would contribute to enhanced interest and meaningfulness.

9. When you are assessing social studies content, draw on a range of genres. Provide students with opportunities to choose among informational texts, poetry, biography, and so forth, making sure that the selection matches the goal in each case.

Effective Practices at Different Grade Levels

In this section, we offer concrete examples of the ways teachers at different elementary grade levels can integrate social studies and literacy according to the criteria for effective instruction we have described earlier. Integrating reading, writing, speaking, and listening into social studies (when it matches the social studies and literacy goals) can enhance understanding, appreciation, and life application of the content.

Kindergarten

Kindergarten offers rich opportunities for the integration of social studies and literacy through reading social studies–based informational texts; writing various forms of communication; and speaking and listening in the discussion of public issues, the influence of historical figures on our lives today, and choices we make when we have limited resources.

Marcia Harris and Virginia Walden, who taught full-day junior kindergarten (4- and 5-year-olds), incorporated literacy into each of their social studies units. One example was a 6-week unit they developed called Where Am I?, which taught students content from geography (as well as from economics, history, and civics), and naturally integrated literacy in various ways in the domains of reading, writing, speaking, and listening.

Marcia and Virginia taught the lessons for each unit during circle time, a half-hour whole-class period at the beginning of the day. In the afternoon, during story time, Virginia read books that often aligned with the topic of the morning lessons to reinforce the concepts. For example, a key understanding taught early in the unit is that maps are made from an aerial perspective (bird's-eye view), rather than from a side or profile view. To reinforce the difference between aerial and profile views, Virginia read Mouse Views (McMillan, 1994), which illustrates how objects look different from differing perspectives. During and after reading, referencing the text and discussing the pictures in the book, she engaged students in a discussion to help them understand that objects look different, depending on one's perspective. The unit also involved the creation of an imaginary neighborhood. To help children grasp the abstract concept of an address, the teachers placed two rectangular pieces of laminated paper, positioned perpendicularly, on the floor to represent the two streets. One by one, each child in the class selected a house on Blue Jay Street or Cardinal Street. The houses were first represented by chairs (that students sat in to indicate they were "at home"), then by milk cartons, and finally by addresses. Children next announced their addresses to the class (e.g., "I live at 6 Blue Jay Street"), and then play-acted in scenarios in which they would visit one another for play dates at their imaginary address, deliver pizza, and so forth. The imaginary neighborhood served as a teaching reference for many activities throughout the unit. Figure 15.4 shows the children's "houses" on Blue Jay and Cardinal Streets.

In addition to teaching the geographic concepts of location and cardinal directions, and the civics concept of government services, the building of the neighborhood provided students an opportunity to practice writing personal correspondence. At the classroom's writing center, students were encouraged to write messages and draw pictures to one another in the form of letters. They addressed envelopes in two ways: They wrote their names and the names of the recipients, and they affixed photocopied photographs of themselves and the recipients. Now that the students had "addresses," they could put their letters in envelopes and address them for delivery to their homes on Blue Jay and Cardinal Streets.

Students also developed speaking and listening skills through many of the circle time activities, particularly when participating in a classroom discussion about an imaginary neighbor on Cardinal Street who did not take care of her property: Sloppy Sally. Students offered ideas about how to get Sally to mow her lawn (because the long

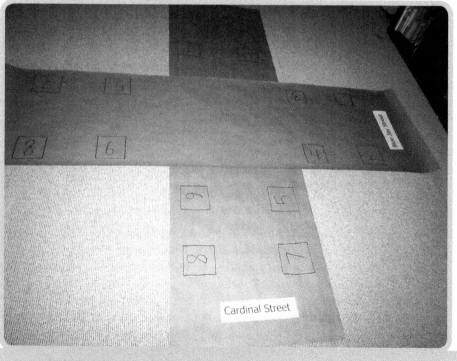

FIGURE 15.4. Children's houses on Blue Jay and Cardinal Streets.

grass and weeds were bothering neighbors' allergies), to dispose of the broken cars on her lawn, and to clean up the dog poop. They tried tactics such as directly speaking to Sally (who was played by one of the teachers) and writing her letters, as well as calling the police to intervene, until she finally complied with their requests to clean up her yard.

A culminating event in this unit was a field trip to the local city of Birmingham, Michigan. To prepare for the trip, Marcia asked students to hypothesize what they thought they would see in the city, writing down their responses in a bulleted list on chart paper. Virginia read *The City* (Douglas, 1982), which describes some of the physical and cultural features of cities. The students then compared the list they generated to what was described in the book. On the field trip, students were placed in small groups; with an adult, each group participated in a scavenger hunt, where the students were given an address and had to locate and name the business at the address, reading numbers and street signs to assist them.

In summary, Marcia and Virginia integrated literacy and social studies in a number of ways that were natural and often blurred the boundaries between the two domains. Activities that they used included the following:

- Reading maps, particularly interpreting symbols.
- Writing and addressing personal correspondence.
- Reading texts for new knowledge (e.g., how maps are made, the features of a city, how mail is delivered).
- Locating particular businesses and residences by reading addresses.
- Speaking and listening with others regarding public issues.

This unit reflects effective literacy and social studies integration because, among other things, (1) it taught new knowledge about absolute location, perspective, government, and taxes; (2) it taught new skills, such as map reading, interpretation of primary documents, using illustrations in a text to describe its key ideas, and writing personal correspondence; (3) it featured ideas that had meaning and application to the students' world beyond school; and (4) it naturally integrated the two domains by incorporating literacy where it was appropriate and where it would enhance the social studies concepts taught.

Grades 1 and 2

In the lower elementary grades, when students' reading and writing skills are progressing and they are becoming fluent readers and writers, there are many ways they can develop these skills in the context of social studies. Moreover, the development of students' knowledge and skills in social studies relies on their literacy skills. For grades 1 and 2, we have selected a unit on families as a topic to illustrate how a select set of literacy skills can be naturally integrated to enhance meaning and apply processes that promote powerful social studies instruction. The topic of families has become and continues to be somewhat controversial (due to the fact that people define *families* differently). We believe that its potentially controversial nature is a positive aspect, as it can help students develop flexible thinking and use such literacy skills as perspective taking, writing to persuade, speaking persuasively, and so forth. During the unit, it is important to focus on families in general terms and then have students apply what they are learning to the study of their own families. For a description of a comprehensive unit on families, see Alleman and Brophy (2002). Here we describe how a particular teacher enacts a unit on family that integrates literacy and social studies.

Barbara Knighton has taught first and second graders in a school that serves primarily working-class and lower-middle-class students of mixed racial and ethnic backgrounds. (Recently she moved to a fourth-grade classroom.) From her years of experience in teaching in the early grades, she has developed a good sense of first and second graders' trajectories of development in different areas and skills. This has enabled her to create benchmarks that help her assess progress and individualize instruction throughout the year. She describes her philosophy about integration as follows:

> I don't have separate conversations in my head or separate plans for integration because I look at things much more holistically than most other teachers do. I don't weed things out and say "this would be good for integration." Instead when I am planning activities and throughout the day when I am teaching, I always keep in mind what I am doing that day, that week, and during that part of the school year. I am always looking for connections and ways to get double duty for some of my activities—design them so as to promote progress toward important goals in two different subjects . . . (Brophy et al., 2010, p. 181)

She begins her family unit by having the students participate in a "gallery walk." She arranges a series of pictures, photographs, and a display of artifacts connected to big ideas she wants students to acquire during the unit. After introducing family, she asks the students to take a walk around the display area and to be thinking, "What do I wonder about?" After Barbara piques students' curiosities, she elicits their responses. She encourages each student to write a different "I wonder" statement on a 3 × 5 card. The "I wonders" are posted on the bulletin board and sorted according to topic. Oral language development is evident throughout this learning opportunity, which sets the stage for the entire unit. Each day, Barbara acknowledges the "I wonders" that fit the day's topic, therefore making the lesson personal as well as purposeful. Barbara often adds her own "I wonders" to ensure that instruction adheres to her overall plan and to model the use of writing to pose questions.

Barbara uses children's literature and personal vignettes as springboards for looking at a range of family structures. For example, *All Kinds of Families* (Simon, 1976), *What Kind of Family Do You Have?* (Super, 1991), *Families are Different* (Pellegrini, 1991), *Heather Has Two Mommies* (Newman, 2009), and *The Family Book* (Parr, 2003) are among the sources she has used. She explains the differences between fiction and nonfiction, and she encourages students to listen to each reading with clearly defined questions they should consider.

To enhance participation in discussion and to build a stronger sight vocabulary, Barbara posts word cards reflective of family structures. Following class discussion, students are asked to engage in expository writing by describing their own families. The posted word cards provide visual prompts and serve as an aid for reluctant writers and spellers.

During another lesson, the students study resources available for families who for various reasons cannot completely satisfy their basic needs. To promote visual literacy, Barbara uses a map of the local community that includes sites where families who need assistance can go for help. The types of assistance are explained and laced with multiple concrete examples. As a follow-up, Barbara asks the families to go on a short ride or walk with their students—and together, using the map Barbara provided, to locate the actual sites. Barbara also explains that these sites offer volunteer opportunities for families who want to provide some local service and enact citizenship skills.

Other topics included in the unit are changes in family life over time, geographic influences on family life, timelines to represent significant events in individuals' and families' lives, family celebrations, how families teach and learn, family support, and family ancestors. Figure 15.5 shows a timeline Barbara created of her own life. Barbara plans and executes a family celebration as a culminating activity. For this session, students review the material and information from the unit. They revisit posters and charts that are subsequently displayed during Family Night. Students create invitations to take home and brainstorm a list of things to tell and share with their families. Barbara models the format for Family Night, underscoring each student's responsibilities for Family Night. Families are guided by their children to various centers/exhibits set up to represent the unit. Family members are encouraged to have conversations about these with their children to add insight to their understandings.

In summary, Barbara's family unit naturally integrates the skills of reading informational text, writing informative/explanatory texts, participating in collaborative conversation, and asking and answering questions about texts read aloud.

FIGURE 15.5. Barbara's timeline.

Upper Elementary Grades

In the upper elementary grades, students' reading and writing skills are more advanced; thus there are more opportunities for students to integrate literacy and social studies, particularly during independent work. The disciplines of social studies (e.g., history, geography, economics, and civics) rely on the reading and interpretation of text-based resources—primary sources (such as political documents, letters, maps, and charts) and secondary sources (such as textbooks). As such, for students to make sense of the social studies concepts and big ideas, they need to draw upon (and further develop) their literacy skills. We present one example below.

Andrew Dickman is a fifth-grade teacher who incorporates literacy into his social studies instruction. In one 4-week unit called Convergence of Three Civilizations, Andrew teaches students content from across four of the core disciplines of social studies (civics, economics, geography, and history), helping his students develop a stronger understanding of exploration and migration while integrating content-area literacy in a variety of ways.

Andrew teaches social studies each afternoon for approximately 45–55 minutes. He begins each lesson of this unit by presenting an image (e.g., a painting) to preview content and engage students. He asks students to make observations and explain what they think the artist is trying to communicate. The content of these images includes themes of migration and interaction among diverse groups of peoples.

Andrew also teaches students about perspective, a historical thinking skill, during these discussions, using the perspectives of Native Americans, Africans, and Europeans. After reading a primary or secondary source from one of these three perspectives, students summarize the main ideas, and record their findings on one-third of a Venn diagram. After students complete their section of the Venn diagram, Andrew puts "experts" together to teach one another about the differing perspectives. As one student teaches about his or her perspective, the other two students are asked to listen and then paraphrase the information shared in the appropriate section of their Venn diagram. After each student has an opportunity to share his or her findings, the students are asked to identify patterns among the perspectives. In doing so, they categorize and reorganize information on their Venn diagrams. Students learn perspective by reading, writing, speaking, and listening about the content of their assigned primary or secondary source. Figure 15.6 shows an example of student work.

In another lesson, Andrew uses a variety of informational texts in order for his students to learn what life was like in Africa, the Americas, and Europe prior to the 16th century. He assigns students a series of questions to guide their reading, and then he asks the students to complete a chart with information about (1) how people made a living, (2) the family structures, and (3) the growth of towns and trade. In order to complete this task, students use sources such as *Slavery* (Grant, 2009), *Kids Discover: America 1492* (Sands, 2009), and *Ancient West African Kingdoms: Ghana, Mali, & Songhai* (Quigley, 2002). He reminds his students of the various text features, including pictures, captions, and boldface words, that will enable them to complete the task effectively.

In summary, Andrew integrates literacy and social studies in several ways: reading images and making predictions, reading texts for new information, using graphic organizers, summarizing orally and in writing, speaking and listening to others for information, and comparing and contrasting information.

Describe the meeting of Africans, Americans, and Europeans after 1492.

1. Each student will fill in the circle associated with the perspective he or she read about, for example, the American perspective.
2. In your small group, discuss the similarities among the three groups.
3. Record the similarities in the overlapped areas.

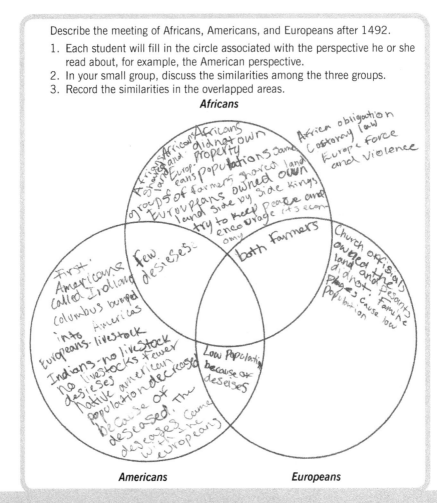

FIGURE 15.6. Venn diagram showing similarities and differences among Americans, Africans, and Europeans.

LOOKING FORWARD

Research suggests that there is promise for increased student motivation and achievement in both social studies and literacy when the subjects are:

- Integrated in ways that teach new knowledge and skills (Alleman & Brophy, 2010).
- Integrated in ways that that have meaning to the students, particularly in their lives beyond school (Alleman & Brophy, 2010).
- Integrated in ways that that are natural (Alleman & Brophy, 2010).
- Contextualized.

Further research is needed in the following areas:

- Determining ways to assist teachers in designing integrated curriculum that is effective and manageable.
- Determining ways to integrate social studies with literacy in ways that do not result in literacy overshadowing social studies.
- Studying the influence of curricular integration of literacy and social studies on student achievement in both areas.
- Determining the similarities and differences between effective curricular integration for the lower elementary grades and for the upper elementary grades.

QUESTIONS FOR REFLECTION ●

1. How can integrating literacy and social studies enhance meaningfulness? What examples have you used or observed?

2. How can integrating literacy enrich the social studies experience? What examples have you used or observed?

3. How can integrating literacy with social studies add useful affective dimensions that make learning more interesting and personalized? What examples have you used or observed?

4. What are some of the knowledge and literacy skills students need to be successful in social studies learning?

5. How can integrating literacy with social studies enhance authentic application of the skills and social studies content?

6. How can integrating literacy in social studies lessons and units provide natural reasons for reading, writing, and so forth? What examples have you used or observed?

7. What steps can teachers take to ensure that integrating literacy does not detract from social studies goals as the primary focus?

8. How can a lesson or unit be constructed so that it is recognizable as social studies, with its aims and purposes evident? What examples have you used or observed?

9. How can we ensure that big ideas in social studies continue to serve as the focus when literacy is included?

10. When should separate instructional attention be given to social studies and literacy?

SUGGESTIONS FOR ONGOING PROFESSIONAL LEARNING ● ● ● ● ● ●

In this section, we present possibilities for professional learning to develop effective strategies for integrating social studies and literacy. We provide four examples of ongoing professional learning sessions on topics emphasized in this chapter: analyzing classroom examples of integration, generating examples of effective integration, meeting diverse students' needs through integration, and collectively brainstorming an example of curricular integration. We describe the examples of ongoing professional learning in the context of professional learning communities (PLCs). We suggest both background preparation for a PLC meeting and activities teachers can use in a meeting. (Ongoing professional learning is covered in more detail by Peterson, Chapter 21, and Sailors, Russell, Augustine, & Alexander, Chapter 22, this volume.)

Analyzing Classroom Examples of Integration

Reading about effective real-life examples of integration and discussing these with colleagues can help teachers visualize what this kind of teaching looks and sounds like. In PLCs, teachers read one or more of the examples of classroom practice at various grade levels from this chapter (we suggest that teachers read the example from the grade they teach or an adjacent grade level). Teachers discuss the ways each snapshot of practice reflects effective integration, as well as ways it might be expanded or improved to make instruction more effective. In the analysis, teachers can refer to the section in this chapter on challenges to effective integration (they will be better able to overcome these challenges if they can recognize them and strategize ways to overcome them). They then draw connections between the example of classroom practice and their own instruction.

Generating Examples of Effective Integration

In advance of a PLC meeting, teachers read the section on this chapter on criteria for effective integration. They then bring examples of their own teaching that they think meet (some) criteria for effective integration to the PLC meeting. Together, they then complete Figure 15.7, drawing upon examples of their practice. For the non-example, they think about how to turn it into an example. Teachers then discuss their examples, exchange strategies for meeting the criteria, and offer suggestions to one another.

Meeting Diverse Students' Needs through Integration

In PLCs, teachers exchange strategies they have used to meet diverse students' needs through integration. As background for a PLC meeting, teachers could do the following:

1. Read the sections in this chapter on meeting diverse students' needs.
2. Create a portrait of the students in their classrooms, and the students' diverse strengths and needs.
3. Consider ways in which integration of literacy and social studies may be adapted to meet the needs of their students through differentiation.

At the PLC meeting, teachers then share both their portraits and differentiation strategies. Teachers respond to one another with suggestions, alternative approaches, and other examples from their teaching practice that might be relevant and helpful.

Collectively Brainstorming an Example of Curricular Integration

In this example, we suggest a possible PLC meeting in which teachers target a particular skill and brainstorm how to design integrated social studies–literacy instruction

Criteria for effective integration	Example from your classroom that reflects this criterion	Example from your classroom that reflects this criterion	Example from your classroom that reflects this criterion	Non-example from your classroom
Each integration activity must be a useful means of accomplishing a worthwhile social studies goal.				
The activity must represent social education content appropriately and not distort the integrity of the subject matter.				
The activity's benefits to social education must justify its costs (for both teacher and students) in time and trouble.				
The activity must be geared to the appropriate level of difficulty.				
The activity must be feasible for implementation within the constraints under which the teacher must work (e.g., space and equipment, time, and types of students).				

FIGURE 15.7. Examples of effective integration. Based on Alleman and Brophy (1993, p. 291).

that effectively teaches that skill. We focus our discussion on a reading skill drawn from the Common Core State Standards; however, teachers can (and should) select whatever standards they want to target in their teaching. In advance of the PLC meeting, teachers read each standard and generate possible teaching examples that target the specific standard to share at the meeting.

The reading standard we have selected is "Analyze multiple accounts of the same event or topic, noting important similarities and differences in the point of view they represent" (Reading Standards for Informational Text K–5: Craft and Structure, 6). At the meeting, teachers share the various resources they selected that present different accounts of the same events. One example is this inquiry question: "Who fired the first shot at the Battle of Lexington Green?" Historians do not know the answer to this question and can only make best guesses, based on their evaluation of the credibility of the sources available. Multiple, competing accounts exist, some of which are more reliable than others (see VanSledright, 2002, for these sources). For whatever standard selected, teachers can then share strategies and offer feedback to one another about effective ways to integrate social studies and literacy.

RESEARCH-BASED RESOURCES

Allen, J., & Landaker, C. (2005). *Reading history: A practical guide to improving literacy.* New York: Oxford University Press.

Chick, K. A. (2008). *Teaching women's history through literature: Standards-based lesson plans for grades K–12* (NCSS Bulletin No. 107). Silver Spring, MD: National Council for the Social Studies.

Fogarthy, R. (1991). Ten ways to integrate curriculum. *Educational Leadership, 49*(2), 61–65.

Kellough, R. D. (1995). *Integrating language arts and social studies.* Englewood Cliffs, NJ: Prentice-Hall.

Lindquist, T., & Selwyn, D. (2000). *Social studies at the center: Integrating kids, content, and literacy.* Portsmouth, NH: Heinemann.

Melber, L. M., & Hunter, A. A. (Eds.). (2009). *Integrating language arts and social studies: 25 strategies for K–8 inquiry-based learning.* Thousand Oaks, CA: Sage.

National Council for the Social Studies. (yearly). *Notable social studies trade books for young people.* Silver Spring, MD: Author.

Sandmann, A. A., & Ahern, J. F. (2002). *Linking literature with life: The NCSS standards and children's literature in the middle grades* (NCSS Bulletin No. 99). Silver Spring, MD: National Council for the Social Studies.

REFERENCES

Alleman, J., & Brophy, J. (1993). Is curriculum integration a boon or a threat to social studies? *Social Education, 57*(6), 289–291.

Alleman, J., & Brophy, J. (1998). Assessment in a social constructivist classroom. *Social Education, 62*(1), 32–34.

Alleman, J., & Brophy, J. (2002). *Social studies excursions, K–3. Book two: Powerful units on communication, transportation, and family living.* Portsmouth, NH: Heinemann.

Alleman, J., & Brophy, J. (2010). Effective integration of social studies and literacy. In M. E. McGuire & B. Cole (Eds.), *Making a difference: Revitalizing elementary social studies* (NCSS Bulletin No. 109, pp. 51–66). Silver Spring, MD: National Council for the Social Studies.

Alleman, J., Knighton, B., Botwinski, B., Brophy, J., Ley, R., & Middlestead, S. (2010). *Homework done right: Powerful learning in real-life situations.* Thousand Oaks, CA: Corwin Press.

Anderson, E., & Guthrie, J. T. (1999, April). *Motivating children to gain conceptual knowledge from text: The combination of science observation and interesting texts.* Paper presented at the annual meeting of the American Educational Research Association, Montréal.

Anderson, T., West, C. K., Beck, D. P., MacDonnell, E. S., & Frisbie, D. S. (1997). Integrating reading and science education: On developing and evaluating WEE science. *Journal of Curriculum Studies, 29*(2), 711–733.

Baker, J. A. (1988). The social context of school satisfaction among urban, low-income, African-American students. *School Psychology Quarterly, 13*(1), 25–44.

Barton, K. C., & Levstik, L. S. (2004). *Teaching history for the common good.* Mahwah, NJ: Erlbaum.

Beane, J. (1997). *Curriculum integration: Designing the core of democratic education.* New York: Teachers College Press.

Bennett, L. (2007). Motivation: Connecting each student with the world. *Social Studies and the Young Learner, 19*(3), 4–6.

Boyle-Basie, M., Hsu, M., Johnson, S., Serriere, S. C., & Stewart, D. (2008). Putting reading first: Teaching social studies in elementary classrooms. *Theory and Research in Social Education, 36*(3), 233–255.

Brophy, J. (1999). *Teaching* (Educational Practices Series No. 1). Geneva: International Bureau of Education.

Brophy, J. (2010). *Motivating students to learn* (3rd ed.). New York: Routledge.

Brophy, J., Alleman, J., & Knighton, B. (2010). *A learning community in the primary classroom.* New York: Routledge.

Brophy, J., & VanSledright, B. A. (1997). *Teaching and learning history in elementary schools.* New York: Teachers College Press.

Cooper, P., & McIntyre, D. (1994). Patterns of interaction between teachers' and students' classroom thinking and their implications for the provision of learning opportunities. *Teaching and Teacher Education, 10*(6), 633–646.

Cruz, B. C., & Thornton, S. J. (2009). *Teaching social studies to English language learners.* New York: Routledge.

Delpit, L. (1992). Acquisition of literate discourse: Bowing before the master? *Theory into Practice, 31*(4), 296–302.

Douglas, F. (1982). *The city.* New York: Crowell Junior Books.

Duke, N., & Bennett-Armistead, S. (2003). *Reading and writing informational text in the primary grades: Research based practices.* New York: Scholastic.

Grant, R. G. (2009). *Slavery.* New York: DK Children.

Halvorsen, A., Duke, N. K., Brugar, K. A., Block, M. K., Strachan, S. L., Berka, M. B., et al. (2012). Narrowing the achievement gap in second-grade social studies and content area literacy: The promise of a project-based approach. *Theory and Research in Social Education, 40,* 198–229.

Hess, D. (2009). *Controversy in the classroom: The democratic power of discussion.* New York: Routledge.

Klingner, J. K., Vaughn, S., & Schumm, J. S. (1998). Collaborative strategic reading during social studies in heterogeneous fourth-grade classrooms. *Elementary School Journal, 99*(1), 3–22.

Levstik, L. S. (1993). Building a sense of history in a first-grade classroom. In J. Brophy (Ed.), *Advances in research on teaching: Vol. 4. Case studies of teaching and learning in social studies* (pp. 1–31). Greenwich, CT: JAI Press.

Levstik, L. S., & Barton, K. C. (2005). *Doing history: Investigating with children in elementary and middle school* (3rd ed.). Mahwah, NJ: Erlbaum.

McMillan, B. (1994). *Mouse views: What the class pet saw.* New York: Holiday House.

Moll, L., Amanti, C., Neff, D., & Gonzalez, N. (2001). Funds of knowledge for teaching: Using a qualitative approach to connecting homes and classrooms. *Theory into Practice, 31*(2), 132–141.

Monte-Sano, C. (2008). Qualities of effective writing instruction in history classrooms: A cross-case comparison of two teachers' practices. *American Educational Research Journal, 45*(4), 1045–1079.

National Council for the Social Studies (NCSS). (2008). A vision of powerful teaching and learning in the social studies: Building effective citizens. *Social Education, 72*(5), 277–280.

National Council for the Social Studies (NCSS). (2010). *National curriculum standards for social studies: A framework for teaching, learning, and assessment.* Silver Springs, MD: Author.

National Governors Association Center for Best Practices & Council of Chief State School Officers. (2010). *Common Core State Standards for English language arts and literacy in history/social studies, science, and technical subjects.* Washington, DC: Author. Retrieved from *www.corestandards.org/assets/CCSSI_ELA%20Standards.pdf.*

Newman, L. (2009). *Heather has two mommies.* New York: Alyson Books.

Parker, W. C. (2011). *Social studies in elementary education* (14th ed.). Boston: Allyn & Bacon.

Parr, T. (2003). *The family book.* New York: Little Brown.

Pellegrini, N. (1991). *Families are different.* New York: Holiday House.

Quigley, M. (2002). *Ancient West African kingdoms: Ghana, Mali, and Songhai.* Chicago: Heinemann Library.

Romance, N. R., & Vitale, M. R. (2001). Implementing an in-depth expanded science model in elementary schools: Multi-year findings, research issues, and policy implications. *International Journal of Science Education, 23*(4), 373–404.

Sands, S. (Ed.). (2009). *Kids discover: America 1492.* New York: Kids Discover.

Shanahan, T., & Shanahan, C. (2008). Teaching disciplinary literacy to adolescents: Rethinking content-area literacy. *Harvard Educational Review, 78*(1), 40–59.

Simon, N. (1976). *All kinds of families.* Morton Grove, IL: Albert Whitman.

Sosniak, L., & Stodolsky, S. (1993). Making connections: Social studies education in an urban fourth-grade classroom. In J. Brophy (Ed.), *Advances in research on teaching: Vol. 4. Case studies of teaching and learning in social studies* (pp. 71–100). Greenwich, CT: JAI Press.

Sunal, C. S., & Sunal, D. W. (2007–2008). Reports from the field: Elementary teacher candidates describe the teaching of social studies. *International Journal of Social Education, 22*(2), 9–48.

Super, G. (1991). *What kind of family do you have?* Frederick, MD: Twenty-First Century Books.

Tucker, C., Zayco, R., Herman, K., Reinke, W., Trujillo, M., Carraway, K., et al. (2002). Teacher and child variables as predictors of academic engagement among low-income African-American children. *Psychology in the Schools, 39*(4), 477–488.

VanSledright, B. A. (2002). *In search of America's past: Learning to read in elementary school.* New York: Teachers College Press.

Walker, E. (1992). Falling asleep and failure among African-American students: Rethinking assumptions about process teaching. *Theory into Practice, 31*(4), 321–327.

Wang, J., & Herman, J. (2005). *Evaluation of Seeds of Science/Roots of Reading project: Shoreline science and terrarium investigations.* Los Angeles: National Center for Research on Evaluation, Standards, & Student Testing.

Williams, J. P., Nubla-Kung, A. M., Pollini, S., Stafford, K. B., Garcia, A., & Snyder, A. E. (2007). Teaching cause-effect structure through social studies content to at-risk second graders. *Journal of Learning Disabilities, 40*(2), 111–120.

CHAPTER 16

Integration of Literacy and Mathematics • • • • • • • • • • • • •

Ellen Fogelberg
Patti Satz
Carole Skalinder

OVERVIEW OF RESEARCH

The kind of classroom needed to create budding mathematicians requires teachers who know the standards and curricular expectations, who recognize and create opportunities for literacy integration, and who are intentional in their pedagogy and instructional moves. The National Council of Teachers of Mathematics (NCTM; 2000) states in its *Principles and Standards for School Mathematics*, "Students who have opportunities, encouragement, and support for reading, writing, speaking, and listening in mathematics classes reap dual benefits: They communicate to learn mathematics, and they learn to communicate mathematically" (p. 60). The new Common Core State Standards also support literacy integration by including standards for reading and writing informational text and technical material, as well as including references to the NCTM process standards (problem solving, reasoning and proof, communication, representation, and connections) in the standards for mathematical practice (National Governors Association Center for Best Practices & Council of Chief State School Officers, 2010).

A great deal of research supports the integration of literacy and the disciplines (Bulgren, Deshler, & Lenz, 2007; Guthrie, McRae, & Klauda, 2007; Reutzel, Smith, & Fawson, 2005). Moje (2008) states that literacy is an essential aspect of disciplinary knowledge. According to Draper and Siebert (2009), "Content area literacy instruction is both a complementary and necessary component of good science and mathematics instruction" (p. 106). Fisher and Frey (2011), citing the research of Zwiers (2008) and Short and Fitzsimmons (2007), conclude: "Providing students time to use language as part of their content-area instruction has the power to significantly improve achievement, especially for English language learners" (p. 345). Research in the area of disciplinary literacy is now focusing on determining which literacy skills and strategies disciplinary experts use to read, write, and communicate in their fields (Draper, 2008; Moje, 2008; Moje et al., 2004; Shanahan & Shanahan, 2008). In other words, these researchers are trying to determine the literacy skills students need to be participants in the discourse of each discipline.

Shanahan and Shanahan (2008) make the case for advanced literacy instruction in all disciplines for students to be successful in their subject-matter courses. They describe a model of literacy learning that involves the increasing specialization of literacy development. This model can be envisioned as a pyramid with three levels: *basic literacy, intermediate literacy*, and *disciplinary literacy*. The basic literacy skills needed to decode text, generally developed in the primary grades, form the base of the pyramid. Everyone needs these skills for literacy to develop. The literacy skills at the next level typically develop in the intermediate grades and include components common to many tasks, such as generic comprehension skills (predicting, summarizing, monitoring understanding, etc.), knowledge of common word meanings, and development of basic fluency. Most students develop proficiency in these skills by the end of middle school. At the top of the pyramid, building on the literacy development of the previous levels, sits disciplinary literacy. It begins to develop during middle and high school and involves learning the unique literacy skills disciplinary experts use on a regular basis. For example, mathematicians emphasize close reading and rereading as important strategies for understanding math texts. Historians, on the other hand, emphasize the need to pay attention to the source of the text to uncover biases and to understand how a specific period in history is portrayed and interpreted. Students need to know how experts in the various disciplines read, write, think, and talk about their work, so they can begin to take on the identity of the novice or apprentice in each subject-area course.

Whereas the literacy skills needed to be successful in the primary and intermediate grades are likely to be taught and practiced often in those grades, the trouble with disciplinary literacy is that the skills needed are high-level, difficult to learn, and rarely taught (Shanahan & Shanahan, 2008). In many subject-matter courses, the text itself poses significant problems for students (Moje, Stockdill, Kim, & Kim, 2011). Textbooks used in each subject-area class are organized differently, use different language, have different visual layouts, and require different background knowledge.

Many textbooks include a variety of sidebars containing prose and pictures both related and unrelated to the main topic being covered (Shanahan & Shanahan, 2008). The visual display can be confusing and overwhelming. Moreover, textbooks often expose students to technical words and definitions before students have had a chance to work with the concepts behind the words. "Although definitional meaning is an aspect of learning a word, when it comes too early in the process it can confound rather than clarify" (Fisher, Frey, & Anderson, 2010, p. 153). Finally, some students have difficulty understanding the structure (organization) and features (headings, boldfaced words, etc.) of the text. Helping students label and understand the different structures and how they are integrated also helps them understand the information (Ogle, 1992).

Even if a textbook plays the lead role in mathematics instruction, teachers must prepare students to understand how the text is similar to and different from other texts that they read. For example, math and science texts contain more concepts per line, sentence, and paragraph than other kinds of texts, and the placement of the main idea in math problems differs from the placement in many other texts (Barton, Heidema, & Jordan, 2002). The main idea is typically found at the end of the paragraph or problem, and it is often in the form of a question. For these reasons and more, many students find reading a math textbook difficult. Wallace and Clark (2005) report on a study where researchers rewrote problems in a textbook to help students focus on solving the problems rather than reading the problems. The results of this effort indicated that students *did not* perform better on the altered-language form of the problems than on the original problems. Wallace and Clark hypothesize that the difficulty students have with problems in isolation may lie in the fact that the "problems may be devoid of connections to prior knowledge, have few context clues, and include a variety of sign systems" (p. 70). Buehl (2011) recommends mentoring students to think mathematically not only when solving math problems, but also when reading about mathematical concepts and relationships: "When students do not develop the capacity to access mathematics understandings independently, students become mired in a continuing cycle of dependency on a knowledgeable other" (p. 65). In other words, it is important that teachers uncover the literacy demands of mathematics texts and teach students the skills and strategies they need to be successful.

Although many teachers and students consider a textbook the only text used in mathematics classes, "texts include anything that people imbue with meaning and then use to represent and communicate ideas" (Draper & Siebert, 2009, p. 110). Math texts may include the student book, workbooks or worksheets, supplemental materials (manipulatives), informational concept books, and even problems placed on an interactive whiteboard or under a document camera. Moreover, literacy in mathematics involves more than just reading words in word problems, but also reading and understanding other signs and symbols. In describing some of the language pitfalls and pathways to mathematics, Barnett-Clarke and Ramirez (2004) point out that "not only do students need explicit instruction to read and write mathematical symbols and words, they also need to learn how to express mathematical ideas orally and with written symbols" (p. 57). Pape (2004) investigated middle school students' problem-solving behaviors from a reading comprehension perspective. He suggests that students require linguistic knowledge to represent a problem accurately, and mathematical knowledge to execute a successful solution. He concludes that problem solvers must monitor understanding and use fix-up strategies when the solution doesn't make sense.

According to the National Research Council (NRC; 2001), "An important part of our conception of mathematical proficiency involves the ability to formulate and solve problems coming from daily life or other domains, including mathematics itself" (p. 420). Wallace and Clark (2005) reviewed the research on integration of literacy and mathematics, and found that textbook reading predominates in most classrooms: "Sadly, studies indicate that teachers continue to see reading in mathematics instruction as the reading of individual problems. In some cases, *reading mathematics* is reserved only for advanced students" (p. 71). To change this practice, they propose three reading stances for use in mathematics classrooms: reading problems; reading mathematics, which includes diverse texts; and reading life, which includes texts found in students' everyday lives (newspapers, coupons, websites, etc.). This last stance requires students to "merge their understanding of numbers and language to make informed decisions" (p. 68). They recommend the inclusion of high-quality children's literature and short picture books, which we refer to as *concept books*. They also recommend the inclusion of newspapers, coupons, and websites, so that students can see the practical applications of mathematics knowledge. According to Wallace and Clark, students build knowledge of the world of mathematics through the use of these multiple text sources, learn to think like mathematicians, and see that mathematics plays a role in their everyday lives.

Many teachers use children's literature as a supplemental source for developing engaging problems. Some research indicates that when teachers connect children's literature with numeracy in interactive ways, students understand concepts and sustain that understanding (Raymond, 1995). Although there is limited research on the effect of using literature in math class to improve student achievement (Jennings, 1992), many teacher educators recommend literature as a vehicle for providing a meaningful context for learning mathematics (Moyer, 2001; Whitin & Wilde, 1992). However, for the mathematics learning to be meaningful, students must be engaged in the practices of mathematics while participating in the read-aloud experience (Draper & Siebert, 2009).

Participating in math discussions offers students opportunities to share their thinking, use the language of mathematics, ask and answer questions, pose problems and solutions, justify reasoning, and seek clarification for what is not understood (NRC, 2001). However, students do not necessarily know how to participate in productive math discussions (Smith & Stein, 2011). Teachers must create routines for listening and must work with students to establish norms for discussion. Hufferd-Ackles, Fuson, and Sherin (2004) provide a framework for the development of "math talk" learning communities. The framework outlines a shift from a focus on answers with the teacher as leader to a focus on mathematical thinking with the teacher as coach and assister. It consists of a progression of levels for teachers and students that support evaluation of students' competencies and teachers' decision making about how to support student growth.

According to the *Principles and Standards for School Mathematics* (NCTM, 2000), students are expected to communicate their thinking clearly and precisely to their peers, teachers, and others (p. 60). Initially, students use their own language for describing what they do to solve math problems. However, as students become familiar with the language and conventions of mathematics, they will need the academic vocabulary of mathematics to describe their problem-solving process more precisely and to justify their answers. Having adequate background knowledge and the ability to use the vocabulary of the discipline is closely related to students' ability to access content in academic texts and talk (Nagy & Townsend, 2012). These researchers state that it is not enough for students to study discipline-specific words to understand their meaning and to be able to use that knowledge to understand text. Therefore, Nagy and Townsend (2012) suggest that it is important for students to learn the vocabulary while studying the text, with the teacher providing the necessary scaffolding: "Learning academic language is not learning new words to do the same thing that one could have done with other words; it is learning to do new things with language and acquiring new tools for these new purposes" (p. 93). The research also suggests that students need repeated exposure and many opportunities to use the words to understand them in the context of the new material they are learning (Blachowicz & Fisher, 2000).

In addition to participating in math discussions, writing about the mathematics they are learning allows students to make their thinking visible to others and contribute to the creation of a community of learners. Newell (2006) reports on a meta-analysis that studied the effect of writing on learning in a number of disciplines, including mathematics (Bangert-Drowns, Hurley, & Wilkinson, 2004). This meta-analysis found that writing interventions, in which students were asked to reflect on their understandings and confusions, yielded small, but positive results. Shanahan (2004) also cites research indicating that writing increases the quality of student understanding in mathematics (Buerger, 1997). However, even though communicating mathematically is a goal of the NCTM and is listed as one of its process standards (NCTM, 2000), Wilcox and Monroe (2011) found little evidence of writing and mathematics integration in the research literature. Despite this, several math teacher educators (Kenney, Hancewicz, Heuer, Metsisto, & Tuttle, 2005; Murray, 2004; Van de Walle, 2007; Wilcox & Monroe, 2011) recommend a variety of writing activities that support the construction of meaning in mathematics.

SUMMARY OF BIG IDEAS FROM RESEARCH

The available studies on literacy–mathematics integration are summarized in Table 16.1. These studies support the following big ideas:

- Teachers need to provide literacy instruction to help their students read and write the texts that are used in mathematics.
- Students need learning activities that will help them talk, write, and think about mathematics.
- Students must be able to read, use, and understand the academic vocabulary of mathematics to explain their reasoning, justifications, and solutions to problems.
- In addition to using general comprehension strategies, students need to use close reading and rereading to understand math texts.

TABLE 16.1. Studies on Integrating Literacy and Mathematics

Aspect of integration	Citations
Reading, writing, and talking about mathematics	Barnett-Clarke & Ramirez (2004); Draper & Siebert (2009); NRC (2001); Shanahan & Shanahan (2008)
Talk in mathematics class	NRC (2001); Smith & Stein (2011)
Vocabulary development	Baumann & Graves (2010); Blachowicz & Fisher (2000, 2010); Marzano & Pickering (2005); Nagy & Townsend (2012)
Literature in mathematics instruction	Jennings (1992); Raymond (1995)
Strategy use	Draper (2008); Shanahan & Shanahan (2008)
Writing in mathematics	Bangert-Drowns, Hurley, & Wilkinson (2004); Newell (2006); Shanahan (2004)

EXAMPLES OF EFFECTIVE PRACTICES

Planning for Integration

The framework we use to integrate literacy and mathematics instruction is based on the use of intentional instruction (Fisher, Frey, & Lapp, 2011). The framework design allows the teacher to provide the necessary scaffolds and supports to ensure that all students can be successful in learning mathematics. We include children's literature to increase engagement and to address the NCTM (2000) expectation that students read a range of mathematical texts. To learn how to communicate effectively in mathematics, we create opportunities for students to talk and write about their mathematical learning and problem solving. We teach the vocabulary of mathematics to help students understand the language and concepts of mathematics and to help them describe their mathematical thinking and reasoning more precisely. Finally, we use a variety of student groupings to differentiate instruction to meet individual student's needs.

Intentional Instruction

We began to move away from using whole-class instruction exclusively several years ago. Initially, we likened our practice to a workshop model similar to a reading or writing workshop (Calkins, 2000; Graves, 1983). Since then, we have discovered a better label for what we do—*intentional instruction*. It differs from the traditional model of mathematics instruction, in which the teacher follows the teacher's guide like a script; instead, it positions the teacher to teach responsively. It includes an adaptation of the *gradual release of responsibility* (Fisher & Frey, 2008; Pearson & Gallagher, 1983), which moves from total teacher responsibility for the learning to include guided instruction and productive group work before students assume responsibility for their learning. According to Fisher and colleagues (2011), "The five-part framework for intentional instruction requires that teachers (1) establish purpose, (2) model their thinking, (3) guide students' thinking through the strategic use of questions, prompts, and cues, (4) provide students with productive group tasks that are meaningful and allow students to practice language and consolidate understanding, and (5) assign independent tasks that require students to apply what they have learned" (p. 360). This framework provides the flow for the math class.

One of us—Carole Skalinder, a third-grade teacher—establishes the purpose for each lesson both orally and by putting it on the board. For example, she may write, "Numbers can be written in many ways. Names for 7: 5 + 2; (3 × 2) + 1 . . . " Writing the purpose provides a visual aid for all students, but is especially helpful to students who need many reminders of what they are supposed to focus on during the lesson. She wants to be sure that students get the "big idea."

Carole uses modeling and thinking aloud to demonstrate, explain, and show—not just tell—students whatever she intends for them to learn and do. For example, she may model how she reads the text and do a think aloud about how she figures out the math meaning of common words. Possible areas of mathematics for thinking aloud and teacher modeling include the following (Fisher et al., 2010, p. 151):

- Background knowledge (e.g., "When I see a triangle, I remember that the angles have to add up to 180°.").
- Relevant versus irrelevant information (e.g., "I've read this problem twice, and I know that there is information included that I don't need.").
- Selecting a function (e.g., "The problem says 'increased by,' so I know that I'll have to add.").
- Setting up a problem (e.g., "The first thing that I will do is . . . because . . . ").
- Estimating answers (e.g., "I predict that the product will be about 150 because I see that there are 10 times the number.").
- Determining reasonableness of an answer (e.g., "I'm not done yet as I have to check to see if my answer makes sense.").

Carole also thinks aloud to model how to solve a problem. She may ask questions when thinking aloud: "What operation should be used?", "Should I draw a picture?", "Should I guess and check or make an estimate?", "Does the answer make sense?", "Am I answering the question asked in the problem?" She has noticed that over time students begin to ask, "May I do a think-aloud?" Eventually, when helping each other, the students use a think-aloud instead of just saying the answer: "Well, when I was finding the difference between 86 and 54, I used the number grid. I started here at 54 and counted up by tens to 84. Then I counted by ones to 86." Students begin to listen to others' think-alouds as they begin to compare, discuss, and collaborate.

The framework includes a variety of grouping strategies: the whole class for teacher modeling and setting the stage for the lesson or problem solving; partners for "trying out" what was explained in the demonstration, while the teacher circulates and guides students; and small groups for more intensive guided practice, using questions, prompts, and cues. While the teacher works with small groups, the other students are engaged in collaboratively solving a new, but similar, problem at centers or tables. Each student attempts to solve the problem independently and then shares problem-solving strategies with the group. The students are actively engaged in the process of learning math concepts, vocabulary, and procedures, while reading and solving problems. According to Frey, Fisher, and Everlove (2009), engagement in productive work is a critical component for students in the gradual release of responsibility. The students talk and collaborate with peers, often mimicking the language used in the teacher think-aloud, and consolidate their thinking about the mathematics that was previously modeled and practiced with teacher guidance.

At the end of the math lesson, students may come back to the whole class for a summary discussion. According to Schielack and Chancellor (2010, p. 13), students should be encouraged to do at least one of the following during the summary discussion:

- Share their problem-solving processes and solutions.
- Compare solution strategies and look for different ways of approaching problems and describing solutions.
- Uncover patterns or generalizations that may serve to connect this learning experience to important complex mathematical understandings.

Even though summarizing is considered important to the math lesson, Hull, Balka, and Miles (2011) find it to be the most underused phase in the mathematics lesson. Teachers often run out of time before they get to this part of the lesson. Planning for the summary discussion and putting a time limit on other parts of the lesson may make this practice more common.

The framework for intentional instruction is not linear. A teacher may need to provide additional demonstrations to a group of students who are having difficulty with a problem during the collaborative group work; an individual may need more one-to-one support; or the teacher may need to provide more cues or prompts to scaffold the learning of several students. The teacher finds multiple opportunities for differentiating instruction and meeting the needs of a variety of students, as long as the rest of the students are productively engaged in group work.

Integrating Mathematics and Literature

Literature provides a means for students to encounter mathematical concepts and vocabulary in the context of something familiar, a book. Literature can enrich the students' "pool of mathematical ideas" (Whitin & Whitin, 2000, p. xii) and facilitate their problem posing. Hunsader (2004, p. 618) states that "engagement with literature provides a natural way for students to connect the abstract language of mathematics to their personal world." Several books (Bamford & Kristo, 1998; Bresser, 2004; Columbia, Kim, Moe, & Wincek, 2009; Whitin & Whitin, 2000) and articles have suggested titles and sample lesson for using math-related read-alouds in the math class.

Bintz and Moore (2010–2011) chose literature as the vehicle for selecting an engaging and challenging mathematical task to address a group of teachers' concerns about their students' reading skills and ability to understand probability. Bintz began by telling the fourth-grade students that picture books can be a good way to learn mathematics, and that *Jumanji* (Van Allsburg, 1981) is a great book for learning about probability. He read the book aloud, stopping at the point where one of the characters must roll number cubes and get a 12 to end a game being played. Bintz asked the students what they were thinking and what they would predict would happen next: What sum of the number cubes was the character likely to roll, and why? These questions are not unlike the questions teachers ask when students are reading in language arts to support active learning. It is important to remind students that they can make and evaluate predictions in math class just as they do in language arts because students do not necessarily generalize strategy use to other content areas (Giles, 2010).

Working in pairs, students used number cubes and a data-recording tool to try to determine whether their predictions were correct, or whether they needed to change them. At the end of the lesson, Bintz brought the children back to the whole class for a summary discussion. Even though the students were able to describe the data after participating in the *Jumanji* lesson, they continued to have difficulty explaining why certain numbers occur more frequently than others. Nevertheless, the students were engaged in the lesson, demonstrated their current thinking and understanding, worked and talked with their peers to record the data, and thus provided the teacher with specific information about where to go next. Armed with this knowledge, the teacher could plan extension lessons to develop the critical thinking needed to be able to analyze the data and explain it.

Developing open-ended lessons—and, in this case, a mathematical problem drawn from literature and related to students' everyday lives—allowed the students to approach the problem from an inquiry stance (Draper & Siebert, 2009) as opposed to applying a fixed solution that only required practice of previously learned procedures. The teachers reported that many of the students were more attentive and involved than they usually are in their typical math and reading lessons. It is important to note that just reading a book will not necessarily promote the kind of thinking needed to grapple with complex math tasks unless the teacher carefully chooses the text to create the problems. Draper and Siebert (2009) remind us that "literacy instruction that is focused on developing fluency with the texts that are written and read while doing science and mathematics is not likely to be successful unless that instruction occurs within the context of having students do science and mathematics" (p. 107).

Hunsader (2004, pp. 623–624) developed a tool for evaluating the literary and mathematics content of various trade books. She found great variability in both the mathematical and literary quality of many of the read-aloud books recommended by the publishers of mathematics programs. Therefore, she recommends that teachers use an evaluation tool to determine the mathematical and literary quality of the books they want to use before deciding to allocate time for including them in math lessons. We have adapted Hunsader's criteria to evaluate both types of quality in the trade books we use for our classes. The changes we have made to the math criteria are listed below. To use this tool, a teacher would look for the following to be present in a trade book, whether it is a narrative or informational book:

- Presents math concepts accurately (vocabulary, text, computation).
- Presents math concepts visually.
- Presents math concepts at the appropriate level for the intended audience *and* addresses one or more of the NCTM standards.
- Contains real-world connections to the math concept.
- Presents a math concept that is an essential ingredient interwoven in the story-line, if the book is narrative.
- Provides a rich opportunity for math investigations.

One of us—Patti Satz, a former second-grade teacher—used this evaluation tool to determine the quality of the book *How Pizza Came to Queens* (Khalsa, 1989), a book suggested for ages 6–9. Although it is often recommended as a read-aloud for math class, Patti determined that it would receive a low rating according to our math criteria and a high rating for literary quality. It is a beautifully illustrated book with a storyline that involves an older woman introducing children to the world of pizza making. However, the mathematical content is limited, with few uses of math terms or concepts. The rating would have improved if the book had included measurement vocabulary or fractions in a discussion of the pieces of pizza.

Communicating Mathematically: Adding Talk to the Math Class

Since using literature in math class is most effective when this is done in an interactive way, talk is a necessary ingredient for advancing students' mathematical thinking about the text (or, for that matter, about any text used in mathematics instruction). Whether students are working on problems from the math text or ones developed in relationship to a piece of literature, students gain from talking about the problem and the process for solving it. However, productive conversation needs to be modeled, practiced, and developed in conjunction with teaching math content goals.

We recommend that teaching math talk should begin with explicit instruction about how to talk and listen productively. Initially, the teacher suggests that each student turn and talk to another student sitting nearby. This provides guided practice for having a focused conversation for a short time on a specific topic. The teacher may say, "Turn and share with your neighbor another name for 12." Not only does this allow students to communicate with each other about their thinking, but it releases energy so that they can return to the whole-class discussion.

After modeling how to talk and listen, we recommend occasionally using a "fishbowl" strategy to demonstrate what a focused math discussion looks like. Using a sample math problem, the teacher and a select group of students talk about the problem as the rest of the class listens and observes. Next, the teacher provides guided practice by dividing the class into small groups, with one student from the teacher-led "fishbowl" in each small group. This provides support, as one student has already participated in a focused discussion. As the group discusses a different math problem, the teacher circulates and takes notes about the talk. The groups meet for just a few minutes. Then the teacher brings the whole class together to reflect on the talk. An anchor chart is created to list the talking and listening skills needed for working on a math problem together. The teacher and class discuss what went well and what still needs work. The expectation that math discourse is purposeful conversation will probably need to be reviewed frequently.

Guided by the work of Hufferd-Ackles and colleagues (2004), we look for progress in students' math talk as indicated by the following student behaviors:

- A focus on thinking rather than just answers.
- Listening in order to understand one another.
- Paraphrasing each other's explanations.
- Expecting their explanations to make sense.
- Seeing errors as opportunities for learning.
- Using explanations about a problem as a stimulus for whole-class discussions.
- Understanding that their ideas will give rise to the content of some lessons.

The teacher plays a critical role in the math discussions. The teacher must be mindful of the lesson's objectives and concepts the students are responsible for learning. Similar to a conductor of an orchestra, the teacher must keep the discourse on the right path. The teacher needs to maintain a balance between students' sharing their thoughts and connections, and finding solutions that tie to the mathematical ideas of the lesson. Smith and Stein (2011, p. 8) discuss five practices in orchestrating a math conversation: anticipating student responses, monitoring, selecting, sequencing, and connecting. Once the teacher observes and understands the different practices that children are using while working with their groups, the teacher can choose and sequence those who speak in the whole-class discussion and can guide the class to the main idea of the lesson. This is very different from just calling on random students to share their problem solving. When the discussion goes well, students feel that they have come up with the very idea that the teacher would have taught anyway. They have ownership of the mathematical thinking. (For more about fostering discussion, see Garas-York, Shanahan, & Almasi, Chapter 10, this volume.)

Strategies for Reading Problems and the Math Text

Although literature may provide a context for learning mathematics, students must also interact with the math textbook. Many students report that they seldom read in math class, or read only what is required to get their homework done (Bosse & Faulconer, 2008; Buehl, 2011). Students need strategies and many opportunities to practice using these to understand math problems and the math text (Hyde, 2006). Teachers can address confusions about the layout and organizational structures through discussion, modeling, and labeling of the parts of the text. For most, demystifying the organization simply involves explaining that the text often provides a narrative section to situate the learning, an explanation of the new concept, an example section that may also list procedures for solving problems, and new problems for applying the procedure. Beyond the organization of the text, however, it is important for students to be metacognitive when reading math problems, rereading for clarity, and checking whether the problem makes sense. This is the kind of close reading referred to in the research (Shanahan, 2004).

If students learn to do a close reading of a problem, they are more likely to be able to infer what kind of problem it is and perhaps predict an answer to it—a first step toward solving the problem. Doing a close reading of mathematics text often involves rereading to make sure the meaning of the problem is clear. It also means paying attention to every word in the problem because every word counts in mathematics. While rereading, thinking aloud, and drawing to represent what they think the problem is about, students develop a potential path for solving the problem. Once they solve the problem, students need to ask themselves whether the solution makes sense. Using the framework for intentional instruction, teachers can make sure they are providing the necessary scaffolds for students to develop independent problem-solving methods. Strategies for actively reading math texts include the following:

- Thinking aloud while reading.
- Making connections to other problems.
- Paraphrasing the problem.
- Visualizing and drawing the problem and/or solution.
- Inferring and predicting possible solutions.
- Rereading to understand and check that they are solving the problem as stated.
- Summarizing and explaining their process and solutions.
- Monitoring (checking that both the problem and solution make sense) and using fix-up strategies.

As stated above, each of these strategies must be modeled and explained. To help students remember and use the strategies, we put them on a bookmark that students can keep in their math text for easy access while reading the text. Working in groups, students practice using the strategies as they read the text and work on a variety of math problems. Ultimately, the teacher will watch for evidence of the students using the strategies to understand the text and to explain their thinking. (For more about several of these strategies, see Stahl, Chapter 9, this volume.)

We also use questioning by both teachers and students as an avenue for addressing understanding of mathematics content, text, and processes. Heuer (2005, p. 52) suggests: "In addition to providing feedback about student understanding, questions also serve a mediating function, helping students discover what they know (or don't know) as they attempt to construct mathematical meaning." As with the other strategies, teachers model questioning during think-alouds, and provide guided practice and opportunities for students to use questioning during focused whole-class discussions. According to Johnston (2004, p. 55), "The ability or tendency to ask effective questions contributes a great deal to children's agency, and to their development of critical literacy."

A growing body of research (Blachowicz & Ogle, 2008; Duke, Pearson, Strachan, & Billman, 2011; Pressley, 2006; Reutzel et al., 2005) suggests that students need to be taught how to use strategies in combination because doing so leads to greater gains. Students need to know what the strategies are (content knowledge) and why they are useful; know how to use them (procedural knowledge); and know when particular strategies might be most beneficial for meeting their mathematical needs (conditional knowledge). Again, this takes teacher modeling, guided practice, and group work so that students can articulate their strategy use for purposes of explaining and justifying their answers.

Using Concept Books in Mathematics

Adding concept books to guided reading and the classroom library encourages students to see math in the real world. These books allow teachers to blur the lines between reading and content instruction across disciplines. In addition to math concept books, such as *Which Is the Tallest?* (Pullen, 2004) and *Comparing Sizes and Weights* (Nguyen, 2006), teachers will find that many informational science concept books contain math content. Many students choose these books during independent reading because of their visual appeal and because they build on students' natural interest in the real world. Concept books come in many formats, including books, magazines, and digital versions. Students need support to read and understand these books. Additional strategies for reading concept books include understanding and using navigational features (table of contents, index, glossary); understanding organizational structures (compare/contrast, problem–solution, etc.) and text features (headings and boldface, pictures and captions, etc.); knowing how to activate background knowledge and set a purpose for reading; and knowing how to skim and scan for specific information.

Reading Charts, Graphs, Diagrams, and Other Features

Some standards-based textbooks include supplemental materials, such as data banks, maps, posters, diagrams, and directions for playing math games. As with other forms of text, students need demonstrations and support for reading them. In some cases, students read charts and tables from bottom to top or may determine their own starting point. For example, Carole Skalinder was working with one of her third-grade students to read a number grid. In the hundreds chart, the numbers go from 1 to 100 in rows of 10. As students read down the grid, the numbers go up in value. However, when explaining the grid, teachers often say, "We are counting up," meaning that "We are counting higher." Without clarification, students can become confused.

Students can begin creating graphs and charts as early as kindergarten. They can graph such things as how many students get hot or cold lunch, how many letters each child has in his or her name, and how many students like a particular kind of treat. The more students create their own graphs and charts, the easier it is for them to read these features when they meet more sophisticated models in their textbook. However, with each new form, teachers must again teach how to read the graph or chart, so that students understand the information and can learn how to create similar graphs and charts on their own.

Teaching and Using Academic Language: Vocabulary Learning in Mathematics

Many of the challenges of math texts are related to the vocabulary found in them. Math texts introduce new, technical vocabulary, along with using familiar words in unfamiliar ways (Kenney, 2005). According to Nagy and Townsend (2012), "Attention to academic vocabulary may be an important first step in raising teachers' awareness of the need to better support students' understanding and use of the language of the disciplines" (p. 96).

Baumann and Graves (2010) define *academic vocabulary* in two ways: *content-specific words* and *general academic vocabulary*, "the broad, all-purpose terms that appear across content areas but that may vary in meaning because of the discipline itself" (p. 6). Pierce and Fontaine (2009) state the importance of students' understanding both types of words in mathematics: "Proficiency in mathematics has increasingly hinged upon a child's ability to understand and use two kinds of math vocabulary words: math specific words and ambiguous, multiple-meaning words with math denotations" (p. 242).

Frey and Fisher (2009, pp. 14–15) describe a subject-area vocabulary initiative that consists of five big ideas for teaching the general, specialized, and technical vocabulary necessary for students to be successful in the disciplines: (1) Make it intentional; (2) make it transparent; (3) make it useable; (4) make it personal; and (5) make it a priority.

1. *Make it intentional.* Start by selecting the words that are *critical* to the understanding of the lesson and unit. This may mean making adjustments in the word lists provided by the chosen math program or text. In addition, the math program may not identify the general words that have a specific math meaning. It is important to include discussion and modeling to help students to understand the math meaning of these words in the context of the math lesson itself.

Occasionally, Carole Skalinder starts a lesson by having students list everything they already know about a word. In one lesson, she asked her students what they knew about the word "digit." As Carole went around the classroom, she invited each student to say something. Examples included the following: "A digit can be a number," "5,000 has four digits," "A digit can be odd or even." By the end of the discussion, even the most challenged math learner was able to come up with a pretty accurate description of a digit. This practice uncovers students' previous learning and allows the teacher to build upon current understanding.

Beck, McKeown, and Kucan (2002) recommend providing *student-friendly definitions* prior to using dictionary or glossary definitions. A student-friendly definition includes an explanation of what a word means and examples of the word used in sentences. Mathematics teachers may include the use of visual aids to foster understanding of the word. Next, students are asked to generate their own sentences using the words. Finally, the words are prominently displayed on word walls for ready reference. The researchers also recommend that students be actively involved in using the words to begin processing them at deeper levels. Therefore, we include math terms in word-sorting activities and math games to increase opportunities for using the words.

2. *Make it transparent.* Teachers often model word-learning strategies to make the process transparent and to support independent word-learning practices. Teacher think-alouds and guided practice can lead students to use context clues for determining probable definitions. Teachers model how they do a close reading of a problem to understand the common words and unusual syntax found in math problems. For example, students are often confused by the word *each*, as in "There are five dogs in each of 20 pens . . . " or the phrase *times as much as*, as in "One amount is 10 times as much as . . . " Simple explanations, physical demonstrations, and repeated practice often provide enough support for students to understand an unusual word or phrase. However, it will take many exposures for students to figure out the meanings of unusual phrases before they do so independently. It is important for teachers to be aware of possible confusions and to be prepared to address them.

The many homophones that students encounter in math class also present challenges. Words such as *some, ate,* and *way* are words used in everyday language that sound the same as the common math words *sum, eight,* and *weigh.* We create charts (public displays) of homophones to help students recognize the different spellings and forms of the words, and to aid them in understanding these words in a mathematics context.

3. *Make it useable.* Frey and Fisher (2009) stress the importance of students having multiple opportunities to use new words in authentic ways. Collaborative group work becomes the vehicle for students to use the new terms while completing a task. We use concept sorts and design other activities where students use the academic language to talk about and solve problems. For example, after posing several problems over several weeks, Carole Skalinder asks students to identify themselves as "experts" in using particular strategies for solving problems. The class then develops a chart with the students' names and the strategies for which they have identified themselves as experts. For the rest of the year, students can go to one of the "experts" if they need help or want to learn an alternative strategy for solving particular problems. As the students are teaching each other, they have multiple, authentic opportunities to use and hear the mathematics words.

4. *Make it personal.* Designing opportunities for students to use the vocabulary terms in new situations allows them to take ownership of their learning and to demonstrate their emerging understandings (Frey & Fisher, 2009). One of our fifth-grade teachers, Amy Kipfer, uses a math journal, which she calls "Math Musing," for students to record math vocabulary words with examples and drawings (see Figure 16.1). The students then have a ready reference for the technical words needed for math learning. Representing the terms with words and drawings helps solidify the learning. The journal also becomes the place for students to try using the words in questions, musings, and reflections.

5. *Make it a priority.* We include math concept books in our classroom libraries and use them in our guided reading lessons, to give students multiple opportunities to read books that interest them and to provide a context for seeing the math vocabulary in a variety of texts. Frey and Fisher (2009) describe a whole-school reading program that places emphasis on the importance of students reading widely and often. Creating daily time for independent reading, and including math concept books and real-world texts (magazines, newspapers, etc.) that reference math in the options for reading, increase students' volume of reading and their awareness that math is all around them.

This five-part plan for vocabulary instruction is comprehensive and supported by the research (Blachowicz & Fisher, 2000; Graves, 2006). It provides teachers with a practical model for helping students learn both types of vocabulary: academic and general.

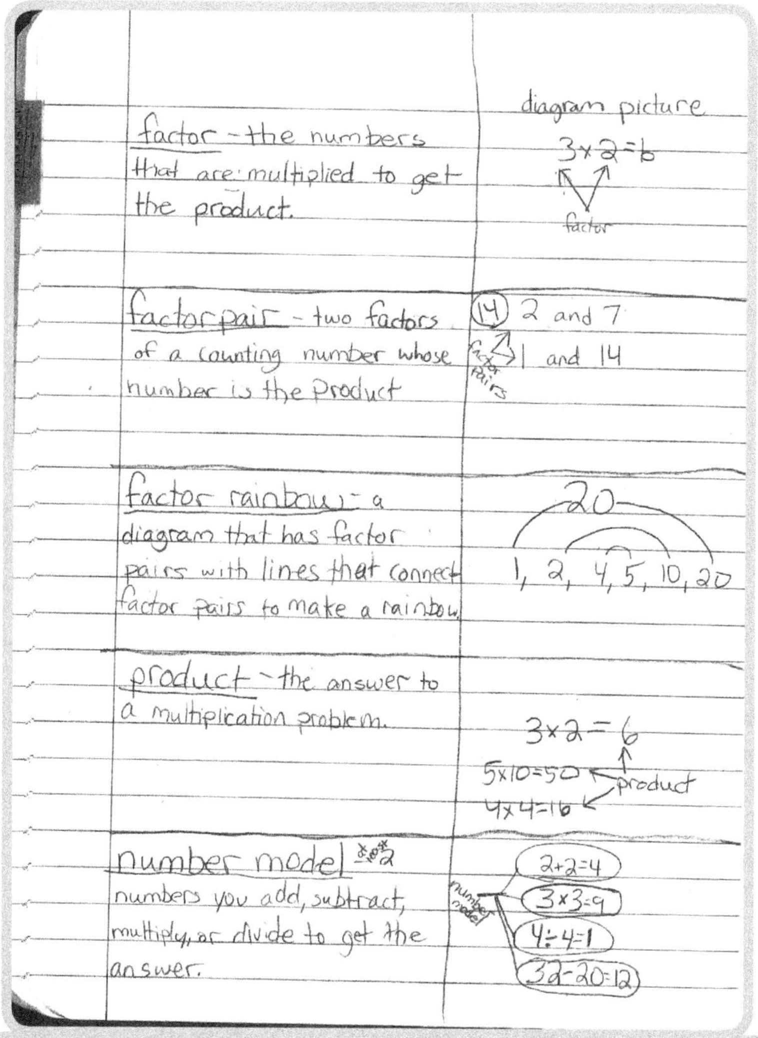

FIGURE 16.1. Journal entry: Vocabulary.

By including an active vocabulary-learning structure in the math program, teachers are also building understanding of math concepts. (For more information on building vocabulary, see Kucan, Chapter 11, this volume.)

Writing to Learn in Mathematics Classrooms

In the introduction to *Writing Next* (Graham & Perrin, 2007), Vartan Gregorian, President of the Carnegie Corporation, quotes from the National Commission on Writing to make the case for the power of writing: "If students are to make knowledge their own, they must struggle with the details, wrestle with the facts, and rework raw information and dimly understood concepts into language they can communicate to someone else. In short, if students are to learn, they must write" (p. 2). Murray (2004, pp. 88–89) identified several benefits to having students write about the mathematics they are doing:

- Thoughtfulness and increased reasoning skills.
- Active involvement in thinking, making sense, constructing, and learning mathematics.
- Questions raised and new ideas explored.
- Use of higher-order thinking while interpreting and explaining data.
- Clarification, reinforcement, and deepened conceptual understanding.

Patti Satz asked fourth-grade students to answer the following question in their math journals: "Are addition and subtraction alike?" One student wrote, "I think that addition and subtraction are related because let's say 4 + 4 = 8. 8 – 4 = 4. They are related because if you add 2 numbers together, it will make a sum. If you subtract a number that equals that sum from the sum, it will equal the other number." This student's response provided Patti with information about the student's understanding and ability to communicate how the additive and subtractive properties are related—an important basic concept in mathematics, and something that teachers need to come back to in the intermediate grades.

In writers' workshop, Carole Skalinder asked her students to generate a list of things they "wonder" about as potential topics for writing. One student generated the following list after writing "I wonder" at the top of the page:

1. How a dog feels.
2. How much (*sic*) milliseconds old I am.
3. How do birds fly?

Later, he elaborated on item 2 during math class (see Figure 16.2). This student used writing for an inquiry project that piqued his curiosity. The writing allowed him to explore mathematics beyond the curriculum, but related to what mattered to him. School has to be a place for exploring what matters to students, even very capable students, to keep them engaged in learning.

Hull and colleagues (2011) advocate for the inclusion of visible thinking as an important avenue for determining student understanding: "Evidence of visible thinking is apparent during mathematical discussions, explanations, demonstrations, drawing, writing and other ways that ideas are conveyed" (p. 2). Students record their thinking

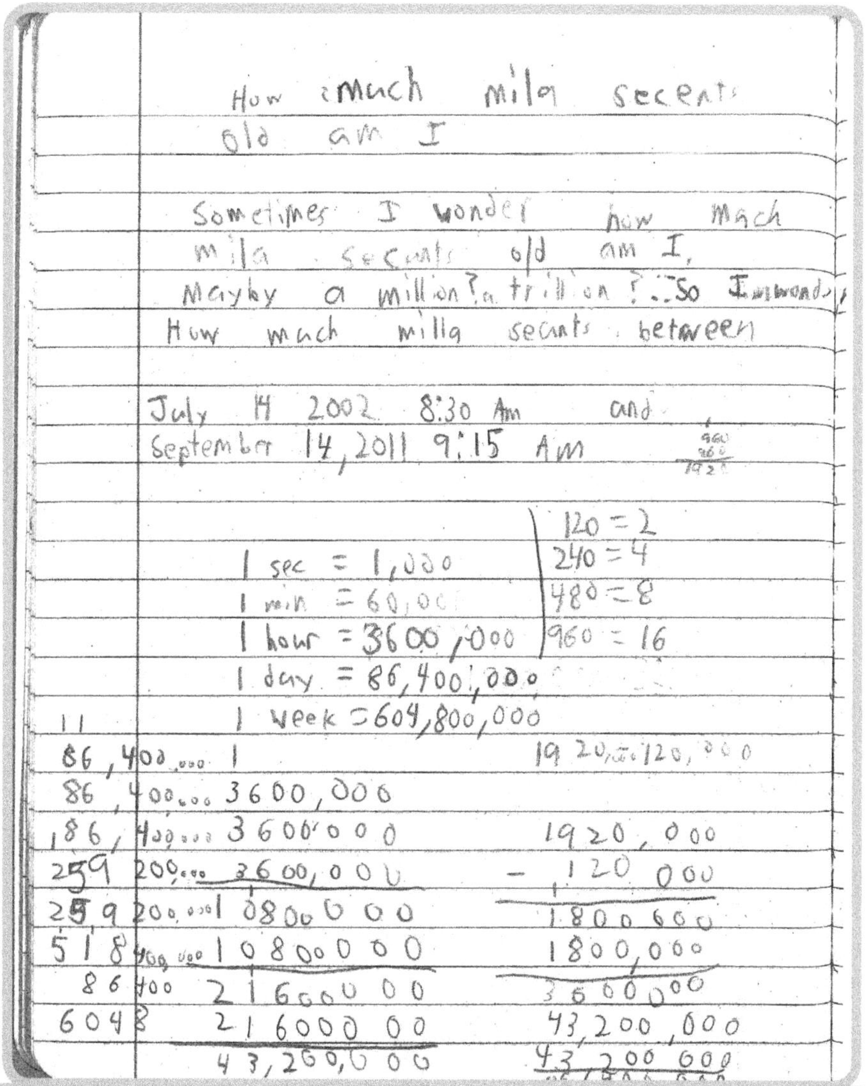

How much mila secents old am I

Sometimes I wonder how mach mila secants old am I, Mayby a million? a trillon? ...So I wonder How mach milla secants between

July 14 2002 8:30 Am and September 14, 2011 9:15 Am

1 sec = 1,000
1 min = 60,000
1 hour = 3600,000
1 day = 86,400,000
1 week = 604,800,000

120 = 2
240 = 4
480 = 8
960 = 16

FIGURE 16.2. Student writing: "How much [*sic*] mila secents [*sic*] old am I."

in math journals, through written examples of problem solving, and by completing projects while using a variety of tools to demonstrate their thinking. For Hull and colleagues, visible thinking is the key to mathematics success. We use all of the expressions of visible thinking as formative assessments and to guide instruction.

The following journal entry is an example of a student's reflection upon discovering the benefit of creating a diagram to solve a problem.

> First I think my groups diagram is good to represent 8 packages with 12 cards in each package. I think this is a diagram that doesn't have any normal math. It has math that you can actually do. I think this is information because you can figure it out real easily, not just figure it out and be done. You need to really think hard—the 8 big squares

represent the eight big packages. The 12 small lines represent the 12 baseball cards that are in the packages.

The journal entry provides evidence for the teacher to know that this student can now comfortably use diagrams to represent the situation and the problem-solving process. "Learning of mathematics is a long-term change in the acquisition and application of mathematical knowledge and skill as exhibited by both understanding and behavior" (Hull et al., 2011, p. 21).

As in any other learning process, we must explicitly teach students what we want them to be able to do and give them models of what good work looks like. Thinking ahead about what students would need for engaging in written explanations of their problem solving, Carole co-created a vocabulary flip chart with her students. It consisted of index cards bound together in a plastic spiral binder. It has a section for problem-solving process words, such as *first, next, then*, and *finally*; it then covers such terms as *to diagram, to model, to show, to represent, to stand for, figured out*. In some cases, they decided to divide the page into quadrants to accommodate related words:

To represent	To show
To model	To stand for

This gave the students a tool to make the expectation for the writing process very concrete and visible. Students kept the flip chart on their desk next to the paper on which they worked out each problem and wrote about their problem solving. As they wrote, they turned pages of the flip chart to remind themselves of the next step and words to go with it.

In another section of the chart, Carole entered other math content words to be used as needed (*perimeter, area, added, subtracted, multiplied, divided, sum, difference*, etc.). The flip chart was created over a period of time, during which Carole provided lots of support and practice, following Fisher and colleagues (2011) "five-part framework for intentional instruction" described earlier in this chapter. Thinking aloud, she modeled using the flip chart to keep track of and explain her thinking for solving a problem. She also explicitly taught the vocabulary for problem solving and reminded the students of the routine for math conversations. This tool made a world of difference in supporting students' understanding of how to write about their problem solving process and solutions. It is important to note that throughout the process of developing and using the chart, the language arts played a prominent role in supporting the development of students' mathematical understanding.

Meeting All Students' Needs

English Language Learners

Students who are English language learners (ELLs) must learn the same mathematics as their English-speaking peers. However, students who are ELLs also have to learn to think mathematically and develop problem-solving strategies in a second language. Coggins, Kravin, Coates, and Carroll (2007) state that in working with ELL students, "a new math concept that underlies a vocabulary word must be systematically built up through experiences, through activation of prior knowledge, and use of informal language. In addition, the formal vocabulary must be purposefully associated with the new concept and frequently practiced" (p. 26). Olivares (1996) suggests that ELL students use visualizing, drawing, manipulatives, and dramatizing as ways to represent what they think the problem is about. Carlo and colleagues (2004) recommend teaching multiple-meaning words and cognates so that students can infer meanings. Finally, the researchers recommend that teachers focus on many aspects of words, including spelling, pronunciation, morphology, syntax, and semantics.

The following example highlights how one teacher used observation and support to bring one of her ELLs into the math talk community. Carole Skalinder told her students that their essential learning for one lesson was to be able *to articulate their thinking* for applying their knowledge of addition facts to figuring out how to add numbers of higher magnitude. "You have to be able to do a 'think-aloud' for how to use little facts to help you figure out bigger ones."

In a preview of the lesson, she quickly posed the question: "Does anyone ever do this? . . . Use a fact such as 2 + 3 = 5 to figure out that 200 + 300 = 500?" Carole and the students briefly discussed this, and she recorded some of the words students used: "Figure out," "Think about," "Know." During math games, she conferred with Simon, an ELL student with very little English fluency. It was very early in the school year, and although he was well liked by his peers, he was not showing any signs of involvement in the math learning community. Thinking that he understood the concept for the lesson, Carole and Simon co-constructed the chart shown in Figure 16.3, using some of the words the class had come up with earlier. They used these simple phrases: "I know . . . " "So then I think. . . . " "So then I figured out . . . " Becoming more and more engrossed, Simon then drew the pictures of the base-10 blocks on the colored strips.

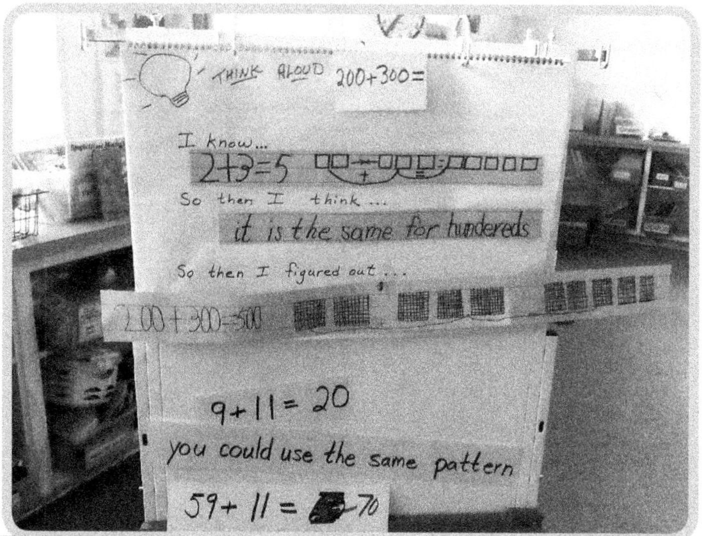

FIGURE 16.3. Photograph of an anchor chart co-constructed by a teacher and an ELL student.

In the next part of the lesson, Simon presented his chart to the class. With the teacher's help in the background, he read it aloud. Now the whole class had concrete help with the task of being able to do a "think-aloud" about the concept. The excitement in the room was electric, and Carole became sure it would stand as an important benchmark in the development of that year's community of learners. Simon became an expert to whom Carole sent "clients" who wanted help. One student decided to write the think-aloud words to help him focus and remember. Simon helped him. This think-aloud frame became a laminated chart to be used generally as a guide for many problem-solving think-alouds.

In this case, the framework for intentional instruction was adjusted to take advantage of a teachable moment that arose from time typically devoted to an activity designed for practice and talk. Carole's observation and subsequent conference with this ELL student provided the impetus for his inclusion in the math community of learners and helped build his confidence for participating in mathematics lessons.

Students with Learning Disabilities

As with ELLs, instruction that is effective with general education students is effective with students with disabilities (Graves & Silverman, 2011, p. 324). However, many of these students have language-based disabilities that make it difficult for them to process, retain, and transfer the information learned about words. Graves and Silverman (2011) suggest using interactive word-learning strategies such as semantic feature analysis, a process used to help students decide what features discriminate one word from another. Carole Skalinder used semantic feature analysis to help her third-grade students understand the different types of triangles (see Figure 16.4 for one student's analysis).

Shape	3 vertices	3 sides	2D	all sides same length	2 sides same	all sides difrent	right angle
Triangle	+	+	+	?	?	?	?
Equilateral triangle	+	+	+	+	−	−	−
isosceles triangle	+	+	+	−	+	−	−
Scalene triangle	+	+	+	−	−	+	?
right triangle	+	+	+				+

FIGURE 16.4. Semantic feature analysis.

In addition to explicit instruction and direct explanation for math-specific words, students with learning disabilities may benefit from using word sorts, word games, and well-designed computer-assisted instruction to practice learning and using the words. Finally, we recommend that teachers give these students more individualized instruction, and extra time and practice for learning new words and concepts.

Fast Finishers and Advanced Thinkers

Carole encourages her third-grade students who are ready for more advanced work to take on some of the responsibility for challenging themselves during group work by using their own curiosity and initiative. She doesn't just leave them to their own devices; she teaches them to look for patterns in their work, or helps them learn how to create similar problems with bigger numbers, negative numbers, fractions, or multiple steps. After meeting with small groups that need more support, Carole checks in with the "investigators," and their work becomes part of the ongoing conversation in the class. On an afternoon in early September, some of the "investigators" were involved in a variety of activities:

- Alex was practicing writing numbers in the Fibonacci sequence that Rebecca had taught him the day before (an extension of a lesson on number patterns and sequences). Significantly, his work in explaining the pattern to two more students provided an authentic context for much-needed practice in word choice and articulation of mathematics concepts.
- Jenny and Mia were are writing number riddles and reading them for others to solve.
- Thomas and Emily were racing to see who could count by ones to the biggest number on their calculators (an extension of a lesson on skip counting with the calculator).

To integrate literacy and mathematics, we suggest that teachers examine their curriculum to uncover the literacy demands within it and provide opportunities for students to use the language arts to support development of mathematical proficiency. Furthermore, to gain more time for addressing some of the literacy demands of mathematics, we have found that it is possible to use some of the language arts time to learn how to read math texts and to do shared writing of mathematics explanations. It is also possible to begin math class with a read-aloud, to use math concept books during guided and independent reading time, and to find time for journal writing of mathematics problem-solving strategies and math reflections.

LOOKING FORWARD

Research suggests that efforts directed toward the following practices will be beneficial in enhancing teachers' effectiveness and improving students' mathematical and literacy abilities:

- Use of an instructional framework to ensure that the necessary supports are available for students to learn mathematics (Fisher et al., 2011).
- Increased use of writing in mathematics classrooms to improve teaching and learning. (Newell, 2006; Wilcox & Monroe, 2011).
- Collaboration with literacy specialists to understand and use the practices and strategies that support the general comprehension of math texts, and to determine the specific strategies mathematicians use for close reading of math text (Draper & Siebert, 2009; Shanahan & Shanahan, 2008).
- Improved math discussions that move from the traditional practice of having students share their work at the end of a lesson, to a more selective process for sharing that pushes understanding of the math concept closer to the purpose for the lesson (Smith & Stein, 2011).
- Addition of children's literature and concept books to the math class, to increase opportunities for students to read mathematics in the real world and to capitalize on students' natural interest in the real world (NRC, 2001; Raymond, 1995).
- Academic vocabulary instruction in the context of reading, writing, and using mathematics language (Nagy & Townsend, 2012).

QUESTIONS FOR REFLECTION •

1. How am I using my mathematics class as a time to build a community of learners? Do my students . . .

   a. Feel safe to take risks?
   b. Understand errors as opportunities for thinking and learning more?
   c. Work collaboratively to solve problems, and at the same time use the vocabulary of mathematics?
   d. Have a voice in whole-class and small-group discussions?

2. What do I do to support ELLs and students with disabilities, to make sure that they can access the content and grow as learners?

3. How do I extend the thinking of my more able math students to make sure they are challenged by mathematics?

4. Does the lesson framework I use foster deep thinking and understanding of mathematics?

5. To what extent do I model and think aloud to help students understand the mathematics language, text, and process?

6. How do I evaluate the literature I am using as read-alouds in math class, to ensure that the time I spend doing this advances the students' mathematical thinking and includes the doing of mathematics?

7. How can I help students learn and remember the mathematics vocabulary?

8. How do I know whether the math talk is improving and helping more students demonstrate their thinking?

9. What kinds of writing opportunities currently exist in my math class? Do I use what I learn from students' writing to adjust instruction and to plan for differentiation?

10. Do I use visible thinking as ongoing formative assessment to determine what students currently understand about a topic, so that I can build on that understanding?

SUGGESTIONS FOR ONGOING PROFESSIONAL LEARNING ● ● ● ● ● ●

One way to improve student achievement in mathematics is to participate in ongoing professional development. According to research (NCTM, 2010), teachers can use analyses of student thinking and student work to refine their instructional practices and respond to students' needs. Participating in study groups or professional learning communities (PLCs) allows teachers to come together to expand content knowledge, to discover new ways for meeting students' needs, and to increase their expertise as mathematics teachers. The following outline presents an example of how a PLC might study a topic in this area.

Integrating Literacy and Mathematics to Improve Student Achievement in Mathematics

Session 1

Discuss this chapter (and Chapter 3 of this volume, by Taylor, on grouping) with your PLC to reflect on your own current practice for using the language arts as tools for improving student achievement in mathematics. You might, as a group, fill out a sheet with these headings: *Talk, Writing, Reading, Visible Thinking*. Reflecting on the math lessons from the past week, each member of the group might list the opportunities they provided under each heading. Then, together, discuss the opportunities provided for students to talk in whole-class and small-group settings, to write collaboratively and individually, and to think visibly about the mathematics learning. Discuss what went well, identify any challenges, and determine what might be needed to increase the opportunities for integration. In the process of doing this, you will probably also end up discussing how you plan instruction. Since teachers are sometimes uncomfortable doing think-alouds, discuss the value of doing them, and talk about when and how you model and think aloud for students. For the next few weeks, keep track of integration efforts and samples of think alouds.

Session 2

Bring the think-aloud notes and planning documents for integrating mathematics and literacy. Use the same chart as in Session 1 and, as a group, list the opportunities for integration. Discuss new additions along with success and challenges. Get ideas from your group about what you might change to enhance the integration while keeping the focus on the important math concepts. Next, as a group, make a list of the think-alouds everyone did. Again, discuss what went well and what was challenging. Some teachers in the group may ask to observe a teacher who is comfortable doing think-alouds. Arrange dates and times for observing each other. Everyone in the group should decide on a different area to try another think-aloud and keep notes for the next meeting.

Session 3

Bring your notes on the think-alouds and any additional opportunities for integration that you used since the previous meeting. Again, list the think-alouds, and this time everyone should take a few minutes to reflect in writing about their efforts to integrate literacy and mathematics. Discuss any changes in students' interest, active engagement, and/or use of talk during math class. In pairs, share your reflections. After a few minutes of sharing, you can discuss burning issues and seek ideas from your colleagues. This part of the session should only take about 15 minutes. For the rest of the time, discuss the think-alouds, and again look for support from colleagues for making think-alouds feel less improvisational and more like a regular practice in your class.

- If everyone is feeling more comfortable doing think-alouds, try having students do think-alouds in partnerships and/or in groups. Be sure that a safe classroom environment exists before doing this. Bring examples of your and your students' think-alouds to the next session. For the last 15 minutes, refer back to the integration chart and list the new ways that teachers integrated math and literacy.
- If some group members have not used literature in math class, this would be a good time to make it a focus for the next session. Everyone should bring a piece of literature or book that he or she used for problem solving, or one that seems to have potential for math problems.

Session 4

In groups of three, discuss the think-alouds used since the previous meeting. If teachers have examples of students' thinking aloud, include them in the discussion. Talk about the work involved in preparing students' for thinking aloud and the grouping strategy used: whole class, small groups, pairs, or triads. Again, discuss what worked well and what was challenging. Get suggestions from your colleagues for improving the use of think-alouds by students, and make notes of any changes you will make. Allow about half of the session time for group members to discuss the read-alouds and problems they used or want to use with the books. Try to evaluate the literature for both math and literary quality: For example, is the book's mathematics content correct and accurate? Is the book's mathematics content intellectually and developmentally appropriate for its audience? Does the plot exhibit good development, imagination, and continuity? Are the characters well developed? Everyone should try to use a children's book or excerpt from a book prior to the next session and keep notes on the book, how well it fit with the mathematics unit of study, and how the students responded to the book. Bring examples of the problems created and students' efforts to solve the problem. Again, note the grouping used for the literature and math integration.

Session 5

In groups of four, discuss the literature–math lesson and how it went. Examine student work from the lesson for engagement, problem rigor, and student problem-solving efforts. Note challenges, and seek support from colleagues for reducing the challenges. Consider what is a good balance in adding literature and keeping the pacing of the math program. Spend the next half of the session focused on the student think-alouds—what went well, what additional changes need to be made, and what the next steps should be. Perhaps the next session could be used to address challenges of providing for flexible grouping. Teachers should keep track of the various groupings used between this session and the next, noting the purpose of the grouping and where it fit into the lesson.

Session 6

After discussing the advantages and disadvantages of the various grouping strategies you and your colleagues have tried, and the literature–math lessons you have conducted, discuss how to provide more opportunities for students to work together to talk and write about mathematics. Some of you may want to try doing a shared writing of a problem explanation during writing time. Some may want to take a week from their regular writing workshop to do a math writing workshop where they can explore the various ways mathematicians write: explanations, reflections, quick writes to keep track of thinking, and journal entries for math words. Everyone should commit to trying writing for math and bring examples to the next session.

Other Possible PLC Topics

Future topics for PLCs might include going deeper with talk in the math class; choosing examples from student work to move the collective thinking of the class to the big ideas of the lesson; how to have a productive whole-class math discussion; and meeting the needs of struggling students and ELLs. This chapter provides many topics to choose for extended study.

RESEARCH-BASED RESOURCES

Altieri, J. (2010). *Literacy + math = creative connections in the elementary classroom*. Newark, DE: International Reading Association.

Fogelberg, E., Skalinder, C., Satz, P., Hiller, B., Bernstein, L., & Vitantonio, S. (2008). *Integrating literacy and math: Strategies for K–6 teachers*. New York: Guilford Press.

Hull, T., Balka, D., & Miles, R. (2011). *Visible thinking in the K–8 mathematics classroom*. Thousand Oaks, CA: Corwin Press.

Hyde, A. (2006). *Comprehending math: Adapting reading strategies to teach mathematics, K–6*. Portsmouth, NH: Heinemann.

Kenney, J., Hancewicz, E., Heuer, L., Metsisto, D., & Tuttle, C. (2005). *Literacy strategies for improving mathematics instruction*. Alexandria, VA: Association for Supervision and Curriculum Development.

Sammons, L. (2010). *Guided math*. Huntington Beach, CA: Shell Educational Publishing.

Smith, M. S., & Stein, K. S. (2011). *5 practices for orchestrating productive mathematics discussions*. Reston, VA: National Council of Teachers of Mathematics.

Van de Walle, J. (2007). *Elementary and middle school mathematics: Teaching developmentally* (6th ed.). Boston: Pearson/Allyn & Bacon.

Whitin, P., & Whitin, D. J. (2000). *Math is language too: Talking and writing in the mathematics classroom*. Urbana, IL: National Council of Teachers of English.

Professional Journals

The International Reading Association publishes *The Reading Teacher* and the *Journal of Adolescent and Adult Literacy eight times each year*. For more information, go to *www.reading.org*.

The National Council of Teachers of Mathematics publishes *Teaching Children Mathematics* and *Mathematics Teaching in the Middle School* ten times each year. For more information, go to *www.nctm.org*.

Language Arts, a journal for elementary teachers, is published six times a year, and *Voices from the Middle*, a journal for middle school teachers, is published quarterly. The National Council of Teachers of English publishes both. For more information, go to *www.ncte.org*.

Websites

Read–Write–Think (*www.readwritethink.org*) is a nonprofit Thinkfinity website maintained by the International Reading Association and the National Council of Teachers of English). It provides free lesson plans, interactive student materials, and Web-based resources for teachers.

REFERENCES

Bamford, R., & Kristo, J. (1998). *Making facts come alive: Choosing quality nonfiction literature K–8*. Norwood, MA: Christopher Gordon.

Bangert-Drowns, R., Hurley, M., & Wilkinson, B. (2004). The effects of school-based writing-to-learn interventions on academic achievement: A meta-analysis. *Review of Educational Research, 74*(1), 29–58.

Barnett-Clarke, C., & Ramirez, A. (2004). Language pitfalls and pathways to mathematics. In R. Rubenstein & G. Bright (Eds.), *Perspectives on the teaching of mathematics: Sixty-sixth yearbook* (pp. 56–66). Reston, VA: National Council of Teachers of Mathematics.

Barton, M., Heidema, C., & Jordan, D. (2002). Teaching reading in mathematics and science. *Educational Leadership, 50*(3), 24–28.

Baumann, J., & Graves, M. (2010). What is academic vocabulary? *Journal of Adolescent and Adult Literacy, 54*(1), 4–12.

Beck, I., McKeown, M., & Kucan, L. (2002). *Bringing words to life*. New York: Guilford Press.

Bintz, W., & Moore, S. (2010–2011). What children taught us about rigor. *Teaching Children Mathematics, 17*(5), 288–298.

Blachowicz, C., & Fisher, P. (2010). *Teaching vocabulary in all classrooms* (4th ed.). Boston: Pearson/Allyn & Bacon.

Blachowicz, C., & Ogle, D. (2008). *Reading comprehension: Strategies for independent learners* (2nd ed.). New York: Guilford Press.

Blachowicz, C. L. Z., & Fisher, P. (2000). Vocabulary instruction. In M. L. Kamil, P. B. Mosenthal, P. D. Pearson, & R. Barr (Eds.), *Handbook of reading research* (Vol. 3, pp. 503–523). Mahwah, NJ: Erlbaum.

Bosse, M. J., & Faulconer, J. (2008). Learning and assessing mathematics through reading and writing. *School Science and Mathematics, 108*(1), 8–19.

Bresser, R. (2004). *Math and literature, grades 4–6*. Sausalito, CA: Math Solutions.

Buehl, D. (2011). *Developing readers in the academic disciplines*. Newark, DE: International Reading Association.

Buerger, J. R. (1997). *A study of the effect of exploratory writing activities on student success in mathematical problem solving*. Unpublished doctoral dissertation, Columbia University.

Bulgren, J., Deshler, D. D., & Lenz, B. K. (2007). Engaging adolescents with LD in higher order thinking about history concepts using integrated content enhancement routines. *Journal of Learning Disabilities, 40*(2), 121–133.

Calkins, L. (2000). *The art of teaching reading.* Boston: Allyn & Bacon.

Carlo, M. S., August, D., McLaughlin, B., Snow, C. E., Dressler, C., Lippman, D. N., et al. (2004). Closing the gap: Addressing the vocabulary needs of English-language learners in bilingual and mainstream classes. *Reading Research Quarterly, 39,* 188–215.

Coggins, D., Kravin, D., Coates, G., & Carroll, M. (2007). *English language learners in the mathematics classroom.* Thousand Oaks, CA: Corwin Press.

Columbia, L., Kim, C., Moe, A., & Wincek, J. (2009). *The power of picture books in teaching math, science, and social studies: PreK–6.* Scottsdale, AZ: Holcomb Hathaway.

Draper, R., & Siebert, D. (2009). Content area literacy in mathematics and science classrooms. In S. Parris, D. Fisher, & K. Headley (Eds.), *Adolescent literacy, field tested: Effective solutions for every classroom* (pp. 105–116). Newark, DE: International Reading Association.

Draper, S. (2008). Refining content-area literacy teacher education: Finding my voice through collaboration. *Harvard Educational Review, 78*(1), 40–59.

Duke, N., Pearson, P. D., Strachan, S., & Billman, A. (2011). Essential elements of fostering and teaching reading comprehension. In S. J. Samuels & A. E. Farstrup (Eds.), *What research has to say about reading instruction* (4th ed., pp. 51–93). Newark, DE: International Reading Association.

Fisher, D., & Frey, N. (2008). *Better learning through structured teaching: A framework for the gradual release of responsibility.* Alexandria, VA: Association for Supervision and Curriculum Development.

Fisher, D., & Frey, N. (2011). Best practices in content-area literacy. In L. Morrow & L. Gambrell (Eds.), *Best practices in literacy instruction* (4th ed., pp. 343–360). New York: Guilford Press.

Fisher, D., Frey, N., & Anderson, H. (2010). Thinking and comprehending in the mathematics classroom. In K. Ganske & D. Fisher (Eds.), *Comprehension across the curriculum: Perspectives and practices K–12* (pp. 146–159). New York: Guilford Press.

Fisher, D., Frey, N., & Lapp, D. (2011). What the research says about intentional instruction. In S. J. Samuels & A. E. Farstrup (Eds.), *What research has to say about reading instruction* (4th ed., pp. 359–378). Newark, DE: International Reading Association.

Frey, N., & Fisher, D. (2009). *Learning words inside and out: Vocabulary instruction that boosts achievement in all subject areas.* Portsmouth, NH: Heinemann.

Frey, N., Fisher, D., & Everlove, S. (2009). *Productive group work: How to engage students, build teamwork, and promote understanding.* Alexandria, VA: Association for Supervision and Curriculum Development.

Giles, C. (2010). Making the most of talk. *Voices from the Middle, 18*(2), 9–15.

Graham, S., & Perrin, D. (2007). *Writing next: Effective strategies to improve writing of adolescents in middle and high school. A report to Carnegie Corporation of New York.* Washington, DC: Alliance for Excellent Education.

Graves, D. (1983). *Writing: Teachers and children at work.* Portsmouth, NH: Heinemann.

Graves, M., & Silverman, R. (2011). Interventions to enhance vocabulary development. In A. McGill-Franzen & R. L. Allington (Eds.), *Handbook of reading disability research* (pp. 315–328). New York: Routledge.

Graves, M. F. (2006). *The vocabulary book: Learning and instruction.* New York: Teachers College.

Guthrie, J. T., McRae, A., & Klauda, S. L. (2007). Contributions of Concept-Oriented Reading Instruction to knowledge about interventions for motivations in reading. *Educational Psychologist, 42,* 237–250.

Heuer, L. (2005). Graphic representation in the mathematics classroom. In J. Kenney, E.

Hancewicz, L. Heuer, D. Metsisto, & C. Tuttle, *Literacy strategies for improving mathematics instruction* (pp. 51–71). Alexandria, VA: Association for Supervision and Curriculum Development.

Hufferd-Ackles, K., Fuson, K., & Sherin, M. (2004). Describing levels and components of a math-talk learning community. *Journal for Research in Mathematics Education, 35*, 81–116.

Hull, T., Balka, D., & Miles, R. (2011). *Visible thinking in the K–8 mathematics classroom*. Thousand Oaks, CA: Corwin Press.

Hunsader, P. (2004). Mathematics trade books: Establishing their value and assessing their quality. *The Reading Teacher, 57*(7), 618–629.

Hyde, A. (2006). *Comprehending math: Adapting reading strategies to teach mathematics, K–6*. Portsmouth, NH: Heinemann.

Jennings, C. M. (1992). Increasing interest and achievement in mathematics through children's literature. *Early Childhood Research Quarterly, 7*(2), 263–276.

Johnston, P. (2004). *Choice words*. Portland, ME: Stenhouse.

Kenney, J. (2005). Mathematics as language. In J. Kenney, E. Hancewicz, L. Heuer, D. Metsisto, & C. Tuttle, *Literacy strategies for improving mathematics instruction* (pp. 1–8). Alexandria, VA: Association for Supervision and Curriculum Development.

Kenney, J., Hancewicz, E., Heuer, L., Metsisto, D., & Tuttle, C. (2005). *Literacy strategies for improving mathematics instruction*. Alexandria, VA: Association for Supervision and Curriculum Development.

Khalsa, D. K. (1989). *How pizza came to Queens*. New York: Clarkson N. Potter.

Marzano, R., & Pickering, D. (2005). *Building academic vocabulary: Teacher's manual*. Alexandria, VA: Association for Supervision and Curriculum Development.

Moje, E. B. (2008). Foregrounding the disciplines in secondary literacy teaching and learning: A call for change. *Journal of Adolescent and Adult Literacy, 52*(2), 96–107.

Moje, E. B., Peek-Brown, D., Sutherland, L. M., Marx, R. W., Blumenfield, P., & Krajcik, J. (2004). Explaining explanations: Developing scientific literacy in middle-school project-based science reforms. In D. Strickland & D. E. Alverman (Eds.), *Bridging the gap: Improving literacy learning for preadolescent and adolescent learners in grades 4–12* (pp. 227–251). New York: Carnegie Corporation.

Moje, E. B., Stockdill, D., Kim, K., & Kim, H. (2011). The role of text in disciplinary learning. In M. Kamil, P. D. Pearson, E. Moje, & P. Afflerbach (Eds.), *Handbook of reading research* (Vol. 4, pp. 453–487). New York: Routledge.

Moyer, P. (2001). Using representations to explore perimeter and area. *Teaching Children Mathematics, 8*(1), 52–59.

Murray, M. (2004). *Teaching mathematics vocabulary in context*. Portsmouth, NH: Heinemann.

Nagy, W., & Townsend, D. (2012). Words as tools: Learning academic vocabulary as language acquisition. *Reading Research Quarterly, 47*(1), 91–108.

National Council of Teachers of Mathematics (NCTM). (2000). *Principles and standards for school mathematics*. Reston, VA: Author.

National Council of Teachers of Mathematics (NCTM). (2010). *Mathematics professional development* (Professional Development Research Brief). Reston, VA: Author. Available at *www.nctm.org*.

National Governors Association Center for Best Practices & Council of Chief State School Officers. (2010). *Common Core State Standards*. Washington, DC: Authors. Retrieved from *www.corestandards.org*.

National Research Council (NRC). (2001). *Adding it up: Helping children learn mathematics*. Washington, DC: National Academy Press.

Newell, G. E. (2006). Writing to learn: How alternative theories of school writing account for student performance. In C. MacArthur, S. Graham, & J. Fitzgerald (Eds.), *Handbook of writing research* (pp. 235–247). New York: Guilford Press.

Nguyen, J. (2006). *Comparing sizes and weights*. Washington, DC: National Geographic Society.

Ogle, D. (1992). Problem-solving and language arts instruction. In C. Collins & J. N. Mangieri (Eds.), *Teaching thinking: An agenda for the twenty-first century* (pp. 28–39). Hillsdale, NJ: Erlbaum.

Olivares, R. (1996). Communication in mathematics for students with limited English proficiency. In P. C. Elliot & M. J. Kenny (Eds.), *Communication in mathematics, K–12 and beyond* (pp. 219–230). Reston, VA: National Council of Teachers of Mathematics.

Pape, S. (2004). Middle school children's problem-solving behavior: A cognitive analysis from a reading comprehension perspective. *Journal for Research in Mathematics Education, 35*(3), 187–219.

Pearson, P. D., & Gallagher, M. C. (1983). The instruction of reading comprehension. *Contemporary Educational Psychology, 8*(3), 317–344.

Pierce, M., & Fontaine, L. (2009). Designing vocabulary instruction in mathematics. *The Reading Teacher, 63*(3), 239–243.

Pressley, M. (2006). *Reading instruction that works: The case for balanced teaching* (3rd ed.). New York: Guilford Press.

Pullen, R. (2004). *Which is the tallest?* Washington, DC: National Geographic Society.

Raymond, A. M. (1995). Engaging young children in mathematical problem solving: Providing a context with children's literature. *Contemporary Education, 66*, 172–174.

Reutzel, D. R., Smith, J. A., & Fawson, P. C. (2005). An evaluation of two approaches for teaching reading comprehension strategies in the primary years using science information texts. *Early Childhood Research Quarterly, 20*(3), 276–305.

Schielack, J., & Chancellor, D. (2010). *Mathematics in focus, K–6: How to help students understand big ideas and make critical connections*. Portsmouth, NH: Heinemann.

Shanahan, T. (2004). Overcoming the dominance of communication: Writing to think and learn. In T. Jetton & J. Dole (Eds.), *Adolescent literacy research and practice* (pp. 59–74). New York: Guilford Press.

Shanahan, T., & Shanahan, C. (2008). Teaching disciplinary literacy to adolescents: Rethinking content-area literacy. *Harvard Educational Review, 78*(1), 40–59.

Short, D. J., & Fitzsimmons, S. (2007). *Double the work: Challenges and solutions to acquiring language and academic literacy for adolescent English language learners: A report to the Carnegie Corporation of New York*. Washington, DC: Alliance for Excellent Education.

Smith, M. S., & Stein, K. S. (2011). *5 practices for orchestrating productive mathematics discussions*. Reston, VA: National Council of Teachers of Mathematics.

Van Allsburg, C. (1981). *Jumanji*. Boston: Houghton Mifflin.

Van de Walle, J. (2007). *Elementary and middle school mathematics: Teaching developmentally* (6th ed.). Boston: Pearson/Allyn & Bacon.

Wallace, F., & Clark, K. (2005). Reading stances in mathematics: Positioning students and texts. *Action in Teacher Education, 27*(2), 68–79.

Whitin, D., & Wilde, S. (1992). *Read any good math lately?: Children's books for mathematical learning, K–6*. Portsmouth, NH: Heinemann.

Whitin, P., & Whitin, D. J. (2000). *Math is language too: Talking and writing in the mathematics classroom*. Urbana, IL: National Council of Teachers of English.

Wilcox, B., & Monroe, E. (2011). Integrating writing and mathematics. *The Reading Teacher, 64*(7), 521–529.

Zwiers, J. (2008). *Building academic language: Essentials for the content classroom*. San Francisco: Jossey-Bass.

CHAPTER 17

Integration of Literacy and the Arts ● ● ● ● ● ● ● ● ● ● ● ● ● ● ● ● ● ●
Creating Classrooms That Perform

DOUGLAS FISHER
NAN L. MCDONALD
NANCY FREY

There is a great deal of pressure to improve student achievement in the area of literacy. Efforts have focused on high-quality instruction and intervention, appropriate instructional materials, and professional development and coaching for teachers (Fisher & Frey, 2007; Taylor, 2011). In some cases, this has resulted in the elimination of, or significant reduction in, instructional time devoted to science, social studies, and arts education (Burroughs, Groce, & Webeck, 2005; Lewis, 2008), despite the evidence that learning content has a reciprocal relationship with learning to read and write (e.g., Guthrie et al., 2009).

Other chapters in this volume have focused on the ways in which science (see Cervetti, Chapter 14) and social studies (see Halvorsen, Alleman, & Brugar, Chapter 15) can be taught so that literacy improvement occurs simultaneously with content learning. This chapter focuses on the role that the arts can play in literacy learning. Importantly, integration of the arts within the general curriculum does *not* take the place of specialized sequential instruction in each of the arts—an education each student deserves. But students benefit not only from receiving a high-quality arts education, but from applying these essential visual and performing arts concepts to their learning across the day.

The inclusion of integrated arts within classroom literacy instruction has been shown to be a valuable and highly memorable way for our students to learn and achieve (Hetland & Winner, 2000; McDonald, 2010; McDonald & Fisher, 2006). When engaged in arts-based activities, students learn by doing and creating. Furthermore, "hands-on and minds-on activities with and through the arts allow students to explore content in new ways" (McDonald & Fisher, 2006, p. 6). Active engagement in arts activities can increase important literacy skills because students read, write, speak, and listen as they participate in the arts, and the arts themselves encourage new types of literacy to emerge (Armstrong, 2003; Jensen, 2005).

THE ARTS DEFINED

As a starting place, we need to take a brief look at the content of each of the four arts and consider the kinds of activities students can do in each. The four arts—music, visual arts, theatre, and dance—each contribute to students' experiences in school, and potentially their literacy learning.

Music

Within musical contexts, students can learn to do many things. They can sing, play instruments, perform, improvise, and compose music; read and notate music; listen to, analyze, describe, and evaluate music; and understand the relationships between and among music, the other arts, and disciplines outside the arts. They can also learn to understand music in relation to history and culture (Music Educators National Conference [MENC], 1994). For a practical classroom teacher–created list of specific activities students can do involving music connected to literacy instruction, see the "Activities Students Can Do in the Four Arts" box.

Visual Arts

Within the visual arts, students learn about art through understanding and applying media techniques and processes; using knowledge of structures and functions; choosing and evaluating a range of subject matter, symbols, and ideas; understanding the visual arts in relation to history and cultures; reflecting upon and assessing the characteristics of their work and the work of others; making connections between the visual arts and other disciplines (MENC, 1994). Again, see the "Activities . . . " box.

Theatre

Within the contexts of the art of theatre, our students learn in a variety of ways: script writing and recording improvisations based on personal experiences, heritage, imagination, literature, and history; acting by assuming roles and interacting in improvisations; designing by visualizing and arranging environments for classroom dramatizations; directing by planning classroom dramatizations; researching by finding information to support classroom dramatizations; comparing and connecting art forms by describing theatre, dramatic media (such as film, television, and electronic media, and other forms); analyzing and explaining personal preferences and constructing meanings from

Activities Students Can Do in the Four Arts

Drama	Art	Music	Dance
Reader's theatre	Found art	Songs	Movement response
Role playing	Painting	Instruments	Pantomime
Pantomime	Sketching	Chants/raps	Movement to poetry
Puppets	Crayons	Listening to music	Movement to ideas
Masks and	Paper-mâché	Poetry and music	Keeping a beat
characters	Clay/sculpture	Rhythmic response	Movement to words
Scriptwriting	Scratch art	Found instruments	Games
Finger plays	photography	composing	moving with props
Action to words	Textiles	History of music	Nonverbal
Scenery design	Artist study	Writing song lyrics	communication
Lighting design	Torn paper art	Music of the world	Body percussion
Sets and costumes	Mosaics	Symbols of music	Dances of the world
Tableaux of scenes	Pastels/chalk	Reading music	Dances of different
Creative drama	Charcoal	Studying composers	eras
games	Water color	Styles of music	Popular dances
	Pottery	Science of sound	Created dances
	Crafts	Environmental sounds	Gestures—no words
	Jewelry	Sound effects	Movement tableaux
	Tie-dye	Music and mood	
	Print making	Musical theatre	
	Stamp art	Performing music	
	Vegetable stamps	Writing about music	
	Murals	Writing about	
	Stencil art	musicians	
	Fashion		
	History of art		
	Art of many cultures		
	Computer art		
	Writing about art		
	Studying artists' styles, lives		
	Science of color		
	Dioramas		

From McDonald and Fisher (2006, p. 3). Copyright 2006 by The Guilford Press. Reprinted by permission.

classroom dramatizations and from theatre, film, television, and electronic media productions; and understanding context by recognizing the role of theatre, film, television, and electronic media in daily life (MENC, 1994). Once again, see the "Activities . . . " box.

Dance

Through the art of dance, students can do the following: learn about and demonstrate movement elements and skills as they perform dance; understand choreography; understand dance as a way to create and communicate meaning; apply and demonstrate critical and creative thinking skills in dance; demonstrate and understand dance in various cultures and historical periods; make connections between dance and healthful living; and make connections between dance and other disciplines (MENC, 1994). Once more, see the "Activities . . . " box.

OVERVIEW OF RESEARCH

The preceding section has focused on the four arts and how they can be implemented in the classroom. But this chapter is focused on the impact that the arts can have on literacy learning. In this section, we turn our attention to some common areas of instructional attention in literacy for elementary teachers, and we synthesize a number of studies suggesting that the arts have an impact on student learning. Table 17.1 contains examples of studies for several areas of instructional attention. We define each of these instructional areas and provide examples of the types of arts that may improve achievement.

Oral Language Development

Often considered the most basic literacy skills, listening and speaking are the bases from which teachers build students' reading, writing, and thinking. Over time, young children move from babbling and cooing, to saying individual words, to combining words in sentences, to speaking in front of their peers. The interaction between speaking and listening should be fairly obvious, so suffice it to say that classroom time should be devoted to these skills on a regular basis. Students actively use oral language, of

TABLE 17.1. Studies about Integrated Arts and Literacy

Literacy component	Citations
Oral language development	Fisher (2001); Fisher & McDonald (2004); Gilles, Andre, Dye, & Pfannenstiel (1998); Grant, Hutchinson, Hornsby, & Brooke (2008); McDonald & Fisher (2002); Podlozny (2000); Smith (2000); Souto-Manning & James (2008)
Concepts about print	Fisher & McDonald (2001); Fisher, McDonald, & Strickland (2001)
Sense of story and text structure	Fisher (2001); Foye & Lacroix (1998); McDonald & Fisher (1999); McDonald, Fisher, & Helzer (2002)
Phonemic awareness and phonics	Fisher (2001); Fisher & McDonald (2001); Fisher et al. (2001); Gromko (2005); Smith (2000); Yopp & Yopp (1997)
Background knowledge and vocabulary	Duncan et al. (2010); Fisher (2001); Fisher & McDonald (2004); Foye & Lacroix (1998); Gilles et al. (1998); McDonald & Fisher (1999); McDonald, Fisher, & Helzer (2002); Medina (1993); Souto-Manning & James (2008)
Fluency	Fisher & McDonald (2001); Gromko (2005); Register (2004); Smith (2000)
Comprehension	Burger & Winner (2000); Butzlaff (2000); Cosenza (2006); Gilles et al. (1998); McDonald et al. (2002)
Writing	Logue, Robie, Brown, & Waite (2009); McDonald & Fisher (1999); Oken-Wright (1998); Shaw (2008)

course, every time they sing the words to a song. Furthermore, a child's personal confidence in using language is increased by his or her participation in the overall sound of group singing. Shy students will participate without the fear of being singled out. Much learning transpires as new words are learned and used through speaking and singing (Smith, 2000). Similarly, oral language is developed as students perform dramas that they have created or read (Podlozny, 2000). They are also provided practice with oral language development when they describe what they see visually while viewing and analyzing a painting or statue (Souto-Manning & James, 2008).

Concepts about Print

One of the early predictors of reading success for young children is their understanding of the ways in which print functions (e.g., Reutzel, Fawson, Young, Morrison, & Wilcox, 2003). This construct, known as *concepts about print* (e.g., Clay, 1985) includes the knowledge that print, not pictures, contains the message; the way to hold a book; the difference between upper- and lowercase letters; left-to-right print orientation; top-to-bottom directionality; and the use of punctuation marks (see Johnson & Kuhn, Chapter 8, this volume). Music is an excellent way to explore concepts of print. For example, when teachers use Big Books or large charts with songs, chants, or poetry written on them, they can physically point to and model the left-to-right, top-to-bottom orientation and directionality that characterize the English language (Fisher & McDonald, 2001). Similarly, as teachers encourage students to follow along with the song text in their music books, students simultaneously hear the words and see them on paper. As students listen and sing, they begin to realize that the print contains meaning, and that there are similarities within the print and the meaning. Movement can also be used to reinforce concepts about print. Students can become better observers of subtle differences in print through participation in movement games, such as mirroring hand gestures, creating letters with their bodies, or walking sentences in which they pause between words.

Sense of Story and Text Structures

Another important task for early readers is to discern the sense of story contained in narrative texts and structures used in informational texts. The earliest stories that children are likely to encounter are oral traditions and read-alouds. Understanding how stories work (in terms of their structure) "provides an inner model of the rhythms and patterns of written language" (Yaden, Smolkin, & Conlon, 1989, p. 208). As children begin to master the sense of story, more complex series of events are introduced. Of course, children also read informational texts that contain information about the biological, physical, and social world. They need to understand the difference between narrative and informational texts, and the arts can provide a route for students to master these differences (Fisher & McDonald, 2000). Theatre and dance are ideal ways for students to practice with story and informational sequences (Foye & Lacroix, 1998). Instructional routines such as readers' theatre provide students with practice in analyzing the structure of a text (narrative or informational) as they create their performances. Furthermore, students can focus on text structures when they have a lot of practice with sequencing visual arts information. Music also contributes to students' understanding of stories and text structures. Songs that students learn each have a story to tell, and teachers who integrate their curriculum enjoy building on this knowledge. In addition, several songs specifically address sequences. For example, the song "I Had an Old Coat" tells the story of a ragged old coat that gradually wears out and is made smaller and smaller into a jacket, a shirt, a vest, a tie, a patch, a button. Finally, when nothing is left of the old coat, the singer simply makes up a song.

Phonemic Awareness and Phonics

As explained by Johnson and Kuhn in Chapter 8, phonemic awareness is believed to be a necessary precursor to reading (Adams, 1998) and, along with instruction in letter–sound knowledge, is an important component of a balanced early literacy program. Chants and songs are great ways to practice phonemic awareness and phonics (Smith, 2000). Several resource books provide teachers with examples that they can use to develop this skill (e.g., Blevins, 1999; Yopp & Yopp, 1997). For example, the song "Rags" (Blevins, 1999, p. 8) reinforces the idea that words that sound the same are often spelled the same:

Rags

I have a dog and his name is Rags.
He eats so much that his tummy sags.
His ears flip-flop,
And his tail wig-wags,
And when he walks,
He goes zig-zag.

In addition, word play during theatre can serve to reinforce students' phonemic awareness, while symbol systems and illustrations can reinforce students' phonics knowledge.

Background Knowledge and Vocabulary

Background knowledge and vocabulary are necessary for later reading and writing experiences. As Rosenblatt (1995) notes, readers bring a great deal of history to the text as they read. This transaction between the readers and the text is highly dependent on what the readers already know. Classroom teachers often use thematic and interdisciplinary instruction to tie their lessons together, build, and build upon background knowledge. Once attention is focused on the importance of vocabulary through professional development, classroom teachers provide vocabulary lessons that are integrated into their thematic lessons (Hairrell, Simmons, Rupley, & Vaughn, 2011). As discussed by Kucan in Chapter 11, there are many effective strategies for building vocabulary knowledge. One is the use of song (Medina, 1993). As Gilles, Andre, Dye, and Pfannenstiel (1998) point out, students acquire new vocabulary and are introduced to fresh content each time they sing a song. For example, in the delightful story song "The Crocodile," some students may not be familiar with the song text's words, phrases, and concepts, such as "crocodile," "tame as tame can be," "down the Nile," and "bade them all goodbye." In his book *Building Background Knowledge for Academic Achievement: Research on What Works in Schools*, Robert Marzano (2004) argues that our building of background and vocabulary knowledge is based in part on the number and quality of our academically oriented experiences. This is a profound statement. We know that background knowledge and vocabulary are critical for reading comprehension and are directly linked with student achievement. As such, teachers must ensure that students have multiple high-quality interactions with academic information. The arts are ways to provide students with these multiple interaction opportunities. For example, after reading a piece of text, students who create a visual image of the information are more likely to remember it (Soundy & Drucker, 2010). Likewise, when songs, visual arts, performances, and texts are combined, students develop a stronger connection with the material, are more likely to remember it, and will probably have a deeper understanding because of the varied ways that the information was presented and received (Burnaford, Brown, Doherty, & McLaughlin, 2007).

Fluency

Development of reading *fluency*—the ability to read words automatically at an appropriate pace, with appropriate inflection, tone, and voice (Rasinski, 2010)—can also be supported by arts education. Fluency requires students to understand and interpret text, to make connections between the text and their background, and to analyze critical aspects of the text. Teachers can easily incorporate musical activities to provide opportunities  for increasing reading fluency (Gromko, 2005). They can also provide students with dramatic experiences that build an often-neglected aspect of fluency: *prosody*. Prosody relates to the rhythm, stress, and intonation rather than just the speed of reading. The arts provide students with multiple opportunities to practice reading fluently, reading quickly enough for the task at hand, and reading with appropriate prosody. For example, readers' theatre provides students with an opportunity to develop their fluency in anticipation of presenting to their peers (Young & Rasinski, 2009). (Fluency development is covered in greater detail by Johnson and Kuhn in Chapter 8.)

Comprehension

When it comes down to it, what is reading for? We don't read to be able to decode or to see how fast we can process the words. We read to understand, learn, think, evaluate, and enjoy ideas. We call this process *comprehension*. Although it sounds easy, teaching comprehension and modeling comprehension strategies are complex and extremely important. Students need regular instruction in comprehension, and they need teacher modeling so that they can adopt the strategies that good readers use as they read texts, such as questioning, summarizing, visualizing, inferring, predicting, clarifying, and so on. In the language of the Common Core State Standards, we need to teach students to "read like detectives" so that they uncover the information found in texts (Fisher, Frey, & Lapp, 2012). The comprehension strategies listed above can all be reinforced through the arts. In fact, students are often introduced to comprehension strategy instruction while looking at visual art, so that they can notice their questions, inferences, and questions. Similarly, while listening to a song, students can visualize the words and practice that aspect of comprehension. Of course, as in all other aspects of literacy instruction, it's not sufficient to use the arts alone to teach literacy. Rather, there is evidence that integrated arts improves comprehension and keeps students paying attention (e.g., Soundy & Drucker, 2010). As texts become more difficult and information is presented in ways that challenge students thinking and reading skills, teachers can use drama to help students understand. (For more on comprehension strategies instruction, see Stahl, Chapter 9.)

Writing

Writing activities cannot be separated from reading activities, as writing instruction is a necessary companion to reading instruction. To become literate, children need systematic instruction in both reading and writing. There are a number of ways in which teachers can and do contribute to early writing instruction for students through the arts. (Writing development and instruction are covered in greater detail by Troia in Chapter 12.) For example, a teacher might use the chant "Miss White Had Fright." After students clap and speak the chant together, they can write replacement lines for the third line of the chant. The following sentence frames could be provided for students to write a new text line for the chant: "Saw a _____ on a _____" or "Saw a _____ in a _____" or "Saw a _____ with a _____." Further integration could be accomplished if students are provided an opportunity to perform their new chants adding their own ideas and creative movements. They could also write out and illustrate their new verses and create a class book entitled "Miss White's Frightful Night."

SUMMARY OF BIG IDEAS FROM RESEARCH

- The components of literacy, such as phonemic awareness, phonics, fluency, vocabulary, comprehension, oral language development, and writing, can be addressed with and through the arts. In other words, the arts complement high-quality literacy instruction.
- When students participate in a wide range of integrated arts activities—including readers' theatre; dramatic interpretations of text, characters, and storyline; group performances; songs and chants; creative movement to poetic text; illustrations of storylines and events in text; and visual art projects and displays linked to original student writing—their literacy skills are developed and reinforced.
- When students are involved in active synthesis and transference of content information through the arts, their knowledge and understanding is strengthened (McDonald, 2010).
- Learning with and through arts infusion enlivens literacy instruction, increases student involvement, and deepens both the meaning and memory of the content learning at hand.

EXAMPLES OF EFFECTIVE PRACTICES

This section provides descriptions of three lessons that have been created, planned, taught, and evaluated by real classroom teachers in high-poverty urban schools, who reflect on the results in their own words. As such, the needs of struggling readers, English language learners (ELLs), and students with disabilities are a part of the planning and implementation process for each of these teachers. These teacher contributors teach within Title I school sites in both Northern and Southern California. Our contributors are not arts specialists, and they acknowledge that their arts infusion activities cannot and do not take the place of specialized instruction and processes specific to each of the arts. Their overriding goal in these lessons is to utilize the creative avenues the arts provide to increase participation and memory of the literacy learning at hand.

How to Read and Dramatize a Poem: Using Theatre in Second Grade

The first lesson focuses on the development of poetry comprehension through the use of theatre techniques. Developed by Nan McDonald and Joanne Orlando of the San Mateo/Foster City (California) School District, the students use pantomime and tableaux to embody the meaning of a poem. As described in detail below, the purpose of this lesson is to connect these outward demonstrations to the use of mental images during reading.

Literacy Skills Focus

- Oral language development, background knowledge and vocabulary, comprehension, fluency, sense of story/sequence, phonemic awareness (rhyming words).

How Arts Are Infused into This Lesson

- Pantomime (wordless action) as a means of retelling the story of a poem.
- Tableau (still characterization/action) as a means of retelling the story of a poem.
- Visual images in video and photographs that retell the story of a poem.
- Use of a camera to capture scenes and to retell and remember the story and the actions created for it.

Ideas Students Need to Know

- Poetry has rhythm.
- Poetry can tell a story.
- A *pantomime* and a *tableau* are different ways of acting something out (with and without movement).
- Using pantomime can help with the comprehension of a poem.
- We form mental images as we read to understand.

Materials and Resources

- Mary Hoberman's poem "Sick Days" (1991, p. 13), written on chart paper.
- Props that suit the poem "Sick Days."
- Digital camera, computer, and data projector.

Teaching Procedure

DAY 1: READING A POEM WITH YOUR MIND, VOICE, AND BODY

Discuss how poems are best understood—especially that poems are meant to be recited aloud, that lines and punctuation tell us when to speed up or slow down, and that listening is an important part of experiencing a poem together. These help us to make pictures in our own minds as we read. In addition, remind students that we reread poems to gain a fuller meaning of the poet's message. Rereading also gives us a feel for a poem's rhythm and rhyme, if it has any. In fact, we read poems with our minds as we listen, our voices as we recite, and our bodies as we feel the rhyme and rhythm. Then read aloud Mary Ann Hoberman's poem "Sick Days" (1991, p. 13), inviting students to listen for the story of the poem:

Sick Days

On days when I am sick in bed
My mother is so nice;
She brings me bowls of chicken soup
And ginger ale with ice.

She cuts the crusts off buttered toast
And serves it on a tray
And sits down while I eat it
And doesn't go away.

She reads my favorite books to me;
She lets me take my pick;
And everything is perfect—
Except that I am sick!

Discuss the meaning of the poem. Then have the class retell the story. Reread the poem aloud again for the students, this time noting how the poet uses rhythm and rhyme. For example, the rhythm is steady and unhurried, so it should not be read too quickly. Point out that Hoberman's use of rhyme is meant to be soothing, as when a parent is rocking a baby. The unhurried and soothing nature of the poem reflect the ways that parents care for a sick child. Guide the students in saying the poem together, then again in boys' and girls' groups, and then in groups on the two sides of the room to get the rhythm of the poem.

Next tell the students, "We are going to dramatize the poem by using pantomime." Explain that the term *pantomime* describes planned movement that conveys meaning, and model several examples (waving hello, pointing to an object, rocking a baby). Write *pantomime* and a short definition on a word chart so that they can read it. Then divide the class into groups of three, and have the students in each group pantomime (dramatize the meaning with movements) a stanza of their choice from the poem. Encourage the students to use classroom objects as props. Later, have students dramatize their stanza for the others as you read the poem aloud. There will be some groups that have the same stanza as other groups, but a different dramatization.

DAY 2: FROM PANTOMIMES TO TABLEAUX

Reread the poem "Sick Days" from the chart to refresh the students' memory of the story and its use of language, and briefly discuss how poems are best enjoyed when read with one's mind, voice, and body. Invite students to return to their groups from the previous day. After practicing their pantomimes, invite the groups to perform the entire poem while you video-record it for them. Play back the video for students to watch and analyze, focusing especially on how movement helps convey the meaning of the poem. Next introduce the concept of *tableau* to them, using a Venn diagram to illustrate the similarities and differences with *pantomime*. Note that both use gestures to convey meaning, but that while pantomime relies on movement, tableaux are still, as in photographs and paintings. Point out that *tableau* is a French word, and that an *-x* is added to make it plural, just as we use *-s* and *-es* in English words.

Move students back into their groups and ask them to choose a tableau that retells their stanza, reminding them that they should first pantomime and then "freeze-frame" one part of it. After the members of each group have agreed on a tableau to symbolize their stanza, ask each to perform it again while you take a digital photograph. Load the photos in sequence onto the computer; then play the tableaux back for the class as you recite the poem for them. Ask the audience to discuss how the tableaux helped represent the poem, and invite them to offer suggestions for others that the groups might use. Guide group members in critiquing what they liked about their scene and what they might do differently. Close the lesson by reminding students that as readers, we create images as we read, and that pantomimes and tableaux are two ways in which we can construct these mental images of what we read.

As classroom teacher Joanne Orlando reflected on this lesson, she noted,

"The use of the theatre activities helped my students understand literacy content because they were all actively involved as participants in creating their project from start to finish. By using the arts-infused process to create a product, they were able to clearly understand the skills they were taught, and to learn from other groups engaged in the same processes and performances."

Animal Adaptations through Music in Second Grade

A challenge for many younger learners is in learning and using science vocabulary. Terms such as *adaptation, organism, camouflage,* and *environment* are not typically a part of their speaking vocabulary. In addition, science terms are often labels for complex concepts. In this unit, teacher Adrienne Laws of the San Diego (California) Unified School District has chosen to use music as a means to reinforce and extend the vocabulary learning of her science students. All of her students are ELLs, and several of them also have been identified as students with disabilities. As we will see in this lesson, chants posted on charts around the classroom provide students with additional practice, and students are able to use the knowledge gained from their musical as they research, write, and complete oral presentations with partners.

Literacy Skills Focus
- Background knowledge and vocabulary, oral language development, writing.

How Arts Are Infused into This Lesson
- Use body percussion (claps, snaps, etc.) to accompany a chant.

- Perform chants (rhythmic speech pieces) about animal characteristics and their ways of adapting.
- Create and perform whole-body movements to show how animals move.

Ideas Students Need to Know

- Mammals, reptiles, and amphibians have unique characteristics.
- Some animals are warm-blooded, while others are cold-blooded.
- Animals adapt in order to survive and thrive in their environments.

Materials and Resources

- Chants, songs, and poetry about animals.

Teaching Procedure

Chants, songs, and poetry are often featured in science textbooks designed for primary-grade students. These genres augment the informational reading these learners use during science instruction. Locate these materials in your science textbooks, or consult any of the numerous websites available with these materials. The purpose of these activities is to reinforce and extend student learning in science by using body percussion and chants as a mnemonic device for learning and recalling new technical vocabulary.

After identifying suitable chants, songs, and poems that align with the science content being taught, write the words for each piece on chart paper. During a series of individual lessons, help students learn a different chant (rhythmic speech piece) about animals each day. For example, students might perform the words in a military boot-camp cadence: "I'm a snake, so long and thin; I have scales and shed my skin!" Later, students can clap or snap along, create and add animal movements, then perform the chants again.

Display the lyrics and other posters of the animals around the room, so that students can revisit them. Invite pairs of students to research one animal from each group, using the Internet and other sources. In addition, students should design and develop a new chant, song, or poem to accompany their animal. Then let each pair present its findings to the class. Encourage students to use a variety of details, such as whether the animal is warm-blooded or cold-blooded, and to make their descriptions interesting. Remind them to tell how each animal adapts to survive in its environment, and ask them to teach their new chant to the class.

In reflecting on this lesson, Adrienne Laws said,

> "Partnering students allowed for a greater experience of success in the written portion of the lesson, as well as during the oral component. The students were introduced to challenging science vocabulary and were able to remember it because it was embedded in a rhyming chant."

Colonial Life: Analysis Using the Visual Arts in Fifth Grade

The study of history can be challenging for many students who have a hard time grasping a central truth: that the people of previous eras were once as alive as they themselves are now. Instead, they view historical figures as static and unchanging. For example, it may be difficult for them to recognize that U.S. presidents were once children, or that people led full lives beyond a singular event that made them a part of history.

Fifth-grade teacher Colleen Crandall of the San Diego (California) Unified School District has developed a social studies lesson to make history come alive to her students, all of whom live in poverty and many of whom perform below grade level in reading. She has designed activities using the visual and theatre arts to teach about the lives of ordinary and extraordinary people of colonial American times. The lesson provides creative opportunities for her students through discussion of artworks, writing, and dramatic tableaux.

Literacy Skills Focus
- Background knowledge and vocabulary, comprehension, analysis of narrative, oral language development (listening and speaking).

How Arts Are Infused into This Lesson
- Students use the visual arts to analyze narrative paintings of the period.
- Students recreate scenes within historic paintings through dramatic tableaux.

Ideas Students Need to Know
- We can gain a sense of the lives of people of other times by analyzing the art and artifacts of their lives.
- The artist's perspective plays an important role in how we see people from other eras.
- We can use what we know about a time in history to dramatize the characters in the historic artworks through the use of tableau and dialogue.

Materials and Resources
- Portrait paintings of the period, widely available in textbooks, school libraries, and district resource centers. In addition, you can search the Colonial Williamsburg website devoted to history (*www.history.org*) to locate the *A Day in the Life* DVD series for use by teachers.
- Computer and data projector.

Teaching Procedures

Explain to students that before photography was invented in the mid-19th century, people relied on portrait paintings of family members to preserve images of loved ones. Wealthier families could afford the services of professional portrait painters, while middle-class families relied on itinerant artists who would travel from town to town selling their services. Portraiture was not confined to paintings, but could also be found as jewelry and even in needlework.

Show students a formal portrait, such as one painted of George Washington in 1780 by Charles Willson Peale. An interactive version of this portrait can be found at *www. history.org/history/paintings/george_washington*. Invite students to examine each quadrant of the portrait to note what artifacts are visible. For example, Washington is in military uniform and rests his left hand on a cannon. Think aloud for them as you speculate on the perspective of the artist. For example:

> "I can see from the uniform and weapons that the artist wants to show Washington as a strong military leader. He doesn't surround Washington with his wife and children because that would emphasize a family man. I think the artist chose these artifacts deliberately."

Ask students to add their ideas, and then use the interactive tools on this website to read about the artifacts in the painting. Next, compare this to "The Reverend Ebenezer Devotion and Martha Devotion," a double portrait of a rural Massachusetts minister and his wife, painted about 1770 by an itinerant artist (*www.library.csi.cuny.edu/dept/ history/lavender/graphics/devpair.html*). Invite students to similarly examine the artifacts found in these paintings. For example, the minister is surrounded by books and has a Bible in his hand. His wife holds the same Bible in one hand, and has a fan in another, suggesting that she enjoys a comfortable life.

Then ask students to work in groups to write dialogue for each of the three paintings viewed. What might each person say about their lives if they could speak? After asking for student examples, provide other group portraits for them to consider. For instance, assign one group the painting titled "Isaac Royall and His Family," painted by Robert Feke in 1741 (*www.library.csi.cuny.edu/dept/history/lavender/graphics/iroyal.html*). This composition of five members of a wealthy Massachusetts family includes trappings of their station, including a prominently featured Oriental rug. After carefully analyzing the artifacts in their paintings, ask the groups to write dialogue that might have been spoken by the people in their paintings. Next, have each group form a tableau representation of the selected historic painting, and practice reproducing the relative positions and dialogue. Each character in the tableau will talk to the audience of classmates about who the character is and what he or she is doing in the scene of that historic painting. Finally, give each student the opportunity to answer questions about his or her character within the tableau performance; this will provide further exercise for oral language, fluency, and comprehension skills.

In her reflection, Colleen Crandall said,

> "The historic paintings gave the students a character from that time period to 'become' and take on the ideas and thoughts of a person. My students were able to synthesize things they had learned as they interjected those ideas into the character they played in their tableau. I was thrilled the students got into the parts of the characters as well as they did, since they had never done this before. In the future, I would like to have students do a tableau around the writing of the Constitution, and have them be the representatives from different colonies and their wives too. What would it have been like for these women?"

LOOKING FORWARD

There are four major areas of focus in the professional literature on integrated arts:

- The arts should not be sidelined or only used by "experts." Rather, classroom teachers should find opportunities to integrate music, visual arts, movement and dance, and drama and performance into their classes. Not only does this engage learners; it also improves achievement.
- As other chapters have emphasized, students deserve a comprehensive approach to literacy. The arts should not be used to focus on one isolated aspect of literacy instruction. Rather, teachers should plan lessons in which the arts build students' oral language; concepts about print; sense of story and text structure; phonemic awareness and phonics; background knowledge and vocabulary; fluency; comprehension; and writing.
- Leveraging what students know and what they experience can create memorable learning situations. When students are allowed to perform in whatever way is appropriate for a lesson, they are more likely to remember that information than they are if it is presented in skill, drill, and low-level repetitive lessons.
- Integrated arts do not replace students' right to arts instruction from teachers with specialization in the arts. The cultural heritage of our world depends on students' understanding of the arts in and of themselves. Integrated arts taps into that knowledge and provides students relevant experiences from which to learn. Classroom teachers should continue advocating for specialized arts instruction for every child.

By integrating the arts into literacy instruction across content areas, we can leverage an array of skills that students bring to our classrooms. Although much has been written over the past three decades about the need to broaden the ways in which students learn and demonstrate their understanding, tasks that exclusively involve reading and writing still predominate. Students who might otherwise express their learning through movement, music, and visual arts have little opportunity to do so. Purposeful, integrated arts instruction allows students to utilize all modalities more fully to learn about the world. In addition, they learn about themselves as they discover other expressive modalities.

But a rationale for integrated arts instruction should not be confined to student expression. It should also be viewed as a powerful instructional tool. This neglected channel can be a conduit for real learning to occur. We are discouraged by the relative dearth of integrated arts research in the last decade, as the profession has turned its attention to basic skills achievement. Focusing on literacy achievement should not mean reduced focus on the arts, as the arts have been shown to boost achievement (Hansen, Bernstorf, & Stuber, 2004). We argue that using aspects of the visual and performing arts has tremendous potential for reaching hard-to-teach students, as well as to expand learning for high-achieving ones. A recommitment to integrated arts across content instruction can reinvigorate and raise the rigor of curricula. In doing so, we can provide our students with new opportunities to perform.

QUESTIONS FOR REFLECTION •

1. What are the four arts, and how I can use them in my classroom (or help someone else use them in his or her classroom)?

2. What does it mean to integrate the arts? Why does this matter, and how might it influence literacy achievement?

3. What are some ways in which the arts could be used to develop students' oral language?

4. What are some ways that the arts could be used to reinforce students' understanding of concepts about print, phonemic awareness, and phonics?

5. How might the arts be used to develop and activate students' background knowledge and vocabulary?

6. Which of the arts might be most useful in helping students develop fluency, vocabulary, and writing?

7. How can the arts be used to improve student performance in science, social studies, and math?

SUGGESTIONS FOR ONGOING PROFESSIONAL LEARNING • • • • • • •

As classroom teachers, we may seek to develop customized ways to infuse the arts into our literacy instruction across the curriculum. Although professional development courses, workshops, and examples of integrated arts lessons may initially help us see what is *possible*, the leap from modeled lessons (done with adult teacher participants) to *what can and does actually work in real classrooms* may be unclear. This reality suggests a need for practical examples by real classroom teachers (nonspecialists in the arts) who have successfully infused arts-based activities into literacy contexts across their own classroom curriculums.

Session 1

Discuss with colleagues the ways in which they have integrated the arts into their lessons. What lessons or units of study have been particularly useful? Which aspects of literacy have been developed through the arts?

Session 2

Discuss the content of this chapter, and create a grid with instructional focus areas in the left-hand column and the four arts across the top (see the chart on the next page). Analyze the chapter for examples in specific areas, and then share with colleagues other ideas you have for integrating arts.

Literacy component	Music	Visual art	Movement and dance	Theatre and drama
Oral language development				
Concepts about print				
Sense of story and text structure				
Phonemic awareness and phonics				
Background knowledge and vocabulary				
Fluency				
Comprehension				
Writing				

Session 3

Observe a colleague teaching literacy through the arts, or invite a colleague into your classroom to observe your lesson. Share notes following the observation. What was the level of student engagement? Did students understand the content? What literacy skills were practiced? Use this discussion to refine a lesson together.

Session 4

Discuss the lesson that you developed with a colleague. Invite others to join the discussion about the lesson and the successes and challenges you experienced. Plan another lesson together, this time using a different art form.

RESEARCH-BASED RESOURCES

Cornett, C. (2010). *Creating meaning through literature and the arts: Arts integration for classroom teachers* (4th ed.). Upper Saddle River, NJ: Merrill/Prentice Hall.

Hancock, M. (2007). *A celebration of literature and response: Children, books and teachers in K–8 classrooms* (2nd ed.). Upper Saddle River, NJ: Prentice Hall.

Katz, S., & Thomas, J. (1992). *Teaching creativity by working word: Language, music and movement.* Upper Saddle River, NJ: Prentice Hall.

McDonald, N. (2010). *Handbook for K–8 arts integration: Purposeful planning across the curriculum.* Boston: Pearson/Allyn & Bacon.

McDonald, N., & Fisher, D. (2006). *Teaching literacy through the arts.* New York: Guilford Press.

Piazza, C. (1999). *Multiple forms of literacy: Teaching literacy and the arts.* Upper Saddle River, NJ: Prentice Hall.

Smith, S. (2001). *The power of the arts: Creative strategies for teaching exceptional learners.* Baltimore: Brookes.

REFERENCES

Adams, M. J. (1998). *Phonemic awareness in young children.* Baltimore: Brookes.

Armstrong, T. (2003). *The multiple intelligences of reading and writing: Making the words come alive.* Alexandria, VA: Association for Supervision and Curriculum Development.

Blevins, W. (1999). *Phonemic awareness songs and rhymes.* New York: Scholastic.

Burger, K., & Winner, E. (2000). Instruction in visual art: Can it help children learn to read? *Journal of Aesthetic Education, 34*(3–4), 277–293.

Burnaford, G., Brown, S., Doherty, J., & McLaughlin, H. J. (2007). *Arts integration: Framework, research, and practice.* Washington, DC: Arts Education Partnership.

Burroughs, S., Groce, E., & Webeck, M. L. (2005). Social studies education in the age of testing and accountability. *Educational Measurement: Issues and Practice, 24*(3), 13–20.

Butzlaff, R. (2000). Can music be used to teach reading? *Journal of Aesthetic Education, 34*(3), 167–178.

Cosenza, G. (2006, Winter). Play me a picture, paint me a song: Integrating music learning with visual art. *General Music Today,* pp. 7–11.

Clay, M. (1985). *The early detection of reading difficulties* (3rd ed.). Auckland, New Zealand: Heinemann.

Duncan, K. A., Johnson, C., McElhinny, K., Ng, S., Cadwell, K. D., Zenner Petersen, G. M., et al. (2010). Art as an avenue to science literacy: Teaching nanotechnology through stained glass. *Journal of Chemical Education, 87*(10), 1031–1038.

Fisher, D. (2001). Early language learning with and without music. *Reading Horizons, 42*(1), 39–50.

Fisher, D., & Frey, N. (2007). Implementing a schoolwide literacy framework: Improving achievement in an urban elementary school. *The Reading Teacher, 61,* 32–45.

Fisher, D., Frey, N., & Lapp, D. (2012). *Teaching students to read like detectives: Comprehending, analyzing, and discussing text.* Bloomington, IN: Solution Tree.

Fisher, D., & McDonald, N. (2000). "With stars in their eyes": An integrated arts unit on the night sky. *Telling Stories: Theory, Practice, Interviews and Reviews (The Journal of Teachers Encouraging a Love of Literature), 4*(2), 15–22.

Fisher, D., & McDonald, N. (2001). The intersection between music and early literacy instruction: Listening to literacy. *Reading Improvement, 38,* 106–115.

Fisher, D., & McDonald, N. (2004). Stormy weather: Leading purposeful curriculum integration with and through the arts. *Teaching Artist Journal, 2,* 240–248.

Fisher, D., McDonald, N., & Strickland, J. (2001). Early literacy development in our musical classrooms: A sound practice! *General Music Today, 14*(3), 15–20.

Foye, M. M., & Lacroix, S. E. (1998). Making connections through integrated curriculum. *National Association of Laboratory Schools Journal, 22*(3), 1–4.

Gilles, C., Andre, M., Dye, C., & Pfannenstiel, V. (1998). Constant connections through literature: Using art, music, and drama. *Language Arts, 76,* 67–75.

Grant, A., Hutchinson, K., Hornsby, D., & Brooke, S. (2008). Creative pedagogies: "Art-full" reading and writing. *English Teaching: Practice and Critique, 7*(1), 57–72.

Gromko, J. (2005). The effect of music instruction on phonemic awareness in beginning readers. *Journal of Research in Music Education, 53*(3), 199–209.

Guthrie, J., McRae, A., Coddington, C., Klauda, S., Wigfield, A., & Barbosa, P. (2009). Impacts of comprehensive reading instruction on diverse outcomes of low- and high-achieving readers. *Journal of Learning Disabilities, 42*(3), 195–214.

Hairrell, A., Simmons, D., Rupley, W., & Vaughn, S. (2011). An investigation of fourth-grade teachers' use of vocabulary instruction in social studies. *Journal of Reading Education, 36*(3), 19–26.

Hansen, D., Bernstorf, E., & Stuber, G. (2004). *The music and literacy connection.* Reston, VA: National Association for Music Educators.

Hetland, L., & Winner, E. (2000). The arts and academic achievement: What the evidence shows. *Arts Education Policy Review, 102*(5), 3–6.

Hoberman, M. A. (1991). *Fathers, mothers, sisters, brothers: A collection of family poems.* Boston: Joy Street Books.

Jensen, E. (2005). *Arts with the brain in mind* (2nd ed.). Alexandria, VA: Association for Supervision and Curriculum Development.

Lewis, A. (2008). Effects of NCLB's focus on reading and math. *Education Digest, 73*(8), 71–72.

Logue, M., Robie, M., Brown, M., & Waite, K. (2009). Read my dance: Promoting early writing through dance. *Childhood Education, 85*(4), 216–222.

Marzano, R. (2004). *Building background knowledge for academic achievement: Research on what works in schools.* Alexandria, VA: Association for Supervision and Curriculum Development.

McDonald, N. (2010). *Handbook for K–8 arts integration: Purposeful planning across the curriculum.* Boston: Pearson/Allyn & Bacon.

McDonald, N., & Fisher, D. (1999). Bug suites: An uncommonly integrated performance unit for fourth through eighth grade. *Telling Stories: Theory, Practice, Interviews and Reviews (The Journal of Teachers Encouraging a Love of Literature), 3*(2), 17–25.

McDonald, N., & Fisher, D. (2002). Strings attached: An introductory unit in musical listening. *Music Educators Journal, 88*(5), 32–39.

McDonald, N., & Fisher, D. (2006). *Teaching literacy through the arts.* New York: Guilford Press.

McDonald, N., Fisher, D., & Helzer, R. (2002). Jazz listening activities: Children's literature and authentic music samples. *Music Educators Journal, 89*(2), 43–49, 57.

Medina, S. L. (1993). The effect of music on second language vocabulary acquisition. *FEES News National Network for Early Language Learning, 6*(3), 1–8.

Music Educators National Conference (MENC). (1994). *Dance, music, theatre, visual arts: What every young American should know and be able to do in the arts: National standards for arts education.* Reston, VA: Author.

Oken-Wright, P. (1998). Transition to writing: Drawing as a scaffold for emergent writers. *Young Children, 53*, 76–81.

Podlozny, A. (2000). Strengthening verbal skills through the use of classroom drama: A clear link. *Journal of Aesthetic Education, 34*(3–4), 239–275.

Rasinski, R. (2010). *The fluent reader: Oral and silent reading strategies for building fluency, word recognition and comprehension.* New York: Scholastic.

Register, D. (2004). The effects of live music groups versus an educational children's television program on the emergent literacy of young children. *Journal of Music Therapy, 41*(1), 2–27.

Reutzel, D. R., Fawson, P. C., Young, J. R., Morrison, T. G., & Wilcox, B. (2003). Reading environmental print: What is the role of concepts about print in discriminating young readers' responses? *Reading Psychology, 24*, 123–162.

Rosenblatt, L. M. (1995). *Literature as exploration.* New York: Modern Language Association.

Shaw, D. (2008). Corresponding with artists. *Arts and Activities, 142*(5), 44, 71.

Smith, J. (2000). Singing and songwriting support early literacy instruction. *The Reading Teacher, 53*, 646–649.

Soundy, C. S., & Drucker, M. F. (2010). Picture partners: A co-creative journey into visual literacy. *Early Childhood Education Journal, 37*, 447–460.

Souto-Manning, M., & James, N. (2008). A multi-arts approach to early literacy and learning. *Journal of Research in Childhood Education, 23*(1), 82–95.

Taylor, B. M. (2011). *Catching schools: An action guide to school-wide reading improvement.* Portsmouth, NH: Heinemann.

Yaden, D., Jr., Smolkin, L., & Conlon, A. (1989). Preschoolers' questions about pictures, print convention, and story text during reading aloud at home. *Reading Research Quarterly, 24*, 188–214.

Yopp, H. K., & Yopp, R. H. (1997). *Oo-pples and boo-noo-noos: Songs and activities for phonemic awareness.* New York: Harcourt Brace.

Young, C., & Rasinski, T. (2009). Implementing readers theatre as an approach to classroom fluency instruction. *The Reading Teacher, 63*(1), 4–13.

PART IV

Essential Collaborations for Effective Schoolwide Literacy Instruction

Developing and Implementing a Framework for Ongoing Schoolwide Reading Improvement • •

BARBARA M. TAYLOR

$\mathbf{A}$s educators know all too well, the stakes are high and pressures are great to improve students' reading scores. Thus almost all schools today are likely to be involved in reading improvement efforts of one sort or another.

This book can serve as a useful resource for a wide variety of schoolwide reading improvement efforts. In the first section of the current chapter, an overview of the research on effective school-based reading reform is presented. References are made to the other chapters in the book that support the multiple components of successful reading improvement efforts. Also, relevant quotations are provided from teachers and administrators involved in a successful school-based reading reform effort at Northwood Elementary, an urban school in which 50% of the students receive subsidized lunch and 15% are English language learners (ELLs). After not making adequate yearly progress (AYP) for several years in a row, the school made AYP for 8 consecutive years during and after its focused reading reform effort. Also, students' mean reading scores at the school increased from year to year. For examples, across a 3-year period during the reform effort, grade 3 students' mean comprehension score went from the 47th to the 56th percentile.

In the second section of this chapter, a general research-based framework for schoolwide reading reform is provided, and action steps for such an effort are briefly described. Ideally, this chapter will confirm positive strategies and actions your school is already engaged in to improve students' reading abilities, and will also give you ideas for next steps or new directions your school might take on its quest to help all students become the best readers they can be.

OVERVIEW OF RESEARCH

Focus on Organizational Change

For a schoolwide reading improvement effort to succeed, teachers and administrators need to begin with or develop an explicit framework and process for change. Because this work is challenging at a collective level, leaders of schoolwide reading improvement efforts need to pay close attention to the actions needed to initiate and sustain a focus on reading instruction reform over 3 or more years (Taylor, Raphael, & Au, 2011). Also, strategies will need to be collectively developed to deal with organizational issues that undoubtedly will arise on the multiyear journey. Furthermore, a collaborative sense of ownership among staff members must evolve in order for the effort to be successful.

Develop Vision, Commitment, and Ownership of the Change Process

Vision of, commitment to, and ownership of a school reading improvement plan must be in place for a school staff to sustain a successful, effective effort over time. Research suggests that members of a school community must develop a shared vision for and establish a long-term commitment to literacy improvement (Lipson, Mosenthal, Mekkelsen, & Russ, 2004; Taylor et al., 2011). The vision incorporates a framework for change that may come from an external partner or may come from within the school. Staff members need to understand from the start that the process for change will occur over more than 3 years and evolve over time. Typically, the vision for improvement undergoes modifications and becomes clearer over time as well. Also, collective teacher and administrator ownership over the process must develop. The commitment and ownership by teachers and administrators tends to become stronger and more universal as students' reading scores increase and as teachers develop increased perceptions of collective efficacy related to their abilities to effect change.

At the end of 3 years of a reading reform effort, a third-grade teacher at Northwood Elementary reflected:

> "I think that staff members at this school have really come together with their beliefs, and teachers have really opened themselves up to learning. We are comfortable with and trust each other. We share ideas and listen. It's very helpful for teachers to collaborate, be on the same page, get other ideas, and simply share struggles and successes. Most importantly, we've seen a lot of progress, and that's what it is all about."

Provide Leadership

Once a school has an initial level of commitment to a shared process of ongoing reading reform, strong leadership is essential to keep the reform effort moving forward with success (Taylor et al., 2011). Leadership is needed that is shared across a principal, a teacher facilitator/coach, and teacher leaders who initiate and help staff members collectively refine a process of continuous reading improvement within their school (Taylor, Pearson, Peterson, & Rodriguez, 2005). Typically, there is at least one key teacher leader who is instrumental in initiating and sustaining the reform effort as a facilitator and peer coach (Au, Raphael, & Mooney, 2008a; Timperley & Parr, 2007). Also, it is vital that leadership team members collectively inspire and support their colleagues as they all become increasingly engaged in and committed to the school literacy improvement effort over time. External partners are also valuable for bringing "outside eyes," ideas, and support to the process.

A first-grade teacher at Northwood reflected on the people providing leadership for the reading improvement effort at her school:

> "We have a lot of leaders. The first person who comes to mind is the literacy coach, who is very knowledgeable and encouraging. I go to her when I have questions or when I want to find out things I don't know. The principal really believes in what we are doing, and I also feel comfortable going to her for support. When the person who visits our school as an external consultant comes to my classroom, she gives me numerous good ideas, listens to any concerns I may have, and helps me reflect on my growth as an effective teacher."

The principal also commented on the importance of the leadership team: "This group has played an important role in identifying professional development needs and planning our next steps toward continuous improvement."

Ongoing professional development for effective school leadership is an important component in effective school-based reading improvement efforts (Taylor, 2011). The updating of leaders' knowledge about effective reading instruction is a component of this learning, but instruction on how to become effective leaders also needs to be stressed.

Engage the Staff in Deliberate Use of Data

In a schoolwide reading improvement effort, use of data is essential to promote change (Au, Raphael, & Mooney, 2008b; Lai, McNaughton, Amituanai-Toloa, Turner, & Hsaio, 2009). Regularly used data at the student, teacher, and school levels serve as important change agents (Taylor, 2011; Taylor et al., 2005). As teachers see students' reading scores increase after they have been making substantial changes in their instruction, all participants are motivated to continue with the reading improvement effort. Also, teachers raise expectations and benchmarks for students as students' reading abilities increase.

A second-grade teacher talked about her use of assessments:

> "The assessments really drive what and how I teach my students as individuals. I use the assessments that are part of our schoolwide assessment plan to understand students' strengths and weaknesses and to identify students who need targeted instruction in specific skills and strategies. Really good things are happening with our focus on data. People are regularly looking at students' performance on assessments, and kids are making fantastic growth."

Strive to Develop a Collaborative School Community

To be successful with a schoolwide literacy improvement effort, teachers and administrators must become a collaborative school community (Langer, 2000; Lipson et al.,

2004; Taylor et al., 2011). Successful teams of teachers and administrators collaborate in numerous ways. They collaborate as they develop a shared vision. Teachers share in the decision making for their schoolwide reading program. They also participate in a number of collaborative teaching and learning communities. This in turn leads to a sense of ownership and collective efficacy that helps them sustain their literacy improvement efforts.

A first-grade teacher shared her enthusiasm for collaborative work at Northwood:

"We all work very well together. Also, if I'm struggling with something, I'm very comfortable going to other teachers for advice or tips, and people are very willing to help. I think as a staff we are going in the same direction and working toward the same goal of helping all students become good readers. We feel like we are all on the same team, and this is a key factor that helps us move forward in our improvement process. The study groups have given us a chance to learn together, to talk about our successes, and to decide where next we should focus our energies. And looking at data together is very valuable because we use [them] to plan our instruction."

A reading specialist with 25 years of experience commented:

"I really enjoy our study groups because we learn new ideas and share what is working and what is not. This is the first time in 25 years that we've had sufficient time to communicate and collaborate during professional development sessions. We now have the best collaboration and learning I've seen in this building."

Focus on Ongoing Professional Learning

In schools involved in schoolwide reading improvement, teachers must have the opportunity and support to engage in ongoing, focused, challenging, job-embedded professional learning. The overall goal of this learning is to translate it into increasingly effective reading instruction within the classroom. Research on school-based reading reform suggests that professional development in literacy needs to be long-term, research-based, and well planned (Taylor et al., 2011). Teachers learn about research-based literacy curriculum and instruction from external partners or literacy leaders within their schools. However, the importance of teachers' going from simply learning about new instructional materials or techniques to focusing on reflection and change in thinking and in teaching is crucial. Peer modeling and coaching; self-reflection; and dialogue related to pedagogy, curriculum, and assessment are techniques that foster reflection on practice. Teachers learn together in school-based professional learning communities (PLCs) in which, ideally, processes for how to learn from one another have been deliberately put into place (Lai et al., 2009). Teachers also learn by participating in peer coaching (Peterson, Taylor, Burnham, & Schock, 2009). (For more on professional learning, see Peterson, Chapter 21, and Sailors, Russell, Augustine, & Alexander, Chapter 22, this volume.)

A third-grade teacher reflected on her professional learning experiences related to the reform effort:

"From the study groups and grade-level meetings, I get valuable new ideas. Also, when I'm struggling with how to help particular students, I can ask others in these groups what they have found helpful in similar situations. I also like the study group meetings with teachers from other grade levels because it helps us develop a common language for our students."

A second-grade teacher also talked about study groups:

"It is so valuable to have the time to meet for an hour twice a month. We look at the latest research and talk about how our learning is impacting our instruction and our students. I've learned so much and I think that this learning has contributed more than anything else to the success we see our students are making."

A first-grade teacher talked about the value of peer coaching and visits to other teachers' classrooms:

"Our literacy coach has been a really good resource for me. I've have been happy to have her come into my classroom, and I've learned a lot from her. I have also enjoyed and learned a lot from observing in other first-grade classrooms. Along with study groups, peer coaching experiences have really changed how I teach reading and have made me a better teacher. I have a lot more confidence in myself as a teacher and in my students' abilities to succeed. I also hold higher expectations for them and for myself than [in] the past."

Successful professional learning within schools is tailored to meet the needs of teachers and students (Taylor et al., 2011). Teachers are not primarily attendees at traditional top-down, one-size-fits-all professional development sessions. They are active participants with choices and responsibilities related to their professional learning, and they provide more effective reading instruction as a result.

A second-grade teacher at Northwood commented, "I was happy I was able to select the study group that I felt would help me the most. Too often we are asked to go to one-size-fits-all workshops."

Focus on Effective Literacy Instruction

To help all students achieve at high levels in reading and writing, teachers in schools that have engaged in successful schoolwide reading improvement efforts (Taylor et al., 2011) focus on providing sound, balanced instruction (e.g., see Part I of this book) and developing coherent reading curricula (e.g., see Part II of this book). Teachers in these schools also provide challenging, motivating learning activities for all students (e.g., see Roehrig, Brinkerhoff, Rawls, & Pressley, Chapter 1).

Establish Curriculum Coherence and Balanced Instruction

Studies on schoolwide reading improvement suggest that through ongoing, school-based professional learning related to evidence-based, effective reading instruction, teacher participants within schools began to teach from a more coherent perspective than in the past (Taylor et al., 2011). In some schoolwide reading improvement projects reviewed by Taylor and colleagues (2011), teachers especially focused on coherent curriculum development (Au et al., 2008a; Timperley & Parr, 2007). In others, teachers focused on continual reflection on teaching effectiveness (Lai et al., 2009; Taylor, Pearson, Peterson, & Rodriguez, 2003). In all cases, effective instruction—as opposed to adherence to prescriptions for teaching or use of particular purchased materials—was the goal. Also, in all projects, teachers focused on providing balanced reading instruction, including the teaching of basic reading skills and more advanced reading strategies related to word recognition and comprehension processes (Mosenthal, Lipson, Torncello, Russ, & Mekkelsen, 2004). In three studies in which external school improvement models were implemented, external partners provided the initial research-based instructional building blocks that evolved into locally owned reading programs within schools (Lai et al., 2009; Raphael, Au, & Goldman, 2009). In other studies, locally developed, site-specific, research-based frameworks for effective reading programs within schools evolved over time (Fisher & Frey, 2007; Mosenthal et al., 2004).

As an ELL teacher at Northwoods explained,

> "Coherence and collaboration are the things that help me become a more successful teacher. In planning sessions we discuss what is going to be taught in reading for the coming week, and through this dialogue I am able to plan for and shape my instruction to best support what is being taught in the classroom. I am able to ensure that I am providing effective support and differentiation to students I teach, based on their skill levels."

A third-grade teacher described her growth at providing balanced, differentiated instruction:

> "One thing I've learned is to be less dependent on the teacher's manual for our core reading program; I use it more as a resource or guide than a script. Also I have gotten better at identifying and understanding the skills of each student, so I focus on their strengths and weaknesses as individuals."

Provide Students with Opportunities for Complex Thinking and Motivating Learning Activities

To help all students achieve well in reading and writing, teachers need to teach with an instructional emphasis on complex thinking. Across studies focused on successful schoolwide reading reform (Taylor et al., 2011), teachers emphasized reading comprehension and students' interactions with texts. Collectively, these studies stressed a common theme: that teachers taught basic skills, but also made a concerted effort to go beyond the basics. They focused on teaching students to be strategic learners who had good comprehension of what they read. They gave students ample opportunities to engage in high-level discussions about text, and students engaged in collaborative learning, inquiry learning, and wide reading.

The principal at Northwood commented on teachers' increased focus on complex thinking and motivation:

"Teachers are thinking more about the roles of motivation and engagement. They are also considering the amount of and quality of the strategy instruction and high-level questioning they provide in their lessons. They are reducing the amount of time they spend on teacher talk to let the children to do more talking, and they are encouraging the children to be more actively engaged in questioning and in self-monitoring their reading. I know this because of the classroom visits I make on a daily basis, and because of the examples of classroom practice that teachers bring up at whole-group meetings and study groups."

The literacy coach at Northwood described the growth she had seen in students:

"Schoolwide, we have seen all of our students grow in reading at a faster pace than in the past. They have deepened their comprehension of what they are reading as well as their ability to engage in dialogue with others, not only during lessons but informal times in the classroom as well. Overall, we've seen our students thinking at higher levels."

A second-grade teacher reflected on changes in her practice:

"I now encourage students to periodically ask themselves lower- and higher-level questions as they read, and to ask clarifying questions as needed. Last year I did most of the questioning, but this year the majority of students in my class are dis-cussing their own questions about the books they are reading with others in their group. And many of these questions get students to really think and have good discussions about their books."

SUMMARY OF BIG IDEAS FROM RESEARCH[1]

Focus on Organizational Change

Develop Vision, Commitment, and Ownership of the Change Process

- Begin with either an external or internal framework for change.
- Develop a shared internal vision for and ownership of success.
- Commit to a long-term improvement process.
- Make modifications to the improvement process over time.

Provide Leadership

- Designate an onsite teacher leader.
- Ensure the principal's support and involvement.
- Establish a leadership team.
- Develop shared leadership over time.
- Seek external support.
- Provide ongoing professional development for leadership team members.

---

[1]This section is adapted from Taylor (2011, p. 83).

Engage the Staff in Deliberate Use of Data

- Regularly use student data to inform instruction and promote change.
- Regularly use data on classroom instruction and school-level climate and collaboration to inform practice.

Strive to Develop a Collaborative School Community

- Strive to develop a positive school culture and sense of collective efficacy.
- Develop a collaborative vision for teaching, student learning, and professional learning.

Focus on Individual Change

Provide Teachers with Opportunities and Support for Effective Professional Learning that Leads to Changes in Teaching

- Develop school-based PLCs.
- Have external partners or literacy leaders within the school provide some of the professional development on research-based literacy curriculum and instruction.
- Ensure that professional learning is ongoing, deliberate, and well planned.
- Reflect on practice that is linked to instructional change or modification.
- Tailor professional learning to a school's unique needs.

Focus on Effective Literacy Instruction

Establish Curriculum Coherence and Balanced Instruction

- Teach from a coherent perspective throughout the school.
- Focus on curriculum development and coherence.
- Focus on dimensions of effective instruction.
- Provide balanced reading instruction.

Provide Students with Opportunities for Complex Thinking and Motivating Learning Activities

- Develop strategic readers.
- Focus on high-level thinking.
- Use collaborative learning experiences.

EXAMPLES OF EFFECTIVE PRACTICES[2]

The process for schoolwide reading improvement described in the remainder of this chapter is based on the Center for the Improvement of Early Reading Achievement

---

[2]This section is adapted from Taylor, Frye, Peterson, and Pearson (2003).

(CIERA) School Change Framework. Research has found that this approach to school-wide reading improvement is effective in enhancing students' reading growth (Peterson & Taylor, 2012; Taylor, 2011; Taylor et al., 2005; Taylor, Peterson, Marx, & Chein, 2007).

Get Started via a Leadership Team

As a group, committed volunteer teachers and administrators who want to see a significant reading improvement effort unfold at their school develop a tentative reading improvement plan as a starting point. This plan gives others a general idea of the purpose of and process for such an effort. The leadership team engages in the following activities:

1. Review research on effective schools, school improvement, school-based collaboration, and shared leadership. (See the *Overview of Research* in this chapter, and see other chapters in Part IV of this book.)

2. Review research on effective reading instruction and effective teachers of reading. (See Parts I, II, and III of this book.)

3. Discuss questions such as the following: How can the teachers and administrators in our school begin to develop or improve upon a collaborative approach to leadership within the school? How can the staff make the reading achievement of all students a schoolwide priority in which teachers are driven by a shared responsibility for all students' success? What should be included in a student assessment plan, in which all teachers monitor students' progress via a variety of assessments and use these data to inform their instruction? What should constitute a schoolwide reading plan, in which teachers are supported as they implement a balanced reading program that develops thinkers as well as readers? What should be included in a parent partnership plan, in which staff members foster relationships and partnerships with parents and the community to improve the reading achievement of all students?

4. Look at data on students' reading abilities and individuals' growth. Also look at data on the time spent on reading instruction in classrooms, as well as at the balance and quality of this instruction, the level of school collaboration, the quality of the school climate, the degree to which there is shared leadership, and the quality of parent partnerships. Determine needs across all of these areas that will promote improvement of reading instruction and students' achievement in reading.

5. Develop an initial, tentative plan for ongoing, school-based, collaborative reading improvement and professional learning (see other chapters in Part IV of this book). The plan should help the school staff develop a strong sense of community and should provide ongoing opportunities and support for teachers to learn, based on their individual needs. The plan should include ways to support individual teachers in this ongoing learning process.

6. Present the initial plan for schoolwide reading improvement to the rest of the staff, make modifications based on teachers' input, and move forward with a plan that at least 80% of teachers vote to accept. Keep in mind that developing a culture of collaborative improvement and ongoing professional learning takes time and patience.

Allocate the necessary resources, make a commitment, and remain focused on the plan. Avoid being tempted to take on too many other new initiatives that are also presented.

7. After a revised plan is agreed upon, rotate members on the leadership team on a regular basis, and ensure that all teachers within the school are represented. Clarify leadership team members' roles and responsibilities, so that all staff members understand the value of this team to the improvement effort.

8. Ensure that there is a respected lead teacher who is able to devote at least half of his or her time to serving as facilitator of the improvement effort and as a peer literacy coach for teachers. This person could be a retired teacher if resources do not permit the selection of a current staff member to the position (see Sailors et al., Chapter 22, this volume).

9. Also, get help from an external consultant who can work alongside the building facilitator/coach if possible. Again, a retired teacher may be a good option in a time of significant budget restraints.

Maintain Momentum in the Reading Improvement Effort

1. The leadership team meets regularly (e.g., at least once a month) to keep the improvement effort moving forward and to provide leadership to the professional learning activities. If possible, the team regularly gets get support from an external consultant who can be a useful "outside pair of eyes."

2. The literacy facilitator/coach and external consultant visit classrooms and offer peer coaching/support to all teachers. The building coach and consultant provide demonstration teaching and modeling of effective practices as requested by teachers.

3. The principal works with teachers who are reluctantly involved with the improvement effort. He or she strives to listen to teachers' concerns and recommendations before moving on to problem solving.

4. Staff members develop a schoolwide reading assessment plans to maximize the productive use student data. Data are collected at least three times during the school year to identify students who are reading above, at, and below grade level (see Weber, Chapter 19, this volume).

5. Teachers participate in data retreats at least three times a year. At these meetings, teachers within grade levels look at standards and benchmarks developed by the state, district, and/or school (see Weber, Chapter 19; see also Resnick & Hampton, 2009). These standards and benchmarks help teachers identify students who are reading above, at, and below grade level. Teachers talk about what they are doing with their students for core instruction, interventions, and supplemental motivating instruction based on this data. They also discuss needed changes in small-group assignments for individual students.

6. Teachers participate in less formal grade-level data meetings at least once a month, as supplements to the more formal data retreats. At these monthly meetings, teachers bring data or work samples to share, and they ask colleagues for ideas about how to help individual students or groups of students progress.

7. Both the leadership team and the grade-level teams regularly examine data on the quality of reading instruction and school climate, as well as data on students' reading abilities and growth. At grade-level and whole-group meetings, teams look at data on classroom reading instruction—what content is being taught, how lessons are taught, how much time is spent on different aspects of reading instruction—to determine instructional strengths as well as changes that are needed. At whole-group meetings, staff members look at data on school climate, collaboration, leadership, and parent partnerships, and determine strengths as well as needed changes.

8. The leadership team looks at data across grade levels to identify strengths and weaknesses in the schoolwide reading program, and brings this information up at whole-group meetings for discussion and action (see the next section; see also Walpole & Najera, Chapter 20, this volume).

9. The leadership team asks all staff members to evaluate the schoolwide reading improvement effort every several months and to recommend modifications. Agreed-upon adjustments are put into place.

Make Adjustments to Improve the Schoolwide Reading Program

1. The leadership team considers and proposes adjustments to the amount and blocks of time devoted to reading instruction, the approaches used by teachers within grade levels to collaborate in the delivery of reading instruction, the use of pull-in or push-out models for supplemental instruction, the placement and duties of instructional aides, and the interventions in place for struggling readers (see Taylor, Chapter 3, and Walpole & Najera, Chapter 20).

2. Staff members work toward alignment of school, state and/or district standards, instruction, and assessments in reading (see Weber, Chapter 19).

3. At whole-group meetings, staff members regularly discuss the schoolwide reading program under the guidance of the leadership team (see Walpole & Najera, Chapter 20).

4. Teachers have opportunities to visit the classrooms of colleagues at their grade level, as well as at grade levels other than their own (especially the grade level below them toward the end of the school year). This helps teachers envision how to make improvements to and increase the coherence of the schoolwide reading program.

Improve Parent Partnerships

1. The leadership team discusses the strengths and weaknesses of the school's current involvement with parents. Members keep in mind that what is important is the concept of parent partnerships, not simply parent involvement (see Roberts, Chapter 23, this volume).

2. The leadership team organizes the development of and administration of a parent survey. The purpose of this survey is to determine what parents feel they need in order to become increasingly involved in their children's schooling.

3. The leadership team devises an initial plan to develop or improve partnerships with parents. This plan is refined and implemented after input from all staff members at a whole-group meeting.

4. The leadership team asks parents and teachers whether the plan for improving partnerships with parents is succeeding and what modification need to be made.

5. The leadership team also studies data from parent feedback or attendance at scheduled events to determine which aspects of the program have been successful and which have not.

SUGGESTIONS FOR ONGOING PROFESSIONAL LEARNING[3] • • • • •

Engage in Study Groups to Improve Reading Instruction

Study Group Basics

1. *Study group topics.* With support from the leadership team, teachers plan study groups with specific foci. These study groups are a core component of ongoing improvement of reading instruction at the school (see Peterson, Chapter 21, for more on PLCs). Study group activities include reading about and discussing research-based reading instruction practices (see resources on specific reading foci in Parts I, II, and III of this book). After an initial meeting and before the next meeting, teachers within a group all try out the same set of new teaching techniques they are studying. At subsequent meetings and based on new techniques being implemented, study group members engage in learning activities such as the following:

- Examination of student work, to determine how to improve teaching.
- Lesson planning and study.
- Examination of effective instruction through classroom visits or video viewing.
- Video sharing of members' teaching, to promote reflection on practice.

2. *Study group routines.* Groups meet for an hour twice a month. Roles of leader, timekeeper, and recorder rotate among group members. Each group develops an action plan that includes goals for students' progress and teachers' successes. Each group keeps meeting notes that are shared with the rest of the school.

3. *Extra support.* Study group members get support from the building coach or external consultant, who is available to offer demonstration teaching and peer coaching on the topics being studied.

4. *Time spent on a particular topic.* Groups remain on a specific topic/technique or set of related techniques for at least six sessions. Thus it is important to select a topic, technique, or set of techniques that warrants six sessions or more of study.

5. *Evaluation of the process.* Members regularly evaluate their learning sessions: What went well? What needs to be done to make the study group more productive?

6. *Reflection.* Members reflect on improvements in instruction. This is a crucial aspect of study groups that is often overlooked. Members should ask themselves

---

[3]This section is adapted from Taylor et al. (2003).

questions such as these: How has my teaching improved as a result of my study group work? What impact does my related teaching have on my students' reading abilities?

7. *Evaluation of progress in students' reading and in instruction.* Members look at data on students to identify their progress, and they look at data on students and on teaching to identify areas of instruction in need of further attention.

8. *Additions to a study group plan.* Members add new techniques relevant to the study group topic as the group feels ready for new challenges.

Study Group Actions Related to a Specific Focus of Study

1. Members review relevant research on effective reading instruction and effective teachers of reading. They use data on students' and teachers' needs to select study group foci (see relevant topics in Parts I, II, and III of this book). Each particular study group begins with one focus; teachers participate in the study group that best fits their needs. The formation of cross-grade-level study groups is encouraged as a way to foster greater cross-grade understanding and collaboration.

2. Members ask key questions to help groups reflect on the effectiveness of instruction related to their focus area. Questions deal with the content of instruction, the process of instruction, time allocations, and individual needs. Possible questions: Am I teaching important aspects of X? Am I using research-based processes to teach X? Am I spending the right amount of time on X? Am I meeting individual needs related to X?

3. Members learn, implement, and reflect on the effectiveness of new research-based techniques in a focus area. They ask questions to reflect on teaching that deal with the purposes of the lesson, the teaching of the lesson, the timing of the lesson, and other aspects of teaching. Possible questions: What new techniques am I trying? Why am I teaching this? How will it help my students developing their ability in X? What is my plan for teaching? Did I spend the right amount of time on the lesson? How could I have taught differently, provided more scaffolding as students were engaged in activities, or involved students more actively to be more effective in my teaching?

4. Over 3 months or more (at least six sessions), study group members continue to implement and reflect on the effectiveness of one or several new research-based techniques related to their focus area.

5. Members assess and share students' progress related to the study group focus and use this data to inform their teaching. Sample questions: How are our students doing in X (e.g., phonemic awareness)? What do we need to do differently to help students be more successful?

6. Members reflect on/refine their teaching by asking questions on instructional process (see Part I of this book) and content (see Parts II–III of this book). Sample questions: How should we adjust the process, or the way we teach? How should we make adjustments to the content we teach? What have we learned or observed in the study group that will help us make these changes?

7. Members strive to meet individual needs. Sample questions: For which students must we adjust our instruction to meet their needs? What resources can we draw from

to help us make these necessary instructional changes? What should we do to provide additional support to some students to meet their needs better?

8. Members continue to implement and reflect on the effectiveness of a new research-based technique or set of techniques over multiple months. They also decide when to move to a new technique within the focus area as the group feels ready for a new challenge. Examples of questions for reflection: Are we ready to focus on learning a new technique to teach X? What should we do next to refine our abilities to use this new technique in our teaching? How will this new technique improve our teaching?

Engage in Professional Learning via Peer Coaching

1. The literacy coach/facilitator spends a majority of his or her time visiting colleagues in classrooms as a peer rather than as an expert (see Sailors et al., Chapter 22, for more on coaching). During these visits the coach either models techniques that teachers are learning about in study groups, or watches colleagues teach reading lessons and supports them as they reflect on and refine their instruction. Scheduled follow-up conversations are key to fostering reflection, and ideas for next steps related to the modeled or observed instruction are discussed.

2. All teachers have a strong understanding of the steps involved in the coaching cycle. These include the sharing of information before a coach's visit, the scheduled visit, and a postvisit conversation about practice in which the teacher does most of the talking.

3. Ideally, a brief meeting is conducted prior to the coach's visit. During this session, the purposes for the lesson are described, and information regarding the students is communicated to the coach. The teacher may ask the coach for specific feedback on an area of focus during the lesson. If a teacher does not have time for a previsit meeting, the teacher completes a short form stating the purpose for the lesson and any specific area of focus for the lesson on which he or she would like feedback (e.g., effective higher-level questioning, strategy instruction, etc.).

4. The coach takes notes during the visit. These are useful as a source of data to refer to during the follow-up coaching conversation. Coaches use a coaching protocol similar to the one in Figure 18.1.

5. After the visit, the coach schedules a time to talk with the teacher about the lesson. Together, the teacher and coach reflect, using the coaching protocol. The literacy coach asks questions to engage in a conversation with the teacher about what went well, what the teacher felt he or she needed help with, and what the teacher might do next to move his or her instruction forward. The coach offers suggestions selectively, but refrains from telling the teacher what should or should not be done. The goal of the meeting is for the teacher to do the most of the talking, and for the teacher and coach together to identify possible "next steps" the teacher can work toward to enhance his or her instructional practice.

6. As a component of an ongoing program of professional development for coaches, one literacy coach watches another coach (perhaps in another building) have a conversation with a teacher. The purpose of this observation is to provide feedback to the coach being observed. Together, the coaches reflect on what was effective in the coaching

Teacher _____   Coach _____

Date _____

Pre-Observation Notes

Purposes of the lesson:

Special area to be focused on as requested by teacher:

Observation Notes (especially related to lesson purposes)

Things the students were doing well:

Things the teacher did well:

Ideas to make the lesson even more effective:

(continued)

FIGURE 18.1. Peer coaching protocol.

Post-Observation Conversation Notes

Discussion of purposes:

Discussion of things the students were doing well:

Discussion of things the teacher felt went well:

Discussion of ways to make the lesson even more effective:

Follow-Up Notes

Teacher goal setting/next steps:

Coach support:

FIGURE 18.1. *(continued)*

conversation and how the coach who was observed might improve his or her questioning to guide a teacher to deeper self-reflection in the future.

LOOKING FORWARD

As schools continue to work on schoolwide literacy improvement, it is important that staff members pay particular attention to the following questions, which focus on some of the biggest challenges they will face in their improvement efforts. In addition, more research is needed on these questions.

- What approaches are most beneficial in developing collaboration among school staff members as part of an effective schoolwide literacy program?
- How do school staff members learn to work with parents as partners in the schoolwide literacy program?
- How does a school continue to sustain and improve its schoolwide literacy program, once external partners are no longer involved?
- How does a school literacy program continue to evolve to prepare students for the future, especially taking into account the ever-increasing role of technology in students' reading and writing endeavors?

QUESTIONS FOR REFLECTION[4] •

1. Is your school ready to embark on a school-based reading improvement effort?
2. What support will your school need, and what changes will need to take place, in order for your school to embark on such an effort?
3. Does your school have the necessary administrative and teacher leadership capacity, and would you have sufficient teacher buy-in, to succeed with a significant schoolwide reading improvement effort such as the one outlined in this chapter?
4. Do teachers at your school feel energized by the concept of collaborative, school-based, intellectually stimulating, reflective professional development? Why or why not? If not, what are the barriers?

FINAL THOUGHTS

Research-validated school improvement models can be identified and used by schools in their reform efforts to improve students' literacy abilities (Taylor et al., 2011). External partners, such as university faculty and researchers, can assist schools in this important work by providing initial knowledge and support. However, teachers, administrators, and district office personnel need to recognize that the drive, creativity, and hard work necessary for long-term change must come from within individual schools, and school staff members need to have ongoing support for their efforts.

---

[4]This section is adapted from Taylor (2011, pp. 93, 117).

Teachers and administrators within schools with successful reading improvement efforts work together to make choices and enact change. Teachers teach with rigor and integrity, and they develop and continue to build upon effective strategies for improving student achievement. Teachers are in touch with their students, colleagues, profession, and society.

Redesign efforts need to be understood and embraced by teachers and carried into daily classroom activities through conceptually integrated strategies rather than superficial change actions. School reform succeeds not with mandates for change, but with a framework, contexts, and coordinated, collaborative actions that invite change.

RESEARCH-BASED RESOURCES[5]

Leadership and School Change

Allington, R. L., & Walmsley, S. A. (Eds.). (2007. *No quick fix: Rethinking literacy programs in America's elementary schools* (RTI ed.). New York: Teachers College Press.

Fullan, M. (2005). *Leadership and sustainability: Systems thinkers in action.* Thousand Oaks, CA: Corwin Press.

Goddard, R. D., Hoy, W. K., & Hoy, A. W. (2004). Collective efficacy beliefs: Theoretical development, empirical evidence, and future directions. *Educational Researcher, 33*(3), 3–13.

Hawley, W. D., & Rollie, D. L. (Eds.). (2007. *The keys to effective schools: Educational reform as continuous improvement* (2nd ed.). Washington, DC: National Education Association.

Taylor, B. M. (2011). *Catching schools: An action guide to schoolwide reading improvement.* Portsmouth, NH: Heinemann.

Professional Learning

Hasbrouck, J., & Denton, C. (2005). *The reading coach: A how-to manual for success.* Longmont, CO: Sopris West.

Walpole, S., & McKenna, M. C. (2004). *The literacy coach's handbook: A guide to research-based practice.* New York: Guilford Press.

York-Barr, J., Sommers, W. A., Ghere, G. S., & Montie, J. (2006). *Reflective practice to improve schools: An action guide for educators* (2nd ed.). Thousand Oaks, CA: Corwin Press.

REFERENCES

Au, K. H., Raphael, T. E., & Mooney, K. (2008a). Improving reading achievement in elementary schools: Guiding change in a time of standards. In S. B. Wepner & D. S. Strickland (Eds.), *The administration and supervision of reading programs* (4th ed., pp. 71–89). New York: Teachers College Press.

Au, K. H., Raphael, T. E., & Mooney, K. S. (2008b). What we have learned about teacher education to improve literacy achievement in urban schools. In L. Wilkinson, L. Morrow, & V. Chou (Eds.), *Improving the preparation of teachers of reading in urban settings: Policy, practice, pedagogy* (pp. 159–184). Newark DE: International Reading Association.

Fisher, D., & Frey, N. (2007). Implementing a schoolwide literacy framework: Improving achievement in an urban elementary school. *The Reading Teacher, 61*(1), 32–43.

---

[5]This section is adapted from Taylor (2011, p. 118).

Lai, M. K., McNaughton, S., Amituanai-Toloa, M., Turner, R., & Hsaio, S. (2009). Sustained acceleration of achievement in reading comprehension: The New Zealand experience. *Reading Research Quarterly, 44*(1), 30–56.

Langer, J. A. (2000). Excellence in English in middle and high school: How teachers' professional lives support student achievement. *American Educational Research Journal, 37*(2), 397–439.

Lipson, M. I., Mosenthal, J. H., Mekkelsen, J., & Russ, B. (2004). Building knowledge and fashioning success one school at a time. *The Reading Teacher, 57*(6), 534–542.

Mosenthal, J., Lipson, M., Torncello, S., Russ, B., & Mekkelsen, J. (2004). Contexts and practices of six schools successful in obtaining reading achievement. *Elementary School Journal, 41*(5), 343–367.

Peterson, D. S., & Taylor, B. M. (2012). Using higher order questioning to accelerate students' growth in reading. *The Reading Teacher, 65*(5), 295–304.

Peterson, D. S., Taylor, B. M., Burnham, R., & Schock, R. (2009). Reflective coaching conversations: A missing piece. *The Reading Teacher, 62*(6), 500–509.

Raphael, T. E., Au, K. H., & Goldman, S. R. (2009). Whole school instructional improvement through the standards-based change process: A developmental model. In J. Hoffman & Y. Goodman (Eds.), *Changing literacies for changing times.* New York: Routledge.

Resnick, L. B., & Hampton, S. (2009). *Reading and writing grade by grade.* Washington, DC: National Center on Education and the Economy.

Taylor, B. M. (2011). *Catching schools: An action guide to schoolwide reading improvement.* Portsmouth, NH: Heinemann.

Taylor, B. M., Frye, B. J., Peterson, D. S., & Pearson, P. D. (2003). *Steps for school-wide reading improvement.* Washington, DC: National Education Association.

Taylor, B. M., Pearson, P. D., Peterson, D. S., & Rodriguez, M. C. (2003). Reading growth in high-poverty classrooms: The influence of teacher practices that encourage cognitive engagement in literacy learning. *Elementary School Journal, 104,* 3–28.

Taylor, B. M., Pearson, P. D., Peterson, D. S., & Rodriguez, M. C. (2005). The CIERA School Change Framework: An evidence-based approach to professional development and school reading improvement. *Reading Research Quarterly, 40*(1), 40–69.

Taylor, B. M., Peterson, D. S., Marx, M., & Chein, M. (2007). Scaling up a reading reform effort in 23 high-poverty schools. In B. M. Taylor & J. Ysseldyke (Eds.), *Effective instruction for struggling readers, K–6* (pp. 216–234). New York: Teachers College Press.

Taylor, B. M., Raphael, T. E., & Au, K. H. (2011). Reading and school reform. In M. L. Kamil, P. D. Pearson, E. Moje, & P. Afflerbach (Eds.), *Handbook of reading research* (Vol. 4, pp. 594–628). New York: Routledge.

Timperley, H. S., & Parr, J. M. (2007). Closing the achievement gap through evidence-based inquiry at multiple levels of the education system. *Journal of Advanced Academics, 19*(1), 90–115.

CHAPTER 19

Improving the School
Literacy Program ● ● ● ● ● ● ● ● ● ● ● ● ●
Developing Coherence in Curriculum, Instruction, and Assessments

CATHERINE M. WEBER

In an era of high-stakes testing, there is a strong push for data-based decision making; however, it can be difficult for teachers and schools to know which data to collect and how to use them to increase students' literacy achievement levels. To improve the school reading program, educators must work together as a professional learning community (PLC) to build coherence within and across grade levels to ensure success for all students. This chapter begins with an overview of research related to schoolwide curricular coherence and assessment data. It then unpacks ways that school teams can work together to improve literacy teaching and learning schoolwide.

OVERVIEW OF RESEARCH

Despite decades of research on effective literacy instruction, an achievement gap remains, particularly for students from diverse backgrounds living in poverty (Kennedy, 2010; Timperley & Parr, 2007). Recently, literacy scholars have begun to examine factors beyond classroom instruction that can contribute to or impede improvement, including the whole-school context. Researchers have consistently found that curricular coherence within and across grades increases student achievement (Bryk, Rollow, & Pinnell, 1996; Hallinger & Murphy, 1986; King & Newmann, 2001; Newmann, Smith, Allensworth, & Bryk, 2001; Strahan, 2003). The key to creating a trajectory of continuous growth is to build a schoolwide system of accountability that addresses literacy curriculum, instruction, and assessment, as well as ongoing professional learning.

Whole-School Collaborative Community

To build a coherent schoolwide literacy program, all members of the school community must be equal stakeholders in students' successes and function as a schoolwide PLC. Stoll, Bolam, McMahon, Wallace, and Thomas (2006) describe a PLC as "a group of people sharing and critically interrogating their practice in an ongoing, reflective, collaborative, inclusive, learning-oriented, growth-promoting way; operating as a collective enterprise" (p. 223). (For more on collaboration, see Walpole & Najera, Chapter 20, this volume. For more on PLCs or study groups, see Peterson, Chapter 21.) Although each member of an effective school community has different roles and responsibilities, each contributes substantively to children's literacy learning. For instance, principals and administrators focus on policy decisions related to scheduling, external initiatives, staffing, and strategic use of resources (e.g., time, money, personnel). They support instruction as well, particularly by supporting those who work directly with students (Cobb, 2003). Teachers and curriculum leaders provide literacy instruction to students in the classroom and support individualized learning. They also work with administrators to make decisions about curriculum, instruction, and assessment (Cooter, 2003). Parents are also important stakeholders who support student learning by bridging the gap between home and school (Walker-Dalhouse & Risko, 2008). Stakeholders may also include external partners, community members, teaching assistants, students, and others who support literacy teaching and learning either directly or indirectly.

Common Vision of Students' Success

Each of these stakeholders must hold a belief that all students can learn (Au, Raphael, & Mooney, 2008; Hopkins & Reynolds, 2001; Stoll et al., 2006), and must have rigorous expectations for what students should know and be able to do. Coherence built around a weak idea or low-level practices will impede a school's progress, resulting in static or even decreased student achievement. Scholars (Au, 2005; Bryk et al., 1996; Copland, 2003; Fullan, 2003; Hallinger & Murphy, 1986; Pressley, Mohan, Raphael, & Fingeret, 2007; Purkey & Smith, 1983; Rowan, 1990; Stoll et al., 2006) suggest that all stakeholders in a school collaboratively develop a common vision for success and clearly articulate goals for student learning. Having a common vision sets the foundation for curricular coherence within and across grade levels by making public what is expected of the school's graduates. From there, staff members at each grade level can articulate their contribution to the school vision. Au (2005) uses the metaphor of a staircase to describe curricular coherence, with each step representing the student learning goals established by teachers at each grade level. The staircase ensures curricular alignment, uniform rigor, and coherence within and across grade levels (Au & Raphael, 2011).

High-Functioning School Infrastructure to Support Students' Literacy Learning

To develop curricular coherence within and across grade levels, a school must create an infrastructure that supports collaboration among members of the school community. A high-functioning infrastructure should address (1) school organization, (2) high-quality literacy leadership, and (3) coherent professional development (Raphael, Au, & Goldman, 2009). (For an overview of effective schoolwide reading improvement, see Taylor, Chapter 18, this volume. For coverage of effective professional learning within schools, see Peterson, Chapter 21, and Sailors, Russell, Augustine, & Alexander, Chapter 22.)

School Organization

Schools need to have high-functioning structures in place that allow for collaborative conversations at multiple levels (e.g., within grade levels, across grade levels vertically, and within the whole school). The teams must meet on a regular basis to discuss curriculum, assessment, and instruction; they also must have systems for tracking what has been done, current projects, and future goals. Moreover, they need clear feedback loops within and across the various groups to create schoolwide coherence. Grade-level teams, for example, may meet weekly to create assessments to monitor student progress, collaboratively score student work, and make instructional decisions together to improve student achievement across classrooms (Newmann et al., 2001; Vissher & Witziers, 2004). Vertical teams might meet monthly to share successes, challenges, and instructional needs across grade levels (Cobb, 2003; Lambert, 1998, 2002). The purpose of these meetings is to build curricular coherence by examining gaps, overlaps, and trends across grade levels. Whole-school meetings may occur quarterly and provide the entire faculty with time to publicize grade-level goals, present student achievement data, and make instructional decisions (Au et al., 2008; DuFour, 2004). In this context, the school community analyzes the developmental progression of curriculum across the grades and makes adjustments as necessary to ensure high levels of achievement at every grade. (For more information on whole-school meetings, see Peterson, Chapter 21.)

High-Quality Literacy Leadership

Creating structures that enable collaboration is necessary, but not sufficient. To build curricular coherence, collaborative school communities must focus on the functionality of a number of structures. That is, to what extent are these structures moving the school toward higher levels of coherence, rigor, and student achievement? School leaders play an important role in building and strengthening the school's infrastructure and increasing its productivity. Spillane (2003, 2006) and others (e.g., Timperley, 2009) suggest schools adopt a distributed leadership model, in which each individual in the school assumes a formal or informal leadership role (e.g., literacy coach, grade-level team member, vertical team representative). From this perspective, teachers, administrators, and other members of the school community are empowered to create and sustain schoolwide change (King & Newmann, 2001). (For more on school leadership and school change, see Taylor, Chapter 18.) Individuals with more formal leadership roles, such as principals or curriculum leaders, equip other leaders and teachers to build, strengthen, and maintain an effective schoolwide literacy program. For example, in addition to being a content expert, a literacy coach may support teachers as they become leaders by engaging them in curriculum development and shared decision making about resources, materials, and use of data (King & Newmann, 2001). He or she may provide protocols for interacting and help teachers work together effectively to build coherence in curriculum, instruction, and assessment within a grade level. (More information about the role of the literacy coach is provided by Sailors et al. in Chapter 22.)

Coherent Professional Development

To create and sustain coherence in the schoolwide literacy program, teachers and administrators must reconceptualize professional development. Research has shown that traditional, decontextualized, "one-shot" workshops are an ineffective way to change classroom practices or improve student achievement (Cooter, 2003; International Reading Association, 2004; Joyce & Showers, 1983). Schools need to shift from disjointed presentations to a model of professional development that consists of collaboration and ongoing learning situated in the context of practice (Brown, Collins, & Duguid, 1989; John-Steiner & Mahn, 1996; Putnam & Borko, 2000). Teachers need sustained opportunities to learn new material, implement ideas in their classrooms, and participate in mutual critique of their practice with colleagues in a PLC (King & Newmann, 2001; Lawless & Pellegrino, 2007). To build a coherent reading program, educators must work together to address challenges, define problems of practice, and collectively set and achieve goals related to curricular alignment over a long period of time (Au & Raphael, 2011; Bryk et al., 1996; Copland, 2003; Mason, Mason, Mendez, Nelsen, & Orwig, 2005; Newmann, King, & Youngs, 2000; Rowan, 1990).

King and Newmann (2001) believe that sustained professional development focusing on school goals is critical for improving student achievement. They argue that professional development influences a school's capacity for providing effective instruction, including (1) program coherence; (2) professional community (e.g., purpose, collaboration, and inquiry); and (3) teachers' knowledge, skills, and dispositions. Increasing a school's capacity for providing effective instruction improves its instructional quality (e.g., curriculum, instruction, assessment), which leads to improved student achievement. Scholars (see Cooter, 2003; King & Newmann, 2001; Newmann et al., 2000, 2001) agree that developing teachers' capacity to make data-driven decisions about curriculum, instruction, and assessment will lead to systemic change and schoolwide coherence.

Multifaceted, Data-Driven Decision Making

Schools need to have clear purposes for collecting, analyzing, and using data. According to Earl and Katz (2006), "Synthesizing and organizing data in different ways stimulates reflection and conjecture about the nature of the problem under consideration and provides the vehicle for investigation and planning focused improvement strategies" (p. 3). If a school is to develop high-level curricular coherence, it must also create assessment systems that generate data about the program's effectiveness. Assessment systems should address both student and teacher learning.

Student Learning

The goal of any literacy program is to improve student achievement and engagement on high-level literacy tasks. Assessment systems allow educators to monitor students' progress toward desired goals. It is important that each of the school's stakeholders understand which data inform which decisions, so they can use data responsibly for the intended purpose. For example, standardized tests provide educators with different information than classroom-based assessments and serve different purposes for informing literacy instruction and school improvement. Stiggins and Duke (2008) propose three levels of assessments that provide teachers, administrators, policymakers, and parents with information about student achievement: classroom, program, and policy. They also suggest that schools ask three key questions about assessment prior to designing or implementing a data collection plan: (1) What instructional decisions are to be based on the assessment results? (2) Who will be making those decisions? (3) What information will help them make good decisions? Table 19.1 presents uses and examples of each assessment level. Classroom-level assessments are most closely aligned to instruction and are used to monitor student progress and teacher effectiveness on daily or weekly lessons. (For more on classroom-level assessments, see Valencia & Hebard, Chapter 5.) Program-level assessments provide information about the overall success of the school's reading program, alignment across grades, and schoolwide coherence of literacy teaching and learning. Policy-level assessments inform policymakers (e.g., district, state, federal) about resource allocation and overall school progress, usually on an annual basis. These assessments are not intended to inform ongoing instruction, nor are they sensitive enough to measure incremental student achievements.

TABLE 19.1. Levels and Uses of Assessments

Level of assessments	Use for assessments	Examples of assessments
Classroom level	• Support and verify learning • Inform and guide instruction for teachers • Student goal setting and self-assessment • Monitor students' progress on an ongoing basis (e.g., daily, weekly) • Focus on each individual student's achievement	• Informal reading inventories • High-level tasks • Writing portfolios • Conversations with students
Program level	• Evaluate program effectiveness across classrooms • Develop plans for whole-school improvements • Create or change programs to better meet student and teacher needs • Focus on achievement standards (e.g., common challenge for many students that needs to be addressed)	• School benchmark assessments • Quarterly writing prompts (given schoolwide)
Policy level	• Provide institutional accountability • Enable district leaders or policymakers to make decisions about resource allocation	• National Assessment of Educational Progress (NAEP) • Districtwide assessments • State standardized tests

Instructional Effectiveness

As previously discussed, both teachers' knowledge and their capacity to deliver effective instruction affect student progress. Thus it is important to use student achievement data, as well as other sources of information, to make decisions about improving teachers' learning. For example, classroom-level assessments are reflective of an individual teacher's knowledge and skills. If data demonstrate that most students in the class are struggling in a particular area, it may indicate that the teacher needs support related to content or pedagogical practices. Program-level assessments provide a snapshot of the entire school. Looking across these data may reveal schoolwide trends of strengths and challenges that indicate a need for targeted professional development in specific areas. Many schools use data retreats (described in detail in the following section) as a systematic way of analyzing and using data. Strategically using data as a basis for identifying professional learning needs allows schools to be responsive in strengthening and developing teachers' expertise. Thus improving literacy teaching ultimately improves student learning.

Data Retreats

Data retreats (Sargent, 2012) are an exemplary model for how to engage school teams in ongoing, systematic data analysis. They are collaborations among educators, including administrators, as well as representative teachers from various grade levels and subject areas. Teams range in size from 5–25 people, depending on the size and needs of individual schools. School teams focus on improving student learning by clearly articulating their visions for student success and using data as a means for understanding where they are and where they want to go on the path to improvement. Each retreat includes eight steps that guide school teams through data collection, analysis, and use (see Figure 19.1) over a 2- to 3-day period.

Step	Activity
1	Prepare the team
2	Collect data
3	Analyze data in four lenses: • Student data • Professional practices data • Program and structures data • Family and community data
4	Pose hypotheses
5	Develop goals
6	Design strategies
7	Design evaluation
8	Develop roll-out and sustainability

FIGURE 19.1. Data retreat process.

The first steps of the process, preparing the team and collecting data, are done prior to the actual data retreats. School teams work together to develop norms and engage in leadership development, as well as to collect various kinds of data (e.g., student, professional practice, program and structures, family and community) that form the bases for the data retreat. They organize data into summary tables to make the data easily useable during collaboration with colleagues.

During the data retreat, school teams analyze data by observing, discussing, and documenting themes and patterns they notice across the data. They then pose hypotheses about why these patterns are occurring in the data. For example, teachers may notice that they focus much of their instruction in one area and students are performing at high levels, while another area of reading may not receive as much attention and students are struggling. The hypotheses should focus on the factors that contribute to or impede student success, and on ways that teaching and learning can be altered to improve achievement. From these hypotheses, school teams develop goals for teaching and learning, and design strategies for meeting the goals. Goals and strategies should relate directly to the improvement needs identified through data analysis. After the retreat, school teams engage in ongoing evaluation of their plans and focus on sustainability. This may include keeping a chart that delineates goals, dates for completion of these goals, strategies to move forward on goals, indicators of progress toward goals, people responsible for meeting the goals, and resources needed to accomplish the goals.

SUMMARY OF BIG IDEAS FROM RESEARCH

This section summarizes key ideas from the research on assessment and curricular coherence, and Table 19.2 presents specific articles to support each idea.

- Effective schools collaboratively develop a vision and goals for student success that reflect rigorous expectations and emphasize high-level cognitive demands.
- For schools to create coherence in the school literacy program within and across grade levels, they must develop a strong infrastructure that enables teachers and administrators to meet on a regular basis to engage in ongoing inquiry about curriculum, assessment, and instruction.
- A successful school engages the entire school and surrounding community (including parents) as equal stakeholders with a long-term commitment to students' literacy achievement.
- An effective school adopts a distributed leadership model in which the principal, curriculum leaders, and teachers work collectively to make decisions about literacy teaching and learning. Each member of the school community has clearly articulated roles and responsibilities for helping each student achieve the school's vision of success.
- School communities should engage in ongoing inquiry about curriculum, assessment, and instruction to build coherence within and across grade levels.

(For a related summary, see Taylor, Chapter 18.)

TABLE 19.2. Summary of Big Ideas from Research on Schools with Coherent Literacy Programs

Citation	Collaborative school community	Common vision and high expectations for student learning	Purposeful school organization and use of resources	Distributive instructional leadership	Ongoing professional development	Collaborative decision making
Au (2005)	×	×	×	×	×	
Au, Raphael & Mooney (2008)	×	×	×			
Brookover et al. (1978)		×		×		
Bryk, Rollow, & Pinnell (1996)	×	×	×	×		×
Copland (2003)	×	×				×
Earl & Katz (2006)	×					×
Fullan (2000)	×		×	×	×	
Fullan (2003)	×	×		×		
Hallinger & Murphy (1986)	×	×		×		
Hargreaves & Fink (2006)	×					
King & Newmann (2001)	×	×	×		×	
Louis, Marks, & Kruse (1996)			×	×	×	×
Mason, Mason, Mendez, Nelsen, & Orwig (2005)	×		×			×
McLaughlin & Talbert (2001)	×					×
Newmann, Smith, Allensworth, & Bryk (2001)	×	×	×	×	×	×
Pressley, Mohan, Raphael, & Fingeret (2007)	×	×				
Purkey & Smith (1983)	×	×	×	×	×	
Rowan (1990)		×	×	×		
Spillane (2006)	×			×		
Strahan (2003)	×				×	
Taylor, Pearson, Peterson, & Rodriguez (2005)	×	×			×	
Teddlie, Kirby, & Stringfield (1989)				×		
Wellisch, MacQueen, Carriere, & Duck (1978)	×		×			

EXAMPLES OF EFFECTIVE PRACTICES

Members of a collaborative school community must work together to improve literacy teaching and learning. In this section, strategies are presented for school teams to use as they work together to build coherence in literacy curriculum, instruction, and assessment within and across grade levels. Illustrative examples are shared from schools engaged in systematic literacy improvement, using a model for change that emphasizes multiple levels of development in an iterative process (see Au, 2005; Au & Raphael, 2011; Raphael et al., 2009). The process involves (1) creation of a school infrastructure to support improvement in teaching and learning; (2) articulation of a schoolwide philosophy and vision related to students' literacy learning; (3) teachers' creation and implementation of assessments and instruction that are aligned with curricular objectives within and across grades, as well as creation of a developmental progression of students' achievement benchmarks tied to data-driven instructional decision making; and (4) development of schoolwide capacity for sustained change within schools through professional learning, achieved via within-building and cross-site professional learning activities. This model for schoolwide literacy improvement supports a school by engaging the community in a series of whole-school processes (e.g., developing norms, creating vision) and grade-level or department tasks (e.g., developing pupil benchmarks, conducting classroom-based assessments), leading to curricular coherence in the target area (e.g., reading, writing).

Examples of Whole-School Collaboration

Research suggests (Au, 2005; Bryk et al., 1996; Hallinger & Murphy, 1986; Purkey & Smith, 1983) that educators work collaboratively within an effective school community to create a common vision for student success. This requires the entire staff working together to determine what its members want their students to know and be able to do when they graduate from their school. Au (2002) suggests that schools first address philosophy (teachers' beliefs), which is foundational to the school's vision.

School Philosophy Related to Literacy Curriculum, Instruction, and Assessment

In any given building, members of the school community hold various philosophies about instructional approaches, assessment, and perhaps even what constitutes literacy (see Kamil & Pearson, 1979; Weber, 2010). Schools can bring these personal philosophies to the surface by engaging in a whole-group conversation that asks each individual to share his or her beliefs about (1) teaching, (2) learning, and (3) literacy (Au, 2002). After each member has an opportunity to jot down two or three ideas for each of the prompts, they can share these in cross-grade-level groups. This allows various perspectives to be represented. For example, kindergarten and fifth-grade teachers may hold different beliefs about teaching, learning, and literacy. Heterogeneous grouping creates natural opportunities to discuss these various perspectives and begin shaping a schoolwide philosophy related to an effective literacy program. Each small group can share its ideas with the whole group, and the entire school community can look for themes across groups to start developing a shared philosophy. This process requires trust, communication, and willingness to compromise, so that each person's ideas are valued and represented in the philosophy. Newmann and his colleagues (2001) stress the importance of such activities for building coherence across the school literacy program, arguing that schools must have "unity of purpose, a clear focus, and shared values for student learning" (p. 10). See Table 19.3 for an example list of ideas that Chambers Elementary School generated as the basis of the school's philosophy statement related to an effective literacy program. The ideas generated by the faculty are truncated into a concise statement that captures the overall philosophy of the school.

School Vision of Students' Literacy Abilities

Building from the school philosophy, schools should develop a clear vision for the readers and writers graduating from their school (Au, 2005; Au et al., 2008). The *philosophy*

TABLE 19.3. Chambers Elementary School Philosophy: Actions Leading to Effective Literacy Instruction

Beliefs about teaching
- Cultivate predisposition to learn
- Encourage appreciation and respect for diversity of others
- Create inquiring minds
- What we give students should be relevant and authentic
- Have fun and enjoy
- Positive
- Hands-on learning and cooperation
- Continuing process—doesn't stop after graduation
- Provide students with a base for their own learning
- Interactive
- Holistic—not focused only on cognitive development

Beliefs about learning
- Helping students gain tools to help inside and outside of classroom
- Independent and self [-guided] learners
- Learning should be shared between student and teacher
- Problem-solving skills
- Project-based learning
- Students should know their own goals for learning
- Applicable to real-life situations

Beliefs about literacy
- Literacy is a survival tool—[as] critical as food, clothing, and shelter
- Opens doorways to learn about anything
- Should be fun and encourage lifelong readers with the abilities to make connections
- Relevant to students' lives
- Reflection, not just recognition
- Enhances self-esteem; promotes awareness of self and others
- Allows for active participation in the world around them (students)
- Making meaning from text
- Communicating through reading, writing, and speaking
- Interactive experiences with text

is what educators believe about literacy teaching and learning, whereas the *vision* is what students will know and be able to do as a result of being educated at the school. The school vision should be broad and represent the culmination of a student's learning experiences from each grade level. This shifts the focus from isolated teaching to schoolwide coherence, in which each faculty member is contributing substantively to every student's success. Newmann and his colleagues (2001) suggest that "students are more likely to engage in the difficult work of learning when curricular experiences within classes, among classes, and over time are connected to one another" (p. 15). Similar to the process of creating the school's philosophy, educators can meet in heterogeneous groups that represent multiple grade levels and perspectives (e.g., special education, bilingual education, administration, etc.). Members of the PLC share individual ideas about the graduating student and collectively determine which ideas

> **Chambers Elementary School Ideas about Vision**
>
> What students should know and be able to do upon graduation from Chambers:
>
> - Write for a variety of purposes and a multitude of audiences.
> - Demonstrate confidence in literal skills to express ideas through writing, reading, and speaking.
> - Read with understanding, [and then] be able to write about it, talk about it, and represent [it] in some medium.
> - Be self-motivated and fluent readers.
> - Think critically about what they read.
> - Fill out high school applications of their choice.
> - Continue to question and explore ideas and find solutions.
> - Connect what they know to what they are reading and move beyond.
> - Discuss intelligently events in the world around them.

should be included in the school's vision statement. See the accompanying box for an example of ideas that Chambers Elementary School generated related to vision.

A vision statement is the overall goal that educators and students strive for as they engage in literacy teaching and learning; it represents the desired outcome of the coherent staircase curriculum (Au & Raphael, 2011). The vision must be broad, but also specific. For example, the faculty at Avery Elementary School created the following statement: "The literacy vision for an Avery graduate is the acquisition of necessary skills and strategies to communicate effectively in all realms of literacy for the purpose of being a critical thinker, problem solver, and advocate in a continuously changing world." Figure 19.2 shows a working vision statement developed by the school community at Danbury Elementary.

Examples of Grade-Level Collaboration

For schools to realize their vision of student success, educators must engage in ongoing collaboration in large-group and small-group settings. Large-group activities enable educators to build schoolwide curricular coherence; however, much of the work related to curriculum, instruction, assessment, and data-driven decision making is done within grade-level teams. Teachers at each grade level work together to develop coherence in curriculum, instruction, and assessments across classrooms, and also work with other grade levels to create schoolwide coherence. Within grade-level teams, teachers (1) set

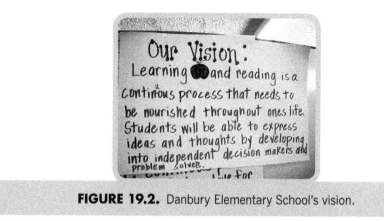

FIGURE 19.2. Danbury Elementary School's vision.

high-level year-end goals for literacy learning; (2) develop data systems to monitor student progress toward goals and reflect on the effectiveness of instruction; and (3) analyze and use data to inform instructional decisions.

Goal Setting for Literacy Learning within Grade Levels

The school's vision serves as the overall goal for student learning upon graduation; however, each grade level should articulate their contribution to students' learning. Grade-level teams can begin to articulate year-end goals by discussing the following questions:

1. What do we want our students to know and be able to do by the end of the year?
2. What literacy skills will our students need to have as they enter this grade in order to accomplish the year-end goal?
3. What skills and/or strategies will we need to teach to help our students reach these goals?

The year-end goals should be broad enough to cover the entire year, but specific enough to be measureable. O'Neill (2000) provides guidelines for developing such goals, which he refers to as SMART: Strategic, Measurable, Attainable, Results-oriented, and Time-bound. Each grade-level goal forms a step in the staircase curriculum described above (Au & Raphael, 2011).

The teachers at Avery Elementary School created year-end goals for comprehension instruction at each grade level (K–8) that lead to the realization of their vision. The goals build upon one another and become increasingly complex as they continue through the grades. For example, in kindergarten, the goal is "Students will be able to sequence a story that has been read to them, including characters and settings." By fifth grade, "Students will be able to interpret author's purpose, summarize big ideas, analyze details in all texts (including graphic sources), and make informed decisions." When students are in eighth grade, preparing to graduate, they "will be able to apply research heuristics (e.g., sourcing, contextualization, subtext, and corroboration), using multiple sources to analyze and critically interact with text across the curriculum."

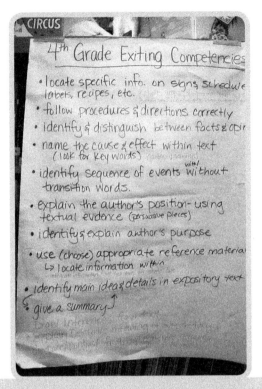

FIGURE 19.3. Caddock Elementary School's brainstorming chart for end-of-year goals.

Teachers developed these goals by brainstorming to create lists of what they believed their students should know and be able to do by the end of the year. The lists serve two purposes: the creation of SMART goals, and the beginning of an instructional roadmap. The items on each list are strategies and skills at each grade level that the teachers will teach throughout the year to help students reach the goal. Figure 19.3 shows the year-end goals of the fourth-grade teachers at Caddock Elementary School.

In addition, each grade level should create a list of expectations related to literacy knowledge and abilities that students should know and be able to engage in at the beginning of the year in order for teachers to be able to accomplish all that they need to teach during the year. This activity is critical for building coherence across grades and is discussed in detail in the section about cross-grade collaboration. Figure 19.4 shows an example of beginning-of-year (entering) and end-of-year (exiting) expectations for student learning from the fourth-grade team at Somerset Elementary School.

Developing Data Systems

Setting high-level goals for student learning is necessary, but not sufficient for schools to develop coherent curriculum within and across grades. Data systems must be created to monitor students' progress toward year-end goals, as well as teachers' effectiveness in teaching students to reach these goals. Progress-monitoring data provide teachers with information about students' performance on tasks related specifically to what is taught in the classroom.

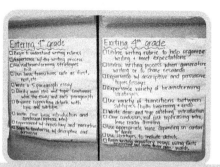

FIGURE 19.4. Somerset Elementary School's entering and exiting expectations for fourth-grade student learning.

ASSESSMENT TASKS AND EVALUATION CRITERIA

At Avery Elementary School, teachers at each grade-level work collaboratively to create assessments that are linked directly to their end-of-year goals. All of the teachers in a grade level administer parallel assessments three times per year. The cognitive demands and rubrics remain the same throughout the year (based on year-end outcomes), but the topic and text change (e.g., sports, music, etc.). At the beginning of the year, baseline data provide teachers with information about what students know and are able to do as a result of previous learning experiences. Midyear data provide a "temperature check" of students' progress toward year-end goals and enable teachers to adjust instruction accordingly. End-of-year data provide information about how many students have met the goal; they also allow teachers to reflect on their instruction and set future goals.

For example, in second grade at Avery Elementary School, the year-end comprehension goal is "Students will be able to read and summarize a text, including the big idea with support from the text, as well as [to] make meaningful connections and inferences." Teachers developed an assessment that addressed each part of the goal and created a criteria chart that articulated the cognitive demand expected at each data collection point (in this case, fall, winter, and spring). See Figure 19.5 for an example of the criteria chart. On the left side of the chart are the general criteria that will be assessed throughout the year. The other three columns display the expected student responses for each administration of the assessment, based on the different texts students read. The second-grade team is still working on creating its spring assessment.

Assessments may simply be high-level tasks that encompass multiple learning goals. For example, third-grade teachers may ask students to "Read two advertisements about breakfast cereals (Lucky Charms and Cheerios). Evaluate which you think is a better choice to buy and why. Use the categories (taste, price, nutritional value, toys/games, and look of the box) to help guide your analysis. Write an explanation of your choice with reasons." The criteria used to evaluate responses include students' abilities to do the following:

- Compare and contrast ideas/claims from both advertisements and how they are supported in the text.
- Identify relevant information.
- Read a table (nutritional information).
- Look at pictures and text about the cereal to gather information.

General Criteria for Meeting the End-of-Year Benchmark	Fall	Winter	Spring
Summary in logical order ➤ Who (name characters) ➤ Problem ➤ Plan for resolution ➤ Resolution	*CHARACTERS:* Oscar is an owl. *PROBLEM:* He is lonely because he doesn't sleep like other owls. *PLAN FOR RESOLUTION:* His friends wanted to help him, so they decide to have a dance party to keep him awake so he gets real tired. *RESOLUTION:* Oscar stayed up and danced all night. The party worked and now he is happy because he sleeps like the other owls.	*CHARACTERS:* Beth and Kim *PROBLEM:* The garden is a mess and Mrs. Miller is not feeling well. *PLAN FOR RESOLUTION:* Clean up the garden and go to the park to ask people to help. *RESOLUTION:* Clean up the garden with the help of others and it looks beautiful.	*CHARACTERS:* *PROBLEM:* *PLAN FOR RESOLUTION:* *RESOLUTION:*
Inferences ➤ Analyze the character's reaction based on events	Oscar is happy at the end. He hangs out with friends and isn't lonely any more.	Mrs. Miller is happy because she waves to the kids and smiles from her front porch.	*INFERENCE:*
Connection ➤ Make a connection of putting yourself in the character's shoes to analyze how you would solve the problem, how you would feel, etc.	(I have felt like Oscar because . . . I would _____ to solve Oscar's _____ problem, etc.) have	I am helpful like Kim and Beth. This is why . . . Will accept: They are nice, helpful, caring. Not acceptable: Garden	*INFERENCE:*

FIGURE 19.5. Excerpt from the criteria chart for Avery Elementary School's second grade.

- Evaluate information about each product.
- Agree or disagree with the authors.
- Write an argument that supports their opinion with evidence.

This type of task is easy to administer and provides a lot of information to teachers about students' abilities related to year-end goals. It is also relevant to students' lives and has value beyond school. As reported in the online magazine *Parentdish*, "A study by Yale University's Rudd Center for Food Policy and Obesity found that cereals marketed to children have 85 percent more sugar, 65 percent less fiber, and 60 percent more sodium than cereals advertised to adults" (Martin, 2010). This task requires students to engage in high-level reasoning about real-world issues that directly affect them—childhood obesity and advertising of products specifically marketed to children.

GUIDELINES FOR ADMINISTERING ASSESSMENTS

To ensure uniformity across classrooms, teachers at each grade level should develop guidelines for administering the formative assessment tasks they co-create (see Airasian, 2000). Guidelines for the data system may include (1) a timeline for administering assessments (e.g., window of dates in the year); (2) time allotted for each task in class (e.g., timed, untimed, length of time); (3) support (or lack thereof) from a teacher during each task; (4) directions to students (e.g., oral instructions, written prompts); and (5) materials needed (e.g., prompts, texts, videos). Having clear guidelines reduces subjectivity and allows for equal comparisons across classrooms at each data point, as well as valid comparisons across data points.

RUBRICS FOR SCORING ASSESSMENTS

In addition to clear guidelines for administering, grade-level teams must develop clear expectations for scoring student assessment tasks. All teachers in a grade level can work collaboratively to determine the criteria that will be used to assess student work and create anchor pieces that are representative of the criteria. At Chambers Elementary School, teachers at each grade level began developing rubrics by defining what it meant for a student to meet the expectation of a task related to an end-of-year goal. They created a list similar to the one described above about breakfast cereals, and unpacked the skills and strategies embedded within each of the criteria. For example, to meet the criteria "Compare and contrast ideas/claims from both advertisements and how they are supported in the text," students would need to (1) use information from both advertisements, (2) analyze claims, (3) determine relevant information, and (4) make comparisons. Once the criteria for meeting the standards of the task are clear, teachers can collect and analyze student work according to the rubric. Using student work samples as a basis for discussion, teachers can articulate criteria for "still working" on the goal and "exceeding" the goal.

Collaborative scoring of student work can serve as a professional development experience in and of itself, as teachers learn from one another through discussion about expectations for rigor in students' work and related instructional strategies to improve student learning. It also provides an opportunity to build coherence across classrooms when teachers look at each other's student work.

Analyzing and Using Data

DuFour (2004) suggests that use of data will improve practice when teachers have an opportunity to develop formative assessments together, analyze students' work on these assessments, and compare student performance across classrooms. This process provides teachers with (1) snapshots of student performance within a grade level; (2) opportunities to share ideas, resources, and strategies with colleagues; and (3) data to inform instructional decisions. (For more on classroom-based formative assessment, see Valencia & Hebard, Chapter 5.)

Examples of Cross-Grade Collaboration

As previously discussed, each grade level works collaboratively to develop expectations for end-of-year goals, as well as expectations upon entrance to the grade level. This creates coherence within the grade level; however, each grade level must communicate with its adjacent grade levels (above and below) to build coherence across grades. Vertical meetings provide opportunities for teachers to make their practice public and negotiate expectations for literacy teaching and learning across grade levels. To build a staircase curriculum, each grade's exiting expectations should align with the next grade's entering expectations. In cases where there is a disconnect, teachers can discuss and determine in which grade level specific skills and strategies should be taught. There are often misconceptions about what is expected of students. The expectation may be low at one grade level because teachers do not realize how much students know from previous grades. In other instances, the expectation at a grade level is appropriately high; however, the teachers are unable to teach what they need to because the previous grades had low expectations. Clarifying such occurrences makes everyone's ideas transparent and allows for negotiation of expectations during adjacent-grade-level conversations. The process of sharing and negotiating expectations ensures high-level learning at every grade level.

For example, at Somerset Elementary School, teachers created charts with entering and exiting pupil performance expectations for each grade. They aligned the charts developed for grades PreK–8, so that they could see the progression of expectations across grades. Teachers in adjacent grade levels used sticky notes to make comments, ask questions, or probe for clarification. The adjacent-grade teachers then discussed whether or not they saw gaps (e.g., missing concepts or skills, discrepancies in rigor) or overlaps (e.g., the same concepts being taught in multiple grades). These teachers collaboratively made adjustments to the expectations to ensure strong coherence from grade to grade. The process of whole-school alignment is discussed further in the section about ongoing inquiry and collaboration.

Meeting All Students' Needs

Teachers use data to improve instruction, group students, and address the needs of diverse learners in their classrooms (Brunner et al., 2005; Datnow, Park, & Wohlstetter, 2006; Wayman & Cho, 2008; Young, 2006). Engaging in student achievement goal setting and strategic data collection, as described above, ensures uniform rigor both within and across grade levels. The process makes expectations for learning transparent to all members of the school community and provides a roadmap for instruction.

Assessment data gathered at the beginning of the year provide teachers with information about students' abilities coming into the grade level. Midyear assessments provide information about progress toward end-of-year goals, and end-of-year data let teachers know whether students have met the goals or not. Each data collection point creates a broad-strokes picture about whole-class progress, but also brings individual students' strengths and instructional needs to the surface.

Individual student data enable teachers to tailor instruction to meet the needs of all learners through whole-class, small-group, and individualized instruction (Newmann, 1996). (For more on grouping practices to meet students' needs, see Taylor, Chapter 3.) Having clear learning goals makes explicit what students should know and be able to do by the end of the school year. The standard of rigor does not change for students who are struggling (e.g., fifth graders reading at a third-grade level), but the instruction and scaffolds to help struggling students achieve the goals may be different. The same is true for students excelling beyond grade-level expectations: Teachers should push those students further so that, regardless of their competencies in the fall, they make at least a year's growth in a year's time. This model of competency-based instruction uses data to inform next steps for literacy teaching and learning, rather than an "X marks the spot" notion of grade-level expectations.

In addition, students should engage in self-assessment and personalized goal setting (Au et al., 2008; Hopkins & Reynolds, 2001). Effective teachers create learning environments in which students have opportunities to develop as independent learners. Such a teacher assumes the role of an instructional coach, facilitator, and participant in the classroom, rather than a pedantic teacher (Newmann, 1996; Taylor et al., 2005). (For more on developing independent learners, see Roehrig, Brinkerhoff, Rawls, & Pressley, Chapter 1. For more on teacher coaching and student-centered learning, see Peterson, Chapter 4.)

LOOKING FORWARD

Curricular coherence is not a new idea. As Ananda (2003) asserts, "[The notion that] standards and assessments must be properly aligned is neither new nor controversial. But the need for alignment has acquired new urgency with the escalating use of student assessment results to determine sanctions and rewards for schools, teachers, and students" (p. 1). Race to the Top funding and value-added assessment systems are examples of this urgency related to alignment and coherence. As educators, we need to investigate further ways to (1) analyze and use data responsibly and effectively to inform decision making; (2) build collaborative school teams capable of engaging in ongoing inquiry that leads to sustainable school improvement; and (3) create school contexts to facilitate high-level learning for all students that is coherent across grade levels. In particular, further research should focus on multifaceted data collection, analysis, and use across each of those areas. For example, we need to develop models for evaluating schools, teachers, and students that consider many factors that impede or improve student achievement (e.g., context, resources, student assessments, school artifacts, classroom observations). Research suggests that the following practices will support schools in their efforts to create curricular coherence in their school literacy program and a trajectory of sustainable growth in student literacy achievement:

- Distribute leadership across grade-level/department teams and leadership teams to support curriculum development and coherence (Cobb, 2005; Johnston & Caldwell, 2001; Taylor et al., 2005).
- Use multiple data sources as a basis for instructional planning (Cobb, 2003; Mokhtari, Rosemary, & Edwards, 2007; Stiggins & Duke, 2008).
- Plan coherent professional development that addresses specific needs of teachers and leaders, as evidenced by data (e.g., student achievement data, conversations within a PLC) (Cooter, 2003; Johnston & Caldwell, 2001; King & Newmann, 2001; Taylor et al., 2005).
- Make a long-term commitment to creating and sustaining schoolwide curricular coherence (Au, 2005; McLaughlin & Talbert, 2001; Newmann et al., 2001).

QUESTIONS FOR REFLECTION •

Whole-School PLC and/or Literacy Leadership Team

1. Does our school have a clear vision of what students should know and be able to do when they graduate? To what extent does it drive our school's literacy program?

2. In what ways does each grade-level and/or department team's collaborative goals contribute substantively to the school's vision for student literacy learning?

3. To what extent are literacy achievement expectations for student success rigorous and focused on high-level cognitive demands across grade levels?

4. In what ways does our school infrastructure allow for consistent meetings of various groups within our PLC (e.g., the whole school, grade levels, departments) to discuss curriculum, assessment, and instruction? Are those meetings productive? In what ways can we maximize their effectiveness to create a coherent schoolwide reading program?

5. In what ways can we improve the use of data at multiple levels to improve schoolwide coherence of literacy curriculum, assessment, and instruction?

Grade-Level Teams or Departments

1. To what extent have we made clear goals for what we want our students to know and be able to do by the end of the year? How do these goals build from year to year across grades?

2. To what extent have we addressed the multiple layers of assessment (e.g., summative assessments, ongoing formative assessments, daily high-level tasks, quarterly benchmarks, etc.) to monitor students' progress toward year-end goals?

3. To what extent are the data we have being used to guide instruction? What other data do we need to collect to be able to meet the needs of all learners more strategically?

4. To what extent are the relationships among our pupil performance goals, assessments, data analyses, and instructional plans coherent and clear?

5. In what ways can we improve our grade-level collaboration related to curriculum development, data collection and analysis, and data-driven instruction decision making?

SUGGESTIONS FOR ONGOING PROFESSIONAL LEARNING • • • • • •

Wayman and Cho (2008), as well as other scholars (Halverson, Grigg, Prichett, & Thomas, 2006; Massell, 2001), suggest that collaborating in regard to data increases the conversations that teachers and administrators have with one another, students, and other community members about education. In addition to grade-level and vertical team meetings, whole-school PLCs need regular times to meet throughout the year to discuss curricular coherence (see Figure 19.6 for a sample ongoing collaboration schedule).

McLaughlin and Talbert (2001) suggest that schools set specific times for meeting and collaboration in which educators engage in inquiry cycles about data collection, analysis, and use for improving instruction. For example, in the Oakley School District, all schools have 3 days per year (at the beginning, middle, and end of the school year) dedicated as "staircase check-in days," which are focused on creating and maintaining coherence across grades to ensure student achievement of the school vision for student achievement in literacy. During those whole school meetings, grade-level teams share (1) end-of-year goals; (2) assessment tasks and rubrics; (3) student data and analyses of trends; (4) plans for targeted instruction based on data; and (5) strengths and challenges related to curriculum, assessment, and instruction. Figure 19.7 shows an example of guiding questions that a school might use as staff members assess rigor and coherence across grade levels. These discussions enable the school community to develop a diagnostic view of what constitute data, what the data indicate, and what data need to be collected. These data inform school teams about instructional needs, as well as professional development needs.

	Professional learning and collaboration activities related to curriculum coherence
Weekly	• Grade-level or subject-area department meetings
Monthly	• Vertical team or cross-grade meetings • Literacy grade-level team meetings • Professional development options (e.g., PLCs focused on content—see Chapters 8–17; PLCs focused on teaching processes—see Chapters 1–7; professional book club discussions)
Quarterly	• Whole-school professional collaboration on curriculum coherence

FIGURE 19.6. Sample schedule for ongoing collaboration.

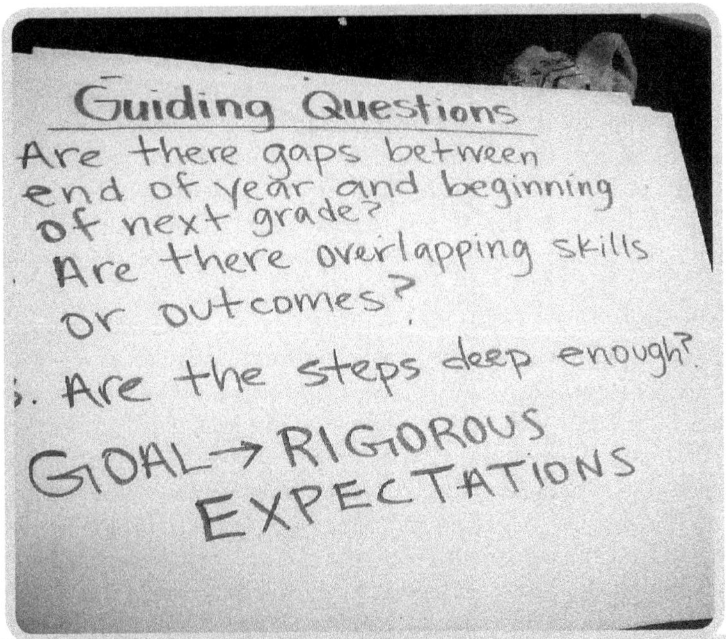

FIGURE 19.6. Guiding questions for whole-school alignment.

RESEARCH-BASED RESOURCES

Afflerbach, P. (2007). *Understanding and using reading assessment, K–12.* Newark, DE: International Reading Association.

Airasian, P. (2000). *Classroom assessment: Concepts and application.* Columbus, OH: McGraw-Hill.

Barr, R., Blachowicz, C., Bates, A., Katz, C., & Kaufman, B. (2006). *Reading diagnosis for teachers: An instructional approach* (5th ed.). Boston: Allyn & Bacon.

Caldwell, J. S., & Leslie, L. (2008). *Intervention strategies to follow informal reading inventory assessment: So what do I do now?* Boston: Allyn & Bacon.

Herman, J. L., Aschbacher, P. R., & Winters, L. (1992). *A practical guide to alternative assessment.* Alexandria, VA: Association for Supervision and Curriculum Development.

McKenna, M. C., & Stahl, K. A. D. (2009). *Assessment for reading instruction* (2nd ed.). New York: Guilford Press.

Morrow, L. M., & Gambrell, L. B. (Eds.). (2011). *Best practices in literacy instruction* (4th ed.). New York: Guilford Press.

Serafini, F. (2010). *Classroom reading assessments: More efficient ways to view and evaluate your readers.* Portsmouth, NH: Heinemann.

Taylor, B. M. (2011). *Catching schools: An action guide to schoolwide reading improvement.* Portsmouth, NH: Heinemann.

REFERENCES

Airasian, P. (2000). *Classroom assessment: Concepts and application.* Columbus, OH: McGraw-Hill.

Ananda, S. (2003). *Rethinking issues of alignment under No Child Left Behind* (Knowledge Brief). San Francisco: WestEd.

Au, K. H. (2002). Elementary programs: Guiding change in a time of standards. In S. B. Wepner, D. S. Strickland, & J. T. Feeley (Eds.), *The administration and supervision of reading programs* (3rd ed., pp. 59–79). New York: Teachers College Press.

Au, K. H. (2005). Negotiating the slippery slope: School change and literacy achievement. *Journal of Literacy Research, 37*(3), 267–288.

Au, K. H., & Raphael, T. E. (2011). The staircase curriculum: Whole-school collaboration to improve literacy achievement. *New England Reading Association Journal, 46*(2), 1–8.

Au, K. H., Raphael, T. E., & Mooney, K. (2008). Improving reading achievement in elementary schools: Guiding change in a time of standards. In S. B. Wepner & D. S. Strickland (Eds.), *The administration and supervision of reading programs* (4th ed., pp. 71–89). New York: Teachers College Press.

Brookover, W. B., Schweitzer, J. H., Schneider, J. M., Beady, C. H., Flood, P. K., & Wisenbaker, J. M. (1978). Elementary school social climate and school achievement. *American Educational Research Journal, 15*(2), 301–318.

Brown, J. S., Collins, A., & Duguid, P. (1989). Situated cognition and the culture of learning. *Educational Researcher, 18*(1), 32–42.

Brunner, C., Fasca, C., Heinze, J., Honey, M., Light, D., Mandinach, E., et al. (2005). Linking data and learning: The Grow Network study. *Journal of Education for Students Placed at Risk, 10*(3), 241–267.

Bryk, A. S., Rollow, S. G., & Pinnell, G. S. (1996). Urban school development: Literacy as a lever for change. *Educational Policy, 10*(2), 172–201.

Cobb, C. (2005). Literacy teams: Sharing leadership to improve student learning. *The Reading Teacher, 58*(5), 472–474.

Cooter, R. B. (2003). Teacher "capacity-building" helps urban children succeed in reading. *The Reading Teacher, 57*(2), 198–205.

Copland, M. A. (2003). Leadership of inquiry: Building and sustaining capacity for school improvement. *Educational Evaluation and Policy Analysis, 25*(4), 375–395.

Datnow, A., Park, V., & Wohlstetter, P. (2006). Achieving with data. Retrieved from *http://newschools.org/files/AchievingWithData.pdf*.

DuFour, R. (2004). What is a "professional learning community"? *Educational Leadership, 61*(8), 6–11.

Earl, L., & Katz, S. (2006). Leading schools in a data rich world: Harnessing data for school improvement. Retrieved from *https://eed.alaska.gov/nclb/2008wc/Focus_On_Leadership.pdf*.

Fullan, M. (2000). The return of large-scale reform. *Journal of Educational Change, 1*, 5–28.

Fullan, M. (2003). *The moral imperative of school leadership.* Thousand Oaks, CA: Corwin Press.

Hallinger, P., & Murphy, J. F. (1986). The social context of effective schools. *American Journal of Education, 94*(3), 328–355.

Halverson, R., Grigg, J., Prichett, R., & Thomas, C. (2006). The new instructional leadership: Creating data-driven instructional systems in schools. Retrieved from *www.cew.wisc.edu/docs/resource_collections/HalversonEtAl_TheNewInstructionalLeadership.pdf*.

Hargreaves, A., & Fink, D. (2006). *Sustainable leadership.* San Francisco: Jossey-Bass.

Hopkins, D., & Reynolds, D. (2001). The past, present, and future of school improvement: Towards the third age. *British Educational Research Journal, 27*(4), 459–475.

International Reading Association. (2004). *The role and qualifications of the reading coach in the United States: A position paper.* Newark, DE: Author.

John-Steiner, V., & Mahn, H. (1996). Sociocultural approaches to learning and development: A Vygotskian framework. *Educational Psychologist, 31*(3–4), 191–206.

Johnston, C., & Caldwell, B. (2001). Leadership and organisational learning in the quest for world class schools. *International Journal of Educational Management, 15*(2), 94–102.

Joyce, B., & Showers, B. (1983). *Power in staff development through research on teaching.* Alexandria, VA: Association for Supervision and Curriculum Development.

Kamil, M., & Pearson, P. D. (1979, Winter). Theory and practice in teaching reading. *New York University Education Quarterly,* 10–16.

Kennedy, E. (2010). *Narrowing the achievement gap: Motivation, engagement, and self-efficacy matter.* Annual Proceedings of the Reading Association of Ireland.

King, M. B., & Newmann, F. M. (2001). Building capacity through professional development: Conceptual and empirical considerations. *International Journal of Educational Management, 15*(2), 86–93.

Lambert, L. (1998). *Building leadership capacity in schools.* Alexandria, VA: Association for Supervision and Curriculum Development.

Lambert, L. (2002). A framework for shared leadership. *Educational Leadership, 59*(8), 37–40.

Lawless, K. A., & Pellegrino, J. W. (2007). Professional development in integrating technology into teaching and learning: Knowns, unknowns, and ways to pursue better questions and answers. *Review of Educational Research, 77*(4), 575–614.

Louis, K. S., Marks, H. M., & Kruse, S. (1996). Teachers' professional community in restructuring schools. *American Educational Research Journal, 33*(4), 757–798.

Martin, E. R. (2010). Kids' cereal advertising still a problem. *Parentdish.* Retrieved from *www.parentdish.com/2010/01/25/kids-cereal-advertising-still-a-problem.*

Mason, B., Mason, D. A., Mendez, M., Nelsen, G., & Orwig, R. (2005). Effects of top-down and bottom-up elementary school standards reform in an underperforming California district. *Elementary School Journal, 105*(4), 353–376.

Massell, D. (2001). The theory and practice of using data to build capacity: State and local strategies and their effects. In S. H. Fuhrman (Ed.), *From the capitol to the classroom: Standards-based reform in the states* (pp. 148–169). Chicago: University of Chicago Press.

McLaughlin, M. W., & Talbert, J. E. (2001). *Professional communities and the work of high school teaching.* Chicago: University of Chicago Press.

Mokhtari, K., Rosemary, C., & Edwards, P. (2007). Making instructional decisions based on data: What, how, and why. *The Reading Teacher, 61*(4), 354–359.

Newmann, F. (1996). *Authentic achievement: Restructuring schools for intellectual quality.* San Francisco: Jossey-Bass.

Newmann, F. M., King, M. B., & Youngs, P. (2000). Professional development that addresses school capacity: Lessons from urban elementary schools. *American Journal of Education, 108*(4), 259–299.

Newmann, F. M., Smith, B.-A., Allensworth, E., & Bryk, A. S. (2001). *School instructional program coherence: Benefits and challenges.* Chicago: Consortium on Chicago School Research.

O'Neill, J. (2000). SMART goals, SMART schools. *Educational Leadership, 57*(5), 46–50.

Pressley, M., Mohan, L., Raphael, L. M., & Fingeret, L. (2007). How does Bennett Woods Elementary School produce such high reading and writing achievement? *Journal of Educational Psychology, 99*(2), 221–240.

Purkey, S. C., & Smith, M. S. (1983). Effective schools: A review. *Elementary School Journal, 83*(4), 426–452.

Putnam, R. T., & Borko, H. (2000). What do new views of knowledge and thinking have to say about research on teacher learning? *Educational Researcher, 29*(1), 4–15.

Raphael, T. E., Au, K. H., & Goldman, S. R. (2009). Whole school instructional improvement through the standards-based change process: A developmental model. In J. Hoffman & Y. Goodman (Eds.), *Changing literacies for changing times* (pp. 198–229). New York: Routledge.

Rowan, B. (1990). Commitment and control: Alternative strategies for organizational design of schools. *Review of Research in Education, 16,* 353–389.

Sargent, J. K. (2012). About data retreat workshops. Retrieved from *www.cesa7.org/schoolim-prove/Data/Data_Retreats/Data_Retreat_Process.asp*.

Spillane, J. P. (2003). Educational leadership. *Educational Evaluation and Policy Analysis, 25*(4), 343–346.

Spillane, J. P. (2006). *Distributed leadership.* San Francisco: Jossey-Bass.

Stiggins, R., & Duke, D. (2008). Effective instructional leadership requires assessment leadership. *Phi Delta Kappan, 90*(4), 285–291.

Stoll, L., Bolam, R., McMahon, A., Wallace, M., & Thomas, S. (2006). Professional learning communities: A review of the literature. *Journal of Educational Change, 7,* 221–258.

Strahan, D. (2003). Promoting a collaborative professional culture in three elementary schools that have beaten the odds. *Elementary School Journal, 104*(2), 127–146.

Taylor, B. M., Pearson, P. D., Peterson, D. S., & Rodriguez, M. C. (2005). The CIERA School Change Framework: An evidence-based approach to professional development and school reading improvement. *Reading Research Quarterly, 40*(1), 40–69.

Teddlie, C., Kirby, P. C., & Stringfield, S. (1989). Effective versus ineffective schools: Observable differences in the classroom. *American Journal of Education, 97*(3), 221–236.

Timperley, H. S. (2009). Distributing leadership to improve outcomes for students. In K. Leithwood, B. Mascall, & T. Strauss (Eds.), *Distributed leadership according to the evidence* (pp. 197–222). London: Routledge.

Timperley, H. S., & Parr, J. M. (2007). Closing the achievement gap through evidence-based inquiry at multiple levels of the education system. *Journal of Advanced Academics, 19*(1), 90–115.

Vissher, A. J., & Witziers, B. (2004). Subject departments as professional communities? *British Educational Research Journal, 30*(6), 785–800.

Walker-Dalhouse, D., & Risko, V. J. (2008). Learning from literacy successes in high-achieving urban schools. *The Reading Teacher, 61*(5), 422–424.

Wayman, J. C., & Cho, V. (2008). Preparing educators to effectively use student data systems. In T. J. Kowalski & T. J. Lasley (Eds.), *Handbook on data-based decision-making in education* (pp. 89–104). New York: Routledge.

Weber, C. M. (2010). *Juxtaposing words and images: Using digital narratives to capture teachers' conceptions of literacy.* Unpublished doctoral dissertation, University of Illinois at Chicago.

Wellisch, J. B., MacQueen, A. H., Carriere, R. A., & Duck, G. A. (1978). School management and organization in successful schools (ESAA in-depth study schools). *Sociology of Education, 51*(3), 211–226.

Young, V. M. (2006). Teachers' use of data: Loose coupling, agenda setting, and team norms. *American Journal of Education, 112,* 521–548.

CHAPTER 20

Improving the School Reading Program ● ● ● ● ● ● ● ● ● ● ● ● ● ●

A New Call for Collaboration

SHARON WALPOLE
KRISTINA NAJERA

During the time that we have been involved in school-based improvement efforts, collaboration among teachers as grade-level teams and between teams, coaches, and specialists has emerged as a central component of professional learning in schools. It may be that the era of Reading First (RF), which introduced grade-level team meetings as a vehicle of intensive professional development (PD) efforts guided by coaches, got the collaboration ball rolling. At the conclusion of RF, that ball was handed off to even more comprehensive collaborative efforts: response to intervention (RTI), which typically involves team-based collaborations to design increasingly more intensive instructional interventions, and Race to the Top, which typically requires professional learning communities (PLCs) reflecting on instruction and an intense focus on turning around chronically low-performing schools. Alternatively, the push for greater collaboration may be the result of No Child Left Behind accountability structures—which require us to demand success for all children, and which highlight the relative performance of children according to their socioeconomic status, their racial and ethnic backgrounds, and their status within special education. As schools find children or groups of children who are not thriving, teachers must collaborate to identify possible explanations and to address them. At first blush, collaborative problem solving seems like a common-sense approach to a complex problem; more heads are surely better than one. In practice, though, collaboration can be very difficult. It is a shift for many teachers. In this chapter, we share practical lessons from research that may make the road to collaboration smoother.

OVERVIEW OF RESEARCH

Let's start by clarifying what we mean by *collaboration*. Interestingly, dictionaries contain two strikingly different definitions. Collaboration can be an act of working together to create something, or it can be an instance of treason, when one party works secretly with an enemy. It is useful to remember the treasonous definition; before collaborations become part of a school's culture, individual teachers and groups of teachers may function as independent nations, and their work together may be seen as somewhat treasonous. In schools, perhaps positive collaborations may be viewed initially as enemy invasions. Positive collaborations typically involve individuals who bring very different perspectives to a task, and those different perspectives may at first be seen as enemy tactics as teachers protect their own interests. What do individuals with different roles and goals actually do when faced with complex problems? They don't immediately or naturally collaborate.

It is not uncommon to confuse the terms *cooperation* and *coordination*, or to substitute them for *collaboration*. Figure 20.1, drawing on the work of Mohammed, Murray, Coleman, Roberts, and Grim (2011), compares and contrasts these terms. Cooperation is easy. Coordination is slightly harder. And when we call a relationship collaborative, the plot thickens. Think about regular education and special education teachers really working together for the first time. What about reading specialists and special educators? How about principals and coaches? Speech–language pathologists and kindergarten teachers? Teachers of English language learners (ELLs) and reading specialists? Collaboration, rather than cooperation or coordination, is costly in terms of time and effort; it also includes a level of risk that may be uncomfortable to some, or many, teachers.

Collaborative efforts in schools take more time to plan and maintain than coordinated or cooperative efforts. They require conscious efforts at trust building. They may require a creative and uncomfortable restructuring of roles and responsibilities. Because they demand the processing of multiple viewpoints, collaborative efforts yield decisions more slowly (Mohammad et al., 2011). Given that fact, it makes sense to review research on collaboration to maximize its yield. It also makes sense that not all intensive teacher collaboration leads to changes in instruction—let alone changes in student achievement (for a discussion, see Carlisle & Berebitsky, 2010).

Cooperation	Coordination	Collaboration
Share information as needed	Share goals and leverage resources as needed	Set a framework for decision making; share responsibility for implementation
Make independent decisions	Share goals, but maintain independent responsibilities	Work together, evaluating the effects of decisions

FIGURE 20.1. Cooperation, coordination, or collaboration? Based on Mohammed, Murray, Coleman, Roberts, and Grim (2011).

You may be surprised to know that a strong collaborative culture may thwart specific efforts at instructional change. Collaboration is a type of shared or distributed leadership. If teachers are empowered to collaborate and are in fact accustomed to doing so, they are likely to oppose ideas that appear to come from the "top" or from those who are not part of the collaboration group. In a recent study of a model of literacy coaching aimed at implementation of *questioning the author* (Beck & McKeown, 2006; Beck, McKeown, Hamilton, & Kucan, 1997)—an instructional strategy with strong empirical support—most (but not all) schools with strong histories of teacher collaboration effectively resisted the efforts of coaches whose jobs were to initiate this new type of instruction. The researchers speculated that the collaborative teacher networks had already chosen their focus areas, and that they were not willing to address those contained in the initiative. Perhaps a lesson, then, is that when teachers engage in extended collaboration, they must consent before any new PD initiatives are launched (Matsumura, Garnier, & Resnick, 2010).

Furthermore, a strong collaborative culture does not necessarily translate to improved student achievement. Brinson and Steiner (2007) found that although their school leadership team, which included teacher leaders, improved its ability to communicate effectively and make decisions toward common goals, student performance did not improve. It was not until the team participated in a 2-day data retreat that performance improved. The authors attributed this improvement to *collective teacher efficacy* (CTE). Teachers with CTE perceive that the efforts of the entire faculty will affect student achievement. Therefore, they are willing to put more effort into the planning and implementation of new ideas. In this school, teachers believed that their efforts as a group contributed to improved achievement. They also received extensive, sustained PD under the guidance of the principal to help them improve practice. Brinson and Steiner provide several recommendations for building CTE:

- Develop instructional knowledge and practices.
- Provide opportunities for collaboration and skill sharing.
- Identify the reasons for success and provide feedback on performance.
- Include teachers in decision making.

For schools where collaboration is not the norm, leaders interested in creating collaborative PD environments should approach the initiative with respect and patience. When teachers feel supported as they build instructional knowledge, participate in decision making, and engage in opportunities to share skills and experiences, they are more likely to try new strategies and techniques, and therefore to change their instructional practices. In fact, a collaborative school culture has been associated with higher reading and math scores in third and fourth grades (Sherblom, Marshall, & Sherblom, 2006). In addition, Duke's (2006) synthesis of characteristics of successful elementary school turn-around cases revealed some essentials: a high value on teamwork and collaboration, a commitment to data-driven decisions, a focus on shared responsibility, and a system for distributed leadership. None of these essentials can be realized without collaboration. Logically, then, collaboration may be necessary but insufficient for real school improvement. For this reason, it is important to appreciate researchers' emerging understanding of the stages and process of collaboration. (For more on schoolwide reading improvement, see Taylor, Chapter 18, this volume. For more on PLCs, see Peterson, Chapter 21.)

Stages of Collaboration

Initial efforts at teacher collaboration may fail because they are simply too idealistic. It may be useful to think of the development of collaboration among teachers in stages. In all disciplines, the term *stages* refers to a sequence of competencies through which individuals tend to pass in order and during which behaviors are similar. For example, emergent readers rely on picture cues and syntax to recognize words. Once they master the alphabetic principle, they move to the beginning reading stage, where they focus much of their attention on sounding out words. Finally, as they build their sight vocabularies and consolidate their decoding knowledge, their attention is spent not on picture cues or decoding, but on the development of fluency. Any elementary teacher knows that it is not possible to bypass the decoding stage and take an emergent reader directly to fluency. Why, then, do we expect teachers to move automatically from independent, closed-door work into fruitful collaboration?

Weick (1979) suggested stages in the formation of a climate of collaboration among teachers, and Dooner, Manzuk, and Clifton (2007) used these stages to understand a 2-year teacher collaboration. The stages are depicted in cyclical form in Figure 20.2. Teachers enter any collaboration with their personal goals in mind. The first stage in collaboration, then, is to explore these personal goals to see whether the group's individual ends overlap enough to move to the second stage, *common means*. During this stage, goals and norms for meetings are set, and means (e.g., reading professional literature, observing one another, analyzing data, common lesson planning) for reaching goals are established. As teachers participate in the common means, though, tensions *must* arise. Tensions and disagreements, both personal and professional, are necessary to movement to the next stage, *common ends*. Differences must be revealed, and either resolved or acknowledged. If they are suppressed or ignored, they will only reemerge later, thwarting collective efforts.

During the common-ends stage, the group refocuses on its collective goals. This time, though, the group members' understanding of one another and of the issues that they are collaborating about is different. They leverage this enhanced understanding, personal and professional, to preserve their group's foundations and to work through the tensions. The final stage, *diverse ends*, can be either positive or negative. When a collaborative group reaches this stage, either it may disband (and members go their own ways with the ideas explored), or it may reach the truly collaborative goal of successful adaptations for individual teachers.

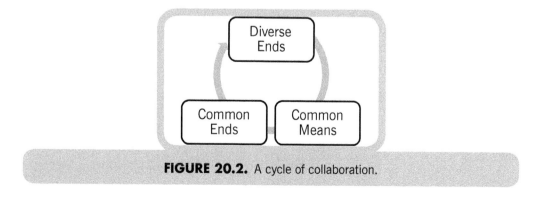

FIGURE 20.2. A cycle of collaboration.

This idea of a collaborative cycle is represented in Figure 20.2. Although it comes from the literature on PLCs (again, see Peterson, Chapter 21), it is typically temporary and interest-based. However, the notion of a cycle may also be useful in those ongoing collaborations that are not voluntary. Think, for instance, of grade-level teams. They are not voluntary. Typically, members do not have control over the focus of their collaborations; they may meet for a purpose set by an administrator or a coach (e.g., common lesson planning or data analysis). Thinking of their collaboration in terms of a cycle, though, may still be helpful. In fact, it may be essential to the efficacy of involuntary collaborations.

Figure 20.3 reshapes Weick's (1979) cycle for a standing collaborative team. In the first stage, members *build community* by getting to know one another. In a grade-level team, it may be helpful to do this by setting up an external ice-breaking task first—one that is *not* about the experiences members share by nature of their work together. From our experience, we recommend distributing community building across time, rather than devoting whole sessions to building community. Time set aside during every meeting of a group for the sole purpose of community building reminds all members that their own identities are assets to the collaboration, and that the identities of others in the group are interesting and important.

As community is built, team members must infuse collaborative efforts with ideas. Some ideas come from members themselves, and draw from areas of expertise and experience. Examples may range from suggestions that have worked in the past to lesson plans or demonstrations. Other ideas come from outside the group. Examples may include new standards and assessments, curriculum, or professional readings. Wherever ideas originate, collaborative groups must have strategies or protocols for dealing with them. The best strategies will anticipate and invite cognitive conflict (disagreement over ideas) and prevent or deflect affective conflict (personal disagreements). It is natural, as collaborative teams *grapple with ideas,* for conflicts to emerge. We have to learn to see conflicts as helpful to learning and to change. They are also helpful, in

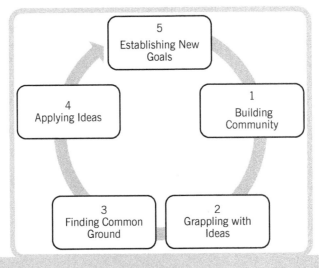

FIGURE 20.3. The cycle of collaboration for a standing collaborative team.

a recursive way, as a means for group members to get to know one another better as professionals. This is because they reveal important commitments and biases. Meeting norms and protocols help teachers navigate these conflicts in a respectful way.

As new ideas are infused into a collaborative team, they will incite both conflicts and solutions. The trick is to have strategies for *finding common ground*. Conflicts tend to arise between two individuals or between two groups. In some cases, the groups find common ground over time, accepting that the ideas have more in common than they seemed to at first glance. In other cases, what appears to be a conflict over the merit of a new idea is really a conflict over whether its implementation is too time-consuming or difficult. Either way, an essential strategy is moving from the world of ideas into the world of instruction. Many conceptual disagreements can be solved after team members have actually tried to do something new. Trials can be speeded by the creation of shared lesson plans.

It may seem counterintuitive, but after new ideas have been tried, they can be more universally applied. Strategies for wider *application* include targeted reflection by the teacher or teachers who tried something new. They can also include moving a targeted instructional strategy to a new student target (maybe a different group) or to a new classroom. Teachers can work together to consider how an instructional strategy would be different for a different grade level, a different grouping format, or a different achievement profile.

Finally, the team members have to consider ways to move on. When a group has built some community, successfully sought new ideas, resolved conflicts, applied ideas to real classroom situations, and reflected in ways that make implementation reasonable, the stage is set for *establishing a new focus*. Although there will be strengths on which to build this time, group members must anticipate a return to the start of the cycle—with all of its stages.

Although a collaborative group's dynamics may be cyclical, it is also useful to understand how individuals respond to change initiatives. Change can be hard for people to accept, incorporate, and master. The *concerns-based adoption model* (CBAM; Hall & Hord, 2006) is one framework that helps us understand the need to acknowledge where individuals are in the change process and to think about how to help them move toward being more engaged and comfortable. The CBAM comprises two components: the *stages-of-concern* continuum and the *levels-of-use* continuum. In the stages-of-concern continuum, individuals range from being unaware of the need for and options for change to being actively engaged in the change process. In the levels-of-use continuum, individuals may start out resisting the change, but with time, training, and coaching they can become willing to explore the change, then become more comfortable with it, and perhaps eventually become expert at it. Collaborative efforts to improve literacy opportunities for all students should attend to teachers' stages of concern and acknowledge the transformations required. Furthermore, this model suggests that full implementation of any change initiative may take a few years as individuals move from early concerns to active engagement.

Researchers have made the CBAM concrete by considering differences in implementation of new instructional strategies as a function of individual teacher differences. For example, in their Teacher Learning Cohort initiative, Brownell, Adams, Sindelar, Waldron, and Vanhover (2006) selected a group of teachers who embraced the collaborative initiative but still differed in their implementation. They learned that high implementers were teachers who were more knowledgeable about curriculum and pedagogy, more positive and proactive in their approaches to management and student behavior, and more student-focused in their beliefs about teaching and learning. Perhaps the lesson here is that just as individual students respond in different ways and at different rates to the instructional opportunities we offer to them, individual teachers will respond in different ways and at different rates to the collaborative communities we build with them.

The lessons shared by Vaughn, Hughes, Schumm, and Klingner (1998) may be helpful to school-based collaborative teams. These researchers were trying to support general education teachers serving the needs of special education students, and they were not immediately successful. They began with the idea that a shared respect among participants and a new knowledge base would lead to instructional changes. The researchers shared instructional ideas, and teachers chose the ones that they wanted to implement. Then they came back together to reflect. After participating in this collaborative effort, teachers reported that they enjoyed it, but the research team doubted that it had led to systemic changes in instruction. The PD was too focused on the reflective process.

The researchers next tried entirely site-based work, with needs assessments driving the selection of instructional strategies for each site. That too failed to change instruction because it was too content-oriented. Finally, they struck a balance between content and process. This time, they chose just four instructional practices supported by research, included in-class coaching and demonstration lessons, and set up time for teachers to engage in collaborative problem solving. What was different about this final iteration was that the teachers were not collaborating to choose instructional strategies to implement. All of them were implementing the same strategies. Their collaborative efforts, then, were targeted toward solving the problems of practice that these new strategies revealed. This approach—balancing content and community—was the most successful in terms of changing practice. To say that it was the most successful, though, is not to say that it was perfect; two teachers remained chronically low implementers, even with all of this support. Clearly, both the pace and process of the collaboration matter.

Furthermore, the most successful collaboration efforts are those in which (1) leadership is distributed to ensure shared decision making; (2) responsibility for implementing instruction that improves achievement is shared among staff members; and (3) knowledge of effective delivery of instructional strategies is built through sharing skills, providing feedback on performance, and identifying the reasons for success.

Process of Collaboration

After studying the efforts of state-level stakeholders collaborating to inform special education policy, Mohammad and colleagues (2011) proposed seven supports for collaboration. These include setting a goal or vision for the collaboration, carefully formulating a collaborative team, gathering resources to facilitate the work, establishing effective communication norms, beginning with a process that can be revisited, including ongoing evaluation data, and adapting to the needs of the individual site. We think that these supports provide a planning template that can go far in facilitating productive collaboration. The steps are listed in Figure 20.4, which we have modified so that it can be used as a planning template.

PLANNING TEMPLATE FOR COLLABORATION

Set a goal and vision.

All members of a collaborative team must know why they are working together and what they hope to accomplish.

What is our goal?

Choose the right team.

If the goal of a collaboration affects others, they must be included on the team from the beginning. Having their input as decisions are made is much more productive than gathering it afterward.

Who should be here?

Gather resources before you start.

Time, money, space, books, data, or personnel resources essential to the collaboration must be acquired up front. It does not make sense to meet without adequate tools.

What do we need?

(continued)

FIGURE 20.4. Up-front supports for collaboration. Based on Mohammad et al. (2011).

Think about constructive, respectful ways to communicate.

Spend time talking about each individual's strengths, empowering the group to acknowledge differences as essential ingredients in collaboration rather than as roadblocks to avoid.

How are we different?

Establish a clear, flexible process.

Norms for how the group will begin its work can be established and then revisited as more information is gathered.

How will we use time?

Be accountable.

Evaluation data, collected across time as the group is working, provides concrete evidence of the extent to which the group's decisions are having the desired results.

How can we know if things are working?

Consider the context.

Problems are different, people are different, and places are different. Collaborations must be informed by the local environment rather than imported or imposed.

How is our situation unique?

FIGURE 20.4. *(continued)*

Even when we acknowledge the stages of collaboration and attend carefully to its process, we may not achieve schoolwide improvement. Also essential are the targets of that collaboration, including both the large contexts and the very specific choices that teacher teams embrace as they solve problems in practice.

Targets of Collaboration

We see two related targets for collaboration: teacher PD efforts and instructional services for children. Regardless of the initial target of any collaborative effort, "the rubber meets the road" when the collaboration influences teachers' instructional decisions and actions. An initial effort to design PD for teachers ended with design of a small-group instruction model that included both support for struggling readers and enrichment for readers with strong skills (Walpole, McKenna, & Morrill, 2011). The model assumed that teachers could use simple informal assessment data to form small groups focusing only on phonemic awareness and word recognition, word recognition and fluency, fluency and comprehension, or vocabulary and comprehension. Once the groups were formed, teachers used a small set of instructional procedures to develop students' skills and strategies, evaluating their success through progress-monitoring assessments every 3 weeks (Walpole & McKenna, 2009). When the small-group model was tested, the extent to which coaches collaborated with grade-level teams was associated with implementation, with management of groups and transitions, and with effective vocabulary instruction for third-grade teachers (Walpole, McKenna, Uribe-Zarain, & Lamitina, 2010).

Teacher study groups (TSGs) are collaborations focused on classroom instruction (Gersten, Dimino, Jayanthi, Kim, & Santoro, 2010). Specifically, TSGs are grade-level groups that meet twice a month with a facilitator. Their purpose is to increase teacher knowledge of research-based content and improve instructional delivery of this content. During meetings, teams discuss research-based strategies, which they learn in a logical and sequential manner predetermined by the researchers, and apply the strategies to the next week's lessons. At the next meeting, teachers describe what worked and what didn't and collaborate to refine application of the strategy. In this manner, teachers share their experiences and take part in the evaluation of their lessons. The TSG approach led to increases in student achievement and to improvements in teacher knowledge and instruction in reading comprehension and vocabulary (Gersten et al., 2010). (For more on TSGs, see Peterson, Chapter 21.)

RTI is a natural target for collaborative efforts that focus on providing necessary instruction to children. A persistent problem in schools is the placement of students in special education environments because their reading achievement is weak—not because of a specific learning disability, but because of lack of access to immediate and targeted instruction. RTI is a partnership of general educators and special educators with the goal of serving students together, flexibly, and as soon as problems are suspected, in order to prevent special education placements. RTI efforts require instruction that is provided in increasingly intensive tiers. Tier 1 instruction is high-quality grade-level instruction, occurring in mixed-ability classrooms. For students whose needs are not being met (as revealed by data), additional, more intensive Tier 2 instruction must be provided. This instruction can be provided by the classroom teacher or by other educators. If the combination of Tier 1 and Tier 2 instruction still does not yield adequate progress, Tier 3 instruction is warranted. Tier 3 instruction almost always occurs outside the classroom in a very specialized curriculum; it can be provided by special educators who are also serving those students already identified for services. In RTI systems, all students have access to all services, personnel, and curriculum materials within a school, regardless of their status. A change from label-driven interventions to a seamless, child-oriented system may seem logical, but in real life it demands extensive, thoughtful, creative collaboration.

There are two general models for RTI. In the problem-solving model, teachers collaboratively design classroom-based interventions for individual students, try them out, collect efficacy data, determine their effectiveness, and generate next steps. This model is useful when the number of struggling students in a school is relatively small. Typically, an RTI problem-solving team including the classroom teacher, a school psychologist, and members of the special education team meets for each RTI case, reviewing data and creating an individual Tier 2 plan for the teacher to use. They reconvene after a period of implementation to review additional data, redesign their plan if necessary, or consider moving the student to a Tier 3 intervention. RTI problem-solving teams pose a collaboration opportunity (and challenge) in the real world of instruction; they might benefit from Mohammed and colleagues' (2011) processes as presented in Figure 20.4.

In the standard protocol model, the school anticipates student needs and develops a system (including personnel, time, curriculum materials, and assessments). Typically, the system is arranged by grade level. For example, a school could design a grade-level reading block for 1 hour, and then a small-group rotation for 45 minutes. Students could be assigned to Tier 3 intervention during that small-group rotation (moving out of the classroom) or to one of three skills-based groups. Each classroom teacher could provide additional instruction in comprehension, in fluency, or in word recognition during small-group time, with students assigned to groups on the basis of their assessments.

Assessment Profile	Teacher Assignment	Instructional Target
Above-grade-level comprehension	Gifted education specialist	Research projects
On-grade-level comprehension	Classroom teacher 1	Literature circles
On-grade-level comprehension	Classroom teacher 2	Literature circles
Weak comprehension, strong fluency	Classroom teacher 3	Reciprocal teaching
Weak comprehension, weak fluency, strong word recognition	Classroom teacher 4	Peer-assisted learning strategies
Weak comprehension, weak fluency, weak word recognition	Reading specialist	Word study and repeated readings
Weak comprehension, weak fluency, weak word recognition	Special educator and paraprofessional	Commercial intervention program

FIGURE 20.5. A standard protocol model for RTI.

For this small-group instruction to constitute Tier 2, collaborative design of the lesson plan for each type of group across classrooms would be required (see Figure 20.5).

Another example of a standard protocol includes creating a Tier 2 intervention block for each grade level, and moving a reading specialist, gifted education specialist, special educator, and paraprofessional into the team. With four grade-level teachers, this opens up the potential for seven small groups, each with a particular assessment profile and a specific instructional target. The groups (identified in Figure 20.5) can be revisited at the end of each marking period. Extensive collaboration will be required to ensure that each teacher supports the placement of his or her homeroom students in a specific group and understands the instructional model for all groups.

SUMMARY OF BIG IDEAS FROM RESEARCH

Research on collaboration, comprising case studies of collaborative efforts, yields useful advice for teams. Below we list the big ideas across settings.

- Collaboration requires an extensive commitment of time and resources.
- Collaboration is a form of shared leadership.
- Collaboration is a cultural shift for most organizations.
- Collaboration proceeds in a cycle.
- Collaboration requires a thoughtful process.
- Collaboration makes sense when the stakes are highest—that is, when schools are planning PD for teachers and inclusive tiered instruction for all students.
- RTI efforts require collaborative skills and structures.

EXAMPLES OF EFFECTIVE PRACTICES

RTI efforts force us to embrace the challenges of collaboration. As we consider our own work in school-based collaborations, we see that they have relied on several up-front assurances. First, they acknowledge that individuals have specialized expertise, developed both through formal study and through experience. Positive collaborations—those yielding creative solutions and products—come from the union of these differences and overcome the initial barriers such differences present. As you consider the strategies for successful collaboration we present in this chapter, we invite you to try on some new language for size. For instance, a classroom teacher's collaboration with other teachers of reading may begin with presenting a problem in which the teacher needs advice from more knowledgeable others. It might sound like this: "You probably can be more creative about this than I am because you *have more specialized training.*" In different dyads, the italicized language can be replaced with other phrases. Consider these alternatives: *have more experience, are more knowledgeable about bilingual education, are trained in special education, are more expert in interpreting assessments, are a fantastic manager, are a children's literature expert, have experience as a supervisor,* or *are accomplished at scheduling.* The possibilities for drawing on the expertise of colleagues are endless. But they begin with an acknowledgment of differential expertise.

Grade-Level RTI Collaborations

RTI, in either the problem-solving model or the standard protocol, is a collaborative challenge for many schools. It requires that classroom teachers, special educators, and reading specialists work together more flexibly and abandon their previous role definitions. One of the strengths that special educators typically bring to the collaboration table is their understanding of the role of curriculum-based measures (CBMs) in evaluating student-level RTI. CBMs were designed originally for special education, but RTI efforts begin in the general education classroom. Special educators, then, are in a strong position to help general education colleagues collect, interpret, and use CBM data in instructional decision making. They may need support, though. Simple discussion protocols such as the following, suggested by Capizzi and Barton-Arwood (2009), can break the ice and empower truly collaborative decision making:

1. Have you had students in the past with similar problems?
2. What strategies have been successful in the past?
3. Are there any new materials or techniques that we should try?

General education teachers, though, tend to have a deeper understanding of the general education curriculum and its grade-level high-stakes testing requirements. Their expertise, and the demands on them to serve an increasingly diverse group of learners, are also factors to consider in RTI collaborations. The teachers may bring paraprofessional partners into the mix, creating a new set of opportunities to serve student needs in creative ways.

In one school, leaders decided that they wanted to implement RTI to decrease special education referrals and increase the use of data-based decision making. (For more on data-based decision making, see Valencia & Hebard, Chapter 5, and Weber, Chapter 19, this volume.) They started by identifying team members for each grade level (special and general educators, reading specialists, and instructional leaders) and using a planning template, similar to the one in Figure 20.4 (above), to lay the groundwork for effective collaboration prior to implementation. Each grade-level team, referred to as a *progress-monitoring team* (PMT), then identified up-front supports such as the team's goal, the resources needed, a description of each member's strengths, a process for solving problems, and a process for collecting and analyzing data and making instructional decisions about needed supports and interventions. The PMTs met regularly to make decisions regarding moving students between instructional tiers.

Each time a PMT met, team members followed the process for solving problems. They started by defining the problem as specific to a skill area. For one group of students, the problem was oral reading fluency. Next they analyzed the problem, considering multiple explanations for why these target students' fluency was not improving. They speculated that it could be because of low engagement during Tier 1 fluency instruction, a lack of feedback during repeated readings, or inappropriate text levels. They developed a plan to implement 3 weeks of 15-minute daily sessions of repeated readings in text that was one grade level below the students' placement. After considering multiple alternatives, they agreed that they would implement the plan during their small-group rotations, and would replace a wide-reading center with a repeated-reading treatment, facilitated by the grade-level team's paraprofessional. To retask the work of this individual was costly to all of the teachers on the team, so they had to agree that the need was real, that the approach was consistent with research, and that the efficacy of their efforts could be documented. Classroom teachers first coordinated their reading rotations so that the paraprofessional could move from one room to another every 15 minutes. Teachers selected reading materials that were consistent with their goals for content-area instruction. A special educator created a lesson plan template and a CBM recording form. An instructional coach took responsibility for training the paraprofessional and for providing formative feedback once the intervention was launched.

What the team found was that four of five students in each classroom demonstrated growth with their relatively low-cost intervention, and that they had more thinking to do for the students who did not respond. Throughout the implementation of this initiative, the school's leaders realized that thinking about how to collaborate was critical for helping teams to make informed instructional decisions to meet the needs of all of their students.

State-Level PD Collaborations

The RF program brought intensive PD support to states, districts, and schools. Our own collaborative relationship was most visible in RF efforts. Sharon Walpole was active in many states' PD; Kristina Najera provided technical assistance for RMC Research, one of the institutions available to assist the states. After several years of involvement with the RF program, both of us could see that some states had developed effective and efficient PD collaborations, and that the collaborations informed and changed instruction in many classrooms. Sharon's work in her home state of Delaware began in the second year of RF. She worked with district-level personnel to avoid the appearance of a "top-down" approach to change. Eventually, she brought RF literacy coaches together monthly to analyze classroom instruction, learn about research-based literacy instruction for small groups, and plan implementation of effective instructional strategies.

Though the coaches became experts at analyzing and identifying their schools' needs, they needed to know more about research-based strategies for vocabulary and comprehension instruction. This was where Krissy came in, and this was where the collaboration broadened. Since Sharon and Krissy had worked together before, the hand-off was seamless. Krissy provided 2-day PD sessions for both coaches and district leaders. During the first day and half of the second day, coaches and district leaders engaged in activities, including reading research articles, to deepen their understanding of research-based instructional strategies. On the second half of the second day, principals joined the coaches and district leaders to develop short- and long-term plans for implementing the instructional strategies they had learned in the PD sessions, such as using interactive read-alouds to deliver embedded (Biemiller & Boote, 2006) and extended (Beck & McKeown, 2007; Maynard, Pullen, & Coyne, 2010) vocabulary instruction. After these sessions, coaches and principals returned to schools and collaborated with teachers in grade-level team meetings to discuss the implementation of instructional strategies. The coaches reported achieving high levels of implementation, leveraging their own understanding of small-group instruction, and expanding their work to more complex targets and more district involvement.

District-Level Curriculum Collaborations

The most challenging collaborations in which we have participated come when individual district leaders realize that their general approach to tiered instruction is not working for large groups of their children and reach out for alternatives. They move from problem solving into a standard protocol. This kind of collaboration is challenging because the members of the district collaborative team are typically the individuals who have developed and championed the existing approach. They have also garnered district resources (funds and time) to enable it. At some level, then, they must come to grips with the fact that their decisions did not yield the desired outcomes—that they were wrong. This realization is likely to be coupled with guilt, and in some cases also with blame. Given those realities, process is most important. Figure 20.6, derived from the work of Dooner and colleagues (2007), provides some practical suggestions for how to navigate this type of collaboration by anticipating and embracing its stages.

Our experience with these district-level standard protocol efforts has typically involved a questioning of their approach to differentiation. In order to achieve true differentiation, teachers need an assessment system that reveals student needs, curriculum materials that can address a wide range of needs, and an instructional schedule embodying the philosophy that all students deserve some teacher attention each day in small groups. None of these issues is a trivial matter. Each imposes demands on teachers and on the system in general. District officials tend to think of improving small-group instruction as a finite target, but it spills over into other aspects of teaching and learning.

Recently, Sharon and her colleague Michael McKenna engaged in a multiyear small-group project with a district. The district serves very high numbers of ELLs, and its schools have moderate to high numbers of students qualifying for federal lunch subsidies. The district's leadership is strong, and realized that the district reading teachers would be powerful advocates for (or against!) change. The first year's collaboration, then, was with these specialists. By the middle of the first year, they were pilot-testing some new instructional strategies and evaluating their efficacy. By the end of the first year, they were comfortable with the new strategies and supportive of the change effort. The second year's collaboration, then, was with grade-level teams and principals. Its aim was to move these small-group practices inside the classroom, reserving the reading specialists' and ELL specialists' efforts for students with the most intensive needs. Those second-year targets were met fairly successfully, but the reading teachers and ELL specialists became somewhat disenfranchised because their instructional roles were no longer specific. In the final year, the work of the reading teachers, ELL specialists, and special educators was the target, and each member of the team brought a strong vision of what his or her role should be. There were honest and deep differences in opinion among the members of the collaborative team, and individual schools ended with different visions of the specialists' work. This collaboration, then, which started with an effort to expand teachers' visions of small-group instruction, became a full-fledged discussion of tiered instruction—involving individuals with very different roles and expertise, and requiring both district-level and building-level administrative buy-in.

Strategies for Building Community	• Begin with a news-from-home session, where members tell about things happening in their lives after school. • Begin with a news-from-my-classroom session, where members briefly share one success they have experienced since the group's last meeting. • Ask members to give book talks, either from their own recreational reading or from new children's literature. • Use a mental team-building exercise. Board games like Pictionary, Scruples, or Scattergories are naturals.
Strategies for Grappling with Ideas	• Start meetings with a recap of the previous session's content, including any cognitive conflicts that were revealed, and then set goals for the day's session. • Set up norms for brainstorming. Target sharing of as many ideas as possible, then sorting ideas into action categories—"consider now," "consider in the future." • Set up norms for discussion. Include turn taking, note taking, and periodic summarization. • Set up norms for discussing readings. Begin by addressing the authors' argument, referring directly to the text, to establish a shared understanding. Then move to participants' response to those ideas. Focus attention on what is similar to previous ideas and what is different.
Strategies for Finding Common Ground	• Provide a common lesson plan that all team members can implement individually, with a follow-up discussion about what they learned. • Use one team member's class profile (with achievement data) as a case study, assigning each group member responsibility for planning one aspect of instruction. • Use classroom videos from some or all members of the team to illustrate an issue. Allow each teacher who was video-recorded to debrief fully before a more open discussion.
Strategies for Applying Ideas	• Engage in lesson study, which takes real examples from the classrooms and engages the group in problem solving to improve the plan, to improve the implementation, or to make either planning or implementation easier. • Think through how to adapt a lesson plan to a different grade level, achievement profile, or teacher. • Consider ideas for sharing responsibility for planning lessons or for organizing materials to make the initial trial implementation smoother or easier.
Strategies for Setting New Goals	• Set a new goal that builds on successes, or one that provides a deeper look at a new conflict that has emerged. • Begin a second collaborative cycle with data analysis. If data drive the new focus, then no one member of the team is imposing a goal on others.

FIGURE 20.6. Concrete strategies to improve the functioning of district-level collaborative groups. Based on Dooner, Manzuk, and Clifton (2007).

LOOKING FORWARD

Collaboration efforts in instructional delivery and in PD, while still tentative in many schools, are the wave of the future in school improvement. Thanks to the efforts of the U.S. Department of Education to fund research in teacher quality and schoolwide improvement efforts, we are likely to see more and more case-based evidence of the process of collaboration. We will be looking for this evidence and incorporating lessons from this research into our ongoing collaborations; we invite you to do the same.

A challenge for researchers in the area of collaboration is the time that must be devoted to one project, but there is simply no substitute. We have to follow collaborations over time, document their processes, and measure their effects. We know that teacher collaborations and shared leadership efforts can yield positive feelings of efficacy and changes in school culture. We need to know, however, that teacher collaborations are associated with concrete changes in instructional delivery, and then whether these changes are associated with achievement gains for students. We need to know whether achievement gains for students change teachers' beliefs about teaching and learning.

Schools require collaborations to be fruitful in advance of our research efforts. For schools, our vision for the future of successful collaboration requires development of three things: a common language, a culture of collaboration, and collaboration networks.

Development of a Common Language

Collaboration is one of the six principles recommended by the International Reading Association Commission on RTI to help educators plan and implement RTI initiatives (International Reading Association, 2010). Ehren, Laster, and Watts-Taffe (2009) describe the components of collaboration that are important to RTI initiatives. They state that successful collaborations require participants to create shared language for communicating the teams' vision and goals as well as the results of collaborative efforts. Furthermore, they must share the language and the process of collaboration with parents and students, particularly when introducing initiatives, such as RTI, that may be unfamiliar to them. Communicating the language, process, and results of collaboration to parents is an issue that deserves further attention.

Development of a Culture of Collaboration

Collaboration among teachers must become the norm, as it is at Adlai E. Stevenson High School in Illinois, a Blue Ribbon School and a model of teacher collaboration (Honawar, 2008). At this school, each teacher has access to team members' materials, strategies, ideas, and expertise. Teachers meet weekly to discuss strategies that improve teaching and learning, create assessments, analyze data, and construct lesson plans. Teachers have constant access to each other, as their desks are arranged together in an open office space where they meet between classes, as well as before and after school. Furthermore, responsibility for student learning is shared, and leadership is distributed. For instance, teacher teams play an active part in the hiring process. Schools interested in creating a culture of professional learning through informal and formal collaboration must be willing to devote time and resources to the effort, to engage in a research-based process for developing effective teacher teams, and to change deeply held beliefs about school culture (DuFour, 2004).

Development of Collaboration Networks

Collaboration networks are PLCs in which teachers use technology to share knowledge and cooperatively develop new understandings (Bacigalupo & Cachia, 2011). Teachers use social media and Internet sites, such as Edutopia and Classroom 2.0, to connect with other teachers, share ideas, and locate effective teaching practices and resources. For collaboration networks to be successful, district and state leaders must allocate the time and resources needed to help teachers learn with and from one another. Bacigalupo and Cachia (2011) claim that the future of collaboration will involve combining the use of collaboration networks and in-person collaboration to develop teachers with a great deal of content and pedagogical knowledge. However, research is needed to determine the effects of using technology to collaborate.

QUESTIONS FOR REFLECTION •

As you embrace your own collaborative responsibilities, think about these questions:

1. Am I committing the time and resources needed to engage in effective collaboration in delivery of literacy instruction and in PD?

2. To what extent am I honoring the different skills and expertise that each member of my team brings?

3. How can I facilitate a shared understanding of our team's vision and process?

4. What can I do to ensure that our discussions are respectful, even when individuals truly disagree?

5. How can we build formative evaluation into our collaboration schedule?

SUGGESTIONS FOR ONGOING PROFESSIONAL LEARNING • • • • • • •

As you build your collaboration skills, here are some things that you can try.

1. For a new collaboration, use Figure 20.3 as a guide. Set aside a full session just for planning, with all team members present. Step back and set up your work before you begin it.

2. For an ongoing collaboration, use Figure 20.4 to conduct a needs assessment. Have a frank discussion about the current functioning of your team, identify areas for improvement, and specify an improvement process.

3. For a completed collaboration, use Figure 20.2 to conduct a retrospective analysis. Engage the team in a reflection meant to reveal strengths and weaknesses in their process and to construct a set of lessons learned for future collaborations.

RESEARCH-BASED RESOURCES

The Center on Instruction (*http://centeroninstruction.org*) provides extensive resources for school-based teams. These include research summaries, practitioner guides, professional development modules, and examples from the field.

The National Center on Response to Intervention (*www.rti4success.org*) provides tools specific for planning, implementing, and continuously improving RTI efforts. These are likely to be targets for collaborative teams. Resources include tools, webinars, and training modules.

If you would like to read research on schoolwide improvement that includes collaborations, consider these case studies:

Harn, B. A., Chard, D. J., Biancarosa, G., & Kame'enui, E. J. (2011). Coordinating instructional supports to accelerate at-risk first-grade readers' performance. *Elementary School Journal, 112,* 332–355.

Kame'enui, E. J., Simmons, D. C., & Coyne, M. D. (2000). Schools as host environments: Toward a schoolwide reading improvement model. *Annals of Dyslexia, 50,* 33–51.

Lipson, M. Y., Mosenthal, J. H., Mekkelsen, J., & Russ, B. (2004). Building knowledge and fashioning success one school at a time. *The Reading Teacher, 57*(6), 534–542.

Mosenthal, J., Lipson, M., Torncello, S., Russ, B., & Mekkelsen, J. (2004). Contexts and practices of six schools successful in obtaining reading achievement. *Elementary School Journal, 104*(5), 343–367.

Simmons, D. C., Kuykendall, K., King, K., Cornachione, C., & Kame'enui, E. J. (2000). Implementation of a schoolwide reading improvement model: "No one ever told us it would be this hard!" *Learning Disabilities Research and Practice, 15*(2), 92–100.

Taylor, B. M., Pearson, P., Clark, K., & Walpole, S. (2000). Effective schools and accomplished teachers: Lessons about primary-grade reading instruction in low-income schools. *Elementary School Journal, 101*(2), 121–165.

Taylor, B. M., Pearson, P., Peterson, D. S., & Rodriguez, M. C. (2003). Reading growth in high-poverty classrooms: The influence of teacher practices that encourage cognitive engagement in literacy learning. *Elementary School Journal, 104*(1), 3–28.

Taylor, B. M., Pearson, P., Peterson, D. S., & Rodriguez, M. C. (2005). The CIERA School Change Framework: An evidence-based approach to professional development and school reading improvement. *Reading Research Quarterly, 40*(1), 40–69.

REFERENCES

Bacigalupo, M., & Cachia, R. (2011). *Teacher collaboration networks in 2025: What is the role of teacher networks for professional development in Europe?* Seville, Spain: European Commission Joint Research Centre Institute for Prospective Technological Studies.

Beck, I. L., & McKeown, M. G. (2006). *Improving comprehension with questioning the author: A fresh and expanded view of a powerful approach.* New York: Scholastic.

Beck, I. L., & McKeown, M. G. (2007). Increasing young low-income children's oral vocabulary repertoires through rich and focused instruction. *Elementary School Journal, 107,* 251–271.

Beck, I. L., McKeown, M. G., Hamilton, R., & Kucan, L. (1997). *Questioning the author: An approach for enhancing student engagement with text.* Newark, DE: International Reading Association.

Biemiller, A., & Boote, C. (2006). An effective method for building meaning vocabulary in primary grades. *Journal of Educational Psychology, 98,* 44–62.

Brinson, D., & Steiner, L. (2007, October). *Building collective efficacy: How leaders inspire teachers to achieve.* Chicago: Center for Comprehensive School Reform and Improvement.

Brownell, M. T., Adams, A., Sindelar, P., Waldron, N., & Vanhover, S. (2006). Learning from collaboration: The role of teacher qualities. *Exceptional Children, 72,* 169–185.

Capizzi, A. M., & Barton-Arwood, S. M. (2009). Using a curriculum-based measurement graphic organizer to facilitate collaboration in reading. *Intervention in School and Clinic, 45,* 14–23.

Carlisle, J. F., & Berebitsky, D. (2011). Literacy coaching as a component of professional development. *Reading and Writing, 24,* 773–800.

Dooner, A. M., Manzuk, D., & Clifton, R. A. (2007). Stages of collaboration and the realities of professional learning communities. *Teaching and Teacher Education, 24,* 564–574.

DuFour, R. (2004). What is a "professional learning community"? *Educational Leadership, 61*(8), 1–6.

Duke, D. L. (2006, Fall). Keys to sustaining successful school turnarounds. *ERS Spectrum,* pp. 21–35.

Ehren, B. J., Laster, B., & Watts-Taffe, S. (2009). *Creating a shared language for collaboration in RTI.* Retrieved January 16, 2012, from *www.rtinetwork.org/getstarted/buildsupport/ creating-shared-language-for-collaboration-in-rti.*

Gersten, R., Dimino, J., Jayanthi, M., Kim, J. S., & Santoro, L. E. (2010). Teacher study group: Impact of the professional development model on reading instruction and student outcomes in first grade classrooms. *American Educational Research Journal, 47,* 694–739.

Hall, G. E., & Hord, S. M. (2006). *Implementing change: Patterns, principles, and potholes.* Boston: Pearson/Allyn & Bacon.

Honawar, V. (2008, April 2). Working smarter by working together. *Education Week,* pp. 7–8.

International Reading Association. (2010). *Response to intervention: Guiding principles from the International Reading Association.* Newark, DE: Author.

Matsumura, L. C., Garnier, H. E., & Resnick, L. B. (2010). Implementing literacy coaching: The role of school social resources. *Educational Evaluation and Policy Analysis, 32,* 249–272.

Maynard, K. L., Pullen, P. C., & Coyne, M. D. (2010). Teaching vocabulary to first-grade students through repeated shared storybook reading: A comparison of rich and basic instruction to incidental exposure. *Literacy Research and Instruction, 49,* 209–242.

Mohammed, S. S., Murray, C. S., Coleman, M. A., Roberts, G., & Grim, C. N. (2011). *Conversations with practitioners: Supporting state-level collaboration among general and special educators.* Portsmouth, NH: RMC Research Corporation, Center on Instruction.

Sherblom, S. A., Marshall, J. C., & Sherblom, J. C. (2006). The relationship between school climate and math and reading achievement. *Journal of Research in Character Education, 4*(1 & 2), 19–31.

Vaughn, S., Hughes, M. T., Schumm, J. S., & Klingner, J. (1998). A collaborative effort to enhance reading and writing instruction in inclusion classrooms. *Learning Disability Quarterly, 21,* 57–74.

Walpole, S., & McKenna, M. C. (2009). *How to plan differentiated reading instruction: Resources for grades K–3.* New York: Guilford Press.

Walpole, S., McKenna, M. C., & Morrill, J. (2011). Building and rebuilding a statewide support system for literacy coaches. *Reading and Writing Quarterly, 27,* 261–280.

Walpole, S., McKenna, M. C., Uribe-Zarain, X., & Lamitina, D. (2010). The relationships between coaching and instruction in the primary grades: Evidence from high-poverty schools. *Elementary School Journal, 111,* 115–140.

Weick, K. E. (1979). *The social psychology of organizing* (2nd ed.). Reading, MA: Addison-Wesley.

Professional Learning • • • • • • • • • • • •
Professional Learning Communities, Whole-School Meetings, and Cross-School Sharing

DEBRA S. PETERSON

Scenario 1

A local elementary school sets 2 days aside for professional development during the school year. One day is focused on reading. Two external guest speakers are invited to present to the whole group about various components of reading. The staff listens to the speakers and participates in activities during the sessions. Then the teachers meet in grade-level teams to organize their assessment and curricular materials for the beginning of the school year. Discussions address issues of scheduling, testing procedures, organization of materials, and so forth.

Scenario 2

A local elementary school provides 1 hour each week for teachers to meet in teacher-led study groups or professional learning communities (PLCs). In their PLCs, teachers read and discuss research articles related to reading instruction; share anecdotes about their application of research-based practices to their daily instruction; analyze student work and assessment data, to determine whether the changes in instruction are resulting in increased student achievement; and share videos of their instruction for reflection and feedback from their colleagues.

Both of these scenarios describe common approaches to professional development. Yet decades of research on effective professional development show that Scenario 2 incorporates more of the characteristics that support a positive and collaborative school climate, lead to changes in instruction, and increase students' reading achievement (Taylor, 2011; Taylor & Peterson, 2006; Taylor, Raphael, & Au, 2011). Effective professional development is:

- Ongoing.
- Job-embedded.
- Collaborative.
- Informed by research.
- Informed by the principled use of data.
- Supportive of reflection on instruction.

OVERVIEW OF RESEARCH

Ongoing Professional Development

True professional development isn't only about increasing what teachers know about a topic, skill, or strategy. It should also include ways for teachers to *apply* what they are learning to their daily instruction (Duffy, 2004). This transformation or refinement of instruction can be difficult, and it generally requires significant time and support. This means that models of professional development that are conducted over time are more effective than "one-shot" experiences. Cox and Hopkins (2006) looked at characteristics of the professional development component of Reading Recovery, a one-on-one intervention program for struggling first-grade readers, and identified the ongoing nature of the training as one of the factors that makes the program effective for transforming teachers' practice as well as improving students' reading achievement. They stated that "professional development should emphasize ongoing, coherent, collaborative, and systematic work with teachers in both knowledge development and delivery of literacy instruction" (p. 265).

Doubek and Cooper (2007) also stressed the need for ongoing professional development. In their study, schools and districts worked to close the achievement gap and reverse the effects of institutional racism. As teachers were building their expertise in teaching reading to culturally and linguistically diverse students, they were also working to build partnerships with community stakeholders and parents. (See Roberts, Chapter 23, this volume, for more information on working with parents as partners.) This kind of effort takes intentional focus and sustained vision over time, and it cannot be accomplished without ongoing learning. Sailors (2009) has also emphasized the need for ongoing professional development, especially when educators are learning complex concepts and techniques like those involved in comprehension strategy instruction.

Job-Embedded Professional Development

Since a major goal of effective professional development is to help teachers refine their reading instruction, it makes sense to embed the professional learning into the daily lives of teachers in their own classrooms. Allington and Cunningham (2007) have emphasized the critical role of job-embedded professional development in shaping schools that effectively meet the needs of all their students: "Elementary schools will change only when new strategies and new knowledge become incorporated into everyday practice" (p. 189). Application of new learning is more likely to occur when it can be immediately implemented in relevant and meaningful contexts. Valli and Hawley (2007) state that school-based professional development is more effective because learning is connected to real-life challenges and situations: " . . . the most powerful opportunities to learn are often connected with the recognition of and solution to authentic and immediate problems" (p. 89). Coaching models, as discussed by Sailors, Russell, Augustine, and Alexander in Chapter 22, are particularly strong in providing job-embedded professional learning because the coach and the teacher can focus on specific lessons, materials, or students as they are applying the new instructional strategies or techniques. Study groups or PLCs are another way to provide job-embedded professional development that can have a direct impact on instruction and student achievement (DuFour, Eaker, & Many, 2006; Joyce & Showers, 2002; Murphy & Lick, 2005; Taylor, Pearson, Peterson, & Rodriguez, 2005). PLCs are described in more detail later in this chapter.

Collaborative Professional Development

Research has also demonstrated that professional development is more effective when it is a collaborative process (Cordova & Matthiesen, 2010). Learning in isolation is difficult, especially when teachers are attempting to change strongly held behaviors and beliefs. When teachers are actively involved in designing, facilitating, and implementing their own professional development, they enhance their sense of collective efficacy and experience the empowerment of working together to increase students' growth and achievement in reading. (See Taylor, Chapter 18, and Walpole & Najera, Chapter 20, for more on collaboration.) Valli and Hawley (2007) have recommended that teachers should be involved in the development of their own professional learning: "Engagement in the process increases educators' motivation and commitment to learn, encourages them to take instructional risks and to assume new roles, and increases the likelihood that what is learned will be meaningful and relevant to particular contexts and problems" (p. 88). Teachers can use their students' assessment data (as discussed by Weber in Chapter 19) to determine students' needs across the school or at a specific grade level, and can then select an area of research and inquiry based on student need for their PLCs. This moves the work that is done in the PLC from an abstract academic exercise to a meaningful, concrete, problem-solving process.

Teachers can also collaborate in their PLCs by sharing the leadership of the group. Murphy and Lick (2005) recommend that teachers rotate their roles within the group from session to session. Roles might include responsibilities like discussion leader, timekeeper, or note taker, but could also include such tasks as finding the research article the group will read next, bringing in a video of instruction or student work to share, or providing the snacks. When teachers share the responsibilities for the group, they feel a greater sense of ownership and accountability for the group. Such sharing also adds to the sense of collective efficacy and collegiality across the school culture. Fullan (2005) found that the more collaborative professional development became a part of the school culture, where leadership for the professional learning was not dependent on a single individual (e.g., literacy coach, principal), the more likely it was to be sustained in the face of institutional change (e.g., staff turnover, changing demographics).

Professional Development Informed by Research

In a recent review of research, Dillon, O'Brien, Sato, and Kelly (2011) highlighted the fact that effective professional development should be informed by evidence-based research. There is a wealth of knowledge available from research on what constitutes effective reading instruction, as evident in Parts I–III of this book. There is also a great deal of research-based information about teaching reading to students who struggle, as well as how to challenge students who are performing above grade level. The professional learning that teachers do together should be informed by this research, so that their decisions and efforts lead to the most potent and powerful instruction for *all* their students across the developmental continuum.

One common but ineffective approach to professional development is to study a different topic or area of reading each time a PLC meets. This leads to surface-level knowledge of various topics, but does not result in lasting and meaningful change. Research has shown that selecting a substantive topic of study (one that has evidence demonstrating that it is effective in increasing students' reading knowledge), and sustaining that focus of study over time, can lead to deep learning and changes in instruction (Taylor, Pearson, Peterson, & Rodriguez, 2003; Taylor et al., 2005; Taylor & Peterson, 2006). Not all reading topics or techniques are substantive or research-based. Educators need to be discerning consumers of research, especially with the proliferation of ideas available electronically. Critically analyzing the source, reliability, and validity of all information is vitally important. The resources provided in this book will be helpful as schools strive to select research-based practices to study and implement. When educators rigorously study a substantive, evidence-based topic across many months and apply their learning to daily instruction, they can see marked improvement in their students' achievement (Taylor et al., 2011).

Professional Development Informed by the Principled Use of Data

Effective professional development should address needs that become evident through the analysis of student assessment data, student work, and teacher observation (Taylor & Pearson, 2005). Assessment results should include multiple sources and types of data. These might include performance measures (e.g., portfolios of students' work samples, running records, checklists) and teacher-developed assessments, as well as standardized test scores. Assessment data should include measures or documentation of what students can do in all areas of reading, not just in phonics and fluency. Once an area of need is identified, the staff members should select topics of study that will help them meet that need more effectively. For example, based on the previous year's assessment data and the state's reading standards, the staff may identify the need for students to better understand and use the information they gain from their content-area reading. Topics for PLCs might include ways to build students' academic and content vocabulary; explicit instruction in text features for informational texts (both print and digital); or comprehension strategies for informational text, such as reciprocal teaching (Oczkus, 2003; Palincsar & Brown, 1984, 1986). (For more information on reading in the content areas, see Part III of this book.)

Assessment data are not just used to determine topics of study for PLCs. Ongoing data collection or progress monitoring is needed to determine whether the changes teachers are making to their instruction are actually helping students. This cycle of assessment and instruction is similar to the reflective process that is recommended with frameworks like response to intervention (RTI) (Fuchs, Fuchs, & Vaughn, 2008; Johnston, 2010; Vaughn, Wanzek, & Fletcher, 2007). In Tier 1 of RTI, classroom teachers identify students' specific needs, make refinements to their instruction, measure students' progress, and make further refinements to instruction. Assessment data should be used in a similar manner with the ongoing, job-embedded professional development that teachers engage in during their PLCs.

Professional Development Supportive of Reflection on Instruction

Reflecting on instruction is an essential component of effective professional development programs or models (Peterson, Taylor, Burnham, & Schock, 2008; Pinnell & Rodgers, 2004; Stover, Kissel, Haag, & Schoniker, 2011; York-Barr, Sommers, Ghere, & Montie, 2006). This process of reflective inquiry leads teachers to refine their instructional practices and their beliefs about what students can do. As teachers reflect on particular lessons with specific students, they can identify teaching strategies and techniques that were effective with those students. They can then apply those strategies to future lessons and continue to build on the positive progress that their students are making. If those same techniques or strategies are less effective with other groups of students, then teachers can change their practice or adapt their strategies. This produces differentiated instruction that can more effectively meet the various needs and learning styles of diverse students.

The process of reflective inquiry is difficult and is often neglected because of the day-to-day pressures of teaching. Most teachers try to do it as they are preparing for the next day or driving home from work, but true reflection requires time and concentration. Although individual teachers can engage in reflective inquiry on their own, a collaborative process of reflection has been shown to be even more powerful for strengthening instruction and improving student performance (Peterson et al., 2008; Taylor & Peterson, 2006). Pinnell and Rodgers (2004) discuss two kinds of group reflection: *coached reflection* and *collaborative reflection*. Coached reflection happens when two colleagues observe each other's instruction and engaging in reflective coaching conversations. They may then co-plan and co-teach a second lesson, followed by further reflection and refinement of instruction. This cycle may be repeated many times as the colleagues continue to learn from each other. (For more information about reflecting on instruction with a literacy coach or peer, see Sailors et al., Chapter 22.) Collaborative reflection is done with a small group of colleagues. PLCs can serve as excellent venues for collaborative reflection. York-Barr and her colleagues (2006) list the following benefits of reflection in small groups:

1. Professional learning is strengthened because colleagues have the opportunity to share from their various experiences, perspectives, and areas of expertise.
2. The collaborative reflective process increases the professional and social support of the individuals within the group.
3. The collegial relationships contribute to schoolwide collaboration in reading instruction, as well as to cohesion between the core curriculum and interventions

for struggling readers or supplemental instruction for students who require more challenge.

4. The commitment of the group to learn and work together leads to an increase in the collective efficacy and collaborative culture of the entire school.

5. The climate of the school becomes more supportive, understanding, and positive.

SUMMARY OF BIG IDEAS FROM RESEARCH

The characteristics of effective professional development discussed above are strongly supported by research. Table 21.1 lists eight research studies that demonstrated how effective professional development was used schoolwide to facilitate reading reform and increase students' growth and achievement in reading. Several of these studies were conducted with schools that served culturally and linguistically diverse student populations in low-income communities. These studies illustrate the importance of professional development in refining instruction and increasing student performance. For more information on reading reform, see Taylor and colleagues (2011).

TABLE 21.1. Studies Focused on Professional Development as a Means to Reading Reform

Citation	Ongoing	Job-embedded	Collaborative	Informed by research	Informed by principled use of data	Supportive of reflection on instruction
Au, Raphael, & Mooney (2008)	×	×	×	×	×	×
Cox & Hopkins (2006)	×	×	×	×	×	×
Kennedy & Shiel (2010)	×	×	×	×	×	×
Langer (2001)	×	×	×	×	×	×
Lipson, Mosenthal, Mekkelsen, & Russ (2004)	×	×	×	×	×	×
McNaughton, MacDonald, Amituanai-Toloa, Lai, & Farry (2006)	×	×	×	×	×	×
Taylor, Pearson, Peterson, & Rodriguez (2005)	×	×	×	×	×	×
Timperley & Parr (2007)	×	×	×	×	×	×

EXAMPLES OF EFFECTIVE PRACTICES

PLCs or Study Groups

PLCs are ongoing, job-embedded, teacher-led small groups where grade-level teachers, specialists, administrators, and coaches can read and discuss research, analyze assessment data, share and reflect on instruction, and encourage one another in instructional change (DuFour et al., 2006; Joyce & Showers, 2002; Lieberman & Miller, 2007; Murphy & Lick, 2005). The purposes of PLCs are as follows:

- Professional learning.
- Analysis of data.
- Collaborative planning and problem solving.
- Reflection on and change to instruction (both classroom-based and schoolwide reading instruction).
- Increased collective efficacy across the school community.

Generally, PLCs should meet weekly for an hour before or after school. The PLCs should be small groups of approximately 5–7 people. If the groups become too large (10 or more), sharing becomes difficult, and members can feel less involved and engaged. Groups can consist of grade-level teams or cross-grade colleagues. Specialists, such as teachers of English language learners (ELLs) or special education students, should also be included. Schools can form PLCs after analyzing student data, identifying targeted areas of need, and selecting topics of study that will enhance reading instruction in those targeted areas. Once small groups are formed, each group should develop an action plan (Murphy & Lick, 2005; Vogt & Shearer, 2011). The action plan should clearly and specifically state these things:

- The areas of need as identified from student data.
- The activities and professional learning the group will engage in to meet the identified areas of need.
- The application of new learning to daily instruction.
- The methods and tools the group will use to measure student progress.
- A timeline for study, implementation, assessment, and reflection.

A sample form for a PLC action plan is shown in Figure 21.1.

An example of an agenda for a typical PLC meeting is included in the box on page 539. Each component of the agenda is then described in more detail, and examples from actual PLC conversations in several different schools are then presented, to further illustrate the kinds of professional conversations and reflection on instruction that can occur in PLCs.

Example of a Circle Share in a PLC

The first example comes from a grade-level PLC in a suburban school. It is made up of five kindergarten classroom teachers, one teacher of ELLs, and the principal. The group members have been focusing on refining their instruction in phonemic awareness,

Study group topic: _____ Date: _____

Leader: _____ Note-taker: _____ Grade level(s): K 1 2 3 Other __

Members present: _____

1. Based on your school's student assessment data (*state, local, and schoolwide data*), data on classroom teaching practices (*observations by a coach, lesson plans, surveys*), and your review of current research on best practices (*research articles, books on evidence-based strategies and techniques*), what are the specific student needs your PLC is addressing?

2. What are the proposed goals for your PLC as a whole, and how will each member implement instructional change? **Be as specific as possible!** *Remember the goal is to change or enhance a classroom practice to improve student performance in the area or areas specified above.*

Goals:	Who is responsible?	Classroom application:	Resources needed:	General timeline/ target dates:
1.				
2.				
3.				

(continued)

FIGURE 21.1. Sample form for a PLC action plan. Adapted with permission from *Catching Schools: An Action Guide to Schoolwide Reading Improvement* by Barbara M. Taylor. Copyright © 2011 by Barbara M. Taylor. Published by Heinemann, Portsmouth, NH. All rights reserved.

3. What data on your own teaching practices (*video sharing, lesson plans, teacher reflection journals . . .*) are you planning to collect to see whether your goals and actions are making a difference for student learning?

4. What student data will you collect to show your group's impact on students' achievement in reading?

5. How is your group making connections to previous topics or professional learning?

6. What are some of your PLC's successes or accomplishments so far?

Revised on: _____ _____ _____
               Date   Date   Date

FIGURE 21.1. *(continued)*

Example of an Agenda for a PLC

5 minutes: Circle share—each member shares what he or she has been doing in his or her classroom related to the focus area of the study group (e.g., vocabulary instruction).

10–15 minutes: The group discusses a research article, book, or book chapter related to the focus area of the study group (e.g., Beck, McKeown, & Kucan, 2002).

15–20 minutes: One person shares a 7- to 10-minute video clip of his or her instruction, showing how he or she is applying what the group has been studying. The group discusses the video clip using a discussion guide or video-sharing protocol (discussed later in the chapter).

15–20 minutes: One person brings copies of students' work for the group to study and discuss. The discussion should be guided by a protocol for looking at student work.

5 minutes: The group members decide on what they will implement in their classrooms before the next study group meeting. (All members of the group should be implementing the same instructional skill, strategy, or technique.) They also decide on roles for the next meeting (e.g., who will be the discussion leader, who is bringing a video, who will share student work, who is bringing treats!) and identify the article or chapter that should be read before the next meeting.

---

the alphabetic principle, and integrating informational texts into their literacy block. They have been meeting together twice a month for the past 8 months. In this session, they start out by having a *circle share*. A circle share is a brief time where each person tells about what he or she is doing in his or her classroom and how it is affecting student learning. Much of the subsequent conversation revolves around *interactive writing*, which is an activity where a teacher works with a small group of students to write a sentence about a book they have read together. The teacher guides the students through each sound and letter in each word of the sentence. The teacher models the writing on a whiteboard or a chart, while all the students write on their papers, whiteboards, or journals. The teachers in this PLC are discussing how the work with interactive writing has transferred to the students' independent writing during free-choice time.

KINDERGARTEN TEACHER 1 (discussion leader): Let's share successes in our instruction and be specific about the impact on students' learning.

KINDERGARTEN TEACHER 4: I think the interactive writing has been the biggest success for me. I think back to the end of January, when I was trying to have the students write in their journals, and it was just like pulling teeth. Now when I have them writing independently, they will go back to their seats and write for half an hour, and they usually won't ask for my help any more. That was 3½ months ago when we started on interactive writing. It is amazing that they have made so much progress.

KINDERGARTEN TEACHER 1: Yesterday at free-choice time, I told the children that they could write in their journals, and I had 10 kids go off and write. They really wanted to write. I think that interactive writing has really got them interested in writing.

KINDERGARTEN TEACHER 3: Yes, it really lets us know where they are at. The new ELL student I have, up until really this last week, acted like "I don't know what to do," but now he is finally writing sentences. All the sentences are alike. They are "I like _____," "I like _____," but he's got sentences with three words, capital letters, and a period at the end. That is real progress.

KINDERGARTEN TEACHER 4: My students are much more interested in writing than drawing. When I give them the option to draw a picture to go with what they wrote in their journals, they just want to keep writing. I say, "Go for it!"

KINDERGARTEN TEACHER 5 (note taker): I love the subtleties you can teach during interactive writing. I use the sentences students come up with, and some things come up that I wouldn't have thought to teach. Someone wrote *Don't*, so I had to talk about how that is a short way to say, "Do not," and show them how they can use the apostrophe. Of course, apostrophes aren't in our curriculum, but I had to talk about it. Then the next day I saw a girl write in her journal and use the word *don't* with the apostrophe. That wouldn't have happened without interactive writing. That is exciting—those little things that you aren't sure they catch until you see them apply them.

KINDERGARTEN TEACHER 2 (timekeeper): My kids get so excited to think of the sentences for interactive writing. They will ask, "Can I write in my journal because I didn't get to write the sentence I was thinking of in small group, and I want to do it?"

ELL TEACHER: We do interactive writing and make small posters of their sentences that we hang around the room. They enjoy reading their sentences or reading sentences that their friends from the other class have written.

PRINCIPAL: Yes, and when you post their writing, it adds to the print-rich environment.

Discussion of a Research Article

Reading and discussing research constitute a critical activity of effective PLCs. Your school may want to develop a generic discussion guide to help your PLCs get started with discussion of a research article or book chapter. As you write your discussion questions, remember that you want to stimulate higher-order thinking among your colleagues. The discussion should also result in some specific action that each member of the group will implement in his or her classroom. The questions you generate may look like some of the following:

1. What were some of the key ideas in this article?
2. What questions have been raised by reading this article?
3. Do you agree or disagree with the author(s)? Why or why not?
4. How do the ideas in this article connect to other articles or chapters you have read?

5. What are some new ideas or strategies that you are going to try from this article? Why did you select those ideas or strategies?
6. What follow-up actions will you take as a result of discussing this article?

Purposes of Video Sharing

Ideally, it would be beneficial to visit many teachers' classrooms to observe their reading instruction. This would allow teachers to see specific skills, strategies, techniques, and teaching routines in the context of real life with real students. Unfortunately, very few teachers have the opportunity to observe their peers because of the teaching demands and schedules of their school day. Video sharing is an alternative and effective way to see another teacher's instruction. The purposes of video sharing in a PLC are these:

- To refine teaching techniques related to the focus or topic being studied.
- To reflect on one's own teaching related to the focus or topic of the PLC.
- To learn by watching someone else teach.

An example of a video-sharing protocol is provided in the box below.

Example of a Video-Sharing Protocol

Step 1. A teacher selects a 7- to 10-minute clip of him- or herself teaching a part of a lesson related to the study group topic.

Step 2. The teacher gives the group a 1-minute description of what has happened earlier in the lesson.

Step 3. The teacher asks for some specific feedback from the group. For example, the teacher might ask the group to watch how he or she prompts students to elaborate on their oral responses to higher-order questions.

Step 4. The group watches the video clip and focuses on four guiding questions:
- What were the children able to do that was related to the study group focus? What things were going well?
- What was the teacher doing to help children develop and be successful in relation to the focus area?
- What else could have been done to help children develop and be successful in relation to the focus area?
- What did you learn that will help your teaching?

Step 5. The group gives feedback to the teacher by discussing the four guiding questions.

Example of Video Sharing in a PLC

This example is an excerpt from a PLC discussion in a school in a rural community. The group is made up of one classroom teacher from each grade (K–3), a special education teacher, and a literacy coach. The group has been meeting for about 6 months and has been studying higher-order questioning and student-led discussions. The grade 3 teacher has just shared a video of one of her small groups of students leading their own discussion of a chapter book. After watching the video, the group members reflect on the instruction by using the video-sharing protocol. The video-sharing questions are *italicized*.

KINDERGARTEN TEACHER (discussion leader): *What were the things the children were able to do well?*

GRADE 2 TEACHER: They stayed on the topic.

SPECIAL EDUCATION TEACHER: They had good eye contact.

KINDERGARTEN TEACHER (discussion leader): They were respectful to each other.

GRADE 1 TEACHER: Everyone got a chance. They allowed each other to talk.

KINDERGARTEN TEACHER (discussion leader): They had good higher-level questions. When she said, "Do you think he is a responsible person?", that was a good higher-level question. "If you were Darren what would you do?" That was another good higher-level question.

SPECIAL EDUCATION TEACHER: When they were predicting, they didn't just copy each other. They all had their own answers.

KINDERGARTEN TEACHER (discussion leader): *What was the teacher doing to help them be successful?*

GRADE 2 TEACHER: It was obvious that the teacher had to do a lot of modeling to get them to this point.

LITERACY COACH: Yes, you need to model, model, model, and give them guided practice.

GRADE 1 TEACHER: I like the use of the role cards that the teacher gave the students. The students had the cards to hold, and it gave them a visual way to focus on what they were supposed to be doing.

GRADE 3 TEACHER: Yes, I want them to get to a point where they don't need the cards, but for now it is helpful for them until they get better or more comfortable at leading their own discussions.

KINDERGARTEN TEACHER (discussion leader): *What else could have been done to help the students be even more successful?*

GRADE 1 TEACHER: We saw them go through the rubric to see if they all did their jobs. Those rules are on the rubric. You could always make a chart and have that up in your room.

GRADE 2 TEACHER: I think the steps they went through were beneficial. It was like reteaching and reinforcing the process. I think the progression was good. The kids were reinforcing each other.

GRADE 3 TEACHER: Sometimes it is hard to get kids to tell that they don't understand what a word or a part of the text means. It's hard to get kids to stop and think about what they don't understand.

GRADE 1 TEACHER: Have you tried giving them sticky notes or note cards to mark places in the text that are tricky or confusing?

GRADE 3 TEACHER: I have tried that, and sometimes it is hard to get them to use their sticky notes. I will try it again with this book.

KINDERGARTEN TEACHER (discussion leader): *What did you personally learn from the video?*

GRADE 2 TEACHER: It can be done!

GRADE 1 TEACHER: It helps you see the foundation we give the kids to help them as they go up through the grades. All of this is at our level. It is not frightening to use it if we can modify it to our level.

SPECIAL EDUCATION TEACHER: It reminds me that you have to teach them the social skills of cooperative learning. You have to really teach them that.

KINDERGARTEN TEACHER (discussion leader): Yes, and then it can spill over into all parts of the day. It is a life skill.

Purposes for Looking at Student Work

Collecting and analyzing student work with peers constitute still another important activity for PLCs. Student work can illustrate the growth that students are making in their daily reading and writing. This is an excellent activity to inform the members in the PLC about the impact of their instruction on student learning. The purposes of looking at student work in PLCs are as follows:

- To reflect on how the application of the new learning occurring in the PLC has impacted students' growth in reading and writing.
- To measure and document students' progress over time.
- To reflect on further refinements or differentiation of instruction that may be needed to ensure that all students are making progress in their reading and writing.

An example of a protocol for looking at student work is given in the box on page 544.

Example of Looking at Student Work in a PLC

This conversation comes from a PLC in an inner-city school. The group has been meeting for approximately 8 months. It is a cross-grade group, including one general education classroom teacher from each grade (K–3). It also includes the media specialist and the literacy coach. The group has been studying higher-order talk and writing about text all year long. They are particularly focused on how to support their students who are ELLs because they have a large population of students from linguistically diverse backgrounds. A grade 2 teacher has brought in students' response journals for the group to analyze. Notice how the group members use the protocol for looking at student work

---

Example of a Protocol for Looking at Student Work

1. A teacher shares copies of student work from his or her classroom.
2. The group asks clarifying questions about the lesson and the teacher's purpose for the activity.
3. The group discusses:
   - The skills/strengths that are evident in the work.
   - The needs that are evident in the work.
   - The surprises that they discovered in the student work.
4. The group helps the teacher reflect on what he or she will do next in his or her instruction to move these students to the next level.
5. Each group member decides on something he or she learned from the discussion that will be applied to future instruction.

Adapted with permission from *Catching Schools: An Action Guide to Schoolwide Reading Improvement* by Barbara M. Taylor. Copyright © 2011 by Barbara M. Taylor. Published by Heinemann, Portsmouth, NH. All rights reserved.

---

to guide their discussion and to foster reflection on how the changes they have made in their instruction have resulted in improvements in students' performance. Key reflection question are *italicized*.

GRADE 2 TEACHER: We were reading a book about a boy who's learning how to swim and how someone helps him to get over his fear of the water. After our discussion of the story, I asked the students to write about a time that someone helped them. Many of my students focused on learning to swim in their writing, but the answers seemed to me a little bit more in depth than we usually would have had because of the conversation we had before we wrote. I'd be grateful if you could help me by checking to see if they focused on something they were taught by someone else, if they seem to make a connection with the story, and telling me if you have any other ideas on how to hold students accountable for what goes on in their student-led discussions. I know the conversations are beneficial in themselves, but if there's a way to transfer that to written work that they are doing independently.

[The group members pass around the students' journals and read their responses. Once everyone has had a chance to read each piece, the discussion continues.]

KINDERGARTEN TEACHER (discussion leader): *What strengths do you see?*

GRADE 1 TEACHER (note taker): Details. Good details. It was also sequential. They used *first, second, third*.

KINDERGARTEN TEACHER (discussion leader): That's one of my big responses, too. I was really impressed to see the sequencing. I don't know if you had discussed that, but that's great. One student even did *first, second, finally*, and knew those sequencing words.

LITERACY COACH: Did that sequencing also appear in the story or the conversation about swimming?

GRADE 2 TEACHER: No, she transferred that from the work that we've done in the past on how to write a paragraph. I was really thrilled to see her doing that on her own.

KINDERGARTEN TEACHER: I think they also stayed on topic. They obviously had a main idea, then they had the supporting details underneath. So, as far as your question, I think they did a very nice job responding to the story and the discussion.

GRADE 3 TEACHER: By reading it, they seemed very excited about their responses. The length that it was and the details that they gave, I think they thought it was fun to write down their experiences.

MEDIA SPECIALIST: It appears the conversation beforehand really got them into that, because if that was only 10 minutes of writing, a lot of kids in 10 minutes will finally just choose a topic to write about. "What new thing did I learn?" and they'll still be thinking about what thing they should write about. I think that's a lot of work, and they were really into the topic when it got to the writing part.

KINDERGARTEN TEACHER (discussion leader): It's a great connection to their lives, and I think that's another reason why they wrote so much, because they got to write about themselves in connection to a story that you were reading in class. [pause] *What do the students need help with?*

GRADE 1 TEACHER: Mechanics, spelling—the constant battle.

LITERACY COACH: Given your directions to them, regardless of spelling and mechanics, do you feel that this was a successful writing activity?

GRADE 2 TEACHER: I feel it was successful because I didn't have anyone come back and tell me, "I don't know what to do," or "I don't know what to write." They all went and wrote and wrote. I didn't have anyone come up to me and actually say, "I'm done," either. I know that's not a big deal, but it was nice to just have them close their books once they were done and go on with another topic. So, yeah, I felt that they fulfilled the task that was requested of them.

LITERACY COACH: And do you think that was because of the way you prepped it with the conversation? Or was it because of the topic itself and how it was related from the text you read to self?

GRADE 2 TEACHER: I think the conversation had an impact on this, just because of the level of detail, and also that I didn't have anyone confused on what in the world could they write about. Even with life experiences, usually I have at least one student out of the groups who—not always the same student, either—who will ask me, "I don't know what to write. None of this has ever happened to me before." But with the conversation, we didn't have anyone who was clueless about what they could write about.

KINDERGARTEN TEACHER (discussion leader): *What could have been done to improve instruction or help students?* [pause] I don't know if you'd rather have us talk about some more ideas to respond to your question earlier, because I think that they've accomplished the task.

GRADE 2 TEACHER: Yeah, I'd really appreciate it if you have other ideas for things that they could do—you know, just in general, as a written or some kind of activity to go along with the conversation.

MEDIA SPECIALIST: I think, too, for the mechanics of student-led discussions . . . in the book we read earlier, they suggested taping the students' conversations and having the kids look at the tape. If you're wanting them to see if they followed the rules that they set, that kind of mechanics, you know, that might be a way that they could then write about what they saw in the video—"How well did we do in following what we said we were going to do?", "Was everyone sharing?", "Were we taking turns without raising hands?"—that kind of thing. So, about the mechanics of it, you could do a writing job and then even come back and have another conversation about what they saw on the video of themselves.

KINDERGARTEN TEACHER (discussion leader): I like that idea. Even something as simple as having them list the rules down and give themselves a smiley face, or a flat face, or a frown for how they thought they did, and then giving them a little space to write on how they think it went today.

MEDIA SPECIALIST: I think even in the older grades, when they talked about high schools doing this, they do a rubric after every conversation that they have—just on themselves, just real quick—"How did we do today as a group?" to keep themselves on track.

KINDERGARTEN TEACHER (discussion leader): *If this was not your student work, what instructional practices did you learn that could be put into practice at this time?*

GRADE 3 TEACHER: You see the evidence of how well a conversation works, when applying it to writing as well. It's a great tool.

MEDIA SPECIALIST: For me, it's just the reminder that student-led discussions and writing can be connected so closely. You know, I get so wrapped up in getting the conversation going that I forget afterwards that that'd be a good time to plug in some of the writing parts.

LITERACY COACH: That also connects with the comprehension, which is your ultimate goal anyway—writing in response to literature or writing in response to discussion.

KINDERGARTEN TEACHER (discussion leader): Especially for our ELL students. They get to use the vocabulary.

MEDIA SPECIALIST: I know I've said this before, but even just in having the conversation, they have to come up with the words to say. If one student brings up a good word, it give the other students a chance to say, "What do you mean by that?" or "What are you talking about?" in a nonthreatening way to everybody. Vocabulary is being built as the conversation is going on and as the writing is happening. The two are intertwined.

GRADE 3 TEACHER: Vocabulary is going to be easier to use once they've talked about it, and then they can use it in their writing, too.

LOOKING FORWARD

As emphasized throughout this chapter, research strongly suggests that individual schools and districts move toward professional development that is:

- Ongoing.
- Job-embedded.
- Collaborative.
- Informed by research.
- Informed by the principled use of data.
- Supportive of reflection on instruction.

Schools that are already participating in ongoing, job-embedded professional development through study groups or PLCs may want to collect data on how this type of professional development is changing or enhancing their daily reading instruction, school climate, and continuity of services, and is ultimately leading to students' growth. Policymakers, parents, and other stakeholders will want evidence that investing in teacher knowledge, collaboration, and reflection results in "value added" for student achievement.

QUESTIONS FOR REFLECTION ● ● ● ● ● ● ● ● ● ● ● ● ● ● ● ● ● ●

The following reflection questions may help schools as they apply the ideas in this chapter to their current professional development models:

1. How is the professional development at your school similar to the professional learning described in this chapter? How is it different?

2. If you are currently using study groups or PLCs, how effective have they been in changing instruction and increasing students' reading performance? How do you know this? What evidence do you have to support your ideas?

3. How rigorous are the study and learning taking place in your professional development? How are topics of study selected? How long do groups study a specific topic? How are groups determining that a strategy or instructional technique is "research-based"?

4. What supports are in place to help teachers apply what they are learning in their professional development to their daily teaching? What else may need to be added?

5. How efficient are your PLCs? What norms of behavior, roles, routines, or protocols for discussion do you have in place to help make the most of your professional learning time? What else might need to be added or reviewed?

6. How are you providing time and opportunities for cross-grade sharing within your school? How are you currently fostering collaboration between grade-level teachers and specialists? What are some possibilities for increasing these opportunities?

7. What is your school or district currently doing to foster cross-school sharing? What else could be done?

SUGGESTIONS FOR ONGOING PROFESSIONAL LEARNING • • • • • •

How to Increase the Effectiveness of PLCs

Here are some lessons learned from over 10 years of work with schools as they implemented PLCs as their primary method of engaging in ongoing, job-embedded, collaborative professional development (Taylor, 2011; Taylor & Peterson, 2006; Taylor et al., 2003, 2005):

- Meet weekly in your PLCs. If this is not possible, meet at least twice a month. Schools where PLCs only met once a month found that their groups were not as effective. They reported that the participants lost their focus and momentum when there were large gaps of time between the PLC sessions.
- Rotate the leadership roles of the group (leader, note taker, timekeeper, etc.) each session.
- Have an agenda and stick to it!
- Refer to your action plan and use it to guide your focus.
- Use protocols for video sharing and looking at student work.
- Focus on research-based practices, and select techniques that are worth studying over time. For example, teaching students how to do a routine of comprehension strategies for reading content-area material, such as reciprocal teaching (Oczkus, 2003; Palincsar & Brown, 1984, 1986), will take concerted effort and study across many months, but it will also have a positive impact on student learning. Focusing on one-time activities like worksheets or "make-and-takes" will not result in significant instructional changes or increased student achievement.
- It is not necessary to read a new research-based article every session. Talk about an article over several sessions. Dig deep into the material and reflect on it over time as you grow in your expertise and knowledge.
- All members should be studying, trying out, or refining the same set of techniques or strategies. Working on the same strategies or techniques allows for deeper sharing and reflection. When colleagues share tips, they are talking about things they have actually tried and tested in their own instruction.
- Transfer what is learned in PLCs to everyday teaching.
- Increase the use of data—data on students and data on teaching—to guide instruction.
- Ask a coach or a colleague to come in to model a lesson or to give suggestions as a peer. Share the results of that coaching conversation in the next PLC.
- Meet in cross-grade study groups to build community.
- As a staff, eliminate practices that aren't working, and seek out new models for delivering instruction that may be more effective.

Whole-School Sharing

It is important for individual PLCs to share the things they are learning and doing with their colleagues across the entire school. This builds schoolwide enthusiasm and momentum for reading reform. It holds small groups accountable for their own professional learning, and their individual successes with students add to the collective efficacy and positive tone of the entire school culture. Purposes for whole-school sharing include the following:

- First and foremost—celebrate success!
- Provide opportunities for individual PLCs to share what they are learning or to model a new strategy for the whole group.
- Provide time for staff to discuss schoolwide issues related to reading instruction and to collaborate across grades. It is vitally important to including the specialists (special education teachers, speech pathologist, Title I teachers, ELL teachers, etc.) in this work. (See Walpole & Najera, Chapter 20, for more information on collaborating with specialists.) Schoolwide issues might include such topics as using assessment data to differentiate instruction within the general education reading block (for students below, at, and above grade level); examining the literacy block and time spent on reading instruction across the grades; better serving the needs of students who are ELLs; increasing motivation and student engagement; or fostering partnerships with parents and the community. (Again, see Roberts, Chapter 23, for working with parents as partners.)

An Example of an Agenda for Whole-School Sharing

5–10 minutes: Share classroom or school successes. Be creative! This may take many forms. For example, it may involve one teacher sharing a success story for an individual student or small group, or a grade-level team sharing about a new or refined teaching technique and how it is working in team members' classrooms, or all teachers displaying their most recent progress-monitoring data on trifold display boards.

15 minutes: Individual study groups share or summarize their progress and challenges. Again, this can take many different forms. An example might be to form small sharing groups made up of one member from each of the different study group teams.

30–40 minutes: In small groups, work on a schoolwide focus area or a new strategy; discuss ways to align assessments with instruction; or read and "jigsaw" a research article and discuss how the information applies to your school reading program. For example, if your school serves a large population of ELL students, you may want to have that as your focus for whole-school sharing. All participants could consider what they are learning about reading instruction in their individual study groups and explicitly connect that to meeting the needs of ELLs.

5 minutes: Set a goal for everyone to work on before the next whole-school meeting.

Tips for Whole-School Meetings

- Schedule whole-school meetings once a month. Remember, this is not another "staff meeting" where the miscellaneous items of day-to-day business are addressed. The meeting should have a specific goal or purpose related to schoolwide reading instruction. Communicate that purpose to the participants, so that they all know why they are there and what they should accomplish during the hour.
- The meeting should be planned by the leadership team (principal, literacy coach, grade-level or department representatives, and specialists). This provides an opportunity to gather input from people working with various groups of students throughout the school, and to bring up issues of which the administration or the literacy coach may not be aware.
- Have an agenda and stick to it. Use discussion guides and protocols, so that all the participants know what they should be doing or discussing. Use roles like leader and timekeeper, so that the meeting moves along in an efficient manner.
- Plan for the participants to be *actively* involved. Distribute responsibility for various parts of the agenda to different individuals or teams. Break the whole group into smaller groups for discussion or sharing.

Possible Schedule of Topics for Whole-School Meetings

- *August.* Look at your students' assessment data from the previous year. Make sure you are analyzing multiple forms of assessment data, including state-mandated standardized tests; district-mandated assessments; school-based assessments, including screening, progress-monitoring, diagnostic, summative, and formative assessments (e.g., teacher-developed activities, projects and tests, student work, portfolios, teacher observation). (For more information about schoolwide use of data, see Weber, Chapter 19.) Once students' strengths and needs have been identified, select a topic of study for a grade-level or cross-grade PLC. For example, if the school has a large population of ELL students, and the data on their oral and written academic vocabulary demonstrate a need for improvement, then a cross-grade PLC could be formed to focus on research-based practices for vocabulary instruction with ELLs (e.g., Helman, 2009). If the first-grade data reveal a need for improvement in students' word recognition strategies, then a grade-level PLC could be started to focus on refining instruction on word recognition strategies (e.g., explicit modeling of strategies, coaching students to apply the strategies as they are reading leveled readers). Remember that grade-level PLCs should include any specialists who are working with that grade level, if possible. Allow teachers some choice in the PLC topics they select, so that everyone feels motivated and interested in the small groups.
- *September.* Work together in small groups to develop group norms or expectations for professional behavior (e.g., starting on time, being prepared, respecting all viewpoints and opinions). Introduce and practice using the protocols for video sharing and looking at student work, so that all participants know what to expect in their small PLCs.
- *October.* Ask all staff members to bring their most recent assessment data and look at how those data can be used not only to group students or place them in various interventions, but to inform daily instruction in the general education classroom. How are

teachers planning to differentiate instruction during whole-class, small-group, and independent work time?

- *November and December.* Members of each PLC could share what they are learning and applying to their daily instruction. What are the successes and challenges? The participants can form small cross-grade groups to read and discuss a research article on an important schoolwide topic (e.g., meeting the needs of diverse learners, building partnerships with parents and the community).

- *January.* All staff members should bring their progress-monitoring data. Celebrate successes! Discuss elements of the schoolwide reading program that may need to change (e.g., interventions, delivery models, time spent on reading). Make plans for adaptations and refinements to the reading program for the remainder of the school year.

- *February, March, and April.* Individual PLCs or grade-level teams share what they are learning and applying to their daily instruction. A group may demonstrate an instructional strategy or technique, bring in copies of student work to show how students have increased their ability to apply a reading strategy (e.g., produce written summaries of informational text, compare and contrast reptiles and amphibians), show videos of students answering higher-order questions in student-led discussions, or the like. Participants can also form small cross-grade groups to read and discuss a research article focused on an important issue related to the schoolwide reading program.

- *May or June.* Participants should bring in their end-of-year data on all students. Celebrate the growth students have made throughout the school year! Summarize the learning that has occurred in the PLCs, and set some goals for professional learning for the next year.

Cross-School Sharing

In our work with schools, Barbara Taylor and I found that cross-school sharing was a valuable way to increase professional learning and to raise expectations for students (Taylor, 2011; Taylor & Peterson, 2006). Approximately four times a year, leadership teams from each of 20–30 schools would come together to talk about issues related to schoolwide reading reform. They would share what was working in their specific contexts through panel discussion groups, poster sessions, or formal presentations. For example, at one quarterly leadership team meeting, each school brought a poster depicting the meaningful, challenging, differentiated independent activities that it was using in its leveled reading groups. Participants could stop and ask questions about the things they saw pictured in the displays, and could make connections with staff at other schools for further dialogue. Panel discussion groups were also very effective for sharing information. Panel members were recruited from various schools (i.e., inner-city, suburban, small-town, and rural) and from various positions (e.g., principals, literacy coaches, special education teachers, grade-level teachers). Participants wrote their questions about reading reform on notecards, and then questions were posed to the panel members by a discussion facilitator. Questions included the following:

- How are teachers finding the time to collaborate?
- How are teachers differentiating their instruction within their classrooms to meet the needs of all learners?

- How and when are interventions taking place?
- What are schools doing to increase parent partnerships?
- How are you integrating science and social studies topics into your reading block?
- What is your school doing to support students who receive special education?

Three times a year, all the staffs from the 20–30 schools would come together for literacy institutes. During the breakout sessions at the institutes, individual teachers or teams would give formal presentations about a reading strategy or technique that they were using in their classrooms. Presenters would bring video recordings of their instruction, share student work, demonstrate teaching methods, and explain teacher-made rubrics or instructional plans. Their colleagues from other schools could ask them questions about how they planned their instruction, assessments they used based on their new instruction, PLC resources they used to learn about the instructional strategies, and challenges they had experienced as they implemented the new techniques. This was an effective means of motivating and energizing everyone involved. For example, many teachers were inspired to begin student-led discussion groups in their classrooms after they attended a session led by a teacher who shared his experiences working with inner-city second graders in student-led discussions.

RESEARCH-BASED RESOURCES

Brock, C., Youngs, S., Oikonomidoy, E., & Lapp, D. (2009). The case of Ying: The members of a teacher study group learn about fostering the reading comprehension of English learners. In L. Helman (Ed.), *Literacy development with English learners: Research-based instruction in grades K–6* (pp. 178–195). New York: Guilford Press.

Cordova, R. A., & Mathiesen, A. L. (2010). Reading, writing, and mapping our worlds into being: Shared teacher inquiries into whose literacy count. *The Reading Teacher, 63*(6), 452–463.

DuFour, R., Eaker, R., & Many, T. (2006). *Learning by doing: A handbook for professional development communities at work.* Bloomington, IN: Solution Tree Press.

Helman, L. (Ed.). (2009). *Literacy development with English learners: Research-based instruction in grades K–6.* New York: Guilford Press.

Joyce, B. R., & Showers, B. (2002). *Student achievement through staff development* (3rd ed.). Alexandria, VA: Association for Supervision and Curriculum Development.

Kennedy, E., & Shiel, G. (2010). Raising literacy levels with collaborative on-site professional development in an urban disadvantaged school. *The Reading Teacher, 63*(5), 372–383.

Lipson, M. L., Mosenthal, J. H., Mekkelsen, J., & Russ, B. (2004). Building knowledge and fashioning success one school at a time. *The Reading Teacher, 57*(6), 534–542.

Murphy, C., & Lick, D. (2005). *Whole-faculty study groups: Creating student-based professional development* (3rd ed.). Thousand Oaks, CA: Corwin Press.

Peterson, D. S., Taylor, B. M., Burnham, B., & Schock, R. (2008). Reflective coaching conversations: A missing piece. *The Reading Teacher, 62*(6), 500–509.

Stover, K., Kissel, B., Haag, K., & Shoniker, R. (2011). Differentiated coaching: Fostering reflection with teachers. *The Reading Teacher, 64*(7), 498–509.

Taylor, B. M. (2011) *Catching schools: An action guide to schoolwide reading improvement.* Portsmouth, NH: Heinemann.

REFERENCES

Allington, R. L., & Cunningham, P. M. (2007). *Schools that work: Where all children read and write* (3rd ed.). Boston: Pearson/Allyn & Bacon.

Au, K. H., Raphael, T. E., & Mooney, K. (2008). Improving reading achievement in elementary schools: Guiding change in a time of standards. In S. B. Wepner & D. S. Strickland (Eds.), *The administration and supervision of reading programs* (4th ed., pp. 71–89). New York: Teachers College Press.

Beck, I. L., McKeown, M. G., & Kucan, L. (2002). *Bringing words to life: Robust vocabulary instruction.* New York: Guilford Press.

Cordova, R. A., & Matthiesen, A. L. (2010). Reading, writing, and mapping our worlds into being: Shared teacher inquiries into whose literacy count. *The Reading Teacher, 63*(6), 452–463.

Cox, B. E., & Hopkins, C. J. (2006). Building on theoretical principles gleaned from Reading Recovery to inform classroom practice. *Reading Research Quarterly, 41*(2), 254–267.

Dillon, D. R., O'Brien, D. G., Sato, M., & Kelly, C. M. (2011). Professional development and teacher education in reading instruction. In M. L. Kamil, P. D. Pearson, E. Moje, & P. Afflerbach (Eds.), *Handbook of reading research* (Vol. 4, pp. 629–660). New York: Routledge.

Doubek, M. B., & Cooper, E. J. (2007). Closing the gap through professional development: Implications for reading research. *Reading Research Quarterly, 42*(3), 411–415.

Duffy, G. G. (2004). Teachers who improve reading achievement: What research says about what they do and how to develop them. In D. S. Strickland & M. L. Kamil (Eds.), *Improving reading achievement through professional development* (pp. 3–22). Norwood, MA: Christopher-Gordon.

DuFour, R., Eaker, R., & Many, T. (2006). *Learning by doing: A handbook for professional development communities at work.* Bloomington, IN: Solution Tree Press.

Fuchs, D., Fuchs, L., & Vaughn, S. (Eds.). (2008). *Response to intervention: A framework for reading educators.* Newark, DE: International Reading Association.

Fullan, M. (2005). *Leadership and sustainability: System thinkers in action.* Thousand Oaks, CA: Corwin Press.

Helman, L. (Ed.). (2009). *Literacy development with English learners: Research-based instruction in grades K–6.* New York: Guilford Press.

Johnston, P. H. (Ed.). (2010). *RTI in literacy: Responsive and comprehensive.* Newark, DE: International Reading Association.

Joyce, B. R., & Showers, B. (2002). *Student achievement through staff development* (3rd ed.). Alexandria, VA: Association for Supervision and Curriculum Development.

Kennedy, E., & Shiel, G. (2010). Raising literacy levels with collaborative on-site professional development in an urban disadvantaged school. *The Reading Teacher, 63*(5), 372–383.

Langer, J. A. (2001). Beating the odds: Teaching middle and high school students to read and write well. *American Educational Research Journal, 38*(4), 837–880.

Lieberman, A., & Miller, L. (2007). Transforming professional development: Understanding and organizing learning communities. In W. D. Hawley with D. L. Rollie (Eds.), *The keys to effective schools: Educational reform as continuous improvement* (2nd ed., pp. 74–85). Thousand Oaks, CA: Corwin Press.

Lipson, M. L., Mosenthal, J. H., Mekkelsen, J., & Russ, B. (2004). Building knowledge and fashioning success one school at a time. *The Reading Teacher, 57*(6), 534–542.

McNaughton, S., MacDonald, S., Amituanai-Toloa, M., Lai, M., & Farry, S. (2006). *Enhanced teaching and learning of comprehension in year 4–9: Mangere Schools.* Auckland, New Zealand: Uniservices.

Murphy, C., & Lick, D. (2005). *Whole-faculty study groups: Creating student-based professional development* (3rd ed.). Thousand Oaks, CA: Corwin Press.

Oczkus, L. D. (2003). *Reciprocal teaching at work: Strategies for improving reading comprehension.* Newark, DE: International Reading Association.

Palincsar, A. S., & Brown, A. L. (1984). Reciprocal teaching of comprehension-fostering and comprehension-monitoring activities. *Cognition and Instruction, 2,* 117–175.

Palincsar, A. S., & Brown, A. L. (1986). Interactive teaching to promote independent learning from text. *The Reading Teacher, 39*(8), 771–777.

Peterson, D. S., Taylor, B. M., Burnham, B., & Schock, R. (2008). Reflective coaching conversations: A missing piece. *The Reading Teacher, 62*(6), 500–509.

Pinnell, G. S., & Rodgers, E. M. (2004). Reflective inquiry as a tool for professional development. In D. S. Strickland & M. L. Kamil (Eds.), *Improving reading achievement through professional development* (pp. 169—193). Norwood, MA: Christopher-Gordon.

Sailors, M. (2009). Improving comprehension instruction through quality professional development. In S. E. Israel & G. G. Duffy (Eds.), *Handbook of research on reading comprehension.* New York: Routledge.

Stover, K., Kissel, B., Haag, K., & Shoniker, R. (2011). Differentiated coaching: Fostering reflection with teachers. *The Reading Teacher, 64*(7), 498–509.

Taylor, B. M. (2011). *Catching schools: An action guide to schoolwide reading improvement.* Portsmouth, NH: Heinemann.

Taylor, B. M., & Pearson, P. D. (2005). Using study groups and reading assessment data to improve reading instruction within a school. In S. G. Paris & S. A. Stahl (Eds.), *Children's reading comprehension and assessment* (pp. 237–255). Mahwah, NJ: Erlbaum.

Taylor, B. M., Pearson, P. D., Peterson, D. S., & Rodriguez, M. C. (2003). Reading growth in high-poverty classrooms: The influence of teacher practices that encourage cognitive engagement in literacy learning. *Elementary School Journal, 104,* 3–28.

Taylor, B. M., Pearson, P. D., Peterson, D. S., & Rodriguez, M. C. (2005). The CIERA School Change Framework: An evidence-based approach to professional development and school reading improvement. *Reading Research Quarterly, 40*(1), 40–69.

Taylor, B. M., & Peterson, D. S. (2006). *The impact of the School Change Framework in twenty-three REA schools* (Research Report No. 1). Minneapolis: University of Minnesota, Minnesota Center for Reading Research.

Taylor, B. M., Raphael, T. E., & Au, K. H. (2011). Reading and school reform. In M. L. Kamil, P. D. Pearson, E. Moje, & P. Afflerbach (Eds.), *Handbook of reading research* (Vol. 4, pp. 594–628). New York: Routledge.

Timperley, H. S., & Parr, J. M. (2007). Closing the achievement gap through evidence-based inquiry at multiple levels of the education system. *Journal of Advanced Academics, 19*(1), 90–115.

Valli, L., & Hawley, W. D. (2007). Designing and implementing school-based professional development. In W. D. Hawley with D. L. Rollie (Eds.), *The keys to effective schools: Educational reform as continuous improvement* (2nd ed., pp. 86–96). Thousand Oaks, CA: Corwin Press.

Vaughn, S., Wanzek, J., & Fletcher, J. M. (2007). Multiple tiers of intervention: A framework for prevention and identification of students with reading/learning disabilities." In B. M. Taylor & J. E. Ysseldyke (Eds.), *Effective instruction for struggling readers K–6* (pp. 173–195). New York: Teachers College Press.

Vogt, M., & Shearer, B. A. (2011). *Reading specialists and literacy coaches in the real world* (3rd ed.). Boston: Pearson/Allyn & Bacon.

York-Barr, J., Sommers, W. A., Ghere, G. S., & Montie, J. (2006). *Reflective practice to improve schools: An action guide for educators* (2nd ed.). Thousand Oaks, CA: Corwin Press.

CHAPTER 22

Professional Learning with and from a Literacy Coach • • •

A Poem in Two Voices

MISTY SAILORS
KATIE RUSSELL
HEATHER AUGUSTINE
KERRY ALEXANDER

Growing evidence suggests that coaching is more than just a trend; there is real value in the role that coaches play inside a well-developed literacy program. Although coaching is not new (Cassidy, Garrett, Maxfield, & Patchett, 2010), it has been rediscovered by a new generation of teachers and teacher educators. While many in the field tell anecdotal stories about the effects of coaching on teachers' attitude, knowledge, and practice, there has (until recently) been a scarcity of evidence to demonstrate coaching's effectiveness in improving instructional literacy practices and student literacy learning (Sailors, 2009).

However, with the emergence of a new (and embryonic) field of research, evidence is beginning to suggest that coaching is (and should be) more than a passing fad. A growing body of research is also demonstrating that the coaching of classroom literacy teachers has a direct impact on students' literacy achievement (Sailors & Shanklin, 2010). In this chapter, we first review the research to date on literacy coaching. We then present a "poem in two voices"—the ways in which a coach and a teacher work together to build an understanding of who they are as professionals, what they know (and want to learn) about teaching, and how they structure an environment for children that leads to literacy learning.

OVERVIEW OF RESEARCH

The verdict is in: The use of coaching as a means of professional development for class-room teachers can have a large influence on the teachers (improved practices) and on their students (improvement in literacy achievement). These claims are supported by three bodies of research: (1) the impact of literacy coaching on instructional practices and student achievement, (2) the nuanced aspects of coaching, and (3) the professional development of coaches. We review each of these in this section.

Improved Instructional Practices under the Guidance of a Literacy Coach

Recent studies have documented the effectiveness of coaching in improving the instructional practices of classroom teachers; they have also examined various models of coaching. For example, Biancarosa, Bryk, and Dexter (2010) conducted a 4-year longitudinal study of a schoolwide reform model known as the Literacy Collaborative. This model of coaching requires a full year of professional development for the participating coaches. The reading achievement of K–2 students in 17 schools was assessed twice during each year of the study. The model demonstrated positive effects on students' literacy learning over the course of the study, with lingering effects in subsequent follow-up studies.

Similarly, Matsumura, Garnier, Correnti, Junker, and Bickel (2010) investigated the effects of a program called Content-Focused Coaching (CFC) on new teachers in an urban district with high turnover rates among its teaching staff. Analysis of data indicated that the CFC program predicted significantly higher school-level gains on the state assessment for English language learners than gains in non-CFC classrooms. Teachers' self-reported and observed instruction in the CFC schools surpassed that of comparison teachers on measures of reading instruction.

Sailors and Price (2010) explored the role of coaching as a means of professional development in improving comprehension instruction in elementary and middle school classrooms. They tested the effects of two models of professional development (workshop only and workshop plus coaching) on instructional comprehension practices and the reading achievement of students in low-income schools. A random-effects, multilevel, pretest–posttest comparison group design and a multilevel modeling analytic strategy were used to explore the effectiveness of the two models. The full-intervention group (teachers who were coached) outperformed the partial-intervention group (workshop only) on all teacher observation and student achievement measures.

Likewise, Neuman and Wright (2010) studied the effects on prekindergarten teachers' early language and literacy practices when these teachers were engaged in either traditional university coursework or on-site coaching. Teachers from six urban areas who received coaching support outperformed teachers in the coursework-only group and the control group on environmental classroom measures. The effects were still evident 5 months after the completion of the study. These results suggest that carefully controlled and implemented models of coaching have benefits.

The Nuances of Coaching

While there are clear demonstrations that coaching has positive effects on learning, other studies have begun to examine the relational aspects of coaching and its importance to successful implementation of coaching programs. For example, several studies have indicated that the more time coaches spend with teachers, the more teachers appreciate their coaches and subsequently improve their practices (Bean, Cassidy, Grumet, Shelton, & Wallis, 2002; L'Allier, Elish-Piper, & Bean, 2010). Other studies have also indicated that the relationship between coaches and teachers is important, as is the relationship between coaches and their school and district leaders (Matsumura, Sartoris, Bickel, & Garnier, 2009).

Bean, Draper, Hall, Vandermolen, and Zigmond (2010) examined the relationship between coaches' distribution of time and student achievement. Examining the time distribution of tasks of 20 Reading First coaches, these researchers found that in schools where coaches spent more time on the task of coaching itself, significantly greater percentages of students were proficient in reading in first and second grades. In addition, these schools had significantly lower percentages of students at risk for academic failure as a result of coaching. The study also examined the effectiveness of coaches' work as perceived by teachers; it found that teachers valued coaches, and that there were significant relationships between the time allocated to working with teachers and teachers' views of coaches.

Others have demonstrated the importance of negotiating the roles and responsibilities of coaching. For example, Stephens and Vanderburg (2010) used qualitative methods to capture the practices of coaches that teachers found most helpful in a statewide reading initiative. Teachers reported that they appreciated the way coaches supported teachers' collaboration and provided them with ongoing support and research-based teaching practices. In addition, Ippolito (2010) investigated the work of middle school literacy coaches from an urban district and examined the balance of coaches' behaviors, identified as either *responsive* or *directive* coaching interactions. He found that coaches attempted to balance these two ways of interacting with teachers during single coaching sessions, particularly by using protocols to balance responsive and directive moves.

The construction of identity by new and beginning coaches also has an impact on the successful implementation of a coaching program. In the field of math, for example, Chval and her colleagues (2010) examined the roles, expectations, and interactions of first-year mathematics coaches as they developed new identities and negotiated their roles across K–7 classrooms. The research team found that the coaches' roles and identities were shaped not only by their own views of the coaching position, but also by the expectations of teachers and principals.

Finally, coaches have a variety of "tools" (see Taylor, Chapter 18, this volume, for a discussion of the multiple components of collaboration and support present in effective improvement efforts) at their disposal to support teachers. Coaches use traditional tools (such as demonstration lessons, co-teaching, critical/responsive feedback, and conferencing) as well as student assessments to support teachers (Denton, Swanson, & Mathes, 2007; Sailors & Price, 2010). A growing number of coaches are successfully using media-based tools to support teachers, including Web-mediated coaching (Pianta, Mashburn, Downer, Hamre, & Justice, 2008), virtual coaching (Denton et al., 2007), and hypermedia coaching (Powell, Diamond, & Koehler, 2010). Finally, general human skill tools, including listening and other "people skills" (Quatroche, Bean, & Hamilton, 2001), are important parts of a well-developed coaching program.

The Professional Development of Coaches

The benefits of coaching (for both teaching and learning), as well as the nuanced aspects of coaching, are important. Equally important, but less studied, is the role played by the professional development of coaches. Only a few studies to date have looked at this topic. Recent research seems to indicate that coaches need and want professional development focused on helping them negotiate their roles and responsibilities in schools (Chval et al., 2010; Ippolito, 2010). Other studies have found that coaches express a desire for professional development aimed at improving their research-based knowledge (Blamey, Mayer, & Walpole, 2008). Still other studies have illustrated that coaches need and want professional development focused on practical knowledge of activities to conduct with teachers, such as activities that can be enacted during demonstration lessons (Blamey, Meyer, & Walpole, 2008). And, finally, coaches have indicated a desire for professional development that focuses on improving their personal attributes (Gibson, 2005), so that they can have effective relationships with classroom teachers (Gibson, 2006) and school leaders (Mangin, 2009; Matsumara, Sartoris, Bickel, & Garnier, 2009).

SUMMARY OF BIG IDEAS FROM RESEARCH

- Literacy coaches matter! Carefully constructed models of coaching lead to improvement in teachers' practices and in the achievement of their students.
- Teachers appreciate the time and work of their literacy coaches, especially when a good relationship exists between them.
- Coaches need and want high-quality professional development for themselves, so that they can continue to improve their own practices.

EXAMPLES OF EFFECTIVE PRACTICES

Although the "process" aspects of coaching continue to be examined by research, there is scant evidence to demonstrate the kind of learning that transpires during interactions between coaches and teachers. In this section, we present the voices of a literacy coach and a teacher (two of our coauthors) in the form of a dialogue poem (see the box on pp. 560–564). However, before we begin this poem, we introduce the two voices in it: Heather Augustine and Kerry Alexander.

Meet the Coach: Heather

I am a "30ish"-year-old female who has been in education for 10 years. I taught second, third, and fourth grades (a total of 6 years) and was a literacy leader at my previous school. I have been in my literacy coaching position for 4 years, having received a year of professional development in CFC (West & Staub, 2003). I received my undergraduate degree in applied learning and development from the University of Texas at Austin, where I specialized in reading. I received my master's degree in education from the same university and hold a reading specialist certification in Texas. One day I see myself educating school administrators on how best to support teachers and plan relevant professional development. I would also like to write books for teachers.

I believe that teaching is a political act. I also believe that the work of teaching involves the heart, and I do what I do because I care about teachers and children; I "care" in the sense described by Nel Noddings (2003). That is, I think that teachers and students must have someone to "feel with" them as they take risks, struggle, and succeed. I also believe that teaching involves reflexivity. I try to be reflexive in all that I do; I was once told that teaching is not about "do-overs," but is about "do-betters." I see teaching experiences as opportunities to learn, and I encourage that in others around me. I balance my time among planning effective literacy lessons with teachers, working in classrooms with teachers and their students, planning and offering relevant professional development, and meeting with administration to advocate for teachers and students. Most of the time, I am "fired up" about something. Often I find myself frustrated with the many obstacles that get in the way of good teaching. My husband often jokes about how I will avoid conflict in other areas of my life, but when it comes to education, I will stand my ground and share my beliefs.

Meet the Teacher: Kerry

I am also a "30ish"-year-old female. I have been in education for 3 years. My teaching experiences started at the school where I currently teach, as an English as a second language fourth-grade teacher. I received my degree in applied learning and development from the University of Texas at Austin in 2009, where I specialized in reading—just as Heather did! Eventually I see myself as a reading or writing specialist, working with small groups of students. I would also love to work with teachers; I feel I am good at facilitating learning and honest dialogue among colleagues.

I teach from the heart. I tend to extend past (and through) a topic, skill, or idea, searching for the greatest connection to my students lives. I take winding paths through what I have to teach (curriculum), following the voices and words of my students, and though I stay true to what I have to present, I often find myself discussing "kid business" (Fairbanks, 2000) with them—paying respect to the whole brain. I am also a "yes-sayer," often signing up for learning groups, though not necessarily all in my district. I can get in a bit over my head, but I know that these experiences lead to great opportunities for my children. I often have interns in my classroom observing and teaching with me because I know that the building of ideas lends to greater learning for all involved. Finally, I spend my quiet time mentally revising what I have done, how it is presently going, and what I am about to do. I use what I learn from real classroom life to rework and retool my practices, and though I'm not immune to "teacher guilt," it can be alleviated by strong reflective habits—which keep me on my toes.

The Partnership: Heather and Kerry Working Together

Heather and Kerry have worked together for the past 3 years as a teacher–coach pair at their elementary school. We present the learning that has taken place within and across the partnership over these years in the poem that appears on the next five pages. The poem is formatted to represent the two voices speaking: Heather (literacy coach) and Kerry (fourth-grade teacher). Inspired by a Newbery Medal winner (Fleischman, 1988), this poem is intended it to be read aloud by two people. It should be read from top to bottom, with one person taking the left-hand part (teacher) and the other taking the right-hand part (coach). When both readers have boldfaced lines on the same level, those lines are to be read simultaneously or in chorus.

A Poem in Two Voices: Teacher (*left*) and Coach (*right*)

I came into teaching because I was interested in very young children.	**I came into teaching because I was interested in very young children.**
I was interested in how my daughter was growing.	
	I've always been fascinated by emergent literacy and loved to watch toddlers discover print and stories in the world around them.
I found myself in a reading specialization cohort at the local university.	**I found myself in a reading specialization cohort at the local university.**
I had some credits from Austin Community College, the University of Kansas, and the Savannah College of Art and Design.	
	I came to Austin after having nearly completed my degree at Texas A&M Kingsville.
That experience changed my life. It taught me about good teaching.	**That experience changed my life. It taught me about good teaching.**
I learned about cultural relevancy, the rights of a child as a learner, and teaching the whole child in an assessment-based environment.	I learned to examine my assumptions and now think differently about these children who come from a low-income community. I learned to value children's individual strengths and needs, and to have high expectations for all. I also learned about myself.
I value cultural relevancy, respect for individual differences, and high expectations for all students.	**I value cultural relevancy, respect for individual differences, and high expectations for all students.**
Not a day goes by that I don't try to meet all the children where they are—with what they bring. Regardless of economics, or the academic nuances between each learner, I know my job is to find their whole self and teach with it, not to fill it or change it. All this while holding tight to real literacy goals—	I use texts that are relevant to our students, where they can see themselves represented in the characters. I see each student and teacher as a unique individual with strengths and needs, and strive to meet them where they are and help them reach where they want to go.

individual and whole-class. We aim high, while treading a path eked out of their "funds of knowledge" (Gonzalez, Moll, & Amanti, 2005), armed with great literature.

I found my way to Houston Elementary. The school has become a family to me.

I have jumped into this community with both feet. My daughter is now in kindergarten and at the school. I can't be part of something without putting my whole self into it. It just wouldn't seem authentic otherwise.

I trust her and what she has to offer me as a learner.

Heather is a mighty coach, but gentle and humble and human. She has taken her role to a place that would exhaust others, but she lives this life as an educator each hour of the day. Heather is a big influence . . .

We are from the same roots.

She encourages me. Because of her, I encourage others, too.

Heather offers her vulnerabilities to us so we can all learn, and with clear and organized language, she challenges us and stands firmly behind what she believes in. She knows that it takes time for a good thing to brew, and she promotes the same tenacity and dedication in us that she has.

She inspires me.

I found my way to Houston Elementary. The school has become a family to me.

I feel like I grew up in that time, and with that growth came a passion for having a voice for children and teachers. I fell in love with the community. I belong here.

I trust her and what she has to offer me as a learner.

Kerry keeps me connected to whom I was when I first came to teaching. She reminds me that authenticity is worth more than anything else, and that the children crave and deserve it just like teachers.

We have the same belief systems.

She encourages me. Because of her, I encourage others, too.

I wasn't sure *encourager* was the right word, so I looked it up in the dictionary. It fits Kerry: (1) to inspire with courage, spirit, or confidence; and (2) to promote, advance, or foster.

She inspires me.

I like the way Heather speaks with us. In planning, during a professional development course, one on one . . . she's so clear and purposeful. You can almost see her turn on the wisdom, collecting resources in her mind. That's how I try to teach with my own students: clear and purposeful, pulling from everything I know and believe. In a way, I think she models best practices when she's with teachers. I try and emulate the thoughtfulness, the mindfulness.

Kerry focuses on the greater good, even in the midst of scrutiny and mandates that don't make much sense. She often reminds her colleagues why we are teachers and that it is really about the kids—they are all that really matter.

I learn from her.

I learn from her.

I've learned how to be a real teacher in a real school from Heather. During my first year, Heather came into my classroom and modeled guided reading while supporting a whole-class independent reading time. She helped students find reading "nooks," and then came back often to check on our progress—not in a looming, "Are you doing it right?" kind of way, but in a "Do we need to amend anything? How's it working?" kind of way. I was never worried I was wrong in those beginning days. I was trusted.

I've learned a lot about the writing process from Kerry. She is a part of the Heart of Texas Writing Project and has opened my eyes to see writing workshop like I see reading workshop. I always felt confident about managing a reading workshop, but really struggled with managing writing workshop and feeling like I was meeting the needs of all my students. I learned from Kerry how to grow a community of writers who understand the purpose of writing on a much larger scale.

She taught me how to really guide the children's thinking in a whole-class setting, what questions would pack the most punch, and how to set a clear purpose for reading each day.

She's helped me to see what growing a community of learners who love writing and see its purpose in interacting with the world, and even changing it, looks like.

I learn with her.

Heather and I have worked through writing instruction together. For the past 3 years, we've been learning about, hunting for, and continuing to revise our writing strategies on a regular basis. We reread trusted sources, dig into new resources, and come up with a new plan. Often it involves a push-and-pull between the natural process of authentic child writing and the rigidity of test writing. Sometimes we have to stop and take a breath; we have had to learn to retrust our own learning process in how to teach writing effectively—and maybe accept the idea that we may have taken a few wrong turns. We allow ourselves to change our minds and to try teaching practices we may never have considered.

We have to support one another in this learning and growing.

We are part of a learning community. Here at our school, everybody is learning!

If you look closely inside our school, you'll find pockets of like-minded teachers and teachers with special energy.

We represent all grades; we all tend to be motivated and interested in learning. Our learning groups are formed naturally, on their own—out of interest and need, mostly. We need each other's support in order for our students to be successful! We meet and reflect and debrief on our practices as often as we can. This job demands it. When a teacher on our campus asks for help, the wisdom and

I learn with her.

One of the things Kerry and I have learned together is how to make change, both in the classroom and on our campus. We've often brainstormed and struggled together over how to help inspire a student to try on a new attitude about reading or writing. We've tried together to find just the right text, or topic, or spot in the room for a student to be successful and feel successful. We've also spent time thinking and planning together how to help our colleagues try out best practices, try out new books that we've seen kids love, and be more open and honest in planning meetings.

We are both committed to making an impact that's bigger than just making it through the day.

We are part of a learning community. Here at our school, everybody is learning!

Even though our school is large, there are pockets of like-minded people who get together to think, learn, and solve problems.

nurturing are quickly palpable. We meet before school or after, or during lunch—in the copy room, the office, wherever. We bring books, quotes, ideas, and even chocolate—whatever is needed to start that teacher's engine again.

A like-minded support group is essential when a busy teacher devotes even more of his or her time to becoming a better teacher, because we know teaching requires such a huge time investment.

It's how we decided to start a book study, join a social justice teacher inquiry group, go to a Saturday writing conference, take a university class, and apply for graduate school. It usually has nothing to do with the mandates; it is really all about us—and what we are interested in and struggling with in our teaching. Heather is a master at building support for this kind of learning, aligning our ideas and questions with real plans.

Kerry's the kind of teacher who is willing to open her classroom and share her learning with all teachers.

She's courageous and stands up for what she believes in.

She's courageous and stands up for what she believes in.

Heather stands up and fights. I see Heather daily with her "game face" on, poking into classrooms or chatting with teachers in the hallway. She braids friend, mentor, and educator together to create a strong, encouraging bundle. It's not uncommon to hear her say, "Just do what's right for the kids. You know what that is. I know you do." Then the ball is back in my court.

Kerry has courage.

Teachers have so many decisions to make each day about what is most important, how to treat students, and how to deal with issues. In a school like ours, there is quite a dilemma: There are different people all telling teachers what to do, when to teach what, how to teach, in hopes of helping students improve their performance on mandated assessments. Kerry and I choose to spend time with people who are willing to join us in trying to make sense of the mandates and do what's best for kids.

It's this kind of give-and-take with Heather.

We spend a lot of time learning together how to negotiate this world of competing agendas.

Modeled after *Joyful Noise: Poems for Two Voices* (Fleischman, 1988).

Summarizing Thoughts

It is clear from the dialogue poem in the box that there is mutual respect between this teacher and this coach, and that much learning takes place between the two as a result. Each brings uniqueness to the relationship, and in turn, each is changed by the interaction with the other. There is value in the similarities and the differences each offers to the other. In addition, these two professionals have engaged in co-constructed knowledge building both inside and outside the school. Obviously, Heather and Kerry support each other within the school setting—in the classroom, in professional meetings and workshops, and in informal settings (such as the hallway and teachers' lounge). However, what may make this relationship unique (and stronger as a learning relationship) is the way in which these two seek out and attend outside professional development opportunities. They both attend workshops sponsored by the Heart of Texas Writing Project (*http://ows.edb.utexas.edu/?q=site/heart-texas-writing-project*), book study groups and the Austin Social Justice Teacher Inquiry Group (*www.facebook.com/groups/Asjtig*). In addition, they do outside readings, sharing with each other when they come across a great piece in *The Reading Teacher, Elementary School Journal*, or a new professional development book by one of the great figures in our field. Perhaps their shared "roots" (through their teacher preparation program) are what lead them to seek out these learning opportunities.

Moreover, Heather and Kerry seem to trust each other, both professionally and personally. There seems to be a balancing or equalizing of power within this relationship. Perhaps this balancing of power is a result of the climate at the school that Heather has helped to build. It may also may be due to their shared dedication to (and respect of and for) the students, which creates the drive to trust and grow together as professionals. Regardless, Heather and Kerry are learners and are working to grow actively as professionals, together.

Finally, this powerful learning relationship between Heather and Kerry may be due to their involvement in a *community of practice* (Lave & Wegner, 1991). A community of practice is a group of people who share an interest, an expertise, and/or a profession. Communities of practice can be intentionally designed by the members to gain knowledge, or can evolve naturally because of the common interest in a particular area by the members of that community. The members of such a community learn from each other and have opportunities to develop both professionally and personally by sharing information and experiences with the group. (For more on collaborative learning, see Peterson, Chapter 21; for more on collegial collaboration within schools, see Walpole & Najera, Chapter 20.)

There are three components to a community of practice (Wenger, McDermott, & Snyder, 2002). First, the domain of knowledge created within a community of practice creates common ground and inspires members to participate. This knowledge also guides learning and gives meaning to the actions of the members. Second, the notion of community creates the social foundation for learning that takes place within the community of practice and fosters the members' interactions and willingness to share. And third, while the domain of knowledge provides the general area of relevance for the community, the practice is the specific area in which the community creates, shares, and preserves its knowledge.

Learning is a natural outcome of the interactions between people and their environments within a community of practice (Lave & Wenger, 1991). The fact that Heather and Kerry belong to several communities of practice (they came through the same teacher preparation program, teach at the same school, and share professional development experiences) may explain some of the learning that takes place. Interestingly, the shared source of conflict (mediating the pressures that accompany high-stakes testing) may be the driving force that creates an environment for these communities of practice to grow.

As members of these various communities of practice, Heather and Kerry have a similar domain of knowledge ("Literacy can be defined as *A, B*, and *C* . . . "), share the same social foundation (both are committed to improving the educational experiences for children from low-income and minority communities), and share a practice ("Literacy instruction is this, but not this . . . "). Understanding the ways in which membership inside these communities of practice shapes Heather and Kerry's relationship offers valuable insight into the way they work together, learning from and with each other.

LOOKING FORWARD

Research seems to suggest that coaching is an effective mechanism for the professional development of both teachers and coaches. Attention to the following points may enhance the ways in which teachers and coaches build relationships that lead to co-constructed learning, meaning making, and improved instructional practices:

- Technology is a powerful tool that can be used to enhance existing professional learning relationships, especially through the use of social networks (Lloyd & Duncan-Howell, 2010).
- Trust is often cited as key in relationships between coaches and teachers, and it takes time and effort to build (Costa & Garmston, 2002).
- Finding common ground on which to build learning opportunities can lead to co-constructed knowledge (DuFour, 2005).
- Development of a community of practice, in which learning is an outcome of a shared domain of interest, is important (Lave & Wegner, 1991).

Future Research Questions

Although the literature on coaching continues to grow, there remain lingering questions that research could address:

- How do coaches and teachers develop learning relationships that are conducive to learning communities?
- What are the school structures that support learning relationships between coaches and teachers?
- What influence do these learning relationships have on student reading achievement?
- What is the role of culturally responsive coaching in developing these kinds of learning relationships?

QUESTIONS FOR REFLECTION ●

1. As a coach, what kind of relationship do I have with your teachers? As a teacher, what kind of relationship do I have with your coach?

2. What do I value about teachers at my school? My coach? What do we learn from each other? With each other?

3. At a school level, how is learning supported by the administration? By the coach? By teachers? Is this learning a one-way street, or is it co-constructed? In what ways?

4. What spaces can I create so that learning is co-constructed and encouraged at my school?

5. What is the role of professional development (and how it is structured at my school) in creating an environment that is conducive to co-constructed learning at my school with my teachers?

SUGGESTIONS FOR ONGOING PROFESSIONAL LEARNING ● ● ● ● ● ● ●

There are several ways in which teachers and coaches can critically examine how to support each other's learning. A professional learning community, or PLC, is one mechanism that offers such support; teachers and coaches can learn a great deal from and with each other in the context of a PLC. Through carefully structured interactions and activities within a PLC, coaches and teachers can create environments that support individual and group learning. (Ongoing professional learning is covered in more detail by Taylor, in Chapter 18, and Peterson, Chapter 21.)

Examining the Learning Relationships within the PLC

The PLC can offer support to its members as they become more aware of (and critical about) the relationships that exist between teachers and coaches. The following PLC sessions are intended to support this self-evaluation and reflection of relationships within teams of teachers and across the coach–teacher relationship.

Session 1

Discuss this chapter, focusing on the poem. Compare/contrast the experiences of Heather and Kerry. How are they similar? Different? How do they match the experiences you have had as a teacher? As a literacy coach?

Session 2

Engage in a writing extension of Session 1: Write your own dialogue poem with your coach/teacher. You can start by brainstorming activities that you do together, and then move on to what you have learned from and with each other. Be sure to think about the role of the school in creating/supporting your learning relationship.

Session 3

At a campus meeting or a meeting of your local school district, perform the dialogue poem you wrote in Session 2. Performances such as this carry weight in keeping your district (and community) informed of the work that you are doing and the progress you are making.

Session 4

At another PLC meeting, think about other learning relationships that exist both inside and outside classrooms, including student–teacher, student–coach, administrator–coach, reading specialist–coach, and student–teacher–coach. Extend the writing activity from Session 2 by brainstorming activities (within one of these relationships), thinking about what you do together and what you have learned from and with each other. Be sure to think about the role of relationships in creating/supporting learning within each pair or triad.

Creating a Community of Practice

PLCs can offer support to members as they work together to create (and strengthen) communities of practice. The following PLC sessions are intended to support the creation (and strengthening) of a community of practice.

Session 1

Revisit the poem in this chapter in detail. Focus on the topics Heather and Kerry talk about. Look critically at the verbs they use to discuss those topics and their experiences. Are there particular metaphors and/or similes that offer insight into their individuality? Into their relationship? Into the way they "fit" in their community of practice?

Session 2

Return to the dialogue poem you wrote in the earlier Session 2 (see the section "Examining the Learning Relationships within the PLC"). Identify the topics in your dialogue poem. How do each of you "fit" into your community of practice? What domain of knowledge does the community share? What is the shared social foundation? What is the shared practice?

Session 3

Revisit the answers you provided in Session 2 (just above). What are some ways in which the members of your community of practice can actively work to improve its domain of knowledge? How can members of the community of practice actively engage those who seem to be on its margins?

Session 4

Again, revisit the dialogue poem you wrote earlier. Identify and discuss the sources of conflict for the community of practice. How do the individuals in your community negotiate those sources of conflict individually? What role does the community of practice play in negotiating those conflicts?

RESEARCH-BASED RESOURCES

The following resources may provide you with additional support in (1) strengthening your domain of knowledge about coaching, (2) building relationships that support effective coaching and learning, and (3) building and strengthening communities of practice.

Strengthening Your Domain of Knowledge about Coaching

Allen, J. (2006). *Becoming a literacy leader: Supporting learning and change.* Portland, ME: Stenhouse.

Bean, R. M., & Dagen, A. S. (Eds.). (2011). *Best practices of literacy leaders in schools.* New York: Guilford Press.

Toll, C. A. (2008). *Surviving but not yet thriving: Essential questions and practical answers for experienced literacy coaches.* Newark, NE: International Reading Association.

Vogt, M., & Shearer, B. A. (2011). *Reading specialists and literacy coaches in the real world* (3rd ed.). Boston: Pearson/Allyn & Bacon.

Walpole, S., & McKenna, M. (2004). *The literacy coach's handbook: A guide to research-based practice.* New York: Guilford Press.

Building Relationships That Support Effective Coaching and Learning

Kissel, B., Mraz, M., Algozzine, B., & Stover, K. (2011). Early childhood literacy coaches' role perceptions and recommendations for change. *Journal of Research in Childhood Education, 25*(3), 288–303.

Lapp, D., Fisher, D., Flood, J., & Frey, N. (2003). Dual role of the urban reading specialist. *Journal of Staff Development, 24*(20), 33–36.

Rainville, K. N., & Jones, S. (2008). Situated identities: Power and positioning in the work of a literacy coach. *The Reading Teacher, 61,* 440–448.

Walpole, S., & Blamey, K. (2008). Elementary literacy coaches: The reality of dual roles. *The Reading Teacher, 62*(3), 222–231.

Building and Strengthening Communities of Practice

Fullan, M. (2001). *Leading in a culture of change.* San Francisco: Jossey-Bass.

Johnston, P. H. (2004). *Choice words: How our language affects children's learning.* Portland, ME: Stenhouse.

Wenger, E. (1999). *Communities of practice: Learning, meaning, and identity.* Cambridge, UK: Cambridge University Press.

Wenger, E., McDermott, R., & Snyder, W. M. (2002). *Cultivating communities of practice.* Boston: Harvard Business Review Press.

REFERENCES

Bean, R. M., Cassidy, J., Grumet, J. E., Shelton, D. S., & Wallis, S. R. (2002). What do reading specialists do?: Results from a national survey. *The Reading Teacher, 55*(8), 736–744.

Bean, R. M., Draper, J. A., Hall, V., Vandermolen, J., & Zigmond, N. (2010). Coaches and coaching in Reading First schools: A reality check. *Elementary School Journal, 111*, 87–114.

Biancarosa, G., Bryk, A. S., & Dexter, E. R. (2010). Assessing the value-added effects of literacy collaborative professional development on student learning. *Elementary School Journal, 111*, 7–34.

Blamey, K. L., Meyer, C. K., & Walpole, S. (2008). Middle and high school literacy coaches: A national study. *Journal of Adolescent and Adult Literacy, 52*, 310–323.

Cassidy, J., Garrett, S. D., Maxfield, P., & Patchett, C. (2010). Literacy coaching: Yesterday, today and tomorrow. In J. Cassidy, S. D. Garrett, & M. Sailors (Eds.), *Literacy coaching: Research and practice* (pp. 15–27). Corpus Christi, TX: Center for Educational Development Evaluation and Research.

Chval, K. B., Arbaugh, F., Lannin, J. K., van Garderen, D., Cummings, L., Estapa, A. T., et al. (2010). The transition from experienced teacher to mathematics coach: Establishing a new identity. *Elementary School Journal, 111*(1), 191–216.

Costa, A. L., & Garmston, R. J. (2002). *Cognitive coaching: A foundation for Renaissance schools* (2nd ed.). Norwood, MA: Christopher-Gordon.

Denton, C. A., Swanson, E. A., & Mathes, P. G. (2007). Assessment-based instructional coaching provided to reading intervention teachers. *Reading and Writing, 20*, 569–590.

DuFour, R. (2005). *On common ground: The power of professional learning communities.* Bloomington, IN: Solution Tree.

Fairbanks, C. (2000). Fostering adolescents' literacy engagements: "Kid's business" and critical inquiry. *Reading Research and Instruction, 40*, 35–50.

Fleischman, P. (1988). *Joyful noise: Poems for two voices.* New York: HarperCollins.

Gibson, S. A. (2005). Developing knowledge on coaching. *Issues in Teacher Education, 14*, 63–74.

Gibson, S. A. (2006). Lesson observation and feedback: The practice of an expert reading coach. *Literacy Research and Instruction, 45*, 295–317.

Gonzalez, N., Moll, L. C., & Amanti, C. (2005). *Funds of knowledge: Theorizing practices in households and classrooms.* Mahwah, NJ: Erlbaum.

Ippolito, J. (2010). Three ways literacy coaches balance responsive and directive relationships with teachers. *Elementary School Journal, 111*, 164–190.

L'Allier, S., Elish-Piper, L., & Bean, R. (2010). What matters for elementary literacy coaching?: Guiding principles for instructional improvement and student achievement. *The Reading Teacher, 63*, 544–554.

Lave, J., & Wenger, E. (1991). *Situated learning: Legitimate peripheral participation.* Cambridge, UK: Cambridge University Press.

Lloyd, M., & Duncan-Howell, J. (2010). Changing the metaphor: The potential of online communities in teacher professional development. In J. O. Lindberg & A. D. Olofsson (Eds.), *Online learning communities and teacher professional development: Methods for improved education delivery* (pp. 60–76). Hershey, PA: Information Science Reference.

Mangin, M. M. (2009). Literacy coach role implementation: How district context influences reform efforts. *Educational Administration Quarterly, 45*, 759–792.

Matsumura, L. C., Garnier, H. E., Correnti, R., Junker, B., & Bickel, D. D. (2010). Investigating the effectiveness of a comprehensive literacy coaching program in schools with high teacher mobility. *Elementary School Journal, 111*, 35–62.

Matsumura, L. C., Sartoris, M., Bickel, D. D., & Garnier, H. E. (2009). Leadership for literacy coaching: The principal's role in launching a new coaching program. *Educational Administration Quarterly, 45,* 655–693.

Neuman, S. B., & Wright, T. (2010). Promoting language and literacy development for early childhood educators: A mixed-methods study of coursework and coaching. *Elementary School Journal, 111,* 63–86.

Noddings, N. (2003). *Caring: A feminine approach to ethics and moral education* (2nd ed.). Berkeley: University of California Press.

Pianta, R. C., Mashburn, A. J., Downer, J. T., Hamre, B. K., & Justice, L. (2008). Effects of Web-mediated PD resources on teacher–child interactions in pre-kindergarten classrooms. *Early Childhood Research Quarterly, 23,* 431–451.

Powell, D. R., Diamond, K. E., & Koehler, M. J. (2010). Use of a case-based hypermedia resource in an early literacy coaching intervention with pre-kindergarten teachers. *Topics in Early Childhood Special Education, 29*(4), 239–249.

Quatroche, D., Bean, R., & Hamilton, R. L. (2001). The role of the reading specialist: A review of research. *The Reading Teacher, 55,* 282–294.

Sailors, M. (2009). Improving comprehension instruction through quality professional development. In S. E. Israel & G. G. Duffy (Eds.), *Handbook of research on reading comprehension* (pp. 645–658). New York: Routledge.

Sailors, M., & Price, L. (2010). Professional development that supports the teaching of cognitive reading instruction. *Elementary School Journal, 110,* 301–322.

Sailors, M., & Shanklin, N. (Eds.). (2010). Coaching, teaching, and learning [Special issue]. *Elementary School Journal, 111*(1).

Stephens, D., & Vanderburg, M. (2010). The impact of literacy coaches: What teachers value and how teachers change. *Elementary School Journal, 111,* 141–163.

Wenger, E., McDermott, R., & Snyder, W. M. (2002). *Cultivating communities of practice.* Boston: Harvard Business Review Press.

West, L., & Staub, F. C. (2003). *Content-Focused Coaching: Transforming mathematics lessons.* Portsmouth, NH: Heinemann.

CHAPTER 23

Partnering with Parents • • • • • • • • •

KATHRYN ROBERTS

Involving parents in their children's educations is an essential part of school success (e.g., Hoover-Dempsey et al., 2005; Neuman & Dickinson, 2001), and it plays a particularly important role in literacy success (e.g., Brown, Palincsar, & Armbruster, 2006; Durkin, 1966; Hewison & Tizard, 1980; Leseman & de Jong, 1998; Purcell-Gates, 2000; Sénéchal, 2006; Weigel, Martin, & Bennett, 2006). Two fundamental assumptions that must be embraced if family literacy initiatives are to succeed are "It takes a village to raise a child," and "We're all in this together." This chapter describes both the positive effects of family literacy interventions and, to some extent, the details of how several have been operated. Although it may be tempting to jump right into an action plan for involving parents with their children's literacy learning, you are much more likely to be successful if you first take an honest look at yourself and your colleagues and ask, "Do we *all* think that *all* of our parents play essential roles in their children's educations?" If the answer is no (which, it would seem, is a more common stance than we might like to believe; e.g., Lareau, 1987; Moseman, 2003), Step 1 is getting your own (figurative) house in order. This chapter can help you do that. Abundant research is included to support the importance of family involvement, and the *Questions for Reflection* and *Suggestions for Ongoing Professional Learning* sections of this chapter can help you structure your discussions and learning. Once you have solid buy-in from the school staff, Steps 2 through infinity (really, the sky is the limit) involve evaluating what you're doing well, planning areas for improvement, carrying out your plans, tweaking based on what happens, and repeating. Ideally, this chapter will provide both motivation and practical ideas for getting started.

OVERVIEW OF RESEARCH

Why Parents and Families Matter

Getting parents involved is more than just getting them to do assigned tasks with their children and attend conferences. Research shows that successful students tend to have parents who feel safe and empowered when interacting with schools (Griffith, 1998); who talk with their children more frequently, using a wider range of vocabulary (Hart & Risley, 1995); who read with their children regularly (e.g., Bus & van IJzendoorn, 1995; Sénéchal, 2006); who model engagement in their own literate activities (Morrow & Young, 1997; Weigel et al., 2006); and who emphasize the importance of school and academic success (e.g., Seginer, 1983). For a variety of reasons, many parents cannot or do not engage in these behaviors, and a disproportionate number of their children also have other factors that place them statistically more at risk for reading (and school) difficulties. For example, in the United States, these factors include cultural minority status, single-parent homes, low socioeconomic status (SES), and lower levels of maternal education (e.g., Dickinson & Snow, 1987; Griffith, 1998; McWayne, Campos, & Owsianik, 2008). As educators, it is our job not only to communicate the importance of these activities and support parents as they engage in them, but also to help build bridges between home literacies (which do not always mirror school literacies, but are valid nonetheless) and school literacies, and to examine our own practices for unintentional barriers to participation.

Teachers can often spout off an uncanny amount of information regarding specific academic strengths and areas for growth for each child in their classrooms. Parents often share some of that same knowledge, but in addition, they often have an encyclopedic fund of information ranging from their child's interest *du jour* (e.g., a parent once told me about her son's *avid* interest in vacuum cleaners, and janitorial catalogues turned out to be just the thing to pique that reluctant reader's interest) to the inside scoop on how the child feels about certain school situations. For example, thanks to a tip from a parent, I learned that a child I had mentally labeled as a reluctant writer did not like our school's writing paper because it ripped when she erased mistakes. A switch to a photocopied version of the lined paper was just the trick to get her going. Teachers who view families as equal contributors not only stand to gain valuable information, but are also likely to be successful at engaging parents as partners in their children's educations (Jayroe & Brenner, 2005), and thus are more likely to have students who are successful learners.

Although it is certainly true that parental involvement is an influential factor for older students (Fan, 2001), it seems that the effects of the home on literacy learning in particular are strongest before children are reading conventionally (Bus & van IJzendoorn, 1995; van Steensel, McElvany, Kurvers, & Herppich, 2011). For this reason, many of the specific parent–child studies cited in this chapter are situated in early childhood/primary grade settings. However, the research presented on the factors that influence parents' decisions to become involved—arguably *the* most important factor determining the success or failure of a program—are much more widely applicable across grades.

Who Participates and Why?

In a phone survey of a racially and ethnically diverse sample of 234 low-SES parents of second and third graders, nearly all parents reported that they believed it was important to help children with their schoolwork at home; the few exceptions were attributed to children not needing help, children not asking for help, or parents' own perceived inability to help (Drummond & Stipek, 2004). Beyond working with students at home, many parents believe that being involved in other ways, such as conferences or volunteering, is also important (McWayne et al., 2008). Why, then, can it often feel like an uphill battle to engage parents?

According to a model of parental involvement created and tested by Hoover-Dempsey and colleagues (Hoover-Dempsey & Sandler, 1995, 1997; Hoover-Dempsey et al., 2005), three umbrella constructs play significant roles in determining whether and to what extent parents become involved in their children's educations: parents' role construction, parents' sense of efficacy for playing a role in their children's school success, and invitations/demands/opportunities for involvement. (For explanations of each, see Figure 23.1.) Once parents make the decision to become involved, the ways in which

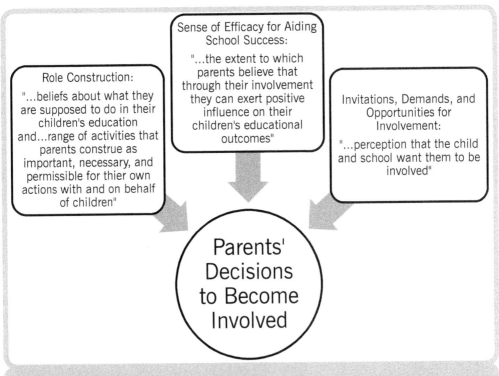

FIGURE 23.1. Three broad constructs that play important roles in determining parents' involvement in their children's educations. From Hoover-Dempsey, K. V., and Sandler, H. M. (1997) Why do parents become involved in their children's education? *Review of Educational Research, 7*(1), 3–42. Copyright © 1997 by the American Educational Research Association. Adapted by permission of Sage Publications.

they enact that decision tend to be influenced by an additional set of factors, including their knowledge of the domains of interaction (e.g., algebra, letter naming, creative writing); competing demands placed on their time and resources (e.g., meal preparation, child care, employment, transportation); and the particular demand or invitation for involvement (e.g., a plea from a child to engage in a take-home activity, a letter from a teacher announcing a conference, an invitation from another parent to attend a school function) (Hoover-Dempsey & Sandler, 1995, 1997). In short, what Hoover-Dempsey and colleagues learned through a rigorous process of gathering information from parents is that if we want them to be involved, we need to be sensitive to these issues and incorporate our knowledge of them into our planning. Figure 23.2 lists several principles for effective family involvement, as well as suggestions for successfully enacting them and avoiding related pitfalls.

SUMMARY OF BIG IDEAS FROM RESEARCH

Family Influence

Parents Are Kids' First, and Perhaps Most Influential, Teachers

- To a large degree, parents control the amount and content of language children hear in the home before formal school entry. Parents who engage their children in higher-level discussions (as opposed to speaking mostly in directives to them), and who talk to their children more frequently, tend to have children with significantly larger vocabularies (e.g., 500 words for those with less exposure vs., 1,100 words for those with more by age 3), as well as children who tend to be more successful in later schooling. These gaps, which are strongly correlated with SES, tend to persist even with the intervention of schooling and teachers (Hart & Risley, 1995). This means that in the vast majority of cases, we cannot make up for a lack of literacy involvement in the home solely through school-based initiatives; parental involvement is essential.
- Factors such as engagement in literate activities (e.g., playing alphabet memory games, writing a grocery list together), reading aloud to children and interacting with them about the text, reading in the presence of children, and the amount of environmental print in the home are all predictive of later reading achievement (e.g., Hood, Conlon, & Andrews, 2008).

Parents Matter for Big Kids, Too

- Although it is true that parental involvement declines as children grow older (Green, Walker, Hoover-Dempsey, & Sandler, 2007), this decline is less pronounced for interactions centering around literacy. As opposed to more technical subjects such as mathematics and the sciences, in which parents' knowledge may become outdated or insufficient in the upper grades, parents and children of all ages are likely to continue using a fairly stable set of comprehension skills to access a wide variety of content, both new and known (Chiu & McBride-Chang, 2010). This means that although parents may become less able over time to help children with topics like biological sciences, they are more likely to remain able to help with many literacy-related tasks.

Principle	We need to . .	We need to avoid . .
Build parental self-efficacy	Give specific ideas for how to help: • "Every 4–5 pages, stop reading and ask your child to tell you what has happened so far." To the degree possible, help parents find support if they lack some of the skills or knowledge needed to participate. Invite parents to participate by sharing their unique skills and knowledge with the class. For example: • Teaching words or phrases in a foreign language • Gardening • Musical talents	Vague requests to work with kids: • "Make sure your child is understanding what she reads." Blame: • "They should know this stuff!" Expectations that all parents should be involved in the same way (e.g., reading a book to the class).
Be respectful of competing demands	Offer logistical support for at-school activities: • Arrange for bus transportation or some sort of travel voucher for public transportation. • Provide child care for siblings. • Provide meals if activities are held near a mealtime. • Offer a variety of days and times for participation (i.e., days, evenings, weekends). Provide off-site ways to get involved: • Home visits • Activities based in neighborhoods • Meetings by phone • Take-home activities • Communication logs	To the extent possible, requests for involvement that are not mindful of competing demands: • Invitations for parents only, unless there is also on-site child care • One-time-only events • Events held only during regular working hours (during which family or friends are less likely to be able to help with transport and child care) • Events that conflict with mealtimes, bus pickup and dropoff times, and other events requiring parental supervision • Events that present only one way to participate (e.g., if a parent cannot attend workshops, not offering an alternative way to get the information)
Support positive role construction	Work to create a shared definition of parent roles (which is not the same as convincing parents to take on our vision for their roles): • Share our expectations for parent involvement, and ask parents about theirs. • Explain why we ask them to do certain things. • Explain why they are uniquely suited to do certain things. Ask parents what they view as important in helping their children succeed, and add those things to your family involvement agenda whenever possible.	Thinking that parents are disengaged or do not care about their children if they do not participate in specific ways. Thinking of parental involvement as a one-way street (we tell them what to do).

(continued)

FIGURE 23.2. Principles for effective family involvement, ways to enact these principles, and ways to avoid pitfalls.

	Be open and inviting to share our roles as teachers—truly seeing parents as partners. Encourage parents to invite their peers to participate.	
Provide sincere invitations to get involved	Create inviting spaces for adults to make it clear that school is their place, too: • Appropriate-sized furniture • Adult lending libraries of parenting resources • Prominently posted pictures of children and families interacting at school • Welcoming environmental print, in multiple languages, if possible (e.g., "Welcome, parents! We're so glad you're here! Please stop and say hello in the office before joining your child in his or her classroom.") Welcome new children and new families: • When a new child enrolls, include a welcome note to the child and his or her family members in a newsletter. • Make a point of personally welcoming the family (e.g., "We're so glad that all three of you are joining our classroom family!") Be sure that children have the chance to invite participation, as well: • Provide children with a lending library of family activities that they can invite parents to engage with. • Have children write invitations to such things as school performances.	Environments that make adults feel like intruders: • Child-sized seating options only • Environmental print sending the message that parents are not a part of the group (e.g., "ATTENTION: ALL PARENTS **MUST** CHECK IN AT THE OFFICE AND PICK UP A VISITORS' BADGE!!!")

FIGURE 23.2. *(continued)*

• Parents can continue to influence their children's motivation and attitudes toward literacy as they grow older by doing such things as modeling activities that involve reading and writing for their own enjoyment (e.g., getting lost in a book or writing the annual holiday cards), successfully using print as a means to an end (e.g., using written text to acquire a new skill), and talking about the general importance of taking school seriously (Hoover-Dempsey & Sandler, 1995).

Cooperation Is a Two-Way Street

• Although it is important to make specific suggestions to parents, so that they feel confident as they support their children (e.g., Cohen, Kulik, & Kulik, 1982; Drummond & Stipek, 2004), it is also important to remember that relationships with parents hinge on good communication. Everyone's insight matters, and involvement with parents should not serve as a series of one-sided directives, but should instead empower parents to share their insights, concerns, and ideas for collaboration (Griffith, 1998; Hoover-Dempsey & Sandler, 1995; Jayroe & Brenner, 2005).

- When parents have a role in determining the content and structure of family literacy interventions, the interventions may be accepted as having greater social validity, and families may be more likely to view the goals, process, and outcomes as important (Jayroe & Brenner, 2005; Waldbart, Meyers, & Meyers, 2006). Consequently, parents are also more likely to engage fully in the intervention (e.g., Miltenberger, 1990), thus increasing the probability of favorable results.

Factors Influencing Parental Participation

- Parents who get involved tend to make the decision to do so because they feel that they should, that they are capable, and/or that someone (e.g., children, teachers, administrators, peers) wants them to be involved (Hoover-Dempsey & Sandler, 1997).
- When parents do not appear to be involved, it is important to remember that they may be involved in ways that are not visible to teachers (e.g., reading with their children at night, but not attending parent outreach meetings), or may be engaging in literacy activities that do not closely mirror traditional classroom literacies but are valid nonetheless (Green et al., 2007).

EXAMPLES OF EFFECTIVE PRACTICES

Classroom Examples

Now that we have discussed the importance of parental involvement in children's literacy educations and what makes parents more or less likely to participate, let's take a look at what these principles look like in action. This section highlights two examples of successful (in terms of both attendance and child outcomes) family literacy programs. Note that these illustrative examples are focused on particular constructs of literacy; however, abundant research shows that well-designed interventions focusing on nearly all constructs of literacy can be successful. (For more on print-rich environments and resources, see Sailors, Kumar, Blady, & Willson, Chapter 2, this volume.)

Project FLAME

Project FLAME (Family Literacy: *Aprendiendo, Mejorando, Educando* [Learning, Bettering, Educating]; Shanahan, Mulhern, & Rodriguez-Brown, 1995); addresses the literacy needs of working-class Hispanic (and other language minority) families by providing literacy instruction to parents of 3- to 9-year-old children. The parents enrolled in the program are not yet fluent in English. The primary goals of the project are to give them the necessary skills and self-efficacy to support their children's literacy learning, and to foster relationships between families and schools. The program was initially led by graduate students, but later part of that role was transferred to "graduates" of

Topic	Parents learn to . . .
Creating Home Literacy Centers	• Make and use a literacy center (e.g., stocking it with provided materials; logistics and ideas for use).
Book Sharing	• Share books with children in effective ways (e.g., talking about books; sharing books if they have limited literacy skills).
Appropriate Book Selection	• Select books to meet children's needs and interests, using specific quality criteria.
Library Visit	• Navigate the library. Apply for a library card.
Book Fairs	• Select appropriate books in English or Spanish (which are then purchased with coupons).
Teaching the ABCs	• Teach letters and sounds via games, songs, and other language experiences.
Children's Writing	• Understand and encourage emergent writing.
Community Literacy	• Model and scaffold literacy during everyday activities.
Classroom Observations	• Visit a classroom (observing how children are taught in school).
Parent–Teacher Get-Togethers	• Talk with teachers and principals about children's education.
Math for Your Child	• Play math games and engage in other math activities.
How Parents Can Help with Homework	• Monitor and help children with homework, particularly when they have limited related skills and/or knowledge.

FIGURE 23.3. Project FLAME: Parents as Teachers sessions. Based on Shanahan, Mulhern, and Rodriguez-Brown (1995).

the program. Three session types are used in order to address all goals of the program: twice-weekly classes in English as a second language for parents, twice-monthly Parents as Teachers classes (see Figure 23.3 for a list of session topics with summary descriptions), and arranged interactions with the school (e.g., observing in a classroom, meeting with a teacher to discuss hopes and concerns). The program, which had served over 300 families at the time the research on the program was published (1995) and which continues today, consistently resulted in gains in children's cognitive development, preliteracy and literacy skills, and English and first-language vocabulary skills. The adults in the program showed improvements in English proficiency and attitudes toward teaching their children. In addition, parents reported that after the program they had more print available in their homes, interacted around literacy more often with their children, read and wrote more themselves, understood their role as their children's first teachers, provided more opportunities for everyday literacy experiences, understood the importance of connecting with teachers, understood the expectations of parental involvement in U.S. schools, and felt more comfortable inter-acting with school personnel ("Project FLAME: Family literacy: *Aprendiendo, mejorando, educando*," 2003; Shanahan et al., 1995).

Project FLAME's creators offer the following insights on their program and its success:

- Parents who view themselves as successful learners are more likely to view themselves as capable of helping their children (Nickse, Speicher, & Buchek, 1988). When parents have skill gaps, helping them to improve their own literacy skills makes it more likely that they will have the necessary confidence and skills to help their children.
- Interventions should be based on sound research and theory, but should also be able to accommodate topics and concerns raised by the participants. It is, however, important to negotiate the content of the sessions without compromising their integrity. For example, in this program, parents wanted to focus on crafts without an academic goal. Facilitators then worked crafts into the sessions, showing parents how to engage in particular crafts that also served literacy learning goals.
- Using the parents' first language is a great instructional support. If this is possible, it supports learners (both adults and children) as they acquire the new language and literacy skills (Moll & Diaz, 1987).
- Plan logistics with parents, not for them. To support parents' attendance, inquire about their daily schedules and competing demands for their time, and do your best to work within or around those constraints.

Reading and Writing at Home (Lire et Écrire à la Maison)

Saint-Laurent and Giasson (2005), working with the parents of Canadian first graders from primarily French-speaking homes, took a slightly different approach from that described above for Project FLAME. They led workshops focused on teaching parents about specific literacy activities that they could engage in at home with their children and about how to adapt their interactions as children became more proficient readers and writers. In addition, in response to research indicating that positive experiences with literacy increase both parents' and children's motivation to spend time together on literate activities, the researchers gave explicit attention to making home activities enjoyable. A socioeconomically diverse sample of 108 children and their parents from 12 classrooms were enrolled in the study; 53 of the families attended the workshops, and 55 did not. Researchers, partnering with the teachers of the classrooms in the workshop condition, co-led eight workshops on such topics as the importance of book reading; playing with letters; being a model for reading and writing; and listening and assisting emergent, beginning, and developing readers. Topics were presented separately as the school year progressed. During each workshop, parents were invited to give feedback on the literacy activities presented in the previous session, discussed the new topic, viewed a demonstration of new suggested activities, and participated in guided practice with children or other parents. At the end of each session, the content was summarized, and parents and session leaders engaged in the planning of a related at-home literacy activity.

Before the intervention, there were no statistically significant differences between students in participating and nonparticipating groups on measures of phonological awareness, concepts about print, invented spelling, total literacy scores, attitudes toward reading, or differences between groups on a measure of family literacy. After the intervention, the students in the group in which parents had received the intervention outperformed their counterparts on all measures administered, including a reading test, a writing test (with six subtests), and measures of attitudes toward reading. Differences were also found between groups on measures of family literacy (i.e., book reading, modeling of literate activities, available text, library visits). (Note that for reasons related to ecological validity and appropriateness of content, the authors decided not to use all of the same assessments at pre- and postintervention; this makes the interpretation of results a bit more difficult, though the general trend is quite clear.) Effects were statistically significant, favoring the intervention group, for family literacy scores, students' reading scores, and students' writing scores. Specifically, in the case of writing scores, children whose parents had participated in the workshop produced sentences with more complex structure, stronger vocabulary, more accurate spelling, and greater length of text. Finally, parents participating in the program, unlike their counterparts, reported that understanding how to help their children reduced their level of stress and made literacy activities more frequent and enjoyable.

The authors of this program offer the following insights on the program and its success:

- Depending on their other obligations, some parents found it more convenient to meet during the school day, while others found it easier to meet in the evening. Parents who met during the day practiced activities with their children, while those who met at night practiced with each other. The time of day and whether they practiced with their children or other adults had no effect on the outcome of the intervention, so making sure that the time is convenient to parents, and thus making it more likely that they will attend, should take precedence over the decision to involve or not to involve children. (For an interesting contrast of these two participation models, see also Doyle & Zhang, 2011.)
- There were no differences in the effects of the intervention related to SES, which may be due to the level of support given to parents both through modeling and through provision of materials for use at home. If the goal is for an intervention to be universally implemented, parents need both instructional and material support.
- The authors presented the program as one to prevent literacy failure, and many of those parents who declined to participate or dropped out attributed their choices to not being worried that their children might fail. As a result, the authors suggest a more positive spin when the program is introduced, focusing on literacy success.
- Teachers were heavily involved in the implementation of the workshops, and endorsed the workshops' content, importance, and connection to classroom learning. Parents may be more likely to participate in programs supported by their children's teachers than ones run by people more distant from their children's everyday lives (e.g., district personnel, principals, researchers alone, or other outside individuals; Hoover-Dempsey & Sandler, 1995).

School-Level Examples

Most of the literature on family–school partnerships focuses on specific interventions in which parents are taught to do specific things with their children or are provided with materials to use in the home, and on the outcomes of those interventions. Very little research has focused specifically on the characteristics of a school or district that make it particularly welcoming to family involvement. However, in the research on specific successful interventions, there is a clear trend toward schools' positioning themselves as "our" space (including parents, children, and staff), as opposed to "their" place (a place limited to children and staff). Following are two examples of successful family literacy programs that made attempts to connect with parents and create a sense of collective responsibility in general, as opposed to the specific academic interventions.

Bridges to Literacy

The goals of the Bridges to Literacy program were to "enhance the quality of children's literacy interactions with family members and simultaneously increase involvement at schools" (Waldbart et al., 2006, p. 775). In order to accomplish these goals, university and school personnel planned a high-quality, research-based intervention in which they supported parents in learning developmentally appropriate ways in which to facilitate their children's literacy learning. In addition, program leaders made a concentrated effort to welcome parents into the school as valued members of the team by seeking their input when designing the intervention; working in meetings around parents' schedules; inviting parents to observe (and later discuss) literacy interactions in children's classrooms; giving parents the opportunity to choose picture books to be purchased for the school library; talking with parents (via telephone, during classroom visits, in the pickup/dropoff line, and on home visits) as equal partners in their children's educations; and making clear their appreciation of families' presence in the school through such gestures as providing refreshments and a dedicated "family center." In addition, bringing families into the school was not left to teachers on their own. The administrator of the building was an enthusiastic and dedicated collaborator— even going so far as to walk the neighborhood, going door to door to welcome new families into the school "family."

Although it was not possible to isolate the particular factors responsible for participation rates, these things, combined with an engaging intervention, prompted a staggering 42% of parents in the focal classroom to participate in the program. This is impressive, given that the rate of participation is traditionally much lower in populations similar to Bridges to Literacy's target population: low-SES parents from predominantly African American neighborhoods. It is also encouraging that the program received high praise from participants, which is likely to lead to even higher turnouts at subsequent sessions as the word spreads through the community (Edwards, 1994).

After-School and Summer Literacy Program, Davis Elementary School

Davis Elementary is a small, rural, low-income school that as of 2001 was characterized by poor test performance, high teacher turnover, low parental involvement, and run-down facilities. At the time of the study, the student body was 100% African American, and 97% of students received free lunch. The school had all of the red flags signaling a

school in danger of failure, and the school was in fact failing. Beginning in the spring of 2001, researchers from a local university and classroom teachers banded together to try to increase student achievement by actively involving parents in more meaningful ways (Jayroe & Brenner, 2005). The group members had their work cut out for them: Parental participation at the school was extremely low for such things as PTA meetings, conferences, and family information nights, and parents were seen by teachers and administrators as uninterested, uninvolved, and uncommitted to their children's academic success.

Taking advantage of a small amount of grant funding, the school set out to involve parents directly in their children's educations by hiring parents at the rate of $50 per week to work as assistants in an after-school and summer tutoring program. Some might see this as a risky move, considering the volunteers' low levels of education (nine parents with high school diplomas, one parent with a GED, six who had attended some community college or were currently attending). However, patience paid off, and the program was a success—benefiting the parents, the children enrolled in the program (75 struggling PreK–3 readers), and other children in the participating parents' households. The participants in the program, including parents, teachers, and researchers, attributed much of their success to the design of the program, which included the following:

- Treating parents as valued members of the instructional team. Parents, teachers, and university faculty worked together to plan sessions; parents were paid a small stipend; parents were involved directly with the children (as opposed to, for example, making photocopies); and parents were invited and trusted to borrow all program materials for use at home.
- Providing professional development to parents, to give them explicit instruction in how to work with children and materials.
- Allowing time and space for group discussions in which teachers were exposed to parents' ideas about such things as discipline and what it means to interact with children around literacy, and parents were exposed to the ways in which teachers expected to interact with children.
- Parents becoming aware of the extent to which "their" school was failing, and using the tools they had acquired through the program to take action not only during the program, but also at home.

LOOKING FORWARD

If we are going to create a support system for our learners that extends bidirectionally between home and school, it is time to let go of several assumptions that are limiting at best and damaging at worst:

- We have to believe that all parents want the best for their children and are willing to do what they can to help, *if* they truly believe that they are needed, that they are capable, and that their actions will make a difference (e.g., Hoover-Dempsey et al., 2005).
- We absolutely must get beyond the idea that teachers and schools should have sole discretion over the content and structure of home–school interactions. Families have valuable and unique contributions to make to the process (Jayroe & Brenner, 2005), and if we lose sight of that, it can sometimes be difficult to hear them over the sound of our own (well-intentioned) voices.
- We also need to be sure to provide the necessary support, both instructional and material, to set parents up for success. The self-efficacy that comes from instructional support for specific interventions is highly correlated with higher levels of participation, and, by extension, higher levels of success (Hoover-Dempsey, Bassler, & Brissie, 1992). However, even the best-planned and most instructionally supportive interventions are likely to fail if they depend on specific materials (books, pencils, paper, etc.) to which families do not have access.
- As educators, most of us are fiercely dedicated to seeing the strengths in our students and making sure that others see them too. We need to offer support for the development of this mentality in the adults who are raising our students. They too have strengths that can be built upon to help their children; and just like our students, they too are more willing and productive when we focus on strengths as opposed to dwell on weaknesses (Edwards, 2009; Jayroe & Brenner, 2005; Nickse et al., 1988).
- Family literacy interventions focused on a variety of topics—from sound–letter knowledge, to comprehension, to beginning writing, and many, many more—have been successful, as the examples provided above have made clear. The key does not seem to be the specific topic of the intervention, but rather the ways in which it is carried out. Although we do have some recommendations from research (described in this chapter) to guide us, we need continuing studies of both the best ways to get parents involved and the effects of that involvement—including studies with methods that proved to be ineffective, so as to avoid wasting precious time and resources through redundancy.
- Parental participation, both at home and at school, begins to drop off sharply as the elementary years draw to a close (Griffith, 1998; Keith, 1991). This is perhaps due to changes in such factors as efficacy that are related to the difficulty of schoolwork content (Chiu & McBride-Chang, 2010). Or perhaps (as many secondary teachers have confided to me) it is due to other factors, such as the number of students per teacher or parents' feeling that their children should become more independent. The waters are pretty murky in this area of research, but it is clear that we need to collaborate with parents in order to come up with beneficial, manageable ways in which parents can be involved with schools in ways

that benefit older students. This involvement is likely to look very different from involvement at the elementary level, and we should try to embrace those differences in a responsive way, rather than trying to fit "square pegs" (elementary-appropriate practices) into "round holes" (middle and secondary schools).

QUESTIONS FOR REFLECTION ●

1. In what areas of literacy learning would my students most benefit from one-on-one interactions? Are those the areas in which I am asking parents to get involved? Why or why not?

2. How important to students' learning are the things that I ask parents to do? To what extent do I explain to parents both what they might do *and* why? To what extent do I make clear the results of their involvement?

3. To what extent are the ways in which parents participate in my classroom dictated by the teacher? By the parents? By both in collaboration? If there is little collaboration, how could I create a space for that?

4. When and how do I invite parental input? Who participates when I invite input? Is there something that I can change to remove possible barriers to participation?

5. When I ask parents to participate, to what extent do I prepare them to be successful? How sure am I that they know what the expectations are and how to carry out the activity? How responsive am I to cultural differences in interaction modes and expectations? How sure am I that families have the required resources? How can I increase instructional and material support?

SUGGESTIONS FOR ONGOING PROFESSIONAL LEARNING ● ● ● ● ● ● ●

Becoming Familiar with Community Supports and Possible Constraints

Session 1

Investigate your community (virtually or via a "field trip"), and determine the availability of potential resources for alleviating some of the time-consuming and emotionally draining barriers to parental involvement (e.g., lack of child care, lack of transportation, insufficient income to meet daily needs, illiteracy, unfamiliarity with the English language, few job qualifications). Questions for small-group or professional learning community (PLC) discussion might include these: How can families access these services? How can we make families aware of these services?

Session 2

Nearly all parents want to see their children be happy, healthy, and successful. Why, then, do some parents appear to be uninvolved in their children's educations? In small groups or PLCs, brainstorm possible competing demands for parents' time and resources. Next, brainstorm a list of the ways in which you would like parents to participate willingly in school events or engage with their children at home. What resources to parents need in order to do those things? What barriers exist? How could you restructure the activities to avoid obstacles and provide supports for participation? It may help to use a chart such as the one in Figure 23.4.

Session 3

Choose one opportunity for family participation that has not been particularly success-ful in terms of attracting parents. With your PLC or small group, discuss the following: Who *did* participate? Why do you think they chose to do so? Who did not participate? What do you think deterred them? How could you restructure the opportunity to get more families involved? (Hint: In addition to using a chart like the one in Figure 23.4, you might find it helpful to discuss the different points at which you have contact with parents, such as the invitation to engage, perhaps the actual activity itself, and follow-up. It might also be helpful to poll parents themselves about why they make decisions to participate or not to participate.) Make a plan to revise one activity, based on this discussion.

Session 4

Take a close look at the ways in which you, as individuals and as a school, invite parents to participate. For each, ask yourselves the following: How do we structure participa-tion? Do we typically give directions, seek input, or engage in both? Are the things that parents are asked to do clearly related to the success and well-being of children? When we ask parents to participate at home or school in ways that require resources from them (transportation, supplies, time, etc.), are we sensitive to the ease or difficulty with which they can obtain them? How can we restructure these opportunities so that they involve input from all parties, clearly and directly benefit children, and are sensitive to parents' capacities to give of their time and other resources? Based on this discussion, make a plan to revise one activity, or outline a new activity that might be more respon-sive to these concerns and give it a try. Soliciting feedback from parents after events as to how well they think you responded to these factors is likely to be beneficial in plan-ning future interactions.

Event/Activity	Resources Needed	Possible Obstacles	Supports We Can Provide
Parent–teacher conferences	Transportation Child care Comfort in building Comfort talking to teacher	Lack of transportation Lack of child care Not speaking English Fear of criticism	Allow parents to ride in on bus Run special bus route Provide child care with advance notice Translate invitations Ask other parents or community members to volunteer as translators Hold some conferences as home visits Regularly find and communicate positive news about students

FIGURE 23.4. Example of a planning sheet for events with parents.

RESEARCH-BASED RESOURCES

Allen, J. (2010). *Literacy in the welcoming classroom: Creating family–school partnerships that support student learning.* New York: Teachers College Press.

Edwards, P. (2003). *Children's literacy development: Making it happen through school, family, and community involvement.* Boston: Allyn & Bacon.

Edwards, P. (2009). *Tapping the potential of parents.* New York: Scholastic.

Epstein, J. L., Sanders, M., Sheldon, S., Simon, B. S., Salinas, K. C., Jansor, N. R., et al. (2009). *School, family, and community partnerships: Your handbook for action* (3rd ed.). Thousand Oaks, CA: Corwin Press.

Henderson, A. T. (2007). *Beyond the bake sale: The essential guide to family/school partnerships.* New York: New Press.

REFERENCES

Brown, A. L., Palincsar, A. S., & Armbruster, B. B. (2006). Instructing comprehension-fostering activities in interactive learning situations. In R. B. Ruddell & N. J. Unrau (Eds.), *Theoretical models and processes of reading* (5th ed., pp. 780–809). Newark, DE: International Reading Association.

Bus, A., & van IJzendoorn, M. H. (1995). Mothers reading to their three-year-olds: The role of mother–child attachment security in becoming literate. *Reading Research Quarterly, 40,* 998–1015.

Chiu, M. M., & McBride-Chang, C. (2010). Family and reading in 41 countries: Differences across cultures and students. *Scientific Studies of Reading, 14,* 514–543.

Cohen, P. A., Kulik, J. A., & Kulik, C.-L. C. (1982). Educational outcomes of tutoring: A meta-analysis of findings. *American Educational Research Journal, 19,* 237–248.

Dickinson, D., & Snow, C. E. (1987). Interrelationships among prereading and oral language skills in kindergarteners from two different social classes. *Early Childhood Research Quarterly, 2,* 1–25.

Doyle, A., & Zhang, J. (2011). Participation structure impacts on parent engagement in family literacy programs. *Early Childhood Education Journal, 39,* 223–233.

Drummond, K. V., & Stipek, D. (2004). Low-income parents' beliefs about their role in children's academic learning. *Elementary School Journal, 104,* 197–213.

Durkin, D. (1966). *Children who read early.* New York: Teachers College Press.

Edwards, P. (1994). Responses of teachers and African-American mothers to a book-reading intervention program. In D. Dickinson (Ed.), *Bridges to literacy: Children, families, and schools* (pp. 175–208). Cambridge, MA: Blackwell.

Edwards, P. (2009). *Tapping the potential of parents.* New York: Scholastic.

Fan, X. (2001). Parental involvement and students' academic achievement: A growth modeling analysis. *Journal of Experimental Education, 79,* 27–61.

Green, C. L., Walker, J. M. T., Hoover-Dempsey, K. V., & Sandler, H. M. (2007). Parents' motivations for involvement in children's education: An empirical test of a theoretical model of parental involvement. *Journal of Educational Psychology, 99,* 532–544.

Griffith, J. (1998). The relation of school structure and social environment to parent involvement in elementary schools. *Elementary School Journal, 99,* 53–80.

Hart, B., & Risley, T. R. (1995). *Meaningful differences in the everyday experience of young American children.* Baltimore: Brookes.

Hewison, J., & Tizard, J. (1980). Parental involvement and reading attainment. *British Journal of Educational Psychology, 50,* 209–215.

Hood, M., Conlon, E., & Andrews, G. (2008). Preschool home literacy practices and children's literacy development: A longitudinal analysis. *Journal of Educational Psychology, 100,* 252–271.

Hoover-Dempsey, K. V., Bassler, O. C., & Brissie, J. S. (1992). Explorations in parent–school relationships. *Journal of Educational Research, 85,* 287–294.

Hoover-Dempsey, K. V., & Sandler, H. M. (1995). Parent involvement in children's education: Why does it make a difference? *Teachers College Record, 97,* 310–331.

Hoover-Dempsey, K. V., & Sandler, H. M. (1997). Why do parents become involved in their children's education? *Review of Educational Research, 67*(1), 3–42.

Hoover-Dempsey, K. V., Walker, J. M. T., Sandler, H. M., Whetsel, D., Green, C., L., Wilkins, A., et al. (2005). Why do parents become involved?: Research findings and implications. *Elementary School Journal, 106*(2), 105–131.

Jayroe, T. B., & Brenner, D. (2005). Family members as partners in an after-school and summer literacy program. *Reading Horizons, 45,* 235–253.

Keith, T. Z. (1991). Parental involvement and achievement in high school. In B. A. Hutson & S. B. Silvern (Eds.), *Advances in reading/language research: Literacy through family, community, and school interaction* (Vol. 5, pp. 125–141). Greenwich, CT: JAI Press.

Lareau, A. (1987). Social class differences in family–school relationships: The importance of cultural capital. *Sociology of Education, 60,* 73–85.

Leseman, P. P. M., & de Jong, P. F. (1998). Home literacy: Opportunity, instruction, cooperation and social-emotional quality predicting early reading achievement. *Reading Research Quarterly, 33,* 294–316.

McWayne, C., Campos, R., & Owsianik, M. (2008). A multidimensional, multilevel examination of mother and father involvement among culturally diverse Head Start families. *Journal of School Psychology, 46,* 551–573.

Miltenberger, R. G. (1990). Assessment of treatment acceptability: A review of the literature. *Early Childhood Special Education, 10,* 24–39.

Moll, L. C., & Diaz, S. (1987). Change as the goal of educational research. *Anthropology and Education Quarterly, 18,* 300–311.

Morrow, L. M., & Young, J. (1997). A family literacy program connecting school and home: Effects on attitude, motivation, and literacy achievement. *Journal of Educational Psychology, 89,* 736–742.

Moseman, C. C. (2003). Primary teachers' beliefs about family competence to influence classroom practices. *Early Education and Development, 14,* 125–154.

Neuman, S. B., & Dickinson, D. (Eds.). (2001). *Handbook of early literacy research* (Vol. 1). New York: Guilford Press.

Nickse, R., Speicher, A. M., & Buchek, P. C. (1988). An intergenerational adult literacy project: A family intervention/prevention model. *Journal of Reading, 31,* 634–642.

Project FLAME: Family literacy: *Aprendiendo, mejorando, educando.* (2003, July 17). Retrieved September 30, 2011, from *www.uic.edu/educ/flame/index.html.*

Purcell-Gates, V. (2000). Family literacy. In M. L. Kamil, P. B. Mosenthal, P. D. Pearson, & R. Barr (Eds.), *Handbook of reading research* (Vol. 3, pp. 853–870). Mahwah, NJ: Erlbaum.

Saint-Laurent, L., & Giasson, J. (2005). Effects of a family literacy program adapting parental intervention to first graders' evolution of reading and writing abilities. *Journal of Early Childhood Literacy, 5,* 253–278.

Seginer, R. (1983). Parents' educational expectations and children's academic achievements: A literature review. *Merrill–Palmer Quarterly, 29,* 1–23.

Sénéchal, M. (2006). Testing the home literacy model: Parent involvement in kindergarten is differentially related to grade 4 reading comprehension, fluency, spelling, and reading for pleasure. *Scientific Studies of Reading, 10,* 59–87.

Shanahan, T., Mulhern, M., & Rodriguez-Brown, F. (1995). Project FLAME: Lessons learned from a family literacy program for linguistic minority families. *The Reading Teacher, 48*, 586–593.

van Steensel, R., McElvany, N., Kurvers, J., & Herppich, S. (2011). How effective are family literacy programs?: Results of a meta-analysis. *Review of Educational Research, 81*, 69–96.

Waldbart, A., Meyers, B., & Meyers, J. (2006). Invitations to families in an early literacy support program. *The Reading Teacher, 59*, 774–785.

Weigel, D. J., Martin, S. S., & Bennett, K. K. (2006). Contributions of the home literacy environment to preschool-aged children's emerging literacy and language skills. *Early Childhood Development and Care, 176*, 357–378.

Author Index

Subject Index

Page numbers followed by *f* indicate figure, *t* indicate table.